Ten Years at War: The Peter Kemp Trilogy
Copyright © 1957, 1958, 1961 Peter Kemp
All rights reserved.
ISBN: 9798576784073

v. I

NOTE FROM THE PUBLISHER

Contained in this volume are three books from Peter Kemp detailing his service in the Spanish Civil War, World War Two, and the anti-colonial terror wave that followed that conflict. For nearly a decade, Peter Kemp was on the front lines of events that determined the course of history. Both his father and his brother would die while he was far away. His first marriage would fail. His mother would miss him dearly. He would travel the world, risking everything, enduring near-fatal injuries, being shot at and returning in kind.

But his life could have gone in a different direction. By all accounts, Kemp was very comfortable before the wars that rocked the world. His family was well-to-do. He studied the classics at one of the most prestigious schools in the world and was preparing for a career as a lawyer. His most notable achievement before his adventures began was crashing a sports car into a telephone pole. It was a life of charm and ease that many would envy, yet he left it all behind.

Kemp was a man of principles. He fought for those principles and paid dearly for them. Details of his later life are scarce; it is reasonable to assume that his service to the nation he loved continued outside of the public record.

In times like these, when courage and duty are minimized in favor of the vulgar or small, it is helpful to remember that giants like Peter Kemp walked among us, not allowing themselves to be merely swept around by the forces of history. Our hope is that these books, sadly forgotten for decades, will allow a new generation to learn about this great man, to honor him, and to apply his lessons to their own lives.

Thank you Peter!

Mine Were of Trouble

Peter Kemp

TO CYNTHIA

The thoughts of others
Were light and fleeting,
Of lovers' meeting
Or luck or fame.
Mine were of trouble. . . .
                                        A. E. Housman

In having thus complied with your wishes I only hope that your sons
will support if necessary with their lives our present glorious
Constitution both in Church and State, love their king and hate all
republics and republicans.

                        Letter from Nelson to Revd Mr Priestly,
                                        8 March 1801

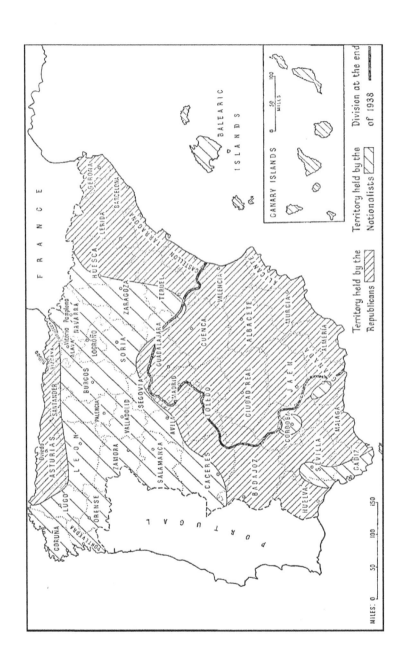

FRANCE

CORUÑA
LUGO
PONTEVEDRA
ORENSE

ASTURIAS
Oviedo
SANTANDER
VIZCAYA
Bilbao
ÁLAVA
Vitoria
NAVARRA
Pamplona
LOGROÑO
HUESCA
LÉRIDA
GERONA
BARCELONA
TARRAGONA

LEÓN
BURGOS
PALENCIA
VALLADOLID
SORIA
ZARAGOZA
TERUEL
CASTELLÓN

ZAMORA
SEGOVIA
GUADALAJARA
CUENCA
VALENCIA

SALAMANCA
ÁVILA
MADRID
TOLEDO
ALBACETE
ALICANTE

CÁCERES
CIUDAD REAL
MURCIA

BADAJOZ
JAÉN
ALMERÍA

CÓRDOBA

HUELVA
SEVILLA
MÁLAGA
CÁDIZ

PORTUGAL

BALEARIC ISLANDS

CANARY ISLANDS

0   50   100
MILES

Territory held by the Republicans

Territory held by the Nationalists

Division at the end of 1938

MILES: 0   50   100   150

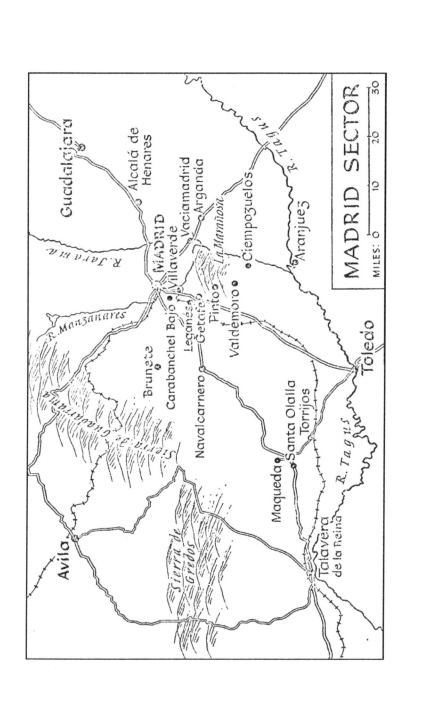

MADRID SECTOR

MILES: 0   10   20   30

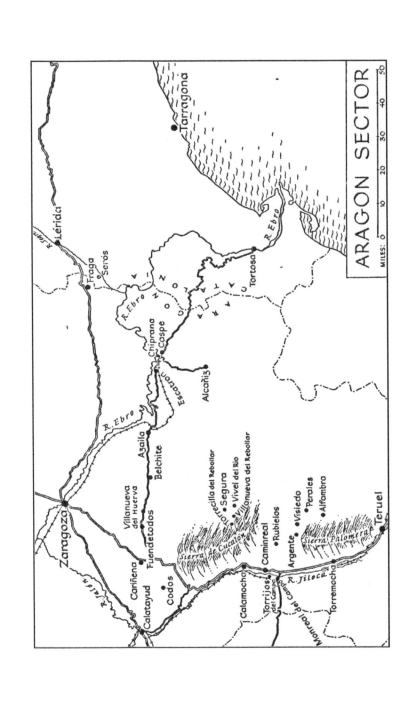

ARAGON SECTOR

MILES: 0 10 20 30 40 50

TABLE OF CONTENTS

PROLOGUE

It is hard now to recall the atmosphere of 1936. When I came down from Cambridge in June of that year the pattern of European politics was confused and obscure. The foundations of peace seemed in danger of collapse, but as yet few were convinced that another World War was inevitable, or could foresee the alignment of the Powers if it should happen. The bewilderment of the peoples of Europe was reflected in the mistakes and hesitations of their rulers.

Hitler had achieved supreme power in Germany, but the full horrors and dangers of his rule were not universally apparent; indeed, he was often applauded in Germany and outside for 'cleaning up the mess' of the Weimar Republic and for his suppression of Communism. But the recreation of the Wehrmacht, Germany's withdrawal from the League of Nations and her military occupation of the Rhineland gave warning of what was to come.

In a France weakened by a succession of shortlived and ineffective governments and resentful that victory in 1918 had brought neither security nor stability, the German occupation of the Rhineland induced a shock of indignation and protest. Monsieur Flandin, taken by surprise, was unable to act with the necessary decision. Having approached the British Government for assurances that Britain would support French military action against the German coup and being unable to obtain them, he acquiesced in a situation which all Frenchmen deplored, and of which most were terrified. The national disapproval was reflected in the subsequent elections, which returned to power a Front Populaire government under the nominal leadership of Monsieur Léon Blum, but with powerful, though less obvious, Communist affiliations. The national unity welded by German action was succeeded by anger and disintegration, by strikes and mass demonstrations in which supporters of the Front Populaire clashed bloodily with Anciens Combattants, Action Francaise and Croix-de-Feu. The general opinion in England was that 'the French are at loggerheads'.

The Italian people, elated by their success in Abyssinia in the face of British and French opposition, were embittered rather than discouraged by the policy of Sanctions. They become progressively and aggressively anti-British and increasingly truculent towards their French and Balkan neighbors. The Axis was being forged.

In South-eastern Europe Jugoslavia, plunged into crisis two years earlier by the murder of King Alexander, was continually disturbed by further Ustashi and I.M.R.O. activities. The former were fomented by Italy, the latter by Bulgaria. Throughout the country Croats, Macedonians and Mussulmans were reacting against the dominance of Serbia. Albania was ruled by King

Ahmed Zogu with Italian financial and economic aid. In October of 1935 King George of Greece had been restored to his throne by a plebiscite of his people.

Russian policy had been radically altered by two important events a couple of years earlier: in internal affairs the murder of Kirov in Leningrad on December 1st, 1934, put an end to all hopes that Stalin might follow a more liberal policy; there ensued a merciless repression, beginning with the trial and execution of Zinoviev and Kamenev and culminating in the virtual elimination of the Bolshevik 'Old Guard' in the great purges of 1936-38. In the words of Greta Garbo in the film, *Ninotchka*, there would be 'fewer, and better, Russians'. The other event, which had a vital effect on Soviet foreign policy and on Communist activity throughout Europe, was the inauguration, at the Seventh Congress of the Komintern in 1934, of the doctrine of the Popular Front. In the future, Communists abroad were to combine with all parties—Socialist, Liberal, Radical and even Conservative—who would join them in a 'Popular Front for Peace and against Fascism'.[1]

The control of the various Popular Fronts was to be in the firm but unobtrusive hands of the Communists. Within the next two years Popular Front governments were established in France and Spain.

The Spanish monarchy had fallen five years before in April, 1931, when King Alfonso XIII went into voluntary exile to avoid the risk of civil war; shortly afterwards Don Niceto Alcalá Zamora became President of the Spanish Republic, with Don Manuel Azaña as Prime Minister. A Socialist government controlled the country for the next two years. Its rule was interrupted briefly by an attempted coup d'état on August 10th, 1932, led by General Sanjurjo, the 'Lion of Morocco', which was quickly suppressed. Sanjurjo had commanded the Guardia Civil in 1931 and by his defeatist attitude had precipitated the departure of King Alfonso; now he declared for the King, but was captured and sentenced to death, reprieved at the last moment by Azaña and sent to prison in Spanish West Africa.

In 1933 the Socialist government was superseded by a coalition of right-wing parties under the leadership of Señor Gil Robles. In 1934 the parties of the left attempted armed revolution, which broke into civil war in Asturias among the inflammable miners of that province. After heavy fighting this revolt was suppressed, the instigators being treated with leniency. A succession of right-wing Governments continued until the elections of February 1936, which put a Popular Front government into power, with Señor Casares Quiroga as Prime Minister.

---

[1] Dr. I. Deutscher, *Stalin* (Oxford, 1949) p. 419. See also Mr. Arthur Koestler in *The God that Failed* (Hamish Hamilton, 1950). pp. 70-71.

This Government proved unable to control the extremists of the right or of the left, and preparations for civil war began on both sides throughout the country.[1]

Such was the state of Europe when I came down from Cambridge, not yet twenty-one years of age, with a Degree in Classics and Law, a restless temperament, no money, and what the Trinity College Magazine once described as a 'deplorable tendency to simper'.

---

[1] See Madariaga, *Spain*, pp. 300-352 (Cape, 1942).

CHAPTER ONE

I remember very well the morning I left London. It was a cold, wet day in November 1936 and in the Temple gardens the trees, now bare of their leaves, swayed and dripped sadly in the bleak wind. I had been awake since dawn and had breakfasted lightly, for I was too excited to feel hungry; now that the one suitcase that was all my luggage stood by the door of the flat and I took a last look around. In an hour the charwoman would arrive and in the evening the two barristers with whom I shared the flat would return from their chambers; by then I should be across the Channel, on my way to Spain and the Civil War.

As I stood at my bedroom window, looking down on the puddles in King's Bench Walk, a green sports car with a long bonnet turned the corner by the library and stopped immediately beneath me. The door opened and the lanky figure of Daughleigh Hills stepped on to the pavement, making signs for me to hurry down. A year younger than myself and one of my closest friends at Cambridge, he had suggested, on hearing of my plans, that he should drive me in his new Aston Martin to the boat at Newhaven, where I would say good-bye to my mother and father. I turned from the window, took leave of my Number 2, Paper Buildings, and carried my luggage down to the waiting car.

It had taken me almost a month to make my final decision to go to this war and abandon, at least temporarily, my efforts to become a barrister. Even then I had no idea how to carry out my decision. I knew no Spanish, I had never been to Spain and I did not know anyone on the Nationalist side. Of course, if I had been willing to join the International Brigade and fight for the Republicans it would have been simple; in every country there were organizations, ably directed by the various Communist parties, for that very purpose. But the Nationalists were making no effort to recruit in England.

Luckily, at this point I received an invitation through a friend to see the Marqués del Moral, who occupied a position in the Nationalist Agency in London. Del Moral, an Englishman by birth who had distinguished himself as a young man in South Africa, received me with some reserve:

'So you want to go to Spain. Why?'

'To fight, sir.'

'Good.' He relaxed a little of his severity.

'Well now, I can give you a letter to a friend of mine in Biarritz, the Conde de los Andes. He runs a courier service across the frontier and I dare say he'd send you as far as Burgos. Better not let him know you're going to fight, though. With all this talk of Non-Intervention the French authorities wouldn't be so tolerant of his couriers if they thought he was passing through volunteers for our side—though they don't seem to mind how many go through to the Reds.' He smiled rather sourly. 'Can you get a journalist's cover? I suggest a chit from some editor saying you are authorized to send him articles and news.'

'I think I can manage that. But what do I do when I get to Burgos?'

'I'm afraid I can't help you there; you'll have to look after yourself. But it shouldn't be difficult. After all, it is the G.H.Q.'

Very soon afterwards I was in Northcliffe House, asking to see my friend, Collin Brooks, then editor of the Sunday Dispatch. At that time Lord Rothermere's newspapers were supporting the Nationalists. An accessible and genial person, Brooks listened attentively while I told him of my project and of my conversation with del Moral.

'Boy,' he said, beaming at me through the thick lenses of his glasses, 'there's anything from fifty to five hundred pounds in this! Good luck to you and send us anything you can.'

When I left his office I carried a piece of paper, signed by him, which read, as far as I can remember:

'To Whom It May Concern. Mr. Peter Kemp is authorized to collect news and transmit articles for the Sunday Dispatch from the Spanish Fronts of War.'

We were silent as the car splashed through the suburbs. I was going over in my mind the events of the past fortnight; everything seemed to have happened so quickly since I had made my decision and written, in some trepidation, to tell my father. A retired Chief Justice of the Bombay High Court, he disapproved, I knew, of many aspects of my life at Cambridge and in London—he had visions of my rowing in the University boat and getting a double First in Classics and Law, and he was justly disappointed when I gave up rowing after my first year and barely achieved an honours degree at the end of my third.

I was surprised, therefore, by his generous reaction to my letter. He came to see me in London, announced that he had told his Bank to open a monthly credit for me in Burgos, gave me a great deal of sound advice and finally took me on a tour of the Army and Navy Stores—'To see you get the right equipment for this sort of thing.' I have no idea what equipment we bought, but I remember a bulky 'medicine chest' which seemed to contain chiefly iodine, quinine and cascara and which I lost within a month of my arrival in Spain. I also bought Hugo's *Spanish in Three Months Without a Master*. I rejected my father's offer of his .275 sporting Männlicher carbine as being likely to cause trouble with Customs.

The ensuing days I spent in a state of joyful excitement and in the preparations for my journey. One incident only remains in my memory. I was having tea with a friend in her house; we had often discussed the idea of my going to Spain and now, with my departure imminent, I suppose I had acquired a certain glamour in her eyes. After a while her father came into the room, an old professional soldier, now retired, with a distinguished record in the Great War and several lesser wars before it.

'Daddy!' she shouted, for he had become very deaf, 'Peter Kemp is going off to Spain!'

'Spain!' the old gentleman roared back, 'Spain! What's he want to go to Spain for?'

'He's going to fight in the war, Daddy.'

'What! What!' The Colonel turned on me. 'You're going to Spain to fight?'

'Yes, sir.'

'You damned young fool! You know what fighting means? It's hell! You bloody young idiot! Ever read Napier's Peninsular War?'—I hadn't—'You damned well read it. Icicles hanging from their noses. Icicles, frost-bite, hunger! It's hell, I tell you. You make me sick.'

*   *   *

We passed through East Grinstead and left the traffic behind. The wind tore across the bonnet in great gusts from the southwest, slapping viciously at the side curtains, while the rain beat in a fierce deluge on the wind-screen. Exhilarated by the roar of the engine and by our need for haste, Hills urged the car on through the Sussex countryside towards the coast. The vibration of the wheel in his hands, the hiss of the tyres on the wet tarmac and the splash of mud against the wings—all are still vivid in my memory. More vivid still is a wild moment when he took a sharp curve at close on eighty, skidded sideways towards a telegraph pole and a ditch and straightened out, apparently without effort, on the rim of disaster. I was nervous on corners since the night, a few months previously and shortly before my Tripos examinations, when I had failed to take a double bend at Melbourne, just outside Cambridge, and run a 'Speed Six' Bentley through a wire fence and a concrete wall into a telegraph pole, damaging myself only slightly but dislocating the telegraph and telephonic communications between London and Cambridge for twenty-four hours. 'Dear Peter,' began the typewritten letter from my father a week later, 'this deplorable termination of your career at Cambridge. . . . Sometimes' he concluded, 'I think that God must have made you for a bet.'

'Peter,' said Hills suddenly, 'what the devil is this really in aid of?'

'Meaning what?'

'Well, all I know at the moment is that you're going to Spain, that you're going there to fight and that you're going to fight against the Government or the Reds or whatever you like to call them. Just why are you going? And why particularly do you choose to fight for the Insurgents? Or don't you really mind which side you fight for?'

'Certainly,' I answered tartly, 'I mind very much which side I fight for. Nothing in the world would induce me to join the other side. Moreover,' I added pompously, 'you know the interest I took in politics at Cambridge.'

'Yes, I remember you were too conservative for the Conservative Association, so you formed a splinter union of your own.' He grinned. 'I don't care about politics myself—we've had too many politicians in the family. Still, if you hold strong political views I dare say it's quite a good idea to go and fight for them.'

'My reasons aren't entirely political—in fact, I think the political motive is about the least important, except that it determined what side I chose. You see, quite frankly this war has broken out at a particularly opportune moment for me. I've finished my time at Cambridge and taken my degree, but I haven't yet started on a career, and I have still some months to play with before I commit myself irrevocably to a job that will tie me down for the rest of my life. This war isn't likely to last more than six months; it's a splendid chance for me to go out on my own, to see a strange country and get to know its people and language, also to learn something about modern warfare— God knows that's likely to be useful enough! Above all, it's a chance to learn to look after myself in difficulty and danger. Up till now I've never really had to do anything for myself. I mean I've always known where my next meal was coming from and that, provided I look both ways before crossing the street, I'm not likely to be in any danger.

'But there's another thing, just as important: If you've read the news reports published at the beginning of this war, before the imposition of censorship, you'll know that there were appalling scenes of mob violence throughout Government territory, wherever the Reds took control. Priests and nuns were shot simply because they were priests or nuns, ordinary people murdered just because they had a little money or property. It is to fight against that sort of thing that I am going to Spain.'

I stopped for breath after this recital. Reviewing them now, I find my words embarrassingly naïve; perhaps I really was trying to justify my decision to myself, to convince myself for the last time that it was the right one. On that stormy November morning I did not know what most of us have learned since, that you do not practice to go to war for only a few months, and that it is much easier to get into a war than to get out of it.

'At least,' I finished, 'the experience is bound to be useful, and anyway I've nothing to lose.'

We must have done that drive in almost record time, but when we reached Newhaven we found that we had hurried for nothing. Owing to the gale the day service had been cancelled, and I had to wait until evening for a boat.

I found my mother and father by the jetty. They had driven from Cooden to see me off, but wisely decided to say good-bye then and there, rather than wait around the whole day. We all hated prolonged leave-takings—the forced cheerfulness, the trivial chatter and embarrassed silences with the tension mounting hour by hour. I realized that what for me was a gay adventure meant for them the start of a long period of separation and anxiety. I was deeply moved by the way they were taking everything, by my mother's cheerful and uncomplaining courage and my father's generous acceptance of a plan which must have appeared to him to be crazy. When we had said a spirited farewell, standing beside their car on the front and raising our voices above the wind and sea, I started to walk towards the hotel where I had left Hills. I turned once to look back at them. I still remember my father's broad figure in a dripping mackintosh and old fisherman's hat, standing by the open door of the car, his stern, sad face gazing intently after me. I never saw him again.

To pass the time Hills suggested a visit to friends of ours, David and Anthony Holland, who lived nearby at Balcombe. Although impatient to start my journey, I lingered gratefully by the fire in the bright, comfortable drawing-room, savouring—as I then felt for the last time—the cozy warmth of an English country house and the cheery hospitality of my friends. Truly one is never so drawn to England and things English as at moments of departure and return.

As we were leaving, their father said to me: 'Here, I would like to give you this.' He took something from his pocket. It was a small black idol about four inches long, roughly carved in wood and worn smooth and shiny with age and frequent handling. The face had an expression of unusual benevolence and charm.

'I bought him in the Congo a few years ago. He's a lucky fellow. Keep him in your pocket.'

Thereafter I always kept him in my pocket wherever I went, until the day, two and a half years later, when I was carried to the hospital on a stretcher, barely conscious and at the gate of death. In the following days of pain and oblivion he somehow disappeared.

*   *   *

The Conde de los Andes, seated at a heavy mahogany desk in his study, was brief and businesslike.

'I will apply for your salvoconducto today. It will be waiting for you at the Spanish frontier the day after tomorrow. Be here then at half past ten in the morning and one of my cars will run you to Burgos.'

I walked out into the sunshine and strolled along the cliffs, delighting in the fresh breeze on my face and the sight of the long green waves rolling in from the Atlantic and bursting in foam on the black rocks below me. I pranced with joy as I reveled in the thought of my new freedom and the adventures that lay before me.

In this mood of elation I took the bus to Bayonne that afternoon after an excellent lunch and, certainly, rather too much wine with it. After wandering round the town and the port I went into the cathedral and there, sitting in the cool, dark silence, I began to reflect on the events in Spain which had led to the explosion of civil war.

My thoughts raced across the pages of recent Spanish history as I sat with my head in my hands. Slowly a drowsiness overcame me, induced by my tiredness and the wine I had drunk at lunch. When I awoke it was night and the cathedral was deserted and in darkness, except for a few faint lights by the alter. I made my way to the door where I had entered. It was locked. So, too, were the other doors I tried. I called out, softly at first as I felt the impropriety of raising my voice in a cathedral, but louder afterwards until in the end I threw away all restraint and shouted at the top of my voice. After a time—it seemed like ages to me—I heard a shuffling and muttering and a cross little figure appeared, shaking a large bunch of keys. My French is mediocre in the best of circumstances and, feeling the fool I did, I was more tonguetied than usual. I stammered, '*Je me suis endormi*' several times, grinning ingratiatingly, pressed some money into the sacristan's hand and fled.

Two days later at half past ten on a bright, clear morning I rang the bell at the Conde de los Andes's villa. Under a brown teddy bear overcoat I wore riding breeches, puttees and ammunition boots, relics of my service at the Cambridge University Officers Training Corps. I carried in my pocket my O.T.C. Certificates A and B, which I hoped might give me some prestige in the eyes of the Spanish military authorities. At half past eleven a large black touring-car drew up, driven by a well-dressed man who introduced himself to me in perfect English as the courier, Señor Pascual Vicuña. When the car had been loaded with my suitcase and a number of brief-cases, parcels and newspapers I climbed in beside him and we drove away.

We followed the coast road south to St. Jean-de-Luz and Hendaye. I sat back happily, admiring the dappled pattern of fields and woods on our left, which rolled away to the dark line of the Pyrenees that stretched eastwards in a broken contour ahead of us.

As we drove, Vicuña with great tact and courtesy questioned me on my reasons for traveling to Spain; but I had resolved to keep strictly to my journalist's cover until we were over the frontier. He told me that he often went to London, where he preferred to stay at the Dorchester, although on his last visit he stayed at that new block of flats in Piccadilly, Anthenæum Court—did I know it? I seemed to remember that he had a son and two daughters at school in England.

He was a great admirer of the English and their way of life. It was a pity that, at the present, there was so little understanding in England of the Nationalist cause—there was so much Red propaganda about. He was convinced that if the British Government really understood the issues being fought out in Spain they wouldn't hesitate to send help to the Nationalists. After all, it was really England's battle that was being fought almost as much as Spain's; because if the Reds were to win—of course this was unthinkable, but if they were to win—Communism would triumph in Spain, then France would go Communist too, then where would England be? The Reds had perpetrated appalling crimes in Spain, as I should soon find out for myself.

This theme, most of which accorded with my own views, was one which I was to hear repeated constantly and with rising vehemence by all kinds and classes of Spaniards during the next two and a half years.

While we waited at Hendaye for the French authorities to stamp our passports and examine the luggage I stood at the barrier of the International Bridge, gazing across the River Bidassoa to the green hills on the Spanish side. Two months earlier they had been the scene of some of the bitterest fighting of the year, when General Mola's Carlists, after a long and bloody assault, had stormed the dominating fort of San Marcial and secured the key town of Irun and the western gateway of the Pyrenees. A few of the defending forces—Basque Republicans and Asturian miners—escaped westwards to San Sebastian, whence they were evicted nine days later. The remainder, after burning Irun, crossed over into France to be disarmed and interned in squalor and destitution until the outbreak of the Second World War. The International Brigade was their only way out of Spain, apart from swimming the Bidassoa, and harrowing accounts were received in London of the frightened mass of refugees desperately making their way along it to safety—which I am told inspired some witty if heartless young secretary at the Foreign Office to comment: 'That's what comes of putting all your Basques in one exit.'

I could see the square fort on a hill to my left, with the red and gold colors of Nationalist Spain floating from its walls. The Nationalists had paid for their victory with some of their best blood, the gallant and devoted Carlists from Navarre and Álava who had rallied to a man to Mola's colours on the outbreak of war. Boys of fifteen and old men of seventy alike rose to defend la Fé and la Tradición, following in the steps of their ancestors who had fought under Zumalacarregui[1] in the last century. They, with no military training whatever, were taught how to load and fire a rifle as they were brought by the lorry to the front. There they were shot down in hundreds on the almost impregnable slopes around San Marcial.

The French officials, after some five minutes' delay and no awkward questions, allowed us to proceed; we passed under the barrier and across the International Bridge, alongside the railway where the trains no longer ran.

Just beyond the Spanish barrier we halted; Vicuña went into the control hut to report and to collect my salvoconducto while I studied the crowd of

---

[1] Famous Carlist commander in the First Carlist War.

10

civilians and officials gathered around. There were the Civil Guard (*Guardia Civil*) in green uniforms, yellow belts and cross-straps and shiny black tricorn hats; *Carabineros*, or frontier guards, in lighter green and flat peaked caps; soldiers with the tasseled forage caps and soiled, ill-fitting khaki uniforms that characterized the Nationalist Army of the Peninsula in the Civil War, many of them loafing about with their round mess-tins in their hands and hunks of bread in their mouths; civilian officials with brassards and the air of busy authority common to minor functionaries in all countries. With some complacency I reflected that my last major obstacle was passed; now I was in Spain. It would not be long before I, too, should be wearing a uniform. The great adventure had begun, In my mind I could already hear the sound of gunfire and the bullets whistling past.

These ingenuous thoughts were shattered by the reappearance of a bewildered Vicuña with the news that my salvoconducto had not arrived. I had appalling visions of being returned ignominiously to France to wait until it should turn up and another courier be available to take me. However, after a quarter of an hour of shoulder-shrugging, gesticulation and excited chatter between Vicuña and the officer in charge, I was given another pass, allowing me to go as far as Burgos.

We drove through the gutted and blackened ruins of Irun and along the road to San Sebastian. We drew up at the Hotel Continental shortly after two, in excellent time for a drink before lunch according to Spanish hours. It took me a little time to accustom myself to the Spanish habit of lunching past two and dining at half past ten or later; but once I became used to them I grew to prefer these hours to the English: indication, perhaps, of a slothful nature.

After lunch with Vicuña's mother, a sweet, white-haired old lady with whom I was unable to converse because of her ignorance of English and mine of Spanish, we continued our journey towards Vitoria and Burgos. Unlike Irun, San Sebastian had suffered no damage from the war, the only signs of which, apart from the uniforms in the streets, were slogans plastered on houses and walls: the 'ALISTAOS A LA FALANGE' and 'ARRIBA ESPAÑA' of the Fascists and the Carlist 'DIOS PATRIA Y REY', the last on a red and yellow background, the former on red and black. The red and yellow was the flag of Spain under the monarchy, but the Republic had changed it to red, yellow, and purple. Red and black were the colours of the Falange, but also those of the F.A.I., or Anarchists, on the Republican side— which sometimes caused confusion in battle, since flags were carried in action by both sides. These exhortations were interspersed with others of a more practical kind: 'IPIDAN SIEMPRE DOMECQ! VINOS Y COÑAC DOMECQ' ('Always order Domecq's wines and brandy').

Our roads led inland, rising gently at first among broken, wooden hills with white, red-roofed homesteads dotted on the sides, then climbing and twisting steeply through deep gorges amid thickly forested mountains, until at length, shortly before Vitoria, we were on the Meseta, the flat plateau of central Spain. At Tolosa, Villafranca and Vitoria we were stopped by controls and made to show our passes; at Vitoria control was manned by young Requetés of fifteen or sixteen years old, very self-important but very smart in their red berets and khaki uniforms.

During the journey I told Vicuña of my true purpose in coming to Spain. His eyes lit up and he exclaimed: 'You will be very welcome with us, and I am sure we can arrange for you to join a fighting unit. In any case, I will introduce you to some friends of mine on the General Staff when we get to Burgos.'

We reached Burgos at seven and parked outside the Hotel Norte y Londres. The hotel was full, but I found a room in a house nearby kept by two women; like James Pigg's cupboard it smelt strongly of cheese, but was clean and comfortable. Outside, the air was bitter, a breath of ice that went right through my overcoat and clothes, and I was glad to return to the warmth of the hotel.

I stood in the lounge waiting for Vicuña to join me and watching the chattering crowd pass through the hall. There were women of all ages, most of them wearing some kind of medallion or badge attached to their dress by a red and yellow ribbon, and men in smart uniforms, or in civilian clothes with red Requeté berets or blue Falange forage caps. A tall, broad-shouldered, fair-complexioned man of about thirty-five came up and introduced himself.

'May I join you? I can see you're English. My name is Rupert Bellville. Have a drink?'

Bellville was already well-known in England as an expert on Spain, an aficionado of bullfights and a bold amateur pilot, flying his own aircraft. Finding himself in the south of Spain at the outbreak of the Civil War, he had enlisted in a Falange unit and taken part in operations at Andalusia. Horrified and disgusted by the frequent spectacles of atrocities committed by some of the anarchists and communists in the villages and countryside of that backward region, he was little less shocked when required himself to take part in firing squads to execute the criminals; eventually he left his unit. What had especially sickened him, apart from a natural revulsion at the shooting of prisoners, was that the victims went on twitching and writhing for some minutes after death and he could never believe that they were really dead. Certainly the execution of prisoners was one of the ugliest aspects of the Civil War, and both sides were guilty of it in the early months. There were two main reasons for this: first, the belief, firmly held by each side, that the others were traitors to their country and enemies of humanity who fully deserved death; secondly, the fear of each side that unless they exterminated their adversaries these would rise again and destroy them. But it is a fact, observed by me personally, that as the war developed the Nationalists tended more and more to spare their prisoners, except those of the International Brigades: so that when, in 1938, the Non-Intervention Commission began to arrange exchanges of prisoners of war, they found large numbers of Republicans held by the Nationalists, but scarcely any Nationalist soldiers in Republican prison camps.[1]

Bellville had attended the funeral of Calvo Sotelo, the Monarchist statesman whose murder by Republican police was the signal for the outbreak of the Civil War five days later. There were about eight thousand people present; the Government had forbidden the Fascist salute, but on this occasion the feeling was so intense that, although only a few were Falangists, nearly everyone was making their salute. Shock Police (*Guardias de Asalto*) posted in side streets on motor cycles, shot up everyone they saw saluting. Bellville estimated that there must have been several hundred casualties.

'Now I have my aeroplane here,' he said, 'but I can't get permission to move nearer the front. There's nothing at all in this place except wives and sweethearts sitting around on their bottoms and discussing the latest rumours.'

At that moment we were joined by a dark-haired woman of about thirty-five, with a quiet, grave manner, whom Bellville introduced to us as the Duquesa de Lécera. She greeted me with a smile of great charm: 'And what do you want to do in Spain?'

'I want to fight,' I answered, feeling rather embarrassed.

She looked me up and down coolly: 'That is very nice of you. I don't think you will find it difficult.' She glided away.

Vicuña arrived and Bellville left us. I did not see him again for some time, but one day in the following September he sprang into prominence in the world's news. the Nationalists had launched their final assault on Santander, whose fall was expected hourly. Bellville had his aeroplane in San Sebastian when a report came through that the town had surrendered. Resolved to be the first to welcome the victorious army, he and a Spanish friend of a similar temperament, Ricardo González, of the famous sherry family, loaded his aircraft with crates of sherry and brandy, took off from San Sebastian and soon afterwards landed on the airfield at Santander. A swarm of blue-clad soldiers surrounded the aircraft and Bellville and González climbed out with glad shouts of 'Viva Franco!' and 'Arriba España!' when they realized with astonishment and dismay that these were Republican militiamen and that Santander was still in enemy hands. They were brusquely marched to prison, transferred to Gijón, in Asturias, just before the fall of Santander and for a week or two were in grave danger of summary execution. Fortunately González was able to pass as an Englishman, having been educated in England; he was released in order to arrange their exchange for two

---

[1] Statement by Mr. Hemming of the Non-Intervention Commission to the author.

Republican prisoners held by the Nationalists. Meanwhile, Bellville stayed in prison, encouraged from time to time by his captors with stories of what was going to happen him should González fail to organize the exchange satisfactorily. In the end the Nationalists handed over two senior officers of the Republican army and he was released.

Vicuña was accompanied by a major and three captains from the Comandancia Militar, one of whom spoke English. He was Captain the Conde de Elda, and he wore, in addition to field boots and spurs, the broad blue and gold sash of the General Staff. After some curious and powerful cocktails of brandy and vermouth we dined in a small, crowded restaurant near the hotel, on river trout and the local vin rosé. Elda said:

'The military situation of the Reds is very precarious. Any day now Madrid will be in our hands.'

It was nearly two and a half years before his words came true.

CHAPTER TWO

After the initial failure of the *Movimiento*, as the Nationalists termed their rising, in large areas of the Peninsula and in the fleet, the Nationalists soon improved their position by a rapid succession of victories and, when I arrived in Spain, were at the gates of Madrid.

Indeed, when I left England I wondered whether I should be in time to see any action before the war was over.

Ever since the elections of February 1936, which established the Popular Front Government, both the extreme Right, led by the Army, and the extreme Left political parties had been preparing to seize power by force.[1] The tension increased through the spring and early summer months. Some idea of what this meant is shown in the words of Don Salvador de Madariaga, a Liberal authority by no means well disposed to the Nationalist cause:[2]

'. . . One hundred and sixty churches totally destroyed and two hundred and fifty-one set on fire or otherwise attacked;[3] two hundred and sixty-nine persons murdered and twelve hundred and eighty-seven injured; sixty-nine political premises destroyed; one hundred and thirteen general strikes and two hundred and twenty-eight partial strikes, as well as many more other cases of other forms of violence.'

On June 16th, in the Cortes, the Government was indicted for its leniency towards this crime and violence by Señor Gil Robles, leader of the Right-wing Acción Católica, and by Señor Calvo Sotelo, leader of the monarchist Renovación Española; as Calvo Sotelo sat down after speaking the Communist Dolores Ibarruri, 'La Pasionaria', shouted: 'That is your last speech!'

At noon on July 12th a certain Lieutenant Castillo of the Guardia de Asalto[4] was murdered in the street, apparently by three Fascists. In the early hours of the following morning, July 13th, Calvo Sotelo was taken from his bed by uniformed Guardias de Asalto and murdered. The Government took no action except to imprison the ninety men of Lieutenant Castillo's company.

---

[1] Madariaga, *Spain*, p. 369.

[2] *Spain*, p. 351.

[3] Eye-witnesses have told me how the looters in Andalusia, at least, would in all simplicity uncover themselves before entering the church, genuflect before the alter, and only replace their hats after leaving the building pillaged and in flames.

[4] 'Shock Police', a well armed, well trained force organized by the Popular Front Government as a possible counter to the old Guardia Civil, of whose loyalty to the government was doubtful.

In the afternoon of July 17th the garrison of Melilla in Spanish Morocco revolted. They were followed immediately by the entire Army of Morocco, consisting chiefly of the Spanish Foreign Legion and the Regulares or Moorish troops.

The same afternoon General Franco arrived in Morocco by air from the Canary Islands, where he had been Governor and Commander-in-Chief. He put himself at the head of the rebels. The details of his flight had been arranged in London by a certain Major Hugh Pollard, one of those romantic Englishmen who specialize in other countries' revolutions. Pollard had taken an active part in the escape of Porfirio Diaz from Mexico in 1911, and in the revolution in Morocco of 1913 which deposed the Sultan Abdul Aziz and placed Mulay Hafid on the throne. Now on this particular operation he took an English pilot named Beeb and his own daughter, Diana, aged eighteen.

The Nationalists started with the great advantage that the most important of the fighting Services, the Army, was on their side.

Its spearhead was the Army of Morocco, of which a brief description might be helpful. The Foreign Legion, or Tercio, was founded in the early 1920s by General Millán Astray with the help of some of the ablest officers of the Spanish Army, including General (then Major) Franco. Its inspiration derived from two sources: historically and romantically from the tercios of the Duke of Alba in the 16th century, the core of the Spanish infantry in the days when 'Spanish discipline' was a byword in Europe;[1] militarily and practically from the French Foreign Legion, whose methods were studied first hand by Millán Astray and his assistants. But the Spanish Foreign Legion differed in one important respect from the French: it was composed almost entirely of Spaniards, although prior to the Civil War it was the only unit of the Spanish Army in which foreigners could enlist. Service was for a minimum of five years and was confined to Spanish possessions overseas. During the Civil War its strength increased from six banderas, or battalions, to twenty; even then about ninety per cent of the rank-and-file and nearly all of the officers were Spaniards, the remainder being Portuguese, with a few French and some Germans and White Russians.

The Regulares were Moorish troops, recruited by the Spanish Government and officered by Spaniards; although mercenaries they could show great courage and devotion. They were skilful and dangerous fighters, especially in the attack. There were also the Mehala, the troops of the Jalifa,

---

[1] A Tercio in the sixteenth century was a Regiment of Spanish infantry. The Spanish Foreign Legion is also called *El Tercio*, 'The Regiment', in the same way as in the British Army the Household Calvary and Foot Guards are known as 'The Brigade'. But the Requetés in the Civil War also organized their fighting units into *tercios*, each approximately of battalion strength.

the Viceroy in Spanish Morocco of the Sultan. They had a leavening of Spanish officers and were useful in skirmishing and mountain warfare.

Señor Madariaga states that, with few exceptions, every Army officer who was free to do so joined the Rebels. There were, however, exceptions; some of them, among the senior ranks, altered vitally the course of the war. Moreover, in the Peninsular barracks at the time there were only cadres of the regiments because the conscripts had already been dismissed. The officers of the Air Force were about equally divided in their sympathies; but, because most of the aircraft were in territory that remained in Republican hands, the Republicans had control of the air, which they retained until early in 1937. Fortunately for the Nationalists the Spanish Airforce was not strong enough to make this a decisive factor.[1]

Much more serious for them was the failure of their rising in the fleet. The Navy would have gone over to the Nationalists in its entirety but for the Communist cells which had been organized in many ships. In those ships the Communists, with their flair and training for leadership, persuaded the seamen to murder their officers and throw them into the sea. The Nationalists were left with the old battleship España, the cruiser Almirante Cervera; two new cruisers Baleares and Canarias, which were still under construction; the old cruiser República; the destroyer Velasco, and four gunboats. The difficulty was that all these ships were in El Ferrol in the north-west, except República and the gunboats, whereas the Republican fleet was based on Cartagena, able to command the vital Straits of Gibraltar and prevent the transport to Spain of the Army of Morocco. The Republicans had the old battleship Jamie Primero; the cruisers Libertad, Miguel Cervantes and Méndez Nuñez; sixteen destroyers, and twelve submarines. Their difficulty was that the crews, having murdered their officers, were unable to sail or fight the ships effectively until, later on, they were trained and officered by Russians.

On land both sides depended largely on volunteer 'paramilitary' organizations. With the Nationalists there were the traditional Requetés, or Carlists, and the Fascist Falange, the later founded by José Antonio Primo de Rivera, a son of the famous Dictator. It is worth nothing that the Falangists numbered less than five thousand in all Spain at the beginning of the war and were then of very little importance; their numbers were swelled by volunteers after July 18th, and they played an important part in the Nationalist campaign in Andalusia in the early days. Later, of course, they achieved overwhelming political power; but this was certainly not due to their fighting efficiency,

---

[1] But Toledo, which had declared for the Nationalists, was reduced (except for the Alcázar) in the first week, largely by Republican air attacks: the first instance in the war of the bombing of an open town.

which was regarded almost with derision by the various units of the Army and by the Requetés.

The Requeté movement drew its main strength from the Basque provinces, especially from Navarre, although its name originates in Catalonia. It was a product of the nineteenth century. Nominally the first Carlist War (1833-39) was fought on the issue whether King Fernando VII should be succeeded by his daughter Isabella, or by his brother, the Infante Don Carlos. Spanish law permitted women to succeed to the throne; Salic law, imported by the Bourbon Dynasty in the early eighteenth century, excluded them. Thus the Carlists, while claiming to uphold Spanish tradition, were ignoring it in this vital matter; despite this inconsistency, they believed sincerely, even fanatically, in their ideal, for which they gladly gave their lives. In reality, the war was a struggle between the Liberales, supporters of Isabella, who wished to centralize authority, reduce local rights and destroy the political power of the Church, and the Carlists, whose ideals are embodied in the words of a famous song: 'Dios, fueros, patria y Rey' (God, our rights, our country and King). It was also a war between the large towns and the countryside; the latter, especially in the Basque provinces, Old Castile and Catalonia was strongly Carlist in sympathy. It was a cruel war, ending in victory for the Liberales and in the disastrous reign of Queen Isabella.

Nevertheless the Carlist movement remained alive, almost a faith in itself. In spite of another defeat in the Second Carlist War (1870-76) it persisted in the Basque provinces and in isolated pockets of Catalonia and Old Castile, and as a political faith it still exists today.[1]

After the 1936 elections and throughout the succeeding disorders the Requetés prepared for another war. In the towns and villages and among the wooded mountains of Navarre and Álava, in country house and farmstead, in cottage and hovel the red beret and ancient rifle of a father or grandfather hung above the hearth in memory of one or other of the Carlist wars. Obsolete as they were, the weapons were taken down and cleaned, ready for instant action. Within three weeks of the outbreak of war thirty thousand Requetés rallied to General Mola in Pamplona. The women enlisted as Margaritas, as nurses for all duties short of bearing arms. Only the very young and very old remained to do work in the countryside.

---

[1] This despite the fact that the Carlists have recognized Don Juan, son of King Alfonso XIII, as rightful King of Spain, thus aligning themselves with the legitimists.

Once again a Carlist song catches the spirit of those weeks:

Cálzame las alpargatas, dáme la boina, dáme el fusil,
Que voy a matar más Rojos que flores tiene el mes de Abril.[1]

Such was the shortage of troops that these had to be thrown into battle
at once, without training or discipline, without adequate arms or equipment,
against the fortresses around Irun and San Sebastian, and over the
Guadarrama passes of Somosierra and Alto de Leon, towards Madrid. It was
a glorious thing to die in defense of La Tradición and el ideal, and so they
died, holding their lives cheaply and taking no care to protect themselves
from the fire of the enemy. A Company in the attack was led by the captain
and the chaplain, one grasping his pistol, the other his missal; all in their
scarlet berets presenting a superb target. So perished in the first few months
of the war the finest flower of Spain.

Afterwards the Nationalist command, knowing the value of their courage
and enthusiasm, sent the Carlists some of the best officers in their army.

The Republican paramilitary organizations were provided by the various
workers' Unions. Of these the principal were the Anarchist F.A.I.
(Federación Anarquista Ibérica); the Anarcho-Syndicalist C.N.T.
(Confederación Nacional del Trabajo), and the Trotskyist P.O.U.M. (Partido
Obrero Unificación Marxista). After the Movimiento one of the first actions
of the Madrid Government was to throw open the State arsenals and
distribute arms to these 'Popular Militias'. Less wisely, they opened the
prisons. These, as Señor de Madariaga points out,[2] had been emptied months
earlier of their political prisoners by an amnesty of President Azaña, and so
could disgorge only common criminals. The latter were immediately enrolled
in the various militias, and were responsible for much of the violence and
horror that disgraced Republican Spain in the early months of the war.

Women, too, enlisted in the militias and fought beside their menfolk,
often with even greater courage and resolution. They were also employed as
jailers to guard female political prisoners, several of whom told me that they
suffered much worse treatment from the *milicianos* than from the men.

Of the police forces the Civil Guard were nearly all on the Nationalist
side, although in a few places, notably Barcelona, their sense of loyalty to an
established Government proved stronger than their natural antipathy to mob
rule. The Shock Police and Carabineros, on the other hand, joined the
Republicans, whom they provided with a much needed nucleus of officers
and N.C.Os.

---

[1] 'Put on my shoes for me, give me my beret and my rifle, and I'm going to kill
more Reds than there are flowers in April.'

[2] *Spain*, p. 378.

On July 18th the Prime Minister of the Republic, Señor Casares Quiroga, resigned. President Azaña replaced him shortly afterwards with Señor Giral and a Ministry of his own friends.

But this Government, having armed the Unions, found itself at their mercy. The various militias did as they pleased, terrorizing the population. On September 4th, 1936, Señor Largo Caballero, the militant extreme Left Socialist, became Prime Minister. His Foreign Secretary was Señor Alvarez del Vayo, his Finance Minister Dr. Negrín—both of them loyal agents of Moscow.

The leader of the Nationalist rising was to have been General Sanjurjo. He was killed in an air crash on July 20th, taking off from Lisbon to fly to Spain. A Governing Junta was established in Burgos under General Cabanellas, consisting of himself, Generals Franco, Mola, Queipo de Llano and Varela, with two other senior officers. In the early days of the war 'La República honrada' was a favourite slogan of the Army, whose leaders maintained that they were in revolt, not against the Republic itself, but against the President and Government in Madrid, who were leading the country towards anarchy and communism.

Of the Army officers I knew, either personally or by repute, scarcely any had Falangist sympathies; some were Monarchists, but the majority preferred to 'leave that sort of thing to the politicians and get on with winning the war'. This also summarized the attitude of the Requetés, whose political leadership in any case was inept. The Falangists, on the other hand, never lost sight of the main chance, and schemed throughout the war to infiltrate their people into key positions of government. General Mola insisted on flying the flag of the Republic until his Requeté allies obliged him to change it for the old monarchist colours. It was only after this event that he became a legend as a 'Requeté' General.[1]

Cabanellas, although the senior General, was no more than a figurehead; after the death of Sanjurjo the choice of a leader rested between Mola and Franco; although Mola seemed to have the better claim it was Franco who, for reasons still imperfectly known, was recognized as Generalissimo and 'Chief of Operations' of the Nationalist forces. That was on October 1st, 1936; he did not become 'Head of State' until six months later.

On July 19th, 1936, the day after the revolt in Morocco, the Movimiento exploded throughout the Peninsula. The result was neither the immediate

[1] H.R.H. The Infante Don Alfonso de Orléans-Borbón, a cousin of King Alfonso and a General in the Spanish Air Force, has told me that when he reported to Mola in Burgos at the beginning of August 1936, Mola refused to see him and sent him under escort to the French frontier; and that he did the same to Infante Don Juan a day or two earlier.

success the conspirators had expected nor the fiasco that the first Republican broadcasts proclaimed. General Cabanellas took over Zaragoza, General Mola rose in Pamplona with four hundred soldiers and General Queipo de Llano captured Seville with a hundred and eighty-five men and a prodigal use of bluff. The Basque provinces of Navarre, part of Álava, the whole of Old Castile and Léon, Galicia in the northwest, and the western region of Aragón went over to the Nationalists. But in Madrid the people's militias and Shock Police stormed the Montaña barracks and, after a bloody battle, overwhelmed the Nationalist garrison under General Fanjul. In Barcelona the Army Commander sided with the Republicans and, with the help of Civil Guards and Shock Police, suppressed the military rising, whose leaders, Generals Goded and Burriel, were captured and shot. The Republicans held all Catalonia, the eastern half of Aragón, and all of New Castile and the Mancha, the whole Mediterranean seaboard from the French frontier to Gibraltar, a large part of the province of Estremadura on the Portuguese frontier and all Andalusia, except Cadiz, Jerez, Seville, Cordova and a small pocket around Granada. In the Balearics, Majorca went over to the Nationalists; but Minorca, with the naval base of Mahón, remained in Republican hands. In the north the remaining Basque provinces of Guipúzcoa, Vizcaya and part of Álava joined the Republicans, together with Santander and Asturias; however, Oviedo, the capital of Asturias was held for the Nationalists by General Aranda, who withstood an intensive siege until he was relieved in October, 1937.

Thus, although the Movimiento had achieved considerable initial success, it had met with some serious reserves. The most important of these were the failures in Madrid and Barcelona and in the fleet, and the loss of Catalonia and the two Basque provinces of Guipúzcoa and Vizcaya with their heavy industries and raw materials. Apart from Andalusia, where the Anarchist tradition was strong among the peasantry, it is reasonable to say that the agricultural districts were for the Nationalists, the cities and industrial areas were for the Republicans. Thus, Catalonia was lost to the Nationalists. The Basque provinces would not have gone over to the Republicans but for the attitude of the Basque Separatists. These, being deeply religious Catholics, had no sympathy with the Communist miners of Asturias, nor with the anti-clerical Unions of Santander, nor even with the industrial workers of their own provinces. But, in the belief that they could secure a more complete autonomy from the Madrid Government than from the Nationalists, they allied themselves with the former and declared and independent Basque Republic under the Presidency of Señor Aguirre. At the end of December, 1936, a young Navarrese officer with whom I was serving said: 'For me the saddest thing about this war is that not only is Spaniard fighting Spaniard, but Basque is fighting Basque.'

The loss of the fleet, and with it the command of the Straits of Gibraltar, might have proved fatal for the Nationalists but for the prompt action of General Franco in Morocco. Using six Junkers 52 transport aircraft, borrowed for him from the Germans by a certain Major Arrauz of the Spanish Air Force,[1] he immediately ferried troops across the Straits to Spain, took Algeciras and La Linea and pushed a column, under Captain Castejón of the Foreign Legion, up to Seville to secure General Queipo de Llano's hold on the city. By the end of July, after a naval action in the Straits in which the Nationalist gunboat, Dato, escorting a convoy of troops from Morocco, beat off a strong Republican squadron, the control of these waters had passed to the Nationalists; thereafter their communications between Morocco and the Peninsula were secure.

Castejón wasted no time in Seville, but sent flying columns of the Tercio and Regulares, aided by Falange auxiliaries, through Andalusia; within a very short time he had occupied the whole province as far as Málaga in the east and the Portuguese border in the west. This included the valuable mines of Rio Tinto near Huelva, and Peñarroya near Cordova. With reinforcements arriving by sea and air from Morocco Franco's forces advanced northwards to Mérida, which they captured on August 9th, and Badajoz, which fell to them on August 15th. These towns were taken by storm, with very heavy casualties on both sides. By the capture of Badajoz the Nationalists secured the whole Portuguese frontier; more important, their Southern army under Franco was able to join with Mola's forces in the north.

The latter, having secured the Guadarrama passes of Somosierra and Alto de León and held them against the sporadic attacks of the undisciplined *milicianos* from Madrid, turned to attack Irun and San Sebastian. Their object was close to the French frontier, isolating the Republican territories in the north, and secure for themselves the railway link with France. Tolosa, the capital of Guipúzcoa, fell on August 15th, Irun on September 5th, and San Sebastian eight days later. After these successes the northern front was stabilized, with most of Guipúzcoa and Álava in Nationalist hands, including the capitals of both provinces.[2]

After the capture of Mérida and Badajoz the Nationalists launched their attack up the Tagus valley against Madrid. At first it seemed as though nothing could stop it. Oropesa fell on August 29th, Talavera on 3rd September. The only opposition came from the *milicianos*, who fought with courage but without discipline or military training. They were, moreover, handicapped by the lack of any organized command; some units appointed their own commanding officers and took orders from them alone: in others

---

[1] My authority for this statement is H.R.H. the Infante Don Alfonso de Orléans-Borbón.

[2] Vitoria is the capital of *Álava*.

there were no officers, each man acting as he pleased. It was easy for the veterans of the Tercio and Regulares to outflank them, shoot up their rear communications and drive them back in disorder upon the next defended village.

On September 22nd the Nationalists reached Maqueda, where the road to Toledo branches southward from the main road to Madrid. In the Alcázar, or citadel, of Toledo a small Nationalist force was holding out, having withstood more than two months of unremitting siege. The defenders, who numbered about a thousand men—regular officers, Civil Guard, cadets from the Toledo Military Academy and volunteers—had won the admiration of the world by their heroic resistance against repeated attacks supported by artillery and air bombardment, by mines and by ferocious reprisals against their own families. Now they were on the point of collapse, their ammunition and food running out, their medical supplies long ago exhausted.

The victorious Nationalists at Maqueda were faced with the problem whether to continue their advance on Madrid, the main military objective, and allow the garrison of the Alcázar to be overwhelmed and massacred, or to divert their effort to the relief of Toledo. Considerations of prestige and military honour impelled them to the latter course. On September 29th the 5th Bandera of the Tercio and a tabor[1] of Regulares entered Toledo, fighting their way up the steep ascent from the Puerta Visagra to the Plaza de Zocodover. The siege of the Alcázar was over. Colonel Moscardó staggered from the ruins of his fortress to greet General Franco, saluted and delivered his report, in a phrase now famous throughout Spain: 'Sin Novedad en el Alcázar' ('Nothing to report in the Alcázar.').

From Lieutenant Noel FitzPatrick and Lieutenant William Nangle, two British officers serving with the 5th Bandera, I have learnt something of that frantic advance on Toledo and the final battle. It is not a pretty story. On the eve of their assault on the city the Nationalists found the bodies of two of their airmen, shot down the day before, who had fallen alive into the hands of the *milicianos*. They were mutilated beyond description. When the Nationalist troops attacked the next day they took no prisoners. FitzPatrick told me that the gutters by the streets leading down from the Alcázar to the city gates were running with blood.

The diversion to relieve Toledo cost the Nationalists one vital week. Had they pressed on directly from Maqueda to Madrid there is little doubt that they would have taken the city without difficulty. The Republican Government, after announcing over the radio that Madrid would be defended to the last, fled to Valencia on November 7th, accompanied by the Soviet Ambassador. But already foreign help had begun to arrive for the Republicans—French Potez aircraft, supplied by M. Pierre Cot and flown by

---

[1] Equal to a battalion.

officers of the French Air Force, batteries of French '75s' and Russian tanks mounting 37 millimetre guns. The Nationalist advance was slowed, but not halted. On the 7th of November their troops held the whole bend of Manzanares, and it is said that one tabor of Regulares penetrated as far as Puerta del Sola. The next day the entire attack was thrown back in confusion. The International Brigades, volunteers from all over Europe raised by the various Communist parties and trained in Southern France, had arrived; they were sent immediately into battle with all necessary support from aircraft, artillery and tanks. Within a few days they had expelled the Nationalists, whom they outnumbered heavily, across the Manzanares into the outer suburbs of Madrid. A prompt withdrawal saved the Nationalists from envelopment and annihilation; only in the University City were they able to maintain a precarious hold across the river in the capital itself—a hold which cost both sides innumerable casualties in the next two years.

During the succeeding weeks the Nationalists, as yet ignorant of the strength that opposed them, launched a series of futile attacks against the city. These cost them casualties they could hardly spare among their best troops, but gained them no appreciable advantage. In effect the front was already stabilized when I arrived in Burgos in the middle of November.

*   *   *

Thus began the second phase of the Civil War—the phase of foreign intervention. To meet the threat of the International Brigades and increased French assistance to the Republicans the Nationalists invoked the help of Italy and Germany. Both supplied arms and technicians: obsolescent tanks, aircraft, anti-aircraft and anti-tank artillery, together with skeleton crews whose task was to train Spaniards in the use of their weapons; they were gradually withdrawn as Spaniards became qualified to replace them. A very few squadrons of bombers, with their fighter escorts, were flown by Germans throughout the war. Occasionally the Germans would send some new weapon to Spain for testing, after which it was withdrawn.

The Italians supplied fighting troops, maintained at a constant strength of about two divisions, with all supporting arms, including tanks, artillery and aircraft. They also provided officers for two 'Mixed Divisions', in which the rank-and-file were Spaniards, the senior officers Italians; it was not a happy arrangement. In addition, they maintained a few squadrons of Savoias in the Balearics to bomb the Republicans' Mediterranean ports. The war material they supplied was chiefly aircraft, flown by Spaniards as soon as they were trained, and small arms, especially automatic weapons.

The Russians did for the Republicans roughly what the Germans did for the Nationalists—they supplied technicians and war material of all kinds. In return they exacted a far greater measure of control over Republican policy and strategy than the Germans were able to obtain from Franco; the price of Russian co-operation was Russian direction of the war and the complete domination by the Communist Party of all Republican political and military organizations.[1]

Thus, not for the last time, Russia showed her allies her interpretation of the word 'co-operation'.

---

[1] Dr. Isaac Deutscher (*Stalin*, pp. 422-5) states that Stalin ordered the purges of the Trotskyist P.O.U.M. and of the Anarcho-Syndicalists: 'He made their elimination from the Republic's administration a condition of the sale of Soviet munitions to the Government. He dispatched to Spain, together with military instructors, agents of his political police, experts at heresy-hunting and purging, who established their own reign of terror in the ranks of the Republicans . . . he put Antonov-Ovseenko, the hero of 1917 and the ex-Trotskyist, in charge of the purge in Catalonia, the stronghold of the "heretics" only to purge Antonov-Ovseenko himself after his return to Spain.'

CHAPTER THREE

In the course of our dinner party on the night of my arrival in Burgos I abandoned forever my journalist's cover and asked my friends if they could help me join the Nationalist Army. They explained that the only units in which a foreigner might enlist were the Foreign Legion and the Requeté and Falange militias. I was strongly advised not to join the Legion as a private soldier—advice which I was subsequently glad I took; the politics of the Falange were not attractive to me, but the ideals of the Requetés fired my imagination. As a result, I was provided next day with letters of introduction from Elda and his friends to the Carlist leaders, Falcode and Zamanillo, in Ávila, together with a pass from the Comandancia Militar and a reservation in one of its cars leaving Burgos in the afternoon.

Burgos, the birthplace of the Cid, seemed a propitious springboard for my adventure. After a visit to the magnificent thirteenth century cathedral I spent the morning wandering through the streets in the bright sunlight and crisp, clean air, wrapped in a naïve, romantic day-dream featuring myself as a modern Campeador. At this time the town was General Franco's headquarters, General Mola having moved south to Ávila; it was also Divisional Headquarters of the 6th Division. Apart from the variety of uniforms in the streets and the posters on the walls there was no evidence of warlike activity; for that, I was told, I must go south to Ávila, Talavera de la Reina and Toledo.

I left Burgos about half past three in the afternoon in an old saloon car with two officers. We followed the Valladolid road south-westwards along the valley of the Arlanzon. The sun setting in our faces flushed the bare brown plains with gold, lit the green of the tamarisks growing beside the river on our left and outlined in sharp, dark contour the plateau rising in the distance beyond. It was dark before we came to Valladolid, the ancient capital of the kings of Castile, where we made a brief halt. At the beginning of the Civil War this was the scene of a coup by the Nationalist General, Saliquet, in which one of my companions had taken part. Saliquet was a stout and elderly officer whose enormous moustache and benign expression, giving him the look of an amiable walrus, soon became a familiar and popular sight in Nationalist territory. In July of 1936 he was living on half-pay on a friends estate near Valladolid. Although the Falangists were strong in the town, the commander of the 7th Division, stationed there, was a Republican. On July 18th Saliquet put on his uniform, collected two or three officers of the garrison and went to see the Divisional Commander, whom he found in his office with his A.D.C.

'You are,' he informed him, 'placed under arrest and relieved of your command, which you will hand over to me immediately.'

The A.D.C. drew a pistol and shot one of Saliquet's companions. The other fired back, killing the A.D.C. The Divisional Commander surrendered. Saliquet and his followers took control of the troops and arrested the Civil Governor, another Republican, who had mobilized the Shock Police. The latter thereupon declared for the Nationalists.

A similar technique was adopted by General Quiepo de Llano to gain control of the troops during Seville. On many occasions during those early days it was the courage and initiative of individual commanders that turned the scale for the Nationalists. At the end of the war, when I was in Madrid, I heard the comment of an Englishman who had witnessed both the Russian and Spanish revolutions: 'If Franco's generals hadn't had more guts than the White Russian generals, Spain would now be Communist.'

It was half past nine when we arrived beneath the battlements of Ávila and drove through a gateway in the ancient walls into the narrow cobbled streets of the town.

We went to the *Comandancia*, where we found a crowd of officers and civilians loitering around the ante-rooms. Forcing a way through, my companions introduced me to the Duty officer, an amiable old major with glasses and a sallow face as creased as a prune. Falconde and Zamanillo, he explained, were not here, but at Toledo, which was now the base for the main assault on Madrid; he would give me a *salvoconducto* at once and my companions would arrange my transport south. Five minutes later I was out of the office, the pass in my hand and his bluff shout of '*Buena suerte!*' ringing in my ears. We called at the Press Bureau, where I found Señor Melgar, the Secretary-General of the Traditionalist party, who confirmed that I should find Falconde and Zamanillo at Toledo and gave me a letter to them. He explained that they were at present engaged in forming a new *tercio* of Requetés from volunteers in the Toledo area; it was to be named the *Tercio del Alcázar* and would be commanded by a regular officer who had taken part in the defence of the Alcázar.

With Melgar I met Harold Cardozo, an old friend of Collin Brooks and the *Daily Mail* correspondent in Nationalist Spain. Cardozo had fought with distinction in the First World War, after which he joined the staff of the *Continental Daily Mail*. Brisk, tough and highly intelligent he was a great war correspondent, in the tradition of Walter Harris, Bennett Burghleigh, Gwynne and other illustrious names of the Balkan and Moroccan wars; he was also one of the kindest-hearted men I have ever known. A good Catholic, he felt a romantic as well as a religious attachment to the Requetés and was once the subject of a question in the House of Commons on his habit of wearing their scarlet beret in Spain; but he never let his sympathies affect the objectivity of his reporting, or cloud his abnormally acute perception. He seemed interested if not impressed by my plans.

'You will find the fighting conducted more or less according to text-book principles. A copy of *Field Service Regulations* should be useful to you.'

As I was leaving he added, 'What about dining with us tonight? Hotel Inglés at nine-thirty. You'll find quite a crowd of us there.'

Ávila was some twenty miles from the front line. Although the town had so far escaped damage I found the atmosphere, if not exactly warlike, at least more serious than at Burgos. A blackout was in force; there had been some air-raids, although these were directed against the airfield and had caused no casualties in the town. The hotels were full but I found a room in a house on the cathedral square. I shared it with another Englishman, James Walford, a quiet, sardonic man, by profession an artist. Through his mother, who was Spanish, he was related to Sir Basil Zaharoff. He knew the country and the language well and was on his way to the front, with the idea of compiling a book of battle sketches.

At nine-thirty I went to find Cardozo at the Hotel Inglés. It was full of British, American and French correspondents, who were trying to cover the Madrid battle from this distant spot with, they told me, very little encouragement from the Nationalist authorities. The British and American journalists were a cheerful and hospitable crowd; one of my happiest memories is the unfailing help and kindness I received from every one of them at different times during my service in Spain. Their job was not made easy for them by the attitude of the military, which seemed to be that all foreign correspondents were spies who must be kept as far as possible from the scene of operations, who were only in the country on sufferance and who ought to be more than satisfied with whatever news the Army cared to issue in the official communiques. This was in marked contrast to the attitude of the Republicans, whose Press and Propaganda services were far superior to those of the Nationalists as their fighting was inferior and who took pains to give journalists and writers all the facilities they required. Although both sides imposed a rigid censorship on all dispatches going out of the country, the Nationalist made virtually no concessions to the Press, while the Republicans laid out enormous sums on propaganda abroad. These factors account in a large measure for the poor Press which the Nationalist received—and of which they ceaselessly complained—in England and the United States.

The dinner was excellent, the wine abundant and the conversation animated everywhere except at the head of the table, where sat the Spanish Press Conducting Officer. An elegant, middle-aged cavalryman with a handsome, dissolute face, he sat through the meal in gloomy silence. 'He sees to have some secret sorrow,' I commented to the American on my right. He laughed:

'Well, in a way I should say he has. You see, he used to live in Biarritz, where he had a very glamorous girl-friend—some titled Spaniard, I forget her name; I guess she used to put the horns on him quite a bit. Anyway, about three months ago, just after this war started, she gave him the bird—finally and for good. So he came to Spain to forget his broken heart in the hell and shellholes of Ávila.' After a pause he went on: 'What got me was our friend's description of their poignant parting scene. When he asked her, "Do they mean nothing to you, those nights of love we spent together?" all she said was, "Don't be ridiculous! Sleeping with you was just like sleeping with my brother!"'

Ávila is one of the highest and coldest towns in Spain; I was reminded of this as I walked back to my lodgings and undressed in the bare stone-flagged bedroom. War in this temperature, I reckoned, was going to be no picnic.

The next morning I breakfasted in the hotel. At a neighbouring table sat a dozen German pilots in the khaki uniforms of the Condor Legion. They were operating from the airfield south of the town, flying Henschel biplane fighters of an obsolescent type. They seemed very gloomy that morning, speaking little and only in monosyllables. Later I heard that they had lost their leader over Madrid the previous day. They had cheered up by the evening, when I next saw them, and were filling the hotel with their noisy singing.

At the Press Bureau Melgar told Walford and me that a car would take us to Toledo the next day, starting at nine in the morning. The direct road, through San Martín de Valdeiglesias and Maqueda, was blocked by the Republicans, and so we should have to go by the route over the Sierra de Gredos to Talavera.

Standing on a mound in the middle of a wide plain, encircled by battlemented walls and associated forever with the name of Saint Teresa, Ávila is renowned as *tierra de cantos y santos* (land of stones and saints). We went for a walk along the top of the famous ramparts. Built about the end of the eleventh century, they have been kept in a fine state of preservation and are, I believe, the most perfect example of medieval fortifications in existence. From the battlements we looked southward across the bare plain beyond the airfield to the horizon where the peaks of the Gredos, as yet only lightly touched with snow, gleamed in the diaphanous sunlight. Walford said:

'I've been thinking I might join the Requetés with you. After all this war concerns me personally; three of my relations have already been murdered in Madrid.'

*   *   *

The Sierra de Gredos, a south-westward extension of the Guardarrama range, forms a barrier, rising to eight thousand feet, between the plains of Old Castile and the valley of the Tagus. The northern face in winter is harsh rock and bare snow, but the southern slopes are thickly covered with pine and fir. On a fine day the sun lights them with a brilliant green, picks out the sparkle of a hundred torrents, glistens from the rock and strikes blinding on the snow. The road across these mountains, with its gravel and dirt surface, its sudden ascents and declivities, its blind curves and hairpin bends flanked by unguarded precipices, might have been designed by some motor-racing enthusiast as a test track for a mountain rally. There is the extra hazard that round each corner you are liable to meet a string of mules with their cursing drivers, a heavy cart loaded with timber or a large lorry, either in the middle of the road or on your side of it. I had a Spanish friend who told me that he made it an inflexible rule on this route to drive on the wrong side round corners; thus, he affirmed, was the only way to avoid collisions—'Provided,' he added, 'that the other driver is a Spaniard. If you were to meet a foreigner you would be completely spoilt.'

Our driver on this bright morning of November 18th clearly had the same idea. A serious young man with a melancholy face and horn-rimmed glasses, who gave the impression of carrying a load of official secrets, the burden of which was intolerable to him, he had arrived at the hotel a couple hours late, picked up Walford and me and a pretty young Margarita on her way to Talavera and driven like a demon to the foot of the pass. This was the famous Puerto del Pico, which was captured for the Nationalists in the first week of September by Colonel Monasterio, who started from Ávila with two regiments of cavalry. This was one of the most brilliant actions by mounted troops during the Civil War, and a remarkable feet in such steep and broken country. We had to take the ascent slowly, with frequent stops whenever the radiator boiled. But once over the pass we picked up speed and whirled downhill, skidding round corners with the tyres screaming, swinging out over precipices, swerving sharply to avoid a cart or lorry, and braking suddenly when it seemed we had lost all control. After some forty minutes of this I noticed that the young *Margarita* sitting beside me in the back was being quietly sick into her handkerchief. We stopped to let her finish this operation in a small copse beside a stream. After further halts—for a puncture and a mechanical breakdown—we ran into Talavera in time for a very late lunch at the only hotel.

During the ensuing months I saw a good deal of this small town. Now I remember it chiefly for its dirt, its ugliness and the cloudy colour and revolting taste of its drinking water. However, it occupied a position of considerable importance to the Nationalists at the junction of their communications between the Madrid front and the north, west and south in Spain. Situated on a bend of the Tagus, it faced Republican territory across the river on the south bank. The enemy used to launch sporadic attacks on the town without achieving any success. It is a measure of their disorganization on this sector that the Republicans made no serious attempt to capture so vital a centre of communications. For the duration of the war it was the depot of the Tercio but, so far as I know, it never contained more than a very small garrison.

Darkness was falling as we left the town. On our way out we overtook a column of Requeté cavalry, wild-looking men, dark and squat, with black beards. They seemed to have come a long way and sat wearily hunched over their saddles, wrapped in their *capotes* against the icy wind from the sierra. Our road ran straight and level, but we were obliged to travel slowly, for the surface was pitted with small shell holes very roughly repaired; there were further traces of September's fighting in the frames and burnt-out lorries and cars on the side of the road. After passing through Santa Olalla we saw ahead of us the dark mass of the castle at Maqueda on its hill commanding the fork where the Madrid and Toledo roads diverged. We bore right, crossing the Madrid-Talavera railway at Torrijos and soon afterwards ran under the walls of Toledo. We turned in at the Visagra gate, climbed slowly up the narrow street and came to rest in the Plaza de Zocodover in front of the ruins of the Alcázar.

*   *   *

It astonishes me even today that Toledo, one of the most fascinating cities in Spain, should be so poorly furnished with hotels. In November 1936, barely two months after its occupation by the Nationalists, we thought ourselves lucky to find a room in the only one open, a draughty, ramshackle building without charm or comfort. We awoke to a raw, grey morning with overcast skies and a chilly drizzle. We set out early for the Requeté headquarters, through narrow, cobbled streets running with muddy water. Like Burgos, the town was thronged with troops—Regular Army and Foreign Legion, Moors in fezes with blue *capotes* over their thin khaki tunics, Requetés and Falange. But the difference is that here the men's faces were lined and battle-weary, their uniforms ragged and dirty; the Madrid front was barely an hour's journey by lorry, and most of them were in Toledo on twenty-four hours' leave. We found the headquarters in a two-storey building, guarded by a pair of sodden sentries in red berets and *capotes*. Inside we climbed a flight of stairs to a large room crowded with people. There was an atmosphere of bustle, even confusion; groups of men stood around in voluble discussion, clerks sat at untidy desks making out orders, passes or lists of stores, orderlies hurried in and out of ante-rooms. Nobody took any notice of us. We approached a young man, wearing the silver fleur-de-lis of a Requeté officer, who was seated at a long table. When Walford explained that we wanted to enlist and had letters for Zamanillo and Falconde he jerked a thumb over his shoulder:

'They're in there,' he said, 'they're very busy. Come back at six o'clock.' He returned to his work.

At that moment a slight, dark woman in a white hospital coat came out of one of the ante-rooms. Walford brightened:

'Blanquita!' he cried; he introduced her as his cousin, the Marquesa de San Miguel, who was working for the Spanish Red Cross in Toledo.

She was a friend of Falconde and took us in to see him at once. Without her influence I doubt if we should ever have penetrated to his office through the crowd of sentries, officers, orderlies and hangers-on that stood in our way. We found him talking with Zamanillo in a small room at the back of the house, but they broke off their conversation when they saw Doña Blanca.

It appeared that Falconde dealt with political affairs, Zamanillo with military organization; our business was therefore with the latter. He asked me about my military training and seemed impressed by my O.T.C. Certificates, which were supposed to qualify me for a commission in the event of war, in the infantry, cavalry, or artillery of the British Army.

'But,' he added, 'I do not know if we can take you as an officer when you speak no Spanish.'

I assured him that I was quite happy to enlist in the ranks. Then I remembered the cavalry we had passed in Talavera. In a war of movement, such as this had been hitherto, it was probable that the cavalry would play an important and exciting part. Now I learned that the Requetés were raising two squadrons in Seville, under a White Russian colonel named Alkon; the horsemen we had seen yesterday were the first squadron, commanded by the Requeté Captain Barrón, who was in Toledo at this moment.

Eventually it was decided that we should enlist in the Requetés immediately, after which we could make up our minds whether to join the cavalry or the infantry. The former seemed to me to offer more exhilarating opportunities, but it might be a while yet before they could come into action; whereas the infantry battalion, the *Tercio de Alcázar*, was already in the line, in the Casa de Campo sector, and fighting hard.

Afterwards we went with Doña Blanca to lunch in a little restaurant below the walls on the northern side of town, the Venta de Aires, where we had the local specialty, partridges richly cooked in olive oil and herbs. We were served by the son and daughter of the house, while the proprietress sat in the background crying quietly to herself all the time. 'She sits there weeping all day,' explained Doña Blanca. 'Before they left Toledo the Reds shot her husband. Poor man, he had never done them any harm.

Next day we reported to Don Aurelio González de Gregorio, the Requeté officer in charge of recruiting in Toledo. He gave us an enthusiastic reception, called us '*Muy bravos*', he said he was proud to have us and made us drink a bottle of dark, sweet Malaga wine with him. We were formally admitted as Requetés without, so far as I remember, the formality of signing a single document. For some reason I have never understood we were not given identity cards, nor—in those innocent pre-World War days—did it occur to us to ask for them; a fact which caused me much difficulty and embarrassment later on, whenever I wished to travel. We drew no pay and we had to buy our own uniforms for the stores had none left.[1] I bought myself a red beret, khaki shirts of very poor quality and a shaggy *cazadora*, a sort of battle dress blouse; on my left breast pocket I had the Carlist emblem embroidered, the Cross of Burgundy, red St. Andrew's Cross surmounted by the Hapsburg double eagle under the royal crown of Spain.

In the evening we saw Captain Barrón of the cavalry, a very quiet man whose age I was unable to guess because the greater part of his face was hidden beneath an enormous pointed black beard in the style of the heroes of the Carlist wars; these beards were much affected by the Requetés, both at the front and in the rear areas, giving the wearers an expression at once of dignity and extreme ferocity. Barrón told us that his squadron had moved nearer Toledo, to Santa Olalla. He suggested that we pay it a visit in a couple days' time; meanwhile he would write to the senior officer there, telling him to expect us.

The following morning we walked up to the Plaza de Zocodover to look at the ruins of the Alcázar. There was nothing but a vast pile of rubble; the cellars, even the foundations, lay bare, with twisted iron girders sticking through the broken masonry and a great pit in the middle where the Republicans had exploded a mine. From the débris rose a foul stench of ordure and decay. The houses all around the square were pocketed with bullet holes, their windows shattered. A young Carlist from Galicia told us: 'We are going to leave it like that as a monument to Marxist civilization.' In fact, no attempt has been made to rebuild the Alcázar, and when I revisited it in the spring of 1951 it looked, and smelt, exactly the same.

In the neighborhood of El Greco's house we were warned to move carefully, for the streets around were exposed to sniping from Republican positions across the river and there had been casualties. The house was supposed to be shut, but we found the custodian, a little troglodyte who reached to my waist, and persuaded him to show us round. Inside I came upon one of the strangest sights of my life: In every room, stacked against the walls like so much lumber, stood these incomparable paintings of El Greco. The Republicans had assembled them thus, intending to send them to Madrid for sale abroad, but had abandoned them in their flight from Toledo.

---

[1] While I was in the ranks I was, of course, given my keep. Later, as a Requeté ensign, I drew a ration allowance which covered my mess bill, and pay equivalent to rather less than £1 per week.

There were some English journalists staying in the town; George Steer of *The Times*, Christopher Holme of Reuters, Pembroke Stephens of the *Daily Telegraph* and an American called Massock. They were all disgruntled because, having come to Toledo for the express purpose of visiting the Madrid front, they had not yet been granted permission to do so, nor did their repeated protests seem to have any effect.

We collected our passes from Captain Barrón and, about four o'clock on a fine afternoon, walked down to the Visagra Gate to stop the first lorry bound for Santa Olalla. We found one soon and settled ourselves in the back, among a pile of vegetables, two furious hens and their owner, an old woman who swore at them throughout the journey with a wealth of obscenity which Walford delighted in translating. Arriving in Santa Olalla at dusk, we found Squadron Headquarters in a small house in the main street. Here we were met by a pert little clerk of about sixteen, to whom we gave our papers. A few moments later we were brought before the senior officer.

Lieutenant (Acting Captain) Carlos Llancia, Marqués de Cocuhuella, was one of the tallest and most powerfully-built men I have ever met. He seemed to flicker with nervous energy. A thin 'eyebrow moustache and cold, dark eyes gave a ruthless expression to his handsome face; but his true nature was a strange mixture of kindliness and cruelty. Although surprised to see us, which was understandable because Barrón's letter had not yet reached him, he became very friendly when Walford told him why we were there. He suggested that we spend the night with the Squadron if we did not mind sharing sleeping quarters with the men. There were two other officers with him: a tall slim lieutenant with a slight moustache, called Medina, and an ensign named Elena, a little man with a high squeaky voice, a childlike smile and the quick jerky movements of a bird. These two came from Seville; Llancia, who spoke halting English, was a Catalan. All three were officers from the Reserve. The men, it seemed, were from Andalusia, most of them over thirty, all of them volunteers. This, said Llancia, made it difficult to apply discipline—an ironic statement in view of all I witnessed later. He added that they were the simplest type of peasant, usually obedient and cheerful but easily depressed, inefficient and inclined to be lazy—on the whole little different than children.

The little clerk, Dominguez, was summoned and told to show us to the barracks and our sleeping quarters. With an authoritative air he bade us follow him and led us to the main street. On the way he told us he had studied English—I fear without much success because he pronounced each word exactly as it would be pronounced in Spanish, and so we were never able to actually converse for more than a sentence or two. The barracks was a bare stone building of two floors, at the eastern end of the village. Outside, the men were lining up for the evening meal, which seemed to consist of *alubias*—a stew of white beans which they collected in their mess tins from a great cauldron—and a mug of red wine each. Our dormitory proved to be a barn. 'I will get some straw and a couple of blankets for each of you,' laughed Dominguez, 'then you'll be quite comfortable.'

After supper with the officers we returned to the barn, where we found our bedding laid out. There were about a dozen troopers there, who greeted us with smiles and friendly chatter, not one word of which I could understand. They had lit a fire outside, which we all sat around while the men sang the high plaintive *flamenco* of their native Andalusia, passing round mugs of wine. As I drank and listened to the strangely thrilling music, watching the firelight throw flickering shadows over the dark, bearded faces, I felt a new elation. The Squadron would be in action any moment now, Llancia had told me. I made up my mind that I would join them, and in their comradeship I would cheerfully endure hardship and danger.

It was early when we went to bed but late before I found my sleep. This was due partly to the thoughts racing through my mind, partly to the strangeness of my bed but chiefly to the thunderous sounds punctuating the stillness as my companions broke wind throughout the night.

*　　　　　*　　　　　*

Back in Toledo Walford told me as he had made up his mind to join the infantry. He left the same evening for Casa del Campo, taking his sketch book with him. I have never seen him since, but I know that he acquitted himself well in the ferocious battle that raged in that sector when the *Tercio del Alcázar* was surrounded and beat off repeated attacks by Republican Infantry and Russian tanks. I owe him much, for I do not know how I should have fared during my first days in Spain without his contacts and knowledge of the language.

After saying good-bye to him I reported to Captain Barrón, who gave me a pass to take me to Santa Olalla in the morning. With him was a short stocky figure with a doughy complexion and a frog's mouth, who spoke in a deep guttural voice. He wore a beret with the two golden fleurs-de-lis of a Requeté Lieutenant-Colonel; he proved to be the White Russian, Alkon. When my Barrón told him that I was joining the Squadron he asked me my nationality; he shook his head sadly when I told him I was English. Later I heard that, like many of his countrymen, he had little love for the English. I met another like him, nearly two years later, in San Sebastian, who informed me that he was so disgusted with the British for the way they had let down his Czar that he had ceased altogether to drink whiskey.

*　　　　　*　　　　　*

Santa Olalla, never an impressive village, had been the scene of severe fighting during the march on Toledo; now it made a sad picture. A dozen private houses and two or three taverns survived intact; in one of the former was located the Squadron Office and Officers' Mess. When I reported I found Llancia talking with a fat little man of about forty, with a sallow complexion and a very gloomy expression. he turned out to be the Squadron doctor. Having been a prisoner of the Republican *milicianos* in Ronda until its capture by the Nationalists at the end of August, he could hardly believe that he was alive. He scarcely ever spoke—never about his experiences as a prisoner.

Llancia explained to me that the Squadron was well below strength, consisting at the moment only of three troops—in total about a hundred sabres; reinforcements of men, horses, and equipment were daily expected. The Squadron's operational duties were, first, the protection of a sector of the Talavera-Toledo road; secondly and following from this, reconnaissance of the few miles of country between Santa Olalla and the Tagus, beyond which lay enemy territory. This road was vital to the Nationalist communications between their rear areas and the Madrid Front. There were Republican forces in the mountains to the north as well as in the country beyond the Tagus to the south; a combined attack from both directions, by cutting off this link at a vital period of the Madrid battle, might inflict disaster on the Nationalists. The road was very thinly held—a small garrison in Talavera, ourselves and a company of Falange militia in Santa Olalla, and a company of soldiers in Torrijos, about sixteen miles to the east. The Squadron was supposed to organize pickets by night and, by day, patrols between these posts to deal with enemy raiding parties and give warning of enemy movements; it was also to act as a mobile reserve in case of attack.

'It is very hard work for so few men,' said Llancia sadly, 'especially when they are not even half trained. But what can we do? All the troops are needed for Madrid; we must hold this long front as best we can.'

Like all of us at this time, he was convinced that a great assault was about to be launched on Madrid; then, he had been assured, our squadron would have its rôle in the battle as part of a mobile column.

I was given a horse, a powerful black beast with a beautiful mouth; also an old Mauser carbine and a sabre, the later of very poor quality steel, with a metal scabbard whose glitter would attract attention from some distance. There was no 'bucket' for the carbine, which had to be carried slung across the back, causing considerable discomfort when riding at any pace other than a walk. The only automatic weapon the Squadron possessed was one old Hotchkiss light machine-gun; I believe, but I am not sure, that there were two people in the Squadron who knew how to use it.

Llancia lent me a Spanish manual of training and indicated to me the movements, mounted and dismounted, which we should use.

During this time I worked hard at my Spanish, studying my Hugo, reading newspapers and carrying on conversations as best I could; but I found it helped me little when I tried to understand the patois of my Andalusian companions. This did not matter so much on parade or patrol, for I soon learned to follow the others, but it made it difficult to enter the life of the Squadron—or would have done had they not been so friendly and determined to make me feel at home.

For the first week I did not go out on patrol, but otherwise took my part in all duties. At six o'clock we were awakened by the beautiful Spanish bugle call of *diana* or reveille. We lined up outside the barracks for breakfast—a piece of bread and a mug of sweet, black coffee. 'Stables' followed. The rest of the morning was spent in drill or training, followed by watering and feeding the horses. *Rancho*, usually some form of stew, was at half past twelve, with a break until half past two. The afternoon was occupied in much the same way as the morning, with water and feed for the horses at half past four. After this there was a lecture, followed by prayers and, at six-thirty, the evening *rancho*. At ten o'clock the bugles sounded *silencio*.

On Sundays there were no parades except one, at noon, for Mass, which was celebrated by the chaplain of the Falange company, there being no chaplain in the Squadron; although a Protestant, I naturally attended. At first I wondered why there was no priest in the village, but I soon found out.

It was usual for one troop to be on patrol while the other two were on training. I was in Llancia's troop; when he was busy with administration we were commanded by Sergeant San Marano, a dark, clean-shaven stocky Reservist, an excellent N.C.O. who took great care of his men.

I had night guard duty about twice a week. This entailed standing sentry in front of the barracks for two hours between *silencio* and *diana*. It would not have been arduous but for the intense cold and the fact that the sentry had to stand motionless throughout his period of duty.

Obviously, I was not very good at this drill; even so I was not much worse than the rest, who were the despair of our officers for their inability to learn the simplest movements, although they were competent enough horsemen. Officers and sergeants carried *fustas*, pliant riding crops, which they laid across the shoulders of any defaulter, mercifully excluding me. This punishment was usually taken in good part by the victim, accompanied by howls of joy from his companions.

But there was a grimmer side to the discipline, which reminded me how far I was from the O.T.C. The day after my arrival two troopers reported for duty incapably drunk; apparently they were old offenders. The following evening Llancia formed the whole Squadron in a hollow square in the main barrack-room. Calling out the two defaulters in front of us he shouted, 'There has been enough drunkenness in this Squadron. I will have no more of it, as you are going to see.' Thereupon he drove his fist into the face of one of them, knocking out most of his front teeth and sending him spinning across the room to crash through two ranks of men and collapse on the floor. Turning on the other he beat him across the face with a riding crop until the man dropped half senseless to the ground. He returned to his first victim, yanked him to his feet and laid open his face with the crop, disregarding his screams until he fell inert beside his companion. Then he turned to us: 'You have seen, I will not tolerate a single drunkard in this Squadron.' The two culprits were hauled, sobbing, to their feet to have half a bottle of castor oil forced down their throats. They were on duty next day, but I never saw either of them drunk again.

The Falange company stationed in the village were Canary Islanders. They were a gay and feckless lot who spent all their money in the taverns and most of their time singing and playing mouth organs, at which they were remarkably skilful. They seemed to regard the war as a joke and anything military as utterly ridiculous. We became very friendly with them, joining at their parties in the evenings and carousing happily together. Although they were horrified that we let ourselves be worked so hard, there was none of the animosity that too often strained relations between Requeté and Falange.

With the villagers we were on excellent terms. They would often invite us into their homes—the few that remained—for a meal or a glass of wine. From them I learned what had happened to the village priest. In August *milicianos* had come to Santa Olalla from Madrid—strangers to the place. After shooting a number of prominent villagers they crucified the priest in front of the rest. The villagers, who were fond of him, would have saved him if they could; but they were powerless before this armed rabble. 'At Alcabón, five kilometers from here,' they told me, 'the *milicianos* burnt the priest alive.' For all I have been able to find out it seems that a very large number, if not the majority, of such atrocities were committed by armed bands who came into the countryside from large towns, rather than by local peasants.

By the end of November I was allowed to accompany my troop on patrols. This was the most satisfying part of our work. We would ride out in the clear, keen air of a December dawn, when the first sunlight was flushing the snowy tops of the Gredos with fingers of rose. Usually we patrolled southward over the brown fields and through the olive groves towards the Tagus. As the morning ripened, the tawny, undulating landscape with its silver olive trees and sunlit hillocks unfolded in brilliant clarity, a pattern of bright light and blue shadow rolling away to the river and the mountains beyond. There lay enemy territory; the enemy would occasionally cross over to raid or ambush, and so we had to move with care.

Sometimes we would split into sections, each under a corporal, to carry out our various tasks of reconnaissance. After being in the saddle all day, with the occasional halt to rest the horses or to eat, we would reform as a troop towards evening and trot back to Santa Olalla in the dusk.

At about three o'clock one morning, about the middle of December, we were awakened by shouts and the sound of distant gunfire. There was a message that the enemy was attacking Talavera. We turned out and made ready to move off. No orders came until, just before dawn, we heard that a Republican force of unknown strength had crossed the river and attacked a guard post between Santa Olalla and Talavera; at the same time artillery had shelled the town. After a brief fight the enemy had retreated and were believed to be making their way back across the river. We were to intercept if possible.

We moved off about seven, one troop to the north-west in case the enemy made for the mountains, the remaining two, including mine, towards the Tagus. We split into groups of three to reconnoitre the country, but took care to keep in touch with Llancia and Squadron headquarters. After we had ridden for two hours without seeing anything Sergeant San Merano halted us while he sent out scouts. We were in a field of water melons, on which we breakfasted—not sharing Mr. Hemingway's views on the only proper use for the Castilian melon.

Suddenly we received orders to mount. We closed in to join the troop in the cover of some olives on a small hill. I noticed my companions pointing and talking excitedly; following their gaze I saw, some distance away to the right, a mass of dark specks moving across a wide gully. What could this be but our enemy? We drew our sabres, formed line and cantered down the hill and up the opposite slope. As we came over the crest San Merano gave the order, 'Charge!' Spurring our horses, we swept downhill in a cheering line, leaning forward on our horses' necks, our sabres pointed. In a moment of mad exhilaration I fancied myself one of Subatai's Tartars or Tamerlane's bahadurs. Whoever, I exulted, said the days of cavalry were past? Preoccupied with these thoughts and with my efforts to keep station I never thought of looking at our target; nor, it seemed, did anyone else. For the next thing I knew we were in the middle of a bleating, panic-stricken, heard of goats, in the charge of three terrified herdsmen. A sharp crack on the elbow from the butt of my carbine shattered my dreams; so ended my first and only cavalry charge.

One morning I was standing in front of a doorway with Llancia and Medina when we heard the sound of an aircraft approaching. As we looked up we saw at the end of the street a bi-plane circling about fifty feet up. We had time to glimpse the red marking on its tail before it banked and dived towards us. As we leapt for the shelter of the doorway bullets began to spatter the street and the walls of houses nearby. The aircraft circled again, fired several more bursts at the barracks, then made off in direction of the river. There were no casualties, but Llancia said gravely, 'You will have to watch out for those birds when on patrol.'

About this time a new Ensign came to us, the Polish Count Orlowski. He was small, dark and beautifully turned out. To my joy, he spoke perfect English as well as Spanish, pronouncing both languages in a careful, precise manner, as though each word were a trip-wire that might set off an explosion. Having served in the Polish cavalry, he was not only a superb horseman but also had a fair knowledge of horsed cavalry tactics; he was horrified by our slovenliness, incompetence, and ignorance. I was now a sergeant, owing my promotion more to Llancia's kindness than my own merit, though he may have been impressed by my O.T.C. certificates. Colonel Alkon was good enough to confirm my appointment on the only occasion he favoured us with a visit.

Much as I enjoyed my life in the Squadron, and fond I was of the officers and men, I was getting impatient at the delay in bringing us into action and at our obvious unfitness for operations. None of the expected reinforcements had arrived—not a man, not a horse, not one round of ammunition. It would clearly be a matter of months before we could hope to operate effectively. My impatience was shared by all ranks throughout the Squadron. Captain Barrón, who was supposed to command us, had not yet put in an appearance.

From time to time I was given twenty-four hours' leave to go to Toledo, where I would collect my letters and money from the Bank. On one of these visits, a few days before Christmas, I dined with a delegation of six British Conservative Members of Parliament which was visiting the Madrid front. There was a Spanish Press Officer in charge of the party, one of the most remarkable characters I have ever known.

Don Gonzalo de Aguilera, Conde de Alba de Yeltes, Grandee of Spain, was a hard-bitten ex-cavalryman of what I believe is known as 'The Old School'. That is to say, he was a personal friend of King Alfonso XIII, a keen polo player and a fine sportsman; he spoke English, French and German perfectly (he told me that he had a Scottish mother); although widely traveled he was no absentee landlord, but spent the greater part of his time looking after his estates near Salamanca; he was widely read, very knowledgeable about literature, history and science, with a brilliant if eccentric intellect and a command of vituperation that earned him the nickname during the Civil War of *El Capitán Veneno* (Captain Poison).

Loyal friend, fearless critic and stimulating companion that he was, I sometimes wonder if his qualities really fitted him for the job he was given of interpreting the Nationalist cause to important strangers. For example, he told a distinguished English visitor that on the day the Civil War broke out he lined up the labourers on his estate, selected six of them and shot them in front of the others—'*Pour encourager les autres*, you understand.'

He had some original ideas on the fundamental causes of the Civil War. The principal cause, if I remember rightly, was the introduction of modern drainage: prior to this, the riff-raff had been killed off by various useful diseases; now they survived and, of course, were above themselves. Another entertaining theory was that the Nationalists ought to have shot all the boot-blacks. (The boot-black is as integral a part of the Spanish scene as the man who sells newspapers.) 'My dear fellow,' he explained to me, 'it only stands to reason! A chap who squats down on his knees to clean your boots at a café or in the street is bound to be a Communist, so why not shoot him right away and be done with it? No need for a trial—his guilt is self-evident in his profession.' For the Requeté ideal he had an amused contempt: 'They call themselves Traditionalists, and what is this tradition that they're always talking about? The Salic Law, imported from France by the Bourbon kings, which has no place whatever in Spanish law or custom.' For the Church, in fact the Christian faith, he appeared to have no time at all; yet he was no Nazi—indeed he hated all 'isms' and was scornful of all authority, except that of the hereditary nobility of Spain.

He sympathized with my impatience to see more active service. 'I'll fix that for you,' he said. 'I'm taking these fellows—he indicated the M.P.s—'to see the Front tomorrow. I'll have a word there with my friend, Colonel Rada. He's Inspector-General of the Requetés, and also commands the Central Sector.'

When I saw him the following evening he said 'It's all arranged. You're going to be attached to Rada's Staff. Your Movement Order will be sent to your Squadron in a few days. I don't know what Rada will do with you—probably give you a motor-bike and let you carry dispatches. Anyway, it ought to be more interesting than what you're doing now.'

About this time I was disturbed to receive a letter from my mother, saying that my father was ill in bed. Although there was no indication that anything was seriously wrong, I worried because he had already taken the greatest pride in his physical fitness and it was very unlike him to take to his bed.

I spent Christmas with the Squadron. On Boxing Day my Movement Order arrived from Rada's Headquarters.

CHAPTER FOUR

I reached Toledo too late in the evening to continue my journey to Getafe, where Rada had his headquarters. Having booked a room at the hotel, I went to one of the cafés on the Plaza de Zocodover, where I found the journalists, Steer, Holme, and Massock, with whom I spent the evening. Both Steer and Holme subsequently quarreled with the Nationalist authorities and were expelled, to return to Spain on the Republican side; they covered the fighting on the northern front during the Nationalist offensive against Bilbao in the summer of 1937. Both played an important part in working up feeling in England against the Nationalists over the bombing of Guernica, of which I shall have something to say later.

I know nothing of the reasons for Holme's expulsion, but Steer, whom I had known before as a man of initiative and courage, could fairly be described as a natural rebel. The incident which precipitated his expulsion is worth recording, as illustrating the fury of an Englishman confronted with Spanish plumbing.

It seems that the Nationalists authorities eventually decided to grant the journalists' pleas for a visit to the Madrid front. They laid on a specially conducted tour, starting from Toledo. There were not only English and American journalists, but French, Italian, German and some South American as well. There were some senior Staff Officers from the Army, to explain the situation as it should be presented. A senior official of the Ministry of Press and Propaganda was in charge. A fleet of cars was assembled, ready to leave from the hotel at 8.30 in the morning. Soon after nine o'clock the party was ready to start, but there was no sign of Steer. After waiting a while in a fury of impatience, they were about to start without him when he appeared on the steps of the hotel with a set, exasperated expression on his face. In clear tones he addressed the assembled party:

'You pull—and pull—and pull—and nothing happens. You pull again . . . and the shit slowly rises. That's Spain for you,' he roared, 'in a nutshell!'

*   *   *

I arrived at Getafe in a lorry in the middle of an artillery bombardment; it was not a heavy bombardment, but scattered shells were falling around the village. A leaden grey sky was fading into the night; it was bitterly cold. I dismounted, retrieved my suitcase and started to walk up the deserted main street. The North wind whistled sadly over the roofs of houses, most of them empty; here and there a few candles flickered through open doorways. An atmosphere of squalor and gloom, rather than of danger, pervaded the place.

I found Rada's headquarters off a side street, in a house that might once have been a rich man's villa. An orderly showed me into a room where several officers were sitting, some of them were Requetés, other in Army uniform. I was greeted in English by a spare, clean-shaven Requeté lieutenant, who gave his name as Espa; he told me he was the doctor:

'The Colonel is busy in his office now; we'll see him at dinner.'

Espa took me across the road to his own house, where we sat in virtual darkness, lit only by one candle, for more than an hour, before going to a tiny, dirty tavern for a glass of vermouth. An occasional shell still exploded nearby, but before long the bombardment had ceased.

'We nearly always have this in the evening,' he explained. 'The Reds have an excellent observation post at the top of the Telefónica building in Madrid. Those guns are Russian "12.40s"; they're good guns, which they handle very well. At the moment this sector is quiet, although of course there's always something happening down the road at Carabanchel Bajo. Our positions there are in houses, right next-door to the enemy.'

Colonel Rada was a cheerful, tubby little man, who spoke with a strong Andalusian accent. This made him almost unintelligible to me, but fortunately Espa was there to translate. After the usual compliments the Colonel said, 'I'm afraid it will be rather dull for you here. If you want to see some action I can send you to Major López Ibáñez, who is in command at Carabanchel Bajo. Report to me at eleven o'clock tomorrow morning if you want to go there.'

But next morning I found the Colonel had gone to a conference with General Orgaz and would not be back until the evening. After lunch I went for a walk in the direction of Madrid, along a path beside some fields. One of our batteries began firing somewhere behind me, I could not see where the shells were falling, but I heard them sighing as they passed on their way above. Enemy artillery replied, their shells whining close overhead to land in or behind Getafe. Other batteries joined in; soon the air was humming with projectiles. Undisturbed by the commotion a peasant continued to work in the middle of the field beside me. To him all that mattered was his field; if other men were fools enough to waste their time in fighting, that was their affair.

Reporting the day after, I found the Colonel with a gaunt, lanky lieutenant in army uniform who fortunately spoke some English. 'Lieutenant Urmeneta,' said Rada, introducing him, 'will conduct you to Major López Ibáñez at Carabanchel. Good luck to you.'

I thanked him. 'Go with God,' he said.

*   *   *

The lorry stopped with a jerk, causing me to bang my head against the windscreen. Urmeneta, sitting beside me in the driver's cabin, smiled, showing an irregular line of yellow teeth with gold stoppings. We jumped down and stood for a moment stretching ourselves in the drizzling rain. A hundred yards ahead of us the road came to an end in a high barricade of sandbags, behind which huddled a sentry. It was a depressing scene—bare, crumbling red-brick buildings, the street torn with shell-holes and littered with rubble, no sound but the occasional sharp impact of a bullet against a wall and the faint rumble of gun-fire to the north.

On the right of the barricade was a small hut built of wood and sand-bags; inside, the smell of gun-oil blended with the reek of cheap tobacco, wet clothes and unwashed men. Three soldiers were lying sprawled about a machine-gun—a pre-1914 Hotchkiss whose barrel pointed through an aperture in a parapet of wooden beams and sand-bags. Looking through this opening I saw a patch of grass-covered open ground, three or four hundred metres wide, and beyond it more houses and another barricade—all that was visible of our enemy.

'It seems quiet enough, doesn't it?' said Urmeneta, 'but don't show your head or you'll have it shot off. People get careless—' we all ducked instinctively as there came a sharp whirr followed immediately by an explosion and the sound of spattering fragments. 'That's a mortar bomb,' he explained. 'We get them all the time. You can't hear them coming till it's too late. Let's go and have some lunch.'

We picked our way through the ruins of houses and along trenches to the dug-out where Urmeneta had his Platoon Headquarters. Several times we passed a strong-point, holding a machine-gun or light Hotchkiss, with a sentry on duty; other men lay around eating, smoking, or sleeping. These posts were strengthened by sand-bags shored with stout wooden beams, and roofed against mortar bombs with iron bedsteads and odd pieces of furniture. Elsewhere, the defenses consisted sometimes of shallow trenches, in which we had to bend ourselves double, or rough barricades; but more often of the walls of houses, the windows being bricked up or blocked with sand-bags or bedding, leaving only a loop-hole for a rifle. For the barricades and parapets every kind of article and material was used—sand-bags, mattresses, bedsteads, furniture of every kind and even, in one place, an old violin.

While we ate, Urmeneta explained our position. By this time the assault on Madrid had given place to a siege, which was to last for more than two years. When the Nationalists were thrown back from the gates of Madrid by the International Brigades in November, they took up fortified positions in the University City, the Casa del Campo, and the suburbs of Carabanchel Bajo and Usera; for the next few months these places were the scenes of bloody fighting as one side or the other tried to improve its position or gain a little ground.

The 8th Battalion of the 27th Regiment of Argel, which Major López Ibáñez commanded, was holding a large part of Carabanchel Bajo. Urmeneta's sector wound in and out of houses and across streets in a confusing series of salient and entrants that I never managed to understand; in some places we were as much as six hundred metres from the enemy, in others no more than ten metres. From many points we could see Madrid, its domes, spires and houses gleaming wetly through the mist, with the high tower of the Telefónica forming a clear and hateful landmark.

The men were conscripts—'Pipis', as they were called in Army slang—from the western province of Extremadura, where the Battalion had its depot; they were admirable soldiers, cheerful and willing, calm in danger, undismayed by the unremitting strain of street fighting. They were fortunate in their officers, especially in Urmeneta, whom they looked upon as a father; although he was the same age as they—only a year or two older than myself—he had a gravity and sense of responsibility beyond his years. A Basque from Pamplona, the capital of Navarre, he had joined the Requetés at the beginning of the war. He had been posted to this battalion after completing an officers' *cursillo* at one of the infantry schools. He was studying to be a lawyer in civilian life.

In the afternoon we went to see Major López Ibáñez. At one point our way lay through a coppice which Urmeneta warned me was a dangerous spot, being exposed to enemy fire. Crouching behind a wall he whispered, 'This is where we run! Keep well down and don't stop running till we've reached that wall on the other side.' We had not gone more than a few yards among the trees when the bullets started to fly around us, hissing through the branches and slapping against the trees. Knowing we had to go back the same way, I was not comforted when Urmeneta told me that the enemy were using a new dum-dum bullet made in Mexico. The Major was a short, thick-set, dark officer who bristled with self-confidence and gruff good humour.

'Where would you like to go?' he bayed. 'We have every kind of position here. You can go to a very quiet one, a very dangerous one, or'—he indicated Urmeneta—'you can stay with this officer.' In very politeness I could do no less than choose to remain with Urmeneta; in any case this is what I preferred.

On the afternoon of New Year's Eve a runner appeared to summon Urmeneta to Company Headquarters. When he returned he looked preoccupied:

'We move tonight to a very bad position, right in the middle of the enemy—are you still sure you want to come?'

'Of course.'

*   *   *

45

It was nearly midnight when, having handed over to our relief, we formed up the street and moved off quietly on foot. I remember that journey well: the silent blackness of the bitter night, the stars twinkling frostily overhead, the whispered orders passed down the column, the muffled clink of arms, the clatter as someone kicked a fallen tile, the muttered curses and occasional quick flash of Urmeneta's torch. How differently would my friends in England be welcoming the New Year!

I had no idea where we were going, and in the darkness it was impossible to keep any sense of direction; it was all I could do to follow the man in front of me. There was a faint grey light in the sky when Urmeneta halted us and went forward to see the Company commander. Returning half an hour later, he said to me: 'You stay here with Platoon Headquarters while I settle the men into our new positions.' I heard them shuffling off into the gloom.

It was daylight when he came back.

'Let's go. Keep close to me. When you see me duck keep well down, and run like hell when I tell you. There are some places that are dangerous to cross in daylight. Above all, when we reach the position don't speak above a whisper. The enemy are very near.'

I kept close behind him, followed by his batman and the two platoon runners. Twice we were fired upon—I never knew from which direction, for I did not stop to look—but we reached the first house of our new position without a casualty. This was a small, single-storey building with a patio opening off a street. It was held by one of the two sections of our platoon.[1] We stopped here for a rest while Urmeneta spoke with the sergeant in command.

Between this and the other house in our position ran a broad, straight street, both ends of which were held by the enemy. This was crossed by a narrow tunnel built on the surface, consisting of a double line of loop-holed sandbags and roofed with planks and sandbags. It was defended by two light machine-guns, one pointing each way; it was just high enough for a man to crawl through on hands and knees, just wide enough for him to edge himself with difficulty past the defenders.

Crawling through the tunnel we came to the main position, held by the remaining section. This was a two-storey building, built round a patio like the first. A gallery, approached by an open staircase from the patio, encircled the upper story, the windows of which were barricaded and loop-holed. In two adjacent rooms, opening off the patio, Urmeneta established his office and sleeping quarters; the latter, where we had our meals, was a bare room about

---

[1] A Spanish infantry platoon is divided into two sections, or half-platoons, of 20-25 men, each commanded by a sergeant. It is confusing that the Spanish word for platoon is *Sección*, and the term for a section, or half-platoon, is *Pelotón*. A *Pelotón* contains three *Escuadras*, each commanded by a corporal, or senior private.

thirteen feet square, lit by a single smelly carbide lamp; it was furnished by a deal table and a few chairs, the rest of the space being taken up by old mattresses, on which six of us slept—Urmeneta, his sergeant, his two runners, his batman, and myself. A half-platoon of Regulares occupied two rooms of a ruined house next to ours; they had nothing to do with the defense of the position, but were there for sniping, reconnaissance and an occasional *coup-de-main* raid. They were happy, giggly little men—some of them fairer in complexion than myself, and one of them red-haired. They soon became very friendly and would bring us cups of sweet mint tea.

Our only line of communications with Company Headquarters and the rear was the tunnel of sandbags. Through this had to come all our food, water, ammunition and supplies; through this we must evacuate our wounded. It could only be done at night, which meant that a wounded man might die before he could receive proper attention, for we had no doctor. Water was so scarce that there was no question of washing, or even cleaning our teeth. In a few days we were all infested with lice. Our food, which consisted chiefly of mule steak and dried codfish, was cooked at Company Headquarters.

The rough sketch,[1] which I drew at the time, gives some idea of our situation. The enemy occupied houses enclosing us on three sides at a distance of between ten and thirty meters. Having pin-pointed the position long ago, they continually dropped mortar bombs and hand-grenades on us by day and night. That was the danger of talking above a whisper: The enemy could hear exactly where we were and would land a shower of bombs all round us. Worse, they seemed to know exactly where our latrine was situated—an exposed and shattered room at one corner of the patio; their attentions did much to expedite the process of nature.

I think there is something in the Spanish character that is stimulated by danger and discomfort; for throughout the ensuing fortnight everyone maintained an astonishing cheerfulness. We learned to take pleasure in the smallest comforts—the arrival of an unexpected bottle of brandy or box of cigarettes would put us in a happy mood for the whole day.

We suffered a daily drain of casualties. Although mortar bombs and hand-grenades could not penetrate the ceilings of the rooms, which were strengthened with beams and sandbags, they could have a devastating effect on the patio. Too often an explosion outside would be followed by the sound of scuffling and childlike whimpering; we would hurry outside to pick up a torn, bleeding figure, which we would rush into the office and lay on a mattress; there he would lie in pain until nightfall—if he did not die first. Even the dead had to be sent out through the tunnel, for there was nowhere we could bury them.

---

[1] See next page.

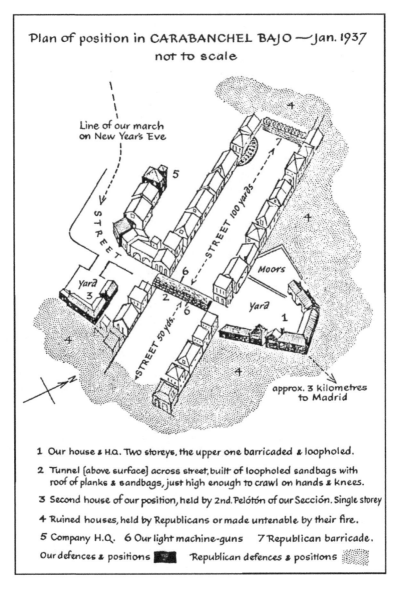

Plan of position in CARABANCHEL BAJO —Jan. 1937
not to scale

Line of our march
on New Year's Eve

STREET

5

STREET 100 yards

Moors

Yard

3

2

6

6

STREET 50 yds.

Yard

1

4

4

4

approx. 3 kilometres
to Madrid

1 Our house & H.Q. Two storeys, the upper one barricaded & loopholed.

2 Tunnel (above surface) across street, built of loopholed sandbags with
   roof of planks & sandbags, just high enough to crawl on hands & knees.

3 Second house of our position, held by 2nd. Pelóton of our Sección. Single storey

4 Ruined houses, held by Republicans or made untenable by their fire.

5 Company H.Q.   6 Our light machine-guns   7 Republican barricade.

Our defences & positions ▓▓   Republican defences & positions ▒▒

There were serious losses from sniping; I think the enemy had machine-guns trained on some of the more vulnerable places. Our men were keen snipers too, and in their excitement would sometimes expose themselves to enemy fire, with fatal results. Urmeneta did not at first discourage this activity, believing it would be good for morale; until one morning when they carried in the senior corporal with a ragged red hole in his forehead and a little white dribble of brain oozing from the back of his head. He had been a pleasant-faced, blonde youth, an excellent soldier, efficient and cheerful, cool in danger, loved by everyone. He seemed to be trying to say something, although he must have been unconscious; all we could hear was a continuous, low-pitched, snuffling moan. Urmeneta bent over him to recite the prayer for absolution, holding his own gold crucifix to the dying man's lips. As he straightened up, one of the soldiers said, 'Mateo was too confident; he would never keep under cover.'

It may be wondered why we tried to hold such a pernicious position, seeing that it cost us so much more than it was worth. I do not know the answer, but throughout this war the most dangerous and useless positions were defended by both sides with absurd tenacity and at great cost. I suppose it was reasons of prestige that prevented either side from voluntarily giving ground.

The fighting in November and December convinced both sides of the folly of attacking fortified houses by day; but we were subjected to frequent night attacks. The first came on the night of January 2nd. About 8.30 Urmeneta and his sergeant were sitting at the table about supper, giving me a Spanish lesson in whispers; all was quiet outside. Suddenly there came a burst of fire from one of our machine-guns upstairs, followed by a series of sharp detonations above and around us. In a moment the whole house was shaking with the blast of mortars and grenades, the night became a chattering cacophony of rifle and machine-gun fire. I snatched my rifle and followed Urmeneta and the sergeant through the door. In the few hideous moments of danger as we raced across the patio and up the stairway of the gallery I saw the darkness lit everywhere with flashes. As I took my post at the loop-hole I became aware of another sound, like hail—bullets striking the walls all round us. At first I could discern no target in the darkness, and confined myself to firing at enemy rifle flashes; but now our men were lobbing grenades, and by the flash of an explosion I could see a shadowy figure on the ground below or on the neighboring roof-top or balcony—a brief glimpse barely sufficient for a snap shot. I blazed away until it occurred to me that I must be wasting a good deal of ammunition, and so must my companions. The same thought seemed to occur to Urmeneta; for, coming up behind me, he shouted in my ear: 'Don't shoot unless you've got a good target—we must conserve our ammunition. That goes for grenades too.' I had lobbed a few grenades, more for practice and to give myself the impression that I was doing something than for their effect. But for every grenade we threw the enemy threw a dozen at us. Fortunately the standard hand-grenade used by both sides was the percussion 'Lafite'. This was a metal cylinder, a little larger than a 'Brasso' tin, filled with high-explosive; once the weighted safety-tape had been unwound, as it would be in the course of flight, the grenade would explode on the slightest impact. But as the case was very thin there was little danger from fragmentation, and the blast effect was limited to a few feet. On this and other occasions during the Civil War I was thankful that the Mills grenade was not in use.

For two hours the battle—or at least the firing—continued; then it died as quickly as it had begun. We tended our casualties, which were four wounded, only one seriously, posted guards and went to bed.

I doubt if the enemy suffered more casualties that night than we did. Had they pressed home their attack and succeeded in forcing an entry, I do not see how any of us could have survived; for they out-numbered us many times. We had these alarms almost every other night. Sometimes, as on this occasion, they were genuine attacks; more often I believe they were started by a jittery sentry or machine-gunner loosing off at a shadow; his companions would join in, and the enemy, thinking we were attacking, would reply. A great deal of ammunition would be wasted over nothing. Men whose nerves were overstrained by constant danger and lack of sleep tend to see shadows.

About this time there was a rumour throughout the army that the enemy were about to use gas; we were all issued with German gas-masks in cylindrical metal containers. The scare soon evaporated, and it was not long before the masks were discarded and their containers used as water-carriers.

One morning, about the middle of the second week in January, an N.C.O. came to the door of our office, asking to speak to Urmeneta. They whispered together; Urmeneta told us to keep quiet, then went down on his hands and knees, his ear to the floor. He stayed there about a minute, then motioned to the sergeant to do the same. When he had finished he scribbled a message for a runner to take to the Company Commander. He looked very worried.

What's wrong, Miguel?'

'I'm afraid the enemy are mining underneath. I heard their picks just now.'

'But are they right underneath this house?'

'No, I don't think so, not yet; I fear they soon will be.'

A new warfare was beginning around Madrid. The Republicans were employing miners from Asturias and Pozoblanco to drive mines underneath Nationalist positions in Carabanchel and the University City, in which they proved themselves extremely skilful. By this means they inflicted severe losses on Nationalists at very little cost to themselves, even forcing them to abandoned some positions. The Nationalists enlisted the most experienced engineers from Italy and Germany in attempts to put a stop to the mining; but they were unable to do more than limit its effect. In their turn the Nationalists began to use flame-throwers, especially in the Usera suburb, to blast the Republicans from their fortifications. I am told by witnesses that their effect at close quarters was devastating.

Happily I did not stay long enough to experience either forms of warfare. On the afternoon of January 13th we received orders to prepare to move out. Soon after dusk we were relieved by an infantry platoon from another regiment. We formed up outside Company Headquarters; at 7 p.m. the whole

Battalion began to move in column up the road to Getafe. We arrived three hours later at the barracks where we were to sleep. Although supper was ready for us we were too tired to be bothered with it, and went straight to bed.

We slept the whole of the next morning. In the afternoon I was ordered to report to Colonel Rada. He received me very warmly and told me to put up the silver *fleur-de-lis* of a Requeté alférez, or second lieutenant.

A fortnight later the entire position we had last occupied at Carabanchel was blown up by a mine; a whole company perished in the ruins.

*   *   *

On January 16th I received from an aunt the following telegram: '*Your father sinking fast come at once.*'

I was all the more shocked by this because the last news I had heard was that my father was much better; nor had I any idea what was the matter with him.

Urmeneta and Major López Ibáñez were full of sympathy; permission for me to leave must, however, come from Colonel Rada. Urmeneta went with me to see him. He was very kind, but seemed doubtful whether even he had authority to give me leave outside the country. However, when I gave him my word to return to his command at the earliest moment, he issued me with a return *salvoconducto* as far as the frontier. Within two hours of receiving the telegram I was sitting in the back of an open lorry bound for Toledo.

As I huddled myself into my overcoat against the bitter wind, I tried to detach my mind from contemplation of the tragic circumstances that must have inspired that telegram, and how to concentrate on my immediate problem—how to get home with the least delay. But I could not concentrate. I thought of the last time I had seen my father, at Newhaven; of our day in London buying my kit for Spain; and, with remorse, of the frequent disagreements, even quarrels, that had previously clouded our relations. I thought of how lonely my mother was going to be, with my brother at sea in the Navy and myself in Spain—for I must keep my word to return to Colonel Rada. I could not doubt for a moment that my father was dying; such a telegram would have never been sent if there were any reasonable hope of recovery. My great fear was that he would die before I could see him.

I had no idea how I was going to get to the French frontier, but decided I was to make for Ávila, where I hoped to find a train. Another difficulty was that I had no civilian clothes, so that I should have to cross France and arrive in England in my Requeté uniform; perhaps my teddy-bear coat and scarf would conceal it satisfactorily.

In Toledo I stopped long enough to draw the rest of my month's allowance from the Bank—about £10 in pesetas—and to have a *café-cognac* to fortify myself against the numbing cold. In Talavera, after various inquiries, I found three men who were leaving for Ávila in a very old, small car; I had difficulty in persuading them to take me, for they were doubtful if the car would get them to Ávila over the snow-bound Gredos. They had grounds for their fears, because we broke down twice on the Puerto Del Pico. Arriving in Ávila about nine p.m. I found there was a train at 11.30 as far as Medina del Campo; there I must change and catch the Salamanca-San Sebastian 'express'. This would at least give me time for a meal, my first since breakfast.

In the Hotel Inglés I found Harold Cardozo, Pembroke Stevens and other journalists. They were naturally eager for a first-hand account of the fighting around Madrid; I willingly answered their questions, stipulating only that my name should not appear in print, because the British Government was beginning to enforce the policy of 'non-intervention' in the Spanish Civil War, and I was anxious to avoid any trouble in getting back into Spain.

I reached San Sebastian the following afternoon, after a cold and uncomfortable journey. There I was lucky enough to meet a friend who gave me pounds and francs for my pesetas, and drove me as far as Irun. I had some anxious moments passing through the French frontier control at Hendaye; I was afraid I should be made to take off my overcoat, thus revealing my Requeté uniform. But I caught the night train to Paris without difficulty, and was home late next afternoon—twenty-four hours after my father's funeral.

*　　　　　*　　　　　*

I stayed a fortnight in England. It was neither easy nor pleasant to explain to my mother why I must return to Spain so soon. It may be that I was wrong to go; let those judge me who have been in a like situation. My mother made no complaint and did all she could to hide her distress. She would be quite alone; for my brother, who had been given only twenty-four hours' leave to attend the funeral, had rejoined his ship before I arrived.

Two days before my departure the local Police Superintendent rung up. Somehow he had heard of my activities in Spain and of my intention to return. He did not propose to try and stop me, but only warned me that I might find myself liable to prosecution under the provisions of the Foreign Enlistment Act of 1880, or some such date. I said I doubted whether the Act applied to Civil Wars, and anyway I would chance it. He was kind enough to wish me luck.

*　　　　　*　　　　　*

The major on duty in the *Comandancia Militar* in Ávila was clearly in a very bad temper. He was not at all impressed by Colonel Rada's *salvoconducto*. A fussy, bald, bespectacled old man evidently dug out from a peaceful retirement, he regarded me with unconcealed suspicion. It was obvious what was going through his mind: what did this damned Englishman think he was doing, asking him for transport to Getafe? Whoever heard of an Englishman in the Requetés? Everybody knew the English were all on the Red side, in the International Brigades. Obviously the fellow was a spy! He might have fooled the Requetés but he wasn't going to fool the Army—least of all an old Regular soldier with forty years' service.

These thoughts he presently expressed to me, forcibly and fast, through ill-fitting false teeth that obscured the details but left the general meaning only too clear. He ended by saying that if I appeared before him again he would put me under close arrest. 'Do me the favour of removing yourself!' were his concluding words.

This was really too bad. I had expected some difficulty in getting back into Spain, but this was the first time I had met with anything but courtesy and helpfulness in the country. I had crossed France wearing the same clothes as before, with an overcoat and scarf over my uniform. In Biarritz the Conde de los Andes warned me that, owing to the 'non-intervention' regulations, I should require a visa from the British Vice-Consul in Bayonne in order to get through the French frontier control. The British Vice-Consul turned out to be a bad-tempered old Swede with a white, pointed, beard. He seemed very suspicious and was only partially satisfied by Collin Brooks's letter; but he gave me the visa. I crossed the frontier without difficulty in one of Andes's cars, which took me as far as Salamanca. This was now Franco's General Headquarters. I arrived there late on Sunday night, the 7th of February.

Next day the Nationalist troops entered Málaga. This offensive was the first occasion on which Italian troops were in action. They played an important part in the fighting, but did not endear themselves to the Spaniards, who had also fought hard, by their claims to have captured the town unaided. Particular indignation was caused by some Italian officers who had the words: *Vincitore di Málaga* printed on their visiting cards. Nevertheless, it was a spectacular victory, for Málaga was one of the principal Republican strongholds as well as the scene of some of the worst excesses of mob violence. Before the final assault the Nationalists cut the roads east of the city and, with their command of the sea, were able to prevent the escape of a large number of leading Republicans. Among those captured and subsequently executed was the infamous García Atadell, leader of the terrible *Brigada de Amanecer* (Dawn Brigade), so called because its members used to drag suspects from their homes in the small hours and shoot them. Some distinguished foreigners were captured at the same time, but later released; these included Mr. Arthur Koestler and his host, Sir Peter Chalmers Mitchell. The latter, a keen Republican supporter, was a little naïve in his efforts to palliate the actions of the extremists in Málaga. He admitted to a friend of mine that some thousands of people had been executed there by *milicianos*: 'But,' he added, 'it was all straight shooting.'

On Monday afternoon I was on a bus to Ávila, hoping to find transport there to take me to Colonel Rada. After my rebuff at the *Comandancia Militar* I decided to try my luck at General Mola's Headquarters. Within twenty minutes I had my *salvoconducto* stamped, and a place reserved for me in the official postal car leaving the next morning.

We crossed the Gredos in glorious spring weather, very different from the blizzard of my last crossing three weeks earlier. In Talavera I lunched with Pablo Merry del Val, a senior official of the Ministry of Press and Propaganda and the younger son of the famous Ambassador. He had been educated in England and still retained the austere manner and appearance of a Sixth Form prefect confronted by a delinquent from the Lower Fourth; he became a very good friend of mine, and I am indebted to him for a great deal of kindness, but I always had the feeling that at any moment he might tell me to bend over and take six of the best.

On the road to Toledo I passed my old cavalry squadron, now in Torrijos; stopping a moment to talk with the men, I learned that Llancia, Elena, Medina and Orlowski had all left for other units. I reached Getafe at 6.30, to be told that Colonel Rada had moved to Pinto, about seven kilometres to the south-east, off the main road to Toledo. I found a lift to Pinto, but Colonel Rada had moved to La Marañosa, twelve kilometres further east, above the Jarama valley. I decided to stay the night in Pinto, where an infantry officer kindly lent me a mattress in his room.

Three days earlier, on 6th February, the battle of the Jarama had begun. This Nationalist offensive, directed by General Varela, had as its objective cutting off the Madrid-Valencia road, and, in particular, the capture of the town of Arganda on that road. This was the last direct supply line remaining to the defenders of Madrid from their bases in the Mancha and on the Mediterranean. Colonel Rada, who was commanding one of the formations under Varela, had launched his attack on Pinto the first day.

The country over which the battle was fought was an undulating plain, covered with scrub, sloping gradually eastwards to the Jarama valley; the most important tactical features were the heights of La Marañosa, six hundred feet above the Manzanares, and the so-called Espolón de Vaciamadrid, a ridge overlooking the confluence of the Manzanares and Jarama rivers. Farmland and olive groves covered the valley of the Jarama on both sides of the river. On the eastern side of the valley were hills thickly covered with olives.[1]

By the time I reached Pinto, on February 9th, the Nationalists had overrun the country to the west of the Jarama and occupied the heights of

---

[1] The battle of Jarama was the last time I saw German crews manning anti-tank guns in action.

La Marañosa and the Espolón de Vaciamadrid; from the latter they were able to shell the Valencia road. On February 11th, they forced the crossing of the Jarama and occupied the hills beyond to a distance of about four kilometres from the river. There they were held by the determined resistance of the International Brigades, including the British, who suffered very severe losses. Heavy fighting followed. The Republicans counter-attacked all along the line, but failed to regain any ground. By February 24th, the battle was over. The Nationalists failed in their main objective, which was the capture of Arganda, but they were able to dominate the Valencia road with their artillery fire and deny its use to the enemy. Thereafter, the only ground communication between Madrid and Valencia was along the Aragón road through Alcalá de Henares and across the country to Cuenca.

The morning of the 10th February was bright, clear and spring-like. As I sat in the back of an open lorry, jolting along a very bad road towards La Marañosa, and looking at the fresh quiet countryside I found it hard to believe that a battle was being fought only a mile or two away. But I was soon reminded of the enemy's proximity by the sight of a battery of anti-tank guns deployed for action by the side of the road, their German crews crouched alertly behind them.

La Marañosa could scarcely be called a village; it consisted of about a dozen houses, on either side of the track from Pinto, and a disused ordnance factory. Immediately to the north the ground rose to the heights where our positions were situated. Colonel Rada's Headquarters was a small house with a garden and a low wall, standing on the left of the road. There I found the Colonel with Espa and others I knew. They seemed surprised to see me back. Rada said he would send me to the Requeté *Tercio del Alcázar*, which was due to arrive in La Marañosa the next day; he could not return me to the 8th Battalion of Argel because they were no longer under his command.

While we were talking there was a small air-raid; Rada took us out into the garden to watch; half a dozen enemy '*ratas*'—Russian fighters—were machine-gunning the area, concentrating on the positions above us, and to the eastward. They dropped three small bombs which landed harmlessly in open country.

As we were sitting down to dinner that evening an enemy battery opened fire, obviously trying to hit Rada's headquarters. The shells fell close around the house, damaging one or two of the other buildings and causing several casualties. There was a feeling of expectancy and tension in the air which made me realize that something important was to happen tomorrow. After dark a *bandera* of the Foreign Legion formed up outside—dark, hard-bitten, grim-looking soldiers with a tremendous pride in their bearing, they were singing the two great Legion songs, *El Himno del Legionario* and *El Novio de la Muerte*, thrilling tunes that moved us all as we heard them chanted with such spirit by these men who were about to die. Indeed, many of them were dead within twenty-four hours; at dawn they went into action, nearly six hundred strong, to force the crossing of the Jarama; by the evening there were barely two hundred left.

Next morning the *Tercio del Alcázar* moved into La Marañosa. I reported to the Commanding Officer in his headquarters opposite Colonel Rada's. Major Emilio Alamán was tall and stout, with a loud guttural voice. He was a fine soldier; skillful, experienced and courageous. He had distinguished himself in the defence of the Alcázar of Toledo, in which he had been wounded. By nature a jovial and good-hearted person, he was clearly still suffering from the strain he had undergone during the siege; this made him liable to sudden and unreasonable outbursts of temper, terrifying in their violence.

He spoke no English and was clearly not very pleased to have a strange Englishman thrust upon him; but he received me well enough. He said that I had better stay with him at Battalion Headquarters for the present. I was allowed a batman and a corner of a room in an adjoining house to sleep in. This room I shared with five others, including a French alférez, a jolly, tubby, middle-aged man with a voluble manner and a passion for his food; he used to spend a lot of time in the kitchen, before and after every meal, giving hell to the cooks. An additional sleeping companion was a tiny mongrel, who hung around the kitchen by day and came to sleep on one or other of our beds at night. We were all fond of him, and would have been fonder but for his habit of making a mess on the bed of his choice. Our chief discomfort was lack of water, for there was no local supply and all our water had to come from Pinto in lorries; there was barely enough to drink, none for washing. The wine, though not scarce, was atrocious.

The first two days were uneventful but for intermittent shelling from across the river; this ceased on the third day. Air-raids continued, usually in the early hours of the morning. They seldom came by day, for two reasons: firstly because we were well protected by anti-aircraft; secondly because the Nationalists were beginning to win command of the air from the Republicans. Credit for this was due primarily to the initiative of one man, the fighter pilot García Morato. García Morato, who commanded a formation of Fiat CR 42 bi-planes, trained his pilots to pitch a perfection far ahead of the enemy. When he brought them into action over the Jarama they chased the Republicans out of the sky.

I usually slept during the night raids, which of course were not comparable with those of the last war. But on one occasion I was awakened in the middle of a raid by infuriated shouts from the Frenchman: '*Merde! C'est le chien qui chie!*' The little dog had chosen his bed that night.

A day or two after my arrival we were joined by a young German officer, Lieutenant Von Gaza. He was something of a mystery, because he claimed to be a lieutenant of machine-guns in the Reichwehr, and was wearing

German army uniform; yet it seemed extraordinary that he should be sent by himself. He spoke English but no Spanish; he was polite but formal in his manner, speaking in a precise, clipped voice and seldom smiling. He told me that he came from East Prussia and that he was an orphan, his parents having been murdered by the Russians in Riga after the First World War. We had one or two Germans in this unit, but Von Gaza held himself aloof from them, causing them grave offence. He soon transferred from us to the Foreign Legion, where he served under Captain Cancela, who subsequently became my own Company Commander and who told me something of his story. He was indeed a Regular Army officer, and came from a Junker family; but, having committed some serious offence which had brought upon him the displeasure of the German military authorities, he was given the choice of a court-martial or service in Spain—but with the proviso that he must not serve with his own countrymen. He was killed by a chance shell two months later, while playing cards in a bungalow with three other officers of his bandera. Cancela told me that he was the best officer he ever had.

There was a German press photographer called Franz Roth, who had taken up his quarters in La Marañosa, with whom I became very friendly; he worked for Associated Press, had travelled widely, and was in Addis Ababa at the time of Mussolini's invasion. He and I used to climb one of the hills overlooking the Jarama to watch the fighting on the other side. Through our binoculars we could see the battle raging among the olives, white puffs of bursting shrapnel in the air, the dark smoke of high explosive between the trees, and the incessant sound of machine-gun fire reaching us faintly from across the valley.

One day Roth asked me to accompany him down to the Jarama. He had heard a report that a company of Frenchmen from the International Brigades had been destroyed by a tabor of Regulares while trying to cross a bridge over the Jarama and that the Moors had castrated their victims. I agreed to go because I felt that this sort of report should be checked, in view of the wild atrocity stories that were circulating about the Moors; anyway I wanted to see the Jarama. We set off on foot in the early afternoon and after about a mile descended into the *vega*, or cultivated plain, of the Jarama. Beside a ruined farmhouse we came upon a German anti-tank gun, with its crew, commanded by an officer. We made to approach and Roth called to the officer in German; but they shook their heads and would not let us come near. The bright sun shone golden on the fields and the olives; it shone also on the huddled corpses of the Frenchmen, heaped around the bridge where we had expected to find them. Most of them had been stripped of their boots and outer garments by the Moors and lay there in their underclothes in every attitude, grotesque and stinking, shriveled by two days' hot sun. With ghoulish intensity Roth probed among the bodies, urging me to do the same. We found no trace of mutilation, but after ten minutes of this grisly business I was violently sick and told Roth I could not go on. My legs would hardly carry me back to La Marañosa, where I drank nearly half a bottle of Roth's brandy before I began to recover. If this is the sort of thing I have to do to prove myself a man, I thought, I think I'll stay a mouse. Roth was quite unmoved.

On the morning of February 15th Major Alamán asked Von Gaza and me if we would like to be posted to one of the positions on the heights of La Marañosa. We were delighted, for we had nothing to do at Battalion Headquarters and felt we were always on the Major's toes. We each took a rifle and pack and set off along a path leading up the hill past Colonel Rada's Headquarters. It took us about twenty minutes to reach our new position. This was on the right of our line, on a ridge overlooking the plain of the Manzanares. Below us, about three-quarters of a mile distant, was a broad belt of olives stretching away to our left. A track led from it straight in front of us for about half a mile to a deserted village. Beyond the village ran the Manzanares. The country between the Manzanares and ourselves was supposedly a no man's land. Von Gaza and I were astonished that no patrols were sent to reconnoiter it at night; we offered to go ourselves, but were told it was unnecessary.

The defences consisted of rough earthworks, with shallow trenches and parapets of earth and stones, bolstered with a few sandbags. There was a Hotchkiss machine-gun and a light machine-gun of the Lewis pattern. About a hundred yards back from the position was a small empty house in a little grove of trees; this was Platoon Headquarters, where we slept.

At dawn on the morning of the 17th we awoke to the sound of heavy firing away on our left. We ran to our trenches and took up firing positions. At first we could see nothing, for the valley below was still hidden in the river mist. But as the haze rolled back in the rising sun, we saw groups of little dark figures moving towards us along the track from the village and across the fields. We held our fire, letting them reach the olive trees undisturbed. Surely, I thought, they can't mean to attack across those open fields in front, with no artillery preparation. It's sheer suicide although they do outnumber us many times. But in a moment they emerged from cover and began to advance at a trot towards us. We waited until they were well in the open, then, at a sharp word from the Platoon Commander, our machine-guns opened up; we joined in with our rifles. The little trotting figures halted and toppled down in heaps. A machine-gun in the olives started firing at us, its bullets flying high overhead; some of the enemy in the open tried to cover the advance of their comrades with light automatic weapons, but in those fields, devoid of cover, they stood no chance against our fire. Soon they were running back for shelter, leaving their dead and wounded strewn among the stubble; many more fell as they ran. It's sheer bloody murder, I said to myself. What criminal staff officers they must have, to send them into battle this way! Possibly, well-trained, experienced troops might have been able to find some dead ground for cover, though I doubt it; certainly no experienced commander should have asked them to do it. It may bet that they counted on surprise, but if so they had planned it very badly. From the sounds of firing I judged that the attack was being pressed on both our flanks. I was a little disturbed that we seemed to have no artillery. But the enemy had; for soon there was a whistle as a shell passed overhead. It was followed by several more, each one landing a little closer. It was fortunate that we could hear them coming, for our earthworks were flimsily built and our trenches much too shallow, so that we had to crouch down each time a shell came over. It was clear that they were shooting at the house, and so the Platoon Commander ordered its evacuation: none too soon, for a succession of shells hit it immediately afterwards, reducing it to a ruin. Then they concentrated on the position itself and their shells began to fall uncomfortably close, one or two of them causing casualties.

Now the enemy were advancing again, threading their way among the bodies that had fallen in their first attempt. Again we opened fire and again they were thrown back, leaving more of their number on the ground. Yet a third time they advanced, fewer of them now, and flagging in their pace.

'Hold your fire!' shouted our Platoon Commander. 'Let them get a bit closer this time.' We kept under cover.

They came on in bounds, one group giving covering fire while another advanced. When the nearest was within four hundred yards, and all were well out in the open, we had the order: 'Fire!'

It was murder. The poor creatures fell in heaps. The survivors turned and ran for cover, dropping their weapons in their haste. When the last few survivors had vanished into the olives, the whole plain in front of us was littered with bodies. Von Gaza told me he saw two officers shot by their own men while trying to stop the rout. Our own casualties numbered some half-a-dozen.

For a while there was a lull and no movement in front of us. Suddenly we heard the sound of heavy engines, and from our right front appeared six Russian tanks, each carrying a 37 millimetre gun in its turret. One after the other they crossed in front of the olives, then turned towards us and began to approach in line. This looked awkward for us, and would have been if any infantry had followed them; but the latter had no fight left in them. If the tanks had preceded the earlier attacks the result might have been very different; even so, we were expecting rough handling. At that moment our artillery, silent before, came into action. It found the range quickly and soon we saw black puffs of smoke bursting all round the tanks. They wavered, then came to a halt. A moment later one of them was enveloped in black smoke as a shell struck it squarely; it began to burn. Then another was hit at the base of the turret. The remaining four turned, spread out and made off.

About midday, when the fighting had died down on our front, a runner arrived with news that the two companies on our left had suffered heavily and were in need of reinforcements; our Platoon Commander was required to send any men he could spare to report to Battalion Headquarters. Von Gaza and I were among those who went. At Battalion Headquarters we found a young man, Felipe Pallejá, a Catalán who spoke good English. He told us that the positions in the centre and on the left had been under heavy fire from artillery and mortars all morning; Major Alamán was up there now and Palleja would take us to him.

The enemy were evidently respecting the hour of the siesta for everything was quiet when we arrived. The Major was in very good heart, although he expected the attacks to be renewed in the afternoon and next day. Most of our heavy machine-guns were concentrated on the centre position; Von Gaza was sent there, where his special knowledge would be most useful. For the moment I was to stay with Alamán.

During the afternoon we were subjected to intermittent shelling, but no new attack developed. It seemed that the enemy were re-grouping for a further assault on the morrow. They had established themselves in the olives. I accompanied the Major on visits to our two positions. These followed the crest of the heights, the centre facing north across the valley of the Manzanares and the belt of olives, the left curving back and facing more to the north-west, towards Madrid. The Major expected the main attack to be launched against the latter, in an attempt to turn our left flank and cut the road to Pinto. It was arranged that Palleja and I should move up there in the evening.

The defences had not been as severely damaged as I had expected; the enemy artillery could not have been of very heavy caliber. Most of the casualties had been from mortars. In places where the parapet had been demolished men were repairing the damage with earth and sandbags. It struck me that the trenches were very badly constructed, being much too shallow to give proper protection, and dug almost in a straight line instead of with traverses. Throughout the Civil War it was my experience that Spanish troops could not be induced to dig proper trenches; this applied even to the Foreign Legion. They seemed to think it indicated cowardice to dig themselves in securely.

We returned to Battalion Headquarters to snatch a meal. There I found the French lieutenant; he had found time during the lull to slip away from his post to give some more hell to the cooks about the soup they had sent up.

At dusk Palleja and I went up to our new station. We found a dug-out to sleep in, which we had to share with eight others; it was a bit cramped, but it would do for the little sleep we were expecting. We went to report to the Company Commander, whose name, if I remember rightly, was Santo Domingo. We found him in his dug-out with another captain, called Frejo, and Father Vicente, the Company Chaplain, a stern-faced, lean Navarrese with the face of a fanatic gleaming behind his glasses. Captain Santo Domingo had a great reputation as a soldier in this *tercio*, and was beloved by his men, whom he led by the sheer force of his own example. He was a man of about forty-five with a strong, gentle face, full of character. Father Vicente, in great spirits, dominated the gathering. He was the most fearless and the most bloodthirsty man I ever met in Spain; he would, I think, have made a better soldier than priest.

'Holá, Don Pedro!' he shouted at me. 'So you've come to kill some Reds! Congratulations! Be sure you kill plenty!' The purple tassel of his beret swung in the candle-light. Santo Domingo frowned:

'Father Vicente , you always talk of killing. Such sentiments do not come well from a priest. The Reds may be our enemies, but remember they are Spaniards, and Spain will have need of men after the war.'

'Of good men, yes. But not of evil.'

'Of good men,' repeated Santo Domingo, 'and of evil men converted.'

I was fascinated, as the argument became heated, to see the roles of priest and soldier reversed; but I noticed that Father Vicente was alone among the party in his condemnation of all Reds as traitors who must be killed. He needn't worry, I thought, we'll have to kill all we can tomorrow, if only to save our own skins.

Captain Frejo spoke: 'It will be a hard battle tomorrow; they must outnumber us by at least ten to one. We have no other defences to fall back on, and if we break the whole Jarama front will fold up.'

'God will not desert us,' pronounced Father Vicente.

None of us felt like sleep; it was long after midnight before Palleja and I returned to our dug-out, to throw ourselves full dressed on the ground. The imminent prospect of a violent, if glorious death, tends wonderfully to concentrate the mind on past misdeeds and future hopes of salvation. I will admit that I said a few prayers that night and even made some resolutions; but I wish I could honestly record that the pattern of my life changed radically after my deliverance. I was not the only one who found it difficult to sleep. I must have dozed, for the next thing I knew was that someone had lit a candle, and my companions were stirring themselves. I put on my belt, pouches, and steel helmet, took my rifle and crawled out into the open. I stood up on the hillside, taking deep breaths of the clear, cold air, which revived me wonderfully after the dusty atmosphere of the dug-out.

It was beginning to get light. I could make out dimly the shape of our own trenches and the position on our right, lined with tense, waiting figures. As the light grew, I stood looking down into a mist-draped valley where the enemy lay hidden in the gloom. Not a sound came from it. Now I could see the tops of the olives beginning to appear through the grey blanket. From the right a single shot broke the stillness.

The next moment the whole valley exploded into countless flashes and the thunderous noise of firing; the air around me was humming with bullets. I ran the few yards to the trench and flung myself against the parapet, with my rifle to my shoulder, as our own line burst out in reply.

All around us the earth was thrown up again by shells and mortar bombs, the air torn by bullets. Once again the enemy machine-guns were firing high, but their artillery already had our range, while mortar bombs were landing on the parapets and in the trenches. As the mist parted we saw that under its cover the enemy had been moving towards us. The plain in front of the olives was full of them, and more could be seen coming up from the river. As Major Alamán had forecast, they were working round on our left flank.

My throat was dry, my face hot and my hands shaking as I feverishly loaded and fired my rifle. With a great effort I pulled myself together and began to fire more slowly, checking my sights, resting my elbows on the parapet and taking careful, aimed shots. This had a steadying effect on me and I began to feel much better. I began, too, to feel a kind of pity for my enemies, exposed in the open to this murderous fire, so that, as I aligned my sights on one of them and pressed the trigger with a slow, steady pressure, as I had been taught, I found myself praying that my bullet might put him out of action, but not maim him grievously for life.

Once again the enemy's planning had let him down. His troops were, indeed, nearer to their objective than on the previous day; so also were they further from cover. Their only chance seemed to be a rapid advance, regardless of casualties. About three or four hundred yards in front of our trenches was a line of low hillocks extending to our left; these, if they could reach them, would afford them some protection, enabling them to concentrate for a final assault. At first they made no progress against our fire. Many fell; some lay down where they were and fired back at us, others turned and ran in all directions, looking for cover, not realizing that this was the most certain way of being killed.

The morning drew on with occasional brief lulls in the fighting, which gave us time to evacuate the dead and badly wounded, dress lesser wounds, repair defences where possible, replenish our ammunition and take a drink from our water bottles. But the mortars in the olives gave us no rest.

The bombardment intensified as a new wave of attackers surged forward, in much greater strength than the first. They had learnt by now to use what little cover there was, and to combine fire and movement more skillfully than before. In spite of their losses, numbers of them reached the shelter of the hillocks, where with rifles and light machine-guns they opened fire on us to cover the advance of their comrades.

The bombardment was reaching a climax. Our ears were throbbing with explosions, our eyes almost blinded with dust; not so blinded, however, that we could not see that the enemy was getting closer, finding his way surely round to our left flank. Bullets from his light machine-guns were slapping against the parapets and whistling by our heads. Sometimes a Requeté, carried away by excitement, would clamber up on the parapet, half out of the trench, to get a better shot; in a moment he would slump back, torn with bullets, or fall forward over the parapet to roll a few yards down the slope in front. Whenever the latter happened—and I personally saw it happen several times—Father Vicente would leap from the trench and run down the hill to where the body lay, the purple tassel of his scarlet beret flying in the wind; there he would kneel, oblivious to the bullets churning the earth around them, while he prayed over the dead or dying man.

Major Alamán was moving along the line between us and the position on our right, limping on his heavy stick, now quite imperturbable in the heat of battle, his harsh guttural voice croaking encouragement to us all. Looking over my shoulder I saw Frejo and Santo Domingo on top of the parados, each standing behind his men, each wearing his red beret and wrapped in a *capote*, unmoved by the bullets flying around him, calmly directing the fire and encouraging the defence. This was the true Requeté tradition. Even when Frejo collapsed with a shattered shoulder and was carried away unconscious with pain, the inspiration remained with us.

My ammunition pouches were empty, the barrel of my rifle was too hot to touch. Near me lay a dead Requeté; I stooped over him to replenish my pouches from his, and to take his rifle. As I straightened up to return to my firing position there was an explosion almost on top of me, which threw me to the ground, where I lay for a moment with my ears singing. Realizing that I was not hurt I got up, adjusting my steel helmet. A bit of it seemed to be pressing against my forehead, and so I took it off; I found a large dent in front, where a piece of metal had hit it. Hitherto I had been inclined to laugh at tin hats.

It was nearly noon. There seemed no prospect of reinforcements for us; our ammunition was running low and the enemy, now within three hundred yards of us, was preparing for the final assault. We were so heavily outnumbered that there could be only one outcome if he reached our trenches. The firing died away and a lull descended, while the enemy collected his forces for the attack and we made ready to meet them.

Then we heard a new sound from the left flank beyond the enemy—the sound of tank engines. In a few moments a column of our own light tanks swept into view—about sixteen of them, each with two machine-guns. They came on fast, fanning out into line abreast, then opening fire together on the enemy's unprotected flank and rear. The battle was decided. The Republicans had no chance. Caught between our fire and the guns of our tanks, they were shot down in swathes as they ran for the shelter of the olives. Few of them reached it; those that did continued their flight to the Manzanares and beyond. Their mortars were silent; even their artillery ceased fire.

I was conscious of Father Vicente beside me; his spiritual duties finished, he was bent on seeing that we did not allow the fleeing enemy to escape unpunished. He kept on pointing out targets to me, urging me shrilly to shoot them down, and effectively putting me off my aim. It seemed to me that he could barely restrain himself from snatching my rifle and loosing off. Possibly recollecting that I was a heretic, and therefore little better than a Red, he soon left me to concentrate on my neighbours. Whenever some wretched militiaman bolted from cover to run madly for safely, I would hear the good Father's voice raised in a frenzy of excitement:

'Don't let him get away—Ah! *don't* let him get away! Shoot, man, shoot! A bit to the left! Ah! *that's* got him,' as the miserable fellow fell and lay twitching.

It had been a very near thing. If our tanks had not arrived, or they had arrived even a little later, we should almost certainly have been overrun. I do not know where they came from; they were German tanks, though the crews were Spanish. As we had been told to expect no reinforcements we were as surprised to see them as the enemy must have been. I have reason to believe that these tanks consisted nearly the whole of General Varela's mobile reserve; if so, he used them brilliantly, to strike at exactly the crucial moment to turn impending defeat into total victory.

Thus ended the two-days' battle of La Marañosa. Although we were shelled heavily that afternoon and frequently during the next few days, we were not attacked again. This had been part of the Republican General Miaja's counter-offensive, which he now switched to other points on the Jarama front. The formation that had carried the brunt of the attack against us was a Spanish brigade with the inspiring title of 'The Grey Wolves of La Pasionaria', named after the notorious Communist Deputy, Dolores Ibarruri. Certainly their fiasco was due to no lack of courage—indeed they showed remarkable bravery in such hopeless circumstances.

Our own losses were considerable. At the beginning of the battle our fighting strength was about three hundred; of these we lost more than a hundred in killed and seriously wounded; I think we were lucky to get off so lightly. Major Alamán, who had contributed notably to it, expressed himself as well satisfied with our performance, and both Colonel Rada and General Varela sent us personal messages of commendation.

By the 24th February the Republican counter-offensive was exhausted. Conducted as it was, it is not surprising that it achieved no success. The battle of the Jarama might have been a decisive victory for the Nationalists if they had had more troops; but at the time of General Varela's original offensive, at the beginning of February, a large part of the Nationalist effort was directed against Málaga.

At the beginning of March I received a letter from my mother, asking me if I could get leave to come to England for a few weeks to deal with some legal business arising out of my father's death. At the same time I heard from my brother, who was in the cruiser *Neptune* at Gibraltar, offering me a passage home in his ship if I could get there by the middle of the month. Colonel Rada gave me leave to go, but advised me to have it confirmed in Salamanca if I wished to return to Spain afterwards. I left for Salamanca the next day.

CHAPTER FIVE

It was something of a shock to find a constable in the uniform of the Metropolitan Police answering me in fluent Spanish; yet this is what happened on the North Front at Gibraltar when I asked my way to the Rock Hotel.

Thanks to Pablo Merry del Val, whom I met in Salamanca, I had no difficulty in getting permission to return to England. In the Gran Hotel I was introduced to a tall, distinguished-looking Spaniard, the Marqués de Manzanedo, who was then serving in the Nationalist Diplomatic Service. A great anglophile, he was extremely kind to me and gave me a lift to Seville two days later. There I took a bus to Algeciras. I crossed the frontier at La Linea in the same disguise I used to cross the French frontier, and with the same success. But in the bar of the Rock Hotel, where I could not very well keep on my overcoat and scarf, I felt considerably embarrassed. There my brother joined me with the news that his ship was sailing in two days' time and that he had the Captain's permission for me to sail in her.

'I'm afraid there's no cabin for you, and I'm damned if I'm going to give up mine, so you'll have to sleep in a hammock. As a matter of fact, I think you'll find it very comfortable.'

I can never forget the kindness and hospitality I had from Captain Benson and the officers of the H.M.S. *Neptune* during the voyage. She was a very happy ship. My brother, Neil, who was in the Fleet Air Arm, piloted the seaplane that she carried; five years older than myself, he had achieved distinction in the Service as a naval historian and writer on naval subjects. Among his fellow-officers he was known as 'Three-plank' because, they told me, when he walked the deck each of his feet covered three planks; they took one look at me and christened me 'Two-plank'.

Neil was right about the hammock. Once I had learnt how to climb into it—it was slung at about shoulder height—I slept in it very well; moreover, because it swung with the motion of the ship, there was no sensation of rolling. But there was one drawback; it was slung immediately over a hatch, usually open, which led down to the boiler-room. This did not worry me when I went to bed loaded with ward-room whisky, but it gave me a fright, on waking with a thick head, to look over the side into a gaping black pit.

It was my brother's last voyage in *Neptune*, she was paying off in England before going out to South Africa. It was a sad blow to hear, in 1942, that she had struck a mine while chasing three Italian cruisers in the Mediterranean, and capsized with the loss of every man on board.

*   *   *

The bearded Swede in the British Vice-Consulate at Bayonne flew into a temper when I presented myself again with Collin Brooks's letter; he abused me as he stamped my passport and almost spat at me as I left his office. There is no doubt, I said to myself, that he isn't in the least deceived. If I have to cross this frontier again I must find another way.

It was now the middle of April. After the failure of their offensive against Guadalajara the Nationalists finally abandoned their efforts to take Madrid. Instead, they began a full-scale offensive against Bilbao. Despite their superiority in aircraft and artillery they were faced by an enemy fully as brave and determined as themselves, well entrenched in positions that they had been preparing all winter; by some of the most difficult terrain in the Peninsula, and by weather that often made operations impossible. It seemed, therefore, that Bilbao would be an unconscionably long time falling.

It would have taken longer still if the Basque Republicans had not wasted their best troops at the end of November, 1936, in a disastrous offensive concentrated on the town of Villareal, the gateway to Vitoria. Some fifteen thousand men, mostly *Gudaris*, or Basque militiamen, were thrown into the attack against a garrison of about six hundred men—Regular Army and Requetés. These beat back all attacks until relieved on December 5th by a column from Vitoria, under Colonel Camilo Alonso Vega. The Republicans renewed their assault on 18th December with disastrous results to themselves; they were forced to abandon their offensive, having suffered appalling casualties. Unfortunately they had not even bothered to organize casualty clearing stations or hospitals, or to provide themselves with medical supplies, such as anti-gangrene serum. In a single night more than four hundred of their wounded died of gas-gangrene.[1]

I saw Orlowski on my way through Paris. He had gone to the *Tercio del Alcázar* after leaving the cavalry squadron in January; he had been slightly wounded in action with them at a place called Cabezafuerte, not far from La Marañosa, but had left just before my arrival, finding the Major's temper too much for him. Through friends of his I had an introduction to the O'Malley-Keyes family, who lived in an enchanting house on a hill at Anglet, near Biarritz; with them I stayed while waiting for my *salvoconducto*, which would allow me to enter Spain. What would have been a period of tedious waiting thus became a delightful interlude.

I arrived in Spain on April 21st in the middle of a political crisis. The only public announcements of it were, first, an official statement that Señor Hedilla, the leader of the Falange, was under arrest; secondly a decree amalgamating the Requetés and the Falange and abolishing all other political parties. The new organization was to be known as *Falange Española,*

---

[1] Lojendio, *Operaciones Militares de la Guerra de España.* (Montaner y Simón, Barcelona 1940), pages 265 and 266.

Tradicionalista y de las Juntas de Ofensiva Nacional-Sindicalista—and, added the Spaniards with their irrepressible love of ridicule, *de los Grandes Expresos Européos*. Parties with more divergent political views than the Requetés and the Falange could scarcely be imagined. Writing of 'this magnificent Harlequin', Señor de Madariaga says it was 'as if the President of the United States organized the Republican-Democratic-Socialist-Communist-League-of-the-Daughters-of-the-American-Revolution, in the hopes of unifying American politics'. Either the Falange or the Requetés would have to dominate; the skill at intrigue of the former, and the political ineptitude of the latter made the outcome certain; the Requetés ceased to exert any serious influence on Spanish politics.

The day after the announcement of Hedilla's arrest the Falangist newspaper, *Arriba*, appeared with thick black borders. Officially the news was hailed as a statesmanlike move to achieve national unity; but public uneasiness persisted, nor was it allayed when General Faupel, the German Ambassador, was sent packing. Clearly there had been a conspiracy. The full details are still imperfectly known abroad, but in brief what happened was this: the Germans were anxious, for their own reasons, to see the war ended quickly. For some months they had been dissatisfied with General Franco, whose strategy they regarded as archaic and likely to lead to an indefinite prolongation of hostilities. But General Franco is a gallego (Galician), with all the obstinacy and subtlety of that race; it was his war, and he was going to run it as he thought fit. The Germans therefore decided to replace him with a creature of their own; Señor Hedilla, as the leader of the most pro-German party, was their ideal tool. He was persuaded by General Faupel to stage a *coup d'état*, which very nearly succeeded. But General Franco reacted vigorously, suppressed the conspiracy, sent Hedilla to prison for ten years and demanded the recall of Faupel. To complete his ascendency he appointed himself head of the new, and only, party. He continued to run the war in his own way, and it was not until March, 1938, that he launched an offensive along the lines advocated by the Germans.

Having made up my mind to be transferred to a unit on the Bilbao front, I went to Salamanca to arrange a posting. From there I was sent to Ávila to see General Monasterio, the ex-cavalry leader, who was now in command of all militia forces. It was an alarming interview. The General, a man of austere appearance, whose face seemed more suited to the wig and scarlet robes of a High Court Judge than the uniform of a soldier, was surrounded by half-a-dozen officers, none of them below the rank of Colonel. They fired a bewildering succession of questions at me in Spanish, to which I could only reply in a high-pitched croak, for I was suffering from laryngitis. Sweating and trembling I left the room, with orders to await my posting in Salamanca.

Architecturally Salamanca is one of the most beautiful cities in Europe. I spent long hours admiring the perfection of the colonnades in the Plaza

Mayor and visiting the University, the two cathedrals, and the Casa de las Conchas. Less beautiful among the sights of Salamanca at this time but, it seemed, scarcely less firmly established, was the figure of General O'Duffy, who commanded the Irish Brigade. I met him through his A.D.C., Captain Meade, a charming man, half Irish and half Spanish, with all the tact and patience that his job required. The General was sitting at a table in a corner of the lounge in the Gran Hotel, a bottle of whisky in front of him; with him were Meade, another officer of his staff, and the Rector of the Irish College at Salamanca. Meade, whom I had met before, came over to my table and asked me to join them; as we crossed the room he whispered to me, 'Please be careful what you say to the General. I'm afraid I must tell you that he loathes all Englishmen.'

A former Chief of Police of the Irish Free State, General O'Duffy launched into Irish politics in the 1930's, forming his own United Party, or 'Blueshirts'. Seeing in the Spanish Civil War a chance to increase his prestige in Ireland, he raised a 'Brigade' of his countrymen to fight for the Nationalists. The 'Brigade' was in fact equal in strength to a battalion, but O'Duffy was granted the honorary rank of General in the Spanish Army. Few generals can have had so little responsibility in proportion to their rank, or so little sense of it. Whatever the ostensible purpose of the Irish Brigade, O'Duffy never lost sight of its real object, which was to strengthen his own political position. He therefore gave the most responsible appointments to his own political supporters, regardless of their military experience; one of the most important he gave to an ex-liftman from Jury's Hotel in Dublin, a man who knew nothing of soldiering and was prepared to learn nothing. In favour of such men as this he declined the service of experienced ex-officers who did not happen to belong to his party. Like some other Irishmen and some Americans—happily a minority—whose minds cherish the memory of past enmity he had a pathological hatred of the English, which he never tried to conceal. To his men he was known as 'General O'Scruffy' or 'Old John Bollocks'.

His secretary and shadow was 'Captain' Tom Gunning, a brilliant journalist who had formerly made a name for himself in Fleet Street. The story Gunning put around was that his Irish Republican sympathies made it impossible for him to set foot in Fleet Street again. Closer inquiry revealed more compelling reasons. A skilful intriguer, he contrived, so long as he remained O'Duffy's secretary, to keep the Irish Brigade divided against itself.

The administration of that unhappy unit was described to me by Lieutenants FitzPatrick and Nangle, who, to their fury, were transferred from the 5th Bandera of the Foreign Legion to serve under O'Duffy, and by Lieutenant Lawler, who came out from Ireland with him. The men were crammed like cattle into the stinking holds of an ancient, unseaworthy ship, with bad and inadequate food and barely enough water to drink.

Disembarking at a port in Galicia, they entrained for Cáceres, which was to be their depot. Their route ran through Salamanca, where they arrived at about ten in the morning, having had no breakfast; they were received on the station by a delegation of the Nationalist authorities, who gave them a *vin d'honneur*, attended by senior Army officers. Lawler said to me: 'I knew it was going to be sheer bloody murder with the boys drinking all that wine on empty stomachs. I tried to see if we couldn't get them some food, but it was no sue. Sure enough, when the time came to get back into the train the boys were so drunk it was all we could do to push them into it. And even that wasn't the end of our troubles! When we'd got them all in, and the train ready to start, the band struck up the Spanish National Anthem, and all the officers and generals came to attention and stood at the salute. And all the time the band was playing, there was one of our lads—drunk as a coot he was— leaning out of the carriage window being sick all the way down the neck of an old general. And the old boy—I was watching him—stood there like a rock at the salute through it all. But I could see he wasn't liking it.'

Misfortune followed them even to the front; their first casualties were at the hands of their allies. One of their companies, marching in column to take up positions on the Jarama, was fired on by a unit of Falange, who unaccountably mistook them for a unit of the International Brigade. The first shots did no harm, but the Company Commander, who had been chosen for his political loyalties rather than his military experience, allowed a minor battle to develop.

It was only fair to add that when the Irish eventually went into action, in the Valdemoro-Ciempozuelos sector, the Spaniards were filled with admiration for the bearing and courage of the troops. Indeed, the quality of the men was superb. They were truly inspired with the ideal of fighting for their faith. With good leadership they could have been the worthy successors of the famous Corps that fought for France in the 18th century:

> On the mountain and field from Berlin to Belgrade
> Lie the soldiers and chiefs of the Irish Brigade.

But they had no chance with the leadership O'Duffy gave them. Quarrels with the Spanish authorities became more frequent and more bitter. In the summer of 1937 the Irish Brigade went home.

*   *   *

Impatient at the delay over my posting, I obtained permission from General Monasterio to move to Vitoria. There I hoped to expedite matters, since it was the headquarters of Generals Mola and Solchaga. The former was in charge of all operations on the northern front, the latter commanded the

Brigadas de Navarra, comprising the Requeté units on that front. Most of the foreign correspondents were concentrated in the town, including Harold Cardozo, who was sharing a flat with a Frenchman called Botteau, the correspondent of the Havas agency; these two asked me to stay with them while I was waiting. I did not see much of them during the daytime because they were usually at the front; the Nationalists had at last relaxed some of their restrictions on the movements of journalists, who were now able to make frequent visits to the front in the company of Captain Aguilera and his colleagues.

The Republicans were countering the Nationalist offensive against Bilbao with a propaganda offensive of their own; at this time it was concentrated on the famous Guernica incident. It was very cleverly handled, and a great deal of money was spent on it abroad—Botteau was told by his head office that the Republicans spent about six hundred thousand pounds in Paris on propaganda about Guernica alone. The story circulated—and widely believed—was that Guernica, an open town, was destroyed by incendiary bombs dropped by Nationalist aircraft; Cardozo was indignant at the success it was having in England. He was in Guernica immediately after its occupation by the Nationalists, and so was able to make a pretty thorough examination. It was clear to him, he said, that the Republicans themselves had set fire to the town before leaving, just as they had burnt Irun, Eibar, and Amorebieta in the course of their retreat through the Basque Provinces; he himself had witnessed the burning of Amorebieta. Certainly Guernica was bombed by the Nationalists, but it was not an open town at the time it was bombed; it was packed with Republican troops, and was, in fact, a Divisional Headquarters. After watching the burning of Amorebieta, he had entered into it the next day, and talked to some of the few inhabitants that were left. Before abandoning the town the *milicianos* had come to their houses and taken all their food and clothing, even what they were wearing, so that they were dressed in pieces of sacking; then they had set fire to the town. 'We know,' those poor people had told Cardozo, 'who burned Amorebieta. So we can guess who burned Guernica.'

It seems to me that nothing illustrates better the superiority of Republican propaganda over Nationalist than the Republican story about Guernica was given immediate and world-wide publicity, and is still generally believed; whereas the Nationalist case scarcely received a hearing.

About the middle of May I fell ill with an attack of jaundice, brought on by influenza, which left me very weak and depressed. I owe a great deal to Cardozo and Botteau for their kindness to me during the three weeks I was ill. I was fortunate in having friends in Vitoria who came to cheer me up; among them were the Duquesa de Lécera, whom I had met my first day in Spain, and an English girl, Gabrielle Herbert, who had been running her own hospital in the Huesca sector of the Aragón front; Huesca was invested on three sides by the enemy, and Miss Herbert's hospital was under direct fire from enemy artillery for several months.

I approached Captain Aguilera about my posting and, as usual, found him sympathetic and helpful. Through him I obtained entry to the headquarters of Generals Mola and Solchaga. Here I met with courtesy, compliments and promises—General Mola was particularly affable—but nothing materialized. I was beginning to despair of ever getting to the front, when I met an Englishman called Edward Earle; a leading Bilbao industrialist, he had financed a *tercio* of Requetés, named the *Tercio de Nuestra Señora de Begoña* after the Virgin who is the Protectress of Bilbao. He promised that I should be taken on its establishment; within a week he had arranged this personally with the commanding officer. Now all I needed was a *salvoconducto* from headquarters in Vitoria to allow me to join them at the front. On June 9th I applied for it, only to be told that I must first produce a certificate signed by Colonel Rada, my last commanding officer, granting me permission to serve on the Bilbao front. This, I felt, was something they might have told me three weeks earlier, when I first applied to them. However there was no help for it but to find Colonel Rada. Nobody seemed to know where he was, but I was advised to go to Salamanca and ask. After two days' inquiry in Salamanca I heard that he was in Ávila; there, to my surprise, I found him, and obtained my certificate without difficulty.

My two days in Salamanca are memorable for one incident: I was lunching at a restaurant with the charming name of 'The Friar's Widow', when a lanky lieutenant of the Foreign Legion came in and sat at my table:

'Excuse me,' he said, 'but you have been pointed out to me as the English Requeté. My name is Noel FitzPatrick and I am English, too—or rather, Irish,' he added hastily. It turned out that we had a number of friends in common in England. He was a most entertaining companion with a highly developed sense of the ridiculous, especially where it concerned himself; I was to see a great deal of him during the next few months and he became and has remained, one of my closest friends. Over lunch he told me something of his pat history, and a great deal about General O'Duffy and the Irish Brigade. He was now in his early thirties.

After leaving Sandhurst he had been posted to a famous line regiment, which he later left, he said, 'with the enthusiastic cooperation of my commanding officer'. He transferred to another regiment; but, deciding not to pursue a career in the regular Army, he was put on the Supplementary Reserve, attached to the Irish Guards. 'At the time the war broke out,' he told me, 'I had a motor business of my own in London. But then I discovered that my secretary, whom I rather fancied, was sleeping with my manager, and I reckoned they were both having a good laugh at me. So I packed it up and came out here. That was in August.' On arrival in Spain he was attached to Major Castejón of the 5th Bandera of the Legion, where he met an old friend and brother-officer, Bill Nangle. They were both mentioned in dispatches during the advance on Toledo, and were among the first dozen to enter the Alcázar when it was relieved. He remained with the 5th Bandera until November 1936, when he and Nangle were transferred to the Irish Brigade. Now he was in Salamanca, trying to arrange a posting back to the 5th Bandera, where Nangle had already preceded him.

*　　　　*　　　　*

On June 3rd, to the grievous loss of the Nationalist cause, General Mola was killed in an air crash. He was a man of great personal integrity and powerful influence, not only with the Requetés but throughout the country; had he survived it is possible that he would have been a check to the ascendancy of the Falange and to the growth of totalitarian rule.

On the 11th June, after an intense bombardment by artillery and aircraft, the Nationalists launched the last phase of their offensive. This was against the defences of the famous 'Iron Belt', the main line of fortifications defending Bilbao. The advanced positions were stormed on the first day, the main defences breached on the second. When I set out from Vitoria on June 19th it was clear that the fall of Bilbao was imminent. Nobody knew exactly where my new unit, which formed part of the Colonel Sánchez González's 5th Navarre Brigade, was operating. Earle thought they were in the region of Las Arenas, a seaside resort about eight miles from Bilbao on the right bank of the estuary of the Nervión. I found Las Arenas clear of the enemy, but there was no sign of my new *tercio*. It was a day of brilliant sunshine, hot inland but cool here with the sea breeze blowing. From up the river came the sound of battle as the *Brigadas de Navarra* stormed the last Republican defences on the heights overlooking Bilbao. The estuary was crowded with boats, from dinghies to small streamers, trying to make their way to safety; they had little chance, for they were within range of Nationalist artillery and machine-guns; most of them were forced to turn back. One steamer alone tried to struggle on. Through my glasses I saw spouts of water leaping up all around her as a Nationalist battery found the range: then one flash after another on board as the shells struck. Smoke and steam poured from her; she heeled over and sank in a vortex of foam.

It was early evening before I found the *Tercio de Nuestra Señora de Begoña*. They were resting in the woods on the heights of Archanda, which they had stormed that afternoon. This ridge was the last enemy line of defence, and now there was nothing between us and Bilbao, which lay beneath. With me, however, it was a matter of 'Go hang yourself, brave Crillon!' for they had fought a bloody battle all day, struggling up the almost vertical hillside through the trees under a murderous fire of mortars and machine-guns from the defences on the top—defences, moreover, manned by fanatical Asturian miners, who did not run away or surrender, but stayed and fought it out to the last man. This *tercio*, already well under strength, had started the assault with a hundred and seventy men; there were barely forty left when I joined them. Among the forty, however, I found my old friend, Father Vicente, from the *Tercio del Alcázar*, who had joined this unit at the beginning of the offensive. Today he had led one wing of the assault, mounted on a white horse and still wearing his scarlet beret with the purple tassel—a perfect target. As so often happens with such people, he was only slightly wounded, in the hand, while the Requetés behind him fell like corn at harvest-time and his fine horse was killed under him. He was at the top of his form, full of sympathy with me having missed the battle. He took me to the Commanding Officer, Major Ricardo Uhagón. 'We shall march down to Bilbao at dawn tomorrow, so I suggest you find somewhere to sleep.' He told his batman to get me a blanket. When he brought it I walked up the hill, past a deserted pill-box, to a small meadow at the top, where some Requetés were standing, sitting, or lying around in the gathering dusk. They gave me a hunk of bread and some sardines from a tin. I was very thirsty; but so was everyone else, and there was no water, nor wine either. A grinning Requeté offered me a canteen full of brandy; like a fool I drank some and became much thirstier. When I handed it back he tilted it to his lips and appeared to swallow most of its contents in three or four gulps.

'Why do you drink it like that?' I asked him. 'It all goes down at once and you get no pleasure from it.'

'Of course I do,' he laughed, 'Now it's all inside me and the pleasure comes from there.' This was the way that nearly all Spanish soldiers used to deal with a bottle of brandy when they got hold of one.

I was terribly cold that night, even with the blanket; after months of sleeping in a bed, and after my illness, the hard ground pressed painfully against my hips and shoulders. I lay awake for hours, feeling ashamed of my softness and very lonely among these strangers.

It was still dark when we were roused and I stood up to stretch my cold and aching body. My Requeté friend gave me some more of his brandy, and this time I was really glad of it. By daybreak we were formed up on the road, awaiting the order to move. The sky was clear and the day promised to be hot.

At six o'clock we had the order to march and moved off in column down the almost vertical, winding road towards Bilbao. I was marching with Major Uhagón at the head. There was no sign of Father Vicente. Our *tercio* led the line of march and we thought we should be the first troops to enter the city; but half way down we heard that the enemy had evacuated it yesterday, and advanced elements of our forces, principally tanks, had entered the previous evening. On the way we passed groups of civilians, looking thin and strained, who watched us apathetically.

Lying in a deep valley, hemmed in by almost perpendicular heights, Bilbao on a fine day has a steamy, relaxing atmosphere. By the time we had reached the river, or *Ría* as the Nervión is locally called, I was already feeling tired. Here we turned left and marched into the Plaza de Arenal; this is a wide square with a small public garden beside it, on the bank of the *Ría*. The bridges had been blown, and sappers were working to construct pontoon causeways. Nearby, field kitchens were working, where we were given a mug of black coffee and a piece of bread. It was Sunday, the 20th of June. After breakfast we formed up in the Arenal for Mass. There must have been well over five thousand troops assembled in the square, facing the church at the eastern end; the *Tercio de Nuestra Señora de Begoña* was in front. The Mass was attended by senior officers of all three services, including the Generalissimo himself. Who should preach the sermon but Father Vicente, his bandaged hand in a sling, his enraptured, ascetic face raised to heaven, his loud, strident voice thrilling with emotion as he poured out his words of faith and triumph in stately measured periods, thundering the repeated refrain of his text:

Contra Dios no se puede luchar! [1]

* * *

Although it wore a sad, neglected appearance Bilbao seemed to have suffered remarkably little damage during the long siege. She is a town accustomed to sieges, having suffered many during the Carlist wars of the last century. The streets were full of broken glass and debris; some of the windows were smashed, others sandbagged and loop-holed for defence, but generally the houses and shops were intact; there seemed to have been remarkably little looting, at least during the evacuation, although there had been more during the early days of the war. Factories and industries were undamaged, though without power. Most serious was the shortage of drinking water, for the enemy had cut off the city's supply and it was a month before it could be restored. The condition of the civilian population was tragic. The first day we were constantly besieged by pathetic, emaciated figures—men and women of every age and class, with wasted flesh, sallow skins, and eyes bright with famine, begged piteously for a little bread. The Nationalists tackled the problem at once, rushing in supplies of meat, potatoes, rice and bread, and opening restaurants where any civilian could get a free meal. The city came back to life very quickly; by the middle of the week power and light were restored and trams were running; even the shops were open, although there was very little in them. There were a few cases of typhoid but no epidemic.

---

[1] Against God no man can fight.

We stayed a fortnight in Bilbao, recruiting officers and men from sympathizers who had remained underground among the civilian population during the Republican régime; we had more applications than the shortage of equipment and instructors allowed us to enlist. I was given a platoon with, fortunately for me, two very efficient sergeants.

*   *   *

In England the summer of 1937 was one of the gayest pre-war years; to me in Spain it was a period of extreme frustration. Having worked so hard to get into a fighting unit on a fighting front, I had arrived too late for the battle. Now I was to spend my time in training and garrison duties on a front that had become stabilized. Moreover I began to receive letters from well-meaning friends and relations at home, urging me to 'think of my future'— in other words, come home and find myself some more permanent and lucrative employment than that provided by the war in Spain. Of course they were right. But having continued so long in the war I could not bring myself to leave it before the end; nor did the promise of financial security appeal to me.

Early in July we moved to Las Arenas, where we were headquartered in luxurious villas belonging to *émigré* Basque Nationalists. This was a relief from the heat, humidity and dirt of Bilbao. We were now about four hundred strong and all our working time was spent in training the recruits.

As an Englishman, my prestige in Las Arenas was very high. This was due to the selfless courage of an English governess, a Miss Boland, who had lost her life while trying to save her employer's family from execution during the Republican régime. They were Basques called Zuburría, who lived in Las Arenas. Miss Boland had been the children's governess and had remained with them after they were grown up. There were four sons, the youngest still a schoolboy, the eldest married just one year. The day before the Nationalists entered Las Arenas, *milicianos* came to arrest the four boys and the wife of the eldest. Knowing that they were going to be shot, Miss Boland went too; in her efforts to save them she was herself executed, the first of them all.

Our training completed, we left towards the end of July for a small village on the border of the provinces of Vizcaya and Santander, near the sea. The village, El Castaño (the Chestnut-tree), was in the mountains a few miles north of Valmaseda. The positions marking the front lay across the top of two peaks connected by a ridge, about half a mile above the hose where we had our Battalion Headquarters. Now we formed part of the 2nd Navarre Brigade under the command of Colonel Muñoz Grande, a magnificent soldier—and incidentally a man of great charm—who later became well-known as the General Officer Commanding the Spanish Blue Division operating against the Russians in 1942. Before leaving Las Arenas we received a large draft of officers who had just finished *cursillos* at infantry schools; this brought our officer strength above establishment. As fully trained officers, the newcomers were obviously entitled to commands in preference to volunteers like myself, and so I reverted to the status of supernumerary officer at Battalion Headquarters.

We stayed idle at El Castaño for nearly a month; we were in reserve, the positions above being held by an Army battalion. Although unsatisfactory to me, it was a pleasant enough existence; having few duties, I spent much of my time bathing in a small cove a mile or two away, or walking in the hills of that lovely country, in company with other officers of the *tercio*. Sometimes I went to Bilbao to have a talk and a drink with Tom Pears, the British Consul, and Charles Purgold, a British resident of San Sebastian, who had come to Bilbao to broadcast to England on the Nationalist radio. Our sector of the front was very quiet, interrupted only by occasional exchanges of artillery fire. Between ourselves and the sea were grouped the Italo-Spanish 'Mixed Brigades' of the *Flechas Negras* and *Felechas Azules*. There was no love lost between the Italians and us. The '*Vincitoria di Malága*' were very much above themselves; not that they had any reason to be, for they had suffered some sharp reverses, because of their own impetuous stupidity, during their advance along the coast during Bilbao. From these they had had to be rescued by neighbouring Spanish units. Spanish soldiers, though they fight stoutly under their own officers, are seldom amenable to foreign command.

During this month we were daily expecting to resume our advance, this time against Santander. The reason it was delayed until the middle of August was the Republican offensive against Brunete on the Madrid front. The Republicans knew that the Nationalists had concentrated a large part of their fighting strength on the campaign in the north; it was only to be expected that they would try to relieve the pressure there, and at the same time exploit the Nationalist weakness before Madrid, by taking the offensive themselves. They had a very able Chief of Staff in General Vincente Rojo, a Regular Army officer, who was the contemporary and—before the war—a friend of my former commanding officer, Major Alamán. He had been caught in Madrid with his family by the outbreak of the Civil War and, to save his family, consented to serve the Republic. This did not excuse him in the eyes of the Nationalists, who would have shot him if he had not escaped from Spain at the end of the war. He was responsible for the planning of the Brunete operations; they were well planned but not well carried out.

On July 6th the Republicans attacked with fifty thousand men in the region of Brunete, north-west of Madrid, and with a further twenty-five thousand in the sector of Villaverde, south-west of the capital. their objective was Navalcarnero, the main centre of communications for the whole Nationalist front. Had they succeeded they would have inflicted a major disaster on the Nationalists. The battle raged savagely in intense heat until

July 26th, and resulted in the total rout and virtual destruction of the Republican forces; it has been estimated that their casualties were in the neighbourhood of thirty thousand. However, the offensive did oblige the Nationalists to withdraw large numbers of troops from the north, and so delayed their attack on Santander.

On August 14 the Santander offensive began; but from the south, and not, as we expected, from the east, where we were stationed. For the moment our orders were simply to stay where we were while the main attack, launched by three Spanish Navarre Brigades and two Italian regular divisions, broke through the enemy defences round the town of Reinosa. For the first two days the Republicans fought stubbornly in terrain particularly suitable for defence; but on the 16th the Navarrese took Reinosa, while the Italians, attacking boldly in the face of determined opposition, stormed the Escudo Pass. These two victories forced the gateway through the Cantabrian Cordillera, and the Nationalists continued their advance against rapidly disintegrating opposition.

On August 22nd the 6th Navarre Brigade on our left occupied the positions in front of them without firing a shot or finding an enemy. At 10.30 the next morning we received the order to advance. We climbed steeply for two and a quarter hours under the blazing sun; then started to advance along a spur leading towards the enemy trenches. We were at the tail of the column, but we should have been in no greater danger had we been at the head; the enemy had fled the night before and there was no sign of them. I noticed that their trenches were skilfully sited and deep. During the afternoon we continued our advance westward along the top of a ridge; on either side of us was a deep valley, with a corresponding ridge beyond it, along which I could see parallel columns of troops advancing. Progress was slow, and when we halted for the night we seemed to have covered only a few miles. Where we rested were some dug-outs, abandoned by the enemy, with dry straw inside. Thinking I should be warmer there, I very stupidly lay down to sleep in one of them; but I found sleep impossible, owing to the attentions of a million fleas.

The advance continued soon after dawn. Our *tercio* was detached to act as a flank guard to the column, which meant that we had to go down into the valley on our left and reconnoitre the villages there—picturesque little mountain hamlets with enchanting, evocative names, like *Nuestra Señora de las Nieves* (Our Lady of the Sorrows). There were no traces of the enemy, but we had plenty of hard work climbing in and out of the ravines that intersected the valley. In the early evening we arrived at a cluster of white, red-roofed houses, surrounded by cornfields and orchards, called The Bridge of Guriezo; here was a crossroads and a bridge over the River Aguera that had not been destroyed. We had orders to halt for the night. Major Uhagón detailed one company for outpost duties; another was sent to patrol the village, on the look-out for enemy stragglers who might be in hiding, and for booby-traps. A series of small explosions soon showed that this last precaution was fully justified; the enemy had laid a few traps in the form of hand-grenades, which were easily discovered and caused no casualties. We need not have worried about enemy stragglers, for the villagers were heartily sick of the Republicans and themselves handed over two *milicianos* who were in hiding. When Uhagón, by nature a kind and gentle person, heard what these men had done in the village, he had them shot out of hand.

The following morning the remainder of the 2nd Navarre Brigade arrived and halted around the village. Nobody seemed to know what the next move would be; but just after lunch news arrived that Santander was on the point of surrender, and our troops were to enter the city the following morning. The previous day the 1st Navarre Brigade had captured the town of Torrelavega, west of Santander, cutting the only escape route to Asturias; a large part of the Republican Army was trapped. Uhagón sent for me and suggested that I should take a fortnite's leave: 'We shall have nothing to do for a while,' he said, 'and so I am sending off any officers I can spare. Start as soon as you like.'

It turned out that the news of the surrender of Santander was a little premature; I have already told how Rupert Bellville and Ricardo González discovered this to their cost.

When we reached Bilbao that evening I found an American friend, Reynolds Packard, the United Press correspondent, and Dick Sheepshanks of Reuters. They were about to leave by car for Santander, which they hoped to enter with the first of our troops; they suggested I should come with them. We started just before one and drove all night, having to make a long detour to the south. About 6 a.m. we were held up for two hours by an Italian picket, but by nine o'clock we had reached a hill looking across the marshes to Santander. A column of Italians was formed up on the road, headed by a squadron of their miniature two-man tanks.

After half-an-hour's wait we saw two men approaching wearily along the road from the city; they turned out to be the Garrison Commander and the Chief of Police of Santander, coming to parley with the Nationalist commanders, General Dávila and General Bergonzoli, who stood apart in a field beside the road. Both delegates looked very white, but whereas the policeman remained quite steady and dignified throughout the brief discussion, the soldier seemed on the point of collapse. The interview was brought to a close when one of them expressed the hope that the Nationalists would spare the women and children; at which gratuitous insult General Dávila ordered them to withdraw.

Squadrons of Nationalist aircraft flew low over the city in close formation, while a mountain battery was assembled and trained on the town in case of resistance. Nothing happened for another hour; then the column beside us formed up to begin their march. The tanks went first, clattering down the steep hill in single file at a dangerous speed, followed by a column of motorcyclists, each carrying a light machine-gun mounted on the handle-bars. Then came the two Italian Divisions, *Littorio* and *XXIII de Marzo*, followed by a nondescript and scruffy Italian militia unit, the *Fiamme Nere*. Spanish troops were entering the town by another route.

We left our car to walk with the leading Italian infantry. It was a hot, glaring day and we were choked by the dust thrown up by the tanks and motor-cyclists. Parties of *Guardia Civil* accompanied our column, some on foot, others on motor-cycles. On our way we met groups of men hurrying away from the town; most of them were wearing blue overalls, clearly militiamen making a last pathetic attempt to escape. They were rounded up by the *Guardia Civil* and made to fall in at the rear of the column under escort; later they were all herded into the bullring to be screened. I was walking with a Spanish friend, a Requeté temporarily attached to the Press Office; we had out-distanced the infantry and were some way ahead of the column when we saw a camouflaged car coming towards us from the town with four militiamen inside. We held it up with our pistols and ordered the occupants to produce their papers; when they failed to do so, we made them get out, disarmed them and handed them over to some police who appeared at that moment. They were too demoralized to resist. My friend, who had his own car, suggested that I should take possession of this one, a fine new Citroën coupé. Thinking it would be useful to my *tercio*, which was very short of cars, I drove it a little way off the road, locked it and rejoined the column. As we neared the centre of the town we found the road lined deep with civilians, who waved to us, pelted us with flowers and cheered as though they had gone mad. I noticed women and girls wearing their best clothes, pathetically shoddy though they were, their faces transported with joy, yet showing the signs of months of fear and famine that no make-up could conceal. Republican rule in Santander had been particularly savage; hundreds of Nationalist supporters were thrown to their death from the top of the cliffs near the lighthouse on Cabo Mayor.

I left the triumphal procession to wander through the town on my own. Almost the first thing that struck me was that the side streets were crowded with dejected militiamen, some of them still carrying arms, but all paralyzed by the suddenness and extent of their disaster. They ignored me, showing neither hatred nor fear at the sight of my uniform. The civilians, on the other hand, were far from indifferent when they saw my red beret; men would come up to me and shake me by the hand, women would embrace me, kissing me on both cheeks—much more often old women than young, I reflected wistfully. Noticing my height and fair colouring they would ask me if I were German. When I replied that I was English their enthusiasm was overwhelming. Some of the Nationalist soldiers were natives of Santander;

there were moving scenes as they found members of their families, or anxiously questioned friends for news of them. I saw no signs of damage in the town, in contrast to the broken glass and debris that had littered the streets of Bilbao.

By half past three I had seen enough, and so decided to return to Bilbao. My new Citroën was full of oil and petrol, obviously in preparation for a long journey. On the outskirts of town I stopped to ask an Italian sentry if he knew whether the coast road was clear of the enemy, of whom a large number must have been trapped between Santander and our troops advancing from the east. He assured me it was clear. For the first twenty-five miles the road was deserted; I saw neither human beings nor animals. The car went beautifully. Leaving the promontory with Santoña and its lighthouses on my left, I drove on without incident until I approached the little fishing port of Laredo. The outskirts and the narrow streets of the town were thronged with men in blue overalls and black berets, carrying rifles slung from their shoulders, pistols and grenades at their belts. It was only when the press in the street forced me to slow down to a walking pace that I realized who these were; I had driven right into the middle of the Republican Army, or a portion of it which had been cut off by our rapid advance to Santander. It was impossible to turn the car; my only hope was to drive on as unconcernedly as I could and hope that I would be taken for the advanced guard of the victorious Nationalists, come to accept their surrender. Of course it would be too bad for me if they had no mind to surrender; wearing my scarlet beret with the silver *fleur-de-lis* and carrying a large 9 millimetre automatic, I was only too obviously an enemy.

Ironically I was reminded of the words of a charming little song from this town, which our Requetés used to sing:

> *Yo no te quiero, chica*
> *Yo no te quiero, no!*
> *Porque los mis amores*
> *Son de Laredo, son!*

Now I knew something of what the former occupants of my Citroën must have felt when we stopped them outside Santander. However, I forced my feature into what I hoped would seem a confident grin and drove on, sounding my horn to clear the way. The *milicianos* stared at me curiously but no one tried to stop me until I was beginning to get clear of the town. Then a couple of men with white arm-bands signaled to me to stop, though without pointing their rifles at me; as I passed them I called out, in what I trusted was an authoritative voice, '*Tercio de Nuestra Señora de Begoña!*' and drove on. In the driving mirror I saw their faces gaping in blank astonishment. I tried this formula on two subsequent occasions with the same success; but I confess I felt relieved when at last I met the advanced units of our 'Mixed Brigades' near Castro Urdiales. It was with some astonishment that I heard the B.B.C. News announce the following day that ten thousand Basque Republican troops had taken up defensive positions on the road between Santander and Castro Urdiales.

I decided to spend my leave in San Sebastian, where I was certain of finding friends at this time of year; but I would go first to Vitoria to collect my mail from England and some pieces of luggage I had left there. Next morning I set out proudly in my new car and reached Vitoria without incident. there disaster overtook me, through my own inexperience and stupidity. I was foolish enough to think that I could get oil and petrol from the Army Service Corps with the excuse that the car was to be used by my tercio. As I had no papers to support my statement, and as the car had a Santander number-plate, it was promptly impounded; moreover I had no identity card, and in the heat of Vitoria and my chagrin at losing my new car I flew into a rage, was very rude to the officer at the depot and was lucky to escape arrest.

I was not disappointed in my expectation of finding friends in San Sebastian. Arriving at the Hotel Continental, I was welcomed almost as a son by the manageress, a generous-hearted French-woman who, at the risk of her own life, had protected many Nationalist sympathizers during the period of Republican rule in San Sebastian. Next, walking into Chicote's Bar for an early drink to help me forget the loss of my car, I found Noel FitzPatrick with another friend of mine, Michael Larrinaga, the son of a well-known Liverpool shipowner; having retained his Spanish nationality, Larrinaga had come to Spain early in the war to enlist in the Artillery. They were sipping two of Perico Chicote's Specials with the air of rapt concentration which is due any masterpiece. Before the Civil War Chicote's in Madrid was already famous; now he had opened in San Sebastian. If there is a world hierarchy of barmen—and I suggest hierarchy as the most suitable word—Perico Chicote must be one of its principal Cardinals; famous in two continents, as much for the warmth of his heart as for the skill of his hand, he radiated through his bar in San Sebastian an atmosphere of *simpatía*, in which past troubles and dangers, future worries and fears alike were forgotten.

In Chicote's the men liked to let their hair down and relax; sweethearts and wives, therefore, though not forbidden, were discouraged. They went to the Bar Basque, where the men usually joined them after their drinks at Chicote's.

I had learnt one thing about the Requetés; for all their courage and endurance, their patriotism and self-sacrificing idealism, they lacked the strict discipline and technical training that are so necessary in modern warfare. This war had altered radically since the early days, and the old qualities of willingness and valour were no longer enough. Only in the Foreign Legion, I was convinced, could I hope to learn first-class soldiering. They were the troops on whom General Franco depended for the most difficult operations. Somehow, I decided, I must join the Foreign Legion; but having worked my way from the ranks to be an officer in the Requetés, I was reluctant to enlist as a private in the Legion and start again. After a great deal of thought I decided to go to Salamanca and see if I could get a posting to the Legion in my present rank.

On my way I stayed a night in Burgos, where I ran into Pablo Merry del Val; with him was Sir Arnold Wilson, Member of Parliament for Hitchin, whom I had met when I was the Secretary of the Conservative Association at Cambridge. One of the most controversial figures of his time, Sir Arnold Wilson had a distinguished and sensational career, mostly in the Middle East; he was an outstanding authority on Persia and Iraq. A man of abnormally forceful personality, absolute integrity and decided political views, he could tolerate no opposition, however sincere; he therefore made numerous and powerful enemies. He was gifted with truly phenomenal mental and physical powers: for instance, he could memorize a book after reading through it once, and his idea of a pleasant summer holiday was to sign on for three months as a stoker in a cargo boat in the Persian Gulf. When the war broke out with Germany he became, at the age of fifty-five, a Pilot Officer and rear gunner in the R.A.F., having passed every physical test that could be devised to stop him. 'I will not,' he said, 'shelter behind a rampart of young bodies.' He was killed the same year, when his aircraft was shot down in flames over Holland. His character was a remarkable mixture of ruthlessness and kindness; personally I experienced the greatest kindness from him, and will always value the memory of his friendship.

Over dinner I told them of my wish to join the Foreign Legion. 'You're in luck,' said Merry del Val. 'General Millán Astray is here in the hotel. I'll have a word with him afterwards and see what can be done.' General Millán Astray, the famous 'Father of the Legion' and its co-founder with Franco, was the most famous, even fabulous, figure in Nationalist Spain, because of his legendary courage and the number of times he had been seriously wounded. A flamboyant personality, with one arm and one eye and a severe limp, he attracted immediate attention in any gathering. In matters concerning the Legion his power was absolute.

Merry del Val spoke to him for a few minutes, then called me over. The General shot questions at me like a machine-gun, concentrating his one eye upon me in a fierce unblinking glare. Apparently my answers satisfied him, for he concluded by saying, 'I will speak personally to the Generalissimo and recommend that you be admitted to the Legion as Alférez. Go to your *tercio* of Requetés and get your discharge. Then wait in Salamanca for your orders from the Legion. Good luck to you!'

CHAPTER SIX

I found Major Uhagón and his *tercio* at Riaño, north-east of León and just south of the famous Picos de Europa, on the borders of Asturias. The war in the north was virtually over and Uhagón thought it unlikely that they would see any action before it finished. I was tempted to linger longer with the Requetés in the delightful village beside a swift and swirling trout stream, where the yellowing birches under the clear September sky made a warm contrast against the grey and sombre grandeur of the eight thousand foot peaks which towered above the valley. But my orders from Millán Astray were to go as soon as possible to Salamanca; and so I said an affectionate farewell to Uhagón and my other friends.

There was a cosmopolitan atmosphere in Salamanca. The long centre table in the Gran Hotel dining-room was reserved for the German military observers, most of them senior officers; a general presided. They were an earnest party, who seemed to take little pleasure in their food or drink, and who kept very much to themselves. At a smaller table nearby sat the newspaper correspondents, among them Randolph Churchill, Pembroke Stevens, Reynolds Packard and his wife and Philby of *The Times*; Churchill's clear, vigorous voice could be heard deploring with well-turned phrase and varied vocabulary the inefficiency of the service, the quality of the food and, above all, the proximity of the Germans, at whom he would direct venomous glances throughout the meal. 'Surely,' he exclaimed loudly, 'there must be one Jew in Germany with enough guts to shoot that bastard Hitler!'

O'Duffy's brigade had gone home; but a few stragglers remained, including my friend, Peter Lawler, a hard-bitten little Irish-Australian who had served with the A.I.F. in the First World War. During the troubles in Ireland he had been an intimate and trusted lieutenant of Michael Collins; in his own part of the country he was still known as 'The Commandant'. At this time he was waiting in Salamanca to collect six months of back pay due to him from the Spaniards, who were responsible for paying the Irish Brigade. When he received it, a month or so later, he returned to Ireland, very bitter against O'Duffy.

Standing one day in the hall of the hotel I was accosted by a Falstaffian figure with a high, bald forehead and a small blonde moustache, who introduced himself in a direct, almost abrupt manner as Archie Lyall, an author and free-lance journalist. He had just come from Santander, where he had been reporting the trials of war criminals by the Nationalists. As a qualified barrister he considered that they had been very fairly conducted and that the sentences on those found guilty had been just. Previously, he had written a multi-lingual vocabulary entitled *Lyall's 25 Languages of Europe*, some travel books on the Balkans, Portuguese West Africa, and Soviet Russia, and a gay little satire, which I had read called, *It Isn't Done: Or the Future of Tabu Among the British Islanders.*[1] He had also founded and administered a donkey hospital in Fez, supported by contributions from rich and charitable old ladies in the United States of America. When I met him he was about thirty-five years of age. An entry under his name in *Who's Who* described his hobbies as 'Reading, travelling and collecting matchbox labels.'

I found him an ideal companion during this time of waiting; for not only was he a witty conversationalist, but he had a remarkable faculty for nosing out the best places in town for food, drink and entertainment; the second of these was important because bars were supposed to close at midnight, after which the only place where we could get a drink was in the *Barrio Chino*, or brothel quarter. Here Lyall found a night club where we could drink and listen to the *guitarrista* and a singer, who gave a brilliant and moving interpretation of García Lorca's lament for Sánchez Mejías.

Sometimes Lawler would come with us; but such occasions had explosive possibilities because of Lyall's tendency to tease Lawler and the latter's quick temper. When Lawler would start to inveigh against O'Duffy and the ruin he had brought so fine a fighting force, Lyall would interrupt with some such observation as: 'But surely you can't expect the Irish to be any use in Spain? There aren't any hedges here for them to shoot behind.' As half an Irishman myself, I would repudiate the slander, but Lawler would storm out, shouting: 'Ye great buckin' whore!'

About this time Pablo Merry del Val suggested that I should accompany him and Sir Arnold Wilson on a quick tour of Castille and the Basque Provinces. My orders to join the Legion might not arrive for another month, but Merry del Val arranged that I should be notified immediately if they came while we were away. With us came Wing-Commander Archie James, Conservative Member for Wellingborough, who was in Salamanca for a brief visit. Sir Arnold Wilson was collecting material for an article he was writing for *The XIXth Century and After*, of which he was then a director.

Arriving in Toledo we went to examine the ruins of the Alcázar. We were looking across the Tagus beyond the Alcántara bridge when a battery of field guns opened fire behind us; we heard the shells bursting across the river. Soon afterwards there came the sound of intense machine-gun fire. 'This takes me back,' said James. We later heard that a *bandera* of the Legion, supported by two *tabores* of Moors, had attacked and cleared the enemy out of the positions from which they had been able to shell and snipe at Toledo.

---

[1] The last of these works was, I believe, the forerunner of the U and non-U controversy; the first enabled a friend of mine to complete the seduction of a Lithuanian chambermaid in the space of fifteen minutes.

Although I did not know it at the time, the bandera was the 14th, which I was to join.

The same evening I was sitting in a café opposite the Alcázar, waiting for the others, when a large party of officers of the Legion came in; by their yellow flashes I knew they were from the 5th Bandera, in which Bill Nangle was serving. FitzPatrick had told me to make myself known; I was anxious to meet Nangle and so I approached the party and asked for him. When he came in a few minutes later, he joined me at my table.

I had heard a great deal about him and his strange career from FitzPatrick. After leaving Sandhurst he joined the Indian Army; but although he was an efficient soldier he found the life monotonous; moreover he was unable to show a proper respect for senior officers. At the end of his tour of duty in command of Fort Alexandra in tribal territory on the Frontier, which is alleged to be the highest fort in the world, he was required to write a report for the Staff at Simla. This he did, couched in the correct official phraseology, but spoiled the effect by adding as a postscript the irrelevant question: 'How much string does it take to go round St. Paul's?' By the time it reached the Staff, Nangle had gone to England on six months' leave. He had sent in his papers but, without waiting for them to be accepted, enlisted in the French Foreign Legion. He was enjoying his new life when the Prince of Wales, with whom his family had some influence, intervened with the French authorities; to his disgust Nangle found himself discharged. Now he had been just over a year in the 4th Bandera, where I discovered from his brother-officers, he was greatly respected and liked. He suffered from recurrent attacks of *cafard*, which had first come upon him during his service in the Sahara and which made him an awkward, sometimes dangerous companion. Family reasons obliged him to return to England in December of 1937, so that it was nearly six years before I saw him again.

When we had completed our tour of the north I returned to Salamanca. On the 26th October I received orders posting me to the First Tercio of the Legion, with the rank of alferez.[1] I was to sign on and draw my uniform at Talavera, then report to the headquarters of General Yagüe, General Commanding the Legion, at Illescas, on the road between Toledo and Madrid.

*   *   *

---

[1] I have already explained (Chapter 2) that the Legion was usually referred to as 'El Tercio'. In fact, at this time its official name was La Légion, and it was divided into two Tercios, each containing ten *banderas*, including one of tanks. The depot of the 1st Tercio was at Melilla in Morocco, that of the 2nd at Dar Riffien, near Cueta.

Harold Cardozo once told me that there were two ways of breaking into London journalism: the first, and hard, way was to serve an apprenticeship on the staff of a provincial newspaper; the second was to solicit influence. The trouble about the latter was that the editor and staff were inclined to look on you as a badly house-trained puppy; you were an object of resentment and any mess around the office was automatically attributed to you.

The same was true, though I did not then appreciate it, of the Spanish Foreign Legion. This was the *corps d' élite* of the Spanish Army; during the war it attracted the most efficient officers of the Regular Army and the most adventurous of the reservists and volunteers. Selection was strictly by merit. Apart from one or two, who had risen from the ranks, non-Spanish officers serving with banderas were virtually unknown. FitzPatrick and Nangle were two exceptions; now I was a third. Naïve as I was, my reception came as a surprise; rather than gratitude for having come so far from home to fight in their cause I encountered at first only distrust and resentment from my fellow-officers; I was made to feel a gate-crasher. It was two months before they accepted me as one of themselves.

At the depot in Talavera I found a sour-faced captain, who made me sign a document committing me for the duration of the war, and issued me my uniform. Very proud of myself in my new green forage-cap with its red-and-gold tassel, I reported to Major Merino, General Yagüe's adjutant, at Illescas. Merino, a broad-shouldered man with a domed forehead, a sympathetic manner, and a quiet, commanding personality, told me that I had been posted to the 14th Bandera, which was now at Getafe. I arrived there on the night of October 31st, very tired after two days of travelling and virtually no sleep. The Bandera was quartered in the infantry barracks. I reported to the commanding officer, Major Alfonso de Mora Requejo, whom I found on the point of going to bed; he told me to report again at nine o'clock the following morning. I found a billet at a private house in the town. After impressing on my landlady that I must be called not later than eight next morning, I went straight to bed.

I awoke to find an agitated legionary standing over me. '*Mi Alférez*,' he began, 'the *Comandante* sends me to ask why you have not reported at nine o'clock as he told you. He requests that you come at once.' I looked at my watch; to my horror I found it was half past nine. Angrily I asked my landlady why she had not called me.

'Oh well,' she said serenely, 'we knew you were tired, and you were sleeping so soundly that we didn't like to wake you.'

'This is a fine start,' I thought as I threw on my clothes and followed the legionary out of the house.

Major de Mora, now in his early thirties, was a small, lightly-built man with finely chiseled features, a strong jaw, prominent nose and clear grey eyes, above which dark, curly hair receded from a high forehead. A lieutenant in the 4th Bandera when the war started, he had won the Medalla Militar—a rare distinction for a junior officer—at the storming of Badajoz in August 1936. His company led the assault on Puerta de la Trinidad—a gateway to the same walls that had caused Wellington's troops such terrible casualties—in the face of an intense concentration of rifle and machine-gun fire; of the whole company one officer and fifteen men remained to enter the city. Standing on the ramparts and waving the Nationalist flag to encourage his men, Mora was struck by a bullet that exploded the magazine of the pistol he carried on his hip. Two years later he was being treated daily by the Medical Officer for the still open wound; yet I, who saw him almost every day, knew nothing of his disability until told of it by another officer at the end of the war. A strict disciplinarian despite his quiet manner, he was a superb commander and a brilliant tactician. In battle, even when things looked blackest, I never saw him ruffled nor lose for one moment control of the situation; his mere presence in action filled us with confidence. At this interview, however, I felt no confidence at all. Dismissing contemptuously my apologies and excuses Mora gazed at me coldly.

'We require discipline in this unit,' he observed. 'I have assigned you to the 56th Company, which is the machine-gun company. Do you know anything about machine-guns?'

'No sir, but I can learn.'

'You'd better. Report now to Captain Almajach.' He ordered a legionary to conduct me to my new Company Commander.

Captain Gutiérrez Almajach was one of the best company commanders in the Legion. Of medium height and well-built, he wore a perpetual half-smile on his thin lips, which gave a first impression of humour, even of joviality; but his eyes behind the thick glasses were hard, and the half-smile more often than not turned into a sneer. Infinitely painstaking, ruthlessly efficient, undismayed in danger, he was at the same time the most bloody-minded man I have ever known. The legionaries feared him for his cruelty but respected him for his competence and courage. He chased me rigorously and unremittingly, as a result of which I learned much more than I would have done from some milder commander.

By the look he gave me when I reported to him I thought that he was going to summon the sanitary squad; then he asked my nationality, and I was certain of it:

'I shit on Englishmen,' he said simply.

The 14th Bandera was a newly-formed unit, composed partly of veterans from older banderas, partly of officers and other ranks fresh to the Legion. The four company commanders were all veterans. The leading company, the 53rd (in the Legion the companies are numbered consecutively throughout the Corps), was commanded by Captain Eduardo Cancela, a slender, handsome gallego with a rich, rakish laugh, a warm heart and a gay and gallant manner, which he fully maintained in battle; he it was who told me of Von Gaza's death near La Marañosa. He was the one officer who from the first accepted me as a friend and comrade. I shall have more to say of him later. The 53rd was the happiest company in the Bandera, nor was it by any means the least efficient.

A small dark officer, Captain Rodríguez, commanded the 54th Company. He had a likeable, ugly face and a pleasant, quiet personality. For some reason I never saw much of him or his company.

The 55th Company, when I arrived, was under the command of Captain José Luengo, a strange, erratic creature with sandy hair and pale blue eyes who always gave me the impression of being detached from his surroundings. He was an officer of many years' seniority in the Legion; but his career in Morocco and Spain had been punctuated by a series of distressing incidents, which eventually convinced his superiors that he would never be amenable to discipline. His eccentricities were a byword in the Corps; among them I remember the story of an occasion during manœuvres in Morocco when his commanding general, having expected to find him at the head of his platoon, and having commented unfavorably on his absence without leave, saw him the next day fighting a bull in the Ring at Málaga. Fearless in battle, he was unfortunately too much inclined to bring the atmosphere of the battlefield into the bar; after a few drinks in a café he would draw his pistol and, slowly and with great dignity, shoot out the lights one by one. He was universally loved in the Bandera, and even Mora had a soft spot for him; but eventually he went too far and was dismissed from the Service by a court-martial.

These three were rifle companies; the machine-gun company, as I have already said, was commanded by Captain Almajach. The officers of each rifle company had their own separate mess; those of the machine-gun company messed with Bandera Headquarters, that is to say with the *Comandante*, the Chaplain and the two Medical Officers. When I joined there was no Second-in-Command and no Adjutant.

The Chaplain, whose name I never knew because he was always addressed as *Páter*, was a Regular Army padre. He was a podgy, serious-minded man in his late thirties. A very devout, conscientious and kind-hearted person, he had to endure a good deal of teasing on account of his home town, Cuenca, which is a regular butt for Spanish comedians, in much the same way as Wigan used to be on the English music-hall. His chief and almost only relaxation was *julepe*, a card game at which most of the officers in the Bandera used to gamble—sometimes for much too high stakes; I was warned against learning this game by the amount of quarrels and bad blood that I saw it engender. Although he deplored my religion—he shook his head, deeply shocked, when I told him that clergymen of the Church of England were allowed to marry—he was unfailingly courteous to me, showing me many small kindnesses and always taking my side in arguments with other officers over Britain and the policy of the British government. He was greatly relieved when I assured him that I was not a Freemason; he had been convinced that all Protestants were Masons—a belief shared by most of the other officers. It was a waste of time trying to explain to Spaniards that English Freemasonry was a different thing from the Continental variety, which they abhorred because of its connection with the Popular Front governments in France and Spain. My friend FitzPatrick told me that what eventually finished his career in the Legion was his admission, in the course of an argument, that he was a Mason.

The senior of the two medical officers, Lieutenant Larrea, was also of the Regular Army and very like many of his opposite numbers in the R.A.M.C. A big man with a loud voice and bluff, hearty manner, he irritated me at first by his frequent attacks on England and the English, a country and people of which he knew nothing, and by his use of me as a target for his witty sallies or outbursts of bad temper. Later, when I found my way around, he became a good friend; indeed, it was impossible to dislike him, for he was fundamentally a conscientious and good-hearted man. When he was not baiting me he was baiting the Padre, his chief weapon being a flow of language that would have horrified many people not in Holy Orders. He was, I thought, unduly severe on the troops. On one occasion he shocked me by sending a man to the Punishment Squad for a fortnight because he asked to be sent to hospital for gonorrhea: 'Damned scrimshanker!' he exclaimed. 'Whoever heard of sending a man to hospital for a dose of clap?' His assistant, Alférez Ruíz, was a friendly little officer with a small moustache. He was cheerful, hard-working and very much liked.

The senior of my two fellow-officers in the machine-gun company was Lieutenant Noriega, a small, wiry, grey-haired man of many years' service, who had risen from the ranks. In general, legionaries do not like their ranker officers, but Noriega was an exception, for he treated them with a perfect blend of severity and kindness; they knew that he would never call upon them to do anything that he was not able and willing to do himself. Quick to discern and despise inefficiency or cowardice, they found neither in Noriega. He had a taciturn manner, a dry sense of humour and a remarkable knowledge of the world. Before joining the Legion he had been a seaman and had served aboard Pierrepoint Morgan's yacht. Subsequently, he had smuggled arms to one or other of the belligerents in the Gran Chaco war— I think to the Paraguayans.

Another officer, Alférez Colomer, a Catalan from Gerona, was about the same age as myself. He was a noisy, rancorous little man, for ever bickering with his brother-officers and bullying his men. He had been badly wounded in an earlier battle, which had perhaps affected his temper; but he always seemed to me to have a chip on his shoulder. His contentious nature was, literally, the death of him: one day, after I had left the Bandera, he became very drunk after a battle, and challenged another officer to a stupid competition to see which of them could pick up more of the unexploded hand-grenades lying in front of their trenches. Colomer picked up one too many; it blew his head off.

Among the Regular Officers in the Bandera were several who had been cadets at the Military Academy at Zaragoza when Franco was Commandant. Respected as an efficient soldier, he was equally feared as a martinet; many were the traps he laid for the unwary or undisciplined cadet. For instance, when he noticed one of them approaching down the street he would sometimes turn to look in shop window, apparently absorbed by what he saw; if the cadet was foolish enough to pass him without saluting, thinking himself unobserved, he would not have gone many paces before he would hear that dreaded, soft, high voice calling him back; betrayed by his reflection in the plate-glass window, he might be on the mat next morning.

He was just as severe on matters not strictly military but reflecting indirectly on the health and efficiency of the cadet. A model of rectitude in his own private life, he was also well aware of the temptations to which young men so easily succumb in a city. He therefore made it an order that every cadet, when walking out in the evening, must carry in his pocket at least one contraceptive. He would frequently stop cadets in the street and demand that they show him this armour; heavy was the penalty for him that failed to produce it.

As in all the banderas, with the exception of the extra one—the Jeanne d'Arc, composed entirely of French volunteers—the men in the 14th were ninety per cent Spaniards. The remainder were mostly Portuguese—good soldiers, although even the Spaniards found it hard to understand their speech. There were a few Germans—poor soldiers and despised by the rest—a White Russian and a Turk. The Turk was even harder to understand than the Portuguese, but as he hardly ever spoke it did not matter. I soon found that my command of Spanish was not nearly so good as I had thought, nor as good as it needed to be, especially when it came to the flow of abuse which a legionary expected as the proper accompaniment to any order given him. I had to put this right when I found that, without it, my orders simply were not obeyed.

The legionaries, like their officers, were all volunteers. Some were attracted by the prospects of adventure and danger which this *fuerza de choque*[1] provided, others by the better pay and food, others by the *esprit de corps* and the extra latitude allowed to legionaries when off duty; the majority were

---

[1] 'Shock Troops'—i.e. Foreign Legion and Moors in the Nationalist Army, International Brigades in the Republican.

impelled to join by a combination of them all. A few had signed on for five years, others for three, but most of them for the duration of the war.

Pay for officers and other ranks alike was about double that of the Regular Army; food was incomparably better. The usual midday and evening meals consisted of soup, followed by fish or *pasta*, a main dish of meat, and pudding or cheese, with wine and coffee; moreover the food was extremely well cooked. At the depots of Ceuta and Melilla it was served to the men on china plates by waiters in white coats. The officers had the same rations as the men, supplemented by a few luxuries bought out of their pay.

Spanish troops, when well led and properly disciplined, show superb qualities of courage and endurance. It was the pride of the Legion that it developed those qualities to their full. From the moment he joined it was impressed on the recruit that he belonged to a corps apart—the finest fighting force, he was taught to believe, in the world; it was up to him to prove himself worthy of the privilege. Battle was the purpose of his life; death in action was his greatest honour; cowardice the ultimate disgrace. The motto of the Legion was '*Viva la muerte*!' It is easy for more phlegmatic nations to deride this 'cult of death'; but it is essentially in keeping with the Spanish character, and it produced the best soldiers of the Civil War—men virtually impervious to cold and hunger, danger and fatigue. As an Englishman I can only say that the thrill of serving with and commanding such troops was one of the greatest experiences of my life.

The turn-out and bearing of the legionary, whether with his bandera or on leave, was expected to be, and was, far superior to that of other units. The greatest freedom was allowed to him when off duty; he was taught to take pride in his individuality; his full official designation was '*Caballero Legionario*'—Gentleman Legionary. In contrast, discipline on duty and the field was extremely strict, even savage by English standards. Orders were executed at the double and usually reinforced by threats or imprecations; the slightest hesitation, laxity or inefficiency was punished on the spot by a series of blows across the face and shoulders from the *fusta*—a pliant switch made from a bull's pizzle, which was carried by all officers and sergeants. More serious or persistent defaulters were sent to the *Pelotón de Castigo*, or Punishment Squad, where they toiled at the most exhausting tasks from before dawn until well after dark under the command of a corporal, usually chosen for his ferocity; in this mobile glasshouse food was meagre, beatings frequent and severe. A dirty rifle was enough to earn a man a month in the *Pelotón*. Insubordination, whether or not in the face of the enemy, was punishable by death on the spot.

Men trained under such discipline were apt to emerge with blunted sensibility, a callous indifference to suffering, whether in themselves or in others, and an unfeeling disregard for the horrible and squalid aspects of war. One of my machine-gun sergeants told me with great satisfaction how his comrades had contrived to spend a comfortable night in the open in pouring rain after an attack in the Casa de Campo: the ground, he explained, was waterlogged but fortunately (sic) it was littered with corpses; these they collected, arranged them in rows, and laid down on them, covering themselves with their greatcoats. FitzPatrick, after the capture of Talavera by the 5th Bandera, found a legionary hammering at the face of a dead militiaman with the butt of his rifle; when FitzPatrick pointed out that the man was dead, the legionary answered serenely, 'I know sir, but look! He has some fine gold teeth.'

*   *   *

The 14th Bandera had been 'bloodied' in action about a fort-night before I joined, in the operation which Archie James and I witnessed from the Alcázar at Toledo. It had come out of the battle well and with improved morale. Now everyone was certain that we would soon be thrown into some great offensive that would see the end of the war.

I had four machine-guns in my platoon, divided into two sections, each under a sergeant. The guns were Maxims, manufactured—and used—during the First World War; they had recently been taken from the Republicans. They were unsatisfactory factory weapons, already worn-out with service and very liable to go out of action through breakage of the firing-pin. There were twelve machine-guns in the Company, and two 81 mm. mortars.

The Bandera remained in Getafe for a week after I joined. My time was spent in routine training, getting to know my men, and learning about the guns under the instruction of one or other of my sergeants. I could have wished that I had been sent to a rifle company, for I knew nothing of the tactical employment of machine-guns, and nothing of their mechanism. Almajach, who would tolerate no inefficiency in his Company, drove me relentlessly with abuse and exhortation to abandon my slovenly Requeté ideals of soldiering and to perfect my fluency in Spanish.

I was *Oficial de Guardia* (Orderly Officer) one night and *Oficial de Vigilancia* another; the latter was a duty only performed when the Bandera was in reserve or resting. The *Vigilancia* was a squad of legionaries with a sergeant and a subaltern, whose duty it was to patrol the streets, to see that there was no rioting or disorderly conduct, and to eject legionaries from bars and brothels by midnight. The service was provided by each company in rotation. Sometimes it meant an energetic evening, when there were brawls between legionaries and soldiers of other units; then the call of '*A mí La Legión!*' would ring down the streets, bringing every legionary within earshot to the rescue of his embattled comrade, and the *Vigilancia* must hasten to separate the combatants. But on peaceful nights the *Vigilancia* and his sergeant could sit in the comfortable parlour of some quiet brothel, sipping coffee and brandy with Madame and listening to her complaints about the rising cost of living, of the pranks of her girls and of the scandalous conduct of the troops—not the gentlemen of the Legion, of course—who frequented her establishment.

On November 7th the Bandera received orders to move. We were to march to Leganés, two kilometres away, there to entrain for Talavera. our final destination was unknown, but it was rumoured that we were going to the Guadalajara front, north-east of Madrid. Within two hours the Bandera was formed in column outside the barracks. The order was given to march, my men shouldered the dismantled guns and the cases of ammunition and we set off for Leganés.

CHAPTER SEVEN

Rumour for once was right; we were bound, eventually, for the Guadalajara front, although it took us a month to get there. After three days' wait in Talavera we were put into another train and journeyed for two days and nights, via Salamanca, Valladolid and Burgos, to a place called Calatayud in Aragón, about fifty miles south-west of Zaragoza. Officers travelled in first-class carriages, five to a compartment, sergeants in second-class carriages and the men, singing lustily all the way, in cattle-trucks, where they must have frozen at night. Calatayud is an ancient town, grouped round the ruins of a Moorish castle, which dominates it from the top of a bare escarpment and from the name (Kalat Ayub, or Ayub's Castle) is derived. The poet Martial was born there. Today it is better known among Spaniards through the words of a bawdy song, which the men were forbidden to sing while we were there because it gave great offence to the inhabitants. Even the first four lines, which are harmless enough, sufficed to upset a Calatayudian:

Si vas a Calatayud
Pregunta por La Dolores
Que es una moza lozana
Y amiga de hacer favores.[1]

After a mug of coffee we embarked in a long column of open lorries—the men huddled in the backs of the vehicles, exposed to the keen wind—and were driven south to the small town of Calamocha, sixty-five kilometres away on the Teruel road. Here we were billeted very comfortably, the officers in private houses; we settled down and relaxed while awaiting further orders. Training duties were very light and we had plenty of leisure. Calamocha is a picturesque little place, hundreds of years old; its most attractive features, I seem to remember, were a church, surrounded by a shallow moat where mules used to paddle, and a humped bridge of stones across a rushing stream.

The people of Calamocha, like all people we met in Aragón, received us with the warmest friendliness and hospitality. The *maños*, as the Aragonese are called colloquially, have the reputation of being hard-headed, plain-speaking, obstinate and even stubborn. They are frugal and straightforward—the North-Country word 'jannock' describes them well;

---

[1] If you go to Calatayud
Ask for Delores
Who is a lusty wench
And fond of doing favours.

they are also, in my experience at least, among the most generous-hearted people on earth. I spent the greater part of a year in and around Aragón, where I noticed that, although the country looked bare and uninviting, the people fared remarkably well for food and drink. They had a great hatred and contempt for the Republicans, which was reflected in their new attitude towards us.

About this time I had a new batman assigned to me, a legionary about my own age named Paulino Albarrán. A peasant from a village near Salamanca, he was sturdily built, with a podgy, fresh-complexioned face, slightly protruding eyes and the expression of a friendly, puzzled little pig, which earned him the nickname of *Tocinito* (*tocino* is bacon, or fat meat). He was one of the best-natured fellows I ever met, but he was a better soldier than servant—at least when he first came to me.

In the afternoons I usually went for walks outside the town. The bare contours and harsh colours of the countryside were softened and refined by the mellow sunlight and clear air of late autumn. The grape harvest was in, and the peasants were making the new wine. One day, walking down a narrow track, I came upon a white-washed farmhouse; in a vineyard beside it was a wine press, where an old man with a white, pointed beard was working, surrounded by his family. When he caught sight of me he called out in a hearty, raucous voice: 'Come here, young man!' As I approached he roared at me. 'You know me? I'm Satan! Oh yes, they call me Satan because of my beard. Also, perhaps, because of the good wine I make. We'll drink some together, you and I!' First he made me sample some of the new must, pouring me out a great beaker of bubbly, purple liquid. When I had drunk this and praised it, while his family stood by, the men with broad and friendly grins, and the girls giggling happily, he went indoors and fetched a dusty bottle. It was tangy and heavy and very strong. He made me drink half of it, sharing the other half between himself and his two sons. Then he fetched another bottle. This he split with me, muttering the while, 'Oh yes, I'm Satan, I am,' and wagging his white beard, now flecked with purple. At last I was able to take my leave and make my way, unsteadily and with several halts to rest, back to Calamocha. At the entrance to the plaza I met the Padre, talking to Sergeant Lorios. 'Holá!' he cried, 'where have you been?'

'Drinking with Satan,' I gasped, and left him standing in the middle of the road.

Curro Lorios, one of the well-known family from Algeciras, had been at school in England and was married to an English girl. Before coming to us he had been attached to the Irish brigade as a sergeant-interpreter, and some of the bitterness and cynicism induced by the experience remained with him to be transferred to the legion. He had a just grievance, in that he should have been an officer; but General Yagüe had refused his application for a commission on the grounds that, at thirty-five, he was too old to be a subaltern. Larios believed the real reason to be that Yagüe, having strong Falangist sympathies, was prejudiced against anyone with an influential name; certainly, there were subalterns in the Legion over thirty-five. Larios left us just before Christmas for the 13th Bandera.

After a fortnight we moved by lorry to Torrecilla del Robollar, a village in the bleak uplands east of the Teruel-Zaragoza road, about twelve miles from Calamocha and three miles from the front line. Our life here was no more exciting than in Calamocha, except that we had to be ready to go into action at an hour's notice. The only event to interrupt the monotony was the Feast of the Immaculate Conception on December 8th, the *Virgen de la Inmaculada* being the Patroness of the Spanish Infantry. After Mass we celebrated the *fiesta* with an enormous lunch, preceded by a party at Bandera Headquarters which all the officers attended; there was also a special lunch for the men. It would have been unfortunate for us had we been called upon to go into action that day—or the next. But calm reigned on all fronts—a calm that preceded one of the worst storms of the war.

Two days later the lorries came for us again. We started off at 5 a.m., down the twisting mountain road to Calamocha and right, along the main road to Calatayud; there we turned left along the main Madrid-Aragón road, and it became clear that we were at last bound for the Guadalajara front. About midday we stopped for lunch at Medinaceli; then we drove north through Almazán and west along the course of the Douro, a large village dominated by a square castle, which stood by itself on a mound. Here we disembarked and once again moved into billets.

There was no question of relaxation now; our second Guadalajara offensive was about to start and we had to be ready to leave at any moment. On December 13th Mora summoned all officers to a conference.

'The operations against Guadalajara and Madrid,' he told us, 'are about to begin. I expect the order to move at any time now. There are three Army Corps taking part: on the left the Army Corps of Castile under General Varela; in the centre the two Italian divisions and the two mixed divisions of *Flechas*, on the right the Marroquí Army Corps, which includes ourselves, under General Yagüe. Together with the 16th Bandera and elements of cavalry, artillery and tanks, we constitute the *Brigada Móvil* of the Army Corps. Our job, once the front is broken, will be to press on ahead of the other forces, capture important points behind enemy lines and hold them until relieved. The 16th Bandera and ourselves, operating in lorries, will form the Brigade's motorized infantry group, under Lieutenant-Colonel Peñaredonda, whom some of you know.'

There was a laugh in the back and a voice said, 'Oh yes, the deaf one.' Mora stared stonily at the speaker and continued:

'I will brief you in detail before we go into action. Meanwhile, here are one or two general points I want you to remember: there seems to be an idea among officers that their proper place in an advance is always at the head of their troops—Company Commanders in front of their companies and Platoon Commanders in front of their platoons; also that an officer has a duty to expose himself to enemy fire the whole time, in order to encourage his men. Both these ideas are nonsense, and I will have none of them in my Bandera. The only time when an officer's place is at the head of his men is in the final assault, as you all know. Otherwise, the Company Commander should be somewhere in the middle of his three platoons, where he can control them all; similarly, the Platoon Commander should be in between his front and his rear *Pelotones*. I want this rule observed. I assure you all that I will deal very seriously with any officer I see exposing himself needlessly, or allowing his men to do so. There will, I have no doubt, be plenty of suitable occasions for the display of courage; otherwise, an officer must keep his vanity and exhibitionism under restraint.'

He went on to deal with technical details: the employment of our machine-guns, the use of covering fire, the importance of keeping touch, the use of runners and the clear and concise drafting of messages in the field.

'One final point; you will see that the rights of the civilian population are scrupulously respected and that there is no looting. If there is any case of an attempt on the virtue of a woman, it will be punished on the spot by death.' He concluded: 'The orders I have just given you for these operations will be observed in any subsequent operations under my command.'

*   *   *

The situation of the provincial capital of Teruel, held by the Nationalists since the beginning of the Civil War, had always been precarious. Only in a civil war would a serious attempt have been made to hold it; for its military value was negligible. Forming a salient from the Nationalist lines and dominated on three sides by the Republicans, its only means of communication and supply consisted of a single road and railway running north-east through Calamocha to Zaragoza and Calatayud. The Republicans could overlook this road from their positions in the Sierra Palomera to the east of it, and were able to keep it under shell-fire. But Teruel was a town of nearly twenty thousand inhabitants, and so could not be abandoned to the enemy.

While General Franco was concentrating his troops for his offensive on Guadalajara, the Republicans were preparing theirs on Teruel. On December 15th they attacked with seventy thousand men. In twenty-four hours they had cut the road and railway to Calamocha and enveloped the city. The Nationalist defenders—a Brigade totaling about three thousand men, with one battery of artillery—retreated inside the perimeter. On December 21st there was fighting in the streets, and the Republican High Command announced the capture of the city—prematurely as it turned out.

The Nationalist were taken by surprise. General Franco immediately abandoned his projected attack on Madrid and moved troops to Teruel. He has been much criticized for this. If he had continued with his original plan he would probably have taken Madrid, an important gain to him and a very serious loss to the other side; whereas the capture of Teruel would bring little military advantage to the Republicans. On the other hand, the capture of Madrid by the Nationalists would not necessarily end the war. Possibly a more certain way, in the long run, was to destroy the Republican army around Teruel, opening the way for an advance to the Mediterranean coast. This, at any rate, seems to have been the Generalissimo's idea.

On December 22nd began the Nationalist counter-offensive to relieve Teruel. General Aranda's Army Corps (Galicia), which had been in reserve near Zaragoza, advanced from the north; General Varela's (Castile), withdrawn from the Guadalajara front, attacked from the south-west. Slowly they forced the Republicans back until, on the last day of the year, they were poised for the final thrust that would break through to the beleaguered garrison. Then it began to snow. The temperature dropped to minus twenty degrees centigrade. Further advance was impossible. Caught in the open by the blizzard at an altitude of over three thousand feet above sea-level, without shelter, without warm clothing and with no possibility of lighting fires, the Nationalists suffered more casualties during the next three or four days from the cold than from enemy action. General García Valiño, commanding the First Navarre Division,[1] told me later that he had three thousand five hundred cases of frost-bite. The Republicans, better protected from the weather, renewed their attacks against the city. On January 8th the garrison was overwhelmed; by the time the Nationalist were able to renew their advance Teruel was in Republican hands.

We in Berlanga de Duero knew nothing of these events but what we read in the scant official communiqués. The tension raised by Mora's conference and the prospect of imminent battle relaxed after a few days, when it became clear that the original plan had been abandoned. We were obliged to settle into a peaceful routine of parades, training and long route marches in snow-blizzards to toughen us. I was getting to know my men, whom I admired for their keenness and efficiency and liked for their wit and cheerfulness; I noticed that there was mutual respect and likening between them and my two sergeants. I was even beginning to understand something about the mechanism and tactics of the guns—though I doubt if Almajach would have agreed about this—when a new hazard was thrust on us, in the form of mules to carry the guns and ammunition. There were thirty-one of them in the

---

[1] The former Navarre Brigades had by now been expanded to Divisions.

company, of which I had eight—one for each gun and ammunition. This seemed to put paid to any idea of our operating as a motorized unit. At first the poor beasts were the objects of bitter complaints and curses. The legionaries detailed to look after them resented the work, nobody seemed to understand the loading of the guns and ammunition, and the mules themselves showed an obstinate, though not unreasonable reluctance to keep formation on parade and on the march; moreover, on the icy roads and streets they slithered all over the place. But as we became used to them we began to appreciate their qualities of strength, endurance and courage. With good treatment they became very tractable, and during the subsequent operations we found that they would carry heavy loads all day over the roughest mountain country, with scarcely any food and very little water; nor did they panic under fire.

Another hazard, but one we could never get used to, was the arrival in Berlanga of Lieutenant-Colonel Peñaredonda—'the deaf one'. He was a tall, well-built officer of about fifty, with a fleshy face and a discontented, almost menacing expression; he was a man of few words, and those were seldom pleasant. He had none of the qualities of the mules except obstinacy, as I was later to find out. For the moment he concentrated on keeping us busy all day, devising exercises and route marches for us and criticizing everything he saw. Naturally, the company commanders whom he criticized passed on the rocket to us, we passed it on to the sergeants and they excelled themselves in passing it on to the men—all in a temperature of twelve degrees below zero. The earlier happy atmosphere evaporated without any corresponding gain in efficiency.

Just before Christmas Captain Luengo left us, much to the relief of the café proprietors of Berlanga. His place was taken by Captain Alonso de Castañeda, a tall, fair man with a handsome face and a dashing manner. He was a regular Legion officer of the same seniority of Mora, intelligent, of independent mind, unorthodox views and a strongly argumentative nature. He loved to poke fun at the Church when the Padre was present; or to cast doubts on the universal depravity of the Republicans or on the sincerity of all Nationalist leaders, when Mora or Cancela were there to argue with him. He took my side in all disputes concerning British policy or behavior, but I felt he did it from contrariness rather than conviction. For all that, he had a sensitive mind, with an intelligent appreciation of literature and a sincere love of poetry. He was an extremely competent soldier.

My billet was a small house near the *Plaza Mayor*, kept by a middle-aged working man and his wife. They had two pretty daughters of about fifteen or sixteen, to the elder of whom Paulino spent his spare time paying spirited but, I fear, wholly unsuccessful addresses. They were all very kind to me, treating me as one of the family. I was lucky to get such a billet, because Berlanga was already full of troops when we arrived—the 16th Bandera, a *tercio* of Requetés and a company of German anti-tank gunners; the latter, I think, were in charge of some new equipment for testing, because they kept entirely to themselves and discouraged all friendly overtures from the Spaniards. Their quarters were in the *Palacio*, a three-hundred-year-old building in the main square. They caused me plenty of trouble one night, about a week before Christmas, when I was officer of the *Vigilancia*.

It was soon after midnight when a panting legionary reported at Bandera Headquarters that a fire had broken out in the Palacio. When I arrived I found the whole building ablaze, lighting up the sky, the square and the surrounding houses; even the castle on its bare mound seemed to be floodlit. The Germans had neglected to inform anybody until the fire was well under way, although they had removed all their ammunition and equipment to a place of safety; I did not see them at all that night, but heard later that they had been finding themselves new quarters. It was lucky for the inhabitants that they had troops in the town, for if they had been left to themselves I think all Berlanga would have been burnt. The Requetés and legionaries worked with a will, the former climbing up walls and clambering over roof-tops with axes and hoses, the latter forming a chain to pass buckets of water from the river and fountain to the two fire-engines. These appeared to date from about the same period as the Palacio, being simple little machines, hand-drawn and hand-operated, each with a crew of four puffing, laughing peasants. The rest of the male population stood grouping in doorways around the square, smoking cigarettes and pointing gaily to the fire. 'Look how it burns!' they cried to me. 'We haven't had a blaze like this for fifty years!' Pained looks greeted my brusque suggestion that they join in the work. The fire was too strong for us to hope to save the palace; all we could do was to try and stop it spreading. Luckily it was a calm night with no wind.

I was on my feet all night, detailing patrols to keep the streets clear of spectators, organizing a water-carrying service and directing operations with a hose from a roof-top. About half-past three I noticed that the legionaries had disappeared, leaving me with my small squad of *vigilantes* and a few Requetés to deal with the fire, which was still blazing fiercely. Putting my sergeant in charge, I ran to the building where two of our companies were quartered, roused them and set some to carry water and others to work the fire-engines, whose crews, tiring of their fun, had gone to bed. By six o'clock the Requetés had gone home, frozen and dead tired; and so I had to find the two other companies and turn them out. I should have had help from the *Vigilancia* of the 16th Bandera, but they were occupied in finding new quarters for two of their own companies, who had been burnt out of their old ones.

About seven o'clock the townspeople, having enjoyed a good night's rest, began to appear to see how things were going—but not to help. On my rounds I came upon two fire-engines standing idle and abandoned. With some difficulty I found the *Alguacil*, who corresponds roughly to the Town

Clerk; he was enjoying a quiet cigarette in a doorway. 'You may be interested to know,' I snapped at him, for my temper was wearing thing by the time, 'that two of your engines are standing over there, abandoned.' He took a puff, removed his cigarette and asked brightly, 'Do you mean that they should work?' However it turned out the engines did not belong to Berlanga, but to firemen from Burgo de Osma, fifteen miles away, who had been summoned when the fire started and had just arrived. I found four of these men strolling along the street, and told them sharply to get their engines working. They nodded genially: 'Certainly, sir! That's just what we're going to do—as soon as we've had a little drink to warm us up.'

I was thankful when my tour of duty ended half an hour later, and I could hand over to another officer. At half past eight I snatched a cup of coffee, shaved quickly and went on parade until lunch time. Somebody finally extinguished the fire in the late afternoon.

Christmas came, bringing a more optimistic tone in the official communiqués but still no orders for us. We began to wonder whether we were to remain forgotten in Berlanga while the greatest and, as we thought, culminating battle of the war was raging barely a hundred miles away.

The New Year opened sadly for me. On January 31st a Press car containing four friends of mine—Dick Sheepshanks, Kim Philby, and two American correspondents, Eddie Neil and Bradish Johnson—was passing through the village of Caude, eight miles north-west of Teruel, during an enemy artillery bombardment, when a 12.40 cm. shell burst beside it. Sheepshanks and Johnson were killed outright. Neil died a few days later; Philby escaped with a wound in the head.

On January 2nd a new alférez, called Campos, came to my company. Being senior to me he took over my platoon and I was put in command of the two 81 mm. mortars. It was a blow to me because I liked and thought I understood my men. They seemed to think so too, for a party of them, under a corporal, came to see me and begged me to ask the Captain to retain me in command. I was fool enough to pass this on to Almajach, who said coldly: 'Of course they want you. They can get away with more under you than they could under a Spanish officer.'

Campos was a tall, flabby young man, a little stupid and morose. He told me that he had been one of the original members of the Falange in Granada, and that he had taken part in the firing squad that executed the poet García Lorca. I prefer to believe him a liar. The Nationalists, including the Falange, strongly denied any responsibility for Lorca's death, attributing to the vengeance of his private enemies, of which he had a large number; certainly he had many good friends on the Nationalist side who would have saved him if they could. His murder was a crime that robbed the world of one of its greatest living lyric poets; the mystery of it has never been satisfactorily explained. I say this with all respect to Mr. Gerald Brenan, who claims to have fixed the responsibility of the *Guardia Civil*.[1] No two versions of the tragedy coincide. Campos's account was not circumstantial enough to convince me even at the time; he was careful not to mention it front of Alonso de Castañeda. The reason he alleged for the execution—that Lorca was a Communist, who was to have led a column against Granada—is too absurd to be worth consideration. In his lines on the death of his friend, Sánchez Mejías, it seems, lies Lorca's own epitaph:

> *Díle a la luna que venga,*
> *Que no quiero ver la sangre*
> *De Ignacio sobre la arena.*[2]

A day or two after the appearance of Campos a Subteniente arrived to join the 56th Company. This rank corresponds roughly though not precisely, to that of Warrant Officer Class 1 in the British Army; the rank, suppressed in the Regular Army, persisted in the Legion. This particular creature was a cocky, officious little man with a shiny red face and pert expression, a squeaky, angry voice and the appearance and manners of a monkey. He started to throw his weight about from the first moment, abusing the N.C.Os. and laying into the men with his *fusta* on the slightest pretext. It was impossible for us to control him, for Almajach approved of him, or at least his methods. With the officers his manner varied between impertinence to us ensigns and a sickening obsequiousness towards the Captain. Day and night the hours were made hideous by his squawks of complaint or abuse.

At last we received orders to move, and on January 10th we left Berlanga in a long column of lorries. To our disappointment our destination proved to be, not Teruel, but another part of the static Guadalajara front—the ruined and virtually deserted village of Almadrones. Situated just off the main Madrid-Zaragoza road, about 65 miles north-east of Madrid, it had suffered severely from bombardment during the Guadalajara battle of the previous March. Few of the houses were undamaged, and the only inhabitants were a handful of miserable, underfed peasants who wandered disconsolately through the dirty streets. We lingered here a week, then set off on foot with our mules and all our equipment and a twenty-mile march eastwards. It was a hard march, across difficult country, but the weather was bright and cold and the men were in excellent spirits, singing lewd songs from the different regions of Spain when neither the Padre nor the Major were around, both of

---

[1] *The Face of Spain.*
[2] Tell the moon it's time to rise,
   I do not want to see his blood
   Where split upon the sand it lies.
                   (Translation—Roy Campbell.)

whom disapproved of the communal bawdry. In the evening we came to the mountain hamlet of Torrecuadrada, about two miles from the front line.

The inhabitants of this region were the poorest I ever saw in Spain, the country the most desolate. It is to the credit of the Falange relief organization, *Auxilio Social*, that as soon as the war was over it directed a great deal of its effort towards improving conditions here. Every morning and evening at meal times the children of the village would gather round our field kitchens, each carrying a little jar or bowl, which the cooks would fill with meat, fish, vegetables and bread. After two days the villagers asked us to stop giving their children meat and fish, which they had never tasted before and which upset their stomachs. Even bread was a luxury to which they were unaccustomed, their normal—indeed their unvarying—diet consisting of a mess of beans or *garbanzos* (chick-peas). The houses were hovels, the streets mean, filthy and dangerously pitted. But the people, though underfed and miserably clothed, were kind and warm-hearted and did all they could to make us welcome and comfortable.

After three days we left Torrecuadrada for the front, to effect what the communiqués called 'a rectification of the line'. This meant occupying and fortifying a range of hills overlooking the valley of Tajuña. The enemy, evidently fearing an attack in strength, had withdrawn beyond the river, and so we were able to occupy the ground without loss. Noriega had gone on leave, and I had taken over his platoon of machine-guns. The work of fortification was extremely arduous, for the ground was hard—in some places it was rock—so that our picks and shovels made little impression. At the end of five days the men's hands were covered with blisters and sores. Much of the work was in view of the enemy and had to be done at night. There was no shelter; we had to snatch what sleep we could lying in the open, each wrapped in his *capote* and blanket, in a temperature well below zero. Luckily the weather was fine. The men worked with a will, their high spirits seemingly unaffected by cold, fatigue or the pain of their hands. My platoon was attached to Captain Cancela and the 53rd Company, an arrangement that gave me great pleasure, for he and his officers were such a gay and friendly crowd that it was impossible not to be happy in their company.

The Tajuña, which separated our new positions from those of the enemy, was barely more than a stream at this point, running through a valley about four hundred yards wide. We had therefore to be careful how we moved during daylight, for the enemy had us well-covered with his machine-guns and would open fire at once on anyone they could see. We suffered half-a-dozen casualties in this way, among them one of my runners, who was shot through the head as he was going to his lunch. He was an efficient and cheerful soldier, which made me rejoice the more when our mortars blew the machine-gun post to pieces that afternoon. On the third night we were favoured with three deserters from across the river, who crept up to our wire in the darkness and shouted to us to let them through. They were Catalans, poor nervous wrecks of creatures, half-starved and wretchedly clad. Under the influence of food and cigarettes they chattered freely to us. According to their account, which their own appearance supported, the enemy opposite us was in a state of alarm bordering on panic, and stood to all night in expectation of an attack. They complained bitterly of well-fed Political Commissars who came from Madrid or Barcelona to give them lectures on The Fighting Spirit or The Meaning of Democracy. I often wondered, but never found out, what happened to deserters after they had been screened—whether they were allowed to live in peace or were conscripted into our army.

On the sixth day we were relieved by an infantry battalion, and returned to Torrecuadrada for a rest. Although glad of the relief, I was sorry to leave my friends of the 53rd for the ill-humor of Almajach, the bickering of Colomer or the unceasing bray of the Subteniente.

On February 1st we left the Guadalajara front for good. We drove east through the day, arriving in the early evening at the small village of Torrijos del Campo, a few miles south of Calamocha. At last, it seemed, we were to take our part in the battle of Teruel.

The following day we were issued with new uniforms, which turned out to be forerunners of the British Army battledress—a green *cazadora*, or blouse, of rough serge; trousers of the same colour and material, which could be pulled in above the ankles, and strapped boots reaching half-way up the calf. We retained our open-necked shirts and tasseled forage caps. Most welcome of all, we were issued with thick, wide-skirted, green greatcoats to replace our worn-out *capotes*. The same day was marred for me by a most unpleasant incident. It was my turn to supervise the Company's midday *rancho*; I was standing by the cauldron in a corner of the village square, the men lined up in a double queue in front of me, the Subteniente and the *Brigada*, or C.Q.M.S., looking on from a distance. Having tasted the food and given the order to carry on, I was watching the distribution when I heard the Subteniente break into a gabble of rage and, out of the corner of my eye, saw him advance on one of the men at the end of the line; at first I paid no attention, being used to his behaviour by now. A moment later I heard the sound of blows as he laid into the man, followed by an angry shout. When I reached the scene I found the Subteniente, flushed and quivering with temper, standing in front of a legionary whose face wore a look of defiance and whose cap was lying on the ground, where the Subteniente had knocked it.

'Now pick it up!' shouted the Subteniente.

'I will not,' growled the man.

'You're under arrest!' I snapped at him. 'You, and you,' I called to two of the other men, 'escort him to the *Vigilancia*. Subteniente, will you please make a report in writing on this incident.

When I told Almajach, he was indignant.

'Did you not have a pistol?' I had, as had the Subteniente for that matter. 'Well, why didn't you shoot the fellow then and there? That's how we deal with insubordination in the Legion! Now we'll have a court-martial on our hands.' I wondered if I should ever make a Legion officer.

CHAPTER EIGHT

On the morning of February 5th a cheerful sun in a clear blue sky brightened the harsh landscape of the Sierra Palomera. Down in the plain that we had left behind, mist still floated in wisps, hiding the valley of the Jiloca and the main road north from Teruel which we had crossed the day before. I was standing on a mountainside, about two hundred yards below the crest of a stony ridge connecting two great shoulders of rock that sloped back towards the plain; the whole formed a wide, semi-circular amphitheatre about half-a-mile in circumference. Now its craggy sides were swarming with troops—green-coated legionaries, Requetés in scarlet berets, khaki-clad infantry and gunners. The whole arena teemed with men, horses, mules, guns and equipment. Colonel Sánchez González's 5th Navarre Division, with the 14th and 16th Banderas, was massed below the crest in preparation for a great attack.

The previous day we had left Torrijos on foot, and crossed the river Jiloca and the Teruel-Calatayud road at the village of Caminreal; then we had struck east and south-east into the hills. Lieutenant Noriega had returned from leave, and so I was back with my mortars. But the fine weather and the certainty that at last we were going into action had raised the spirits of all of us; even the Subteniente was almost amiable. After a march of fifteen miles we halted for the night in the open, near the hamlet of Rubielos. Despite the cold we slept well, waking refreshed and happy in the frosty dawn. By the Major's orders we dumped our blankets and greatcoats before moving up to our assembly point; they would only impede our movement in battle, and they could catch up with us in the evening with the Bandera pack train, which would bring the rations. As we moved in a narrow column up a winding track, I saw Lieutenant Peñaredonda with his A.D.C. standing watching us. Seated on a white horse nearby was a small wizened old man with glasses and a white moustache; on his left breast he wore the crossed sword and baton of a general. I heard someone exclaim:

'Look, there's Papa Vigón! We'll be all right if he's planned this."

General Juan Vigón was the Generalissimo's Chief of Staff, a brilliant soldier whose careful planning was largely responsible for the Nationalist victories. As he caught sight of me Peñaredonda shouted: '*Holá*, Mr Peter! Are you looking forward to today?'

'So we really are going into action, sir?'

'Certainly we are. There are five divisions in this.'

As we stood on the mountainside, waiting for the artillery and air bombardment to begin, I felt the tension in the mass of troops around me. A hush seemed to spread over the whole area; men talked little and in undertones; the clink of weapons or harness sounded unnaturally loud, and the bray of a mule from half-a-mile away seemed like a trumpet call. I heard a strident female voice nearby and saw a girl in Legion uniform talking to a sergeant in the 53rd Company; she was about thirty but looked older, with a leathery, weather-beaten face and short, black hair. These *legionarias* were a common sight in all banderas; they usually acted as camp-followers, cooking, washing and mending for the men and generally making themselves useful; but it was not often that they followed a bandera into action. This girl had been a long time with the Legion; she had a good knowledge of first aid and assisted the *practicante*, or medical orderly, of the 53rd. She was as tough and brave as any of the men.

At this moment a voice behind me said in English: 'Excuse me, but didn't we meet at Cambridge?' Wondering if I was dreaming I turned and saw a lieutenant of artillery of about my own age, with a pleasant, clean-shaven face. He introduced himself as Guy Spaey. He had, in fact, been a contemporary of mine at Cambridge, where he was at King's; we had a number of friends in common. Of mixed Belgian, Dutch and German extraction, he had arrived in Spain in October 1936, and immediately joined the Nationalist forces. At the moment of our meeting he was Gun Position Officer of a battery of 10.5 cm. mountain artillery, attached to Lieutenant-Colonel Peñaredonda's command.

By half past ten the last of the mist had cleared. We heard a droning in the sky and saw a formation of silver, twin-engine bombers, with an escort of bi-plane fighters, approaching from the west; they flew over us towards the enemy lines; a minute later we heard the thunder of their bombs. At the same moment our batteries opened fire all round us, from the mountains on either side and from the foothills and the plain behind; the air was alive with the hiss of shells passing overhead. The aircraft returned to circle over us and made a second run; again we heard the roll of bursting bombs.

For two hours the bombardment raged, the guns keeping up an unceasing barrage while waves of aircraft flew over us to unload on the enemy positions. Not a shell came back in reply, nor was there a sign of enemy activity in the air. When the firing began we all made ready to advance, expecting the order at any moment; but as it became clear that the bombardment would be a long one, we gradually relaxed and made ourselves comfortable. I thought it odd that we had no briefing from de Mora before going into action and that none of us had the least idea of our plan of battle; but I concluded that we should be briefed when the time came. As I meditated I watched another formation of our bombers approaching. They looked almost beautiful as they came on in perfect formation, steady and unhurried, the sun flashing on the metal of their wings and bodies—flashing too, I saw, on a tiny object that fell from the leading aircraft. It took me a second to realize what was happening— then, as I heard Almajach shouting, I roared at my platoon:

'Down on the ground where you are. Hold on to the mules' head-ropes! Keep your faces down!'

As they dropped I saw a bright orange flash; a great fountain of earth erupted from the slope a hundred yards below us. I threw myself on the ground, pressing my face between my arms against the rock. The next moment the whole mountain side seemed to be torn apart in a convulsion of flame. The ground shook as from an earthquake and the air was full of flying metal and boulders. The explosions hammered our ear-drums and tore at our clothes. There followed a horrible silence. I struggled to my feet, deaf and battered by the blast, blinded by dust which hung in a thick cloud over the whole area. Gradually the singing subsided in my ears and I began to hear the groans and whimpers of wounded men, the screams of injured and frightened animals and a swelling roar of fury and indignation from the troops. As the dust cleared I could see that most of the bombs had landed among us—a whole division massed without cover on that mountain side, where the rocky ground added to the force and destruction of the explosions. I called to my men: although shaken they had suffered no casualties, apart from cuts and bruises. I started to examine the mules when renewed shouting made me turn and look upwards. The bombers had circled and were coming back over us, still in perfect formation, with the same unhurried, steady pace. Oh my god I thought, they can't be going to do it again! Please, dear god, don't let them do it again! To my horror, as I fixed my glasses on them I saw the leader unload his bombs, followed by the rest. Men began to run wildly in all directions, up the flanks of the mountain, in a mad, useless and suicidal rush to escape. Again I shouted to my men:

'Stay where you are! Get on the ground and hold on to your mule-ropes!'

Those bombs seemed an age falling. I found myself praying feverishly that I should not be hit, or at least not maimed. Once more there came the splitting detonations in my ears, the scream of flying fragments and the grisly silence after; then the dust and the cries of the wounded. When I got to my feet my legs were trembling so that I could hardly stand, my voice shaking so much that I could scarcely call to my platoon. But they had been spared again; one man was cut in the forehead by a piece of rock and so shaken by the blast that he was sick all day; a bomb had burst a few feet from him. Two of my mules were dead. Another had run away but was soon recaptured. I was astonished at the docility of the mules during the bombardment and after; one had a bomb fragment through the shoulder, but carried his load through the next two days' operations with no sign of pain or fatigue. The Bandera had been very lucky, losing only two legionaries killed and three wounded badly enough to need evacuation. Elsewhere the carnage was heart-breaking—over five hundred casualties, including one hundred and fifty-six killed, in less than five minutes. Our sister Bandera, the 16th, had suffered severely, losing one of their best company commanders, whose foot was taken off at the ankle by a bomb splinter. The whole of the mountain was like some nightmare abattoir, with disemboweled horses, shreds of human flesh and clothing, severed limbs and broken pieces of equipment strewn around. In the midst of it I noticed the girl medical orderly of our 53rd Company moving calmly and efficiently among the wounded, tying tourniquets and bandages, giving morphia pills and exchanging an occasional joke in her hoarse chuckle.

That was the last we saw, or wanted to see, of our aircraft for that day. How the mistake occurred is uncertain. We had white identification panels spread on the crest in front of us, to indicate our forward positions; but it is possible that the troops behind us had also spread them, in which case the aircraft would have taken us for the enemy; or it may have been simply an error of navigation.

The operation was now beginning to be known as the Battle of the Alfambra, or of the Sierra Palomera. The object of the Nationalist was to clear the Republicans from their positions in the Sierra Palomera, which commanded the road and railway north from Teruel, and to advance the Nationalist line eastwards as far as the River Alfambra. The plan was simple. The positions along the Sierra Palomera were too strong to be taken by frontal assault; but behind the mountain massif, to the east, the country opened out into a wide, undulating plateau, interspersed with a few hills and ridges, which sloped gently towards the valley of the Alfambra. This area the Nationalists selected for their battleground. The operation, a pincer movement, was on a larger scale than Colonel Peñaredonda's figure of five divisions had indicated. Preceded by a morning's artillery and air bombardment, the attack was launched simultaneously from three directions: from the south-west, from the direction of Teruel, by General Aranda's Army Corps of Galicia with four divisions; from the north-east by General Yagüe's Marroqui Army Corps with three divisions, and from the north-west by the First Cavalry Division and the 5th Navarre Division, both under the command of General Monasterio. The bombardment destroyed the opposing defences, opening the way for a general advance; Monasterio's cavalry swept across the open country to the banks of the Alfambra, followed, more slowly, by the 5th Navarre Division, while the two Army Corps pressed inwards steadily from the north-east and south-west. On the second day the 5th Navarre Division joined up with General Aranda's troops, completing the envelopment of the enemy in the Sierra Palomera. On the third and last day the cavalry made contact with the two Army Corps advancing from the north and south, completing the occupation of the line of the Alfambra; at the same time the 5th Navarre Division cleared the enemy from the Sierra Palomera, attacking from the rear. During the three days the Nationalists inflicted some fifteen thousand casualties on the enemy and took a further seven thousand prisoners at very small cost to themselves. From that moment the recapture of Teruel was no longer in doubt.

We junior officers knew practically nothing of this plan on that morning of February 5th. Half-an-hour after our disastrous bombing the fire of our batteries slackened and we received the order to advance. We climbed slowly to the top of the ridge behind which we had been sheltering all morning, and moved in single file down a narrow, stony track on the further side; the three rifle companies in our van spread out in open order to cross the flat country in front of us. Away on our left the cavalry were racing ahead, widely extended across the plain. We advance slowly towards a line of low hills. At any moment I expected to hear the patter of bullets falling among us; but the most we encountered were a few 'overs' from far away, and we reached the hills without casualties. The enemy had abandoned their defences under the inferno of bombing and shellfire; and after our experience of the morning I could not blame them. The effect on me had not yet passed off, and it was a long time before it did or before I could watch our own aircraft fly overhead without a shiver of apprehension. To tell the truth, I had been badly frightened and so, I found, had most of us. During one of our many halts that afternoon I overhead Captain Cancela talking to Almajach:

'That girl,' he said, referring to the *practicanta* of his company, 'has certainly got guts. She is still with the Company, and for any woman to want to go on after what happened this morning—well, I can only tell you that I feel like lying down at once if I think I hear an aeroplane!'

Towards the evening we came to a bare, snow-covered ridge overlooking another broad plain, in which lay the villages of Argente and Visiedo. The Republicans had abandoned the ridge and retired to the villages in the plain. We prepared to camp for the night on the bare hillside. An order came that no fires to be lit under any circumstances, and so we opened the tins of sardines and tunny that we had taken with us as emergency rations, and started to eat them in our numbed fingers while we waited for the pack train to bring our greatcoats and blankets. At over four thousand feet above sea-level the temperature was well below freezing, the faint wind a caress of ice.

'What I wouldn't give now,' said Colomer to me, 'for a litre of that red wine which we used to call undrinkable when we were at Berlanga!'

Some of the men had canteens of brandy, *anis* or the rough, aniseed-flavoured spirit called aguardiente, from which they drank despite our orders and warnings that it would only make them feel the cold more. When it became clear that the pack train would never find us in the darkness we lay down in the snow as we were. It was a clear night, and as I lay on my back looking up into the sky the stars seemed to wink at me in mockery of my efforts to sleep. Several times I stood up and paced around, trying to get some warmth and circulation into my body; then I lay down again, hoping to fall asleep before the glow passed off. I must at last have succeeded, for I awoke, without even knowing that I had been asleep, to find a sky a pale rose above the Alfambra valley in front of us. As I stood up I saw that the front of my jacket and breeches were stiff and white with hoar-frost; it was thick in my nose, my eyebrows and my hair, reminding me comically of that old colonel in London who had taunted me, before I first came to Spain, with Napier's description of the Peninsular War and the 'icicles in their noses'. But I was not so amused soon afterwards when I saw a group of legionaries bent over a stiff figure on the ground; he had died in the night from the cold. With the daylight came the pack train and permission to light fires. Gratefully we snatched our mugs of scalding coffee, swallowing them with nips of *aguardiente*—surely the best pick-me-up after such a night. As we started to advance, the warmth of the day and the movement of our limbs put new life into us; in the bright, cheerful sunlight we forgot our misery of the night before. After occupying the village in Argente—or what was left of it—we continued our advance Eastward across the bare plain to Visiedo. There was no sign of the enemy; only the sound of firing from the direction of the Alfambra indicated where he had gone. When we reached Visiedo in the late afternoon we received orders to halt for the night. This village seemed to have suffered less than Argente; a few houses were still standing, some of them inhabited. Best of all, we came upon the abandoned supply depot of one of the Republican divisions; this we put under guard, but not before we had distributed crates of every sort of tinned food to the various companies.

In this village we encountered our only opposition that day: a furious old woman who, about an hour after our arrival, stormed into the room where Mora had established his headquarters, complaining that our men had stolen one of her chickens.

'Villains!' she screamed, shaking her fist at us all, 'Bandits! They thought I didn't see them—but I saw them all right! Liberators, you call yourselves? You're worse than the Reds!'

Mora let her finish—I think she would have scratched his eyes out if he had interrupted. Then he asked her what she thought her loss was worth, paid her the sum she demanded and told the officer of the *Vigilancia* to find the offenders; they did a month in the *Pelotón*. I imagine the Duke of Wellington, who had his troops flogged for similar offences,[1] would have approved of Mora.

Setting out early the next morning we retraced our steps, marching westwards all day until, in the evening we encamped for the night on a ridge of the Sierra Palomera. Here, to my joy, I found Spaey again. I had been worried that he might not have survived the bombing of two days before; but he rode into our camp, leading a spare horse, and asked me to ride back to his lines and dine with him. Neither Mora nor Almajach raised any

---

[1] *Letters of Private Wheeler.*

objection, only insisting that I should be back with the Bandera by first light. I was astonished how well the artillery looked after themselves in such conditions; for not only did we dine extremely well, with the luxury of good cooking and good wine, but Spaey found me a small tent to sleep in. He ordered his servant to call me half-an-hour before dawn with a horse ready saddled to take me back to the Bandera. His battery had been detailed to cover the movements of the 14th and 16th Banderas; although he had not been required to go into action, Spaey had been able to form a fairly clear picture of the course of the battle, which he explained to me. Tomorrow, he said, we were going to clean up the Sierra Palomera from the rear of the enemy, but it was unlikely we should meet with much resistance. We both reckoned we were due for leave when it was over, and agreed to spend it together in Zaragoza.

Next morning, accompanied by Spaey's servant, I cantered the two miles back to the Bandera in the crisp air of another bright dawn. All that day we climbed among the ridges of the Sierra Palomera, rounding up the broken remnants of the Republican forces. They were in no state to offer resistance, and only wished to surrender as quickly as possible. They were all Spaniards. In the evening we arrived exhausted at a ruined monastery in the mountains, where we spent the night. Tired though we were, it was a sleepless night for most of us; the wind howled and whistled among the bare rocks, cutting clean through our greatcoats and blankets. We were thankful when the day brought another sun to warm us. During the morning we completed our sweep of the Sierra, then made our way by steep, winding tracks down to the plain and Teruel-Calatayud road. Late that night we limped into the village of Torremocha, where hot food and comfortable billets awaited us. During the whole operation the Bandera had suffered less than half-a-dozen casualties from the enemy; these had been among the rifle companies on the first and third days. But the cold had killed an equal number of us.

*   *   *

From the stony soil of the Sierra Palomera to the comfortable bed in the Gran Hotel at Zaragoza was the sort of sudden change that we came to accept as natural during the Civil War. Torremocha was little more than three hours by road from Zaragoza, where Spaey and I arrived on forty-eight hours' leave a day or two after our descent from the Sierra. At this period of the war it was a sure place for meeting old friends. When, after soaking for half-an-hour in a hot bath and changing my clothes, I walked downstairs into the great marble lounge of the hotel to meet Spaey, I heard my name shouted from a table across the room. Sitting there, with three whiskies and sodas in front of him was Captain Von Hartmann, a Finnish cavalry officer whom I had met in San Sebastian.

'Goddamit!' he cried in a nasal twang, 'I see you two bastards crossing the room half-an-hour ago, so I order these whiskies. It's Spanish whisky and it's terrible! See if you can drink one.' I couldn't; nor could Spaey when he joined us.

'Neither can I,' said von Hartmann, 'I'm a cavalryman and I know what that stuff's made of. I guess we better settle for brandy.'

At first sight von Hartmann, though short and handsome, looked like the typical Prussian officer of stage and screen, with close-cropped hair, scarred face and monocle. The resemblance was only in his appearance. He had an enthusiastic, volatile temperament, a warm, generous nature, wild courage, and a keen sense of humour. A nephew of the great Mannheim, he had gone to war at an early age, serving in the German Army on the Eastern Front in the 1914 war, first as a cavalry officer, later as an aviator; afterwards he had fought under his uncle in the first Finnish war of Independence. In the early months of the Spanish Civil War he commanded a squadron of mounted Falange on the Santander front; later he was appointed to the command of a cadets' academy near Salamanca. There he became involved in the Hedilla plot, for his part in which he was placed under house arrest and relieved of his command. When we met in Zargoza he had just been released and was about to take over an infantry battalion; I think this leniency was due to his universal popularity. He had more wounds even than General Millán Astray, some of them showing in the scars on his face.

Judged by the standards of the 400 or the Milroy, night life in Zargoza offered poor entertainment. The girls depended for their charm more on make-up and dim lighting than on youth or beauty; the liquor would have given a bootlegger a bad name. But to us it all seemed glamour and gay. It was sometimes exciting as well; for, under the influence of cabaret brandy and, I suppose, war-strain, officers would sometimes become boisterous, then bellicose; pistols would be drawn and bullets start to fly across the room. On more than one occasion a hand-grenade was thrown, with resulting injury and loss of life. Once an Italian tank officer, being refused admittance to a night-club that was full, hurried to his lines and returned half-an-hour later in his small tank, which he drove through the door and on to the dance floor. On the afternoon of February 15th Spaey and I left Zaragoza to rejoin our units. About nine o'clock in the evening we reached the village of Monreal del Campo, some fifteen miles north of Torremocha, where we found Spaey's battery; they told me that my Bandera had moved to Torrecilla de Rebollar, where we had been in December. It was too late for me to reach them that night, but the battery were moving in that direction at dawn and would give me a lift.

After a few hours' broken sleep on the floor of a chilly, unheated room Spaey and I climbed into a lorry in the freezing darkness of early morning. With the rest of the battery we drove north to Calamocha, there turning east up the winding road to Torrecilla in the first grey light. Torrecilla was deserted but a mile or two farther on I found the Bandera commissariat and learned that the Bandera was in action about a mile to the north-east. I could hear the sound of incessant machine-gun fire and the occasional explosions of shells and mortars. With a legionary to guide me I hastened on foot towards the battle.

We followed the road eastwards for a few hundred yards, then turned left to descend a rocky valley studded with shrubs and pine trees. The going was difficult and we made slow progress, but as we stumbled on, the sound of battle grew nearer and seemed to intensify; bullets hissed through the branches above us and a few shells landed on the sides of the ravine. After about twenty minutes, when we had reached the bottom of the valley, they firing slackened. I saw a figure approaching slowly, with his arm in a sling; he was a young Catalan officer, Alférez Mentasi, from the 53rd Company. He was very pale and obviously in great pain, but he smiled a greeting.

'Watch your step up there, Peter,' he gasped. 'It's pretty bad. We've had a lot of casualties. I've a bullet in my wrist and it hurts like hell.'

He stumbled on, and I began to climb the ridge ahead of me, traversing it towards the left. About a hundred yards below the crest I found de Mora, the two doctors, the Padre, and Noriega; with them was the Subteniente, taking surreptitious pulls at a bottle of brandy.

The previous day the Republicans had launched a surprise attack on this sector with two International Brigades—one Canadian and one Anglo-American—supported by two Spanish Brigades. After the Alfambra battle the Nationalist front ran roughly north from the line of the Alfambra, through the road and rail junction of Vivel del Rio and the village of Segura, towards Zaragoza. With their first onslaught the Republicans overran the forward positions of the Nationalists, capturing the village of Segura; their further advance was blocked by a second line of defence in front of Villanueva del Rebollar, four miles east of Torrecilla. The two 'mobile' banderas—the 14th and 16th, under Colonel Peñaredonda—were rushed to the scene, with orders to counter-attack and retake Segura and the lost positions; they were supported by a battalion of infantry and one or two batteries of field artillery. It was an ill-conceived operation. The Nationalist command, which was vested here in General Camilo Alonso Vega's 4th Navarre Division, seemed unaware of the strength of the enemy and of the distance that their own troops must cover between their assault positions and their objective; this was about a mile of difficult going, a large part of it brutally exposed to the defenders' fire. In the event, a force of under two thousand men, with inadequate artillery and no air support, was ordered to attack in daylight an enemy of several times its number—an enemy firmly entrenched on a high ridge, well supplied with automatic weapons and enjoying at least equal artillery support. Under the cover of darkness the plan might have succeeded; but Spanish troops were not trained in night operations.

Between the opposing lines ran two valleys separated by a low pine-covered ridge; scrub and low bushes grew in the valleys and on the lower slopes. At first light that morning de Mora, with his company commanders, had made a personal reconnaissance of the nearer valley—the one I had just crossed—to select a route for his advance. They came under fire immediately. Captain Almajach received a bullet in the foot, which shattered the bone and crippled him for life. Noriega took command of the company. Taking advantage of such cover as the undergrowth afforded, the Bandera advanced down the forward slope against a murderous volume of fire from some hundred heavy and light machine-guns. In spite of casualties it crossed the first valley and reached the low ridge of hills about six hundred yards from the enemy. Here de Mora halted and placed his machine-guns. When I arrived he was about to continue the attack.

I was put in command of a machine-gun platoon on top of the ridge, on the right flank; two of its four guns had already been destroyed by shell or mortar fire. I hurried off to supervise the distribution of ammunition and arrange for the provision and carriage of fresh supplies during the ensuing engagement; then I prepared to bring my two remaining guns into action, to cover the rifle companies' advance. Across the valley I could make out where the enemy positions were located, well concealed among the pines and dominating our own; my orders were simply to maintain as high and accurate a volume of fire upon them as possible. My left-hand gun was emplaced behind a low, broken-down brick wall which had once formed part of a pigsty; it gave cover rather than protection; the other gun was shielded, inadequately, by a rough, shallow earthwork constructed by the crew.

As soon as the rifle companies began to move down through the trees in front, the enemy opened fire all along his line, sweeping the forward slope and the crest of our ridge with a steady rain of bullets, mortar bombs and shells. As I ran from gun to gun, crouching low and taking what cover I could from the formation of the ground, I wondered how any one could survive in the open against such a devastating weight of fire. I flung myself to the ground beside each gun in turn, straining to mark through my field glasses the impact of its bursts on the enemy positions, and passing corrections in elevation and direction to the sergeant in command, shouting my orders to make myself heard above the stammer of the gun. I tried to hold the glasses steady, to give my orders without a tremor in my voice and to ignore the vicious spatter of the enemy's bullets. The legionaries needed no encouragement from me; quietly, efficiently and with occasional jokes they worked the two guns, maintaining a steady rate of fire as if they were on range practice.

It was difficult at that distance to be certain just where our shots were falling, but when I had satisfied myself as best I could that we were firing on target I stationed myself and my two runners in between the guns, where I could control them both. The enemy artillery and mortars were searching for us, their shells throwing up earth and stones around us. Shells from our own guns on the ridge behind whirred close overhead, some of them landing short, uncomfortably near. We had been in action for twenty minutes or half-an-hour when a mortar bomb landed on my right gun, dismounting it and scattering the crew. I hastened to the spot, to find the gunner dead and the sergeant severely wounded in the face and chest; there were no other casualties, but the gun was wrecked beyond repair. I withdrew the survivors of the section behind the shelter of the crest and returned to place myself beside my remaining gun. It seemed only a matter of time before it, too, must be destroyed.

Some fifteen minutes later a runner arrived from Bandera Headquarters with orders for me to cease fire and report to de Mora. On my way down the hill I met the Subteniente, red-faced and puffing, on his way to take command in my absence. I found the Major with his Company Commanders and the other machine-gun officers. It was a grim and gloomy gathering; even Cancela had lost his usual ebullient good humour. The rifle companies had suffered heavily and made little progress; even if they were to reach their objective it seemed impossible that they should capture it against such superior numbers. De Mora, who valued the lives of men he had trained and formed into this fine fighting unit, was unwilling to sacrifice them uselessly in such an ill-planned operation. On his own responsibility, therefore, he halted the advance, having accepted that the 16th Bandera, too, could make no headway; then he sent back a report to Colonel Peñaredonda and Division, requesting at least some air support or more artillery. It must have taken a great deal of moral courage for him to make this decision in the face of his orders. In the event it nearly cost him a court-martial; but it saved the 14th Bandera—and probably the 16th as well—from annihilation.

It began to snow. With numbed fingers we opened tins of sardines and tunny, spreading the frozen contents on lumps of hard bread; I have never been able to eat either of those fish since that time. The enemy had ceased fire; a dispiriting silence pervaded the dismal landscape of the Sierra under the murky yellow sky. In all my life I had seldom, if ever, felt so disheartened. The other officers shared my gloom, but the men, whether from ignorance of our situation or from natural good spirits, seemed in excellent humour. I noticed, with gratitude and almost a feeling of shame, one of the survivors from the crew of the gun I had seen destroyed, an energetic little man with a flair for buffoonery, he darted from post to post cracking jokes with his comrades in a high, squeaky voice that brought shouts of laughter and applause. His unquenchable gaiety, together with de Mora's quiet confidence, put new heart into me.

I was to need it. In the afternoon orders came to continue the attack. Indignant that neither Colonel Peñaredonda nor anyone from Division had thought it necessary to come forward and see the position for himself, we dispersed to our battle stations. I grieved for the men of the rifle companies, sent to futile execution by this heartless lunacy; I could not bring myself to look at de Mora. Strutting in front of my only machine-gun was the Subteniente, a bottle of brandy in one hand; he offered me a swig, which I refused, though unwillingly.

'Come, Mr. Peter!' he shouted, 'Let's see if those *cabrones* in the front can kill us!' Taking me by the arm he swaggered forward about twenty yards down the slope; there he stood and spread his arms, shouting insults towards the Republican lines amid a chorus of titters from the men. Of all the silly ways to get killed, I thought, and cursed myself for not checking the exhibitionism of this drunken mountebank. Yet I felt I must put a good face on it in front of the troops—though I wonder if they would not have respected me more had I bawled him out on the spot. To my relief the enemy chose to ignore us—if they even saw us—and after I minute I said: 'The battle is about to start again, Subteniente. I think you had better go back to Lieutenant Noriega.' He scuttled off down the hill like a bolted rabbit.

As my guns on the left opened fire I threw myself down beside my sergeant and gave the order to engage the enemy, checking our bursts through my glasses. The enemy replied vigorously, his bullets coming from the front and both flanks; they seemed to come at us like hail, with all this hiss and splatter of a heavy storm. Soon his mortars and his artillery joined in, repeating the pattern of the morning's battle. I tried to look as though this were the one thing in life I enjoyed, but with dry throat and thumping heart I doubt if I succeeded. I am inclined to turn red in the face when scared, and I couldn't help laughing when one of the ammunition numbers cried out: 'Look at the colour of the Alférez's face! It's giving away our position.'

It had stopped snowing, but the light was beginning to fade; it was becoming increasingly hard to make out the enemy parapets among the dark pine woods. The Republicans must have found the same difficulty, for I noticed that they were beginning to fire high. Suddenly, ,to my horror, our gun stopped firing; as the crew wrestled with it I heard the sergeant mutter fiercely, '*Percutor!*' with tears of vexation in his eyes. The firing-pin had broken, as too often happened with these old weapons. There was no way of repairing it, nor any means of replacement. I had no alternative but to withdraw gun and crew into cover behind the ridge. When I reported the mishap to Noriega all he said was, 'It doesn't matter, Peter. The Major is breaking off the action.' De Mora had just returned from the rifle companies in front, and from a conference with the commanding officer of the 16th Bandera on our left.

At nightfall we received orders to withdraw. A dejected and depleted Bandera dragged itself wearily back to the ridge it had left that same morning. There, after posting guards, we lay down to sleep in the snow, too weary to eat, too sad to even talk of the day's misfortune.

Thanks to de Mora our losses had been remarkably light in the circumstances—four officers and about a hundred men killed or severely wounded; the 16th Bandera had suffered more heavily, losing a large percentage of officers. We expected to have to renew our attack during the next two or three days, during which I accompanied de Mora on several reconnaissances to try to discover a fresh and safer route for the advance. On the second afternoon de Mora called all officers to a conference, where he gave us our operation orders for an attack at dawn next day—supported this time, by air bombardment and a much heavier concentration of artillery. But that night the attack was cancelled. We were favoured by visits from various senior officers, including the Divisional Commander and General Yagüe himself. They were evidently impressed by de Mora's arguments, for the next orders we received were to dig in on the ridge and stabilize the front.

The ridge we now occupied was high and steep, its reverse slope thickly wooded. Along the top we strengthened the existing trenches, adding new strongpoints. We put two companies into the line, keeping the other in reserve; all our available machine-guns were needed for defence, but we switched round the crews to give everyone a rest. Those of us who were in reserve set about making ourselves as comfortable as possible, building dug-outs in the side of the hill, where we slept warm at night and entertained each other with lavish supplies of drink brought from Zaragoza. My batman, Paulino, built me a roomy dug-out with an ingeniously constructed fireplace and chimney. In the wall he levelled out a wide ledge of earth, spreading it lavishly with dried grass and covering it with a blanket to make it a comfortable bed; he hollowed out smaller recesses for seats all around and put a rough table of packing-cases in the middle of the floor. To me it seemed like a palace. With excellent food, few duties and plenty of rest our spirits soon rose, and I look back on those days as being among my happiest in the Legion.

Each day we saw large formations of enemy bombers, escorted by fighters, flying over us in the direction of Teruel; but they never bothered us. After the recapture of Teruel by the Nationalists, on February 22nd, the enemy abandoned the offensive on our sector, only troubling us occasionally with artillery bombardments by '75s' and heavier field guns; these caused very few casualties, but were alarming because our dug-outs were only thinly covered with earth. One morning a shell from a '75' struck a tree where four or five of my mules were tethered. I ran to the spot, expecting to find a shambles; instead I found all the mules unhurt, apparently not even frightened.

About this time I had another lesson in the workings of chance, in the form of a letter from my brother, once again at Gibraltar. He told me that his new observer, Charles Owen, had a brother who was also in the Legion; did I know him? His family were half Spanish and had lived in Vigo before the war. As it happened, there was a lieutenant in the 55th Company who came from Vigo, a sombre but friendly character called Arrieta; upon inquiry I had found that he knew the Owens well: Charles, the elder, had entered the Royal Navy about the same time as my brother; the younger, Cecil, had joined the Requetés at the beginning of the Civil War, had transferred to the Legion and was an officer in, Arrieta thought, the 14th Bandera. Now that FitzPatrick and Nangle had gone home, Cecil Owen and I must have been the only two British officers in the Corps; meanwhile our only brothers were in the same ship, flying together in the same aircraft. After receiving a citation for the Medalla Militar, Cecil Owen was killed in the Battle of the Ebro at the end of August, serving with the 16th Bandera.

During these days I saw much of Cancela and his officers in the 53rd Company; we would spend almost every evening together talking and drinking sherry, brandy or red wine in one or other of our dug-outs. They taught me to drink wine from the *bota*, the peasant's wine-skin which is held at arm's length to squirt a jet of wine down the throat. Only a little practice is needed to learn this method of drinking, and it is worth learning; a well-matured *bota* will vastly improve the roughest wine; slung from the shoulder it is easy and comfortable to carry. Thereafter I was never without one during my active service with the Legion; the trouble was that no sooner had I nursed my *bota* to maturity than someone would steal it and I would have to mature a fresh one.

Cancela's second-in-command was Lieutenant Torres, a dark, good-looking officer of about twenty-five, whose family operated a fruit-canning factory in Logroño, captain of the great wine-producing district of the Rioja. When I knew him he was a quiet-mannered, serious-minded young man, intending to go into the family business after the war; but he had been a wild youth in the stormy days of the *Frente Popular* government, earning his living in Madrid as a *pistolero* for his political party, the Requetés. All the political parties employed these professional gunmen, he said, to provide bodyguards for their leaders and to intimidate their enemies. On the outbreak of war Torres enlisted in the Requeté Militia, and was severely wounded in the lung. He was a conscientious and competent officer, much respected by the men. With the loss of Mentasti—the wounded officer I had met on my way to join the Bandera at Villanueva—the company had only one other officer, a young Andalusian, Antonio Marchán. A chemist's assistant from Seville, with all the Sevillano wit and *gracia*, he was inspired by a passionate enthusiasm for the spirit of the Legion and for Cancela as the personification of it. Gay, courageous and sincere, he was one of the sweetest-natured men I have ever met. He did not live long.

As a machine-gun officer I was neither very happy nor very efficient. Having resolved for some time to ask for a transfer to a rifle platoon, I now longed to join this cheerful and devoted company. One evening I summoned the courage to ask Cancela if he would take me in Mentasti's place. He readily agreed and promised to arrange it with de Mora as soon as we moved.

After a week of idleness I was ordered up to the line to take command of one of the machine-gun sections. My command post was a strongpoint on a hillock that dominated the position; it was comfortable enough to live in, protected from bullets and mortar bombs by walls and a low, domed roof of wooden beams and sandbags; but a single shell could wreck it. I had to be careful when walking through the trenches, for they were not deep enough to hide me, and we were under continual fire from snipers and machine guns. I soon became used to keeping my head down, but I hated the shelling. We did most of our sleeping during the day, standing to an hour before dawn and dusk and keeping alert at night in case of an attack. In the early hours of one morning, two days after I took over, my sentries heard noises close to our wire, about twenty yards down the slope in front; we fired a few bursts and the noises ceased. In the morning we saw two khaki-clad bodies entangled in the wire. When we retrieved them that evening we found them to be Canadians from the Mackenzie-Papenac Battalion of the International Brigades. Whether they had come to desert or to probe our defences we never discovered. At nine o'clock on the morning of February 28th I was ordered to withdraw my guns and rejoin the Bandera below; by ten o'clock I had completed the withdrawal. Around noon a '75' shell landed squarely on top of my recent command post, blowing it inside out.

CHAPTER NINE

At dusk on the same evening we left the pine-woods of Villanueva for the last time. We marched for eight hours, with only one halt, moving north-westwards along tracks over the Sierra de Cucalon until we reached the small village of Olalla. There were rumours that our High Command was about to launch a great offensive in Aragón in which we were to take part; replacements began to arrive to bring us to full strength, including a captain to take over the machine-gun company—a podgy, middle-aged officer, quiet and soft-spoken, very different from the domineering Almajach.

From Olalla we moved in lorries to Codos, a charming little place in the mountains east of Calatayud. This was a very rich part of Aragón, producing abundance in wine and olives. The sun shone warm on the white almond blossom, announcing the end of winter and the arrival of an early spring; as we drilled in the open in our shirt-sleeves the scented air that filled our lungs made us forget the bitter memories of the winter, and raised our hopes that the end of the war might at last be near. The people were friendly and hospitable. I was billeted with an old peasant and his wife, who gave me an enormous feather bed to sleep in and cooked me some of the best meals I ever had in Spain. They treated me almost like a favourite son, apparently delighted to have an Englishman with them; each evening after supper we sat talking over the fire and drinking a bottle of smooth *anis*, which the old man made himself and matured for many years. When the Bandera left, the old woman wept, and they would accept no payment from me.

Our comfortable time ended abruptly on March 6th, when the lorries came to take us to the front. We passed through the town of Cariñena and continued due east towards Belchite, which the enemy had captured the previous year. We reached the thirteenth kilometre stone at dusk, dismounted from our lorries immediately and moved swiftly off the road into the shelter of thick pine woods. Here we bivouacked for the next two days and nights. The enemy was only a mile or two away, strongly entrenched in fortifications which dominated the area; not only were we forbidden to light fires at night, but we must keep under cover all day. After the usual cold supper of bread, tunny and sardines, we lay down to sleep under the trees.

Next morning we heard the sad news of the sinking of the new Nationalist cruiser *Baleares* by Republican destroyers in the Mediterranean, with the loss of nearly all her crew. This was the first and only Republican success at sea; it showed a remarkable departure from their usual torpid tactics. The destroyers attacked in darkness, in the early hours of the morning, pressed their attack vigorously and, after launching their torpedoes, disengaged without loss. Rumours immediately circulated that they had been commanded by Russians or by Communist ex-officers of the Imperial German Navy; certainly there would be no officers of the old Spanish Navy left to command them. But the Nationalist Press was surely a little naïve when it abused the enemy destroyers for 'fleeing cravenly into the darkness' after discharging their torpedoes.

While Paulino was building me a shelter of earth and brushwood de Mora sent for me to say that he had approved my transfer to Cancela's company. Cancela assigned me to take over his third platoon; Marchán commanded the second and a new officer, Lieutenant Martín, the first. Torres remained as second-in-command of the Company. I had my hands full that day, getting to know the N.C.O.s and men of my new platoon and making myself familiar with their weapons. It was clear that in a very short time we should be in action again, and it was essential that we should feel confidence in each other. I had about thirty men, in two *pelotones*, each commanded by a very capable sergeant. They were a merry, self-confident crowd who seemed to know their jobs and to look forward to the prospect of battle; in addition I had two platoon runners, keen and intelligent lads who were to give me valuable and devoted service in the days ahead. All the rifle companies had been issued with new Fiat light machine-guns—two to each platoon. They were good enough weapons by our standards—light, accurate and giving a fair rate of fire—but they were liable to jam.

The new machine-gun captain asked me to a farewell party in his shelter that evening; it was a spacious structure. Besides the machine-gun officers and myself he had asked a number of others, including Cancela, Arrieta and a young lieutenant called Terceño who was temporarily commanding the 54th Company. De Mora had called a conference of all officers for nine o'clock the following morning. All our talk at first was of the impending attack: this time we should have plenty of support from aircraft and artillery, as well as superiority in numbers; but the enemy positions, we also knew, were extremely strong—considered impregnable by their defenders. The dug-out, lit by a single flickering candle, was filled with an air of tense excitement as we debated our chances of success. Some rash person had ordered a barrel of Cariñena wine, a sweet, heady red wine, not quite so disagreeable as it sounds; under its influence we soon relaxed and forgot our hopes and fears of the immediate future. Our host was determined not to let us go until we had finished the barrel—an impossible task even for so many of us. Much later I remembered getting to my feet with great difficulty, mumbling a slurred good night and then, foolishly, trying to stand to attention and salute. This was fatal. I ended up flat on the floor. Luckily Paulino was waiting outside to haul me to my bed.

My memories of the next week have been impaired, partly by the excitement and exhaustion of those days, partly by the passage of time; but I still remember clearly the aching head and throbbing eye-balls with which I awakened early next morning. However, fires were allowed in daylight and, after a mug of hot coffee, I was able to attend de Mora's conference feeling almost intelligent.

General Franco gave the Republicans no time to recover from their disaster at Teruel. Within a fortnight of the recapture of the town he had regrouped General Dávila's Army of the North in seven Army Corps along a line running from the Pyrenees to Teruel, poised for the greatest offensive of the war. This time the campaign was to be conducted along the blitzkrieg lines advocated by the Germans. Concentrating an overwhelming superiority of aircraft, artillery, tanks and troops, the Nationalists shattered the Republican defences and in less than six weeks swept across Aragón to the borders of Catalonia and the Mediterranean coast; cutting Republican Spain in two, this offensive virtually settled the outcome of the war. There were three phases of campaign: the first, from March 9th to 17th, comprised the breaking of the enemy front south of the River Ebro and the Nationalist advance to Caspe and Alcañiz; the second, from the 22nd of March to the 20th of April, saw the break-through north of the Ebro and the advance to the borders of Catalonia, with the capture of the towns of Lérida, Balaguer and Tremp and the power stations which supplied the industries of Catalonia; the last, which overlapped with the second, brought the Nationalists from Caspe and Alcañiz to the shores of the Mediterranean, south of Tortosa. My story is concerned only with the first phase.

This attack was launched by four Army Corps: on the left, with its left flank on the River Ebro, was the Marroquí Army Corps, commanded by General Yagüe and consisting of the 15th, 5th (Navarre), 13th and 150th Divisions, in that order from north to south. On the left centre with a Corps known as 'Agrupación Garcia Valiño', from the name of its commander; this contained two infantry divisions and General Monasterio's Cavalry Division. On the right centre was the Italian Corps, consisting of two Italian divisions and two mixed divisions. General Aranda's Army Corps of Galicia, with five divisions, formed the right flank of the advance. The 14th and 16th Banderas, under Lieutenant-Colonel Peñaredonda, made up the mobile striking force of the Marroquí Army Corps; for the present we were to operate as part of General Sánchez González's 5th Navarre Division.

At dusk, de Mora explained, we were to move forward to our assault positions, just east of the village of Villanueva del Huerva. The axis of our advance would be the Cariñena-Belchite road. After capturing Belchite we should continue eastward to Azaila, where we should join up with the 15th Division on our left, who would be advancing along the south bank of the Ebro. Our next objective would be Escatrón, after which we should move on the important road junction and enemy headquarters of Caspe. Much of this time we should be operating as motorized infantry in conjunction with tanks. The three rifle companies would take it in turn to lead the Bandera.

The assault would start tomorrow at daylight with an intense bombardment. Our first objective was a hill, known as the *Frontón*, a heavily fortified position of great natural strength. A *Frontón* is a *pelota* court—a Basque game something like fives; this hill was called the *Frontón* because its face rose perpendicularly, like the back of a fives court, dominating the plain across which we should be advancing. If there was any serious enemy resistance left after the bombardment we should have a hard time of it. A screen of tanks would move between one and two hundred yards ahead of us—one section of tanks to each company; a section of tanks consisted of six light German tanks, each carrying two machine-guns, and two of the captured Russian tanks, each mounting a 37 mm. gun; their crews were from the Tank Bandera of the Legion.

*   *   *

The sun had dropped below the horizon behind us when, at the head of my platoon, I followed the rest of the company out of the pine woods and down a winding track that led into a shadowy ravine. We were all in excellent spirits, partly because we were on the offensive again, partly because of our confidence in our commanders and partly because we believed that we were taking the enemy by surprise. Even so, we had no idea how complete our victory was to be; my own private exaltation sprang from the knowledge that at last I was going to get grips with the enemy under a company commander I liked and trusted unreservedly, and from my happiness in my new command. Some leaders have a genius for inspiring confidence by their very presence, making their subordinates feel themselves capable of achievements or endurance beyond their normal powers; de Mora was one of these, Cancela another, as both had proved and were soon to prove again. My platoon was singing *Mi Barco Velero*, a song they had adopted for their own and a popular song of the period; it had a gay, lilting rhythm, well suited to the quick marching step of the Legion. A clear, full moon came up, washing the sides of the valley in silver light and casting deeper shadows in the depths. Overhead we heard the rising drone of an approaching aircraft. An order came down the line to halt and keep close to the cliffs that rose above the road. The aircraft circled overhead for several minutes, then the pulse of its engine increased as it straightened into a run. In front and to the left of us we saw a series of flashes and heard the detonations of a stick of bombs falling on Villanueva del Huerva. We reached the bottom of the valley and started to climb to the further side. In a little while we emerged into open pasture, with hills on three sides intersected by ravines; in one of these ravines we halted for the night.

I slept well, warmly wrapped in my greatcoat and two blankets, awakening before sunrise with the first paling of the sky. The ground, covered with hoar-frost, was thick with troops, some still asleep, others bustling about or stamping their feet for warmth. Paulino brought me some bread and a few slices of smoked ham, which we ate together, washing them down with draughts of rough red wine from my *bota*. The sun rose in a clear sky, its early warmth giving promise of a perfect day of spring. I felt excited and happy. A runner arrived from Company Headquarters with orders for me to report to Cancela. There I found Torres, Marchán and Martín.

'The bombardment will be starting soon,' began Cancela. 'So I'll give you my orders now. We are the left-hand company of the Bandera today. The Comandante is deploying the Bandera in inverted arrowhead formation for this attack—the 53rd and 54th companies leading, with the 55th in the centre and a little to the rear. I am going to use the same formation for our company. Your platoon, Marchán, will be on the right, yours, Martín, on the left, with Peter's[1] in reserve. Torres and I, with Company Headquarters, will be in between the two leading platoons. Watch me carefully for signals. Above all, when you see me stop, halt your platoons immediately and get down on the ground. Keep your men well spaced out, and see that they keep formation and distance at all time. Don't hesitate to check your men whenever necessary'—he laughed—'it will keep their minds off the bullets!'

Soon after nine o'clock the first squadron of bombers flew over us towards the enemy, and our artillery opened fire with a barrage far more powerful than that which we had witnessed in the Sierra Palomera. The bombardment continued for over two hours with constant relays of aircraft and incessant fire from our batteries; if the enemy had artillery it was silent. Beyond the low ridge of hills in front of us, which hid the enemy from view, we could see columns of smoke and dust drifting upwards.

Shortly before noon we heard the rumble of engines as our tanks moved into position; a few minutes later the advance began. We left the shelter of the hills and began to cross a flat, open plain covered with coarse grass. Less than a mile in front of us I saw, for the first time, the bulk of the *Frontón*—a great black mass of rock rising sheer above the plain; a grey pall of smoke hung over and around it; clouds of earth and stones erupting from it as our guns continued their pounding. I deployed my platoon in open order, with one *pelotón* in advance and to the left of the other, myself and the two runners in the middle. I had plenty to occupy my attention, watching Cancela and seeing that my platoon kept station; it was a while, therefore, before I noticed how meagre was the enemy's fire. Our bombs and shells were no longer falling on the *Frontón*, but small units of our fighters were diving on the position, raking the trenches with the machine-gun fire. About two hundred yards ahead our tanks halted; at the same moment a burst of machine-gun

---

[1] I was always known in the Bandera by my Christian name, the double consonant at the end of my surname being difficult for Spaniards to pronounce.

fire passed uncomfortably close. As I saw Cancela halt I ordered my platoon to get down. I saw one of our captured Russian tanks fire three shots from its gun, then move forward; Cancela stood up and waved us on. A few bullets whistled past us and I shouted to my sergeants to keep the men well spread out; someone was hit over to the right—I saw the stretcher-bearers running across. Next moment I was treading on flattened barbed wire, and a line of trenches was gaping a few yards ahead of me; huddled in the bottom and slumped across the further parapet were a few dead bodies; the surviving defenders had fled. I now saw that for the last part of our advance we had been slowly climbing; this was the first line of the *Frontón's* defences. In a few minutes our two leading companies had occupied the whole of the position.

We could not believe that it had been so easy. The 53rd and 54th Companies had less than a dozen casualties between them, of which my company had two, neither of them serious. But when we looked around at the effects of the bombardment we began to understand why we had escaped so lightly; the whole mountainside was blasted into craters; parapets had caved in, trenches were filled with earth and rubble, pill-boxes had collapsed. A few nerve-shattered and tearful prisoners were being given cigarettes by our men before being sent to the rear; they belonged to one of the Republican second-line divisions: 'All the same,' said Cancela, 'if those had been first-class troops we should have suffered heavily.'

Half-an-hour later we formed in column on the Belchite road and continued our advance eastward. Having entered the deserted village of Funedetodos without opposition we halted there for food and rest. This village is the birthplace of Goya; the museum in his house had been gutted by the enemy, but a few of us left our ranks to gaze respectfully at his monument. In our immediate neighbourhood the fighting seemed to have subsided; but the sky was full of aircraft, and from a mile or two away to the south came the sound of intense machine-gun fire and the roll of bursting bombs. We met no more resistance that day. Other troops, who had taken our place in the van of the Division, were sweeping aside such hastily-organized opposition as the enemy could muster. As we marched along the road we saw ahead of us the 'circuses' of our fighters diving in rotation to machine-gun the fleeing Republicans, harrying them incessantly with hand grenades tossed from the cockpits as well as with their guns. Later we heard from prisoners that these grenades, although they caused few casualties, were very demoralizing. In this manner we continued until dark, when we encamped for the night on some high ground beside the road.

Cancela seemed satisfied with our performance that day. 'Of course,' he said, 'you had no chance to prove yourselves in action; but I could see you had your platoons well in hand.'

I awoke with the dawn of another fine, clear day. Before the sun was up we had started our advance along the road. After an hour of marching in columns we bore to the right of the road into open country and deployed in order of battle. Ahead of us lurched a section of our tanks, keeping a constant distance of about a hundred yards between themselves and our foremost files. The other two companies were leading the attack this morning; from our place at the rear it was difficult to see what was going on. Although the country seemed to be flat as a billiard table, no enemy fortifications were visible; however our artillery was firing in support, using high-bursting H.E. as well as percussion fuses, so that we could mark roughly where they were; moreover, our fighter 'circuses' were at work above them. When we approached we ran into small-arms fire; we halted and lay down while our heavier tanks blasted individual strongpoints and the light tanks swept the positions with their machine-guns. A few of our casualties came through to the rear, one or two on stretchers, others walking; among the latter I noticed the Bandera standard-bearer, a tall, fine-looking corporal with long black side-whiskers; he had a bullet in the thigh, but was limping along cheerfully enough, supported on the arm of a comrade, exchanging cracks with his friends in our company.

We remained on the ground for a little more than ten minutes, while the firing in front increased in volume and then subsided. Cancela rose and waved us on at a run. Once again I found myself tripping and stumbling over wire, but the fighting was finished before we reached the trenches. Beyond were several half-ruined shepherds' huts; against their walls about a dozen prisoners were huddled together, while some of our tank crews stood in front of them loading rifles. As I approached there were a series of shots, and the prisoners slumped to the ground.

'My God!' I said to Cancela, feeling slightly sick. 'What do they think they're doing shooting the prisoners?'

Cancela looked at me. 'They're from the International Brigades,' he said grimly.

We were allowed no time to rest. Reforming in column of platoons we struck left to rejoin the Belchite road further east, crossed it and climbed on to a ridge of the Sierra Carbonera. We had eaten nothing all day, and so, when a halt was called to allow the artillery to come into position, we were glad of the chance to swallow some food. Some of us were inhibited from eating by the old theory that if a man were hit in the stomach he would have a better chance of survival if he had eaten nothing; the drawback to this theory is that you cannot fight indefinitely on an empty stomach. My trouble, I found, was rather that as soon as I ever sat down to eat the order would be given for us to move on, and I would have to jettison my food in the scramble to join the platoon.

The spur on which we were halted overlooked the road where it ran through a ravine towards Belchite. Beyond the road rose a steep hill, on the top of which stood an imposing monastery, the sanctuary of the *Virgen del*

Pueyo. This was one of the enemy's strong points for the defence of Belchite. The upper slope of the hill was honeycombed with trenches—no hurriedly improvised defences such as we had stormed earlier in the morning, but a well-planned system of fortifications cut deeply into the rock, with a clear field of fire in all directions. The view my glasses gave me was not reassuring.

A mountain battery was climbing the slope behind us to take up position on our left; I caught sight of Spaey, whom I had not seen since the morning of the battle of Villanueva del Rebollar, three weeks ago. After a while he walked over to join us:

'We shall be opening fire on that monastery soon.'

'Well, let's hope you make good shooting,' we answered; 'we've got to take it.'

'I don't think you need worry. By the time the guns and aeroplanes have finished there won't be much resistance left.'

Behind us, from the west, we heard the drone of aircraft. Following the line of the road from Cariñena appeared a squadron of silver twin-engined Junkers. In three flights they turned towards the monastery; when they were almost over it we glimpsed the flashes of sunlight on the falling bombs. Staring through my glasses I saw the whole hilltop erupt in reddish brown smoke, which blanketed the monastery for nearly a minute. The echoes of the explosion had barely ceased reverberating round the hills when we heard another squadron approaching; at the same time, from our ridge and from other heights across the road on our right, battery after battery of medium and field artillery opened fire. For the next ninety minutes our view of the monastery was hidden in a pall of smoke and dust; no sooner had one bomber squadron dropped its load than another would approach the target, while all the time the guns kept up their fire. At the end it seemed impossible that anyone could be left on that hill or, if they were, that they could still be capable of fighting. When the last bomber had turned away to the south and the shells had ceased to fall on the hill, all that we could see of the monastery through the thinning cloud of smoke and dust was a ruin with rubble spilled all round.

From the hills on our right descended a column of infantry, a khaki snake winding across the slopes towards the ravine. A few minutes later we were on our feet, making our way across broken country towards the foot of the monastery hill. Not a shot came from the top as we panted slowly upwards and picked our way through the torn barbed wire. Only the dead remained to great us, sprawled in the trenches and mangled under mountains of brick and stone.

Two of our companies, including the 53rd, were ordered to occupy the ruins for the night; the rest of the Bandera encamped at the foot of the hill. About five o'clock that evening we heard that the town of Belchite was in our hands.

The late defenders of the monastery included, as well as Spanish units, our old adversaries from Villanueva del Rebollar—American and Canadian contingents of the International Brigades. In their flight they had abandoned their personal belongings, including a large quantity of mail from home, some of it unopened. Cancela asked me to look through the letters in English while he and the other officers examined the Spanish. I had barely started to read when he called me back. I found him convulsed with laughter over a letter from a girl in Valencia to her boy-friend, which he insisted on my reading. It was a witty and salacious letter, every sentence alive with bawdy gaiety that was strangely moving in its cheerful allusions to the squalor and discomforts of that suffering city.

'You say you haven't enough to eat at the front,' she had written, 'so hurry back here as soon as you can get leave. At least I can promise you plenty of crumpet.'[1]

Some of the letters I had to examine were more tragically moving; letters from sweethearts, wives and even, in one or two cases, children. It was horrible to feel that many of these men, who spoke my own language and who had come even further from home to fight for a cause in which they believed as deeply as I believed in ours, would never return to enjoy the love that glowed so warmly from the pages I was reading.

'The radio is on,' a girl from Brooklyn had written, 'and I'm writing letters. Yours comes first of course. They are playing the Seventh Symphony. You know how that music brings us together, how often we've heard it together. Please, oh please, come back to me soon.'

The next day, March 11th, was marked by some ugly fighting in which my own carelessness nearly cost me my life. We had been advancing since dawn, after by-passing Belchite; about midday we went into action against a line of trenches and barbed wire similar to those we had stormed the previous morning. The enemy resisted tenaciously and the bare plain across which we were advancing hummed with bullets—most of them, fortunately, above our heads. We were one of the leading companies and my platoon was on the left. About a hundred yards short of the wire the enemy machine-guns pinned us to the ground. As we lay there, gathering ourselves for the final assault while our tanks blasted the position, as hell burst in the air almost directly over my head; the blast seemed to tear at my breeches and I felt a slight pain in my right thigh, like the slightest touch of a hot iron. I looked over at a jagged rent where a piece of shrapnel had ripped through the cloth, leaving a faint graze on the skin. I had time only to note that there were no casualties in the platoon, before I saw that the tanks were moving forward and Cancela was waving me on to the charge. I shouted to my men and, drawing my pistol, leaped over the remains of the enemy wire, closely followed by my two

---

[1] The Spanish idiom was *No te faltará conejo.*

runners. A figure rose up at me out of the trench in front, levelling his rifle and slamming home the bolt. I aimed my pistol and tried to press the trigger; but nothing happened—I had forgotten to release the safety-catch. Even in that second of hypnotized terror as I watched the rifle come to his shoulder there flashed through my brain the bitter message: 'If ever a man deserved to die, you do now! You're no more use in a rifle company than you were in the machine-guns.' At that moment there came two rifle shots, almost simultaneous, from behind me; the man fell back into the trench. My two runners had been wider awake than I.

By now the Bandera had overrun the whole position; legionaries were moving among the trenches, dispatching with rifle butt and bayonet the few remaining defenders. The enemy were German soldiers from the Thälmann Brigade, good soldiers and desperate fighters, since even their homeland was barred to them. They expected no mercy and received none; I felt a sickening disgust as I watched the legionaries probe among the fallen, shooting the wounded as they lay gasping for water. I resolved to speak to Cancela at the first opportunity; I had not come to Spain for this. We had in our Company a German lance-corporal, known as Egon; I never knew his surname, for he was not in my platoon. He was a very young, quiet boy, with a baby face, fresh complexion and innocent light-blue eyes; he was not very popular with his fellows. Reporting for orders I found Cancela interrogating a prisoner; Egon was interpreting. When he had finished Cancela looked away at the legionaries around him, then motioned the prisoner away, saying '*A fusilarle*'. Egon's face became suffused with excitement: 'Please let me shoot him, sir,' he begged. '*Please*, let me do it.' His eyes were shining and a small droplet of spittle trickled down his chin. Cancela seemed surprised, but he told Egon to take the prisoner away. Trembling with excitement Egon jabbed his rifle into the prisoner's ribs, barking at him in German: 'About turn! Start walking!' They had gone about a dozen paces when the prisoner suddenly bent double and started to run, zigzagging as he went. In that flat country he had no chance. Egon fired two or three shots after him; then the legionaries around him joined in; within a few seconds the fugitive lurched and fell to the ground. Egon ran to him and fired a couple of shots into his head. He seemed a little disappointed.

We spent that night on a desolate, rocky mountainside, so precipitous that it was impossible to find a level place to lie down and sleep. Torres was suffering from acute tonsillitis and the rest of us from sore feet and frayed tempers, inflamed by a biting wind from which there was no cover. I thought it better to defer my discussion with Cancela on the shooting of prisoners to a more favourable occasion.

Such an occasion did not arise the next day, which was the most arduous of the whole offensive; for on that day the Marroquí Army Corps made a spectacular advance on foot of thirty-eight kilometres. Starting from a few miles east of Belchite, the 5th Navarre Division swept though the road junction of Azaila in the early afternoon and reached the south bank of the Ebro at the town of Escatrón late in the evening; by this rapid advance large enemy forces were cut off, with the Ebro at their back, in a pocket between Escatrón and Quinto to the north-west; there they were destroyed at leisure. As the spearhead of the Division, the Bandera covered a full twenty-five miles on foot during the day, marching and fighting from daylight until long after dark with scarcely a pause for rest.

Our manoeuvres followed a familiar pattern: preceded by an advance guard of tanks we marched at a forced pace along the main road; ahead of us flew fighters for reconnaissance and protection. At the first sign of resistance we would deploy across the country in battle order, the tanks extending in line abreast in front of us; if the position was strongly defended there would be a brief artillery preparation before we went into the assault, in the same manner as on previous days. Although we repeated this performance several times that morning and afternoon, our casualties were remarkably light; the speed of our advance had disorganized the enemy, who was throwing in his forces piecemeal in a vain effort to gain time for a stand further east. Only on one occasion did we meet serious opposition—in the morning, at a place between Belchite and Azaila, where the old front line used to run before the Republican offensive against Belchite in August 1937. Here the enemy trenches were deep and well traversed, stoutly reinforced with concrete, well concealed from observation yet commanding an excellent field of fire. They held us up for an hour before we overran them and their garrison of International Brigades.

At about five o'clock we were enjoying a brief rest on the top of a broad escarpment that overlooked the valley of the Ebro. I had taken off my boots and socks and was rubbing my swollen feet with surgical spirit, reveling in its refreshing coolness, when Spaey walked over from his battery.

'Hullo!' I greeted him, 'Your bloody battery dropped some shells pretty close to us this morning.'

'Nonsense! You infantrymen always think it's us when it's really the enemy shelling you.'

'Their artillery has been pretty accurate today for a change,' I observed.

'But not very accurate. You can think yourselves lucky they've got no officers. I'm prepared to bet those are sergeants in command of batteries.'

At that moment Colonel Peñaredonda approached with de Mora and two legionaries, escorting a prisoner, a lieutenant of Carabineros who had surrendered after the last engagement; he was a stocky little man with dark, curly hair, whom fear and exhaustion had made into a pathetic figure. The Carabineros, like the Guardia de Asalto, were especially detested by the Nationalists; few of their officers who were taken prisoner survived. Addressing Cancela, de Mora said:

'The colonel wants some men to shoot this prisoner.'

There was a wild scramble around me as a dozen legionaries leaped to their feet, clamouring for the job with an eagerness surprising in men who a moment earlier had seemed exhausted. Even Peñaredonda was startled.

'Quiet, my children, quiet!' He urged in a pained voice. 'There's nothing to get excited about. This is simply a creature who is about to pass over to the other side.' His unctuous tone barely veiled his satisfaction. He turned to de Mora:

'I think we'd better have an officer.' De Mora caught sight of Torres. 'Will you undertake it?' he asked. Poor Torres, still suffering from his tonsils, turned a shade paler.

When the prisoner had made his confession to our padre, Torres pulled himself together and, with obvious reluctance, approached the man; they spoke together for a moment; then they walked slowly towards the edge of the escarpment, the escort following. The prisoner stood with his back to us on the top of the bluff, gazing across the shadowed valley to the further side where the slanting sunlight touched the hills with gold. Torres stepped back, drew his pistol and shot him once through the back of the head.

It was after midnight when we halted beyond Escatrón, turned off the road and encamped for the night on a cliff-top overlooking a small tributary of the Ebro. After a while Cancela returned from a visit to Bandera Headquarters with news that we were to rest all the next day. 'I'll spit the liver of the man who tries to wake me before eight o'clock!' he announced as he sank to the ground.

It was over lunch the next day that I nerved myself to ask Cancela:

'Where do the orders come from that we must shoot all prisoners of the International Brigades?'

'As far as we're concerned, from Colonel Peñaredonda. But we all think the same way ourselves. Look here, Peter,' he went on with sudden vehemence, 'it's all very well for you to talk about International Law and the rights of prisoners! You're not a Spaniard. You haven't seen your country devastated, your family and friends murdered in a civil war that would have ended eighteen months ago but for the intervention of foreigners. I know we have help now from Germans and Italians. But you know as well as I do that this war would have been over by the end of 1936, when we were at the gates of Madrid, but for the International Brigades. At that time we had no foreign help. What is it to us if they do have their ideals? Whether they know it or not, they are simply tools of the Communists and they have come to Spain to destroy our country! What do they care about the ruin they have made here? Why then should we bother about their lives when we catch them? It will take years to put right the harm they've done to Spain!'

He paused for breath, then went on: 'Another thing; I mean no offence to you personally, Peter, but I believe that all Spaniards—even those fighting us—wish that this war could have been settled one way or another by Spaniards alone. We never wanted our country to become a battleground for foreign powers. What do you think would happen to you if you were taken prisoner by the Reds? You'd be lucky if they only shot you.'

Torres's quiet voice interrupted: 'If it comes to that, what chance would any legionary stand if he were to fall into their hands, especially into the hands of the International Brigades? We know what they did to their prisoners at Brunete and Teruel.'

'We realize you can't feel the same as we do,' concluded Cancela, 'but please, Peter, do not speak to me of this again.'

Nevertheless, I knew this was not the policy of the Nationalist High Command, who already had several thousand International Brigade prisoners in a camp at Miranda de Ebro, and who released all of them a few months later. Spanish prisoners, of course, were decently treated by the Nationalists at this stage of the way, with the exception of regular officers of the armed forces, who were regarded, by a curious process of thought, as traitors. Apart from the difficult question whether International Law can be applied to a civil war, I believe that its rules afford no protection to volunteers from non-belligerent countries. For myself, if I were taken prisoner, I expected no mercy.[1]

While we were enjoying our rest on the 13th, other forces were mopping up the numerous large pockets of the enemy isolated by the last few days' advance. Although doubtless necessary—and certainly welcome to us—this delay gave the enemy time to reorganize his defence and give us a nasty shock a few days later.

The following day remains in my memory for one of the most horrible incidents in my experience.

The horror of it is still with me as I write; nor, I fear, will it ever leave me. I can scarcely bear to write of it now. At noon next day we were still resting on our cliff-top when I was ordered to report to Cancela. I found him talking with some legionaries who had brought him a deserter from the International Brigades—an Irishman from Belfast; he had given himself up to one of our patrols down by the river. Cancela wanted me to interrogate him. The man explained that he had been a seamen on a British ship trading to Valencia, where he had got very drunk one night, missed his ship and been picked up by the police. The next thing he knew, he was in Albacete, impressed into the International Brigades. He knew that if he tried to escape in Republican Spain he would certainly be retaken and shot; and so he had bided his time until he

---

[1] Captain Don Davidson, an English officer of the International Brigades whom I met subsequently, confirmed that I should certainly have been shot if captured.

reached the front, when he had taken the first opportunity to desert. He had been wandering around for two days before he found our patrol.

I was not absolutely sure that he was telling the truth; but I knew that if I seemed to doubt his story he would be shot, and I was resolved to do everything in my power to save his life. Translating his account to Cancela, I urged that this was indeed a special case; the man was a deserter, not a prisoner, and we should be unwise as well as unjust to shoot him. Moved either by my arguments, or by consideration for my feelings, Cancela agreed to spare him, subject to de Mora's consent; I had better go and see de Mora at once while Cancela would see that the deserter had something to eat. De Mora was sympathetic. 'You seem to have a good case,' he said. 'Unfortunately my orders from Colonel Peñaredonda are to shoot all foreigners. If you can get his consent I'll be delighted to let the man off. You'll find the Colonel over there, on the highest of those hills. Take the prisoner with you, in case there are any questions, and your two runners as escort.'

It was an exhausting walk of nearly a mile with the midday sun blazing on our backs.

'Does it get any hotter in this country?' the deserter asked as we panted up the steep sides of a ravine, the sweat pouring down our faces and backs.

'You haven't seen the half of it yet. Wait another three months,' I answered, wondering grimly whether I should be able to win him even another three hours of life.

I found Colonel Peñaredonda sitting cross-legged with a plate of fried eggs on his knee. He greeted me amiably enough as I stepped forward and saluted; I had taken care to leave my prisoner well out of earshot. I repeated his story, adding my own plea at the end, as I had with Cancela and de Mora. 'I have the fellow here, sir,' I concluded, 'in case you wish to ask him any questions.' The Colonel did not look up from his plate: 'No, Peter,' he said casually, his mouth full of egg, 'I don't want to ask him anything. Just take him away and shoot him.'

I was so astonished that my mouth dropped open; my heart seemed to stop beating. Peñaredonda looked up, his eyes full of hatred:

'Get out!' he snarled. 'You heard what I said.' As I withdrew he shouted to me: 'I warn you, I intend to see that this order is carried out.'

Motioning the prisoner and escort to follow, I started down the hill; I would not walk with them, for I knew that he would question me and I could not bring myself to speak. I decided not to tell him until the last possible moment, so that at least he might be spared the agony of waiting. I even thought of telling him to try to make a break for it while I distracted the escorts' attention; then I remembered Peñaredonda's parting words and, looking back, saw a pair of legionaries following us at a distance. I was so numb with misery and anger that I didn't notice where I was going until I found myself in front of de Mora once more. When I told him the news he bit his lip:

'Then I'm afraid there's nothing we can do,' he said gently. 'You had better carry out the execution yourself. Someone has got to do it, and it will be easier for him to have a fellow countryman around. After all, he knows that you tried to save him. Try to get it over quickly.'

It was almost more than I could bear to face the prisoner, where he stood between my two runners. As I approached they dropped back a few paces, leaving us alone; they were good men and understood what I was feeling. I forced myself to look at him. I am sure he knew what I was going to say.

'I've got to shoot you.' A barely audible 'Oh my God!' escaped him.

Briefly I told him how I tried to save him. I asked him if he wanted a priest, or a few minutes by himself, and if there were any messages he wanted me to deliver.

'Nothing,' he whispered, 'please make it quick.'

'That I can promise you. Turn around and start walking straight ahead.'

He held out his hand and looked me in the eyes, saying only: 'Thank you.'

'God bless you!' I murmured.

As he turned his back and walked away I said to my two runners: 'I beg you to aim true. He must not feel anything.' They nodded and raised their rifles. I looked away. The two shots exploded simultaneously.

'On our honour, sir,' the senior of the two said to me, 'he could not have felt a thing.'

I went to examine the body. There was no doubt the death had been instantaneous. When we had buried him I reported to Cancela, who said:

'The Comandante has asked me to give you this message: he wishes you to know that he deeply regrets the shooting of that Englishman; that he considers it a crime, and that the responsibility for it must rest for ever upon the conscience of *that*—he spat the word—'gentleman! You know, he went so far as to send a pair of legionaries after you to shoot you if you did not immediately carry out his order? That is something we shall none of us forget.' He looked hard at me: 'We are all sorry, Peter.'

I excused myself hurriedly.

I was not left long to my thoughts. In a few minutes a messenger came running from Cancela to tell me that the Bandera was on the move. Two hours later we were assembled beside the main road that led from Escatrón to the important town of Caspe, the last town in Aragón remaining in Republican hands. Here we waited until dusk, when a company of tanks rolled up the road from Escatrón. Behind them came a column of lorries, into which we climbed. It was dark when we started towards Caspe, the tanks moving about half a mile ahead of us. A few minutes later we put out our lights. The driver beside me seemed to think that we were bound for Caspe itself, in a sudden dash to take the enemy by surprise; I doubted we should get so far in our lorries, even at night. It was impossible to see anything of the country, for the night was very black.

After half-an-hour the column came to a halt. I heard the sound of small-arms' fire ahead of us. A minute later bursts of tracer fire flew over us from high ground on our right. This was the first time I had been under fire from tracer; I was fascinated to watch the little red bulbs, each seeming to approach ever so slowly, then suddenly accelerating to fly past with a very frightening hiss. I began to wish that someone would order us off the lorries. I heard our tanks moving across towards the enemy positions and saw the flash of tracer from their guns. In half-an-hour the engagement was over and we were on the move again. There was another brief action a mile or two further on, which held us up for a quarter-of-an-hour, while we stayed in our trucks. We finally halted near the hamlet of Chiprana, about eighteen kilometres from where we had started. Leaving our lorries, we climbed to the top of the hills overlooking the road, where we spent a cold and uncomfortable night, alert for possible counter attacks.

We made steady progress next morning, moving well ahead of the 5th Division. We met no serious opposition but came under a good deal of artillery fire in the afternoon, most of it from '75s'. Towards evening we halted on the fringes of the thick olive groves that cover the approaches to Caspe. The sun was setting when a runner from Bandera Headquarters hurried up to me with orders to report at once to the Major. I found de Mora with his company commanders on the top of a knoll overlooking a wide vale, from which a silvery-green sea of olives swept upwards to a distant hill. Briskly he gave me my orders:

'Yours is the leading platoon of the leading company to-night. I want you to make a reconnaissance through those olives ahead of us and try to find out where the enemy are located. Put out scouts in front, but don't let your men get scattered in that close country. Get moving as quickly as you can.' Calling the platoon to attention, I briefly outlined our mission, issued my orders and detailed a pair of scouts to move fifty yards ahead; I took the rest at a trot down the valley. We had hardly started to move through the olives when we were fired on by a machine-gun from the hill in front. As the bullets slapped against the trees I felt a sharp stinging pain across my ribs; realizing that it was only a flesh wound and that nobody else was hit, I looked around quickly for cover. In front of us was a ditch with an earth bank, one of many that intersected the plantations. I ordered the platoon into the ditch while I tried to fix the position of the machine-gun through my glasses; but I could not find it in the falling light. Unwilling to waste time I gave the order to advance, hoping that the gloom would cover us as we went deeper into the trees. Suddenly we came upon a railway, a single track running at right angles to our advance; about twenty yards to the right was a level-crossing where the main road from Escatrón ran over the line. As I halted before crossing the exposed piece of track my senior sergeant caught my arm:

'Listen, sir!' He jerked his thumb in the direction of the road.

From behind us I heard the deep rumble of heavy engines coming up the road towards the crossing.

'We're ahead of our own tanks, sir,' said the sergeant, looking worried.

For a moment I failed to grasp the significance of what he had said. Then I realized that the tanks, seeing us ahead of them, would certainly take us for the enemy; in the half-light they could not see our uniforms, and they must suppose themselves to be the most forward of our troops. This was one of those moments, with which the textbooks deal so light-heartedly, when the young officer must use his initiative. The decision was taken out of my hands by the sergeant himself; bulling out a white handkerchief he ran to the level crossing, planted himself in the middle of the road, and started to wave it, shouting through a cupped hand at the leading tank. This must have had a nervous gunner; I was running to join him when there was a bright flash and a sharp explosion; the sergeant staggered to the side of the road with his hands to his face. A few seconds later the tank lumbered into view, with its turret open and the officer peering out of tis top. When he saw us he halted, horrified at his mistake. At that moment Cancela came to tell me to discontinue the reconnaissance and rejoin the company with my platoon. The sergeant was carried back to the medical officers, who patched him up and sent him off to hospital; miraculously he had escaped serious injury, although he had a nasty gash in the side of the face. I was going to miss him badly. His *pelotón* was taken over by a tall, red-haired Portuguese corporal called Mateu, a good enough soldier but lacking the sergeant's experience.

The Company crossed the railway in extended order and began to move at a rapid pace through the olives that covered the gently rising slope beyond. We were no longer under fire, but I found it an exacting task to keep touch with Cancela on my right in the thick country and gathering darkness; our feet sank heavily into the earth, we fell into ditches and stumbled up banks, sweating and cursing in a frenzied effort to keep pace. The graze on my ribs smarted and irked me where my clothes pulled on the caked blood. I tried to console myself with the thought that it was better to be one of the heroic wounded than one of the glorious dead; but even so, I found my temper running very short. I had no idea where the rest of the Bandera was, nor even in which direction we were advancing. As far as I was concerned, the military situation was, in official language, 'obscure'.

Quite suddenly we halted in the last of the fading light. Ahead of us the hill rose sharply and steeply to a conical mound, falling away gradually to our right in regular, unbroken lines of olives. A hundred yards or so on our left ran a road, roughly parallel with the line of our advance; we could hear tanks moving along it. One of the rifle companies was sent to occupy the mound, supported by Colomer's machine-gun platoon. We stayed where we were, near de Mora, ready for instant action. It seemed that we had run into heavy opposition and would not take Caspe without a fight.

When we were settled I went to Bandera Headquarters to get one of the doctors to dress the graze on my side. I found them in a small hut with the Padre and de Mora; the latter was lying down, looking very tired. Back with the Company I forced myself to eat something, and then lay down to sleep. But I found sleeping as difficult as eating. The air was charged with tension and uncertainty. The night was full of the sounds of impending battle: explosions and bursts of machine-gun fire from over the hill, and the rumble of tanks along the road on our left. At first I was confident that the tanks were ours; but soon afterwards I was disturbed to hear the sound of engines coming down the road from the direction of Caspe. A few minutes later the last of my complacency was shattered by a series of sharp reports, followed immediately by the hiss and explosion of shells among the surrounding olives. The tanks were hostile; moreover they were shooting at us. At first we lay where we were, hoping the bombardment would subside; on the contrary, it increased rapidly in volume, shells raining on the ground around us or bursting in the branches overhead. I heard the clamour of Colomer's machine-guns from the mound, and the thud of grenades. Cancela shouted to the Company to stand to; I felt better on my feet. The shelling continued for half an hour; then it died almost as suddenly as it had started, to be succeeded by a silence almost unnerving in contrast. I doubt if any of us slept for the rest of that night.

We were on our feet again before dawn. De Mora ordered the Company to take up a position over on the right and prepare for a strong enemy counter-attack. Our delay on the 13th and 14th had given the Republicans time to pull the bulk of their retreating forces into Caspe; these they had strengthened with four International Brigades and part of a fifth. Pushed far ahead of the 5th Division, our two Banderas and supporting tanks were now thrown back on the defensive in face of vastly superior numbers; furthermore, the enemy controlled the high ground. Until substantial reinforcements could arrive we should be batting, in the language of Mr. Naunton Wayne, on a very sticky wicket.

In the first faint grey light we moved to our new positions, crossing without incident one very exposed piece of open grounds, bare of olives or other cover. Cancela posted my platoon on the left, Martín's on the right and Marchán's in the centre; at first he had planned to keep mine in reserve, but with the length of the front we had to hold and the danger of enemy infiltration on the left, he felt he could no longer afford the luxury of any reserve but that of his own headquarters. Our orders, Cancela explained, were to hold our positions at all costs; rather than retreat we must die where we stood. Remembering the open ground across which our ammunition supplies would have to reach us, I wondered if we should be able to achieve even that usefully.

As the sun rose we heard the first sounds of battle over on our left, where the rest of the Bandera was engaged. I was relieved to note that the enemy seemed to be very short of artillery; apart from the 37 millimetres of tanks I could hear none.

In trying to describe the action that followed I am at a disadvantage which anybody who has been an infantry subaltern in battle will appreciate: I had little idea of what was happening anywhere but in my own immediate vicinity, and not always a clear idea of that; moreover, my mind was so fully occupied at the time that, even while I was in hospital immediately afterwards, I found it difficult to recollect the sequence of events.

De Mora could not spare us any machine-guns, and so we must depend on our own Fiats and rifles. I was thankful that the olives at least made it difficult for the enemy to use mortars.

Taking advantage of the cover afforded by the banks and ditches, I disposed my platoon with a view to giving the maximum depth to my defence. 'Fire at anything you see moving to your front,' Cancela had said. there was, of course, no time to cut away the olives that blocked our field of fire, giving excellent cover to an attacker. I awaited the enemy's assault, trying to dissemble my anxiety from the men. I did not have long to think about it. One moment we were waiting, the men crouched behind their weapons, myself scanning the olive groves through my glasses: the next, bullets were hissing through the trees, slashing the trunks, spattering earth from the bank in front of us. I heard Marchán's guns go into action a second before my own. All we could see of the enemy was an occasional glimpse of a crouched figure darting from one tree to another. For a while we held them off; but at the end of twenty minutes, when the firing died down, I had lost half a dozen men and we knew the enemy were appreciably closer.

I sent a runner to Cancela with an account of the action; he returned with orders for me to report in person. I found the Captain looking grave.

'There's a hill just above you on your right,' he said, pointing it out to me. 'Take one of our *pelotones*, get up there as quick as you can and hold it at all costs—at all costs.' he repeated.

I was getting to know that phrase pretty well. I ran back to my platoon, made a quick readjustment of my plan of defence, and ordered Corporal Mateu to follow me with his *pelotón* to the top of the hill. There was a small piece of open ground in front of the foot of the hill. As we ran across it a sharp burst of fire came from the left; I felt a searing pain across the front of my throat; a bullet had torn a shallow furrow through the flesh, but I had no time to think about it as we scrambled panting up the hillside. On the top was a small space of open ground before the olives began again on the farther edge; hurrying across it we dug in on the other side. When I returned to Cancela to report my dispositions, he said:

'Go and get that wound dressed.'

I hesitated. It had bled profusely, making a picturesque mess on the front of my jacket, but it was causing me no trouble; I felt that this was scarcely the time to bother with trivialities.

'Don't argue,' he said, 'the sooner you go the sooner you'll be back.' And so I went, running all the way.

Bandera headquarters was under heavy fire from the enemy tanks. It seemed the fuses of the shells were adjusted to explode immediately on impact, so that many of the burst in the trees on striking a branch or even a twig, producing an alarming effect and causing a number of casualties. The sound of fighting seemed to come from all sides. De Mora was looking a little worried. I noticed the Subteniente sitting by himself, huddled despondently beneath an olive tree, peering through the collar of his greatcoat; he looked like an old, mournful, red-faced sheep. Paulino greeted me with a look of friendly concern.

'You again!' laughed Doctor Larrea when I came up to him. I apologized for bothering him because I could see that he and Ruiz had their hands full, with the wounded pouring in from all companies. De Mora, standing near, looked up.

'I think you ought to go to hospital,' he said, 'those throat wounds can be very dangerous.'

I had not the face to follow up this suggestion and ran back to rejoin Cancela. I found the battle had broken out again; I could hear the sound of continuous small-arms fire from ahead and from the right where Marchán and Martín were closely engaged. As I arrived a runner hurried across from Martín with the news that he was under severe pressure, heavily outnumbered, and in danger of being outflanked.

'He's got to stay there,' said Cancela. Sounds of firing came from the hill which I had recently occupied. Cancela told me to take the rest of my platoon up there to join Mateu.

'The position on the left can look after itself; but that hill is vital. We ought to have occupied it before. For God's sake hold on to it, Peter!'

For some reason the enemy had ceased to press his attack on the left, so that my *pelotón* was not engaged when I reached it. We climbed to the top of the hill without difficulty and took up firing positions. Mateu was glad to see us; with his limited firepower he had been unable to stop the enemy closing in. I cursed the thickly-planted olives which prevented my seeing where the enemy were, or at what point they were likely to launch their main attack; their fire seemed to come from straight ahead and from the right, saturating us in a deluge of bullets that was carrying off my men at a frightening rate.

During one of the intervals I found Cancela beside me, come himself to see the situation. I told him quietly that if the enemy were in the strength that I believed them to be, I did not see how we could avoid being overrun. He nodded gravely:

'This is a classic Legion situation, Peter, but don't be dismayed.' He raised his voice in a laugh for everyone to hear: 'We'll enjoy our drinks more in Zargoza when we look back on this day.'

'Well,' I said, 'I certainly hope the girls will look better than they did the last time I was there.' Our poor sallies were acknowledged by a few grins from the men. Suddenly one of them attracted our attention, pointing over to the left, where we saw a figure crawling painfully on his stomach across a piece of open ground, trying to reach the shelter of some trees.

'Shall we shoot, sir?' he asked.

We studied him for a moment through our glasses, then Cancela said firmly:

'He's wounded. Leave him alone.'

He walked back down the hill, leaving me to make my final arrangements to meet the assault which I knew could not be long delayed. Both my Fiats were still in action and I reckoned I had enough ammunition and grenades; on the other hand I had already lost half my men, including one of my runners. However, the rest were in good heart and I knew they would stand by me. I resolved that, before we were finally overrun, I would pull my force back to the edge of the hill and make my last stand there, where we could at least deny the position to the enemy. There was a small ditch which would give us some protection. I warned my sergeant and Corporal Mateu of my intention.

'They're on the move again!' cried the sergeant as a fresh hail of bullets started to fly among us. This would be the final assault. While we poured our full volume of fire into the attackers—or what we could see of them—the legionaries tearing at the bolts of their rifles, slamming them back and shooting as fast as they could, the Fiat gunners firing in long steady bursts, I ran, crouching, from one *pelotón* to the other, checking the fire to see that we were not shooting too high and trying desperately to forecast the point of the enemy's principal thrust. But from what I could make out they were converging on both sides in equal and overwhelming strength. They were getting terribly close to us. The explosions of grenades were added to the crackle of small arms fire. Realizing that if we were going to disengage we must do so at once, I gave the order to retire; in a few seconds we had covered the twenty yards to the edge of the hill. We were now ready for what I reflected grimly was, literally, a 'last ditch' stand. I sent my runner to warn Cancela.

Across the clearing we saw the gaps in the olives fill with figures. I noticed one of them steady himself against a tree and take aim, I thought at me; I fired twice with my pistol and he disappeared. I gave the order to fix bayonets. I remember being fascinated by the sight of the diminutive legionary beside me working feverishly to get his bayonet onto the boss of his rifle, his little monkey face puckered with anxiety, the tassel of his forage cap bobbing up and down like an agitated yo-yo. We were a pitiful remnant, a bare dozen; around us the ground was strewn with the bodies of our comrades. In a few moments—minutes at most—the enemy would close and that would be the end. As I unwound the tape from a grenade and slung it across the clearing I understood that at last I was face to face with death; that there was nothing I could do about it. With that realization there came over me an extraordinary sense of freedom and a release from care. A few yards in front of me I caught sight of the red and yellow colours of a Nationalist flag which had been carried by one of our *pelotones*; it was on the ground beneath the dead body of its bearer. Running forward—I realize now, of course, that this was the most puerile dramatics—I seized the flag and ran back with it; calling encouragement to my men, I waved it in a wide arc. Whether this nonsense had any moral effect I am unable to say: a second or two later there was a soft thud beside me, an anguished shout of warning from my runner—'*Cuidado mí Alférez*!—and a violent explosion.

I was knocked clean backwards clean off my feet to roll over and over down the hill, ending up in a heap in front of Cancela, who, with Torres, was on his way to visit us. I pulled myself up, dazed and shaking, to feel the blood pouring down my left arm. I began to climb back, but Cancela reached the top before me; taking one look at the situation he shouted: 'Down the hill, all of you!'

I feared we should be shot down as we ran, but the enemy was slow to press his advantage. We halted about a hundred yards beyond the foot of the hill, behind an earth bank among the olives, where we found Cancela's headquarters.

Nearly a year later I learnt that our adversaries this day were a British battalion of the International Brigades; Captain Don Davidson, my informant and one of its Company Commanders, told me that their own casualties were very heavy.

Although embarrassed by the enemy's capture of the hill, with the dominating position it gave them, Cancela was determined to hold his ground, covering de Mora's right flank. After pulling the remnants of Marchán's and Martín's platoons, which were in danger of being cut off, he awaited the enemy's next move. But the latter made no attempt to advance further, and confided himself to raking us with small-arms fire. In the end it was our own artillery that forced us from our new positions, coming into action now for the first time; I suppose it had just arrived. A battery of six 77 mm. dual purpose anti-aircraft guns began to fire at the enemy on the hill. Unfortunately, three shells in every salvo landed in our midst. After what we had been through we were enraged as well as unnerved each time we heard the guns fire to know that within a few seconds we were likely to be disemboweled or maimed by one of our own shells; pressing my face into the earth and shrinking as the blast of the explosion swept over me, I cursed a fate that had delivered me from an honourable if uncomfortable death at the hands of the enemy, only to consign me to ignominious and messy annihilation by my own guns. After a grim ten minutes, during which time we had as many casualties, Cancela took us back another hundred yards, where life seemed peaceful in comparison, with only the enemy's bullets to worry us. Soon even these abated, and we reckoned that the guns, with their high rate of fire, must be giving the enemy as bad a time as they had given us.

About twenty minutes later we had our first really happy moment of the day: a section of our tanks appeared through the olives behind us, negotiating the difficult country with remarkable agility.

'It looks as if the worst is over,' said Cancela. He turned to me: 'Now go and get that arm looked at.'

I was glad enough to obey; the blood had clotted and the arm was stiff and painful. I moved warily through the olives, having no wish to be knocked out at this stage of the battle by a sniper's bullet. I came to the edge of the open ground we had crossed early that morning; among the trees on the other side I saw Lieutenant Terceño, who shouted to me not to linger while crossing it; I saw what he meant when a couple of bullets sang past my head as I hurried over. The tanks were still shelling Bandera headquarters, where Larrea and Ruiz were working calmly and efficiently, while the Padre was busy among the rows of wounded on the ground. De Mora looked strained and grim, but he cheered up a bit when I told him about our tanks. The Subteniente was wailing that he had been hit in the chest by a shell fragment that was hurting him horribly. When the girl *practicanta* had cut away the sleeve of my jacket and shirt, prattling happily to me the whole time, Larrea examined the wound; there were no bones broken, but splinters of metal had lodged in my forearm and above the elbow. He looked at me with his hands on his hips:

'This time, damn it, you really are going to hospital! I haven't enough lint and bandages to keep on wrapping up a bloody great bean-pole like you.'

When he had dressed the arm and put it in a rough sling he wrote out a hospitalization order, which he handed to me:

'You'll find a casualty clearing centre somewhere back down the road; just go on walking till you find it.'

De Mora added: 'Be careful for the first part of the way; it's dangerously exposed to fire.'

Accompanied by Paulino, who, I was delighted to see, and hung on to my wine *bota*, I walked away from the battle. We went very carefully at first, for

Paulino told me that several casualties had been hit again as they were being carried back, and a stretcher-bearer had been killed. For the first half-mile bullets flew over us, but afterwards we were pretty safe. About three-quarters of a mile back we passed a culvert where the railway ran over a sunken track. Here Colonel Peñaredonda had established his command post, though he alone knew what control he could exercise at such distance. He greeted me with effusive cordiality:

'Hi Mr. Peter! What's it like up there?'

'Arduous, sir,' I repeated sourly. 'You could see it better from up the road.' And I passed on.

Soon afterwards we came to the main road, where we met a column of cavalry, who hailed us gaily; they were part of General Monasterio's division, just arrived from Alcañiz. With a light heart I realized that the agony of the Bandera was over. A mile further we came to a tent, marked with a red cross, in a small grove of oaks; in a field beside it a battery of 10.5 cm. field guns was in action. I gave my hospitalization order to the medical officer in charge, who told me that I should have to wait some time before an ambulance could evacuate me—he indicated the rows of wounded lying around; I had better make myself as comfortable as I could in the meantime. Paulino spread a blanket for me at the edge of the trees. I fell asleep immediately, undisturbed by the firing of the guns fifty yards away.

In the hospital train at Zaragoza, where the ambulance dropped me late in the evening, I found myself sharing a compartment with Antonio Marchán. In the turmoil of the battle I had neither seen him nor given much thought to the fortunes of his platoon; but I had gathered from Cancela that he had done very well. He had become a casualty soon after me, with a grenade wound in the hand; it was more painful than mine but did not seem to damp his gypsy spirits. Two days later we were reveling in hot baths and clean, comfortable beds in the General Hospital at Bilbao.

The day after we were wounded Caspe fell to an assault from three directions by overwhelming Nationalist forces. The International Brigades, particularly the 14th (British), had fought a gallant and determined action, inflicting terrible casualties on the 16th Bandera and ourselves; our own company had barely twenty men left, out of the hundred and ten with which we had started the battle.

CHAPTER TEN

After three days in hospital my wound ceased to throb and I felt a great deal better. I knew my brother was still in Gibraltar and I was anxious to see him before his ship left for England. The Commandant of the hospital in Bilbao was sympathetic, although he was doubtful if I was yet fit for so long a journey, especially as I should have to hitch-hike; but I convinced him that with my uniform and my arm in a sling I should have no trouble getting lifts, and with Paulino to look after me I should come to no harm. He only insisted that I report to the Red Cross Hospital in Seville for treatment on the way. We reached Seville in two days, riding some of the way in luxury in the car of a Divisional General, which I had stopped on the road outside Burgos. After a night in the Red Cross Hospital, where I had my arm dressed, I made the rest of my journey to Algeciras in a very uncomfortable and dilapidated old bus, which lumbered across country along appalling roads for eight hours; I reached the Rena Christina Hotel in the evening, feeling that the Commandant in Bilbao might have been right.

A telephone call to Gibraltar brought my brother to Algeciras the next day and Charles Owen, his observer, with him. They had borrowed a car in Gibraltar, in which we drove to Seville and, on the way back, to Jerez, where we were taken over the *bodegas* of the Marqués del Mérito—a delicious but exacting orgy lasting more than two hours. Our host was the Marqués nephew, whom I had known in San Sebastian. This young man, much to his grief, was unfit for military service; instead he had worked for the S.I.M., or Military Intelligence, where one of his jobs had been to keep tabs on me. The Nationalists were no more spy-conscious during the Civil War than the British were during the last war, or than the Americans have been since. My position as an infantry subaltern was not one where I could have been very useful as a spy; but the S.I.M. probably thought that any lone foreigner would bear watching. In fact it never occurred to me to offer my services to the British Intelligence authorities, even if I had known how to do so; certainly they never approached me—I suppose I was considered too irresponsible.

After saying good-bye to Neil and Owen I returned to Seville, where I entered the Red Cross Hospital as an in-patient; not only did I need some rest after the past few days, but I felt that I had tried the patience of medical authorities far enough. In the hospital the medical attention was adequate, the nursing conscientious rather than skilful, the food plentiful and excellent; but there was little opportunity for rest. In the first place, I was in a ward with fifteen other officers of about my own age and, like myself, only lightly wounded; secondly, it was now Holy Week, when the processions went on all night and no one seemed to mind how long we stayed out, provided we were back in time for our treatment in the morning. On Easter Sunday there was the usual grand bull-fight, the first of the season. Cancela used to tell me that since he had gone to war he no longer enjoyed watching bull-fights; that the reality of his own escapes from death blunted for him the thrill of watching those of the matadors. I could not agree with him; to my mind the exhilaration derives as much from the flow of colour and grace of movement of cape and body, the grandeur and tragedy of the culmination, and the brilliance of the whole magnificent spectacle, as from the crude physical excitement of watching men risk their lives.

Towards the end of April I was discharged from the Red Cross Hospital with a week's sick leave, which I decided to spend in San Sebastian. Through the good offices of Captain Burckhardt of the German Condor Legion, whom Neil and I had met in Algeciras, I was given a seat in a Junkers 53 transport aircraft as far as Burgos; I hitch-hiked the rest of the way. While I was in San Sebastian I paid a visit to Biarritz to see my friends, the O'Malley Keyes. It was a foolish thing to do: the Spanish authorities made no objection, but as soon as I arrived in France I realized that I was going to have difficulty in getting out again; officers of the Non-Intervention Commission were patrolling the frontier and it was made clear to me that I stood no chance of obtaining a French exit visa to return to Spain. However, at a dinner party one evening at Bar Basque at San Jean-de-Luz a friend pointed out that a simple way was to walk up the disused funicular that climbed La Rhûne, a prominent mountain nearby, along the top of which ran the frontier.

'Plenty of picnickers walk up there to spend the day,' he explained. 'When you get to the top you should be able to find an unguarded spot where you can slip across. Anyway, it's worth taking the chance.'

I agreed, and he promised to drop me in his car at the foot of the funicular next morning.

The Bar Basque at this time must have been one of the liveliest spots in Europe: a gathering place of play-boys and play-girls, journalists, black-marketeers and conspirators of every nationality and political complexion. It seemed to pivot on the sinister but intriguing personality of a Mittel-European barman known as Otto, whose pale face, light eyes and thin lips had been schooled over the years into expressionless immobility; he made it his business to know everybody, and everything about everybody. I remembered meeting Esmond Romilly there, with whom I had been at school at Wellington; although a charming young man of great intelligence, initiative and personal courage, he had early acquired unpopularity with the school authorities for editing, in collaboration with his elder brother, Giles, a subversive newspaper, entitled *Out of Bounds*. When the Spanish war broke out he joined the Republicans. On this occasion I asked him to have a drink, with no other motive than the wish for a friendly chat; he accepted, but kept looking furtively around the bar, hissing in apology: 'This place is full of Fascists!'

On a perfect morning of early summer I left my friend's car at the foot of La Rhûne and started to walk along the track leading to the funicular. In an old machine-gun ammunition case, which did not look as suspicious as it sounds, I carried my uniform, intending to put it on as soon as I crossed the frontier. I had not climbed more than two hundred yards up the railway when I heard a shout and, turning, saw a gendarme coming after me. I waited for him with what I hoped was a smile of polite attention. When he arrived, puffing but amiable, I explained that I was an English tourist out for a day's picnic on the mountain; I indicated my ammunition case, saying that it contained a bottle of wine and my lunch. He beamed and wished me *bon apetit*. I went on my way, a bit out of breath myself. It was a monotonous as well as tiring climb along the sleepers; La Rhûne is about three thousand feet high. Fearing that there might be a guard post in the building at the head of the funicular, I left the track a quarter-of-a-mile short of it and cut across the side of the mountain to the top. A little way down the farther side was a thick belt of woods, already coming into leaf. I imagined that the frontier would run along the crest, but in any case I ought to be safe once I had reached the trees. Trying not to hurry, I began to walk across the crest with as nonchalant an air as I could manage although my heart was pounding uncomfortably. I heard a shout from the funicular building a few hundred yards to my right; pretending not to hear, I walked steadily without turning my head or hurrying my pace. I heard a couple of shots. But by now I was walking down the farther side, among large rocks which I hoped would give me some shelter. I dived into a narrow gully, ran down it for a hundred yards, paused a moment to get my breath, and scrambled over a small spur to drop down the other side to the shelter of the woods. I did not linger there, but hastened downhill for another quarter-of-a-mile, where I struck a small track leading further to the south. Now at last I reckoned I must be in Spain; however, I decided to take no chances and to keep on my civilian clothes until I was quite certain.

When I had cooled off and felt calmer I started to walk down the track. I had gone about half-a-mile when, round a corner, I walked into a Spanish soldier, his rifle slung on his shoulder, his jaws moving rhythmically as he plodded up the hill.

'Good afternoon,' I said. 'I am Alférez Peter Kemp, of the 14th Bandera of the Legion, returning from leave in France. I should be grateful if you would escort me to your guard post, where I could change into my uniform and perhaps get transport into San Sebastian.'

The soldier looked at me in astonishment, his jaw dropping open to reveal a bolus of well-chewed bread. After a moment he nodded and turned on his heel, beckoning me to follow. Half-an-hour later I was drinking a beaker of *chacolí* with the officer in charge of the frontier post of Vera.

At the General Mola hospital in San Sebastian, where I had to report for my final examination before rejoining the Bandera, the doctors found that the wound on my upper arm showed signs of festering. In consequence, it was not until the middle of May that I was allowed to return to duty.

I had no idea where I should find the Bandera after all the operations that had taken place since my departure, but Zaragoza seemed the best place to inquire. There I met an English girl, Pip Scott-Ellis, who had been serving as a nurse with the Nationalist armies since the previous autumn; she had come to Spain with no knowledge of the language, had passed the Red Cross examinations in Spanish within a few months of her arrival and had worked in field hospitals throughout the battle of Teruel and the offensive south of the Ebro. During the latter she had been attached to the Marroquí Army Corps and, with a Spanish friend, Consuelo Montemar, had worked in a hospital at Escatrón under heavy fire from artillery across the Ebro; both girls had been proposed for the *Medalla Militar* for their gallantry during these bombardments.

I found the Bandera resting in the village of Villanova de Alpicat, a few miles from Lérida, just inside the borders of Catalonia. Any regrets I may have felt for the end of my leave were immediately dispelled by the warmth and kindness of my reception by de Mora and my brother officers. Marchán had already returned; and so with my arrival the Company had all its old officers back; but among the other ranks there were many new faces, replacing our losses at Caspe. Colonel Peñaredonda was no longer with us, having been posted to another command. Cancela told me that shortly after I left him our tanks had stormed the hill in line abreast with every gun blazing; when he reached the top the scene of carnage was indescribable. The '77s' had done most of the damage and the tanks had completed the work, so that the company took possession of the hill without another casualty. He had found the flag lying where I had dropped it, the pole broken clean off by the explosion of the grenade that had blown me off the hill; he gave me the flag as a souvenir. Since the fall of Caspe the Bandera had not been in action.

Villanova de Alpicat was a pleasant little village in flat country intersected by canals and irrigation ditches. We had horses and plenty of leisure for riding, good food and plenty of wine. But I had a strong impression that the sympathies of the villagers were not with us, although they were polite enough to our faces. Separatism and Anarchism were the strongest political forces in Catalonia; I felt that these people would not be sorry to see the village change hands.

Towards the end of May we found ourselves in the line again. In this sector the front followed the course of the Segre, a river that flows past Lérida in a south-westerly direction to join the Ebro about half-way between that town and Caspe; twelve miles below Lérida the Nationalists had established a bridgehead across the river at the village of Serós, where the river flows through a deep ravine about three hundred yards wide. throughout the months of June and July this bridgehead was garrisoned by the 14th Bandera. It was an unhealthy and uncomfortable position, consisting of a semi-circle of trenches about half a mile in diameter and nearly the same in depth. It was connected with the ruined village of Serós on the west bank by a narrow iron bridge, which was under constant artillery fire. Our trenches ran along high ground, which rose steeply from the river bank; near the bridge there was a small piece of ground at river level, on which stood a damaged house that served as Bandera Headquarters. Of our three rifle companies two occupied the trenches, the third being disposed around Bandera Headquarters in reserve.

The Republicans were entrenched on three sides of us, at distances of between one and two hundred yards; they were second-line troops of inferior quality and poor morale, but their situation enabled them to shell and mortar us from three directions, inflicting a small but steady drain of casualties. Sometimes it was more unpleasant for the company in reserve than for those in the trenches; enemy artillery was persistent in its efforts to destroy Bandera Headquarters, and although they never succeeded, owing to the steep angle of fire, it was unnerving to be Orderly Officer during a bombardment and have to sit unprotected beside the field telephone while shells rained close around. Otherwise our worst enemies were the flies, the bad water and the heat. I have never seen so many flies before or since; they hung above us in great black clouds, covered our food, polluted our drink and swarmed all over our faces. It says something for the qualities of my brother-officers that during those two months there were no quarrels among us and we managed to have a great deal of fun together.

On the 23rd July my company was occupying the trenches on the left flank of the bridgehead, a hundred yards from the enemy. It was a day of intense heat. During the morning I had mortared the opposing trenches at Cancela's request, trying to silence a troublesome machine-gun. I lunched as usual with the other officers of the Company in Cancela's dugout. Afterwards I remained behind to discuss an operation he wanted me to undertake after dark—to lead a patrol against an enemy working party which we had heard the previous night in no-man's-land in front of us. While we were talking the enemy started to mortar our position—I suppose in retaliation for my effort in the morning. Their trenches were so close we could hear the thuds of the discharges long before the grenades burst; they were using 50 mm. mortars, not the more lethal 81 mm. I excused myself in order to go and see that all my men were taking shelter; then I returned to Cancela's dug-out. He was lying on his bed, and I sat down on a packing-case by the table in the middle of the floor just inside the entrance. I had started to explain my plan, using my hands for gestures, as one does when speaking Spanish, when a grenade burst in the opening beside me. I barely heard the explosion: I was conscious of it only as a roaring in my ears, a hammer blow on the left side of my face and a sickening dizziness as I fell to the floor. My mouth seemed to fill with a sea of pebbles; as it fell open the sea resolved into a deluge of blood and the pebbles into fragments of my back teeth; twice more the floor welled up into my mouth to pour in a widening pool across the floor. I watched with a detached bewilderment, changing to near-panic. 'Oh God!' I prayed, 'don't let me die like this, in terror!' I took a grip on myself, remembering how someone once said to me, 'You're never dead till you think you are'. Cancela, on the bed, was unhurt; he provided a comic interlude by standing over me, exclaiming in tones of sincere and horrified concern:

'Are you hit, Peter? Tell me, are you hit? He pulled himself together; faintly through the singing in my ears I heard his strong voice calling for stretcher-bearers. Slowly I rolled over my back, then painfully raised my head to examine my wounds; my mouth and throat felt numb and soggy, I could not speak, my jaw hung loose—I realized it was shattered; there was a bloody gash across each hand, another at the top of my right arm and something at the back of my head. Cancela examined my body and assured me that the haemorrhage was not internal. Heartened by this news and filled with exhilaration that follows shock and precedes collapse, I motioned away the stretcher-bearers and walked three or four hundred yards down to the Bandera Headquarters. On the way I stopped to rest: leaning against the parapet I looked out north-eastwards along the shimmering band of the river to the old stone citadel of Lérida dancing in the heat haze. Somehow the sight of that harsh and alien landscape drove into my fuddled mind the firm resolve that I would not die there, far away from my home.

At Bandera Headquarters Larrea and Ruiz were busy with other casualties from the bombardment; but as soon as they saw me they shouted to an orderly to lay me on a mattress and make me comfortable. They had their hands full, and it was nearly half-an-hour before they could attend to me. I lay on the mattress, my head propped up on a haversack and greatcoat, watching the black clusters of flies settle on the wounds in my hands and feeling the movement of their buzzing through my jaw; I watched them with interest, even fascination, as though from a long way off. By the time Ruiz came to look at me the flies were congealed into the wounds; he worked on me quickly but with surprising gentleness, cleaning and bandaging while he talked to me about the wonderful time I was going to have in San Sebastian when I was well again. Larrea came to help him, and then they tried to cheer me by a discussion of the joys of leave and love of a cool climate. I was soon to hear what they really thought. After giving me injections of anti-tetanus and anti-gangrene serum and a shot of morphia, they went away to arrange the evacuation of the wounded. After a while I heard them whispering; they probably thought I was asleep, but in fact I seemed to hear everything with increasing clarity:

151

'It's no good sending Peter back,' one of them said, 'he won't live more than a few hours.'

In my mind flooded that view of the Segre and the ruined citadel of Lérida, filling me with the determination to overcome this death that threatened me. Slowly I raised myself on one elbow; painfully I turned my head, caught their gaze and held it. Larrea smiled:

'Send him in the first ambulance.'

*   *   *

The war was over before I saw the Bandera again. In July 1939, I visited them in a village near Madrid to say good-bye for the last time. I was on my way to England, the threat and excitement of another war hanging over me; my former comrades, with years of peace ahead of them, were already falling under the spell of that post-war reaction, called by C.E. Montague 'Disenchantment', which spread throughout England in the twenties and Spain the forties. Now that the stimulus of imminent battle was over, routine training and discipline seemed to have lost much of their purpose. The temporary officers were awaiting demobilization and the uncertainty of civilian life; the regulars could look forward only to the monotony and slow promotion of peacetime soldiering. Now, too, they had time to mourn the good friends they had lost in action—the Bandera had been heavily engaged in bitter fighting in the Pyrenees at the beginning of the year. Antonio Marchán was dead, half his face blown off by a grenade thrown from a trench which he was storming at the head of his platoon. Arrieta was killed by a stray bullet a moment after he had dispatched a prisoner with his pistol.

I last saw de Mora in Madrid in the spring of 1951, when he was a lieutenant-colonel; he had commanded a battalion of the Blue Division in Russia—an experience he seemed to have enjoyed. Cancela, he told me, was a major in an infantry battalion in the Canary Islands. Larrea, whom I saw at the same time, was also a major.

'When I sent you off in that ambulance from Serós,' Larrea told me, 'I didn't expect you to live very long.'

*   *   *

During the weeks that followed I was to experience something of the self-sacrificing generosity that is part of the Spanish nature. In the ambulance that took me to the hospital at Fraga—a ten-mile journey over rough roads pitted with shell-holes—a gunner lieutenant with his left arm shattered by a shell splinter stood over me, bracing his body with his foot against a stretcher on the other side, holding me on to my own stretcher with his remaining arm to prevent me being shaken out by the bumps; there were six of us serious casualties in the ambulance with only one attendant.

In the hospital at Fraga, where I arrived late at night, I met with a stroke of luck that may have been decisive: the medical officer on duty was Captain Tomás Zerolo, one of the most brilliant surgeons in Spain; a Canary Islander by birth, he had taken his degrees in London. Hearing him talk to me in English raised my morale immediately. I had not once lost consciousness since being hit. Now Zerolo explained that he must operate immediately, to clean the wounds and remove fragments of metal that had lodged in them; but, for medical reasons which I could not understand, he dared not give me an anesthetic. He offered me some brandy instead, but my throat was so burnt by white-hot metal from the mortar bomb that I could not bear the thought of alcohol. While he probed the wounds and cut away the burnt and infected flesh, he helped to take my mind off the pain by talking quietly and incessantly of England and the things he loved in London—the roses at Regent's Park, the sweep of the Thames from Chiswick to Greenwich, Ferraro's food at the Berkeley and his favourite night-clubs. When he had finished he bound my jaw together so skillfully that the broken bones eventually knitted of their own accord.

I remained conscious, unable to sleep, all that night, the next day and the following night. Each time I felt the approach of oblivion I would be jerked awake as though by a violent explosion. On the morning of the third day Zerolo came to my bedside with a long face:

'I'm sorry old boy, but I've got to send you to Zaragoza right away. I hate to do it, but I've just had orders to clear this hospital immediately for a heavy intake of casualties.' He tucked an envelope into the pocket of my shirt:

'This is for your doctors in Zaragoza; it explains that there are still pieces of metal in your hands and jaw. See that he understands.'

I was past caring. I did not know that the Battle of the Ebro had begun that morning—the last desperate Republican offensive—and that in a week every hospital in Aragón would be over-flowing with the wounded. Many months later Zerolo told me that he had not expected me to survive the move; I know that his skill on that first evening was decisive.[1]

It was a grim journey: two hours on a stretcher inside a hot and stuffy ambulance, driving at high speed along a road pitted with shell-holes, where every bump sent a spasm of agony through my jaw. I remember little of my first days in the General Hospital in Zaragoza, because at last I began to lose consciousness for long periods of time. I have a vivid picture of the chief dental surgeon, a cross little man with steel-rimmed glasses and a grey goatee beard, who, after probing my mouth for a few minutes, asked how he could be expected to operate on anyone whose throat was so badly burnt. He

---

[1] I was sad to read the news of his death in *The Times*, early in 1956.

seemed to think it was all my fault. Severe urticaria from Larrea's serums added to the pain of my wounds and the discomfort of the heat—it was agony to swallow even saliva, and I dreaded the liquid meals that were forced down my throat. Most of all I dreaded the arrival of the dressing trolley each morning; there was a deep hole in the joint of each of my thumbs, into which they would pour neat surgical spirit. Usually I fainted. I was, however, lucky in the nurse who looked after me, an angel of skill and kindness who never seemed to sleep, for at whatever hour of day or night I rang my bell she was always there to help me.

During my conscious periods I used to have visits from two of my friends: a retired American general, Henry Reilly, a red-faced, white-haired, warm-hearted old man who lived near Paris and was visiting Nationalist Spain as an observer; and Eileen O'Brien, a small, purposeful young woman who represented an organization called the Irish Christian Front. I had met Miss O'Brien in Salamanca the previous September, General Reilly on my last visit to Zaragoza. I could not speak at all, but was happy to listen to them and the news they brought me of the world outside my tiny, whitewashed room. I remember how my spirits would rise at the sight of the General's burly figure staggering into my room beneath a crate of beer—though it was agony for me to drink it—his friendly red face pouring with sweat and his breath coming in short gasps as he panted his indignation against the Spanish Government, who had just issued an edict forbidding civilians to shed their jackets in public; this was published in the newspapers with a preamble full of humourless pomposity of which the Nationalist Government was fond: only Zulus (why pick on them, we wondered) and similar savages, it announced, went about naked; in a civilized country, such as Spain, gentlemen must appear decently clad in jacket and tie—presumably also trousers, though these were not mentioned.

Soon the hospital filled with wounded from the Ebro. A young Requeté officer from Navarre with a mangled leg was brought into my room. He was in terrible pain, his face green and waxy with sweat. Unlike me, he never complained of his wound, but expressed himself delighted to be sharing a room with an Englishman who had come to fight for the cause of Spain. I woke up one day after a long period of oblivion to find that he had gone. Eileen O'Brien told me the reason; the hospital was overcrowded, with fresh casualties pouring in; one of us two had to be moved to another hospital further away. I was unconscious when the order came, but the Requeté contended that, as an English volunteer, I must have priority over him; although he was in no better state than I to travel, he insisted on going. Deeply moved, I begged Eileen to find him and thank him for me. She shook her head:

'I can't. He died on the way.'

*   *   *

At the end of the first week in August I was moved to General Mola Hospital in San Sebastian, which was to be my home for the next three months. Despite the rigours of the journey the climate of San Sebastian was a wonderful relief after the heat of Zaragoza; because it was a base hospital the medical attention was very much better. For the first week I took little interest in my surroundings; although I was no longer in acute danger, I was still in considerable pain and could only sleep after heavy doses of morphia, which I was not denied. I was fortunate in coming under the care of three distinguished doctors: the Catalan doctor Soler, a dental surgeon called Scherman and the famous Irish-American plastic surgeon, Eastman Sheean. Sheean had run his own hospital for the British Army in the First World War, after which he had gone to America, where he had a fashionable and lucrative practice lifting the faces of the ageing rich; but his hobby was travelling round Europe, treating wounded ex-Servicemen without payment; just before coming to Spain he had paid a visit to Turkey for this purpose. He took wonderful care of me, and, when I was better, accompanied me on long walks to help me to recover my strength. The nursing in Mola Hospital was supervised by nuns, devoted and kindly souls whose indifference to the principles of asepsis nearly drove Sheean mad; they had an irritating habit of waking me in the middle of the night, when I had barely managed to fall asleep, to ask if I would like a cup of coffee. The routine nursing was done by enchanting women who, before the war, would never have been permitted by their families to go out without a chaperone; the effect of their charm and beauty on our morale made up for any deficiencies in their knowledge or skill.

At the end of August Scherman told me that he would have to operate on my jaw to remove the broken and septic fragments of teeth, bone and metal that still remained there; he warned me that it would be a painful business because, for some reason that I did not understand, he would not be able to give me any effective anaesthetic. The day before the operation I had a visit from Michael Weaver and George Sheffield, who had been staying with the Hennesseys in Cognac; they brought with them a bottle of Three Star brandy. Next morning, when I was wheeled down to the operating theatre, I took the bottle with me and asked Scherman if I might use it in place of the anesthetic he couldn't give me.

'Certainly! I might even have a nip with you.'

I started with an enormous swig, he with a very small one to encourage me; then he set to work. Whenever the pain became too much for me I signaled him to stop and took a long pull at the brandy. In this way I finished the bottle, feeling comparatively little pain during the operation, although I felt a great deal when the effect of the brandy had worn off. I was quite proud of myself until I remembered that this was the manner in which operations were usually performed before the last century.

A few days later I was moved from the large ward where I had been since my arrival, to a small room with two beds. As I entered it for the first time I was greeted by a shout from the other bed: 'Why, Goddammit, you old bastard!' and saw my friend, Goggi von Hartmann. He had a bullet in the arm—the nineth or tenth wound of his life—which had damaged the main nerve; but he seemed to rise above it. After a lengthy and painful operation, with only local anesthetics, he found it difficult to sleep, even with morphia; he would therefore swear horribly, when awakened in the night by the light being switched on, to find a smiling nun offering him a cup of coffee. We besought the nuns to abandon the practice, but with the obstinacy of the truly pious they persisted—for three nights. On the third night, no sooner had I been awakened with the light in my eyes than I was startled by a couple of deafening reports in quick succession from Hartmann's bed; there was a pungent smell of cordite as the room was plunged into darkness; a shower of splintered glass fell to the floor, followed immediately by a sharp scream and the clatter of breaking cups.

'Next time,' von Hartmann shouted as the door banged behind the fleeing nun, 'I shoot *you*, not the light!'

We made a good recovery from our operations, gaining strength rapidly. By the end of the first week of September we were already on our feet; we began to go around the town, visiting Chicote's every evening and often dining out afterwards. It may seem surprising that hospital discipline allowed us such latitude; but the theory seemed to be that the freedom would benefit our morale without seriously endangering our recovery. For myself, I found that a few glasses of gin or whisky deadened the pain in my throat, making it easier for me to swallow the soft foods that were all that I could manage; from this it was a very short step to drinking far too much. 'You be careful,' said Scherman to me, 'or you'll get yourself a red nose and become a dull fellow.' Von Hartmann throve on the treatment, sometimes staying out all night and slipping back to the hospital just in time for breakfast. One morning he ran straight into the Mother Superior in the entrance hall. Without batting an eyelid he opened the conversation with a cheerful but respectful: 'Good morning, Reverend Mother! I'm just back from early Mass.' The good woman beamed at him:

'Ah Captain, if only you could persuade some of the other boys to follow your example!'

I was less amused one evening a few days later when I had gone to bed early: von Hartmann came in at midnight looking morose and dangerous.

'I have had a fight with two officers of the Legion. They are coming here to kill me.'

'Well they won't get very far,' I said, 'the guards will stop them.'

He shook his head as he finished undressing:

'They will come. But they will get a big surprise when they come in here.' He cocked his automatic and released the safety catch.

'Now,' he said, climbing into bed, 'I have my hand on this all night.' And he had, too; the barrel, where it lay on the pillow, pointed straight at my head.

The Munich crisis came upon us in the middle of September, filling me with particular alarm as I considered the difficulty of my own position. There was general certainty among the Nationalists that, if war were to break out, the French would immediately attack Franco; unable to leave hospital, enlisted for the duration of the Civil War in the Nationalist Army, I was threatened with a very delicate situation, which at best could only land me in a Nationalist concentration camp. Whatever the merits of the Munich settlement, it was for me, personally, an unmitigated blessing. My Nationalist friends evidently considered it was the same for them; I have never been stood so many drinks as I was in Chicote's the night we heard that the immediate danger of war had been averted. Curiously enough, at the end of the crisis the general opinion in Nationalist Spain seemed to be, not that British prestige had suffered a severe blow, but rather that by her initiative Britain had assumed the leadership of Europe.

Early in October I applied for convalescent leave to England; it was clear that I should not be fit for active service for at least another three or four months, and I saw no reason why I should not convalesce as well in England as in Spain. The application would have to be approved by the Generalissimo, and so I went to Burgos to try and pull a few strings there. I was lucky enough to get an interview with the Colonel commanding Medical Services at G.H.Q., who was most sympathetic and undertook to forward my application immediately, together with his own recommendation; I also met with the Duke of Piñahermosa, one of General Franco's A.D.C.s, who promised to speak personally to the great man. Three weeks later I received news that I had been granted two months' leave in England, dating from the day I crossed the Spanish frontier. At the end of November I arrived home.

*   *   *

I never doubted that my application for home leave would be granted, once it came to the personal attention of General Franco. Abused by his enemies, criticized by his allies and even by his friends, he was nevertheless, like all good commanders, devoted to the interests of his subordinates, especially the officers of the Foreign Legion which he had helped to found. The following July, when I was passing through Burgos on my way to England, having obtained my discharge from the Foreign Legion, I was informed by the Duke of Piñahermosa that the Generalissimo wished to see me.

When I had passed through the enormous gates of his headquarters, receiving an impressive salute from the Moorish guard, walked along a curving drive and climbed a flight of stone steps, I was shown into a long, dim ante-room, full of heavy, black furniture. After a lengthy wait, for there were several people before me, Piñahermosa escorted me through a door to a small sitting-room, with another door leading out of it. Knocking on this further door he disappeared, leaving me to seat myself on a small sofa by the window.

Five minutes later the door opened to admit a small, tubby figure, dwarfed by the broad scarlet sash and pendulant gold tassels of a full general. As he came towards me with short, brisk steps I sprang to my feet and saluted: '*A sus ordines, mi General!*'

He told me to sit beside him; then, inkling his dark sombre face towards me and putting his hand on my knee to emphasize his words, he began to speak in one of the quietest voices I have ever heard. He talked for half-an-hour, practically without intermission. He had always admired the English, he said, especially their system of education with its emphasis on self-discipline, breeding the spirit of adventure that had made so small a country the ruler of so great an empire. He regarded the British Empire as perhaps the greatest bulwark against Communism in the world; but he doubted that the British were fully alive to the Communist danger. Whenever any of his friends returned to Spain from a visit to England he made a point of examining them on all aspects of English life: political, social, and economic. It seemed to him that our Universities in particular—perhaps because of their commendable anxiety to preserve intellectual freedom—were paying too little attention to the spread of subversive influences among our youth.

Throughout this interview his tone was informal and friendly, neither didactic nor condescending; sensitive, no doubt, to the embarrassment I should feel if I had to express my own views, he invited no comment. At the end he rose, shook hands gravely, thanked me for my services and wished me luck.

'What will you do now?' he asked.

'Join the British Army for this coming war, I suppose, your Excellency.'

He cocked his head, then gave a wintry smile:

'I don't think there will be a war.'

I wonder what he really thought.

*   *   *

In England I was plunged into a political as well as a social mêlée. The former involved me in such various activities as writing for *The Times* and for monthly reviews, addressing Members of Parliament in a committee room of the House of Commons and speaking at a meeting in Northampton in company with disillusioned ex-members of the International Brigades. I was astonished by the initiative and vitality of Republican propaganda in Spain— fortified, of course, by the growing fear of Germany; certainly the Republicans seemed to have the ear of Fleet Street, where the Nationalist voice was only the faintest of squeaks. I found myself involved in bitter and often painful controversies with some of my best friends; for the Spanish Civil War aroused in ordinary Englishmen an intensity of interest and partisan feeling unusual in people notoriously indifferent to the affairs of other countries. On top of these activities a series of parties with friends in London and with my brother and sister-in-law at Portsmouth scarcely helped my convalescence. My mother did her best to look after me; Sir Arnold Wilson asked me to stay at Much Hadham, where he tried to make me rest, and Archie James put his comfortable house near Brackley at my disposal for rest or writing. Nevertheless, when my leave was due to expire at the end of January I was far from well. Fortunately for me, the Duke of Alba, the Nationalist Representative in London, had observed this himself. He sent for me to say that he had caused my leave to be extended for another two months and forbade me to return earlier. It was typical of that great man that he took such trouble over the welfare of someone who could have been no use or interest to him.

When eventually I was able to return to Spain the Civil War was over. The Battle of Ebro, which had caused the Nationalists some anxious moments and severe casualties, ended on November 16th with the withdrawal of the beaten remnant of the Republican Armies. Two days before Christmas the Nationalists began their offensives against Catalonia; on January 26th they entered Barcelona. Rejecting all peace overtures, whether directly from the Republicans or through the intermediacy of foreign powers, General Franco launched the last offensive of the war on March 26th, 1939; two days later his troops entered Madrid. He was the master of Spain.

ACKNOWLEDGEMENTS

I would like to express my appreciation of the kindness of the Oxford University Press and Messrs. Jonathan Cape in allowing me to reprint extracts from their respective publications, *Stalin* by Dr Isaac Deutscher, and *Spain* by Salvador de Madariaga.

My particular thanks are due to the following friends: Tom Burns and Gavin Maxwell, without whose encouragement and patient help I should never have begun this book; John Marks, Collin Brooks, and Archibald Lyall for their careful reading of my MS. and for much valuable advice; Mrs Michael Hurt and Mrs John Hanbury-Tracy, who, together with my wife, corrected my proofs while I was in Budapest; and Vane Ivanović, aboard whose ships I have done most of my writing.

P.K.

January 4th, 1957

No Colours or Crest

Peter Kemp

TO THE MEMORY OF
MY BROTHER NEIL
14th July 1910—10th January 1941

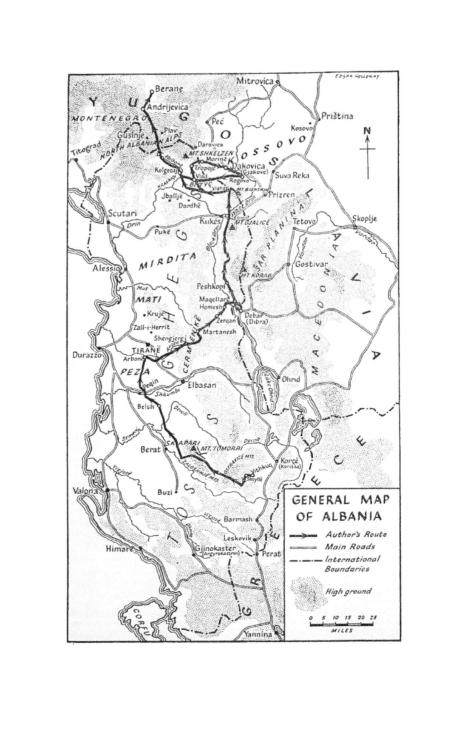

EDGAR HOLLOWAY

Mitrovica

Berane

Andrijevica

MONTENEGRO

YUG

Peć

Priština

Kosovo

Gusinje

Plav

Titograd

NORTH ALBANIAN ALPS

Daravica

O

MT. SHKELZEN

Morinë

Tropojë

Dakovica

(Gjakove)

Kolgecaj

Vlad

Rogovo

Suva Reka

BYTYÇ

Ylahdan

MT BISHTRIK

SS

Jballjë

Dardhë

White Drin

Prizren

O

Scutari

Drin

Puke

Kukës

MT GJALICË

Tetovo

Skoplje

N

MIRDITA

ŠAR PLANINA

Alessio

MAT

Peshkopi

MT KORAB

Gostivar

MATI

Maqellarë

Homesh

Kruje

Debar

(Dibra)

MACEDONIA

Zall-i-Herrit

Zerqan

Martanesh

Shëngjergj

CERMENIKE

Durazzo

TIRANË

Arbonë

PEZA

Peqin

Elbasan

Ohrid

Shkumbi

Lake Ohrid

Belsh

Devoll

SKRAPARI

Devoll

Semeni

Berat

MT TOMORRI

OSTRAVICË MTS

Korçë

(Koritsa)

Vjosë

Vithkuq

Smyllë

Valona

Buzi

E

Barmash

Osum

Leskovik

Himare

Gjinokaster

(Argyrokastron)

Perat

G

R

CORFU

E

Yannina

GENERAL MAP
OF ALBANIA

→ Author's Route

Main Roads

International
Boundaries

High ground

0 5 10 15 20 25

MILES

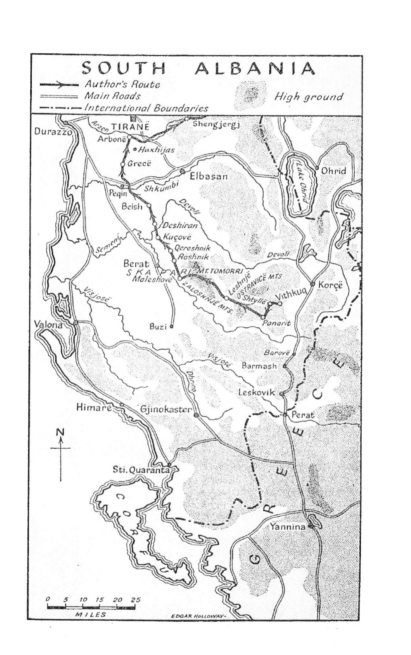

SOUTH ALBANIA

→ Author's Route
═══ Main Roads
·—·—· International Boundaries

High ground

Durazzo
TIRANE
Arben
Arzen
Shengjergj
Haxhijas
Grecë
Shkumbi
Elbasan
Lake Ohrid
Ohrid
Peqin
Belsh
Deshiran
Kuçovë
Devoll
Qereshnik
Roshnik
Semeni
Devoll
Berat
SKA PARI
MT.TOMORRI
Maleshovë
Leshnjë
OSTRAVICE MTS
Korçë
ZALOSHNJE MTS
Shtyllë
Vithkuq
Valona
Visjosë
Buzi
Panarit
Barovë
Visjosë
Barmash
Drino
Leskovik
Himarë
Gjinokaster
Perat
N
Sti. Quaranta
G R E E C E
Yannina
C O R F U

0 5 10 15 20 25
MILES

EDGAR HOLLOWAY·

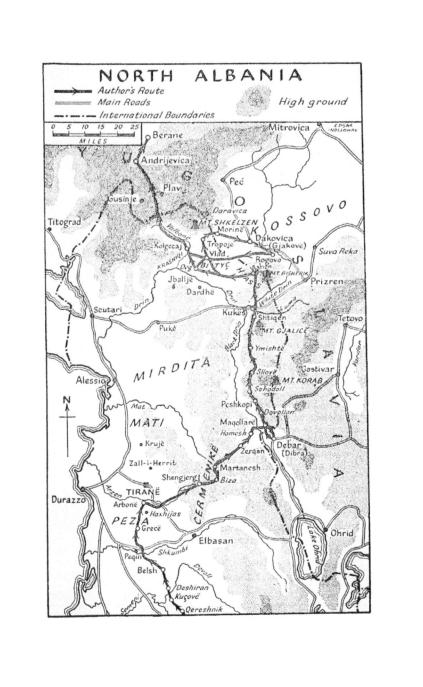

NORTH ALBANIA

→ Author's Route
= Main Roads
–·–·– International Boundaries

High ground

0 5 10 15 20 25
MILES

EDGAR HOLLOWAY

Berane
Mitrovica
Andrijevica
Peć
Plav
Gusinje
Daravica
Titograd
MT. SHKELZEN
Morinë
Dakovica
(Gjakove)
Kolgecaj
Tropoje
Vlad.
Rogovo
MT. BISHTRIK
Jballje
Dardhë
Prizren
Scutari
Drin
Kukës
Shtiqen
Tetovo
Pukë
MT. GJALICE
Ymishtë
Sllove
Gostivar
Alessio
MIRDITA
MT. KORAB
Sohodoll
Mat
Peshkopi
Dovollari
MATI
Maqellarë
Homesh
Krujë
Zall-i-Herrit
Zerqan
Debar
(Dibra)
Shengjergj
Martanesh
Biza
N
TIRANË
Durazzo
Arbonë
Haxhijas
PEZA
Grecë
Ohrid
Lake Ohrid
Elbasan
Peqin
Shkumbi
Belsh
Deshiran
Kuçovë
Qereshnik

KOSSOVO
Suva Reka
Valbona
KRASNIQI
Dhg
BITYÇ
HAS
White Drin
Luma
Black Drin
CERMENIKE
Arzen
Semeni
Devoll
Vardar

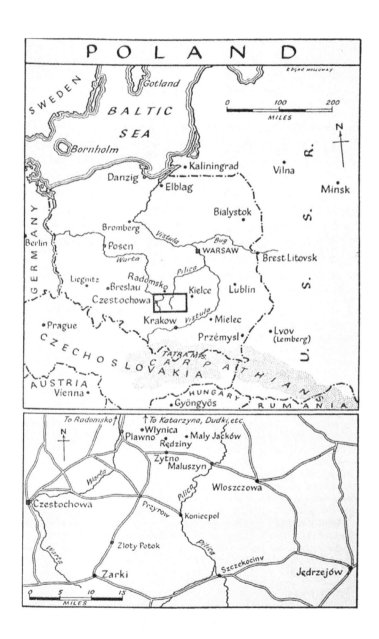

ACKNOWLEDGEMENTS

My particular thanks are to Colonel David Smiley, M.V.O., O.B.E., M.C., some of whose photographs are reproduced in this book; Commander Alastair Mars, D.S.O., D.S.C., R.N., and his First Lieutenant Mr. A. G. Stewart, for their reading and criticism of the passages dealing with my experiences in H.M. submarines; my friend Ihsan Bey Toptani for much valuable help on the chapters concerning Albania; Captain A. R. Glen, D.S.C., R.N.V.R., and to Mr. I. S. Ivonović, aboard whose cargo boats I have done most of my writing; and to the many kind friends, too numerous to mention, who have helped me with their advice, encouragement, and criticism.

PETER KEMP

There's a Legion that never was 'listed,
That carries no colours or crest,
But, split in a thousand detachments,
Is breaking the road for the rest.
Rudyard Kipling

TABLE OF CONTENTS

I

ENGLISH WINTER

'Of course they must let you wear your Spanish Civil War medals,' pronounced my uncle in the brisk, cheerful tones that generations of Indian Army subalterns had learnt not to contradict.

'After all, the whole point of campaign ribbons is to indicate that the wearer is a veteran who has seen active service.'

Seated erect in a hard, high-backed chair, with his long, thin legs sprawled wide in front of him, my uncle quizzed me with bright, twinkling eyes; his head was cocked to one side, his deep-lined bony face creased in the half mocking, half affectionate smile that had at once charmed and disconcerted his Sepoys, his relations, and refractory Frontier tribesmen. My gaze wandered round the bleak sitting-room of the suite in the small hotel near the Brompton Road where he had moved when the approach of war drove him from the sunny comfort of the Italian Riviera: plain, deep red carpet; green, flowered wallpaper; drab chintz-covered sofa and armchairs; white net curtains drawn back from the windows to give a dispiriting view of the grimy, uneven Kensington skyline. The street outside was silent and heavy with the gloom of that impending catastrophe which before the end of the next year was to obliterate this unpretentious little family hotel from the face of London.

It was the morning of Sunday, 3rd September, 1939. Germany had invaded Poland; Britain and France had sent an ultimatum to Hitler; King Carol was digging a ditch round Rumania. Within an hour we should hear the sad, tired voice of the Prime Minister announce the beginning of another world war.

A month previously I had returned to London after nearly three years service in Spain, one of the very few Englishmen to fight in the Nationalist armies, defending a cause which enjoyed little popularity among my countrymen. I had joined the Nationalists almost immediately after coming down from Cambridge, partly out of a desire for adventure and partly from the conviction, fostered by the study of early, uncensored reports from newspaper correspondents on the spot, that the vital issue of the civil war was Communism, and that a Republican victory would lead to a Communist government in Spain. A strong Tory myself, I had served in the Carlist militia and the Spanish Foreign Legion, where my friends—Traditionalists, Conservatives and Liberal Monarchists—had no more sympathy than I for totalitarian regimes. But General Franco's friendship with Hitler and

Mussolini and his establishment of the Falange as the only political party in Spain had erased from most British minds all memory of the Communist threat he had defeated; even the Soviet-German Pact had not wholly revived it.

Now the weight of Republican propaganda, backed by the formidable organization of European Communism, had dubbed Franco a Fascist, while many of my British friends regarded me as, at best, a Fascist fellow-traveller. Even those who sympathized with me feared that Spain would enter the war against us, although I had seen enough of the devastation and war-weariness there to believe that she would remain neutral.

When I had left England for the Spanish Civil War, with all the romantic enthusiasm, ingenuousness, and ignorance of my twenty-one years, I had never imagined that six months after it was over I should find myself involved in another and infinitely vaster holocaust. Now, without thinking of myself as a veteran, I knew enough of war to feel no elation at the prospect; I was conscious only of a grave anxiety at the strength of the forces matched against us, a grim realization of what defeat would mean, and the hope that the experience I had acquired in the face of much disapproval and ridicule might not prove entirely useless to my country.

I left my uncle to go to his club in Pall Mall, and sauntered morosely through dismal, deserted streets to the house in Brompton Square which an aged great-aunt had lent me while she and her husband relaxed in the milder atmosphere of Brighton. Greta, the amiable young Austrian cook, panted upstairs from the kitchen, her plump, round peasant face split in a wide, careless grin.

'Please do not look so sad, sir. I think there will not be a war.'

Poor Greta. She was a wonderful cook. But her naïve optimism did not save her from nearly six years in an internment camp.

I walked across the road to listen to the wireless over drinks with a girl-friend and her mother and sister. When the Prime Minister had finished speaking and we knew we were at war there was absolute stillness in the softly lit grey-green drawing-room; under a picture light above the fireplace a charming portrait of a doll-like little Infanta seemed to mock us from the security of a distant age of privilege and faith. I saw my hostess weeping silently and took her hand in a clumsy gesture meant to comfort.

'Oh, I don't mind for myself,' she whispered, looking past me to her daughters. 'But it does seem so hard that these children should have their lives blighted a second time.' I remembered that she had lost her husband from wounds in the first war. Her son was to be killed in this.

When the siren screamed from the Walton Street police station a few yards away, I knew with shame that I was afraid. In Spain I had experienced heavy air attack and I had seen the damage in the dock area of Barcelona; those bombardments would seem like pigeon droppings, I reckoned, compared to what we could now expect. As we trooped downstairs to join the servants in the basement kitchen I must have cut a pretty poor figure, clutching in each hand a bottle snatched in passing from the drinks tray; and in the forced, embarrassed conversation that followed I was all too conscious of my failure to set a proper example of indifference and courage. When the All Clear sounded I reflected sorrowfully that the last three years had left their mark upon my nerves.

I was never granted permission to wear my Spanish decorations; nor even, at first, a uniform on which to wear them. In July 1938 a mortar bomb had shattered my jaw and severely damaged both hands; now, when I joined the general scramble for a commission, the members of the medical board that examined me told me sympathetically but firmly to come back in six months' time. My consequent feeling of frustration was exacerbated by the sight of friends in uniform and the knowledge that my only brother, five years my senior and a lieutenant in the Fleet Air Arm, was already at sea in the carrier *Courageous*. With humiliation I pictured them battling on the fields of Flanders or leading torpedo attacks on pocket battleships or locked in desperate dog-fights in the sky, while I loitered uselessly in England, put out of action by injuries received in an alien war.

As it turned out, I need not have worried; after six months of peace indistinguishable from war it seemed that we were to have six months of war indistinguishable from peace. While the German armies swept eastward and Stalin agreed with Hitler that Poland must never rise again, in England the British Expeditionary Force prepared to cross the Channel, the Women's Services demonstrated that girls could retain their allure and chic in battle-dress and trousers, and the Committee of the Royal Thames Yacht Club announced that in view of the national emergency, smoking would in future be permitted in the Members' Dining-room at eight-fifteen every evening instead of eight-thirty.

In the interval since my return from Spain I had begun work on a book about the Spanish Civil War for the publishing house of Macmillan; now there seemed to be little point in continuing it. My publishers were evidently of the same opinion, for I received a charming letter from Harold Macmillan saying that his firm would be delighted to discuss the matter again at the end of this war 'should both parties survive hostilities'. As a stop-gap I took a job in the Postal Censorship, where I was employed in the Press Section under the urbane direction of Cosmo Hamilton and the stimulating supervision of his assistant, Benn Levy; Levy was deeply suspicious of my Spanish connection, but never allowed his feelings to affect his natural courtesy or his engaging habit of addressing me, like the rest of us, as 'ducky'.

I remained in London for another two months. I was fortunate in the companionship of Archibald Lyall, author, traveller, and epicure, whose robust sense of humour and Rabelaisian wit kept me from brooding on my disappointment. A conspicuous and impressive figure, tall, blond, and corpulent, with a high, bald forehead above a plump and florid face and a carefully trimmed Mephistophelian moustache, Lyall concealed an able and inquisitive mind behind the mischievously complacent expression of a dissipated baby. We had become close friends two years before, when he was visiting Salamanca, at that time the Nationalist G.H.Q., where I was awaiting my posting to the Foreign Legion. During a period when time had hung heavy on my hands he had shown a remarkable flair for discovering interesting and unusual sources of drink and diversion; and in our joint explorations of the night life of that beautiful but usually placid university town he had proved himself an inspired connoisseur of the picaresque.

His works included several travel books on the Balkans, the U.S.S.R., and Portuguese West Africa; *Lyall's Languages of Europe*, a multi-lingual phrase-book; and an unpublished treatise on women, entitled *The Enemies of Englishmen*. On the strength of *Lyall's Languages* his publishers had recently asked him to compile a phrase-book for the Forces, which he was now preparing in the comparative seclusion of a flat in Mount Royal; it was a practical little hand-book, called *Soldier's Speakeasy*, and catered for all the warrior's needs from '*When does the next train leave for Paris?*' to '*How much is that girl with red hair?*'

He nursed a particular resentment against Hitler for what he regarded as an intolerable interruption of his private life. 'Up to the age of thirty-five,' he explained to me, 'a man can work and drink and copulate; but at thirty-five he has to make up his mind which of the three he is going to give up. I had just passed my thirty-fifth birthday and made all my arrangements to give up work when that bloody Hun started the war.'

He sympathized with my impatience at my enforced inactivity. 'How would it be if I took you to see the Dame one of these days?'

Dame Beatrice Lyall was his mother, a formidable woman of strong mind and noble character, who distinguished herself in the Red Cross in both world wars. She was the only person from whom Lyall felt it necessary to conceal the more lurid details of his life.

'She's got quite a bit of influence and might be able to fix you up in something more active than Postal Censorship. But he went on, tapping my arm urgently, 'there's one thing I must emphasize: from the moment we cross the Dame's threshold I, Archie, am a teetotal eunuch of rather low Anglican views.'

For all her kindness there was nothing she could do against the verdict of the medical board. My bitterness was intensified at the end of September, when *Courageous* was sunk by a U-boat; although my brother was a survivor, picked up by a destroyer after swimming for two hours, the event drove home to me the futility of my own war effort.

Returning from work one evening I ran into Douglas Dodds-Parker, whom I had met in Spain during the summer; because he had also been in Prague at the time of the Sudeten crisis I suspected that he was connected with Intelligence. My spirits rose when he asked me:

'Would you like me to give your name to my people at the War Office?'

Early in October I received a letter from a room number in the War Office, which began, as far as I remember:

'Your name has been given to us by Mr. Dodds-Parker as having qualifications which may be of interest to this Department.'

The department seemed to have no name. But the letter requested me to present myself for interview at the above address, and concluded with regrets that the department was not authorized to defray the cost of my travelling expenses.

The interview took place in a large room full of desks, at each of which sat a Staff Captain. The officer who interviewed me, a solicitor in private life, asked me a long succession of questions, writing down my answers on a buff foolscap form; he recorded minutely every detail of my service in Spain. When he had finished he looked up at me:

'I think we might be able to use you. We haven't a job for you at the moment—frankly we haven't a job for anybody at this stage of the war. But if the war spreads, as we believe it will, we are going to need officers with your special experience. Have you any idea of joining a particular regiment at the moment?'

He went on: 'From what I know about you I should say that you would have a more interesting time with us than you would in regimental soldiering. If I can get authority to recruit you, and if you agree, we would commission you and send you in your commissioned rank to an O.C.T.U., where you would get your basic training and fill in the time until we needed you.'

'That would suit me,' I said.

'Good. Now, supposing we accept you, which would you rather go to— the Horsed Cavalry O.C.T.U. at Weedon, where we have a few vacancies, or an infantry O.C.T.U. at Aldershot?'

'Weedon,' I answered emphatically.

I told him about the Postal Censorship, adding that we were supposed to be moving to Liverpool at the end of the month.

'You might as well go with them. It will take us a month or two to commission you and fit you into a course at Weedon. Leave an address where we can get in touch with you.'

As I rose to go I heard my name called from the other end of the room. Standing by a fireplace was a tall captain, whom I recognized as Peter Wilkinson, with whom I had been at Cambridge; he had been commissioned into the Royal Fusiliers from the University. With him was a trim, dark, wiry officer with a neat, clipped moustache and alert, bright eyes, whom he introduced as Lieutenant-Colonel Gubbins; this officer was to have a profound, even decisive influence on the course of thousands if not millions of lives—among them my own. Speaking in staccato, precise sentences he questioned me about the Spanish War, where we had friends in common. He had just returned from Poland, where he had commanded the British Military Liaison Mission with the Polish Army.

Liverpool in November is perhaps not the most attractive city in the British Isles; but my work in the Postal Censorship had become more interesting, or at least more amusing, since my transfer to a new department, known as 'Impounded Baggage'. This ambiguous title signified that our duties were to examine luggage taken at airports and seaports from travellers between neutral countries and the British Isles. My knowledge of Spanish was more useful here than in the Press Section. In addition to letters, books, and newspapers we often had to censor gramophone records and cinema films, for which purpose we were provided with a gramophone and a cinema projector. We had a room to ourselves at the top of a tower in Littlewoods Pools Building; here, comparatively immune from official surveillance, our director was able to run the department to his own and our complete satisfaction. As relief from the routine work we could censor a few gramophone records, or run through a film. Among the latter we had some quaint examples of the *cinema bleu*. These we found particularly useful for the entertainment of visiting mandarins from civilian or Service Ministries. After a quick run through of *His First Affair* or *La Petite Ingenue* the V.I.P.s would depart in a chorus of sniggers, well satisfied with the work of Impounded Baggage.

A week before Christmas I received a bulky O.H.M.S. envelope with the initials M.I.(R.) stamped on the back. M.I.(R.) proved to be the department that had interviewed me in October; to this day I do not know what the (R.) stood for: Recherché? Revolutionary? Reactionary? The envelope contained, among other documents, an official letter informing me that it was proposed to commission me as a second lieutenant (General List) with effect from 19th January, 1940; that I should report on that date at the 110th (Horsed Cavalry) O.C.T.U., Weedon, Northants, informing them of the time of my arrival; that I should first provide myself with the uniform of my rank, including riding-breeches and field boots, for which I might claim the sum of £40 uniform allowance; lastly—and this was the snag—that I was required to attend a medical board in Liverpool in the first week in January and that I was to inform 'this Department' immediately, should I receive any lesser grading than A.I.

I romped through the medical board with an A.I rating, managing this simply by following the old maxim of not speaking unless spoken to: in other words I volunteered no information about Spain or my wounds because I was asked for none, and took care not to expose my hands or jaw to anybody's attention.

On 10th January, having said good-bye to my colleagues in Impounded Baggage, I went south for a few days' leave, most of which I passed at home. My last two days I spent in London with Archie Lyall, who was about to leave for Belgrade, where he had been appointed Press Attaché. For his new assignment he borrowed my treasured Spanish cloak, which I had bought in Madrid the previous summer.

'You can have it, Archie,' I told him, 'on the one condition that you promise to save it, even though you can't save yourself, if the Germans invade Jugoslavia.'

'Agreed. And will you promise to bequeath it to me if you should croak before I do?'

On this exchange of promises we parted and did not meet again for more than three years; but over the next fourteen months reports reached me from Belgrade of the huge, amorphous figure enveloped in a dark blue cloak with green and crimson lining who was a familiar and popular spectacle at public functions and private parties. He fulfilled his part of the bargain the following year, sending the cloak to Athens in the diplomatic bag the day before the German invasion. From Athens it travelled, via Cairo, to England. Lyall remains my heir to this fetish.

The cavalry barracks at Weedon were built, I believe, in the reign of George II, to quarter troops sent to oppose the advance of Prince Charles Edward's highlanders; sometime before the First World War they were considered to have outlived their usefulness and were condemned as unfit for habitation, even by soldiers. A succession of inter-war governments— alternately abused as 'warmongers' and 'appeasers'—so effectively reduced military expenditure that the War Office had no money to spare for new barracks. In January 1940, therefore, the two-hundred-year-old buildings housed the Officer Cadets of the 110th (Horsed Cavalry) O.C.T.U. The winter of 1939-40 was probably the most rigorous of the war. Standing conspicuously on a hill above the town, exposed to every bitter wind and inadequately heated by diminutive coal fires, our new quarters gave us an icy reception. Our block warmed up a little after we had lived in it for a few days; but during our first week-end—we arrived on a Friday—I remember having to abandon the attempt to write a letter because my fingers were too frozen to hold the pen. We were, however, fortunate in that new washrooms had been installed, with an unlimited supply of hot water.

Each troop of twenty-five to thirty cadets occupied a separate block of barrack rooms. Whereas all the other troops consisted of officer cadets between the ages of eighteen and twenty-one, destined for horsed cavalry regiments, ours—known locally as 'the M.I. Troop'—was composed of men varying in age between twenty and forty, recruited by M.I.(R.) in much the same manner as myself; some of us were already commissioned, the remainder would be commissioned at the end of the course. Drawn from every walk of civilian life, with widely different backgrounds and experience, we were something of a puzzle to our instructors, who treated us with more leniency than they showed to the embryo cavalrymen. This was just as well, for most of us had no previous military training apart from our school O.T.C.s, and some had never been on a horse.

The most distinguished among us was Professor Pendlebury of Pembroke College, Cambridge, an archaeologist whose researches in Crete and Egypt were well-known before the war. A quiet man of great charm and sense of humour, he proved his adaptability by becoming a most efficient soldier. He had a house in Crete, where he was sent, after leaving Weedon, to make certain preparations against enemy invasion. His murder at the hands of Gestapo or *Sicherheitsdienst*, as he lay incapacitated by wounds in a peasant's hut a few days after the German occupation, was a tragic blow to learning and a wanton crime.

The most ebullient, by contrast, was Harold Perkins, a former master mariner who had abandoned the sea before the war to graduate in engineering at the University of Prague and become the proprietor of a textile factory in Poland; on the outbreak of hostilities he was attached to Colonel Gubbins's mission, making his escape with Gubbins and Wilkinson through Hungary and Rumania. A solid ball of muscle, gifted with remarkable administrative ability and physical stamina, he was also blessed with a schoolboy sense of fun which, although it endeared him to our instructors as much as to ourselves, nearly landed him, later in the war, in serious trouble. His work when he left Weedon involved the planning of subversive operations in Poland. He was relaxing from his duties one evening in the room of a senior officer of the Polish Air Force, on the first floor of a famous London hotel; after a few drinks they became involved in one of those friendly free-for-alls which have as their object the removal of the adversary's trousers. Both contestants were successful, and two pairs of trousers—one khaki, the other blue—floated gracefully from the window into the busy street below; a moment later guests in the lobby were astonished to see two trouserless but otherwise impeccably uniformed officers dive down the stairs and out into the street, to return in a few seconds clutching their trousers as they darted for the safety of the first floor.

Perkins's friend, Mike Pickles, had been through a bad time during his escape from Poland, travelling from Silesia across the country to the Baltic States dressed as a peasant and riding mostly in haycarts. He and his Polish companions were overtaken by the advancing Germans, but passed through the lines when the Germans halted, only to meet the Russians. Their worst troubles came from the latter, who were looking for Polish officers and shooting all above the rank of lieutenant; the party was frequently stopped and the hands of each one examined to see if they showed a proper proletarian horniness; luckily, by that time they did.

One of my closest friends in the troop was John Bennett, a barrister who had stood for Parliament in the Socialist interest against Neville Chamberlain; a scintillating but polemic character, he had precipitated a riot at one of his election meetings when, carried away by his own indignant eloquence, he had referred to his illustrious opponent as 'that Edgbaston parrot.'

Whatever the limitations of horsed cavalry in modern warfare, the training filled three of the pleasantest months of my career in the British Army. The full O.C.T.U. course lasted five or six months, but ours was a shorter version; the Commandant, Major R. H. Sheppard, 9th Lancers, himself an outstanding horseman, had devised for us a course at once practical and interesting, cutting out such unnecessary items as sword drill and ceremonial order. The two instructors of whom we saw most were Sergeant-Major Sennett and Sergeant Rourke; under the supervision of Captain Hamilton-Russell, the Equitation Officer, they attempted to teach us the elements of riding and horse mastership, to which the greater—and by far the most useful—part of our training was devoted. They taught us a great deal in a short time, using a balanced blend of patient encouragement and ferocious bullying, the latter reinforced by a superb flow of vituperation and an armoury of blasphemous taunts which had probably been handed down from generation to generation of N.C.O.s since the days of Rupert of the Rhine. We often found it hard to believe that the two warm-hearted and genial fellows with whom we had been exchanging pints of beer and dirty stories in the 'Globe' the previous evening could become next morning the pair of furious and sadistic Tartars who insulted us in the riding school.

For dismounted drill we came under a delightful highlander from the Scots Greys, Sergeant Stewart. These parades could never be wholly dull because of his practice of marching our squad across the square, as far away from himself as possible, and then shouting an order in what, from that distance, sounded like pure Gaelic; each of us would place his own interpretation on the command, and the squad would break up in disorder. An angry bellow would come from the stocky, purple figure at the other end of the square.

'Nae! A' didna say "Whah whooh!" A' said "Whah whu-u-h!"'

Our theoretical training might have been of use to cavalrymen in or before 1919. We heard lectures on tactics from an earnest young officer in the Inns of Court Regiment who took his chief illustration from an incident in the First Battle of Mons; lectures on animal management from the Veterinary Officer, who was inaudible; lectures on Military Law, which were incomprehensible, and lectures on the light machine-gun (Hotchkiss 1913 model).

The R.S.M., who controlled our conduct and discipline, was an austere Yorkshireman known as 'Gentleman Joe' Taylor; formerly an equitation instructor at Sandhurst, he was the personification of smartness and efficiency. Not a single detail escaped his eagle eye—a cliché which might have been coined expressly for him—not the smallest speck of dust in a barrack-room or the faintest blemish on a button, boot, or belt. He had that dour North Country humour which gleams brightest when administering a reprimand or dealing out a punishment.

His strongest weapon was his power to stop our week-end leave, and he used it mercilessly to punish slackness. Week-end leave lasted from Saturday midday until, theoretically, Sunday midnight. In fact, the last train that would get us back in time from London left soon after eight o'clock; if we missed that—and we often did—we had to take a tube to the north of London, and thumb a lift from one of the lorries that travelled by night up the Great North Road and passed through Weedon; it was easy to slip into the barracks unobserved in time for a quick brush-up and shave and a mug of tea before the first parade on Monday morning. But the first parade was always Riding School, when Sennett and Rourke would be at their fiercest, knowing that they had a number of sleepless and hung-over gentlemen at their mercy. Trotting round the riding school on my uncomfortable army saddle with its high bridge, I would hear with sinking heart the merciless order, 'Ride! Quit and cross your stirrups!' Often this exercise would last for forty-five minutes—a severe strain at any time. After half an hour Sennett would call out in a conversational tone:

'You married, Mr. Kemp, sir?'

'No, Sergeant-Major.'

His voice would swell triumphantly:

'Nor you never will be neither if you don't sit down in that there bloody saddle!'

II

OPERATION 'KNIFE'

One morning in the middle of April, shortly after the German invasion of Norway, I was ordered to report to the R.S.M. Expecting to lose another week-end's leave I was cheered to hear him say:

'War Office for you, Mr. Kemp, sir! Report to the Orderly Room right away and draw your warrant.'

Next morning I was sitting at another desk in the room where I had been recruited, receiving from Captains Davies and Kennedy a remarkable briefing. Davies's grim, heavy face was unusually grave; he began impressively:

'It's very possible, Kemp, that you may not feel like proceeding with this operation when you hear what we have to say; we shall quite understand if you don't. It involves going somewhere by submarine.'

Assuming an indifference that I did not really feel, I asked him to continue. Later on I came to realize that a submarine is no more dangerous a form of transport than a surface vessel—often, indeed, safer; but at the time I confess the idea scared me. Although it was clear, even from the communiques, that the German invasion was making uncomfortably good progress, it was not yet certain that the Allies would have to evacuate their Expeditionary Force. German land communications were peculiarly vulnerable to 'paramilitary' or 'partisan' warfare—both terms were new in British Army phraseology at this time; Operation 'Knife' was to be one of the first experiments. Briefly, the plan was to land a party of six officers, of which I was to be one, by submarine at a point on the southern shore of the Sogne Fjord, where Norwegian army officers and local guides would meet us. Our first task would be to make our way south across country on skis to the Bergen-Oslo railway, which we were to blow up in such a manner as to render it unserviceable for a long time. In addition to our own requirements we should take with us substantial supplies of explosives, Bren guns, rifles, grenades, and small-arms ammunition to equip local partisan units. After the destruction of the railway we should reconnoitre a lake farther east to see if it would be possible to land seaplanes. Our subsequent plans would depend on circumstances: we might stay in the country to help the partisans, or try to make our way to the Swedish frontier.

'How does this appeal to you?' asked Kennedy.

I said that it suited me well.

'Then we'd better see if Colonel Brian will take you.' Lieutenant-Colonel Brian Mayfield, Scots Guards, who was to command the expedition, was a regular soldier who had left the Army before the war to go into business. An experienced skier, he had recently been Second in Command to Colonel Jimmy Coats in the '5th Scots Guards'—a composite ski battalion raised by the War Office at the end of 1939, consisting almost entirely of officers from various units of the British Army; intended for operations in Finland, it was disbanded early in 1940.

For a few minutes Mayfield studied the written information about me that Kennedy showed him; then he asked: 'Can you ski?'

I hesitated. 'I used to be able to, sir, some years ago. I haven't tried recently but I expect I should be all right on skis.'

He looked at me thoughtfully: 'I think we'll make you our Bren gun instructor. Do you know about Brens?'

I thought it better to admit straight away that I had never even seen one.

'No matter. They're very easy. I suggest you go along to Wellington Barracks this afternoon and get a bit of instruction. I'll give them a ring and let them know you're coming. When you've finished you can come back here and meet the rest of the boys.'

After the complexities of the Hotchkisses and Fiats that we had used in Spain I was astonished at the simplicity, as well as the lightness, of this new weapon. By half past four that afternoon I was able to report to Colonel Mayfield that I felt myself competent to fire, strip, demonstrate and instruct in the Bren. Easily the most junior of our party, I was delighted to find myself promoted overnight to the rank of Captain, which seemed to be the lowest rank on our Establishment. After me the most junior was Bill Stirling, at this time a captain in the Scots Guards; a man of six foot five and proportionately broad, he would, I thought, find a submarine uncomfortably cramped. Our demolitions officer was Jim Gavin, a regular Sapper and skilled mountaineer who had found time off from his duties before the war to take part in one of the Everest expeditions. The remaining two members of the party were Ralph Farrant, a regular officer in a Line regiment, and David Stacey, who in civilian life had been a stockbroker. Not only was I the most junior, but also I had the least skiing experience—apart from Bill Stirling, who have never been on skis in his life. The others had all served in the '5th Scots Guards'.

Two days later we assembled for our final briefing. We were to leave King's Cross that evening for Rosyth, where we were to embark in H.M. Submarine *Truant*. Our stores were already packed and awaiting us there. When Tommy Davies had finished with us he took us along the corridor to see the Director of Military Intelligence. Unfortunately, the passage of time has driven the General's message from my memory, but I am unlikely to forget his opening words:

'I say, you know, it's frightfully nice of you chaps to go on this show.'

H.M.S. *Truant* (Lieutenant-Commander Hutcheson, D.S.O., R.N.) was one of the new 'T' class submarines—the same class as the unlucky *Thetis*. Completed just before the war, she had an extremely strong hull, enabling her to dive to much greater depths than any previous class of submarine. To that extra strength in her hull we were to owe our lives. Lieutenant-Commander Hutcheson was one of the ace submarine commanders of the early months of the war. On his last patrol with *Truant* he had penetrated the Ems estuary, where he had sunk the new German light cruiser *Karlsrühe*, a piece of skill and daring which earned him an immediate award of the D.S.O.; it must have been an exacting experience, for he was obliged to remain submerged for more than forty-eight hours consecutively while making his escape, during which time the enemy dropped over a hundred depth charges around him.

We were introduced to Hutcheson aboard *Truant*'s parent ship, the Submarine Depot Ship *Forth*, where we arrived in time for the pre-lunch gin session in the wardroom; he was a dark, sallow-complexioned, slightly built man who spoke very little and drank nothing. In my experience of submariners I have observed that, whereas they are strictly abstemious on patrol, they delight in making up for lost time aboard their depot ship, where their hospitality is, even among the Navy, outstanding.

In the early part of the afternoon we went aboard *Truant*, where our stores were already stowed. It proved more difficult to find space to stow ourselves. Carrying her full complement of officers and crew—she had to continue on a routine patrol after landing us—*Truant* had little enough space to accommodate even one or two passengers; Hutcheson and his First Lieutenant had to spend a long time finding odd corners where we could lay our heads among the machinery. It was not easy, for we were tall men; Stirling was only able to straighten out during the brief periods when we were allowed on the bridge. I was provided with a mattress of cushions from the wardroom settees, laid at one end of the engine room; at least I could stretch to my full length, but I was deafened by the thunderous hammering of the diesels all the time the submarine was travelling on the surface.

We cast off about an hour before dusk, gliding beneath the Forth Bridge just after a train had passed over. Hutcheson allowed us to stay on deck until we were clear of the estuary, when he dived to trim; thereafter we were only allowed on the bridge for a quarter of an hour, one at a time—any more of us would be an embarrassment in the event of a crash dive. When we dived to fifty feet for trimming I was amazed at the stillness throughout the boat, and the absence of the sea's motion; in a curious way I found it comforting. Although a passenger, I could feel the unity around me—a feeling that captain and crew were working together as a smooth and perfectly controlled machine. The only other time I sailed in a submarine I noticed the same confidence. It was a most inspiring experience.

When Hutcheson was satisfied with the trim he gave the order to surface; in a few minutes we felt the rise and fall of the sea beneath us and heard the diesels begin their deep, regular pounding. We should be on the surface all night, and all the next day unless we sighted an enemy; we ought to reach the entrance of the Sogne Fjord late the following night or in the early hours of the morning after. We were very cramped in the tiny wardroom where we ate our supper; it was a silent meal, for we were all filled with the strangeness of our surroundings and preoccupied with the uncertainties and hazards that lay ahead. We dispersed to our sleeping quarters soon afterwards. I trod carefully along the narrow passage that ran the length of the engine room, edging past the stokers on duty, each of whom stood silently watching his panel of gauges and controls; at the after end of the compartment, by the bulkhead door leading into the stokers' mess, my improvised bed was laid in a small space just wide enough for me to lie down. Taking off my boots and battle-dress blouse, I managed to stow them out of the way of a burly, broad shouldered seaman who was standing over me on duty by one of the electric motors. He gave me a friendly smile:

"Fraid you won't get much sleep there, sir, not with all this 'ere din.'

'Oh yes I will! I can sleep through anything when I'm tired enough.'

I was tired, for I had slept badly in the train the night before; turning my face to the bulkhead I fell asleep within a few minutes. But I was wrong when I said I could sleep through anything. The two explosions, coming hard on top of one another, penetrated my dreamless unconsciousness; through my slumber I was vaguely aware that the first was somewhere quite near me, the second away forward. Suddenly I was fully alert as I heard the order 'Diving Stations!' relayed on loud-speakers through the boat. I realized that the diesels had stopped. In the tense, pervading silence I waited for the diving hooter to sound. I looked at my watch; it was four-thirty, and so I had slept for nearly six hours. Close by, a muffled voice broke the stillness:

'Gawd! We've 'it a bleedin' mine!'

I looked up from my bed to see a stoker standing above me at the nearest diesel; he was stripped to trousers and singlet and the light glistened on the beads of sweat on his muscular arms. His broad, homely face was set in grim lines and he was murmuring out of the corner of his mouth to his companion in short, jerky sentences. From what I could overhear I gathered that the torpedo compartment, right forward, was flooded, but that the watertight bulkhead was holding. After a short interval I saw the tall figure of the First Lieutenant approaching, his friendly features grave and expressionless. Catching sight of me where I lay on my back—there had seemed to be no point in moving—he stopped and grinned.

'Are you comfortable there?'

'Perfectly, thanks. How long am I likely to remain so? Do we know what's happened?'

'I'm trying to find out the full extent of the damage now. It seems there was a U-boat waiting for us. I should say those were magnetic torpedoes she fired. Fortunately, the first one didn't go off as close to us as the second, and our rudder and screws don't appear to have been damaged. We're lucky not to have been blown up.'

'What are we going to do now?'

'Well, the Captain was hoping we might be able to hunt the U-boat; but I'm sorry to say that's impossible in view of the damage. I'm afraid it looks like home, James—with whatever horses we can get out of her. Ah, well! Pretty adjacent, what?' He turned back to his duties.

The big stoker beside me chuckled in admiring imitation:

'Pretty adjacent, what? Don't nothin' ever worry 'im?'

My brother had often told me that during a crisis aboard ship the perfect passenger keeps out of the way and does nothing unless he is told. I decided to stay where I was; asking my stoker friend to let me know if anything happened, I turned over and tried to sleep again. Half an hour later I was much relieved to hear the diesels start; rightly or wrongly it seemed to me an indication that our immediate danger was over. Soon afterwards I fell asleep.

Someone was prodding me in the ribs. As I sat up in sudden alarm I heard a cheerful voice shouting above the pounding of the engines:

'Breakfast ready in the wardroom, sir!'

It was eight o'clock. Breakfast proved to be a picnic which we had to take in relays, for almost all the wardroom crockery had been shattered by the two explosions. This was the least of the damage we had suffered, in addition to the flooded torpedo room, Hutcheson told us, there was some flooding aft, and several rivets were started amidships:

'If this had been any boat but one of these new T-class,' he said, 'we shouldn't have remained afloat.' He added thoughtfully, 'I wonder if that Hun was really laying for us, or just happened to be there?'

There was serious damage to the machinery, details of which I did not understand. But the batteries of the electric motors were cracked, causing them to give off quantities of chlorine gas from the action of the sea water— unpleasant enough while we were on the surface, extremely dangerous if we should have to submerge for any length of time. Hutcheson had no choice but to turn for home. Much later he told us that he had concluded his signal to *Forth*, reporting the incident, with the words, 'will require at least three weeks' refit and new Commanding Officer.'

Apart from an uncomfortable ten minutes while we dived for trim, and one false alarm when an aircraft flew over us as we were approaching the Firth of Forth, we met with no further incident on the way home; but the strained expressions on the faces of Hutcheson and his officers told us that they looked forward to the end of the trip. Just before dark we limped into Rosyth and berthed alongside H.M.S. *Forth*.

We were filled with gin and plied with questions by incredulous submariners, who seemed astonished that *Truant* had managed to get home in such a condition; meanwhile Bill Stirling telephoned to his home at Keir, near Dunblane, and arranged for us all to stay there while new plans were hatched for Operation 'Knife'.

During the next few days we remained in a state of instant readiness; we heard that the Admiralty were providing one of the large 'River' class submarines to take us on a second attempt. It was a very pleasant interlude. Exhilarated by the recollection of our recent escape and stimulated by the hope of another, more successful venture, we were yet able to relax enough to enjoy the superb hospitality which the Stirlings, undismayed by the imminent conversion of Keir into a hospital, lavished upon us.

Once the decision had been taken to withdraw Allied troops from Norway our own small mission clearly had no further purpose; nevertheless, the order to abandon Operation 'Knife' came as a severe blow. Besides the anti-climax of our return to London, we were saddened by the imminent break-up of a party so closely knit by a common purpose and the experience of a common danger. It was thanks to Stirling's imagination and initiative that our partnership was not, in fact, immediately dissolved. Accompanied by Mayfield he preceded us to London for conferences with Colonel Holland, the head of M.I.(R.), and a number of influential friends of his own; when the rest of us arrived he already had a plan for our useful employment as well as the necessary authority to carry it out.

The invasion of Norway showed clearly the possibilities of partisan warfare. Paramilitary formations known as 'Independent Companies'—the forerunners of Commandos—had been employed in the last stages of the Norwegian campaign; Colin Gubbins had commanded a brigade largely composed of them. In spite of a good deal of angry controversy they were considered to have proved their usefulness. There was, however, no organized instruction in this kind of warfare, no school or centre where troops could be trained in its principles; there was a certain amount of theory—Gubbins himself had written a pamphlet—and there must be an untapped reservoir of officers and men with the necessary qualifications and experience to act as instructors: Indian Army officers who had served on the North-West Frontier, 'bush-whackers' from the West African Frontier Force or the King's African Rifles, Polar explorers, ghillies from Lovat's Scouts, and the like. There should be no difficulty in finding a suitable location for the project; the Scottish highlands abounded in what Boswell has described as 'fine and noble prospects', ideal country for training in irregular or amphibious operations; also in half-derelict houses which in size and architecture might have been designed as barracks.

16

It was Stirling's idea that the six of us, reinforced by a few selected officers and N.C.O.s, should form the nucleus of the new training school; we should begin with cadre courses for junior officers from different units of the Army. Mayfield was to be Commandant, Stirling Chief Instructor. There was no fear, Stirling assured us, of our having to remain instructors for the rest of the war; when the first few cadres were trained there would be a plentiful supply of officers to fill our posts as and when we wished to be released for operational duties; moreover, he added, we should be in a strong position to choose our own operational theatres. By the time the Battle of France opened, Stirling and Mayfield had obtained War Office approval for our Establishment, selected the training area and set the requisitioning machinery in motion; the first cadres would report for training at the end of the month.

Some twenty-five miles west of Fort William as the crow flies—rather more as the road and railway run—stands Inverailort House, a large square building of plain grey stone. It is situated at the head of Lochailort, on the south shore, where the gloom of its natural surroundings matches the chill austerity of its design. The front of the house faces north to the sea loch, whose sombre waters, alternately wrapped in mist and whipped by rainstorms, blend with the leaden tones of walls and roof. The back is overshadowed by a grim black cliff, surmounted by a thick, forbidding growth of trees, which rises from the back door to well above the height of the roof, blotting out the light of the sun at all times except high noon in summer. The rainfall at Glenfinnan, ten miles to the east, is the highest in the British Isles. But on the few fine days at this time of the year the shores of Lochailort and the Sound of Arisaig reveal a wild, bleak beauty of scoured grey rock and cold blue water, of light green bracken and shadowed pine, that is strangely moving in its stark simplicity and grandeur.

In May and June of 1940 the same clear weather that favoured the German offensive in France brought warmth and sunshine to Inverailort, where, at the beginning of the last week in May, we arrived to prepare for the first training course. With the help of the War Office Stirling had been able to recruit some outstanding officers and N.C.O.s to bring our staff of instructors to full strength.

Training in amphibious operations formed an important part of each course, and was supervised by a naval commander. The senior instructor in field-craft was Stirling's cousin, Lord Lovat, to whom I was appointed assistant. In view of his epic career later in the war he needs no introduction here; a brilliant instructor as well as a superb fighting soldier, he taught me in the three weeks I was with him all I know about movement across country and the principles of natural camouflage. Gavin, now a major, was in charge of demolitions; his assistant was another regular Sapper, Mike Calvert, who had just had the satisfaction of seeing himself reported in the official War Office casualty list as killed in Norway; three years later 'Mad Mike', at the age of twenty-five, was one of Wingate's brigadiers. Major Munn, a Gunner officer who had served on the North-West Frontier, instructed in map reading and allied subjects. He brought with him two lean, bronzed, hard-bitten officers of the Guides. They were supposed to instruct in the practice of irregular warfare, but it turned out that their experience had all been the other way—in suppressing guerrillas; they exasperated their pupils by making them climb to the tops of the hills and march along the crests, where they were visible for miles against the skyline. They left us after a few weeks.

Our first students arrived at the beginning of June—twenty-five keen but puzzled subalterns, some of them volunteers, others arbitrarily dispatched by their commanding officers. Among them was Stirling's brother David, later to become famous as the founder of the Special Air Service Regiment in North Africa. Each course was to last a month, with a few days break before the arrival of the next. From this small beginning developed the series of Special Training Schools which was later established throughout Great Britain, in the Middle and Far East, in Australia and the North American Continent.

III

EDUCATION OF AN AGENT

In the year 1941 began with the greatest personal tragedy of my life. On 10th January, the aircraft carrier *Illustrious* was heavily bombed by Stukas in the Sicilian Channel: among the dead was my brother. The previous November he had flown a Swordfish in the Fleet Air Arm attack on Taranto, and torpedoed one of the new *Littorio* class battleships, for which he was posthumously awarded a D.S.C. My mother's telegram reached me in Edinburgh, where I was convalescing after a prolonged illness following my return from Portugal. As I read it again and again, numb and sick with shock, it seemed absurd that so much human misery could be carried on a crumpled piece of buff-coloured paper. My mother, four years a widow, never recovered from the blow. It was a long time before I could bring myself to realize that Neil was dead. Throughout his life he had exercised a profound, even decisive influence on me; it was easier to imagine that the sky should fall than that he should be killed. Not yet thirty-one he had already earned recognition as an historian and writer on naval affairs, and a column and a half of tributes to him in The Times showed that his death was a severe loss to the Service as well as to ourselves. I tried to console myself with the words of Clarendon's epitaph on Lord Falkland:

'And whosoever leads such a life need not care upon how short warning it be taken from him.'

Early in February I was ordered to report in London to Captain Kennedy, one of the officers who had briefed us for Operation 'Knife'. M.I.(R.) was now dissolved and its place taken by a much larger organization, combining elements of M.I.(R.) with other departments that had previously been working along the same lines, but so often at cross purposes that their efforts had seemed directed against each other rather than against the Germans. This new organization, known as S.O.E., became responsible for all subversive activities in enemy-occupied territory. It received its directives through the Minister of Economic Warfare, and was staffed, surprisingly, by senior executives from several large banking and business houses, with a small but useful leavening of Regular Army officers, a few of whom had received Staff College training.

'We're preparing a party,' said Kennedy, 'to go on an operation that I think might interest you. Are you quite fit again?'

I was, except for a sharp attack of gout, an inherited complaint which caused me much annoyance later.

'I can't give you any details about the operation now,' he went on. 'You will join the rest of the party at Lochailort and do the paramilitary course with them as a student. While you're up there you'll be told more about the scheme.'

I arrived at Lochailort on a clear frosty morning three days later. The instructing staff had changed a great deal since I was last there. Mayfield was commanding a brigade in North Africa, Stirling was in Cairo, Gavin on his way to Singapore; Lovat was about to start his spectacular career in Commandos; Calvert was in India.

I had at first supposed that the operation for which we were being prepared would take place in Spain; but my eighteen companions did not seem to have been chosen for their knowledge of that country or language. In fact, we seemed to have no common background. Not all of us could speak Spanish, and the majority of those who could had learnt it in South America; one or two had been to Spain for a short holiday. The majority had been plucked without explanation from regimental soldiering and given a brief interview in London; they had been asked a few obscure questions, such as 'Would you rather be General Wavell or Lawrence of Arabia?' Then they had been ordered to report to Lochailort. They felt they had been better employed in their old units; some, who had been company commanders, were indignant at the change. One officer, known to the rest of us as 'Slogger', was frankly apprehensive; he was a quiet, meticulous man with a nervous manner, a literal mind and no sense of humour.

It was, therefore, a bewildered and resentful audience that assembled in one of the lecture rooms towards the end of February to hear what was in store for us. For the past three weeks we had undergone extremely rigorous training, making forced marches across country carrying fifty-pound rucksacks, sweating up steep hillsides, plunging into deep ravines and across rock-strewn torrents, pretending to blow up bridges with dummy explosives, and once nearly destroying a bridge and ourselves with real explosive that had been substituted in error. We had spent hours listening to lectures on map-reading, demolitions, and German Army Order of Battle; and we had been taught pistol-shooting and 'unarmed combat' by two ex-detectives from the Shanghai International Police. The senior detective had the manner and appearance of an elderly, amiable clergyman, combined with the speed and ferocity of a footpad; lulled by his soft tones and charmed by his benevolent smile, we would be startled to hear him conclude some demonstration with a snarled, 'Then you bring up your right knee smartly into his testicles.'

Now at last we were to know the object of our training: a senior officer of S.O.E. had come all the way from London to tell us. There was some ribald speculation as to whether he would be a banker or a business tycoon;

he proved to be neither, but a rising young lawyer, now wearing the badges of a lieutenant-colonel. His manner jarred on us, probably because he had little military experience. He seemed anxious for us to realize that he was a jolly good fellow, just like one of us, a simple, friendly chap with no nonsense about him. To emphasize this he began his talk with one of the oldest dirty jokes in the legal profession. He continued, in a tone half ingratiating, half patronizing, to explain that it was very probable that the Germans would invade Spain. If they did there would be a surprise for them; we were going to be the surprise. He himself would control our activities from not too far away, and he would be with us all the time in spirit.

We should soon be leaving for Gibraltar, there to await the German invasion. We should be divided into parties of two, each party to be provided with a wireless set, a wireless operator, and quantities of arms, ammunition and explosives. When the German invasion seemed imminent each party would move as fast as possible to a previously determined operational area; it was not quite clear what we should do when we arrived there, but it seemed that there would be anti-German resistance groups with whom we could work and whom we would supply with arms. We might be interested to know that we were already spoken of in the Office as 'Ali Baba and the Forty Thieves'; 'Ali Baba' was the officer detailed to command us inside the country, with whom we should keep in contact by wireless. We should meet him in Gibraltar. Another piece of good news, he told us, was that we were all to be made captains with effect from 16th March. Those of his audience who were already captains received this *bonne bouche* without enthusiasm.

'As for what the future holds for you,' he summed up, as though he had not already made it clear, 'I can only tell you'—his voice took on a deeper, sterner tone—'Hardship shall be your mistress, Danger your constant companion.'

If we had any qualms about the venture he urged us to withdraw from it now, before the irrevocable step was taken.

'Slogger' rose to his feet. This was not at all the sort of thing, he explained in low, precise tones, for which he would consider volunteering. In the first place, he had not been consulted before being sent on this course; he felt himself to be quite unsuited for this kind of operation, and he would be grateful if he could be returned as soon as possible to his work with the Intelligence Corps.

As we suspected, and as it turned out, 'Slogger' had the laugh on us.

After a few days' leave we reassembled at Fawley Court, near Henley-on-Thames, an S.O.E. holding school for operational parties such as ours; the commandant was Major Tommy Lindsay, an Irish Guards officer gifted with the very necessary qualities of tact, patience and charm. Here we discovered that, in addition to being 'Ali Baba and the Forty Thieves,' we were Operation 'Relator'.

We were told to choose our partners for the operational parties. I found myself paired with John Burton, a tall, burly, ginger-haired officer from the Lincolnshire Regiment; it was a partnership that was to last a long time, through operations much more serious than 'Relator'. Burton's quiet, almost gentle manner concealed surprising determination, courage and powers of endurance; despite an austere appearance he combined a sense of humour with a genuine personal humility, while his natural common sense and efficiency provided a valuable counter to the volatility of my own temperament.

At the end of the second week in March we received our embarkation orders. The prospect of a fortnight at sea during the Battle of the Atlantic and at such a time of year filled some of us with dismay; others, like myself, who were good sailors and enjoyed the sea, fortified ourselves with thoughts of comfortable bunks, congenial company and unlimited quantities of duty-free liquor. The reality, when we boarded the tramp steamer *Fidelity* at Liverpool, proved a shock to the most pessimistic of us.

Although she flew the White Ensign *Fidelity* had recently belonged to the French mercantile marine. Her captain, officers and crew were all French; but they appeared on the ships manifest under incongruous Scottish or Irish names and were supposed to pass as Canadians in the event of their being taken by the Germans. Although they spoke no English they gallantly tried to call each other by their assumed names, so that the ship would ring with such cries as '*Merde! Où est ce sale Maconzee?*' At the time of the fall of France her captain had smuggled *Fidelity* out of Marseilles with this volunteer crew; now she was in the service of a similar organization to S.O.E.. Naturally, there was no love lost between the two organizations, which may have accounted for some of our discomfort.

We arrived in Liverpool on a raw, rainy evening and went straight to the Adelphi for dinner. About ten o'clock we were driven to the ship.

We were received on board by Lieutenant-Commander Milner-Gibson, R.N., who was sailing as liaison officer. He was both apologetic and indignant.

'I don't know how to break it to you chaps,' he began. 'Until an hour ago, when I got here myself, nobody in this ship had the least idea that there would be passengers. There's nowhere for you to sleep, but the crew are clearing space in two of the holds, and you'll just have to park your camp-beds there. At least it's a lucky thing that you've brought camp equipment. I'm afraid you're going to be hellish uncomfortable. Of course the Captain's furious, but that's not your fault. Another thing—I don't know how we're going to fit you in for meals, as there's no room in the saloon; I don't even know if there's enough food, because we're sailing tomorrow and there's no time to order extra stores.'

'Oh well!' somebody said, 'I expect we'll survive till Gibraltar on gin.'

'You won't!' he retorted. 'Not unless you've brought it with you. There's no time to get Customs clearance for extra liquor and the ship's officers have barely enough for themselves. The whole thing's a damn disgrace,' he concluded sympathetically, 'and I can assure you I'm going to send in a strong report about it!'

We set up our camp-beds and sleeping bags in the holds, where there was just enough space to accommodate all of us, with two feet between each bed. We turned in immediately, by the light of kerosene lanterns; next day the electricians rigged up a few lights, enabling us to see enough for dressing and moving about, but barely enough for reading. Neither daylight nor fresh air could penetrate to lighten the frosty atmosphere of our dormitories.

After dropping us at Gibraltar *Fidelity* was bound for secret operations in the Mediterranean. She had been converted into something between a 'Q' ship and a flak-ship; her decks and superstructure fairly bristled with guns of varying calibres, from the clumsy four-inch fore and aft to light Oerlikon anti-aircraft cannon, pom-poms, and machine-guns; most of them were concealed behind dummy bulwarks.

The ensuing fortnight was among the most unpleasant in my experience at sea. *Fidelity* was not a happy ship. Officers and crew alike were terrified of their Captain, a stocky, black-bearded pirate with a reputation for ferocity and courage which he seemed resolved to impress upon us all. Slung from a belt round his uniform jacket he carried an automatic pistol, with which he claimed to be a deadly shot and with which he would blaze away at anything that caught his eye—a seagull on the mast, a piece of flotsam on the sea or an offending member of the crew; he would stride about the bridge, his hands in the pockets of his jacket, his beard thrust out aggressively and a malignant expression on his brick-red face, screaming invective at the Officer of the Watch, the guns' crews at practice, the quartermaster at the wheel or anybody unlucky enough to cross his line of vision. During these black moods, and they were more frequent than his bright ones, he would aim savage kicks and blows at the nearest officer or man within reach. He never actually assaulted any of us, contenting himself with abuse. Only to Milner-Gibson was he always polite. I do not ever remember seeing him smile.

For defaulting officers he had a special treatment: when all were assembled for a meal in the saloon the Captain would bellow the offender's name. A trembling 'O'Flaherty' or 'Mackenzie' would present himself at attention in front of the angry little man, who would launch into voluble details of his offence, his character and the less creditable habits of his parents, concluding with three or four heavy slaps across the face in dismissal;

often, as the victim turned to go, a well-directed kick in the seat of the pants would send him sprawling among his colleagues.

The only person who could control the Captain was his mistress, a sharp-faced little blonde with a metallic voice and vicious tongue; he had smuggled her out of Marseilles with the ship and had persuaded our sister organization to invest her with the uniform and two rings of an officer of the W.R.N.S. She was the real ruler of the ship, and she let us know it. Towards us soldiers she showed a particular animosity, reviling us on every possible pretext and resorting, when she felt that words were inadequate, to typewritten announcements on the saloon notice-board; these began usually with the phrase: '*Messieurs les officiers anglais sont avisés que...*' followed by a list of our misdemeanours—chiefly being late for meals, and spilling cigarette ash on the saloon deck. Space in the saloon was so restricted that the eighteen of us were divided into three watches for our meals, the first watch going to lunch at eleven-fifteen, the second at twelve o'clock and the third at twelve forty-five; we changed our mealtimes in rotation. The slightest unpunctuality on the part of any of us would invoke a tirade from this harpy, followed by some such announcement on the notice-board as: '*Messieurs les officiers anglais sont avisés que nous ne sommes pas sur un paquebot et que l'Empire est en guerre!*'

In the early afternoon following our arrival on board we sailed, one of a slow convoy that made its way round the north coast of Ireland and well out into the Atlantic. While we were in port the crew had worked hard to make our sleeping quarters habitable; but despite all their efforts the holds, with their bare iron decks and bulkheads, remained a grim reminder to us that we were not '*sur un paquebot*'. In good weather we should not have been too uncomfortable, but as soon as we entered the Western Ocean we ran into the first of a series of gales which lasted until we had rounded Cape St. Vincent. Through the ill-caulked decks above, rain and sea-water poured in unceasing streams, drenching our beds and clothes and swirling about the floor with each roll of the ship. Because of her heavy armament aloft Fidelity rolled with a savage, plunging violence, sending our camp-beds and their occupants skidding across the floor and often upsetting us into the water which had collected at one or other side of the hold. Seasickness did not affect me, but it prostrated poor Burton, whose bed was next to mine and for whom the whole voyage was unbroken hell. We found buckets for him and other sufferers to be sick into, but no ingenuity could prevent the buckets themselves from overturning and adding their contents to the mess swilling about the floor.

I think we were all haunted by a nagging fear of being trapped in those holds if the ship were torpedoed. However, although the convoy was attacked on more than one occasion, we in *Fidelity* were disturbed by nothing more menacing than the distant explosions of depth-charges.

The Rock of Gibraltar has never seemed so beautiful to my eyes as when it appeared, wrapped in a faint haze, in the shining forenoon of 5th April. *Fidelity* dropped anchor in the bay with the rest of the convoy, a launch drew alongside and a middle-aged lieutenant-colonel, wearing Gunner badges, climbed on deck. In a Canadian accent he introduced himself as our new commanding officer—the 'Ali Baba' of whom we had heard at Lochailort.

The news with which he greeted us killed whatever hopes we might have had for the success of our operation. He had just returned from a visit to Madrid, where he had tried to persuade our Ambassador to let us make a few preparations in Spain for our reception after the German invasion. The Ambassador's answer had been an emphatic refusal to countenance any S.O.E. activity whatsoever.

'Ali Baba' sugared this bitter pill with the news that our Director—the officer who had addressed us so disarmingly at Inverailort—was now in Gibraltar, having followed us from England, V.I.P. fashion, in a battle-cruiser. He was giving a cocktail party that evening for us at the Rock Hotel.

Our quarters had been prepared under canvas on the North Front, on a strip of ground beside the military cemetery, bordering the new and rapidly growing airfield. This was the site of the old race-course, which had disappeared at the beginning of the war, together with such peacetime luxuries as the Calpe Hunt. By the time we had installed ourselves, two to a tent in our operational pairs, it was time to leave for the Rock Hotel and our party with the Director.

Smooth and well-groomed in a Palm Beach suit, he greeted us effusively, hoping that we had had a pleasant voyage. It was a good party, but no one had foreseen the impact of unlimited martinis or whisky upon young men recently accustomed to one glass of Suze a week. Officers gathered in groups of two or three to celebrate their release from the discomforts of *Fidelity* and the tyranny of her Captain and his mistress; soon, flushed faces and raised voices began to indicate the general dissatisfaction with Operation 'Relator', its planners and commanders. In retrospect this appears rather ungrateful, seeing that those we were reviling were paying for our drink; but at the time it seemed to us that we had been brought a long way to execute a plan that was already stillborn.

Our host came to the entrance hall of the hotel to say good-bye; he stood at the head of the steps which led down to the drive, to shake hands with each of us. When my turn came I marched up to him very erect, extended my hand and, trying to look him in the eyes, uttered a thick 'Goodnight, sir! Thank you very much!' Then I did a smart about turn and fell headlong down the flight of marble steps, to land in a heap on the gravel, where I was collected by John Burton and David Muirhead, and bundled into their waiting taxi.

Next morning the whole party assembled in the large mess tent for briefing; we were joined by our wireless operators, who had travelled out separately with their equipment. 'Ali Baba' presided. It was regrettable, he explained that the Ambassador's attitude made it impossible for us to prepare for our task inside Spain; but we must be ready to do our duty whenever the situation should arise. He would now proceed to allot our operational areas. The one to which Burton and I were going was in the western province of Extremadura. It was a part of the country that I did not know. Nothing, it seemed, was known about our proposed collaborators beyond the fact that there was a group of people living there in the mountains who, it was hoped, could be persuaded to work for us against the Germans; for all we knew, they might be remnants of the Republican Army against which I had fought for nearly three years.

It was difficult for us to feel great enthusiasm for such a vague and ill-planned scheme, or to take much interest in its preparation. The method by which it was proposed that we should reach our areas had the one merit of simplicity: as soon as the German invasion began, each party would climb into its lorry—already loaded with arms, explosives and wireless—and drive by the shortest route to its destination; how many of us would get there, or even succeed in crossing the International Zone to La Línea, was anybody's guess. The assembly broke up in a mood approaching alarm and despondency.

Our chief problem during the succeeding weeks was how to fill in time; we had no troops to train, and after our course at Lochailort we required little more instruction ourselves. But 'Ali Baba' wished our establishment to be run on Regular Army lines; he devised a training programme which, sensibly, included wireless instruction—a subject I could never understand—demolition practice, shooting with tommy-gun and pistol, and lorry-driving. At times we were sent to scale the north-western face of the Rock, each carrying a Tommy-gun and a fifty-pound rucksack—a terrifying performance for anyone, like myself, with a poor head for heights. In addition to this collective training we each had separate, specialist duties. Mine was the preparation of an English-Spanish dictionary of military terms, on which I worked every free morning in a room at the Joint Intelligence Centre. It was an uninspiring task, the more so because I was sternly forbidden to include the most interesting phrases from Archie Lyall's *Soldier's Speakeasy*.

The problem of our spare time was more difficult. A large part of the civilian population had been evacuated, but the strength of the garrison had swollen to many times its normal size. We were no longer allowed to visit Spain or Tangier. Apart from the Yacht Club, the Rock Hotel, the Bristol, and a few bars, Gibraltar offered little in the way of evening entertainment. I spent most of my afternoons swimming off one of the beaches on the east side of the Rock, or sailing in the bay of Algeciras with a Cambridge friend of mine from the Meteorological Office, who owned a Star; we had to keep our distance from the Spanish shore, because we were liable to be fired on if we approached too close. In the evening, as the sun was sinking behind the dark hills above Algeciras, reminding me with bitter nostalgia of the Western Highlands where I used to spend my holidays before the Spanish War, Burton and I would stroll out of camp, past the sentries at the concrete road-blocks, towards the harbour and the Yacht Club. We always knew whom we should meet there, just as we knew whom we should see in the Bristol or any of the other bars. The tension of waiting for a hazardous operation and the exasperation of feeling that it could never come off increased our urge to look for relief in gin and whisky, which were plentiful and cheap, in frivolous conversation and forced geniality. Worst of all, I was in love. The pain of separation had been bearable as long as my mind was occupied with thoughts of hazard and adventure in Spain; but now idleness gave me too much time to brood, and the bottle was a simple anodyne.

We often had friends to dine in Mess in our camp, where the food was poor but the drink lavish. The Mess tent, a large marquee, stood on the very edge of the airfield; behind it were the rows of sleeping tents, their guy-ropes almost overlapping; some distance beyond them were the latrines. Every guest night at the end of dinner the darkness would ring with cries of pain or indignation as we and our guests tripped over guy-ropes or the iron staples supporting them, on our tipsy journey to relieve ourselves. My most frequent guest was Hugh Sidebottom, a Newmarket trainer in civilian life, now a Captain in command of the Pack Transport Company on the Upper Rock; a broad, powerfully built man with an inexhaustible fund of good humour and a boisterous but endearing manner, he had the distinction, in which he took great pride, of being the only mounted officer on the Rock. He exulted in his surname and would shake his head sadly over a relation who had changed it to Edgedale.

'Not a true Bottom,' was his comment.

The Navy—chiefly submariners attached to the depot ship *Maidstone* and officers from Admiral Somerville's famous Force H—provided us with some diversion. Theirs were faces we did not see every evening in the bars, for the submariners were often away on patrols and the ships of Force H only put in to Gibraltar for a few days between their visits to the 'Men's End' of the Mediterranean. They meant to make the best of their time ashore. Most of our friends were from the carrier Ark Royal—Fleet Air Arm pilots whose enjoyment of life was not impaired by their slender expectation of survival. It was they who initiated an incident subsequently known as 'The Battle of the Bristol'.

One evening I was dining in the Bristol Hotel with Sidebottom and a captain in the Devonshire Regiment. There were a few Army Officers at tables near us; the rest of the room seemed to be full of pilots from Ark

Royal. Drink was flowing freely; there was a good deal of banter passing across the room, and an atmosphere of vigorous good humour. Just for the fun of it someone slung a glass at the chandelier, shattering the lights. In a moment everybody joined in the party; the air was full of flying glass and crockery, accompanied by war whoops and hunting calls. Crouched behind our table in the darkness, lobbing our plates and glasses and listening to the splintering of others close around us, we wondered whatever could have made us think Gibraltar dull. Soon the stocks of ammunition were exhausted, and we were wiping lumps of goulash and *sole bonne femme* from our hair and mopping wine from our eyes. Within a quarter of an hour peace reigned, light had been restored and the management was graciously accepting our apologies and promises of compensation. There were no serious casualties, but Force H veterans subsequently swore that not even in their battles up the 'Men's End' had they been more terrified.

One way and another, I did not envy the Assistant Provost Marshal his job of keeping discipline on the Rock. He was a dug-out major of a famous cavalry regiment, whose ideas had crystallized in or about the year 1916 into an almost religious and totally humourless veneration of the outward forms and appearance of soldiering; in his trim, perfectly tailored uniform, gleaming buttons and Sam Browne, and strikingly coloured forage cap he was a figure of half affectionate, half ribald fun to the garrison. On one occasion all officers of Fortress Headquarters had to go through a gas chamber wearing their masks as part of an exercise; afterwards Sidebottom jokingly asked him if his gas mask had fitted.

'I should hope so, indeed!' replied the A.P.M. in genuine surprise. 'I had it made for me at Lock's before I came out here.'

Early in May Lord Gort replaced Sir Clive Liddell as Governor of Gibraltar. The appointment of this tough fighting soldier and disciplinarian gave rise to rumours that a German attack on the Rock was imminent. Soon afterwards the news of the German invasion of Crete with airborne troops shook Gibraltar. It was taken for granted that similar tactics would be used at any moment against us. The whole fortress was put into a state of siege. In the galleries inside the Rock work went on with redoubled speed by day and night; extra roadblocks and anti-tank defences appeared on every road; a curfew was imposed at eleven o'clock and severe penalties threatened against all unauthorized persons found abroad after that hour; at any time after dark there was danger of being shot by some trigger-happy sentry.

All units were obliged to take special security precautions; 'Ali Baba's' took the form of issuing an order that one officer and one sergeant should sit up all night in the Mess tent, armed with tommy-guns. The burden of this duty was light enough until about two in the morning, because there were usually several officers carousing in the ante-room; but the small hours dragged intolerably on this farcical guard. Nevertheless, there was an air of tension and grim purpose for at least ten days after the initial shock. It was dispelled, for us, by the arrival of a brief order, signed by the Garrison Commander, announcing that 'in the event of an enemy airborne invasion of the Rock, all tentage will be returned forthwith to Ordnance.'

One afternoon at the end of May we were all ordered to assemble in the big marquee; the Director had something important to say to us. We had not seen much of him lately; on the few occasions when he had dined with us in Mess he had seemed preoccupied and had spoken little. Now, when he walked into the stuffy Mess tent, dressed as always in a Palm Beach suit, we all felt that we were about to hear something dramatic. Standing at the head of the long trestle table and laying his brief-case carefully in front of him, he began to speak in sombre, heroic periods.

In view of the refusal of His Majesty's representative in Spain to countenance any of our preparations for action in that country, he had decided that it was impossible to pursue our original plan. Once the German invasion was under way we could not hope to penetrate the country in uniform; our only chance would be to infiltrate in civilian clothes. He was already working on new plans to this end. He could not, of course, order us to undertake such an operation, but perhaps some of us would care to volunteer.

'It is my duty to warn you,' he continued, 'that if you are caught in civilian clothes in an enemy-occupied country, you will most certainly be—' At that precise moment the crash of a volley from the adjoining cemetery broke in upon his words.

Even those of us who volunteered were not destined to learn details of the Director's new plans. Well on into June we persisted in our hopes that 'Relator' might yet prove feasible, and we remained in a state of readiness to put it into practice, if necessary, at a few hours' notice. But when on 22nd June we heard the news of the German invasion of Russia, all prospect of the operation vanished. We seemed likely to spend the rest of the war kicking our heels within the narrow frontiers of the Rock, for Lord Gort would not allow any officer or other rank to leave, except on a specific military assignment, whether or not his presence on the Rock was necessary. During the ensuing weeks a few members of our party were sent by the Director on clandestine expeditions to North Africa; they ended in Vichy prison camps, where they remained until the North African landings.

Soon after five o'clock on a bright, brassy evening at the end of June H.M. Submarine *Clyde* (Commander David Ingram, D.S.C., R.N.) slid out of Gibraltar harbour between the South and the Detached Moles into the Bay of Algeciras. Standing on the bridge beside Ingram I felt once again the throb of diesels beneath my feet as we pounded westward towards Tangier and the

Straits; I turned my eyes from the glare of the sun on the water to gaze at the white and yellow houses of the town clustered beneath the great blue bulk of the Rock, and wondered grimly whether this second submarine trip of mine was going to end in such an anti-climax as my first.

Clyde was the submarine which the Admiralty had detailed to take us to Norway in place of *Truant* in April 1940. I had not expected to see her again. But when, after the collapse of our hopes for Operation 'Relator', I had approached 'Ali Baba' with the suggestion that I should go on a submarine patrol in order to study the problems of inter-service liaison and Combined Operations, he had raised no objection. My friends from H.M.S. *Maidstone* made the arrangements for me, introducing me to David Ingram over a few pink gins in the wardroom. Ingram, a serious-minded officer of high seniority and long submarine experience, agreed to take me on his next patrol. He told me, confidentially, that *Clyde* was to sail in twenty-four hours' time to hunt a U-boat which was reported on its way to refuel in the Canary Islands.

'If we can catch her at dusk or in darkness,' he said, 'it would be fun to try to board her and take her alive. In that case, you will come in useful with your cloak and dagger stuff.'

I reported on board next morning, armed with tommy-gun, grenades, and .32 automatic. *Clyde* was a considerably larger boat than Truant; as the only passenger I was given a bunk in the comfortable little wardroom. Over lunch, which we ate aboard H.M.S. *Maidstone*, I met the rest of *Clyde's* officers, a quiet, friendly group who seemed genuinely glad to be taking a 'pongo' with them; they seemed to think it would be a good opportunity of studying the breed at close quarters.

For the first few minutes after casting off, while the crew were at 'Harbour Stations', I was asked to stay below; but as soon as we were in the Bay I was invited up to the bridge. As we swung westward into the Straits I watched the houses and streets of Ceuta glimmering on our port beam under the imposing mass of Gebel Musa; to starboard, on the Spanish coast, rose tiers of dark hills clothed in groves of cork trees; high up, a ruined Moorish watch-tower concealed, some supposed, a German observation post.

We were abeam of Tarifa when we sighted the destroyer approaching from the west. She proved to be H.M.S. *Avon Vale*, one of the new 'Hunt' class. Once she had been identified as a friend I turned my attention from her to watch the changing colours on the African shore glow and fade in the evening light. I was vaguely aware that we were exchanging identification signals with her at a distance of a little over a mile on our starboard beam. Then in a flash of alarm I sensed that something was wrong: there was a mistake in the colour of the recognition flares. I heard the Officer of the Watch shout, 'My God, she's opening fire!' Simultaneously with Ingram's snapped order, 'Crash dive!' I heard the whine of a shell close overhead. I was seized from behind and pushed roughly to the opening of the conning tower hatch. Fearfully alive to the danger I almost threw myself down the vertical iron ladder, with the boots of the next man stamping on my fingers. As my feet touched the floor of the control room and the last man off the bridge slammed the hatch of the conning-tower, there was a violent explosion overhead, followed a second later by the faint report of a gun. I heard someone exclaim, 'Bloody good for a second shot!'

The confined space of the control room, the ship's nerve centre, was crowded with men, each concentrating grimly on his job: the First Lieutenant by the hydroplane controls, anxiously watching the angle of our dive; the helmsman tense at the wheel, listening for Ingram's curt directions; petty officers and ratings with their hands on control levers, their eyes on the dials and gauges. Clearly this was no place for me; I made my way to the wardroom and sank onto a settee at the little dining-table. *Avon Vale* was still firing. Sitting in the silence of the wardroom I could plainly hear the bark of her guns and the rising hum of the shells as they flew towards us, to burst with a curious metallic ringing on the water around us. Over the intercom came the warning, toneless and terrifying:

'Stand by for depth-charge attack. Stand by for depth-charge attack.'

Alone, bewildered, and sweating in anticipation, I wondered what action I was supposed to take. Looking up I caught sight of the ward-room steward in the narrow passageway, bracing himself against a bulkhead; following his example, I braced myself between the wall and one of the supports of the table. I was glad to notice, even from that distance, that he also was sweating. I managed a feeble smile and received a cheerful grin in reply.

The shelling ceased; there was absolute silence. I would never have believed that a crowded ship could be so quiet. It was impossible to tell if we were still diving, or even if we were moving. No sound came from *Avon Vale*. Surely, I tried to comfort myself, if she were closing to attack we should hear the sound of her propellers. I have no idea how long we continued thus before the tension was broken by the Captain's voice:

'Flap seems to be over. Up periscope!'

A minute or two later the welcome orders came through the loudspeaker:

'Stand by to surface!'

'Blow number one!'

'Blow all tanks!'

I heard the rush of water sweeping past our sides as we broke surface, and felt a draught of air blow through the boat when the conning-tower hatch was opened. A few minutes later I was on the bridge, watching *Avon Vale* wallow in the swell while signals of explanation and apology flew between us. *Avon Vale* could certainly be proud of her gunnery: with her second shot she had landed a four-inch shell on our bridge as we were submerging; luckily the damage was only to the superstructure, and we were able to continue our voyage.

'Could it be, Peter,' asked Ingram, who had heard of my journey in *Truant*, 'that you are a Jonah in submarines?'

Passing Cape Spartel we altered course towards the Canaries. At first we travelled on the surface by day as well as at night, but we kept a sharp look-out for enemy aircraft and dived whenever we sighted a ship in the distance; we met no enemy, or any ship suspected of trading with the enemy, but it was important for us to escape detection on our outward journey, lest our destination and the nature of our mission were suspected. Because space on the bridge was limited and everyone needed a spell up there for fresh air, I spent most of my time in the wardroom, where the reading matter varied in subject and quality from the stiff, blue-bound *Mediterranean Pilot* to James Hadley Chase's *Twelve Chinks and a Woman*.

Between meals—the food was excellent and included luxuries unknown in our mess at Gibraltar—we spent most of our time sleeping. No liquor was drunk at sea, apart from one whisky every night before supper; known as the 'evening snodgrass' it gave me more pleasure than a whole day's drinking in Gibraltar. At six o'clock each evening we had prayers, attended by all the ship's company who were not on watch; they would crowd into the control room and the compartments next to it while Ingram read the brief service.

'Save and deliver us, we humbly beseech Thee, from the hands of our enemies; abate their pride, assuage their malice, and confound their devices.' The noble language of the Book of Common Prayer filled me with quiet confidence and pride as I stood bunched with the others in the dim and cramped interior of our pulsating steel shell.

As we neared the Canaries the feeling of tension increased. We travelled submerged during the hours of daylight, surfacing only at night to charge the batteries, when we would be thankful for a short spell on the bridge. It was quiet and restful under water—so restful that I passed nearly all the time asleep on my bunk. Although we sometimes submerged for sixteen hours on end I never felt stifled; the everything was damp with the condensation, and we sweated all the time in the heat. We nosed around the Islands, sometimes less than a mile off shore, searching for indications of our quarry. Through the after periscope, which was fitted with a telescopic lens, we could see people bathing, their dark brown bodies glistening in the bright sun, and watch the fishermen in their gaily coloured boats pulling in their nets; but in the three days of our search we found no sign of a submarine. Ingram's orders did not allow him to remain longer. With a feeling of anticlimax we turned for home, reaching Gibraltar ten days after we had set out.

During the next few weeks Burton and I became more and more impatient with our inactivity on the Rock. I heard from the Director that there was talk of dropping operational parties into northern Spain, should the collapse of Russian resistance enable the Germans to launch an attack through the Peninsula. When I pointed out to him that most of my experience of Spain had been in the north, he agreed to have Burton and myself recalled to England on military grounds.

August the 3rd, 1941, was my happiest day on the Rock; that morning Burton and I received orders to embark for England aboard the French liner *Pasteur*, now converted into a troopship. We went aboard in the afternoon, but when we had stowed our kit in our cabin we were curtly ordered ashore and told not to return before midnight. We learnt the reason next day: *Pasteur* was one of the largest and fastest liners in the world; moored at the South Mole, she would be clearly visible to anyone with a telescope in the neighbourhood of Algeciras. All that afternoon long lines of troops could be seen filing aboard her, obviously bound for the besieged island of Malta. When darkness had fallen the fast mine-laying cruiser *Manxman* glided alongside *Pasteur*. By the time Burton and I boarded her at midnight, all those troops had been transferred to *Manxman*, who carried them safely to Malta, in the early hours of 4th August *Pasteur* sailed for England, full of service men and civilians from Malta, with a few soldiers like ourselves from the Rock. She had as escort the battle-cruiser *Renown*, the aircraft carrier *Furious*, and five Tribal class destroyers. Our homeward course took us well out into the Atlantic, but travelling at nearly thirty knots in good weather, we were only a week on the voyage.

The offices of the Spanish section of S.O.E. were in a large block of requisitioned flats off the Marylebone Road. The two staff officers who interviewed us on our return were solicitors in private life, members of the same firm as our Director in Gibraltar. One was an R.N.V.R. lieutenant with a solemn manner and an enthusiasm for the piano, the other an Army captain whose tastes were simpler; he could usually be found around midnight at a night-club called the Nut House, a bottle of whisky in front of him and a blonde on either side.

'We're going to send you on a series of courses,' said one of them. 'We've got some pretty interesting ones now, which I'm sure you'll like. Let me see. There's a nice little three-day course on industrial sabotage at a place of ours down in Buckinghamshire, which starts at the end of September. We'll send you there first. Then at the end of October there's our parachute course up at Ringway, near Manchester. You'll love that. Then early in November you can go to Beaulieu, where we have a very interesting course for agents, lasting a fortnight. By that time we hope there'll be an operation for you. Meanwhile, you'd better go on leave, but keep us informed of your address.'

I took advantage of my leave to get married. Looking back from time's distance I wonder how I could have been so foolish, complacent, and blind to my own character as to ask any girl, at my age and at such a time, to marry me; it is scarcely less remarkable, I suppose, that any girl who knew me well—

and this one did—should have considered me a suitable husband. Our marriage lasted almost, but not quite, to the end of the European war.

Burton and I reported for our course on industrial sabotage at a comfortable house standing, as estate agents would say, in its own park-like grounds. Three days did not seem a very long time in which to learn so extensive a subject; but we were told that with our previous knowledge of demolitions it should be long enough to teach us the bare essentials; so that if we found ourselves in enemy-occupied country we might at least be able to blow up something. Theory was well combined with practice. For instance a lecture on the sabotage of power stations, illustrated by diagrams, explained the most vulnerable points for the placing of charges; afterwards a tour of a neighbouring power station showed us where these points were, what they looked like, and where we might expect to find sentries. On a visit to the railway yards at Bletchley we were each allowed to drive an engine. When my turn came I started the engine without difficulty, and was approaching a tunnel at fair speed when I found that I could not stop; luckily the engine driver could, but he insisted on driving back himself.

The most interesting character among our instructors was an officer known locally as the Mad Major. He had a particular fondness—and a genius—for elaborate mechanisms of destruction, of which he invented or developed a large number. He had a disquieting habit during lectures of exhibiting to us one of his pets with a live charge attached, placing it on the desk in front of him, cocking it, and announcing, 'this will go off in five minutes'. He would then continue his lecture, apparently unconcerned, while we nervously counted the minutes ticking away. During the last half of the last minute the sound of his voice was almost drowned by shuffling and scraping of chairs, especially from the front rows. When only five seconds remained, and every head in the class was down, he would suddenly remember, pick up the infernal machine, look at it for a moment thoughtfully, and toss it nonchalantly through the window to explode on the lawn with barely a second to spare.

For our parachute course we reported, towards the end of October, at Dunham Massey House, between Altrincham and Knutsford in Cheshire. It was by far the best-run course I ever attended. The Commandant was a Major Edwards of the Northumberland Fusiliers, had served with distinction in the First World War; an industrious and efficient officer whose passion was punctuality and whose relaxation billiards, he instilled into me more of the latter than the former. His Chief Instructor, Captain Wooller, was an enthusiastic young athlete with more than a hundred and fifty parachute drops to his credit.

They were supported by an able and energetic staff of N.C.O.s, under whose direction we did P.T. every morning before breakfast to limber us up, and learnt our parachute drill. The ground training, I seem to remember, was divided into two main exercises: jumping from a height of about fifteen feet to learn how to fall when landing by parachute—the theory was that the impact of a parachute landing was equal to that of jumping from the roof of a train moving at the same speed as the wind—and dropping through a hole in a dummy fuselage in order to learn the correct position for leaving the aircraft. The important points, they told us, were to keep the body rigid, the hands pressed close to the sides and the knees and feet together, in order to brace the body against the force of the slip-stream; also to look up on leaving the exit, because if we looked down we should bang our heads on the opposite side. The exit aperture in the Whitley, which we were using in those days for training, was indeed too narrow; I saw a number of such injuries during the course. On landing we must take care to keep our feet and knees together, to let each leg bear an equal part of the shock; otherwise we should risk breaking a leg or an ankle. Above all, once the parachute had opened we must keep our eyes on the ground all the way down, and resist the temptation to relax and admire the scenery.

The day before we were to make our first drop we drove to Ringway Aerodrome and flew in a Whitley to get 'air experience'. This was supposed to give us confidence, but on me it had the opposite effect. When the covers were taken off the exit aperture as we approached Tatton Park, our dropping ground, and we looked through the hole at the fields and trees eight hundred feet below us, while the aircraft lurched and shuddered as the pilot throttled back, my stomach turned over and I wondered how I should ever be able to face my first drop. I spent a sleepless and apprehensive night.

Next morning, while waiting on the aerodrome for our turn, I looked at my five companions and noted with a little satisfaction that none of them seemed happier than I. Our sergeant-instructor fitted our parachutes; they felt surprisingly heavy on the back. He gave us a few words of encouragement. He was coming with us in the aircraft, he said, to dispatch us. We should be dropped singly from a height of eight hundred feet, which should give us about twenty seconds on the way down. Subsequent drops would be from five hundred feet.

'Nah, don't forget,' he concluded with a sudden leer, 'if yer 'chute don't open there's never any blood! There yer lies spread on the grahnd like a jelly. All yer bones broke. But there's never—any—*blood*.'

For a time it seemed doubtful whether we should take off; there was a fresh wind blowing and at that time it was considered unsafe to drop in a wind of more than twenty-five miles per hour. After half an hour we were ordered aboard the aircraft, and arranged ourselves opposite each other across the fuselage, three of us forward of the exit, three aft. I was dismayed to find that I should be the last to drop. The sergeant clipped the static lines of our parachutes to the 'strong-point', a stout wire running along the fuselage just beneath the roof. In this way the weight of the parachutist's body, as he left the aircraft, would pull on the static line attached to the 'strong point', causing the parachute to open.

The flight to Tatton Park took about ten minutes. As the pilot throttled back, the sergeant stood up beside the exit. A red light came on by his head; raising his hand he shouted, 'Action Stations, Number One!' The first man swung his legs over the hole and sat on the edge, his hands gripping the sides, his head up—looking, I thought, like a man on his way to the gallows. The red light was followed by a green one. As the sergeant dropped his arm and shouted 'Go!' Number One, with a last imploring look upwards, disappeared through the hole. The sergeant peered after him, then nodded to us. ''E's okay!'

Between each drop the aircraft made a circuit of the park. When the fifth man had gone, leaving me alone with the dispatcher, I eased over closer to the hole, ready to swing into the 'action stations' position, and gripped the edge with one hand against the bucking of the aircraft. I dared not look down, fearing that if I did I should not have the nerve to jump. I was cold and sweating at the same time. Reason told me that only one parachute in five thousand failed to open, that five people had just dropped before me without mishap, and that I was being a fool and a cissy; but reason failed to comfort me in the face of an unknown experience, against the background of the aircraft's hammering vibration and the startling backfires of the engines. I may add here that, among all the parachutists I know, I have never met one who did not find his first drop a frightening experience.

The sergeant gave me an encouraging smile, then turned to watch the lights above me. The red flashed. Swinging my legs over the edge, I sat tense and rigid, fixing my attention on the sergeant's arm, as I had been told, and not on the lights. During the next ten seconds I felt no sensation, not even fear, so fierce was my concentration. As his arm swept down and his shout rang in my ears, I thrust myself upwards and outwards with my hands and heels, jerking my head back in my anxiety not to look down. For a ghastly two seconds I felt myself falling, then the slip-stream hit me like a battering-ram and I turned a complete somersault. Next moment I felt a strong pull above me, the sensation of falling ceased, and my parachute was floating like a brilliant white mushroom against the sky.

In the first surge of relief I forgot all my instructions about keeping my feet and knees together and my eyes on the ground; I just relaxed and watched the panorama, enjoying the delicious sensation of gliding slowly earthwards. Even when a loud-hailer on the ground sharply recalled my attention to the drill I remained happy in the thought that my troubles were over. I was gravely mistaken. What I did not know was that the pilot had failed to see a red Verey light, fired from the ground while he was on his last circuit, warning him not to drop me; the wind had risen rapidly and was now gusting up to thirty-five miles an hour. The ground, which a moment before had seemed comfortably far away, suddenly rose up to strike me. I took a frantic pull on my liftwebs to ease the impact, then I landed in a sprawl, partially stunned and totally winded, face down on a cinder-track. Before I could get to my feet and run round behind the parachute to let it collapse, it had billowed out in a great gust of wind and was dragging me over the cinders at the speed of a racehorse. Jerking myself onto my back I struck the quick-release plate on my chest and began to tear with frenzied, shaking fingers at my leg-harness, striving to keep my head off the ground. When my legs were free I twisted back onto my stomach in accordance with the drill, my arms extended straight in front of me, and prayed for the shoulder-harness to slip off before all the skin was torn from my face. In a few seconds my parachute and harness were flying across the park and, after ploughing through some fifty yards of cinders I came to rest.

I lay still until two members of the ground staff, who had been chasing me since my landing, arrived to help me up and escort me to Major Edwards and Captain Wooller; they greeted me with deep concern and warm sympathy. During my descent the wind had carried me beyond the edge of the dropping-zone onto the foundations of a new road. My face, hands and knees were lacerated and black with dirt; I was slightly concussed, but not seriously damaged. When my injuries had been dressed, Edwards drove me back to Dunham and ordered me straight to bed.

'According to medical opinion', he told me, 'the first parachute drop is normally equivalent to the loss of eight hours' sleep. I don't know how much you've lost. You are excused P.T. tomorrow.'

In London, when we arrived after completing the course, my greeting from the staff officers of the Spanish section was not such as a hero might expect. Coldly the R.N.V.R. lieutenant said to me, 'Perhaps you would care to read the concluding words of Major Edwards's report on you?'

They ran simply: 'Not once, nor twice, but three times have I seen this officer punctual.'

IV

SMALL-SCALE RAIDING FORCE

Our intensive courses did not lead, as we had expected, to immediate operations; the Spanish Section, lacking opportunities rather than ideas, had no employment for us. The end of 1941 found Burton and me living in London, reporting daily by telephone to receive each time the same answer. Perhaps, we thought, one of the other Country Sections of S.O.E. might have use for us. We approached in turn the French, Norwegian, Polish, Czech, Russian, and—after Pearl Harbour—Far Eastern Sections, all without success; some had no vacancies, others no work.

Towards the end of February 1942 our spell of unemployment came at last to an end. While job-hunting in one of the several buildings in Baker Street that comprised S.O.E. headquarters we met Colonel Munn, who had been an instructor with me at Lochailort in 1940.

'You had better join my old friend, Gus March-Phillipps', he said after hearing our story. 'He is recruiting officers for a scheme of his which should be just up your street. I'll give your names to him.'

A few days later we were interviewed by Major March-Phillipps and his second-in-command, Captain Geoffrey Appleyard. However overworked and misapplied the words 'personality' and 'genius' may be, it is difficult to avoid their use in a description of those two remarkable characters. A regular officer in the Royal Artillery, March-Phillipps had served in India before the war, where he had experienced both the glamour of action with his battery on the North-West Frontier, and the glitter of social life in various hill stations. Wearying of the latter he had sent in his papers and retired to the English countryside to write novels, only to be recalled on the outbreak of war. After winning the M.B.E. in France in 1940 he had been posted as a Troop Commander to Number 7 Commando on its formation that autumn. In the spring of 1941, with the help of Brigadier Gubbins, he had persuaded S.O.E. to allow him to fit out a Brixham trawler, the *Maid Honor*, and sail her with a crew of seven from Poole Harbour to Freetown in West Africa. Such a voyage would have been extraordinary in peacetime; March-Phillipps and his party completed it without incident at the height of the Battle of the Atlantic. They carried out some brilliant *coup-de-main* operations along the African coast, for which March-Phillipps was awarded the D.S.O. He had returned to England at the beginning of the year.

By religion a deeply sincere Roman Catholic, by tradition an English country gentleman, he combined the idealism of a Crusader with the severity of a professional soldier. He was slightly built and of medium height; his eyes, puckered from straining against tropical glare, gave him an enquiring, piercing and even formidable expression, only slightly mitigated by his tendency to stammer. Despite an unusually hasty temper he had a great sense of fairness towards his subordinates. In battle he was invariably calm. He was intelligent, without any great academic ability. Above all, he had the inspiration to conceive great enterprises, combined with the skill and daring to execute them; he was also most fortunate in his second-in-command.

Of calmer temperament but similarly romantic nature, less impetuous but more obstinate, Appleyard combined a flair for organization and planning with superb skill in action and a unique ability to instill confidence in time of danger. Beneath a broad forehead his deep-set blue eyes gazed on the world with a quiet steadiness matched by the low timbre of his voice. He had the agility and stamina of a champion skier, which his extraordinary will-power subjected to inhuman strains.

The son of a leading Yorkshire industrialist, he had entered his father's engineering business on leaving Cambridge, but had been commissioned in the R.A.S.C. in 1939. Having met March-Phillipps for the first time with the B.E.F. in France, he became one of his troop officers in Number 7 Commando. Landed from a submarine near the Loire estuary early in 1941, he collected two of our agents and brought them back to safety in peculiarly difficult conditions; for this he was awarded the M.C. For the *Maid Honor* operation, when he was March-Phillipps's second-in-command, he received a Bar to his M.C.

The scheme which March-Phillipps and Appleyard had conceived, and for which they had already received official approval, was to raise and train a force to carry out small-scale raids on selected points along the enemy-occupied coasts of Europe. The size of each raiding-party would be about a dozen men, the objectives small strong-points or signal stations thinly held and comparatively easy of access by parties of trained and determined men approaching silently under cover of darkness.

The short-term object of these raids was to take prisoners for information, to shake the morale of the enemy and to raise that of our European allies; the long-term object was, by launching a series of small raids almost nightly along the whole length of coast from the Texel to Brest, to force the enemy to redeploy his forces in Europe, and so relieve some of the pressure on the Russian front. March-Phillipps's eventual ambition was to command a chain of small-scale raiding groups operating from bases scattered along the English coast; his immediate intention was to raise a nucleus of officers and N.C.O.s, to train them in the principles of this kind of warfare, and to give them practical experience by leading them himself in raids across the Channel. As we ourselves acquired experience, he explained, we should be able to train and lead others in similar operations. In this way would the force expand.

As I listened to the details of this plan and realized its enormous possibilities the clouds of frustration that had hung over me during the last few months vanished. Glancing at Burton I saw by his expression how much the idea appealed to him. Before we left the office we were enrolled on the establishment of the Small-Scale Raiding Force.

'We've seen a house in Dorset,' Appleyard told us, 'that would do admirably for our headquarters; I think we shall be allowed to requisition it. Our early raids will be mounted from Portland, Poole and Gosport, so that Anderson Manor, which is between Blandford and Poole, is ideally situated. We shan't be able to get down to our training for at least another six weeks, so what would you like to do with yourselves in the meantime?'

The most sensible thing, we decided, would be to get ourselves fit again, and refresh our memories on demolitions and other useful paramilitary activities; and so, two days later, Burton and I left for the Western Highlands.

The S.O.E. paramilitary training centre was now at Arisaig, a few miles north of Lochailort. After reporting there we were sent to one of the outlying establishments, hard by the shores of Loch Morar. Here, under the direction of Major Young and the expert instruction of Captains Gavin Maxwell and Matthew Hodgart, we started a course of hard and intensive training. Carrying tommy-guns and fifty-pound rucksacks we tramped across the hills in dense mist and darkness, trying to find our way by compass, stumbling over invisible obstacles, sinking into bogs and falling into gullies and ravines. On one of these schemes the Adjutant from Arisaig, an enormous Highlander, broke a leg and lay for six hours in the mist on a mountain top before he could be carried down. Our companions on these exercises were a party of Czech officers, whose enthusiasm, skill and stamina inspired us to yet greater efforts; within three weeks we were thoroughly fit, competent at demolitions and accurate with pistol and tommy-gun.

We did some amphibious training in small boats on Loch Morar. Here we encountered a party of Spanish Republicans, a villainous crowd of assassins; we made no attempt to mix with them. Their conducting officer, a Captain Martin, spoke of them with distaste.

'They seemed to take no interest in anything', he told us, 'until, the other day, I brought them down to one of the beaches for a spot of landing practice. They slouched about apathetically until suddenly one of them found a whelk or mussel or something. He let out a shout and all the others started running around like mad. Believe it or not, inside half an hour they'd eaten every living thing on that damn beach that didn't speak to them!'

We were back in London in time to attend March-Phillipps's wedding in the middle of April. His wife, who had the same adventurous nature as himself, had interrupted a stage career to become the first qualified woman parachutist at Ringway.

At the wedding we met some of the other officers who were to form the nucleus of the Small-Scale Raiding Force. Senior among them was Major John Gwynne of the Sussex Yeomanry, in charge of planning. A teetotaler and vegetarian, obstinate, unwavering, and fearless, he fretted constantly under the restraints of his sedentary occupation; eager to lead an operation in the field, he was always planning for himself some desperate venture into enemy territory. With his lean, dark, ascetic face, gleaming eyes, and thinning, almost tonsured hair, he had the look of some medieval inquisitor; he always shaved in cold water.

Captain Graham Hayes of the Border Regiment, a school friend of Appleyard's, had also won an M.C. in Maid Honor. He was a quiet, serious-minded young man of great personal charm, courage, and strength, who had sailed before the mast in a Finnish grain ship, and was a superb seaman.

Another member of our party was Anders Lassen, a cheerful, lithe young Dane with a thirst for killing Germans and a wild bravery that was to win him the M.C. and two Bars, and at last a posthumous Victoria Cross.

In spite of a competing claim by the Ministry of Health we moved into Anderson Manor towards the end of April. This beautiful Elizabethan house had been cleared of its furniture before we took over, and the walls covered with beaver-boarding; nevertheless March-Phillipps, who was a friend of the owner, and who knew only too well the Army's reputation for vandalism, enjoined the strictest care upon officers and other ranks, so that not only was the house preserved from damage, but the handsome gardens were maintained by us in our spare time. In other parts of the grounds we built a pistol range and an assault course with walls, ditches full of barbed wire, Dannert wire entanglements, and a rope slung across the drive between two tall oaks; wearing full equipment we had to climb one tree, crawl along the rope and clamber down the other.

Our basic training was on the same lines as our course at Arisaig, with emphasis on tests of strength and endurance; but we specialized in map-reading exercises, movement across country by night, and boat training both by day and night. Because our raiding parties would be small their only hope would be in surprise; for this reason our raids must take place during non-moon periods. We must train ourselves to see like cats in the dark, and to move as silently. On our first night exercises we were all very uncertain and noisy, but in a surprisingly short time we became accustomed to the work; within two months we were able to find our way in silence over unknown country at a surprising speed, to crawl noiselessly under barbed wire and to stalk sentries on our stomachs, using elbows and feet to propel us. Rock climbing by day and night was an important and for me a terrifying part of our training.

The Admiralty put at our disposal a small, fast M.T.B. under the command of Lieutenant Freddy Bourne, D.S.C., R.N.V.R. Affectionately known as 'The Little Pisser' she was smaller than most M.T.B.s, was armed only with two Vickers machine-guns and had been stripped of her torpedo tubes. There was space to carry a light landing craft, lashed to the after deck. She would take us across the Channel to within a mile or so of our objective, where we could disembark and row or paddle ourselves ashore. We practiced with various types of landing craft, chiefly the eighteen-foot dory and the Goatley pattern assault craft—a flat-bottomed boat with canvas sides, which proved itself surprisingly seaworthy. We practiced in every kind of weather, under all sorts of conditions, until we had perfected our training in disembarkation, landing, and re-embarkation.

Although we were administered by S.O.E. we came under Combined Operations Headquarters for planning, and under Special Service Brigade—the Commando organization—for discipline; this last control was only a formality, because March-Phillipps arranged our training according to his own ideas, almost free from outside interference. Thus, although we were also known as No. 62 Commando and were issued with green berets, March-Phillipps encouraged us to wear civilian clothes when off duty; this was in keeping with his conception of us as successors to the Elizabethan tradition of the gentleman-adventurer. During training our discipline was extremely strict, March-Phillipps and Appleyard demanding the highest standard of efficiency from everyone. There were no punishments, nor were they necessary: we knew that the lives of all of us would depend on the skill and competence of each. Off parade relations between officers and other ranks were easy and informal, almost casual. We were a very happy unit.

Because we had been recruited as the nucleus of a larger force our establishment comprised more officers than other ranks. Besides those whom I had already met there was Captain Lord Howard of Penrith, quiet, intellectual, and conscientious; Captain Colin Ogden Smith, who had been one of March-Phillipps's troop officers in No. 7 Commando; Captain Hamish Torrance, M.B.E., of the Highland Light Infantry, a veteran S.O.E. officer who had seen service in Norway; a young and earnest Sapper, Paul Dudgeon, who had been through Woolwich; Tony Hall, a subaltern from the London Irish; a Yorkshire neighbour of Appleyard's, Lieutenant Warren; Lieutenant Brinkgreve of the Royal Netherlands Army; André Desgranges, a deep-sea diver and ex-petty officer of the French Navy, who had sailed with *Maid Honor* and had received a commission in the British Army on his return; and Brian Reynolds, newly commissioned as an ensign in the Welsh Guards.

Reynolds was an Irishman, well known before the war as a sportsman, bon viveur, and playboy. On the outbreak of the Russo-Finnish war in 1939 he went to Finland as a volunteer in Major Kermit Roosevelt's International Brigade; having exchanged the comfort and cuisine of Buck's for the icy forests of Lapland and Karelia, he endured bitter hardship with that ill-fated band of idealists before making his way to Sweden after the collapse of Finnish resistance. There he turned his unusual abilities to the service of the Allies, smuggling cargoes of ball-bearings on merchant ships through the Skagerrak from Gothenburg to Britain, under constant attack from the German Navy and Air Force; on his last run he lost four ships out of five, but his arrival with the fifth prevented a serious gap in British tank production. He was awarded the O.B.E. As well as courage he had great personal charm and a delicious sense of humour. His death, the day after the European war ended, was one of those futile tragedies in which fate seems to delight: when the Small-Scale Raiding Force broke up he returned to his old activities in the Skagerrak, this time in fast motor boats. Entering Antwerp harbour to celebrate the victory with some friends, he was killed instantly when his M.T.B. struck a mine.

Outstanding among the other ranks were Sergeant-Major Winter, an amiable but extremely efficient soldier who had also served with March-Phillipps and Appleyard in West Africa; Sergeant Nicholson, by far the oldest man in the force, a grey-haired regular soldier with the D.C.M.; Bruce Ogden Smith, Colin's brother, who had joined us as a private; Adam Orr, a Polish Jew who had taken this English *nom-de-guerre* as a precaution in case of capture, and Rifleman Rowe, an irrepressible little Cockney with a salacious wit who had spent some years in a priest's seminary in Belgium before deciding that the Church was not his vocation.

By the end of July we were fully trained, at the peak of our morale and craving action; plans were already completed for our first raids. But there followed a disheartening period of frustration and delay: our M.T.B. was considered unseaworthy in any wind stronger than Force 3; and two or three nights in the week were 'convoy nights', when we were not allowed to be in the English Channel. Because we were restricted to non-moon periods—a fortnight in each month—it was difficult to find a night when the limitations of weather and convoys did not affect us. Keyed up as we were, standing by night after night, sometimes setting out on a raid only to turn back within an hour or so, we all found this period of waiting a heavy strain on our nerves; for March-Phillipps and Appleyard it must have been nearly intolerable.

Early in August the first raid was launched, with about half of our force, against a small strong-point on the Normandy coast. The approach involved some difficult rock climbing, which caused March-Phillipps, who had noticed my clumsiness, to exclude me from the party; Burton, who had injured a calf muscle, was also left behind. With envy and anxiety we watched the party set out in the dusk for Gosport, each of them festooned with tommy-gun, Colt .45 automatic, and hand-grenades. Next morning before breakfast they returned, strained and exhausted but content with their night's work. They had found the target without difficulty and had crawled undetected to the wire perimeter. Trying to force an entry they alarmed the guard, most of whom they slaughtered with hand-grenades and small-arms fire. After inflicting further casualties on the frightened and bewildered garrison they withdrew without loss and were embarked safely aboard the M.T.B. Although they had taken no prisoners we all felt it was an encouraging start.

Our next target was in the Channel Islands—the German-occupied lighthouse and signal-station on the Casquets, a rocky islet about seven miles west of Alderney. About a week after the first raid our party, this time including Burton and myself, assembled in the Conference Room at Anderson; for several hours we studied charts, aerial photographs and, most important of all, a large and perfectly executed scale model in plasticine of the Casquets Rock with the lighthouse and adjoining buildings clearly shown in detail. March-Phillipps issued his operation orders.

Leaving Portland at 9 p.m. we should arrive off the Casquets just before midnight; Appleyard would be navigating. During the last part of the approach the M.T.B. would travel on her silent auxiliary engine. At half a mile's distance she would anchor, and we should man the Goatley and paddle ourselves ashore. It was likely to be a difficult approach and landing, because we could expect a heavy swell and a fierce tiderace round the rocks. Hayes, as coxswain, would be responsible for letting go the kedge anchor to keep the boat off the rocks; Appleyard as bow-man would take the painter ashore and make her fast while the rest of us landed. Hayes and Warren would stay with the landing-craft. Once ashore we should climb in single file up to the wall surrounding the station buildings. Inside, we were to divide into four parties, each with its separate objective: 'A' party, consisting of March-Phillipps, Dudgeon, Howard and Orr, was to tackle the main building, containing the living and sleeping quarters; 'B' party—Burton and myself—was to make straight for the wireless tower, kill or capture any Germans we found before they could use the wireless, and put the transmitter out of action; 'C' party—Appleyard and Winter—were to take possession of the lighthouse tower, and 'D' party—Brinkgreve and Reynolds—were to occupy the engine room. When we had cleared the enemy from our respective buildings we were to report with our prisoners to March-Phillipps. The prisoners would then be shepherded to the landing-craft by a small escort, while the rest of the party searched the buildings for code-books and other documents. Nobody knew the exact strength of the German garrison, but it was believed to number about eight; there would be ten of us excluding Hayes and Warren, so that if we could achieve surprise we should be able to overpower them.

Although we had now a detailed description of our target and were familiar with its every aspect, none but March-Phillipps and Appleyard knew its exact position; not until the raid was over were the rest of us told where we had been. Without this precaution there might have been a security leak;

in fact, owing to engine trouble in the M.T.B. as well as unfavourable weather, it was nearly a fortnight before we could make the raid. During this time we had several false starts, arriving on one occasion within a mile of the rock before thick fog compelled us to turn home.

Wednesday, 2nd September, was a fine day with a fresh breeze. We had spent a large part of the previous night crawling on our stomachs in the rain, practicing silent movement. I did not sleep well afterwards, and awoke feeling tired and jittery; but a brisk run before breakfast with Burton and Appleyard, followed by the news that we should try to do the raid again that night, revived my spirits. We spent the morning in the conference room, the afternoon resting. Although we had the greatest confidence in our commanders and in each other, it was difficult not to contemplate the numerous possibilities of disaster. Once we were in the M.T.B. I should feel all right, but I found this period of waiting very hard to bear. We spent the time between tea and supper in drawing and preparing our equipment. There was plenty of it. I was carrying a tommy-gun and seven magazines, each with twenty rounds, a pair of wire-cutters, two Mills grenades, a fighting knife, a clasp knife, a torch, emergency rations, and two half-pound explosive charges for the destruction of the wireless transmitter; on top I had to wear a naval lifebelt, an awkward and constricting garment which might save my life in the water but seemed very likely to lose it for me in action. We wore battle-dress, balaclava helmets and felt-soled boots.

After a hurried supper we climbed into our lorry. The whole unit turned out in the stable-yard to see us off; Tony Hall, in an old suit and peaked cap, was ringing the mess dinner bell and shouting in the accents of an American railroad conductor:

'All aboard! All aboard! Minneapolis, Saint Paul, Chicago, and all points east!'

We sang lustily, all tension now relaxed, as we drove through the green and golden countryside towards Portland. The lorry swung into the dockyard, drove onto the quay and halted close alongside our boat; we hurried aboard and dived out of sight below. I found myself in the forecastle with Dudgeon, Reynolds, Warren and Orr; March-Phillipps and Appleyard were on the bridge with Lieutenant Bourne; Burton and the rest were disposed somewhere aft. At nine o'clock we sailed.

With the forecastle hatch battened down to show no light, it was oppressively hot in our cramped quarters. The small craft bounced jarringly across the waves, for the wind, which had been Force 3 when we started, was rising to Force 4, with occasional stronger gusts. My companions lay down to sleep on the two wooden seats and the floor; I sat up and tried to read a thriller.

We had hoped to drop anchor off our target about ten-fifteen to catch the slack of the tide; the moon would be rising at eleven-thirty. But one of the motors again gave trouble, forcing us to reduce speed for part of the way. It was after ten-thirty when Appleyard knocked on the forecastle hatch and warned us to be ready to come on deck when summoned. When we had adjusted our equipment and inspected our weapons we switched out the forecastle lights, to accustom our eyes to the darkness outside; half an hour later the hatch was opened and we were ordered on deck.

It was a beautiful, clear night, bright with stars. The wind had dropped and the sea was moderating. Clustered in a body aft of the bridge, standing by to launch the Goatley as soon as we should anchor, we could make out the dim shapes of some rocks on the starboard beam; Appleyard and March-Phillipps were on the bridge, trying to identify them. The M.T.B. had switched from her main engines to the silent auxiliary. Looking round the horizon and shivering in the chill night breeze, I noticed a flickering light at some distance on our port bow, and another—a bright red one—almost directly ahead of us; the latter, I afterwards heard, was Sark. The moon appeared, low in the sky, on our port quarter. Suddenly I caught sight of our target, straight ahead of us; the tall, thin column of the lighthouse, the whitewashed wall and the buildings of the signal-station gleamed palely above the blackness of the rock.

Slowly the M.T.B. moved in, maneuvering to approach from the north-west; at half a mile's distance she anchored. Silently we pushed our Goatley over the stern and dropped quickly into our places, kneeling with our paddles ready. It was five minutes after midnight when March-Phillipps jumped down beside me and called softly:

'Right! Push off! Paddle up!'

Now the moon was higher, casting a sharp, clear light over the choppy water between us and the island; we could see it distinctly and must ourselves be visible, I thought uncomfortably, to any watchers there. I dismissed such thoughts and concentrated on keeping time with the others, holding my paddle well away from the side of the boat; I took comfort from the silence of our movement through the water and from the knowledge that we were a small object and therefore difficult to pick out among the waves. It was hard work paddling, for the north-east flood was running fast.

Some twenty minutes after leaving the landing-craft I saw that we were entering a small bay. There were splashes of white close ahead, where the surf was breaking on the rocks.

'All right, Apple?' whispered March-Phillipps. Appleyard's voice called back from the bows, low, yet to our tensed minds alarmingly clear:

'Okay. Graham, bring her in just to the right of that white splash of surf.'

Hayes, in the stern, could not hear him above the hiss of the sea, and asked him to repeat his orders more loudly. I could see the landing place, a smooth and gently sloping slab of rock, lighter in colour than the rest, in the right hand corner of the bay. As Hayes let go the kedge anchor Appleyard stood up in the bow, the line in his hand. The swell caught us, sweeping us towards the rock; Appleyard leaned forward to jump for the shore. At this moment, the kedge began to drag, holding us back. We paddled up with all our strength to shorten the distance, but we could make no headway against the weight of the kedge. I saw March-Phillipps glance apprehensively at the buildings above us. We were close under the rock; its black mass towered overhead, the signal station standing out clearly against the sky. It would be awkward to be caught in such a place, as it seemed we must be if the enemy up there were alert. As the swell lifted us again and carried us shore wards Appleyard jumped with the bow-line. He landed on the rock, slipped on the wet surface and almost fell into the sea; recovering just in time, he scrambled up the cliff to make fast the painter. One by one we followed him ashore, timing our jumps to the rise of the swell, while Hayes held the boat off the rock with the stern-line and kedge. Encumbered by our weapons we slithered about, trying to get a purchase on the rock, until March-Phillipps hissed angrily:

'Use the rope, you b-bloody f-fools, to haul yourselves up!'

Leaving Hayes and Warren to look after the Goatley and keep a watch on the M.T.B. through an infra-red receiving set, we started to climb the cliff in single file. I followed Burton, who, prostrated with sea-sickness during the crossing, had made a remarkable recovery as soon as his feet touched land. We had avoided the recognized landing points, fearing that they might be set with mines or booby-traps; we were lucky, therefore, to find an easy way up from the shore. Our only obstacle was some coiled Dannert wire, through which we cut our way without trouble. Any noise we made was probably drowned by the rumble of surf and the booming of the sea in the chasms and gullies round the cave. Nevertheless, my heart was pounding with more than exertion as we came into full view of the buildings. Under different circumstances the white-washed walls and dark roofs must have seemed lovely under the pale moonlight: in those critical moments they loomed cold and menacing, silent and lifeless, yet seemingly ready to spring into life to destroy us.

The entrance to the courtyard was blocked by a heavy 'knife-rest' barbed wire entanglement. Motioning us to follow him, March-Phillipps leaped for the wall, heaved himself over it and dropped on the other side. Within a few seconds we were all in the courtyard. This was the moment for independent action. Burton and I tore across the fifty yards of open ground to the door of the wireless tower, where a light was burning. Inside, on the left, a stone staircase led up to the transmitting room. Without a pause we raced up the stairs to a landing on the first floor, where an open doorway led into a lighted room. Burton was through the door in a second, his pistol in his hand; I was hard on his heels, my finger on the trigger of my tommy-gun.

We found ourselves in a deserted room, crammed with wireless sets, generators and equipment; by the operator's stool, which was thrust back from the table, were some signal pads and an open notebook; code-books were on a shelf on the wall above. I stood on guard at the doorway overlooking the staircase, listening for sounds of firing from the other parties; but everything was quiet. Meanwhile Burton went through the room collecting code-books, signal-books and other documents likely to be of interest. I heard a sound from the entrance below; raising my tommy-gun I peered over the low balustrade, and was relieved to see Appleyard looking up at me.

'All clear here,' I said, 'we haven't seen a soul. How's it gone with you?'

'Splendid! We caught the whole damn bunch with their pants down—or rather, with their pajamas on. Two of them had just come off watch and were turning in, two others were filling up log-books, and the rest were in bed. Just as well, after all, that we didn't get here earlier. I've never seen men look so astonished and terrified—not a show of fight among the lot of them. We're taking them down to the boat now.' He came upstairs to join us.

'What about smashing up all this equipment?' I asked. 'Can I use the tommy-gun to blast it?'

'No. There's been no shooting, so Gus wants us to keep as quiet as possible. John had better use his axe while you and I go back to help with the prisoners. When you've made a nice mess, John, pick up that bumf you've collected and join us in the main building.'

We had indeed achieved complete surprise. Like the wireless tower, the lighthouse and engine-room were both deserted; all seven members of the garrison were in the main building. It seemed extraordinary that they had not posted a sentry, but they explained to us that they had not expected visitors. Nothing could better describe their state of un-preparedness than a sentence from March-Phillipps's official report to the Chief of Combined Operations: 'A characteristic of those in bed was the wearing of hairnets, which caused the Commander of the party to mistake one of them for a woman.'

All the following day and night, we were informed later, Cherbourg was calling up the Casquets, and asking all other stations if they had had any signals from the island. It was a month before the Germans discovered what had happened to the garrison. All the prisoners were naval ratings, under the command of a Chief Petty Officer Muenthe. Among them were two leading telegraphists, one of whom had previously been employed on guided missiles and whose information proved particularly valuable.

While some of us made a thorough search of the buildings, collecting documents and destroying arms and equipment—which included an Oerlikon cannon—others rounded up the prisoners and marched them down to the boat. As time was running short the Germans were not allowed to dress; dejected and tearful they were hurried away with over-coats over their pajamas, one of them keeping on his hairnet until we arrived at Portland, where he proved a willing subject for interrogation.

It was one o'clock when I reached the Goatley, to find the prisoners already embarked. The moon was well up, bathing the Casquets and the sea around in brilliant light; our position now would be desperate if enemy patrol craft were to approach. Although the Goatley was going to be seriously overloaded, with the seven prisoners and ourselves, March-Phillipps decided to take the risk rather than waste time sending for the emergency dory. He ordered me to jump in and stand at the bow to help the rest of the party aboard. With the heavy-swell, the jump from the rock to the landing craft varied from five to twenty feet, so that re-embarkation was not easy. The smallest mistake might cause the swamping of the boat and bring disaster on us all. The last man to jump before March-Phillipps and Appleyard was the Pole, Orr; he had his fighting knife in his hand and, as he dropped, the boat lurched and threw him against me. I felt a sharp, biting pain in my right thigh as the blade went in. However, I had no time to think about it; March-Phillipps dropped into the boat and ordered us to cast off. I crawled to my place and began paddling with the others, under a ceaseless rain of invective from our agitated commander.

With nineteen men aboard, the Goatley was dangerously low in the water; but she rode the swell admirably and we reached the M.T.B. safely after thirty-five minutes. The prisoners were hauled aboard first and sent down to the forecastle with Howard and Dudgeon to guard them; I joined them there, helped along by Orr, who was very contrite about the injury he had accidentally caused. The return journey to Portland was uneventful. The prisoners were docile, huddled together in their misery at one end of the forecastle; indeed, there was no comfort for any of us in the cramped and stifling compartment. Orr's knife had penetrated deep and my wound was stiff and painful; when we reached Portland, just before dawn, I could barely stand. After a while an ambulance took me to the Naval Hospital, where I was immediately put to sleep with a shot of morphia. An operation the next morning removed the blood-clots and greatly relieved the pain. I thought I was the only casualty of the raid, but I was wrong: Appleyard, following March-Phillipps into the boat, had seriously damaged his ankle. These accidents, which temporarily put us out of action, in the event prolonged our lives.

During my convalescence disaster struck the Small-Scale Raiding Force. On the night of 12th September one of our parties sailed in M.T.B. 344 to attack a target on the Cherbourg peninsula. March-Phillipps was in command, with Appleyard, whose damaged ankle would not allow him to land, as navigator. This was the second consecutive night that they had attempted the raid, having run into fog the first time when they were within a mile or two of their objective; this part of the coast was heavily defended, and so it might have been wiser to allow a longer interval.

At that time my wife and I had a cottage at Spettisbury, about five miles from Anderson. Although I had left hospital two days before, I was not yet fit for operations. On the morning of the 12th Reynolds and Torrance, who were not included in the raiding party, drove over to us for dinner. It was an uncomfortable meal; conversation was artificial and constrained, for all our thoughts were with our friends crossing the channel on their desperate mission. As we stood in the garden afterwards silently looking down over the vale of the Stour and watching the shadows creep across the meadows beside the river, Torrance put my fears into words.

'Don't telephone, Peter. As soon as we have any news I'll come over myself and let you know.'

I slept little that night: Burton, my close companion for the last eighteen months, was with March-Phillipps and I hated not to be there beside him in the battle; I half hoped that fog would again defeat them and the operation be postponed until I was fit again. All next day I loafed about, irritable and unhappy, with no word from Anderson. Long after dark I heard a truck draw up at the gate, and rushed out to meet Torrance; his thin, dark face was puckered with anxiety and grief.

'We've lost the lot! Apple came back tonight with Freddy Bourne—I've just left them in the Mess. They aren't sure exactly what happened, but the Germans must have been waiting for them. Gus and his party could hardly have landed when the boys on the M.T.B. heard all hell break loose on shore; they were quite badly shot up themselves. God knows if any of the landing force got away, but it looks as if they're all dead or prisoners.'

It was not for many months that we learned the full story of the tragedy. In the small hours of 13th September March-Phillipps landed with eight others, including Burton, Hayes, Howard, Hall, Winter, and Desgranges. They had barely stepped ashore when heavy fire was directed on them from the cliffs above; machine-guns, hand grenades, mortars and cannon blasted their narrow and exposed strip of beach. In the pitch darkness Bourne and Appleyard, aboard the M.T.B., could see nothing but the enemy flashes and the explosions of shells; but they edged their craft as close inshore as they dared in the shallow water, and stood by to pick up the party. As the firing died down they heard a voice, which they believed to be Hayes's, calling to Appleyard to leave them and save the ship while he could. Nevertheless, the M.T.B. continued to cruise around just off-shore, showing signal lights and blowing whistles in a desperate attempt to rescue survivors. She was under continuous fire from the shore and one of her engines was put out of action. With the approach of daylight there was no alternative but to make for home.

March-Phillipps's death was reported two days later in a communique issued by the German High Command. Afterwards, we heard that the

Goatley had been swamped while carrying the party back to the M.T.B. All but March-Phillipps had swum ashore; he was drowned trying to reach the M.T.B., and his body was recovered by the Germans next morning. Letters from the survivors told of the calmness, skill and courage with which he had faced that desperate situation on the beach and organized the withdrawal of his force. All but one of the others were taken prisoner almost immediately, Hall and Howard with serious wounds. Hayes alone managed to escape, swimming away from the beach and landing farther down the coast; he eluded capture for a while, but was eventually handed over to the Germans, placed in Fresnes prison in solitary confinement for nine months, and shot on 13th July, 1943. Burton made his way inland, but was picked up a day or two later and spent the rest of the European war in a prison camp near Kassel; he emerged, however, in time to fly to the Far East and take part in what were officially and euphemistically called 'post-hostilities operations' against the Indonesians in Sumatra.

We had been prepared for casualties, but not for such a catastrophe as this. The death of the gallant idealist and strange, quixotic genius who had been our commander and our inspiration, together with the loss of so many good friends, all in the space of a few hours, was a crippling calamity which nearly put an end to our activities. Indeed, it probably would have done so but for the energetic reaction of Appleyard, who refused to let our grief for our comrades arrest his determination to avenge them. Our masters in London responded with a heartening display of confidence, appointing Appleyard as temporary commander of the Force, with the rank of Major.

Their confidence was quickly justified. Within a month of the disaster Appleyard took a party, consisting of Ogden Smith, Lassen, Dudgeon and half a dozen others to the island of Sark, leading the raid himself in spite of his injured ankle. They spent more than four hours reconnoitring the island; they also captured two Germans. Realizing that the route back to the landing-craft passed close by some German defences, Appleyard ordered the prisoners' hands to be tied behind their backs, to lessen their chances of escape. At the most critical point on the journey one of the two ran away; Lassen gave chase in the dark, caught him and before he could raise the alarm dispatched him quickly and silently with a fighting knife. The remaining prisoner gave no trouble; he subsequently proved a most valuable source of information. For their work on this and previous raids Appleyard received the D.S.O., Dudgeon the M.C.

There was one unfortunate sequel: when the dead prisoner was found, his hands still tied behind his back, the German High Command raised an outcry, maintaining that it was contrary to International Law to tie the hands of prisoners. In retaliation they put chains on some of the prisoners they had taken in the Dieppe raid.

In October the Chiefs of Staff gave orders for the expansion of the Small-Scale Raiding Force. It seemed that March-Phillipps's dream was coming true. Four more large houses were requisitioned to provide bases for us along the south coast—one in the New Forest, another near Dorchester, a third near Paignton and the fourth between Falmouth and Truro. Bill Stirling, recently returned from Cairo, arrived to take command of the whole force, with the rank of Lieutenant-Colonel; Appleyard became second-in-command and field force commander; John Gwynne was at last allowed to train a party of his own to operate deep into Northern France. Two motor gunboats were put at our disposal, but on operations we preferred to use M.T.B. 344 because she was smaller, more difficult to see, and easier to manœuvre. Two navigating officers were added to our establishment. One of them was an R.A.F. squadron-leader, the other a tubby, red-faced Breton fisherman who spoke no English and whose dialect few of us could understand; a cheerful, friendly little man, he took a touching pride in his new uniform of lieutenant R.N.R., especially in his uniform cap, which he seldom, if ever, removed; sharing a room with him I was fascinated to watch him sitting up in bed reading a book, wearing a suit of thick flannel pajamas, his cap set jauntily on the back of his bald head.

With our expansion came an important change of policy, affecting the composition of our raiding force; in future, selected officers and N.C.O.s from the Commandos would be sent to us for a short period of training in the specialized technique of small-scale raiding, after which we should take them on a raid. This was the logical development of March-Phillipps's original idea. Towards the end of October the first cadres arrived at Anderson Manor—all from No. 12 Commando. The officers, Captains Pinckney and Rooney and Lieutenant Gilchrist, each brought six N.C.O.s from his own troop. Reynolds, Sergeant Nicholson and I were ordered to train Rooney's squad in preparation for a raid in the immediate future.

Rooney, a powerfully built, self-confident officer, who knew his men intimately and commanded their implicit obedience, had little to learn from me. In fact, apart from pistol shooting and movement at night, he and his men knew more about the business than I. However, I was to command them on the forthcoming raid, and so we spent the next two weeks together in unremitting training by day and night. In particular we exercised ourselves in night schemes on land and water, in soundless movement and the use of our eyes in the dark. For such intensive practice we were soon to be thankful.

On 5th November, appropriately enough, we were called to the Conference Room for our operational briefing. Our target was to be a German semaphore station on the Point de Plouezec, about fifteen miles north-west of Saint Brieuc on the Brittany coast. This time we had no scale model of the target, but plenty of maps and aerial photographs, as well as some local intelligence about the station and its defences; the latter was to prove inaccurate in some important details.

Our information from all sources indicated that the semaphore station stood on the top of steep cliffs at the end of the point, which jutted north-eastwards from the Baie de Saint Brieuc. The northern and eastern faces were defended by concrete emplacements, at least one of which mounted a gun; the only practicable landing place seemed to be a small shingle beach below the southern face, where a narrow track appeared to lead up the cliff to join a path running inland from the signal station. On this side of the station, we were told, the defences consisted only of a single belt of barbed wire and, beside the track, just inside the entrance, a small concrete guard-house, where we should probably find a sentry. The entrance itself was not protected by barbed wire. According to local information there were neither mines nor booby-traps. The garrison contained about a dozen soldiers; there would be ten of us, so that surprise would be essential.

Appleyard would accompany us in the M.T.B., but he was forbidden to land, for his ankle was now encased in plaster; I was to command the landing-party, with Rooney as second-in-command and Reynolds as coxswain of the dory in which we should paddle ashore. Stirling particularly impressed on us that he wanted no casualties in our party; afterwards he took Reynolds and me aside to emphasize the point.

'Rooney and his chaps,' he began, 'are very keen and will obviously seize any opportunity for a fight. Naturally we want to inflict casualties and take prisoners; but not, I repeat, at the cost of losing men ourselves; it isn't worth it at this stage. If, when you get there, you don't think you can fight without losing men I promise you I shall be quite satisfied with a recce. Remember, Peter, I don't want any Foreign Legion stuff on this party!'

He did not need to worry: with the lives of nine valuable officers and N.C.O.s in my hands I had no mind to stick my neck out on my first independent command.

With the help of Rooney and Reynolds I drafted my operation orders.

In addition to the usual weapons, my landing-party was issued with a Bren gun, a Sten gun fitted with a silencer, and two hand grenades of a new pattern known officially as "Grenades P.E., No. 6'; these grenades had a thin metal casing and contained a heavy charge of Plastic Explosive; they burst on impact with a very heavy blast, and so should be useful if we had to blow our way through the barbed wire. Once we had gained the cliff top, our most difficult problem would obviously be to approach the sentry close enough to kill him noiselessly before he could raise the alarm; that was the purpose of the silent Sten, which we had already tried out and found satisfactory. The Bren gun was to guard our rear while we were making the attack, and cover our withdrawal afterwards.

I worked out a simple plan: immediately after landing, the party was to form a defensive beach-head at the foot of the cliffs, protecting the landing-craft, while I located the track leading to the top. When we reached the top of the cliff Sergeant Nicholson would take up position with the Bren gun, to cover the path inland and to indicate the point where the track led down. This should be about a hundred and fifty yards from the entrance to the semaphore station. The rest of us would approach the target in three groups, one on either side of the path and one in rear; Rooney would lead the left hand party, I the right. The last part of the approach would have to be made crawling on our stomachs. If we could get near enough, Rooney and I would kill the sentry with our knives; if not, Sergeant Broderson would shoot him with the silenced Sten. We should then invade the station, the party on the right pausing to clear the guard-house, while the remainder attacked the main building.

M.T.B. 344 was lying at Dartmouth, ready to take us across on the first night of favourable weather. At midday on Wednesday, 11th November, heartened by the news of far more important landings in North Africa, we set off from Anderson to carry out our raid.

After a brief halt at Lupton House, our new base near Paignton, where we had a hurried meal and put on our operational clothing and equipment, we drove into Kingswear in the late afternoon. Stirling and Sam Darby, our new Intelligence Officer, were on the quay talking to Freddie Bourne, whose boat lay alongside, her engines already running. As soon as the last of us was on board we cast off and started down the estuary. Waving a silent good-bye to Stirling and Darby I settled myself with Rooney and Reynolds in the lee of the dory on the afterdeck. Appleyard took up his usual station on the bridge with Bourne; Rooney's men were below. Savouring my first moments of relaxation since early morning I gazed at the wooded hills above the Dart, watching their colours soften as we drew away in the last clear light of evening; the old castle above Dartmouth stood black against the fading western sky. Soon distance and darkness hid them; only the bright torrent of our wake showed in the blackness of night and water.

I strove to keep myself from worrying about the work that lay ahead of us, reflecting that we had rehearsed every detail of my plan; but now doubts began to crowd upon me. Rooney and his men were superb, but we had worked together only for a fortnight; on this difficult approach the slightest misunderstanding or mischance, impatience or carelessness, would destroy us before we could launch our attack. Moreover, despite all that Stirling had said, I knew that we should look extremely foolish if we were to return without taking prisoners or inflicting casualties; yet I could not overlook his instructions, which I knew came from headquarters, to bring my party home intact.

Fortunately I was not allowed to immerse myself for long in these unhappy droughts. As we cleared Start Point and increased speed to twenty-eight knots against a Force 3 wind and swell from the southeast, the sea began to break green over the whole length of the boat, drenching us through our protective clothing, and freezing us as we lay under the inadequate cover of the dory. Before long I was too numbed to think about my troubles, and looked forward to our arrival off the Point de Plouezec, which would at least put an end to this discomfort.

The journey took us nearly six hours. For some of the time I stood on the bridge with Appleyard, staring in silence through the spray and darkness, unable to make out the horizon in any direction, so dark was the sky. Two or three times I went below with Rooney to see how his men were faring; finding nearly all of them asleep, I envied their composure.

It was not surprising that we had some difficulty in finding our first landfall, the light tower on the Roches Douvres, and wasted an hour making a 'square search' for it; just before ten o'clock we picked it up at a distance of about a mile. From here Appleyard laid a course to bring us directly to the Baie de Saint Brieuc. At half past eleven we switched onto silent engines, altering course again to approach the Point de Plouezec from the east-south-east. The night was now bright with stars, and as we drew near we could clearly distinguish the headland with its off-lying rocks and islands; on top of the point the squat outline of the semaphore station made a dark silhouette against the sky.

At ten minutes past midnight we dropped anchor about half a mile from the shore; Rooney's men filed noiselessly on deck. Now I realized that the hours we had spent rehearsing the launching of the dory had not been wasted; within twelve minutes, without a word having been spoken, we were all in our places and paddling silently towards the shore.

Fifteen minutes later we ran into the cove we had selected for our landing; we were dismayed to find that the beach was not shingle, as our intelligence had led us to believe, but boulders. The tide was ebbing fast, and if we left the dory on this beach we should be unable to refloat her on our return from the raid. While Reynolds stayed in the boat, to keep her off the rocks, I took the party ashore and established my beach-head at the foot of the cliffs; Rooney went off on a reconnaissance of the cove, in the hope of finding a more suitable beach. He returned ten minutes later to tell me that there was nowhere else possible. The only solution was to leave Reynolds to keep the dory afloat while we made our attack. He accepted the disappointment with his usual good nature. In the end we owed to him our survival.

We formed up in staggered file and began to climb the cliff, myself in the lead, Rooney close behind me; but we soon realized that we could not hope to keep any formation. The track, which had looked so plain in the aerial photographs, did not exist, or, if it did, was invisible in the darkness. We set ourselves to scramble up the face, which I judged was nearly a hundred feet high at this point. It was an arduous climb, for the ascent was almost perpendicular and the cliffs were overgrown with thick gorse bushes whose spikes pierced our clothes and tore our hands and faces; it was alarming too, for the surface was slippery grass and loose shale, which we could not help dislodging with the sound, to our strained ears, of an avalanche.

After twenty minutes we reached the top, where we lay down to look around us and regain our breath. About a hundred yards ahead I could make out a hue of telegraph poles running parallel with the cliff face, indicating the track which led inland from the semaphore station. We made for the track, moving swiftly across the open ground that separated it from the cliff top; we joined it about a hundred and fifty yards away from the barbed wire and the guard-house. I was reflecting with relief that at least we had encountered no mines or booby-traps when I saw Rooney staring fixedly at two small notice-boards, one on each side of the track, facing inland. I went to examine them, and read with horror the warning: '*Achtung! Minen.*' Included in the minefields was the route by which we had approached and by which we must return.

I sent Rooney with one of his men to make a close reconnaissance of the defences of the semaphore station. They returned with the gloomy news that the entrance and guard-house were protected by a double line of barbed wire, which also blocked the path, and by two sentries, who seemed very much on the alert. Our best plan seemed to be to work our way across country on the left of the path and try to get through the wire at some distance from the sentries. This, of course, involved the risk of mines; but we had already crossed one advertised minefield without mishap, and so could reasonably hope that the notices were either a bluff or merely warning of an intention to lay mines. Accordingly, after leaving Nicholson with the Bren gun by the path to guard our rear and to serve as a marker for our return, I started to lead the others across the open ground on our left.

We did not get very far. I had covered only a few yards, crouching low and straining my eyes to watch the ground at every step, when I all but trod on a mine. It was laid, with very little attempt at concealment, under a small mound of turf. Abandoning our hopes that the notices might be a bluff, we returned to the path. A frontal attack was the only solution; whatever the risks, they were at least calculable; we must trust to our luck and skill to bring us close enough to the wire to blast our way through it and kill the sentries before the garrison could turn out. Although I knew that Stirling would not blame me if I abandoned the raid at this point, I agreed with Rooney that it would be pusillanimous of us now to return without putting up a fight.

I split the party into three groups, according to my original plan. I took the right side of the path myself, followed by Sergeant Broderson with his silent Sten; Rooney, Sergeant Barry, and another N.C.O. were to move along the left side, abreast of me, while the rest followed a dozen yards behind. I was to set the pace; as soon as I dropped to the ground the rest of the party would do the same, after which we would complete the approach on our stomachs. We had rehearsed all this beforehand, and so detailed instructions were unnecessary at this point; Rooney was carrying the No. 6 grenade which was to blow our way through the wire, and he would have to decide when to throw it.

As we padded slowly up the path I was appalled at the stillness of the night. At a hundred yards distance the voices of the sentries sounded unnaturally clear; Sergeant Broderson's breathing pounded like a steam-engine at the back of my neck, and I feared my own must be as loud; but our felt-soled boots and long hours of practice enabled us to tread silently, and as long as the sentries went on talking we could move forward in reasonable safety, although slowly. Whenever they stopped speaking we halted and stood motionless, holding our breath. Thirty paces from them I dropped onto my stomach and, waiting until all the others were down, began to edge forward inch by inch on my elbows and the points of my toes. I halted frequently to listen and peer through the gloom at the line of wire and the silhouette of the guard-house ahead. Those last yards seemed like miles, and it needed all my self-control to move without haste; in that still air the least sound would carry to the sentries' ears and give us away. I was glad to note that Rooney and the others were watching me carefully, coordinating their movements with mine; I could see Rooney's dark bulk on the other side of the track exactly level with me.

When we were ten paces from the sentries we came upon a pair of low posts, one on each side of the track, with a trip-wire hanging loosely between them. I judged that we were unlikely to get any nearer without being heard, but I decided to wait awhile in the hope that the guards might move away on a round of the defences. For a full fifteen minutes we lay there, listening to the lazy drawl of their conversation, punctuated all too frequently by periods of silence when they would peer towards us and listen. The nervous strain inside me grew almost intolerable, sometimes bordering on panic when I thought of the peril of our situation; we must carry on now, for I could never turn my party back under the noses of this watchful pair. Clearly we had no hope of killing them quietly. I remember thinking how good the earth and grass smelt as I pressed my face close to the ground; overhead a lone aircraft beat a leisurely way up the coast; from the direction of Paimpol came the distant sound of a dog barking.

Out of the corner of my eye I saw Rooney make a slight movement; then I heard a distinct metallic click as he unscrewed the top of his No. 6 grenade. The sentries heard it too; they stopped their conversation, and one gave a sharp exclamation. I sensed rather than saw Rooney's arm go up, and braced myself for what I knew was coming. There was a clatter as one of the sentries drew back the bolt of his rifle; then everything was obliterated in a vivid flash as a tremendous explosion shattered the silence of the night. The blast hit me like a blow on the head. From the sentries came the most terrible sounds I can ever remember: from one of them a low, pitiful moaning, from the other bewildered screams of agony and terror, an incoherent jumble of sobs and prayers, in which I could distinguish only the words '*Nicht gut! Nicht gut!*' endlessly repeated. Even in those seconds as I leaped to action I felt a shock of horror that those soft, lazy, drawling voices which had floated to us across the quiet night air could have been turned, literally in a flash, to such inhuman screams of pain and fear.

Though they were to haunt me for a long time, I had no leisure for such thoughts now. In a moment I was floundering through the wire by the guard-house on the heels of Rooney and Sergeant Barry. The wire, mangled by the explosion, was no longer a serious obstacle. A little dog sped out of the open door of the guard-house and ran off into the darkness, giving tongue in shrill, terrified yelps. The guardhouse was empty. The two sentries were sprawled on the ground, one silent with his hands over his face, the other calling on his mother and his Maker until a burst of tommy-gun fire from one of my N.C.O.s quietened him; the grenade must have landed close beside them, for their clothes were terribly burnt.

I wasted no time here, but followed Rooney's party past the guard-house and on to the open courtyard in front of the main building. As I arrived beside Rooney a German loomed up out of the darkness, firing rapidly at us with a small automatic. Rooney and I replied with our .45s, bringing him to his knees; but he courageously continued firing until a burst from Sergeant Barry's tommy-gun finished him off. A door was thrown open in the station building ahead, revealing a light inside and, silhouetted clearly against it, the figure of a man with a sub-machine gun, poised at the top of a flight of steps. He paid for his folly in presenting such a target, because Sergeant Broderson gave him two bursts from the silenced Sten, toppling him forward on his face; as he tried to rise Corporal Howells riddled him with his tommy-gun.

When my rear party arrived I prepared to send half of them round to the back of the station building, while the rest of us stormed the front. But although only a few seconds had passed since we had started the attack, we no longer had the advantage of surprise; the Germans were organizing their defence and, having turned out the lights, began to pour a heavy fire on us from the windows and the open doorway. The garrison was clearly stronger than we had expected. If we stormed the building we should have to cross the open courtyard under heavy fire, with a grave risk of casualties; in any case it was doubtful if we were strong enough to overwhelm the garrison now that they were alert. We had killed four Germans for certain, without loss to ourselves; I decided to disengage now, before I had the added difficulty of carrying wounded through the minefield and down the cliffs.

I shouted the order to withdraw. We raced back across the wire and along the path to the spot where Sergeant Nicholson was waiting impassively with his Bren gun. As we hurried through the minefield I was in a sweat of terror lest we should have a casualty here at the last moment; I do not know how we could have carried a wounded man down those cliffs to the boat. In fact we were lucky, but the descent was dangerous enough as we slid and fell blindly in the gorse-covered gullies leading down to the beach. I was greatly relieved that there were no signs of pursuit from above, although the semaphore station was in an uproar and we could still hear the sound of small-arms fire when we arrived on the beach. The Germans had sent up alarm rockets, and I wondered whether they would have searchlights to intercept us on our way back to the M.T.B.

When we reached the dory I saw how much we owed to Brian Reynolds. While we were away the tide had been going out fast; but for Reynolds the dory would have been left high and dry on the boulders, where she would have been almost impossible to refloat. For two hours he had stood waist-deep in the icy water, holding the boat off the rocks; I wondered that he had any movement left in his legs, but he seemed active enough.

We stumbled to our places in the boat; but when Rooney called the roll there were two men missing. Both had been with us when we started down the cliff, and so presumably they would join us at any moment—unless they had had an accident on the way down, which was not unlikely. As we sat waiting anxiously, a Verey light shot upwards from the cliff top and fell slowly towards the sea, illuminating the bay, the cliffs and ourselves in a vivid magnesium glare. I began to feel desperate. In such a light the Germans could not fail to see us; my stomach contracted as I awaited the spatter of machine-gun bullets that would announce our discovery. There could be no escape for us once we were seen; was I to lose the whole party for the sake of two men, or must we incur the shame of abandoning two of our companions to certain capture and possible death? Fortunately I was not called upon to make the decision: as the last glow from the Verey light faded we heard a clatter on the pebbles; the two missing men heaved themselves painfully over the gunwhale.

There was no need to urge everyone to paddle his hardest. We were three hundred yards off-shore when another Verey light went up from the signal station, lighting up the tense, sweating faces of my companions as though in the glare of footlights. This time, I thought, they're bound to see us, and I waited, almost resigned now, for the hiss and splash of bullets. But once again darkness enveloped us, allowing us to go our way. Reynolds had a pair of very powerful night glasses, with which he had been able to pick out the M.T.B. from the shore; when the second Verey light expired he sent our homing signal—three green flashes from his torch. We were onboard at half past three in the morning, ten minutes after leaving the shore, and received a warm welcome from Appleyard, who had passed an anxious three hours while we were away. As we turned for home two more alarm rockets went up from the semaphore station, followed by another illuminating flare, but we could see no response anywhere along the coast.

During the homeward journey Rooney and I sat huddled miserably in a pool of water on the bottom of the dory, under the flimsy protection of a tarpaulin. I was feeling the reaction from the excitement of the last few hours; although relieved that I had brought our party back intact I could feel no elation at our small success: instead, I could not rid my ears of the terrible screams that had come from the mangled, wounded sentries, or my mind of the grim memory of our return through the minefield and our wait in the dory under the blazing Verey lights. At the same time I could not shake off a nagging, persistent worry that perhaps I had not acted with sufficient resolution; that if I had pressed home my attack instead of giving the order to withdraw we might have made prisoners of the entire garrison.

At seven-twenty, through the half light of dawn, we made our first landfall on Downend Point; an hour later, on a raw, grey morning, we came alongside the quay at Dartmouth, where Stirling was awaiting us with Darby and a formidable escort of Field Security Police. My spirits sank as I saw the latter and wondered how Darby would take the news that we had no prisoners for him. What he said was:

'Go straight back and get some!'

Stirling listened without interruption to my account of the raid. At the end he said:

'You were fully justified in breaking off the action when you did, in view of the score at the time; I will say so in my covering report. It's bad luck that you couldn't take any prisoners, but you must have given the enemy quite a shock, which is one of our objects.'

Revived by an excellent breakfast in the Y.M.C.A. at Paignton, of scrambled eggs and mugs of tea laced with our rum ration, we drove back to Anderson, arriving in time for lunch. I worked all the after-noon and until late in the evening, composing two reports on the raid—a summary which Stirling wanted to show to the Prime Minister, and a detailed account for Combined Operations Headquarters. Appleyard told me later that the Prime Minister made the simple comment, 'Good!'; and so I suppose that honour, at least, was satisfied.

That was the last raid to be carried out by the Small-Scale Raiding Force from a base in England. During the succeeding months a number of operations were planned for us by Stirling; but on each occasion we were thwarted by weather, by lack of ships or by the overriding priority of other operations, such as the landing of agents by sea along the coasts of Normandy and Brittany—in preparation, as we learnt later, for the Allied invasion. After this change in policy our raids, which kept the Germans on the alert, would be more of a hindrance than a help to the grand design.

A few days after our return from the Point de Plouezec, when Rooney and his men had gone on leave, I was ordered by Brigadier Gubbins to take a party of our officers on the parachute course at Ring way. I had been sleeping badly, with terrible nightmares of those screaming sentries, and I was glad of an opportunity to take my mind off the recent raid. The party included Lassen, Warren, and two Anglo-French officers who were booked to go with John Gwynne on an intelligence mission into France. I was particularly glad, because it was hinted that there might be a parachute operation for me afterwards. Lassen had mixed feelings; on the one hand he was keen to learn about parachuting, on the other he loathed all courses of instruction.

'Tell me, Peter,' he asked nervously when I explained about Dunham Massey, 'is it a much-bullshit place?'

Remembering the report I had received at the end of my last course, I was determined this time to make a favourable impression on Major Edwards. I therefore took particular care to be in time for meals, for parades, and even for early morning P.T.; moreover, with shameless hypocrisy I gave my party short talks on the importance of punctuality. I was rewarded for my sycophancy with a report which concluded: 'He is not entirely the irresponsible officer that he appears at first sight.' I was disappointed in my hopes of a parachute operation. In fact, the only person with the prospect of any action for the moment was John Gwynne. He refused, quite rightly, to give us any details of his proposed mission beyond the fact that it was not planned by Stirling and had nothing to do with Combined Operations Headquarters. He spent much of his time away from Anderson visiting various S.O.E. experimental stations, in particular one concerned with camouflage. He reappeared at the end of his tour with two unusual pieces of equipment. One of them was a lifelike cow's head mask in *papier mâché* with holes pierced through the eyes; the other was a curious arrangement of fine-meshed camouflage netting. He was good enough to reveal to us their purpose. The mask was for road-watching: in other words, he would lie up in a field beside a main road and push his head, enveloped in the mask, through the hedge; thus disguised, he would be able to keep a watch on the road and observe the number and nature of enemy troops using it. The purpose of the netting was even simpler.

'It enables a man to disguise himself at will,' explained Gwynne, 'as a rubbish heap or pile of sticks.'

Not all the products of the extensive research organization maintained by S.O.E. were camouflaged exclusively for protection; almost the whole range of children's joke toys was exploited for some destructive purpose. For instance, imitation turds of horse or camel dung contained small explosive charges which would destroy the tyres of any vehicle that drove over them; and sickeningly realistic dead rats, apparently in the later stages of decomposition, were dropped by the gross over occupied Europe to be smuggled into German barrack rooms and offices. Anyone picking them up by the tail—the natural method when throwing them away—would automatically release a pin, exploding a small but lethal charge.

We were concerned with Gwynne's operation only in that the Small-Scale Raiding Force was to transport Gwynne and his party over to the Brittany coast and provide an escort in case they ran into trouble on landing; once they were safely ashore we should return to England. In early December I spent a week at Paignton with a party including Appleyard, Ogden Smith, Lassen, and Warren, waiting for a chance to land them in France. Once again, however, the weather defeated us, and we all returned in disappointment to Anderson. And so went out the year 1942.

Early in 1943 Stirling conceived the plan of transferring the bulk of the Small-Scale Raiding Force to North Africa, where there were plenty of opportunities for the amphibious operations we were no longer allowed to carry out across the Channel. Among those he took with him were Appleyard, Lassen, Dudgeon, and Philip Pinckney of No. 12 Commando. Together they formed the Second Special Air Service Regiment, following in the footsteps of Stirling's brother, David, who had founded the First S.A.S. in 1941. Operating first from Tunisia, later in Italy, and finally in France, they expanded their activities to include parachute as well as sea-borne raids. They achieved a number of brilliant successes, but at the cost of some of their most valuable lives. Appleyard was killed in Sicily, Pinckney and Lassen in Italy, Dudgeon in France.

Among those who stayed behind with me were Reynolds, Ogden Smith, and the Dutchman, Brinkgreve. After an uneventful and frustrating four months of inactivity we split up towards the end of April. The death of Reynolds I have already recorded. Ogden Smith was parachuted into Brittany with a sabotage party in June 1944; surrounded in a farm-house by a large force of S.S., he and his few companions put up a stout fight for four hours, until they were all killed or incapacitated by wounds. The survivors were shot out of hand by the S.S. In Holland a similar fate overtook poor Brinkgreve.

V

TO THE WILDER SHORES OF WAR

One morning in the middle of May 1943 I was sitting in an office in Baker Street, talking to Lieutenant-Colonel James Pearson, who had been in my troop at Weedon. He had recently returned from a staff appointment in Cairo to take up a post in London concerned with S.O.E. operations in the Balkans.

'We're looking for officers,' he told me, 'who would be prepared to parachute into Greece and Jugoslavia to work with the guerrilla forces there. Would that interest you? If so, which country would you prefer?'

Apart from a brief visit to Greece during my first long vacation from Cambridge, I knew very little about the Balkans; Pearson explained that the present need for British Liaison Officers was greater in Jugoslavia, and so I asked to be sent there. Parachute operations into the Balkans were controlled from Cairo; I should be flown to Egypt about the end of the month. I spent the next three weeks in a basement office in Baker Street, learning about the political and military situation inside the country, reading reports and telegrams from British Liaison Officers already in the field and listening to the views of two of Pearson's staff officers, Major Boughey and Captain Uren.

Hitherto I had believed that Jugoslav resistance centered around General Draža Mihailović and the guerrilla bands, known in the British Press as Chetniks, who had taken to the mountains under his leadership after the German invasion in the spring of 1941. Now I knew that there was another guerrilla leader in the country, a shadowy figure called Tito, who, after the entry of Russia into the war, had rallied the Communists and their sympathizers and taken to the hills in arms against the Germans. For a few months the supporters of Tito and Mihailović had worked together, although with mutual suspicion, for they were fundamentally opposed in outlook and objectives. By the end of 1941 their hostility to each other had flared into open warfare, so that their efforts were wasted in internecine strife. Now British Liaison Officers were being dropped to both sides in the hope of persuading them to concentrate on fighting the Germans rather than each other. Although Mihailović still enjoyed the official support of the British Government, Tito was not without friends in S.O.E.: one staff officer, in fact, so far allowed his enthusiasm to exceed his discretion that he was subsequently tried and convicted under the Official Secrets Act for passing confidential information to the Soviet Embassy in London.

In Boughey's office I met my friend John Bennett, whom I had last seen on the barrack square at Weedon. In June 1940 Bennett had been sent to Belgrade, where he had remained to do valuable work for the Allies until the German invasion in April 1941. For the next two years he had been in charge of the Jugoslav Country Section of S.O.E. in Cairo, a post which he had just left when I met him. When I told him where I was going he shook his head gloomily.

'I don't think you'll enjoy it there; or be able to do anything useful. Nobody can stop this ghastly civil war now. I think you'd prefer Greece. Better still, why don't you try to get into Albania? It's a wonderful country, wonderful people, ideal for guerrilla operations and no civil war. So far as I know we haven't anybody there now, but we ought to have. You'll see Archie Lyall in Cairo, he added. 'Archie should be able to give you a good idea of what goes on in those countries.'

'How did he do in Belgrade?'

'He certainly livened the place up. I remember once the Embassy told him to entertain a delegation of Bishops from England. Archie took them to about the lowest night-club in the place, where the high-spot of the evening is a girl dancing the belly dance. I don't suppose you've ever seen the belly dance, but you can take my word for it that it's all its name implies. Nothing is left to the imagination. The audience applauds the dancer's contortions by shouting "*Mešaj!*" which means, literally, "Mix it!" '

Tired and dirty, in a sticky, crumpled uniform, and sweating in the unaccustomed heat of Cairo, I climbed out of the lorry which had brought me from the airport and walked stiffly up the steps of Shepheards Hotel; I had asked to be taken to Shepheards because it was the only place in Cairo I knew by name. Cringing beneath the supercilious glances of the cool, immaculate officers and their girl friends who were having tea on the terrace, I went straight to the telephone and called a number I had been given in Baker Street; then, as I had been told, I asked to speak to 'Mr. Rose' and gave my name. Having thus established my identity I was told to take a taxi to G.H.Q., where I would be collected.

In Rustum Buildings, the headquarters of M.O.4, as our organization was named in Egypt, I reported to Captain Ionides of the Jugoslav Country Section. He gave me the disappointing news that there was no hope of my being dropped into Jugoslavia in the next moon period, which was in a fortnights time, because all vacancies were already filled; I should therefore have to wait until August. These parachute operations, unlike those of the Small-Scale Raiding Force, could take place only in moonlight, because it was difficult to locate the target in that mountainous region. In the interval, Ionides said, I could stay in his houseboat on the Nile, and occupy my time in learning Serbo-Croat and studying the situation inside the country. He introduced me to Captain James Klugmann, the Country Section Intelligence Officer.

I was surprised to find Klugmann occupying such a confidential position, because when I had last seen him, in 1936, he had been the secretary and inspiration of the Cambridge University Communists. I had innocently supposed that Communists were strictly excluded from S.O.E., for I myself had been required to sign a declaration that I belonged to no Communist or Fascist party before I was enrolled in the organization. However, among my acquaintances at Cambridge there were a number of young men who had joined the Party in a spirit of idealism, only to leave it after the Soviet-German pact of 1939; I assumed that Klugmann was one of them. But I was wrong: like his contemporary, Guy Burgess, he was one of the hard core and today he is a member of the Politburo of the Communist Party of Great Britain.

Although it was impressed upon me from the moment of my arrival in Cairo that when I went into the field I must regard myself simply as a soldier, whose task would be the prosecution of military operations to the exclusion of politics, I could not fail to be aware of the strong political differences which divided the staff officers both in London and Cairo. Nowhere were they more evident than in the Jugoslav Section. Boughey in London had maintained that because Mihailović was the representative of the recognized Jugoslav Government he should be given every support; Major Basil Davidson, on the other hand, the head of the Country Section in Cairo, who later distinguished himself in action with partisan forces in Jugoslavia and in Northern Italy, could not conceal his antipathy to the Chetniks. He wanted me to sign a declaration that I had been subjected in London to indoctrination on behalf of Mihailović; I refused, but the incident warned me of the sort of feeling that was to embitter relations between British officers in the field as well as at headquarters.

With the end of the fighting in North Africa, Cairo had relaxed in an atmosphere of untroubled gaiety; I had plenty of leisure to enjoy it, in the company of Archie Lyall and an old friend from the Spanish Foreign Legion, Bill Nangle. Nangle, who had been a regular officer in the Indian Army before joining the Legion, had at this time just relinquished command of the Indian Squadron of the Long Range Desert Group. He had volunteered for service in the field with S.O.E., but his stubborn refusal to be civil to senior ranks led him to quarrel with the brigadier who controlled the Cairo office, and so he returned to the L.R.D.G. He was killed in action in Italy early the following year.

Lyall had escaped from Jugoslavia, carrying a diplomatic bag to Athens, before the German invasion began. Afterwards he had worked for nearly a year with the S.O.E. organization in Cairo and Jerusalem before returning to Cairo as a major in the Balkan Section of Political Warfare Executive.

He shared John Bennett's pessimism about the future of operations in Jugoslavia, and feared the prospects were no better in Greece.

'I should try for Albania, Peter,' he advised. 'At least the situation there is uncomplicated by civil war. We have two first-class men in there at the moment, Bill McLean and David Smiley, both personal friends of mine. I can't think of a better party for you to join.'

We discussed the failure of S.O.E. preparations against the Germans in Rumania, Bulgaria, Jugoslavia, and Greece before those countries became involved in the war. They had cost us some valuable lives and a great deal of money without inflicting appreciable damage on the enemy.

'I once thought of designing a coat of arms for S.O.E.,' he mused. 'It was to be something like this: Surmounted by an unexploded bomb a cloak and dagger casually left in a bar sinister. The arms supported by two double agents. The motto: "*Nihil quod tetigit non made a balls of it*".'

A day or two later Ionides called me to his office.

'Look, you've a chance of going in during this moon period after all, if you don't mind going to Albania. They're looking for officers at the moment. Come with me now and I'll introduce you to the head of the Section.'

The Albanian Section at that time consisted of two officers, Major Philip Leake and Mrs. Hasluck. The former, a schoolmaster in civilian life, had held an important post with S.O.E. in West Africa in 1941, when March-Phillipps and Appleyard were there with *Maid Honor*, and had worked with them on several operations. A gentle, kindly person with a nice sense of humour, a dry, cynical wit and that 'transcendent capacity of taking trouble' which Carlyle equated with genius, he was a most capable staff officer, well fitted for his post as head of the Cinderella of the Balkan Country Sections.

Mrs. Hasluck, a grey, bird-like woman who made up in energy and determination what she lacked in patience, was an anthropologist who had entered Albania in 1919 and settled near Elbasan in the centre of the country. Until her expulsion by the Italians twenty years later she had lived there very happily, winning the trust of the people and the friendship of many of their leaders. Thereafter she had organized an Albanian office for S.O.E. in Athens and Istanbul, before coming to Cairo to work with Philip Leake. Because of her love for Albania she regarded us B.L.O.s with special affection; we were 'her boys', and when we were in the field we would often receive signals from her, directing our attention to some nearby beauty spot where we could enjoy a picnic.

Among her publications was an English-Albanian grammar, which we were required to study; alas, it was of little use to most of us, who found it scarcely more intelligible than the language it was meant to interpret. Indeed Albanian, which is supposed to be derived from ancient Illyrian, must be one of the most difficult of European languages to learn. Few of us managed to learn it, which was a great hindrance to our work in the field; unable to converse directly with the inhabitants we were nearly always dependent upon interpreters, whom we could trust neither to render faithfully our own words nor to give us a true picture of local reactions.

Most of our knowledge of the current situation in Albania came from signals which McLean and Smiley had sent since their arrival in the country. Dropped to a British headquarters in Epirus during the previous April, their party—known in code as 'Consensus Mission'—had walked across the Albanian frontier about the end of the month, with no knowledge of what they would find on the other side. In the first week of May they were able to establish contact with Albanian guerrillas and set up their wireless. Before describing the situation as they found it I must briefly trace the course of Albanian politics in recent years.[1]

Albania within its present frontiers is about the size of Wales; by far the greater part of it is mountainous. It is a poor country, where under-nourishment is general among the peasantry, who suffer much from tuberculosis in the mountains and from malaria in the marshy coastal plains. The Albanians, or Shqypëtars, as they are properly called, are, in the words of *Chambers's Encyclopedia*, 'the remains of a race which inhabited the Balkan peninsula at the dawn of history, and are of pure Aryan stock.' In spite of nearly five hundred years of Ottoman rule, followed by the frequent attempts of neighbouring powers to absorb their country, they still retain a strong sense of nationality. The race is subdivided into two branches—the Ghegs in the North, the Tosks in the South—speaking slightly different variants of the same language. The river Shkumbi, impassable in winter, divides the two. At this time the social structure in the north was tribal, resembling that of the Scottish highlands before the Forty-five; in the south a rich landowning aristocracy exploited a landless peasantry which since the beginning of Turkish rule had been allowed neither the security of wealth nor the dignity of freedom.

There are three religions in the country, generally confined within geographical limits: in the south the majority of the peasantry is Greek Orthodox, though the land-owning *Beys* are Moslem; the centre and plains are predominantly Moslem, while the north is divided between the Catholic mountaineers of Mirdita and Djukagjin, and the Moslems of Kossovo and the wild north-eastern frontier. But religious differences seemed to be of little importance in comparison with the rivalry of Gheg and Tosk and the age-long hatred of both for their Slav and Greek neighbours.

---

[1] For a fuller account than I am able to give here I would refer readers to Julian Amery's classic study in guerrilla warfare, *Sons of the Eagle* (Macmillan, 1948). pp. 1-71, where they will find a clear, detailed and objective account of Albanian politics and tribal structure, to which I gladly acknowledge my own debt.)

At the end of the Balkan Wars the Ambassadors' Conference of 1913 recognized Albania as an independent State, delineating for it frontiers which were acceptable neither to the Albanians nor to their neighbours. Those boundaries, which were confirmed by the Great Powers in 1926, condemned nearly a million Albanians to live under Greek and Serb rule, without abating the claims of the Serbs and Greeks to most of the rest of Albania; the majority of these irredentist Albanians lived in Kossovo, the borderland between Serbia and north-eastern Albania, a rich and fertile country considered by Albanians to be their natural granary. Nevertheless, Serbia's claim to Kossovo, based on grounds of history and tradition, prevailed over racial and economic considerations.

During the First World War the Albanians, impelled by their hatred of Serbia and Montenegro, contributed troops to the Austrian Army, while various parts of the country were occupied by Serb, French, and Italian forces. The Peace was followed by a period of internal unrest, which was settled, at least nominally, in December 1924, when Ahmed Bey Zogu, subsequently known as King Zog, seized supreme power with the help of the Jugoslav Government and the support of Gheg tribesmen from Kossovo and his own territory of Mati, north of Tirana. Zog, who was not yet thirty when he assumed power, had learnt the art of government in his youth in Constantinople under the tutelage of the Sultan Abdul Hamid. Playing off his rivals against each other, resorting to methods not always applauded by western democracies and relying on a competent gendarmerie trained by British officers, he ruled without interruption for more than fourteen years.

Although he had won his throne with Jugoslav aid, it was upon Italian financial and technical support that he depended during the years of his rule. Albania's foreign policy, the development of her communications and mineral resources, her currency, commerce and education were directly or indirectly under Italian control. So strong was this influence that during my travels throughout the country, from south to north, there were few villages, even in the mountains, where I was unable to exchange a few words of Italian. But Zog was too independent a character to suit Mussolini's imperial ambitions; he retained in his own hands the internal administration of the country, refused to dismiss the British Mission under General Sir Jocelyn Percy and Colonel Frank Stirling which trained and led his gendarmerie, and generally obtained more concessions from the Italians than he gave away. This situation came to an end with the Italian invasion of Albania on Good Friday, 1939. King Zog and Queen Geraldine escaped to Greece with their infant son. Only in the port of Durazzo did the Italians meet organized resistance; there a battalion of gendarmerie and a few tribal levies resisted for thirty-six hours the assault of two divisions supported by heavy naval bombardment. The Albanian Army officer who directed this gallant action was Major Abas Kupi, a stocky, granite-faced, illiterate Gheg from Krujë in the Mati country—the fortress where the national hero, Skanderbeg, raised his revolt against the Turks in the fifteenth century. After the battle Abas Kupi was smuggled by his followers out of the country to Istanbul. Two years later he was back in the mountains of Mati, where he carried on a guerrilla war against the Italians and their German successors until the end of 1944, when he was overrun and driven into exile by the Communists who now dominate his country.

In the summer of 1940, after Italy had entered the war, S.O.E. began to organize from Belgrade an Albanian resistance movement. Foremost amongst its promoters were Colonel Frank Stirling, Lieutenant-Colonel Oakley-Hill—an ex-instructor to the Albanian gendarmerie and a fluent Albanian speaker—and Julian Amery. Recruited from Albanian exiles living in Jugoslavia and from Kossovar irredentists its leaders were Gani, Saïd, and Hasan Kryeziu—three brothers from an influential Kossovar family—Abas Kupi, who had been brought from Istanbul by Stirling, and Mustafa Gjinishi, a leading Communist with a flair for propaganda. Previously the Kryezius had been bitter enemies of Zog and his lieutenant, Abas Kupi, for they believed that Zog had ordered the murder of their eldest brother, Cena Beg, in 1927. But now both parties were prepared to forget their differences and even to ally themselves with the Communists, whom both detested, in the interests of their country.

On 7th April, 1941, immediately after the German invasion of Jugoslavia, Kupi, the Kryezius, and Gjinishi, accompanied by Oakley-Hill led a force of some three hundred Kossovars over the border into Albania. At first the Moslem tribesmen rallied to them, and they advanced westwards towards Scutari, defeating several Italian patrols on the way; but the Catholic clans, who enjoyed a privileged position under the Italians, gave them no support. After the collapse of Jugoslavia even their Moslem allies deserted them. Italian armies occupied the province of Kossovo, which the Axis powers formally incorporated into Albania, thus winning the sympathy of Albanians and Kossovars alike. Within a week Oakley-Hill and his friends were fugitives. He tried to escape to Istanbul with the help of the Kryezius, but the plan miscarried and he was forced into hiding in Belgrade. At length, fearful of the risk he was bringing on his friends, he gave himself up to the Germans.

The leading Albanian conspirators—they were later to become my friends and associates—now scattered in flight. Gani and Saïd Kryeziu were betrayed to the Italians, who imprisoned them in a concentration camp for political offenders on the island of Ventotene; Hasan, who had taken no part in politics before the war, returned to his large estates in Kossovo, where he remained unmolested, but by no means idle, until the end of 1943; Abas Kupi escaped to the Mati country, and Mustafa Gjinishi made his way southward to his native town of Korçë, near the Greek frontier, where he made contact with the principal Albanian Communist leaders.

It was two years before S.O.E. again turned its attention to military operations in Albania. In the meantime such scraps of information as came out of the country were collated by Mrs. Hasluck in her Istanbul office and passed on to Cairo. There was not very much information, but what there was, combined with rumours coming from Jugoslavia, indicated that there were armed bands, or *çetas*, in the Albanian mountains; of the nature of these bands, their politics, location and activities there was little known.

In consequence of the Allied victory in North Africa and the approaching invasion of Italy, S.O.E. began to take a more serious interest in Albania, if only because of the importance to the Axis of her lines of communication. 'Consensus' Mission was therefore dispatched with the primary task of reporting on the situation and strength of the Albanian guerrillas and their potential value to the Allies. From the information they sent out a much clearer picture emerged.

After the outbreak of war between Russia and Germany, the Communists in Albania, as in other Balkan countries, took to the hills for safety. Having established a comparatively secure base in the mountains between Korçë and Gjinokaster they began to form partisan *çetas*, recruited partly from the landless peasantry of the countryside, partly from the young intelligentsia of the towns. Probably their original instructions came from Tito, who maintained two representatives with the Albanian Communist committee; I was to meet these sinister gentlemen, Dušan Mugoša (alias Ali Gostivari) and Miladin Popović, and to note the respect, bordering on veneration, in which they were held by their Albanian colleagues.

Following the general practice, the Partisan leaders declined to call themselves Communists. Their movement, they pretended, was a 'democratic' movement which all who held 'democratic' views were welcome to join. Its true nature, which we came to learn in time, is best described in Julian Amery's own words:[1]

'In practice, exclusive control of the movement was retained in the hands of a small committee, all of whom were Communists. This committee, besides directing policy, appointed the guerrilla commanders, the political commissars, and the regional organizers. The former were most often, and the two latter invariably, Communists; while, in accordance with the best conspiratorial traditions, all three were kept under observation by Party members who held no official position at all. By these methods, seconded by the salutary liquidation of those who disobeyed or disagreed, the Partisan

---

[1] *Sons of the Eagle*, p. 54.

movement presently achieved a degree of discipline and cohesion of which few observers believed Albanians to be capable.[1]

As Amery goes on to point out, the Partisan movement drew its strength entirely from the Tosks. North of the Shkumbi there was little support for Communism; there were, however, various guerrilla groups with which the Communists, for reasons of prestige, wished to ally themselves. Most powerful of these was Abas Kupi with his Mati tribesmen; next in importance was the veteran outlaw, Myslim Peza, who controlled the scrub-covered, malarial hills southwest of Tirana, and who for the past ten years had been defying the central authority; lastly, in the mountains of Martanesh, north-east of Tirana, the hard-drinking old Bektashi abbot, Baba Faja, a bitter enemy of the Italians, commanded a powerful *Çeta*.

The skilful diplomacy, personal charm and evident sincerity of Mustafa Gjinishi were largely responsible for persuading these three chieftains to join the Partisan movement; a conference between all the guerrilla leaders was held at Peza in September 1942, as a result of which their various groups were amalgamated in a single 'National Liberation Movement', subsequently known as the L.N.C. from the initial letters of its Albanian name. The movement was controlled by a Central Council of ten members, predominantly Communist but including the three Gheg chieftains.

This was a triumph for the Communists: it disarmed the suspicions of those who feared the political affiliations of their movement, for it was now clear that the L.N.C. included known anti-Communists; secondly, it enabled them to extend their influence among the Ghegs and to infiltrate their own supporters into the forces of Myslim Peza and Baba Faja, who soon became mere Communist puppets. Abas Kupi alone refused to allow any Communist penetration or to accept Communist nominees in positions of responsibility; although he served on the L.N.C. Council and collaborated in battle with Partisan units, he kept the control of his forces firmly in his own hands.

There was another resistance movement in southern Albania, known as the Balli Kombëtar, or National Front. Recruited largely from local landowners and their retainers, from merchants, teachers and professional men, and from the non-Communist intelligentsia of the towns, the Ballists viewed the L.N.C. with fear and suspicion. The founder of the party was the venerable statesman, Midhat Bey Frasheri, an outstanding figure in the struggle for Albanian independence during the early years of the century; its leaders included some of the ablest politicians in the country. As convinced Republicans the Ballists were opponents of King Zog, but as staunch nationalists they were enemies of the Italians, although they did not take the field against them until the end of 1942. They were lukewarm in their support

---

[1] Communist tactics are, of course, more widely understood today than they were in 1943.

of the British, for they feared, rightly as it proved, that an allied victory would result at best in the loss of Kossovo, at worst in Communist domination of their country. Moreover, they were especially handicapped in undertaking guerrilla operations by the fact that many of their supporters lived in villages near the main roads, where they and their families were peculiarly vulnerable to reprisals. Nevertheless, in order to justify their demands for arms and money they would on occasion go into action against the Italians.

Thus, at the time when McLean's mission entered Albania there were two separate resistance movements in the south of the country, each viewing the other with suspicion, often inflamed to hostility. For a few months after the fall of Mussolini there seemed to be a chance that the two movements would sink their differences for the duration of the war, in a common effort against the Italians. On the initiative of Abas Kupi and Mustafa Gjinishi delegates from the L.N.C. and Balli Kombëtar met in conference at the village of Mukaj, near Tiranë, and agreed to a truce. This triumph of patriotic moderation was shortlived. The extreme Communists, who really directed the policy of the L.N.C., disapproved of compromise, and had only acquiesced in the meeting for fear of offending Abas Kupi; nor did the leaders of the Balli Kombëtar, in their deep distrust of the Communists, put any faith in the agreement.

It gradually became apparent that the arms and money which S.O.E. was dropping so lavishly into Albania were being conserved by L.N.C. and Balli Kombëtar alike for use against each other. In our briefing it was repeatedly impressed on us that, unlike B.L.O.s in Greece and Jugoslavia, we were going to be dropped to an area, not to a faction; we were to ignore politics and consider ourselves only as soldiers, lending our support impartially to any groups or parties in our area that were prepared to fight the enemy. These instructions, which seemed clear and logical to us in Cairo, were to prove quite unrealistic in the field.

My hopes of dropping into Albania during July were disappointed. I was about to leave when, with my peculiar genius for anticlimax, I fell ill with a sudden and crippling attack of gout, which put me into hospital for a fortnight; by the time I was able to walk again the July moon period was over.

At this time S.O.E. parachute operations were launched from Derna; I arrived there in the first week of August after a hot and crowded train journey of twenty-four hours across the desert to Tobruk, followed by an eight-hour lorry ride. We lived comfortably enough in a camp on top of the escarpment overlooking the shell-battered white buildings of Derna and the brassy sea beyond; half a mile up the road was the aerodrome, where a squadron of Halifaxes, commanded by an old school-friend of mine, Wing-Commander Jimmy Blackburn, waited to carry us to our different destinations in the Balkans.

There were four parties, including my own, going to Albania this month; each of the other three consisted of an officer, a wireless operator, and an N.C.O. who was supposed to be an expert in demolitions and sabotage operations. By far the eldest—and the toughest—of us was Major Tilman, commanding 'Sculptor' Mission. Short and stocky, with a prominent nose and chin and a small fierce moustache, he was an experienced and enthusiastic mountaineer who had taken part in the last pre-war Everest expedition; he had volunteered for Albania, he informed us, in order to keep himself in practice for his next Himalayan attempt. He took not the slightest interest in politics, and so, while he was always glad to blow up a bridge or ambush a convoy, his passion for climbing and the frequent opportunities to indulge it left him happily impervious to the bitter quarrels between the different Albanian factions.

Less fortunate in this respect was Major Gerry Field, in command of 'Sapling' Mission; a serious-minded and enthusiastic officer, he had a positive aversion to political controversy and all who engaged in it. He was particularly unlucky, therefore, to be sent to the Valona area where L.N.C. and Balli Kombëtar were expending all their energies in civil strife, in which they were aggressively determined to involve him.

Major George Seymour, Royal Scots Fusiliers, who commanded 'Sconce' Mission, was, like Tilman and Field, a regular soldier. After five gay years of regimental service in India before the war, he had been through some grim experiences in the Western Desert, culminating in the Battle of Alamein, where he had commanded a company of the Argylls under Colonel Lorne Campbell, V.C., and had been severely wounded by a land mine. Although imbued with a professional distaste for politics and politicians he was prepared to tackle both when necessary, confident that they held no problems which could not be solved by an officer with a gentleman's education, a Sandhurst training, and a sound knowledge of King's Regulations.

Tall and thin in appearance, he had the manner of a military dandy of Crimean days, enriched by a vast handlebar moustache which always reminded me of those anglers' stories of 'the one that got away'.

In my own party, which bore the code name of 'Stepmother', I had as paramilitary expert Sergeant Gregson Allcott, R.A.F., a gentle, soft-spoken young man from Eastbourne; my wireless operator, Corporal Roberts, had dropped in the previous month. Although destined for different parts of the country, our four missions were to be dropped together to McLean and Smiley at the village of Shtyllë in the mountains about ten miles south-west of Korçë. We were to take off in two aircraft, Tilman and Field with their parties in one, Seymour and I in the other.

We passed our days in supervising the packing of our kit, choosing our maps, and studying our operational briefs, and our evenings in drinking, dart-playing, and writing letters. We were allowed to take with us one container of personal clothing and equipment, including any special weapons for our own use; I was taking a Colt .45 automatic and a new type of sub-machine gun, named the Welgun after the S.O.E. experimental station where it was designed. The main load of each aircraft would consist of supplies for McLean and Smiley—chiefly explosives, arms, clothing, and money; the money was in gold sovereigns and Napoleons, for gold was at this time the only readily negotiable currency in the Balkans.

Our operational instructions were drafted in the broadest terms. They bade us, quoting from my own, 'kill Germans and Italians, to lower by every possible means their morale, to contain their forces; to ascertain the requirements in arms and supplies of the Albanian *çetas* resisting the enemy and to give every possible encouragement to all parties, irrespective of politics, who were prepared to co-operate against the enemy; to collect as much intelligence as possible, both political and military'. Reading this last sentence I was reminded that the *Encyclopedia Britannica* listed the word 'intelligence' under three headings: 1. Human; 2. Animal; 3. Military.

An unsatisfactory though necessary feature of our letter-writing was that we were forbidden to give any indication where we were going or what we were about to do. An anxious wife or mother could have gained little satisfaction from such stereotyped phrases as 'I am about to go on active operations in the field and I shall be unable to communicate with you for some time. My headquarters will keep you informed of my health and safety,' which was about all we were allowed to say. While we were in Albania we could hope to receive mail whenever supplies were dropped to us, but of course we could send nothing out. We were, however, told to leave the names and addresses of our next-of-kin and of any other friends or relatives we chose; the Welfare Section of our Cairo office would keep in touch with them by a regular series of formal telegrams, assuring them of our safety and health and, in varying degrees, of our affection. Unfortunately, in the course of time and with the transfer of the Cairo office to Italy the telegrams were sometimes misdirected, occasionally with catastrophic results. A certain officer, arriving back in Italy after six months in Albania, complained to a colleague:

'I don't so much mind that they've divorced me from my wife, but damn it, they've engaged me to another girl!'

The outlines of the Halifaxes ranged by the runway looked like monstrous black locusts against the angry light of the dying sun; the ground shook from the thunder of their warming engines, the grass around them was flattened by the slip-streams. As Seymour and I walked towards them from the station buildings an aircraft carrying a party bound for Bosnia began to taxi, gathered speed and floated into the air above the escarpment; a moment later it turned northward over the sea. Beside our own Halifax stood our dispatcher, a cheerful, fresh-faced young corporal. Telling us to follow him he climbed a short ladder under the belly near the tail, leading through a narrow aperture into the reeking metal interior of the fuselage. When the ladder was removed and the hatch closed I experienced a terrifying moment of claustrophobia at the thought of being trapped within that narrow, windowless shell, a feeling of suffocation which lasted until we were airborne.

It was the night of 10th August. Having fitted our parachutes earlier in the day we need not put them on for at least another three hours, and so we could enjoy a certain freedom of movement in the aircraft. We crowded into the fore part of the fuselage for take-off, but afterwards settled ourselves comfortably among the soft bales of blankets and clothing. These bales were known as 'free drops', as distinct from the containers which required parachutes and were carried in the bomb bays. When we had climbed to our cruising height the roar of the engines softened to an even purr, the vibration eased and, stretched among the blankets in the heated, dimly lit belly of the Halifax I fell asleep. . . .

The dispatcher shook me awake.

'You'll be putting on parachutes in about half an hour, sir. The Skipper wondered if you'd like to go forward to the flight deck for a look around.'

Ten thousand feet below us the coast line of Epirus rose white in the moonlight from an indigo sea. It was a clear and lovely night 'clad in the beauty of a thousand stars'. In a few minutes we should be crossing the coast, turning inland towards Korçë and our dropping zone.

'We can be thankful for this,' said the pilot, following my gaze downwards. 'That dropping zone is in a narrow valley with some nasty hills around. I shouldn't fancy going down through cloud to look for the fires. You'd better get back now. Good luck to you!'

The dispatcher helped us on with our parachutes, clipped each static line to the steel wire running along the roof of the fuselage and pushed the metal safety-pin through the clip, thus ensuring that the clip was not torn from the wire by the weight of the parachutist's body as he left the aircraft. Before the introduction of the safety-pin there had been some nasty accidents. We had already arranged the order of our dropping. On the first run-in the aircraft would loose the containers and the 'free-drops'; she would then make a complete circuit and drop us in two sticks: as senior officer Seymour would go out first, followed by his N.C.O.s, Corporals Smith and Hill; on the next run-in Gregson Allcott would drop, followed immediately by myself; Seymour and I had agreed that, as officers, we ought to be first and last out of the aircraft.

We seated ourselves around the exit hatch in our dropping order; the dispatcher lifted back the covers, letting in the night air to blow chill on our bodies; the roar of the engines struck suddenly at our ears. We had about half an hour to wait before we might expect to sight the signal fires marking our dropping zone. With nothing to distract my mind from contemplation of the immediate future, my spirits began to sink; I wondered how I should withstand mentally and physically whatever stresses and dangers might be awaiting me. For all our study of 'Consensus' signals, Mrs. Hasluck's lectures, and such few books on Albania as had come our way I felt that it was into an utterly unknown country that we were about to launch ourselves; nor could I imagine when or how we should return. It was not so much fear that coloured my thoughts as gloom.

A shout from the dispatcher, who had been talking on the intercom, brought me back to the present.

'We've sighted the fires! We're going to circle now to make the first run-in. Remember, when your turn comes to drop don't watch the signal lights, watch my hand. I'll raise it when the red conies on for Action Stations. As soon as I drop it, you go. I repeat—don't bother about the lights. And remember this is a four-engined kite—so brace yourselves for quite a punch from the slip-stream. We'll be dropping you from a thousand feet, so you'll have plenty of time to look around on your way down.'

The floor tilted steeply as the aircraft banked and began to lose height rapidly, pitching sickeningly in the turbulent air; the engines spluttered and flashed as the pilot throttled back for the approach. One of the crew had come aft to help the dispatcher throw out the 'free drops'. The pair of them stood over the hole, their eyes fixed on the two signal lights in the roof above us; neither man was wearing a parachute. The red light flashed on, gleamed steadily for some ten seconds, then changed to green; as the two men hurriedly bundled out the packages I caught a glimpse through the hole of a line of fires flashing past on the ground. When the last package had disappeared the rhythm of the engines swelled as the aircraft rose steeply and began to bank in a wide turn. Sweating, the dispatcher turned to us with a broad smile.

'That's the containers and bundles gone. Now it's your turn!'

Beneath the handlebar moustache Seymour's lips twisted into a sickly grin.

Once again the beat of the engines slowed as we came out of our turn. When the dispatcher's hand went up I gave Seymour what I hoped was a smile of encouragement; but his eyes were fixed on the upraised hand. There was a shout of 'Go!', the hand dropped, and within five seconds Seymour, Smith, and Hill had disappeared through the hole.

'Lovely!' sighed the dispatcher, looking after them.

It seemed to me that the last circuit would never end. Opposite me across the hole sat Gregson Allcott, his hands gripping the side, his feet dangling into space; as soon as his head was clear of the aperture I must swing my legs over the side and follow him, dropping with my back to the direction of the aircraft's flight. Hastily I tried to fix in my mind all the details I had been taught at Ringway—hands pressed to my sides, body stiff, feet and knees together.... Above my head the dispatcher's hand was raised, in those few remaining moments I noticed thankfully that I felt no longer gloomy or afraid; only quite cold and drained of all emotion. I caught the flash of the green light a fraction of a second before I felt the dispatcher's hand come down on my shoulder. Gregson Allcott toppled rather than dropped through the hole. I gave him one second to fall clear, swung my legs over, stiffened, and pushed myself away from the side; I remembered to look up as I dropped.

There were two seconds of nausea when my stomach seemed to leap into my mouth; then something like the fist of a heavy-weight boxer hit me in the small of the back, I felt a violent pull under the armpits and groins and at last I was floating slowly earthwards with a great white canopy billowing above my head. Instead of the rush of air through my ears the only sound was the hum of the Halifax's engines growing fainter in the distance.

The moonlight shone on rocky, scrub-covered hills rising from a long, narrow valley where, immediately below me, flickered a line of small fires. As I drifted lower there came on my ears the sounds of men shouting in the valley, mingled with the faint tinkle of goat-bells from the surrounding hills. I felt as content, even elated, as before I had been sad and frightened. I beamed upon the happy pastoral scene. My complacency was shattered a few moments later when I realized that I was drifting away from the fires, across what seemed to be a dry water-course, towards the side of a mountain...

The next thing I remember, I was standing unsteadily on a piece of sloping, rocky ground, supported on my feet with difficulty by a grinning, dark, shaggy little man; he seemed to my confused mind like a satyr, and I should not have been surprised to see goat-feet, horns and a tail. I tried to collect my wits and remember where I was and to decide whether I was awake or dreaming; my head swam, my eyes seemed unable to focus. The word 'Albania' flickered through my consciousness and I found myself repeating it aloud, to the delight of the satyr, who broke into excited pidgin French:

'*Albanie, oui! Vous êtes en Albanie! Vous venez parachutiste*'—he pointed upwards—'*Vous frappez tête—poum!*' He indicated the rock where I was standing and my parachute and harness strewn upon it. '*Moi*,' he added, tapping his chest, '*Moi Albanais. Moi Stefan.*'

At this moment I heard Seymour's cheerful tones behind me:

'How do you feel, Peter, old boy?'

'What happened?'

'You missed the D.Z. and landed half-way up the hillside. You came an awful smack and hit your head on a rock. It looks as though you've got a bit of concussion. Come along and we'll see if we can get you onto a mule.'

'Would you mind telling me the date?' Somehow it seemed terribly important.

'Certainly! It's nearly midnight, Tuesday, 10th of August, 1943.'

With one of them on either side of me I limped down the hill, over the bed of the watercourse and onto the smooth grass of the valley, where the fires were being doused and all their traces obliterated by the Albanians. On the farther side a bunch of mules were standing, waiting for the containers to be loaded as they were collected from the dropping ground. Hoisting me onto one of the rough wooden pack saddles, Seymour and Stefan led my mule along a narrow track winding towards the eastern end of the valley. After ten minutes we reached the crest of a low col, where we looked down on another, broader valley in which nestled the low white houses of the village of Shtyllë. Approaching up the hill with long, easy strides came a tall, well-built figure in jodhpurs and a wide crimson cummerbund, a fresh-faced young man with long, fair hair brushed back from a broad forehead and wearing a major's crown on the shoulder-straps of his open-necked army shirt. With a charming smile he introduced himself as Bill McLean and bade us welcome to Albania.

'Stefan will take you to our headquarters,' he went on, 'where you'll find the others, as well as some food and drink, which I expect you need. I'll join you as soon as we've finished clearing up the D.Z. Your kit will be collected and brought to you there. Afterwards I'll send somebody to show you where you're sleeping.'

'Consensus' headquarters was in the disused village mosque and school, a single-storey mud and brick building consisting of three large rooms and standing on a low out-crop of rock which overlooked the valley to the south-east. In the largest room, lit by oil lamps and candles, was a long trestle table laden with plates of hot food, bottles of Italian champagne and brandy and flasks of red chianti—brought from Korçë, it was explained to me, by McLean's Albanian couriers on their biweekly visits to the town. Seated at the table on old ammunition boxes and empty parachute containers were members of McLean's headquarters staff, busily entertaining Field, Tilman and their parties. I was glad to hear that I was the only casualty of the evening's drop, although Gerry Field had achieved the remarkable if not unique distinction of being sick in the air on his way down; it must have been a distressing experience, for it seemed that he descended quicker than his vomit.

By this time I was feeling very sick myself; and so after swallowing two or three mugs of hot sweet tea I asked to be shown my bed. Led by Stefan and accompanied by Seymour, who was sharing my lodgings, I climbed the hill to a small wooden house, where an old woman led us into a narrow, low-ceilinged room; there were two mattresses covered with blankets on the floor. Within five minutes I was asleep.

VI

PARTISANS AND PARASITES

For the next thirty-six hours I slept almost continuously. On the morning of Thursday, 12th August, I awoke feeling refreshed and fit again. After a breakfast of hot sweetened milk and maize bread I walked down to the mosque to report to McLean.

If ever an officer could be described as having, in the colloquialism of the time, a 'good war' that officer was Bill McLean. Entering the Army through Eton and Sandhurst he was commissioned in the Scots Greys in 1939 and was serving with them in Palestine when the war broke out. During the Abyssinian campaign he commanded a battalion of Amhara irregulars, with which he inflicted heavy casualties on the Italians. Now, in his twenty-fifth year, he was commander of the British Mission in Albania, one of the most responsible military appointments in the Balkans. Gifted with outstanding qualities of imagination, leadership, courage and endurance he hid beneath a nonchalant and charming personality a shrewd and ruthless mind.

Captain David Smiley, his second-in-command, had left the morning we arrived to lay an ambush on the main road from Korçë to Yannina with a Balli Kombëtar *Çeta*; but in the mosque I found the Sapper, Lieutenant Garry Duffy. A spare dark young man with a serious cast of expression, Duffy was a very brave and competent officer with an uncanny skill at demolitions and the laying of mines—his two chief interests in life. The other British members of headquarters staff were Sergeant Williamson, McLean's wireless operator, Sergeant Jenkins, a big, bloodthirsty paramilitary expert who had dropped in a month previously, and Sergeant Jones, his inseparable companion who lived in the same street in Liverpool. With them I also met my own wireless operator, Corporal Roberts, a quiet young man, brave and intelligent, in whom I soon grew to have great confidence. Squadron-Leader Neel and Flight-Lieutenant Hands, who had dropped to McLean in July, had already left for the north.

McLean had collected a number of camp followers, some of them Albanians, others Italian deserters; there was a carpenter, an armourer, and several Italian cooks, batmen, and house-servants. More important—for security in guerrilla warfare is vitally dependent on mobility—he had hired a band of Vlach muleteers to look after his pack transport. These Rumanian nomads were exceptionally skilled in the management of mules; they were not particularly honest but were expert in the performance of their contractual duties, which they insisted did not include fighting or the exposure of themselves to danger. There were also three Albanian interpreters: Stefan, who had rescued me when I landed—in the daylight he looked splendidly farouche with a pair of fierce black moustaches; Stiljan Biçi, a gentle, timid youth who spoke excellent French; and, dominating them both—indeed dominating all the Albanians in our camp—the sinister figure of Frederick Nosi. Nephew of the respected elder statesman, Lef Nosi, this young man, still in his early twenties, enjoyed a position of great confidence with the L.N.C.; a thoroughly indoctrinated Marxist with unusual qualities of intelligence and judgment and a fluent knowledge of English, he was selected by Enver Hoxha as liaison officer to McLean's mission—as official interpreter and unofficial spy. Few were the messages we sent to Cairo or to each other that Frederick Nosi did not do his best to read.

Marxist theory teaches that the 'historical process' must lead to the emergence of a Communist society and that the wise man, faced with the alternatives of opposing or assisting the process, will choose the latter. Uninhibited by personal scruple or family tradition Frederick Nosi made his choice. Imperturbably brave, infinitely ambitious, he trampled ruthlessly on all who impeded his progress, allowing no considerations of friendship to stand in his way. He terrorized his subordinates, fawned on his superiors and spied on his comrades; towards the majority of his fellow-countrymen he assumed an attitude of supercilious contempt, emphasizing his superiority to them with the frequent use of the phrase, 'we intellectuals'.

One of the first tasks that McLean and Smiley had commissioned after their occupation of Shtyllë was the erection of a large wooden structure, known as 'the barracks', on the southern side of the valley under the lee of a steep mountain. It was a single storey building skillfully camouflaged with parachutes and containing a kitchen and sleeping quarters for the N.C.O.s, a wireless room, and separate store-rooms for arms and explosives, money and clothing. It had cost sixty gold sovereigns to build. The supplies received in drops were stored there under lock and key, to be doled out to the partisans by Smiley, who as quartermaster kept an exact tally of each item down to the last pair of socks.

We lived very well in McLean's headquarters. In addition to what we received by air we could buy as much fresh food as we needed from the friendly inhabitants of Shtyllë and the neighbouring village of Vithkuq; luxuries such as wine, brandy, and the excellent local cigarettes came from Korçë, brought by McLean's well organized courier service. In short the mission had established a well-found and comfortable base; how long we should be able to enjoy it depended on the sufferance of the Italians.

Vithkuq, some three miles east of Shtyllë, was at this time the head-quarters of the L.N.C. Central Council. Although a much larger village it was not so secure a base, for it was accessible by road from Korçë, about twenty miles away, where the Italians maintained a strong garrison. A cart track, winding along a steep mountain-side, connected Vithkuq and Shtyllë; Smiley and Duffy had prepared it for demolition in case of enemy attack.

By the time I arrived various local L.N.C. *Çetas* had been grouped into the nucleus of a striking force, based on Vithkuq and grandiloquently styled 'The First Partisan Brigade'.[1] Totaling no more than eight hundred men, organized in four 'battalions', it was nevertheless formidably equipped with small-arms, heavy machine-guns and mortars captured from the Axis armies in North Africa and dropped to 'Consensus' mission; after a month's intensive training by McLean and his staff it was now ready for action.

The men were of every age from fifteen to sixty. Against a background of peasant misery or artisan squalor the contrast of this free life under arms in the mountains made a strong emotional appeal to each of them. They seemed fit, cheerful and enthusiastic; sitting round their camp fires under the stars they would sing of their courage and endurance, the skill of their officers and the wisdom of their leaders. There were some girls among them, who carried rifles and dressed like the men and whose functions, we were repeatedly assured, were strictly confined to cooking, nursing, and fighting. Dress varied from town or peasant clothes to uniforms captured from the Italians and British battle-dresses issued by Smiley. But all ranks wore the five-pointed red star in their caps. Officers, who wore no other insignia, were saluted with clenched fist and the Partisan slogan, '*Vdekje Fashizmit! Liri Popullit!*' ('Death to Fascism! Freedom to the people!').

The Brigade Commander was Mehmet Shehu, a grim, energetic and efficient soldier who has since become Prime Minister of the Albanian People's Republic. Unlike most of the Partisan leaders he already had some practical experience of serious warfare, for he had commanded a company of the International Brigades in Spain; unlike most of them, also, he spoke good English. A sour, taciturn man of ruthless ambition, outstanding courage, and sickening ferocity—he had personally cut the throats of seventy Italian prisoners after a recent engagement—he tried hard to conceal his dislike and distrust of the British, because he admired the soldierly qualities of McLean and Smiley and valued the help they gave him.

The direction of Partisan military operations was vested in the *Shtabit*, the General Staff of the L.N.C. Central Council. Although, as Commander-in-Chief, Mehmet Shehu was a member, supreme political and military control of the *Shtabit*—and indeed of the whole L.N.C. movement—was in the hands of the Chief Political Commissar, Professor Enver Hoxha, an ex-schoolmaster from the Lycée at Korçë. He was a tall, flabby creature in his early thirties, with a sulky, podgy face and a soft woman's voice. Like Mehmet

---

[1] The term Partisan refers in future to L.N.C. guerrillas, as distinct from the Balli Kombëtar and other resistance groups in Albania and Jugoslavia.

Shehu he was a fanatical Communist, cruel, humourless, and deeply suspicious of the British. He spoke excellent French but no English. Although physically a coward he had absurd military pretentions, which led him two years later, when his forces had made him master of Albania, to arrogate to himself the rank of 'Colonel-General'.

It was only gradually that I came to appreciate the influence exercised by Political Commissars in this guerrilla army; for neither Enver Hoxha nor any of his colleagues would admit to us that the policy of their movement was Communist, even when, later on, they must have realized that it was obvious to us. As the army expanded, every L.N.C. brigade, every battalion and every *çeta* had its own Political Commissar. In theory the responsibilities of the Commissar were limited to political discipline, administration and welfare: in practice, on all matters outside the actual conduct of military operations his authority overrode that of the Commander to whom he was nominally adviser.

When I reported to McLean on the morning of 12th August he took me for a walk, ostensibly to show me the dropping ground, in reality to explain to me in private the political situation in the area and throughout the country and to discuss plans for my own future.

'Relations between the L.N.C. and the Balli Kombëtar,' he told me, 'are daily getting worse. The L.N.C. call the Balli reactionaries, which they may be, and collaborationists, which they certainly are not; they also accuse them of attacking L.N.C. *çetas* when the latter go into their territory to attack the Germans or Italians, and of giving warning to the enemy of ambushes planned by the L.N.C. The Balli accuse the L.N.C., of being Communists and of making unprovoked attacks upon their villages and their *çetas*, they say they're willing to fight the Huns and Ities, but are hindered by the fact that they haven't enough arms unless we give them some; also by the fact that their villages lie alongside or very near the Leskovik—Korçë road, and whenever a convoy is attacked, either by themselves or the L.N.C., one of those villages is burnt in reprisal and its inhabitants slaughtered. The L.N.C., of course, who have no villages, couldn't care less.'

'How much truth is there in the Balli excuses?'

'A good deal in what they say about reprisals. At the beginning of last month, after a series of Partisan attacks on the road, the Germans sent an armoured column down from Korçë to Borovë and Barmash. They went through both those villages with flame-throwers, setting every house on fire with the inhabitants inside; they then surrounded each village and drove the people back into the flames as they tried to escape. There's one little boy of seven in Shtyllë now; both his parents were burnt alive in Borovë and he was twice driven back into the fire before he found a way to crawl out, badly burnt. No wonder the villagers are fed up! They must either take to the hills and lose their property, or stay and be massacred. Sometimes, to escape reprisals, they do warn the enemy of L.N.C. ambushes, and it's hard to blame them.

'It's becoming more and more difficult for us to carry out Cairo's instructions about helping L.N.C. and Balli impartially. In spite of their difficulties the Balli have attempted a few half-hearted and unsuccessful operations, and we've given them some rifles and ammunition, the odd machine-gun and mortar, and a few grenades; but every time we do so Enver raises a howl that we're supporting traitors, collaborationists, and enemies of the Albanian people, and he sulks for a week. Meanwhile the Balli complain that we're arming the L.N.C. for civil war.'

'What are you going to do about it?' I asked gloomily, remembering John Bennett's description of the Civil War in Jugoslavia.

'Well, we're putting pressure on both parties to prove their good faith by undertaking an action against the Germans. If they don't fight they don't get any more arms—or any more sovereigns either, which will shake them! David Smiley left on Wednesday to attack the main road down south, near Barmash, with a Balli Çeta. They're two hundred strong, and David has taken our 20-mm. cannon to support them, so they should be all right. Enver and Mehmet of course are furious and will probably try to sabotage the operation. David should be back tomorrow, so we'll hear then.

'Secondly, David and I have worked out a plan with Mehmet for a large-scale ambush by the whole Brigade on the road, near the same place; there's an ideal stretch where the road runs along the side of the mountain with a sheer precipice below, and if a large convoy comes along we ought to bag the lot. It will be a wonderful blooding for the Brigade and a splendid climax to all our training.'

'When is it to be, and am I in on it?'

'Of course you are, if you like. We've planned it for the end of next week—about the 20th. That brings us to the question of your own future. While you were laid up I discussed with Seymour, Field, and Tilman the areas where they should work. Bill Tilman is going to Gjinokaster, Gerry Field to Valona, and Seymour to Peza to work with Myslim; they'll be moving early next week, as soon as we can get them mules and drivers; Tony Neel went north last month to Abas Kupi in the Mati, and Hands is on his way to Dibra. Have you any ideas for yourself?'

'Well, while I was in Cairo I saw a signal from you suggesting that someone should be sent to the Kossovo area. That's where I should like to go—it's bound to be interesting, that frontier.'

'Right. They haven't come back on that signal yet, but we'll book you for Kossovo if and when they approve. Meanwhile, I suggest you stay with us and help us out in dealing with Enver and the Central Council; there's a lot of political work and it's quite interesting if a bit discouraging at times.'

'What are they like to deal with, those boys?'

'Not very cooperative—suspicious and bloody-minded. It's very hard to get them to agree to anything, and impossible to rely on their carrying out what they do agree to. Apart from our relations with the Balli they're always complaining about something, always demanding more money and more arms. They give us absurd figures of casualties they claim to have inflicted on the enemy in various alleged operations, and get furious when we cast the smallest doubt upon their accuracy; yet they hardly ever bring us an identification disc, as we've asked them to do, nor will they ever warn us in advance of any of their operations, so that one of us can go and observe. The only actions of theirs that David and I have watched have been flops, so of course we don't believe their figures.

'They're incredibly inefficient and sometimes very funny. About a fortnight ago the *Shtabit* came to see us with lists of figures of the oil production from the Kuçovë oil-wells, north of Berat, for which I had asked them. But they wouldn't let us keep them or copy them—sheer bloody-mindedness, of course! However, while I kept them talking, David left the room with some excuse about listening to the wireless, swiped the papers off the tables as he went, made a copy of the lot and returned the original without anyone noticing. The sad thing was that when the *Shtabit* went away they forgot to take the lists with them, so all David's work was unnecessary.'

In brilliant sunlight we stood on the col that separated the two valleys, looking down on the board stretch of grassland and the river bed where I had dropped two nights before. The hills rose steep on either side, the lower slopes covered with scrub and stunted conifer, the summits bare and rocky; at the western end of the valley the blue bulk of a great mountain glittered in the clear air.

'I take off my hat to those Halifax pilots,' said McLean. 'Sometimes they come down to five hundred feet to drop our stuff accurately. God knows how they manage to miss that mountain at the other end, or clear the hills on either side when they make their turns. We had a nasty shock during a drop three weeks ago. There were two Halifaxes, and while the second was making its run-in an Italian aircraft followed it and bombed the dropping ground. Luckily David heard it above the noise of the Halifax and recognized it from the engines as a Caproni. He shouted in French to the Partisans who were on the D.Z. to clear off and take cover, which they did pretty quick; but he forgot that poor Garry Duffy, who was right in the middle flashing the recognition signal, didn't speak French! The Caproni dropped twelve 50-kilo bombs with great accuracy, blowing out more than half the signal fires and making a frightful mess of the dropping ground, but luckily without hurting Garry or anybody else. It was a fantastic sight to see the Halifax and the Caproni making alternate runs, one dropping supplies and the other bombs, and neither of them seeming to notice the other! Needless to say, all the Partisans panicked and ran off, although most of them came back next day to loot our kit and steal our food. You ought to have heard David's language next morning, especially when some Albanian came up to him saying he was the owner of the field and claiming compensation for the damage caused by the bombs!'

'The Ities haven't tried it again?'

'No. The Caproni crashed the same night on landing at Korçë, and all the crew were killed, so I suppose they never had a chance to tell anyone about their exploit.'

We turned and walked back to Shtyllë in silence, listening to the tinkle of goat bells and the distant calls of shepherds. The sun beat strong upon our heads but the air, at three thousand feet above the sea, was sweet and cool, filled with the resinous scent of trees and grass and the tang of wood smoke. As we came to the outskirts of the village McLean took me by the elbow:

'Remember, Peter, be very careful what you say in front of Frederick Nosi. Every word gets back to Enver. Above all, no mention, please, of your part in the Spanish Civil War!'

I spent the following day on 'training walks' with Tilman; in the morning we climbed the hills on the north side of the valley, in the afternoon we scaled those on the south. The exercise left me, as it left others who climbed with that indefatigable alpinist, completely exhausted; for it seemed to be his habit, which I am told he followed throughout his stay in Albania, to climb straight to the top of any peak in his path and straight down the other side, disdaining the tracks used by lesser men and mules.

I was nodding over the dining table after our evening meal when there was a commotion outside and Smiley strode into the room. He gave us all a brief good evening and called for beer.

A regular officer in the Household Cavalry, Smiley had served with his regiment in Syria and the Western Desert and with the Commandos in Abyssinia and Eritrea before coming to Albania. Reserved in manner, economical in speech, he had a shrewd insight and quiet self-confidence which enabled him to make up his mind quickly and speak it with a directness that compelled attention without giving offence. Politics bored him, although he could deal well enough with political problems when they came his way; he was happiest when in action or planning action, when testing a new gun or preparing a demolition. In the most dangerous situations he appeared phlegmatic to the point of indifference, not because he lacked the intelligence to feel fear but because he possessed the priceless self-discipline that can conceal and suppress it.

He had a surprising variety of interests outside his profession, and a remarkably detailed knowledge on such widely differing subjects as the rise and fall of the Mongol Empire and the care and cultivation of cacti and succulents. Square and stocky, with fair hair and very bright blue eyes in a round, tanned, well-polished face, he radiated briskness and efficiency.

Standing in front of us, his feet apart, his head slightly cocked to one side, with the bright, alert look of a bird listening for a worm, he told his story in quick, clipped sentences.

'It was quite successful,' he began, 'but not half as good is it might have been. We got into position on Friday morning—the day before yesterday. The *çeta* commandant and I watched the road all day and made plans for the ambush. In the evening I had a lot of trouble with that bloody man Petrit Duma. He arrived with thirty Partisans, saying he intended to lay an ambush in exactly the same place as ours. Of course this was just to bitch the Balli. I told him so and made him push off, but I had to use a lot of threats. That night I laid sixteen mines on the road, in two places about 250 yards apart and out of sight of one another. The road is cut out of the mountain side and there's no way off it—sheer cliffs above and a ravine below. Perfect for an ambush. While I was laying the mines a Halifax flew over and all the men with me ran away, thinking it was a car, so I had to do all the work myself.

'At six-thirty yesterday morning a Hun troop-carrier full of troops and towing an 88-mm. gun approached from the north. Some of the guerrillas shouted, "A Tank! A Tank!" and ran away. The troop-carrier blew up on my mines, and I've got a photograph of it going up. All the Huns were killed—twelve by the mines and my 20-mm. and six shot while running away. Then the braver guerrillas went onto the road and got identifications from the dead Huns and murdered any wounded ones. They had a wonderful time looting the troop carrier. I tried to get them to push the gun over the ravine, but the mines had damaged the wheels and they couldn't move it. We threw all we could down the ravine. Then we heard a convoy coming from the south and got into position again. There were twenty-three lorries all told, five Germans in the first and two in each of the others. The first was blown to bits on the mines, and all five Germans killed inside it. But by this time all the guerrillas had run away except the two who were with me by the 20-mm. It was heartbreaking, as the remaining Germans ran back down the road, leaving the three of us to destroy the lorries they left behind. I sent two of them up in flames with the 20-mm. and hit a third; but if the *çeta* had stayed there we could have got onto the road and destroyed every one. A bit later a lot more Germans returned and started shooting at us, so we went home; they came too close to be healthy. We got good identifications—all from the 1st Alpine Division.'

The next day we were all invited to attend the ceremony of the 'official inauguration' of the First Partisan Brigade at Vithkuq. The cart-track from Shtyllë followed the contour of the mountain, which rose sharply on the right, and on the left dropped sheer into a deep wooded ravine with a stream at the bottom. Near Vithkuq the ravine broadened into a valley, commanded by a steep hill covered with a monastery, which the Partisans had garrisoned and fortified. It gave me a satisfying feeling of security to see how ideal was this country for defence.

The 'inauguration' turned out to be a parade and march-past at which Enver Hoxha took the salute and Mehmet and other members of the Central Council each in turn made a speech. The speeches, of course, were in Albanian and so we had no idea of what was being said, but all were warmly applauded with clenched fist salutes and shouts of 'Death to Fascism!' After two or three hours of this we sat down on the ground to a *vin d'honneur* and lunch on a lavish scale: There was raki,[1] followed by chianti or beer; pilaff and sheep roasted whole; even coffee and execrable Italian brandy. There were speeches throughout the meal and Partisan songs in chorus at the end of it. The most popular song, which had a stirring, haunting rhythm, commemorated, if I remember rightly, the heroism of a certain Comrade John, who came from Valona; when the rest of his *çeta* ran away he alone stood firm.

The following morning, 16th August, Seymour, Tilman, and Field left for their different areas, each with a string of mules carrying his wireless set and generator and canisters full of stores. At McLean's suggestion I moved my kit and sleeping bag into the mosque, where a mattress was laid for me on the floor of the dining-room.

Once a week the peasants from the surrounding districts came to Shtyllë to sell us mules and horses; any thing from seventy to a hundred animals would arrive, of which not more than ten would be fit for use. When McLean and Smiley had selected those they wanted to buy they would leave the bargaining to one of the camp followers, a Palestinian Arab known as Black George[2]—to distinguish him from the armourer, who was known as Greek George. The price of a mule usually worked out at about five gold napoleons; a horse would cost more. However, I was strongly advised to buy myself a mule to ride rather than a horse, because a mule was surer on the steep and stony tracks across this mountainous country and could see better in the dark. Smiley had a mule named Fanny, to whom he was devoted; whenever he felt depressed or particularly disgusted he would stalk out of the mess and over to the mule-lines, where he would be found with his arm round Fanny's neck, whispering into her ear.

In the course of the next few days we received two supply drops. For their reception we had the help of a detachment of Partisans from the First Brigade, under the command of a certain Xhelal Staravecka, a fierce looking, loud-mouthed braggart in a dirty grey fur hat. He had been a gendarmerie officer under the Italians but had deserted to the Partisans in the middle of a

---

[1] A strong, clear spirit distilled from grapes and drunk as an aperitif.
[2] Black George was a private in the Pioneer Corps who had taken to the mountains in Greece after the British withdrawal.

battle, for which he had been rewarded with the command of one of Mehmet's new battalions. After the German occupation of Albania in September 1943 he deserted again and joined the Germans, perpetrating in his new employment such atrocities against both Albanians and Italians that when I last heard of him, in 1949, he was in the Regina Cocli Prison in Rome awaiting trial as a war criminal.

Hearing that my birthday would fall on 19th August McLean sent a courier into Korçë the day before to buy food and drink for a party. On such occasions he would give the courier a few gold sovereigns or napoleons to change into Albanian paper money at the existing black market rate; it was obviously unsafe to buy from the shops with gold—indeed the couriers ran a considerable risk even in carrying our gold, because they might easily be searched by *carabinieri* on entering or leaving the city.

During these days we had several official meetings with the *Shtabit*, sometimes at Vithkuq, sometimes at Shtyllë. They were the first of many conferences I was to endure with this organization, all of which followed a similar pattern. The first item would be a demand for money. The members of the *Shtabit* rendered no accounts, and gave only evasive answers when we asked for precise statements of their needs; if we did not agree to their demand in full—and some of their figures were outrageous—there was sure to be a period of sulky silence or an outburst of blustering rage from Enver Hoxha. When this had subsided Mehmet Shehu would present his indent for military stores; this matter seldom gave difficulty because we always agreed to pass on his requirements to Cairo. Then the *Shtabit* would give us a report on actions undertaken by its units against Germans or Italians, accompanied by imposing figures of enemy killed, captured, and wounded. The figures were seldom supported by the evidence we had asked for—identification discs and shoulder straps—but the hysteria generated by any signs of skepticism on our part was so exhausting that we developed a technique of smiling politely, congratulating the *Shtabit* and promising to tell Cairo what it had achieved.

The fourth item, which the *Shtabit* clearly enjoyed the most, was complaints. These were divided into complaints against the Balli Kombëtar, and complaints against the British Mission. The one usually led on to the other, with little variation in the form of either: The Balli had refused to allow an L.N.C. *çeta* to pass through their territory on its way to attack an Italian garrison; the Balli had fired on some Partisans who were trying to buy food in a Balli village. (Privately we thought the word 'buy' was good.) The Ballist leader, Abas Ermenje, had betrayed the Partisan plan of attack on Berat to the Italians, causing the Partisans to suffer heavy casualties. There was irrefutable evidence of all these incidents, which we could examine one day. Nevertheless, the *Shtabit* was deeply pained, in fact horrified, to learn that the British Mission had been supplying arms to those Fascist traitors, those enemies of the Albanian people, in particular to that tool of the Italian invaders, the so-called Professor Safet Butkë (the local area commander of the Balli Kombëtar). No wonder there was not enough money or arms for Albanian patriots, when *Monsieur le Majeur* gave so much away to collaborators.

We would reply mildly that we were only carrying out the instructions of the Allied High Command, which were to give arms to all those who were prepared to fight the Axis; if Professor Safet Butkë or any other Ballist would fight, then it was the duty of the British Mission to help them with supplies. It had always seemed to us a great pity, we would add, that the two Albanian patriotic movements could not compose their differences and combine against the real enemies of their country.

Thereupon the whole *Shtabit* would break out in a gabble of angry protest, the gist of which was obvious to us even before Frederick Nosi could translate such parts of it as were not covered by 'Traitors!', 'Fascists!' and 'Collaborationists!' Of course the Balli had no intention of fighting the Germans and Italians; all the tales they told about their battles were lies. Couldn't we understand that they only told us these stories in order to get arms from us with which to fight the L.N.C., who alone represented all true Albanian patriots? This theme, developed with rancorous enthusiasm, would result in a general political discussion, usually lasting into the small hours of the morning.

At our second meeting, however, the *Shtabit* had tangible proof of military success, in the shape of eight Italian prisoners captured in an ambush near Korçë; Smiley had already interrogated them at Vithkuq. They were a captain, three subalterns, two N.C.O.s, and two privates. Smiley obtained from them their names and units and the addresses of their families in Italy; but they refused to divulge any more information.

'I admired their behaviour very much,' he told us afterwards. 'Because they must have had a pretty good idea that they were going to be shot. When we get out of here I'll write to their next-of-kin.' 'Do the Partisans always shoot their prisoners?' I asked him. 'Either that, or cut their throats—which is probably kinder to them as these people are such bad shots. They ambushed a cartload of Huns the other day and took four of them prisoner. One of the Partisans who was there told me they led the Germans into a wood and made them take off their boots, and then lined them up and shot at them with Sten guns. The shooting was so bad that the Germans were able to pick up stones and throw them at the Partisans before being killed. One German ran away, but was caught again.'

'I suppose,' said McLean maliciously, 'the Partisan told you that to show you how brave he was to go on shooting at the Germans while they were throwing stones.'

My twenty-eighth birthday was marked by the first signs I had seen of enemy action. In the morning an Italian two-seater biplane circled over our valley; shortly afterwards we heard the sound of gun-fire from the east. Through our glasses we could see the monastery on the hill near Vithkuq; shells were falling on the slopes around the building and bursting on the walls, while the aircraft circled overhead, presumably spotting for the guns. The shelling, punctuated by the sound of machine-gun fire, continued for most of the morning. At lunch time we heard that the monastery was in Italian hands. Partisan losses had been light.

On the morning of 21st August Smiley and I walked into Vithkuq to see Mehmet Shehu. The Brigade was to leave that evening to carry out the attack McLean had planned on the road near Barmash; we, who could move faster, would leave the following morning. Mehmet Shehu confirmed that his troops were ready, and added the interesting news that the *Shtabit* had departed on the previous day for the region of Elbasan in central Albania. Whatever the defects of the *Shtabit*, its members possessed, as events were to prove, a useful capacity for scenting danger. Back at Shtyllë we spent a busy afternoon in final preparations for the battle.

The target was the same stretch of road that Smiley had attacked eight days before. In retrospect it seems a foolish choice; but Partisan patrols had reported that the sector was still clear of enemy pickets, and. it would be difficult to find a better spot for an ambush. A convoy caught there would be at our mercy because there was no room to turn on the road.

The plan as I remember it was simple. During the night of the 22nd-23rd Mehmet Shehu would dispose his brigade on the heights commanding the road—one battalion on a spur immediately above the road, the remainder across the valley where they would have a clear field of fire. Everyone was to be in position by sunrise. Northbound convoys were to be left alone, but when a large enough convoy appeared travelling southwards it would be shot up from both sides and the road closed behind it by mines. Meanwhile Duffy, with a demolition party of our N.C.O.s, would blow the important bridge at Perat, farther south, closing the road to reinforcements from that direction. With the force and armament at our disposal it should not take long to destroy the largest convoy.

Duffy, whose party had a long way to go, left as soon as our conference was ended. I was to leave at daylight for a meeting on the way with Professor Safet Butkë, the local Balli Kombëtar commander, who had been complaining of increased hostility from the L.N.C. After the meeting I was to meet the others for lunch at a nearby village.

The first sunlight striking on my back as my mule-cleared the ridge above Shtyllë dispelled the bad temper caused by early rising and a hurried breakfast. My companions were Stiljan, the young interpreter, and a Balli guide. I soon learnt that it was impossible to move in Albania without a local guide. For although our maps were good enough they did not show the countless tiny tracks which branched in every direction over the mountains; nor, if we left the tracks, could we have moved very far across that savage terrain, even with the best of compasses; on a long journey it might be necessary to change the guide once or twice a day. It was a waste of time to ask about distances; men would reply vaguely, 'two hours on foot, three hours with mules'. But it was wiser to add several hours to their estimates because their natural politeness would lead them to try and spare a stranger's feelings.

After a couple of hours' ride across desolate, scrub-covered hills our way led down through a forest carpeted with pine needles into a green valley, where we halted to rest our animals and drink from a clear, cool stream. We climbed again through pine forest onto rolling green uplands reminiscent of high pastures in the Alps in summer. About eleven o'clock we came into another valley, where a party of armed men awaited us at the entrance to a small village. As I dismounted, their leader, a tubby old man with a stubbly chin, weak, watery eyes and a worried, nervous manner, came forward and greeted me in French, introducing himself as Professor Safet Butkë.

Obviously distrustful of Stiljan he insisted on talking with me alone. His story ran along the lines I had been led to expect and which I later took for granted from either faction when discussing the other: L.N.C. aggression in his territory was becoming intolerable; they came in bands to steal food and plunder property, taking by violence what they could not secure by stealth; they even tried to conscript young men into their get as. He had tried to avoid bloodshed, but in truth he could not promise to restrain his men much longer if these bandits continued their depredations. Would I please ask Major McLean to use his influence with the L.N.C. to stop their aggression? Another point: the villages near the Korçë-Leskovik road were Ballist. Every time an attack was made on that road one or more of these defenceless villages would be burnt and its inhabitants massacred. It was all very well for the L.N.C. and ourselves to attack the road, because we could escape into the mountains where the enemy could not reach us; but it was Ballist villages that had to suffer. Could we not in future find some place to attack the road far from any villages?

Sadly I rode on my way with Stiljan to the village where I was to meet McLean and Smiley. Safet Butkë sent a strong escort to accompany us as far as the outskirts. I never saw him again. A month later he shot himself in a lavatory.

We joined the Brigade in the late afternoon. The winding column of guerrillas faded slowly along the broad, sandy bed of a water-course; oleander bushes grew thick on the banks and a thin stream trickled sluggishly between. We were in flat, open country with little cover from the air; but we travelled undisturbed. Riding a little ahead of McLean and Smiley I was beginning to feel acutely uncomfortable on my wooden pack-saddle, my feet thrust into improvised stirrups of thick cord. Snippets of Smiley's talk drifted to my ears; he and Mclean were back in London rehearsing the drill for mounting guard.

'You do that, Billy,' I heard Smiley bark, 'and you go straight back to riding-school for the next six months!'

I admired their detachment before an operation that meant so much to them both.

As the sun was setting we began to climb again into the hills. With darkness came a chill wind that whistled mournfully over the bare ridges. It was hard not to lose touch with one another or stray from the track in the impenetrable blackness. Poised on the edge of some escarpment, unable to discern any way down, I was often in despair; but each time my mule carried me with sure feet to the bottom, while I lurched in the saddle, sweating with fright. About midnight we came to a broad plateau surrounded by hills, where we halted.

We were now within half a mile of the road. After a brief conference Mehmet Shehu dispatched one of his battalions, under Tahir Kadaradja, to cross the road and take up position on the spur beyond. A few minutes later the rest of us moved forward towards the hills overlooking the valley and the road. Leaving our mules in the care of our Vlachs we followed Smiley to the position he had already selected for us on the forward slope of one of the hills. We had just settled ourselves to get what rest we could before dawn when we were disagreeably startled by the sound of machine-gun fire from across the valley.

'Oh God!' sighed Smiley, 'Tahir's run into trouble. Unless of course they're shooting at each other.'

Half an hour later Mehmet Shehu and his staff approached over the hill, shining torches with a lavish disregard for concealment which infuriated Smiley.

'Our plan has failed,' began Mehmet angrily. 'Tahir's battalion has been surprised by a German post on that hill. We must withdraw. There is nothing we can do here.'

'Oh yes, there is!' said Smiley and McLean together. 'You can start by wiping out that German post. There can't be many of them.'

Mehmet Shehu shook his head: 'No. It is impossible. My first operation must be one hundred per cent successful.'

'Just what we mean,' said Smiley. 'Look how easy it's going to be to kill those few Germans with all the men you've got—especially in the dark. Then we can have a crack at a convoy tomorrow.'

Mehmet looked at the ground between his feet. 'I have already given the order to withdraw,' he muttered.

We returned to the plateau, where we lay on the ground wrapped in our blankets and sleeping bags. But none of us slept. Mehmet found himself confronted next morning by three furious and disgusted officers. He brought his entire staff with him, feeling, I suppose, the need of moral support. Our reconnaissance had already shown us that the German post consisted of a platoon party of from eighteen to twenty men with a light machine-gun. With such odds in his favour we could hardly believe that Mehmet would refuse to fight. We urged him to overrun the post that night and carry on with the operation as planned on the following morning.

Mehmet remained unmoved by all our arguments. It was useless, he sullenly maintained, to blind ourselves to the fact that the operation had failed. He argued that although a withdrawal would be a blow to the morale of his men, the heavy losses which would result from carrying out our plan would be a bigger blow. At the end of a morning's argument McLean gave up.

'So eight hundred of your "patriotic Albanians", with all the armament and all the training we have given them, are to be frightened away by twenty Germans!' he exclaimed.

Without a word Mehmet turned and walked away, followed by his staff and some plainly audible comments from Smiley.

In the early afternoon I spent two hours watching the road through my binoculars. No convoy passed; a few solitary staff cars and one or two army lorries were the only traffic during my vigil. When I rejoined McLean the Brigade had moved off, leaving us alone with Stiljan, Stefan, our mules, and their drivers.

'You'll be pleased to hear that the Brigade has been in action,' was Smiley's greeting to me.

I looked at him in astonishment, for I had heard no shooting.

'Yes, they killed a solitary German who had wandered into a village near here in search of food. He was unarmed, of course.'

We spent another chilly and despondent night in the same place; but sunrise warmed us and raised our spirits.

'I'm damned if I'm leaving here without having a crack at something,' McLean said to me over breakfast. 'David's got to get back to Shtyllë to receive the drops we're expecting, but if you agree I thought we might try to shoot up a lone staff car. Of course, it's a purely Boy Scout operation, but at least it should work off some of our bad temper.'

Stiljan volunteered to come with us, and one of the Vlachs agreed to guard our mules out of sight of the road. We decided to lay our ambush just before dusk, in order to have the protection of darkness for our escape should the action go against us.

In the early evening we made our way slowly towards the road, while the dying sunlight dappled the hills in a splendid contrast of ochre and indigo. We chose a spot a mile north and out of sight of the German position; here the hills reached almost to the road, and fern and bushes gave plenty of cover without obstructing our view in either direction. Leaving the Vlach with our mules behind a ridge some five hundred yards back, we hid ourselves behind a bank above the road; Stiljan crouched beside me, McLean stood ten yards to our right watching and listening.

The sun had set. In the still, clear light before dusk the land seemed deserted; the only sound I could hear was Stiljan's heavy breathing, showing that he was feeling the same nervous tension as I. We had agreed to attack only a vehicle travelling by itself; but now I remembered that it was the practice for a staff car to precede a convoy at a few hundred yards distance, and I prayed that we should not find ourselves in a trap. Besides our pistols and submachine-guns each of us carried two phosphorus smoke grenades to cover our retreat in an emergency, but I had little faith in their protection if we should run into serious trouble.

Faintly from the south came the sound of a car. We heard it a long way off, the noise of its engine rising and falling on the twisting mountain road. I saw McLean staring through his field-glasses; then he stiffened:

'It's a German staff car, all alone; don't fire till I give the word.'

The car turned the last bend and came into full view, a grey saloon approaching at about twenty-five miles an hour—a perfect target. As I heard Stiljan cock his Schmeizer I pressed forward the safety-catch of my Welgun. Then McLean stood up, his Schmeizer at his shoulder.

'All right, let 'em have it,' he ordered quietly.

We opened fire simultaneously. Within a few seconds the windscreen and side windows were shattered, the body scoured with the marks of our bullets. The car continued on its way for about twenty yards, then slewed in a cloud of dust and came to a halt at the side of the road. The driver sat slumped over the wheel, two men lay huddled motionless in the back, but from the front seat a figure leapt out and, crouching behind the car, returned our fire with his pistol. Changing their magazines McLean and Stiljan continued firing, but at this moment my Welgun jammed; savagely I cursed George, the armorer, to whom I had given it for adjustment three days before and who, it now appeared, had damaged the mechanism. Throwing it aside I drew my .45 and began to fire carefully aimed shots at the place where I imagined the German to be. Suddenly I heard McLean shout.

'Give me covering fire, boys! I'm going down.'

'For Christ's sake stay where you are!' I shouted back; but I was too late. Throwing one of the smoke grenades, which landed well short of the car, McLean scrambled down the slope; Stiljan, urged by me, redoubled his rate of fire. Unfortunately the thick cloud of phosphorus smoke effectively hid the car from our view, although it did not seem to hide McLean from the German; we could hear the crack of his pistol and see spurts of earth fly from the bullets round McLean's feet. I knew McLean was going down not only to finish off the German, but to collect any documents in the car, and I shuddered to think how we should get him away if he were hit. I threw a smoke grenade, hoping to give him extra cover; but by now McLean himself had thought better of it and was climbing back towards us. In a moment he was safe.

'I think we'd better beat it,' he gasped, 'while the score is still in our favour.'

We raced down into a gully and started to climb the ridge beyond which our mules awaited us. It was an arduous journey until we found a gap with a rough track running through it. The mules were grazing peacefully in the shelter of an outcrop of rock, but the Vlach looked thoroughly frightened; he and Stiljan urged us to be on our way at once. I too was anxious to be gone, remembering that one of the first rules of an ambush is not to linger on the scene of the crime. I wasted no time in climbing onto my mule and begged McLean to hurry. We had a wide patch of open ground to cross, and although darkness was falling there was still enough light for us to present a very good target. McLean, however, was in no mood for haste. The danger, he maintained, was over and now was the time to relax and rest before the long journey home. Pulling a tortoiseshell comb from his breast pocket he began to pass it in long, leisurely strokes through the thick blond hair that swept back from his forehead.

'Don't be so damned windy, Peter,' he protested with a careless laugh.

At that moment, with the crackle of exploding fireworks, a burst of machine-gun fire struck the rocks beside us. For a moment McLean stood rigid, the comb still in his hair, the smile frozen on his face; then he gave me a sheepish grin and seized the head-rope of his mule.

'On our way, boys!' He pointed to a low bank beyond the open ground. 'Meet you on the other side of that.'

The Vlach was already making off at the double, followed by Stiljan and our spare mule, which had broken loose. My own mule took fright and started to follow at a trot across the hideously exposed piece of ground. Feeling uncomfortably naked and conspicuous I tried to dismount; but my right foot was caught in the cord stirrup and I could not free it. The air was full of the hiss of the bullets and the angry red gleam of tracer flying all round me as I bent helplessly over the beast's neck, my useless Welgun, which was slung across my back, beating painfully against my hips and elbows with every movement. The machine-gun was firing from the direction of the road; I could not be sure exactly where it was, nor at that moment was I much interested in finding out. The distance was only two or three hundred yards, but it seemed as many miles with the stream of tracer whistling about my head. The Germans must have found it hard to see us in the gathering gloom; they were shooting high, although one or two bursts struck the ground behind me, ricocheting past with an angry whine. At last I was behind the cover of the bank; I fell rather than climbed from my mule, luckily remembering to keep hold of the head-rope. A few seconds later McLean joined me, panting heavily. The rest of our party had disappeared.

Cautiously we peered over the edge. The shooting had ceased and there was no sign of pursuit. We decided to put a safe distance between ourselves and the road, and then to look for a village where we could sleep. Leading our mules we struck northwards away from the road and into the hills. After half a mile we found a track, which we followed for another mile until we felt it safe to halt for a rest. We were about to move on when McLean seized my arm and pointed back down the path:

'There's someone coming!' he whispered, unslinging his Schmeizer.

Listening, with my pistol ready, I heard the sound of hooves striking against rock; a moment later Stiljan's slight figure loomed out of the darkness, leading our spare mule. He had not seen the Vlach since the firing started.

'Never mind,' said McLean. 'He'll have the sense to find his own way back to Shtyllë. Let's get a move on.'

With Stiljan as guide we rode on for an hour without meeting any-one. There was no moon, but the stars gave enough light to follow the track. At last we came to a village. The houses were shuttered and silent, the street deserted; glimmers of light showed behind a few of the doors.

'We should be safe enough here for the night,' said McLean. 'Let's see if we can get anyone to put us up.'

Leaving Stiljan to try one of the houses on our right, McLean and I rode up the street and dismounted in front of a large wooden door. McLean knocked and called several times in a clear voice, 'O Zot i shtepis!'[1] At first there was no reply, but when he persisted a surly voice from within shouted back, brusquely ordering us away; other voices joined in, angry and frightened.

'I'd better try another house,' sighed McLean. 'You go back and see how Stiljan's getting on.'

I found Stiljan engaged in what was obviously a losing argument with an indignant figure in a half-open doorway. As I came up, the door was slammed in the interpreter's face.

'He will not have us, Captain,' explained Stiljan—superfluously in the circumstances. 'They have heard of the shooting on the road and they are very much afraid, and very enraged with us for causing the trouble.'

We found McLean arguing with a group of gesticulating and hostile villagers. As he caught sight of us he shouted:

'For God's sake hurry up and let's get out of here! These people are going to shoot us if we stay any longer.'

Hastily we mounted and rode on our way, the abuse of the peasants following us as far as the outskirts. We tried two more villages in the next

---

[1] Lit.: 'Master of the House!'

hour, but the inhabitants refused to open their doors to us or even to answer our requests for shelter. Finally, about two in the morning, we came to a hamlet with a Greek Orthodox church, where at last we found a friendly reception in the house of the priest. After a few hours' sleep on the floor and a breakfast of warm sweetened milk, maize bread and yoghourt we went on our journey in the dawn.

The sun was sinking below the hills as we rode into Shtyllë. Smiley greeted us with the news that the aircraft which had dropped our stores the previous night had made their runs across the valley instead of down it, with the result that our stores had been scattered all over the hills. He had spent the whole day searching for them, but a great deal had been lost or looted.

'Really Cairo do make some prize bogs,' he snorted. 'All the boots they sent—which I listed as top priority—are size six! They may be some use for the local school children but none for the Partisans. And, believe it or not, all the hand grenades were dropped ready primed, which is bloody dangerous.'

Duffy had returned from Perat, where he had found the bridge too heavily guarded to attempt a demolition. We worked late, drafting signals to Cairo and checking stores; then, utterly exhausted, we crawled to bed, promising ourselves a long lie-in.

At half past seven next morning I was awakened by two most un-welcome sounds: an aeroplane circling low above the house and the explosion of a shell outside. Smiley, already fully dressed, put his head into the dining-room where I was lying on my mattress. He gave me a friendly grin.

'We're being attacked, but never mind.'

I am not normally quick at getting up, but I made an exception that morning, spurred by two more shells which landed considerably closer than the first, blowing in the windows and part of the roof. As I threw on my clothes I reflected savagely that it was exactly a week since my birthday and my first sight of that aeroplane. With the help of their observation post in the monastery and the spotting aircraft overhead the Italians would not take long to reduce the mosque to rubble; the only course for us was to pack up our essential stores and move as quickly as possible to the barracks across the valley; there, under the lee of a steep mountain, we should be fairly safe from shelling. While we were getting ready Smiley mounted the 20-mm. on a rock outside and started firing at the aeroplane; but his gun had no anti-aircraft mounting and he could not bring it to bear on the aircraft as it banked and turned, so that his shells were always bursting below and behind his target.

'Pack it in, David, and let's get weaving!' cried McLean after another salvo had straddled the mosque. 'There's no future in staying on here.'

We moved off in pairs, making use of what cover the ground afforded. We had a few seconds' warning of each salvo, for we could hear the faint thuds as the guns opened fire; we reckoned them to be a battery of 15.5-cm. howitzers placed about five miles away on the road beyond Vithkuq. Reaching the barracks without loss we sent a messenger to Vithkuq to find out from Mehmet whether he expected an attack in force. During the previous month Smiley had prepared a hide-out for our stores among the pine woods in the hills a mile or two north of Shtyllë. The mule lines were alongside the barracks, and so we should be able to move our stores fairly quickly. For the moment there was no hurry.

From the security of the barracks we watched the shells bursting among the houses of Shtyllë and felt ashamed that the unhappy villagers should have to suffer for the hospitality which they had had no choice but to give us; I began to understand the feelings of the peasants who had chased us away from their doors two nights before. Little groups of men, women, and children were streaming out of the village, some struggling up the steep hillsides, others plodding down the track that led past the barracks to the west, all carrying pathetic little bundles of food and clothing. If I had been entranced before I came to Albania by the romance and glamour of guerrilla warfare, this was a sobering reminder of its squalor and injustice.

A small group left the track and came towards us, bearing the frail figure of an old man which they laid under the tree beside us. One of his legs was shattered at the knee. We gave him a morphia tablet and bandaged the ragged, bone-splintered pulp of his leg, which in our ignorance was all we could do; but he seemed to feel no pain and smiled and chattered away happily until he gradually lost consciousness. We made him as comfortable as we could in the shade of the tree, but he died in the afternoon. The next casualty was a boy of fifteen with shell splinters in his stomach. We put him beside the old man, where he lay groaning and crying for water; Smiley told us not to give him any, but when we saw that there was no hope of saving him we gave him a drink. He died in a few minutes.

At the height of the shelling an old man in military uniform came riding slowly down the track from the west accompanied by a girl on foot; when he saw us he hesitated, then turned his horse towards us. At that moment a shell landed about five yards from him, covering him and the girl in a cloud of smoke and dust. Quite unperturbed they came on, the old man smiling happily, the girl and the horse seemingly indifferent to their narrow escape. When he was a few paces from us the old man dismounted, threw his reins to the girl and came rigidly to attention in a smart salute. McLean explained to me that he was Colonel Osman Gazepi, a rich Bey from Leskovik and a strong supporter of the L.N.C.

'He's quite dotty,' added McLean, 'and has no influence in the area, but he's a nice old thing. The girl's his daughter; she's barmy too.'

The girl, who was about twenty-five, was fair-haired, short and broad. She wore a green forage cap embroidered with the red star, a short jacket, a brown kilted skirt, and woollen stockings below the knee. She carried a rifle and bandolier.

The object of their visit was to tell us that the Colonel had decided to place the produce of his Leskovik farm and estate at our disposal. It seemed unlikely to benefit us much, because the farm was burnt and the estate deserted; but we thanked him warmly, and watched him ride away still smiling happily.

Soon after midday the bombardment ceased, the aeroplane flew off towards Korçë and we supposed that the Italians had knocked off for lunch. There were still some things we wished to salvage from the mosque, and so McLean and I set off along the path to the village, forgetting that we could be seen from the monastery. We found the mosque damaged but not destroyed, the rooms full of broken glass and fallen plaster; the stores we wanted were intact. We had hardly started to collect them when we heard the ominous thuds from beyond Vithkuq. We had just time to throw ourselves to the floor before the salvo arrived. Two of the shells went wide; the other two landed on either side of the house, a yard or two away. Dazed by the explosions and covered in debris and plaster we scrambled to our feet and ran from the mosque into the fields below. Deciding to leave further salvage operations until after dark we made our way cautiously back to the barracks for lunch.

The bombardment continued intermittently throughout the afternoon. In the evening the biplane returned in company with a light bomber. For about an hour they bombed and strafed the villages on the other side of the mountains to the north-west; although they circled our valley between their bombing runs, often flying directly over the barracks, they left us alone; this was just as well, because in one of our rooms we had nearly a hundred canisters of explosives, besides ammunition, mortar bombs and hand grenades. Undeterred by this frightening prospect Sergeants Jones and Jenkins mounted a Bren gun outside and loosed off a stream of tracer at them every time they approached.

At nightfall a message arrived from Mehmet telling us that an Italian force of about two battalions, supported by artillery and heavy-mortars, was attacking Vithkuq; the Partisans were engaging them and expected to hold the town. McLean told me to attach myself to Mehmet next morning and bring back a report on the battle at the end of the day.

The morning was bright, with promise of great heat. As guide and interpreter I took Stefan, the fierce-looking Albanian who had rescued me after my drop. There was no splendour about him now; his moustaches seemed to droop lower with every step we took towards the sound of battle. When I struck the cart-track leading to Vithkuq I realized that the fighting was much nearer than we had supposed. From a hill beyond the gorge on my left came the sound of heavy machine-gun fire; I decided to see what was happening there, and started to scramble down the steep slope towards the stream. Stray shells were bursting on both sides of the ravine as we crossed. Stefan's melancholy deepened; from time to time he stopped to glance longingly back the way we had come.

'*Faut nous éloigner d'ici, monsieur le Capitaine!*' he whispered. '*C'est très dangereux.*'

Spurred by my own anxiety I bullied him with threats and taunts into following me. Near the top of the slope we came upon a group of Partisans, who told us they were part of Tahir Kadaradja's battalion; we should find Tahir and the rest of the battalion somewhere on the top.

McLean had nicknamed Tahir 'T for Pig', which was a fair comment on his looks. I found him nervous and unhappy, but he greeted me civilly enough. His battalion, he explained, was holding the left flank of the Partisan defence; the centre and right rested on the hills beyond the ravine I had just crossed. The Brigade had engaged the Italians outside Vithkuq last night, but had withdrawn to this line of hills before daylight. He added that his battalion had just beaten off an attack against their position—that must have been the firing I had heard from the road—but he was not sanguine about his chances of holding on for long—'For you see, *monsieur le Capitaine*, there are many of the enemy, and they are powerful in artillery and mortars.'

I pointed out to Tahir that he held a very strong position with plenty of natural cover and a superb field of fire; but he was doubtful whether his troops would stand up to very much shelling. My immediate object now was to find Mehmet; Tahir had no idea where he was to be found, but supposed he must be with one of the battalions on the other side of the valley. He seemed anxious to be rid of me and sent a runner with us to help us find our way.

There was a lull in the fighting as we crossed the ravine and climbed the hills above the road. By steep and devious paths we came, after two hours, to the battalion headquarters of Xhelal Staravecka, who was holding the left centre of the Brigade. Xhelal was manifestly and unashamedly frightened; as a deserter he could expect no mercy from the Italians. He did not know where Mehmet was, nor could he spare a man to help me find him. Fortunately Mehmet chose that moment to pay us a visit. He seemed worried and preoccupied, but readily answered my questions about the progress of the battle. He claimed to have inflicted heavy casualties on the Italians the previous evening, in what he called 'a highly successful mortar action'. He had abandoned Vithkuq under cover of darkness for fear of being surrounded and trapped in the town. He had launched a counter-attack early in the morning with two battalions, to cut off the enemy in a pincer movement.

'But,' he concluded sorrowfully, 'I was obliged to call off the attack when one of the battalions ran into very heavy enemy fire and was forced to withdraw with the loss of'—he hesitated—'of two killed and three wounded.'

Suddenly the fighting flared up again, spreading all along the line of hills. Shells crashed into the mountain side all round us or burst overhead in the branches in a whirr of flying splinters; two biplanes swooped to rake us from tree-top height, their bullets spattering the pine trunks and ricocheting viciously among the rocks. Throughout the afternoon the Italians shelled the ridge, while the aircraft circled overhead machine-gunning the hill tops and upper slopes. Under cover of this barrage their infantry began slowly but steadily to advance. Although the bombardment was uncomfortable enough it would not have sufficed to break a determined opposition. In addition to the guns which had shelled us at Shtyllë the Italians were using one battery of light mountain artillery for the whole operation—not a very heavy concentration against such formidable natural obstacles defended by so strong a force. Moreover, the hills were thickly wooded and even our forward positions were well concealed by scrub and undergrowth. While, therefore, the artillery and even the aircraft were to a large extent firing blind, the Italian infantry had to advance across open country which was swept, or should have been swept, by Partisan fire.

But although Mehmet himself showed an example of coolness and courage his troops and their officers failed to respond; they were utterly demoralized by the shelling and by the continuous strafing from the air. Xhelal in particular cut a ludicrous figure of impotence and fear; he stamped, gesticulated and shouted, but I could not persuade him to accompany me to his own forward positions, so that I began to wonder if he even knew where they were. Stefan kept up his miserable refrain of '*faut nous éloigner d'ici*,' until I swore to ask McLean to dismiss him unless he shut up.

By evening it was clear that the Partisans were going to fall back. The Italians were pressing close and had brought their 81-mm. mortars into action—weapons far more terrifying and deadly than the artillery. I returned with the bad news to McLean.

Back at the barracks I found that McLean had had a far more alarming experience than any of mine: together with Frederick Nosi he had gone to reconnoitre Vithkuq, and had arrived there just at the time when the Italians were setting fire to the town. The two of them had blundered into a party of the enemy in one of the streets; they had almost been cut off but had managed to get away under fire. McLean told me that Nosi had shown great resource and courage on this occasion.

There was little doubt that the Italians would reach Shtyllë some time the following morning. McLean therefore ordered the mules to be loaded with all the stores they could carry and told Smiley and me to take them up into the woods after dark, where we were to spend the night guarding them; Duffy and Jenkins would leave the barracks before dawn to blow the road between Vithkuq and Shtyllë, where it had been prepared for demolition; McLean himself would go tonight to see Mehmet. We would meet again at the barracks at eight o'clock next morning unless the Italians were already there, in which case our rendezvous would be the village of Panarit, five miles south-west of Shtyllë, on the other side of the mountains.

We had to leave behind nearly sixty canisters of explosives; under Smiley's direction these were cunningly concealed among some bushes two hundred yards from the barracks, and skilfully covered with green camouflage parachutes. Smiley was able to recover them four days later.

After a hurried meal Smiley and I moved off with Sergeant Gregson Allcott, Corporal Roberts, Stiljan, Stefan, a few camp-followers, about thirty mules and half that number of Vlach drivers. It took us two hours to find our way in the darkness, stumbling up a narrow track into the hills and feeling our way through the thick gloom of the woods. At last we had the mules unsaddled and the canisters stowed ready for immediate reloading. Spreading my sleeping bag on the most level patch of ground I could find on the hillside, I tried to snatch a little sleep.

Soon after seven Smiley and I started back for Shtyllë, leaving Gregson Allcott and Roberts to guard our stores. The woods smelt delicious in the early morning air, but we had little heart to enjoy scent or scenery. Shells were already falling among the trees below—probably 'overs', for there was no target in the neighbourhood to interest the Italian gunners; but the aeroplane was circling overhead, and so we must move with care. From the direction of Shtyllë came the crash of shells and the crump of heavy mortars.

We passed safely through the woods where the shells were falling, and took a path that led us out onto the dropping ground. Here we were under the fire of the mountain guns, which must by now be shooting from the hills where I had been the day before; I felt uncomfortably exposed, walking across the open grassland towards the col where I had met McLean on my first night in Albania. As we crossed the col and came down into the valley of Shtyllë we saw that the barracks were still intact; there was no sign of life in them. The Partisans seemed to have faded away, but evidently the Italians were taking no chances; shells and mortar bombs were falling thick in the valley and around the barracks, some of them bursting uncomfortably close to us as we hurried forward. I was frankly scared and several times threw myself on my face when I heard a shell coming our way; Smiley, on the other hand, showed an irritating indifference and walked on, his head held high, as though he were being pelted by urchins with snowballs while mounting guard.

After a quick look round the store-rooms we went outside to watch for McLean. I crouched in a ditch, peering over the top, but Smiley sauntered nonchalantly up and down, his hands in his pockets, among the puffs of smoke and dust and erupting earth. After half an hour of waiting, expecting at any time to find the Italians on top of us, we saw his tall figure striding blithely down the hill. As we had guessed, the Partisans were in full retreat. We must move to Panarit.

'We ought to have an officer with the mules,' concluded McLean. 'Peter, will you go back there now and wait for us until we join you, which I hope will be in a couple of hours. If we don't turn up, or if things get too hot for you, take the stuff on to Panarit. David and I will hang around here for a bit to see what happens.'

I spent an anxious morning waiting for them. A few shells dropped around us, none of them within two hundred yards but near enough to alarm the muleteers and to terrify Stefan and Stiljan, who sat one on each side of me begging me to move away from such a dangerous place. At the end of three hours I gave orders to load the mules and be ready to move at a moment's notice; I was worried that the Italians might cut us off or surprise us, for their patrols were reported to be very near. I had posted Albanian guards but had little confidence that they would give us warning. Another half-hour passed without a sign of McLean or Smiley; I was wondering how much longer I could risk waiting and endangering our stores, when my mind was made up for me: Stiljan came to me with a message from the leader of the Vlachs saying that unless I agreed to leave now they would desert us. I wondered if Stiljan had anything to do with the ultimatum, for he knew that I could not afford to let the Vlachs go; then I reflected that if we were caught by the Italians the English might be made prisoners, but the Vlachs and Albanians would almost certainly be shot. I gave the order to leave.

We climbed through the woods for an hour; then the track led onto a bare and rocky ridge with a superb view to north and east over wild, craggy mountain tops and thick, dark forest. We should now be safe from pursuit and so I ordered a halt, for the ascent had been arduous. We were preparing to go on when we were joined by Duffy and Jenkins, both of them wearing the exhausted but happy look of men who have survived great peril. They had indeed: they had reached their objective that morning, quite unaware that the Italians were in occupation of the heights overlooking the road on both sides. The Italians let them get well under way with their preparations before opening up on them from two directions with machine-guns, light machine-guns, rifles, and even mortars. It is a mystery how they managed to reach cover unwounded; but Jenkins had a bullet through the paybook which he kept in his breast pocket.

We reached Panarit the following afternoon, where we found McLean and Smiley, very despondent over the failure of the Brigade to put up a fight after all the training and armament it had received. I tried to comfort them by pointing out that a month's training was hardly enough to turn a rabble of peasants and artisans into disciplined soldiers who could be expected to stand up to shelling; that by trying to fight 'brigade actions' the Partisans were only sacrificing their natural advantages of mobility and knowledge of the country, in order to meet the enemy on his own ground where his superior training and armament were bound to tell; finally that they would do better for the moment to confine themselves to small, carefully planned 'bullying' actions, dispersing whenever the enemy concentrated against them.

There was, of course, one point that was not yet apparent to me: Enver Hoxha and Mehmet Shehu were not building up their military formations in order to fight Germans or Italians, but in order to gain control of Albania for themselves by force; they were not going to risk serious losses in operations which to them were only of secondary importance.

I suppose it was Stefan who had the last word on those three days of battle. As we jolted down the valley that led to Panarit his spirits rose to their normal exuberance.

'*Monsieur le Capitaine*,' he affirmed, nodding his head in wise appreciation, 'now we know that the Italians are no use. But for their artillery they would never have taken Shtyllë. Their soldiers have no stomach for fighting.'

VII

CLOAK WITHOUT DAGGER

In spite of the set-back of the last week we could at least be thankful that we had escaped with our lives and most of our stores. Much of our personal property had been looted, but if the looters were the inhabitants of Shtyllë we were in no position to blame them; they had suffered far worse than we. Those of them who had taken to the hills returned to find their houses in ashes; those who stayed behind were shot by the Italians.

This dilemma was our constant companion in our efforts to promote resistance: if we were to do our job properly we were bound to put innocent people in jeopardy; they had to stay and face reprisals while we found safety in flight. In the service of our country we simply had to harden our hearts. Whether the leaders of the L.N.C. were as squeamish I do not know; in any case our qualms were no protection to the victims.

Our usefulness in this area was over. Both the L.N.C. Central Council and the First Partisan Brigade had moved north; the Balli Kombëtar were becoming increasingly hostile. It was time for us to split up. On 31st August Smiley, with Sergeants Bell and Jenkins, set out north-east for the Mokra area, near Lake Ohrid, to establish a new headquarters for 'Consensus'; Duffy and my paramilitary expert, Gregson Allcott, left for a reconnaissance in the south; McLean decided to reconnoitre the Greek frontier east of Korçë before rejoining Smiley. Cairo had not yet replied to my request to go to Kossovo; in the meantime McLean suggested that I should move north-west into the Berat area to take on the duties of political liaison officer with the L.N.C. Central Council, at the same time keeping in touch with Abas Ermenje, the Balli Kombëtar leader in that region.

On 6th September I set out with Corporal Roberts, Stiljan, an Albanian servant, three Vlachs, and ten mules; I was riding a small but sturdy horse which I had bought in Panarit. The Vlachs proved excellent servants, efficient, tireless, and cheerful; Dimitri, their leader, a tall gaunt figure with a sardonic cast of expression who wore a splendid shepherd's cloak of grey wool, was a genius at loading his animals so that each could carry the maximum load with the least discomfort. This was important because the mules were heavily laden with stores, including a wireless set, clothing, blankets for the approaching winter, food and two canisters of gold. The wireless set presented the greatest problem in loading; it was about the size of an ordinary suitcase and ran off batteries which had to be charged regularly from a heavy and awkward petrol generator. The set, batteries and engine required two mules to transport them. Roberts and I each wore a canvas money-belt under our battledress, filled with gold. McLean gave me a word of warning.

'Take care you don't let any of the locals see you carrying that money; they're quite likely to bump you off to get it.'

'I can imagine they'd try and steal it, but surely they wouldn't go so far as murder?'

'Wouldn't they? Two months ago David gave two hundred sovereigns to a Partisan commissar, Ramiz Aranitas, to organize a çeta in this area. David's bodyguard—a man called Ali—saw him do it; he followed Ramiz for a mile, then shot him in the back, pinched the sovereigns and disappeared. My God! One of our Italian camp-followers at Shtyllë was shot in the back by a Partisan just for a pair of boots David had given him. You must never walk around this country on your own. That's why, after you've stayed in a house, your host always sends you on your way with an escort.'

I was to spend the night at the village of Leshnjë, some fifteen miles north-east of Panarit, in the house of Kahraman Ylli, a Partisan commissar; he had been warned of our coming, and sent a small party of his followers to guide us all the way. We climbed steadily for the first half of our journey, passing beneath the bare crags of the Ostravicë range whose tallest peaks, rising above seven thousand feet, glittered majestic and bright in the strong, hard sunlight.

At Leshnjë we were greeted by Kahraman Ylli's father. He was a man of fine physique, over six foot tall, with a fierce white moustache; but his features were predatory, his eyes narrow and shifty. He and his two brothers were rich landowners, whose attachment to the Partisan cause sprang partly from Kahraman's influence, partly from the hope of saving their property from confiscation by the L.N.C. While dinner was being prepared we were led into the guest-room and offered raki and mezë—small pieces of goat cheese, slices of hard-boiled egg, onions, and meat balls. Our personal kit was brought in and placed beside us, for this was the room where we should spend the night.

In the morning, when the mules were being loaded for an early start, I noticed that my sleeping bag was missing. I had seen it in the guest-room when I went to bed, but I had not slept in it; no one but our host and our three selves had been in the room since supper. Our host affected deep distress that the property of any guest should have disappeared in his house. I could not conceal my dismay at losing, on the threshold of a winter in the mountains, a sleeping bag at once warm and so light and compact that it could easily be carried in a small haversack. Much later, when I told McLean, he laughed.

'Not one of us has stayed in that house without losing something of value!'

We rode northwards until midday over rough and broken tracks under the enormous grim bulk of the Zaloshnje mountains; then we climbed slowly over a spur of the Tomorri range by a steep path that brought us down to a village nestling in the shadow of Mount Tomorri itself, the highest mountain of southern Albania. Tomorri was an ancient seat of pagan worship before the days when the gods of the Greeks ruled the land; in classical times pilgrims came there to consult an oracle as powerful as the oracle of Dodonian Zeus. Now a Bektashi monastery stood on the slopes. The Bektashi sect, which was influential in Albania, seems to have originated during Turkish times among the Janissaries and contains elements of different religions absorbed into the Islamic faith. In particular, its adherents are not forbidden the use of strong drink.

The area between Tomorri and Berat is called Skapari, a name whose harsh syllables suit well the savage stony country with its bleak mountains and narrow, precipitous valleys. Thick cloud laid the upper slopes of Mount Tomorri and a chill rain blew in our faces as we picked our way down the mountain towards the house of Muharrem Kaplanë, a powerful Bey who under Abas Ermenje commanded the Ballist çetas in this area. I had already sent word to him, asking for a meeting. On the borders of his domain an escort of retainers waited to take me to his house.

A solid stone building with, thick walls loopholed for defence, the home of the Kaplanë family stood on a mountainside overlooking a deep valley rich in grain fields and olive groves. We were shown into a cheerful guest-room with white walls and high windows looking onto a courtyard. The floor was spread with thick, richly coloured rugs; round the walls ran a broad divan strewn with silk cushions. In accordance with custom our arms were taken from us when we entered the house. This gesture signified that as long as we were under his roof our host was responsible with his life for our safety; if anyone were to kill us our host must start *Hakmarjë*—a blood feud—with him and would be dishonoured in the eyes of all his neighbours until he avenged our death with that of the murderer.

The *Hakmarjë* existed throughout Albania, among both Tosks and Ghegs. Whenever a man was murdered his family were obliged to start a blood feud, not only with the murderer but with all the murderer's family, one of whom must be killed to wipe out the stain; a man who left a blood feud unavenged was subject to perpetual dishonour and insult. It was not unusual for as many as twenty members of one family to be killed in the same vendetta in the course of two or three generations.[1] More than once an Albanian has said to me:

'I cannot go with you to that house; I have enemies.'

---

[1] Women and children were generally excluded from the *Hakmarjë*.

While a messenger ran down to the valley to tell our host of our arrival Roberts, Stiljan and I sat in the guest-room with the men of the house, sipping Turkish coffee. This was the time, Stiljan explained, when I must decide whether or not I meant to stay the night; if so, I should start to remove my boots. I had intended to press on after my talk with Kaplanë, for I was in a hurry to catch up with Enver Hoxha; but night was closing in and I had no wish to lose my way in that wild country, which would be only too easy in the dark, even with a guide. I began to undo my field boots, whereupon one of our companions took them off for me while another went to give orders to prepare a meal. We were in for a long wait, Stiljan told me, for they would probably kill and roast a sheep in our honour; meanwhile we must sit and make conversation, however tired we felt, until the food was served.

Muharrem Kaplanë was a well-built man in early middle age, with a grave and courteous manner and a quiet air of confidence and authority. He welcomed us cordially, serving us with raki from his own estate and a rich assortment of *mezë*.

I had asked to see him for two reasons: to hear his views on the situation in Skapari, where it was rumoured that the L.N.C. and the Balli Kombëtar were on the verge of civil war; and to ask him to arrange a meeting with Abas Ermenje, who was reputed to be the ablest and most vigorous of the Ballist leaders. However, it turned out that Abas Ermenje had left the district to attend a conference that would keep him away for a week.

I learned from Kaplanë that rumour had not exaggerated the tension in Skapari; he expected to be fighting against the L.N.C. within two or three days. The trouble had become acute after the failure of Abas Ermenje's attack on the Italian garrison at Berat a few weeks previously; according to Kaplanë the L.N.C. had promised their support but had treacherously withdrawn it in the middle of the battle, leaving the Balli out on a limb. At my insistence he promised to use his authority to restrain his men; but he added ominously that a great deal would depend on the Partisans.[1]

My next meeting was with Mestan Ujaniku, the L.N.C. area commander, who entertained me for lunch the following day in the mountain village of Nishovë. He was a picturesque old man with a huge white moustache and a breast covered with decorations of various countries, which he had apparently awarded to himself, for he had been a brigand until he joined the L.N.C. He welcomed me with a kiss on both cheeks, a painful experience because he had not shaved for some days. His account of the present situation confirmed Kaplanë's, although he placed the blame for it on the Balli, who, he said, had attacked prematurely and without giving warning to

---

[1] Kaplanë was captured by the Partisans at the end of the war and, after months of cruel imprisonment, executed.

the L.N.C. He too promised to urge moderation on his forces, but he seemed to have little confidence in the result.

Civil war would surely have broken out already but for the presence in the area of one Isa Toska, a notorious Albanian quisling, whom Balli and L.N.C. were combining to destroy. This man was a brigand who with Italian help had equipped a strong band of mercenaries and turned his own house into a fortress. Having for a long time terrorized the countryside with murder, robbery, and rape he had incurred the extreme hatred of all the people of Skapari. The Italians, having used him to subdue their enemies, as they used others of his type, now abandoned him to the fury of his countrymen; he was surrounded in his house and, after a few days' fighting, taken prisoner. According to one of Mestan's men who was present, he was blinded and his ears and nose cut off before being shot. This was one of the few occasions when I heard of Albanians using torture, until later on the Communists employed it to punish or extract information from 'traitors'.

Mestan now told me that Enver Hoxha and the Central Council had moved to the Peza area, five or six days' journey to the north-west. Because my first task was to make contact with them I abandoned my plans to see Abas Ermenje and contented myself with sending him a letter. I waved a friendly good-bye to Mestan as we rode out of Nishovë escorted by his Partisans; with his cheerful, easy-going manner, flamboyant uniform and obvious attachment to the old Albanian way of life he seemed an incongruous figure to be holding such a responsible position in an organization controlled by ruthless fanatics who proclaimed their contempt for all tradition. Evidently he thought so too, for when the policy of the L.N.C. hardened in favour of the extreme Left he joined Abas Kupi.

On the evening of 10th September we were approaching the village of Roshnik, six miles east of Berat, when we met a merry group of Partisans. They gave us the news of the surrender of Italy. We embraced each other while raki circulated freely; then it occurred to me that I ought to take some immediate and positive action. Roberts had a wireless 'sked' with Cairo at nine-thirty the following morning; I decided to spend the night in Roshnik, hoping to receive instructions from Cairo. Meanwhile I sent a courier into Berat to find out the situation and if possible make contact with the Italian commander; I also summoned the chief of the local Partisan get *çeta* to meet me.

No instructions came for me over the wireless; moreover my batteries ran out and the charging engine developed a technical fault which Roberts assured me rendered it useless. I was therefore cut off from Cairo until I could find Seymour, who I believed was still in the Peza area at a place called Grecë. When eventually I joined Seymour a week later, I received a message from Cairo ordering me to 'contact the Italian commanders in Berat and persuade them to implement the terms of the Armistice'. By then, of course, it was much too late.

My courier returned early in the morning. It appeared that the Partisans had entered Berat unopposed on 9th September and had invited the Italians to give them arms and to join their ranks. While they were discussing the details a German column swept into the town, causing the Partisans to leave in haste. Now Berat was an important town with a large Italian garrison, and the Germans were not yet established there in strength. During the next two days, therefore, I tried to persuade the Partisans to guide me into the town and put me in touch with their supporters; I hoped to see the Italian commander myself. For two days they vacillated, by which time the Germans were firmly in control. On 13th September we continued our journey north.

During the next three days our route lay through Ballist villages with strange and comic names—Qereshnik, Deshiran, and Belsh. Our Partisan escort proved an embarrassment, for the villagers, though friendly enough to ourselves and willing to provide us with food and guides, would not let us remain in the neighbourhood while we were with Partisans; in consequence we had to keep on the move, and went almost without sleep for three nights. After leaving Qereshnik we came down from the mountains into flat, open country where the going was much easier. Just before dusk we passed through the Kuçovë oilfields, the centre of Albanian oil production on which the Italians had based such hopes before the war; they had been disappointed, and now we rode through a forest of abandoned derricks in a deserted, smelly plain.

We changed guides at every village, but each relay seemed more useless than the last. Even when we lent them mules they held us up by loitering and demanding frequent halts to smoke and rest; at every fork in the path they stopped to argue with each other, chattering like parakeets, and they often lost the way. When we came to the bank of the Devoll river near Deshiran they delayed us for half an hour while they argued who should venture in to test the depth and swiftness of the stream. At last I lost patience and put my own horse into it, leading the string of mules across; but when we reached the other side three of the guides still remained behind, waving their arms and twittering shrilly until one of the Vlachs went back for them with a spare mule.

After the bare mountains the country beyond Deshiran seemed soft and fertile, with newly harvested fields of maize on every side; but the few farms and dwellings we passed were miserable hovels of mud and thatch, where wretched undernourished families lived sunk in apathy, poverty and filth.

At Belsh we took on fresh guides who would see us across the Shkumbi and the main road from Elbasan to Durazzo. This was the only hazardous part of our journey, for the river was broad and deep, the road in constant use and probably guarded; with our long train of mules it would be difficult to escape attention. We planned to make our crossing about midnight, when we could hope that the traffic would have ceased and the guards would be asleep; and we chose a point some two miles east of the town of Peqin, where there were no villages whose dogs might betray our presence.

A bright moon hung in the sky as we approached the bank, shining cold and white and beautiful on the broad stretches of sand beside the river and illuminating faintly the pencil of road beyond. The calm, scented night, the moon and the quiet river carried memories of Andalusia and the *Romancero Gitano*; but the scene that would have stirred Garcia Lorca brought only anxiety to me. If anyone were watching on the road he could hardly fail to see us against the gleaming sand.

I sent across a guide with two Partisan scouts to keep a look-out for us on the other side; then, dividing the mules into three groups, each with a Vlach, I ordered them to follow me at five minute intervals. When all were across I went forward on foot with the guide to reconnoitre the road. On either hand it ran straight and deserted for as far as I could see. I decided to take the whole party across at once, and sent back the guide to bring them on. After a few anxious moments while the mules clattered across the tarmac road we found ourselves on a track climbing gently through low, scrub-covered hills. We continued for an hour, to put a safe distance between ourselves and the road; then I ordered the mules to be unloaded in a small wood and settled down to sleep for the three remaining hours of darkness.

At ten o'clock next morning, 16th September, we rode into Seymour's camp. This consisted of two or three tents pitched in a pine wood among the hills. We were greeted by Bombardier Hill and Sergeant Smith, Seymour's wireless operator and paramilitary specialist. Seymour, they told us, was at the village of Arbonë, some five or six miles south-west of Tirana and six hours' journey from where we were at Grecë, he was engaged in negotiations with General Dalmazzo, G.O.C. Ninth Army and Italian Commander-in-chief in Albania. There were signals awaiting me from Cairo, and others which I must give Roberts to send now that he could re-charge his batteries; I decided to spend the night at Grecë and join Seymour next day.

It was just as well that I made this decision, for a crisis was immediately thrust upon me. Dimitri, the leader of the Vlachs, announced that he and his men could stay with us no longer; with the approach of winter they must get back to their families, who would starve without them. Worse still, the mules belonged to the Vlachs, for the Italian attack on Shtyllë had prevented my buying any for myself and none had been obtainable in Panarit. Not all my entreaties, reinforced by lavish offers of gold, would persuade the Vlachs to stay; courteously, even regretfully, Dimitri pointed out that his original contract with McLean had expired at the beginning of the month, and although they had carried on in order to see us through our journey they could not remain longer; nor dared they sell us their mules, which were their livelihood and which they could not replace at this time of year. I had no choice but to let them go. Their departure left me with one horse and one mule—insufficient to transport even my wireless set; Seymour was very short of mules and there were none to be bought in the district. I could only hope that we should not have to move in a hurry.

Early in the morning a courier arrived from Seymour with messages for Cairo; he was returning immediately and so I asked him to conduct me to Arbonë. I decided to take Stiljan, leaving Roberts to help Smith and Hill, who had more work than they could manage, with the cipher and wireless duties. We travelled for five hours over drab, low hills formed of a kind of black sandstone and covered with stunted mountain oak; we passed no villages or houses, but only an occasional charred ruin. The poor vegetation is attributed to centuries of grazing by goats; the depopulation was caused by an Italian punitive expedition the previous year against Myslim Peza, when nearly every house and village in these hills was burnt.

At noon I reached Arbonë, where I was warmly greeted by Seymour in the house which he shared with Myslim Peza and Colonel Barbi Cinti, who until the surrender had been commandant of the Italian aerodrome at Shijak, near Tiranë. Seymour looked tired and very ill; his moustache flared as bravely as ever but his face was white and sunken, his eyes deeply shadowed. He suggested that I stay with him because there was plenty of work for me in Arbonë. Enver Hoxha and the Central Council were living in a farm-house a few miles back in the hills, but they visited Arbonë daily.

Arbonë was a small village on the southern edge of an open plain bounded on the north by a low wooded ridge, which separated it from Tirana, and on the south by the Peza hills; the plain was bisected by the river Arzen which flowed from east to west between steep banks. From the river's edge to the Peza hills the plain was dotted with Partisans bivouacking with no attempt at shelter or camouflage. Their numbers grew every day with the arrival of fresh Italian deserters from units of the Ninth Army. Colonel Barbi Cinti was working conscientiously to weld the Italians into a composite fighting force, which was to be commanded by General Azzi from the 'Firenze' Division. Azzi proved an unfortunate choice. He explained to Seymour and me that he had never been the same since he had experienced the British bombardment at Alamein; this was understandable but scarcely excused his subsequent conduct: a few months after his appointment to command the Italian Partisans in Albania he absconded to the mountains, accompanied by his Staff, with a considerable sum of money given him by the Allies to feed and equip his men.

For about a fortnight after the surrender of Italy there was one belief held in common by almost everybody in Albania, whether German or Italian, British or Albanian, L.N.C. or Balli Kombëtar: that an Allied invasion of the Balkans was imminent. That this was not so naïve a hope at the time as it seems in retrospect is clear from the pages of Chester Wilmot's *Struggle for Europe*. I have no doubt that had there been an invasion at that time it would have been followed by a general rising in Albania, with the co-operation of most of the Italian army of occupation. We were therefore surprised that our headquarters in Cairo, usually so prodigal of advice and admonishment, failed to give us any directive at this critical moment. Seeing nothing of the larger picture we abused our office savagely for their neglect.

As soon as he heard the news of the surrender, on 9th September, Seymour hurried to Arbonë, where he sent a message to General Dalmazzo in Tiranë requesting his co-operation and asking for a meeting; unfortunately the message was not delivered until the next day, when the Germans were already in occupation of the capital. However, Dalmazzo sent a staff car to Arbonë, which took Seymour, wearing an Italian army greatcoat over his uniform, through the German control posts to Army Headquarters, where he had a long discussion with Dalmazzo's Chief of Intelligence. At the same time, in an adjoining room, Dalmazzo himself was in conference with senior German officers, arranging his own evacuation under German protection to Belgrade; not until Dalmazzo had left Albania did Seymour learn the truth.

This deplorable example was followed by other senior officers of the Ninth Army, including at least two Divisional Commanders; abandoning their men they thought only of saving themselves and their families. The junior officers and rank-and-file, deprived of the leadership they had a right to expect, became hopelessly demoralized. Overcome with terror large numbers allowed themselves to be disarmed and led into captivity by a handful of Germans; others dispersed to farms and houses in the hills, where they worked for the owners in return for their keep; the more virile among them joined the Partisans, who, it must be said, treated them well; a few attached themselves to British missions as cooks, batmen, or grooms, rendering valuable service and often showing great loyalty and courage in the face of severe hardship and danger.

The speed of the German reaction to the surrender surprised every-one in Albania. Within forty-eight hours German troops had occupied every key point in the country; although few they were enough to dominate the people, disarm the Italians and contain the Partisans. In the face of German resolution and Allied inactivity most Albanians outside the L.N.C. followed the old precept, 'When rape is inevitable relax and enjoy it', and adjusted themselves to a German instead of an Italian occupation. Their attitude was reasonable in the circumstances.

Without Allied help they could not hope to expel the Germans, who would in any case be obliged to leave the country if the war continued its present course against them. Better, surely, to bear with patience a temporary inconvenience rather than try to end it prematurely at the risk of property, security and life. Moreover, to many patriotic Albanians it was by no means clear that an Allied victory was in the best interests of their country; they feared—perhaps I should say fore-saw—that it would result not only in the loss of Kossovo but also in their own subjection to Communist rule.

The Germans played cleverly upon these feelings. Firstly they made very few demands on the civilian population, to whom they behaved with courtesy and consideration, and secondly they made much political capital out of the Kossovo question. It is a measure of their success that when they set up a puppet government in Tirana they were able to induce Albanians of high principles and distinction to serve in it. As time went on it became more and more obvious that we could offer the Albanians little inducement to take up arms compared with the advantages they could enjoy by remaining passive. I must confess that we British Liaison Officers were slow to understand their point of view; as a nation we have always tended to assume that those who do not whole-heartedly support us in our wars have some sinister motive for not wishing to see the world a better place. This attitude made us particularly unsympathetic towards the Balli Kombëtar, although the latter was a thoroughly patriotic organization. The Balli refrained from collaboration with the Germans against us; indeed, they gave us much covert help; but they did sit on the fence, hoping to establish themselves so firmly in the administration of the country that the victorious Allies would naturally call upon them to form a government. Indeed, they were naïvely convinced that the British and Americans would be glad to entrust the government to them, in preference to the Communist alternative of the L.N.C. The leaders of the L.N.C. had good reasons for continuing the struggle; but their interests, of course, were not Albania's.

During those days at Arbonë large numbers of German aircraft flew directly over us, taking off from or landing at Tiranë airfield. The plain in front of our house was alive with troops—several thousands of them—who must have been clearly visible from the air and whose camp fires at night could be seen for miles around. Although they were within easy range of German artillery and presented a perfect target for air attack they made no attempt to dig so much as a slit trench for their protection, despite repeated warnings to Myslim Peza and their other commanders from Seymour and myself; nor could we persuade the *Shtabit* to disperse them amid the cover of the neighbouring hills.

I was astonished that we were never awakened in the morning by anything more unpleasant than the singing of the Partisans. After a few days, however, Myslim Peza became alarmed for our personal safety and insisted on moving us to a farmhouse which overlooked the plain from the shelter of the Peza hills—one of the few that had survived the Italian holocaust of the previous year.

Myslim himself had a highly developed sense of personal security, acquired during fourteen years as an outlaw. He never slept twice in the same place; nor, if he could avoid it, would he spend a night in a house, but would move into the hills each evening with an escort. He had recently been appointed Commander-in-Chief of all L.N.C. forces in the field—excluding, of course, those of Abas Kupi. Of all the leaders of the L.N.C. that I met in Albania, with the possible exception of Mustafa Gjinishi, Myslim was the most charming, the most helpful and the most honest. A man of no intellectual ability or pretensions, he understood little of politics—a weakness which his more cunning colleagues exploited to their advantage; but he was a brilliant guerrilla fighter with outstanding qualities of leadership, loyalty and courage.

In his own country his people revered him with a devotion almost amounting to worship; he was known among them as Baba, or Father, and whenever they mentioned his name they would touch their foreheads in the Moslem sign of respect. Peza, where his word was absolute law, was the only region in Albania in which I ventured on journeys without an escort. His frame was slight and emaciated, his dark marmoset's face drawn and sunken; but his small body held enormous strength and inhuman endurance, his black eyes flashed with excitement, enthusiasm, or anger and his thin, delicate hands were never still.

On both of us he bestowed a warm and generous affection, giving us his utmost help in our military and political problems—a refreshing change from the attitude of his colleagues. Himself an enthusiastic and convivial drinker he was delighted to find in Seymour and myself companions who would share his pleasures. We learned to start our work at seven in the morning in order to be finished by eleven o'clock, when we were invariably interrupted. There would be a knock on the door of the room where we lived and worked, and a small procession would enter: first would come Myslim's wife, carrying a roast chicken, followed by Myslim himself, his A.D.C., and his escort, all carrying bottles of raki and plates of mezë. The session would often last two or three hours, while we sat cross-legged on the floor at a low, round wooden table, discussing whatever problems had cropped up since our last meeting. Myslim's wife, who in defiance of Albanian custom sat through these parties with us, was a small slim woman of about forty, dark and wiry like her husband; she always dressed like a man, carrying an automatic at her hip, and had shared her husband's outlawry since its beginning. A less sympathetic participant in these gatherings was Myslim's Political Commissar, a bitter, cantankerous Communist who considered it his duty to the Party to thwart us whenever he had the chance.

We were particularly grateful to Myslim for his 'elevenses' because for a time they provided us with our only meals. The owners of the farm were supposed to feed us in return for our rent; but since it was the month of

Ramadan, which the family strictly observed, they were much too debilitated to cook us any food. In theory our rent included the exclusive use of a large room where we could work undisturbed, but in Albania it is considered most discourteous to leave guests by themselves; however much we desired privacy the good manners of our hosts forbade it. The Albanian code of hospitality does not allow a host to accept payment from his guests; but the demands we were forced to make upon our hosts and the risks to which our presence exposed them put us under an obligation to pay generously. In practice we overcame the difficulty by asking them to accept the money for the benefit of the children.

The first of my tasks when I had re-established contact with Enver Hoxha was to answer a series of questions from Cairo about the political situation in Tiranë. Cairo seemed to attach particular importance to the subject, and so, when I was unable to get a clear picture from the Central Council, I decided without much enthusiasm that I should have to visit Tiranë myself. Since it was impossible for me to go in uniform I signalled Cairo for permission to put on civilian clothes; the only reply I received was a repeat of the original questionnaire. I was now committed.

After a good deal of argument Enver Hoxha reluctantly agreed, on the intervention of Myslim, to provide me with a guide and prepare a safe house where I could stay in the city. He made one stipulation: because he would be responsible for my safety I must only see people approved by himself or by my hosts in Tiranë. He did nothing to raise my spirits by pointing out how conspicuous I should appear in the town, for not only did I look like a foreigner but I even walked like one; to the vast entertainment of Seymour, Myslim, and Stiljan he insisted on giving me lessons in the 'Albanian Walk'. He was not impressed with my progress. On the eve of my departure he turned up at our farm-house with a certain Mehmet Hoxha, ex-Prefect of Dibra, who was lending me a suit of clothes. This gentleman, of whom I was later to see a great deal, was short, broad, and stout—in fact, of quite a different build from mine.

Shortly before midday on 22nd September I set out with my guide, a young Albanian of nineteen or twenty who spoke a little Italian. Mehmet Hoxha's old grey lounge suit hung loosely round my waist, leaving my wrists and ankles to protrude like the stumps of a scarecrow; on my feet were a pair of patent-leather shoes at least two sizes too small for me; my head—and my ears too—were covered by a soft green felt hat. I had grown a sparse blond moustache which drooped discontentedly at the corners of my lip. Seymour tried to console me as he said good-bye.

'I can promise you one thing, old boy: you may not look much like an Albanian, but at least you won't be mistaken for a British Officer.'

It was a day of blazing sunshine; the plain of Arbonë lay shimmering under the noonday heat. We plodded slowly and in silence across the fields, over the narrow bridge spanning the river, and up into the hills. I was surprised to meet no one on the way, until I remembered that this was the time of day when sensible people rested; perhaps that was why my guide had chosen it. After the first half-hour my patent-leather shoes pinched and galled at every step, so that I had to call frequent halts to take them off. At first I was glad when we reached the hills and began to climb in the shade of the woods; but each time I stumbled on the steep and broken track, crying out with the pain that gripped my feet, I longed for the sun-baked but easy paths of the plain.

Every moment I cursed more savagely the foolhardiness that had sent me on this journey; I reflected that I was involving myself and my friends in a great deal of trouble and some hazard in pursuit of information of uncertain value. I preferred not to dwell on the consequences of capture. As a parachutist and saboteur I knew that my chances of survival would be slender enough if I were taken in uniform; in civilian clothes I faced the prospect of a squalid and painful end accompanied by every circumstance of ignominy and ridicule.

Before leaving the cover of the hills we halted in a small copse on the outskirts of Tiranë to cool down, recover our breath, and brush the dust of the journey from our clothes. I carried no papers, and so we had agreed that if we ran into a German picket or were stopped by a patrol I was to look stupid and say only, '*Shqypëtar. Skadokument.*'[1] We trusted that this simple phrase would allay suspicion, because I could not hope to run away in those shoes of Mehmet Hoxha's.

I could feel my heart pounding as I accompanied my guide into the first streets. I tried to look indifferent to my surroundings and pay no attention to the groups of townspeople who passed; they, I noticed, were paying a great deal of attention to me, scanning me closely and gazing after me with expressions of hilarious astonishment. The only people who paid no attention whatever were the few parties of German soldiers who passed us, marching in step, their heads held high, looking neither to right nor left. My guide, who kept shooting me sombre glances out of the corner of his eye, was getting more and more nervous, obviously sharing my own feelings. Suddenly he brightened; following his gaze I saw a lone carozza standing on a corner, with a tired looking horse and sleepy driver. Painfully but thankfully I climbed in and sank back on the cushions as my guide gave an address to the driver. We rattled through dusty side streets, turned into a broad avenue and after a few hundred yards turned off again into a quiet road flanked by prosperous modern villas with bright tidy gardens. At one of these we halted, and after paying the carozza, rang the bell. In a second the door was opened

---

[1] 'I am Albanian. I have no papers.'

and my guide hustled me into the cool twilight of a large, comfortably furnished room.

A tubby, middle-aged man dressed in a Palm Beach suit rose from an armchair and greeted me warmly in English, introducing himself as the owner of the house; for security reasons I was not allowed to know his name, but I gathered that he was a prosperous businessman who owned some copper mines east of Tiranë, and that he was a member of the Greek Orthodox Church. He told me later that he had joined the L.N.C. for patriotic reasons although he detested Communism; he seemed to be a staunch Anglophile and treated me during my visit with exuberant hospitality. After nearly two months in the hills I wallowed in the luxuries of a comfortable bed and a hot bath, of good food and wine, of thick carpets and soft chairs.

My fellow-guests were two members of the Central Council, Ymer Dyshnica and Njako Spiro, both of whom I had met in Shtyllë; they were close friends, who had worked together in France during the first year of the Italian occupation of their country, editing a newspaper for Albanian exiles. Dyshnica was a young doctor of great ability, intelligence and charm;[1] Spiro, by contrast, was a sour-faced, black billed fanatic who would heap abuse and hysterical invective upon all his countrymen who were not members of the L.N.C. I had disliked him in Shtyllë but was forced to a reluctant sympathy when I learned that he suffered from a chronic and incurable disease of the liver.

During the three days I stayed in this house I was occupied with a succession of visitors. Although Enver Hoxha had stipulated that I should meet only people approved by himself or my host, they did their best between them to show me a representative selection of Tiranë opinion. Most of my visitors were professional or business men; none, apart from Dyshnica and Spiro, was a Communist or fellow-traveller; all spoke English, French, or Italian and so I was able to converse without an interpreter.

Hitherto, it seemed, the new occupation had weighed very lightly on the people of Tiranë, who were therefore disinclined to take any active steps against it. The imposition of a curfew, the establishment of check points on the roads, and the compulsory registration of private cars were the only restrictions; civilians were supposed to carry identity cards, but were seldom required to produce them. In the last few days, however, as a result of a number of attacks on Germans in the countryside, the control had tightened considerably; some houses had been searched and the streets were watched by security police in plain clothes. At the same time the German authorities circulated through their Albanian agents grim stories of the ruthlessness of their reprisals and the grim fate that would overtake any Albanian found 'consorting with the enemy'.

---

[1] It is reported that he has been executed by Enver Hoxha.

One of my objects was to find out what aircraft were using Tiranë airfield. Among my visitors was a young man of an illustrious Albanian family, Liqa Bey Toptani; belonging to no political party he maintained good relations with the L.N.C., even with Njako Spiro. Now he volunteered to take me for a drive in his car along the road past the airfield, where I should be able to see all I wanted. On the afternoon following my arrival he turned up with a companion in a small black Fiat saloon; he asked me to get into the back, adding apologetically that I should attract less attention there.

We drove through side streets and into a broad avenue, past the Dajti Hotel, Tiranë's last word in modern luxury, and the chrome stucco palace of King Zog sprawling in its neglected gardens; after half an hour's drive round the town Toptani brought us out on to the road leading towards the airfield.

'You'll easily be able to see the aeroplanes through the fence,' he explained. 'We can drive past very slowly and then perhaps on our way back—' he broke off with a gasp, putting his foot on the brake.

Leaning over his shoulder I saw through the windscreen a car drawn up at the side of the road about fifty yards ahead, with German soldiers standing around it.

'I am afraid it is a control post,' he muttered and began to put the car into reverse. At this moment the car in front began to move on; one of the soldiers noticed us and signalled us to approach. We had no alternative, for behind was a long stretch of straight, open road. As he put the car into gear Toptani whispered to me:

'Sit back and look as stupid as you can. I will do the talking—do not say anything.'

Ramming my green hat well over my cars I huddled in a corner, looking cautiously from under my eyelids for cover in case we had to run. There was not so much as a ditch or a tree; there was nowhere we could flee in safety. I had come to Tiranë unarmed, believing that a gun was more likely to get me into trouble than out of it. I watched Toptani's companion slide his right hand inside his coat and, leaning forward for a moment, saw his fingers close over the butt of an automatic. I felt quite helpless, numb and sick with fear.

A corporal with a slung Schmeizer put his head through the driver's window and spoke quite civilly in German to the two in front; then he came to my window, looked at me searchingly and asked for my papers. I stared back oafishly at him from under the brim of my hat and hissed my piece:

'*Shqypëtar. Ska dokument.*' He gave me a long, puzzled stare and turned back to Toptani. He was clearly dissatisfied about something, and I felt a surge of panic when he turned away as though to shout to his men. At that moment Toptani had an inspiration; from his wallet he pulled out a crumpled piece of paper and waved it in the corporal's face. The German scanned it for a moment and evidently found what he wanted; for he handed it back with a friendly smile and waved us on. When at last we were out of sight and I was mopping my sweaty face Toptani began to laugh.

'Really, that German was very unobservant!'

'Why?' I asked.

'Well, he was asking for the registration paper of this car, which has to have the *Feldkommandatur* stamp on it. Unfortunately there are no papers for this car, but I suddenly remembered that I was carrying a document belonging to another car—a Lancia with a Durazzo number plate. Luckily he only looked at the official stamp and did not notice that this is a Fiat with a Tiranë number plate.'

He stopped the car, and while my two companions pretended to be fiddling with the engines I managed to have a good look at the aircraft scattered on the field. They did not seem very interesting—a few Messerschmitt 109s, half a dozen Stukas, about twenty Junkers 52 troop-carriers, and some old 3-engine Savoias. When we passed the control post on our way back to the town the corporal recognized us and gave us a spectacular salute.

The following evening Dyshnica and Spiro were not present at dinner. My host explained that they had gone back to the hills, adding:

'This evening we received information that the Germans are going to impose a much stricter control in this city; they have already begun to search the houses, section by section. I do not think it is safe for you to stay here any longer. You cannot leave tonight because of the curfew, but you will forgive me if I order your guide to be here after breakfast tomorrow morning to take you back to Arbonë.'

Although I had thoroughly enjoyed my visit I was not inclined to linger after my host's warning. I had the answers to almost all of Cairo's questions and I had been promised some useful introductions in Kossovo should I be allowed to go there. At nine o'clock the next morning, having taken an affectionate leave of my host, I climbed into the carozza which was waiting outside the gate with my guide; after our experience of two days before we had decided that this was a safer method of travel in the city than a car. We returned by the same route as we had entered, making our way out of the city unchallenged. By midday I was back with Seymour in the farm-house, where I thankfully discarded the patent-leather shoes and bathed my blistered and swollen feet. Myslim embraced me warmly and laid on a special celebration in honour of my safe return.

I was alarmed to hear that during my absence Roberts had been taken gravely ill with malaria and bronchial pneumonia. The three N.C.O.s at Grecë had been seriously overworked; not only did they have to deal with a heavy two-way traffic of signals between Cairo and ourselves, but they also had to receive supply drops at all hours of the night. Moreover the dropping ground, although the only possible one in the area, was much too small, with the result that stores were often scattered among the woods on the neighbouring hillsides the N.C.O.s had to spend hours searching for them.

The whole region had a bad name for malaria, against which the only medicine we possessed was quinine. Roberts was a man of frail physique, and for a few days there were fears for his life. However, Seymour had sent an Italian doctor to him as soon as he heard of his illness; when, the day after my return from Tirana, I visited the camp the doctor told me that Roberts was out of danger.

For the next fortnight my time was fully occupied by my liaison work with the L.N.C. Central Council. These duties were exacting, dull and uncongenial. When I had met the Council at Shtyllë I had been able to leave the brunt of the discussion to McLean, speaking only if my advice was asked; now that I was their official link with Cairo they regarded me almost as their servant. They would often fail to turn up for meetings they had arranged; they would fritter away hours of discussion with petty complaints—usually directed against the B.B.C. for some favourable reference to a leading member of the Balli Kombëtar or for failing to denounce one of their political opponents; their claims of military success against the Germans—always unsupported by evidence—grew daily more inflated, their demands on my credulity more absurd. Despite all our protests they refused to allow Seymour or myself to attend any of their operations, leading us to the conclusion that they did not welcome any check on the accuracy of their reports; the few simple requests I passed to them from Cairo were ignored.

Perhaps their most irritating habit was the opening of our letters. Seymour and I kept up a correspondence with Neel in the north and McLean in the east, as well as with our N.C.O.s at Greece. Our letters had to pass through L.N.C. territory, and on every occasion they were delivered with the seals broken and the unvarying excuse that they had been 'opened in error'.

It was sometimes difficult to treat seriously their childish reflections on our own good faith. On one occasion, after I had left the country, a certain British Liaison Officer prepared, at the request of Enver Hoxha, a list of the names and regiments of British officers in northern Albania. The list read something like this:

Lieutenant-Colonel N. L. D. McLean, The Royal Scots Greys.
Major David Smiley, The Royal Horse Guards.
Major Richard Riddell, The Royal Horse Artillery.
Captain Anthony Simcox, The Royal Horse Artillery.
Captain The Honourable Rowland Winn, 8th King's Own Royal Irish Hussars.

When he came to read it to the Central Council the British officer noticed that at each mention of the word 'Royal' Enver Hoxha shot a significant glance round the table at his colleagues, who all nodded in understanding: officers from such regiments must obviously be reactionaries and Fascists. With a disarming smile the B.L.O. ended his recital:

'But *my* regiment is the *Manchester* Regiment—the *People's* regiment!'

The two most serious problems were arms and money. It was quite true that we were very short of arms, for our Italian deserters had brought none with them; but I pointed out to the Council that there was a shortage of arms in every theatre of war at this time, and one or two successful operations with the equipment we had already given them would be more convincing to Cairo than all their eloquence or mine.

Their appetite for money was insatiable. Since my arrival at Arbonë we had already given them three thousand sovereigns to buy food, equipment, and—where possible—arms for their new Italian allies; now they demanded a further fifteen thousand sovereigns. This sum, they blandly assured me, was the bare minimum necessary for the upkeep of their troops—they had just declared 'general mobilization' throughout the territory under their control; for the maintenance of their soldiers' families; for the relief of Albanian refugees from Kossovo and Macedonia, and for the purchase of grain to avert famine in the coming winter. I passed on their request to Cairo, unaware that the E.A.M. in Greece had used identical arguments to obtain funds which they had then misapplied to the use of the Communist Party. Cairo agreed to drop the money, but in small amounts, and to disperse it among the various British missions in the country, hoping thus to control its expenditure. The result was the same: most of the money was diverted to finance the Albanian Communist Party, who took exclusive credit for such relief work as was done.

It was not until much later that we learned how much care the Albanian Communist leaders took to see that the people were kept in ignorance of the source of their relief. When the Partisans entered Tiranë after the German withdrawal at the end of 1944 a certain British Liaison officer with the Partisans arranged a large-scale drop of food and clothing over the airfield to succour the starving population. Enver Hoxha and Mehmet Shehu insisted that the aircraft should not carry British markings. This stipulation was not understood by the R.A.F. The aircraft flew low over the city, their red, white and blue markings clearly visible to the crowds watching from below; as the containers floated down it was seen that each one was brightly painted with an enormous Union Jack. White and almost speechless with rage Mehmet Shehu turned to the Englishman and spat in his face.

'If only I had anti-aircraft guns I would order them to shoot down your planes!'

Enver Hoxha presided at our meetings, acting also as interpreter for me. Mehmet Shehu was still in the south with the First Brigade, so that on purely military matters I dealt with the Chief of Staff, Spiro Moisi, a silent, unassuming little man who understood his own subject and kept silent on others.

The most colourful member of the Council, whom I now met for the first time, was Mustafa Gjinishi, one of the heroes of the 1941 rising and one of the architects of the Mukaj agreement with the Balli Kombëtar. Cheerful and witty, highly intelligent, and incorruptibly honest Gjinishi commanded the affection and respect of all his country-men, of whatever political complexion. Now in his early thirties he had spent much of his adult life abroad and could converse fluently in English, French, Italian, and German. At the invitation of Myslim Peza, who was devoted to him, he came often to our farm-house, where we found him a delightful and stimulating companion. An avowed Communist but a sincere patriot he urged conciliation on the L.N.C., believing the liberation of his country to be more urgent than the struggle for political power. This attitude branded him as a Right deviationist in the eyes of his fellow Communists; his personal courage, his friendship with the British, and his popularity with the Partisan rank and file, to whom his wit and audacity made an irresistible appeal—all aroused the jealousy and suspicion of Enver Hoxha, who saw in Gjinishi his most serious competitor for the leadership of the movement. Enver Hoxha never deviated from Stalinist orthodoxy, particularly in his treatment of political rivals. At the end of August 1944 Gjinishi was murdered in an ambush near Dibra, on the Jugoslav frontier. The incident took place some distance from the battle area; no one saw the murderers or heard of them again.

A very different character was Tito's representative with the L.N.C., Ali Gostivari, alias Ali Dušanović, alias Dušan Mugoša. A tall, heavily-built Kossovar, with a thick, black 'Uncle Joe' moustache, he had seemed to us a ridiculous figure at Shtyllë, earning from McLean the nickname of 'The Shop Assistant' on account of his fussy manner. Now he appeared in a different light, speaking at meetings with an authority that commanded even Enver Hoxha's respect and adopting an angry, hectoring manner whenever his opinions were questioned. To Seymour and myself he was formally polite, affecting an ignorance of any language other than Albanian and Serbo-Croat. However, an incident at the end of September revealed his true attitude with alarming clarity.

One morning Seymour and I were working in our room when we were surprised by the arrival of Sergeant Smith from Grecë; he looked extremely worried. Two days ago Ali Gostivari and another member of the Central Council, whom the N.C.O.s knew by sight and who spoke English, had arrived at the camp, saying that they had come on our behalf to see if the N.C.O.s needed anything; naturally no one had thought to question their statement. They had stayed two nights, during which time they had read through all our papers, interfered with the wireless operators at their work by questioning them about wave-lengths, skeds, and other technical details, asked them numerous leading questions about our work and the reports we sent back—and—here Smith could not control his indignation—had tried to indoctrinate the three of them with Communism.

Myslim, furious, sent for Gostivari as soon as he heard our story. Unabashed, Gostivari assured us that he and his companion had stayed in our camp at the pressing invitation of our N.C.O.s; they had not looked at any of our papers or engaged in any political discussion, apart from a few words of praise for Mr. Churchill.

At the beginning of October Tony Neel joined us on a visit from the Zogist country north of Tiranë; he brought with him an escort of Abas Kupi's men. At the time of the Italian surrender Neel was in the Mati country, maintaining an uneasy contact between Abas Kupi's followers and a force of Partisans under Haxhi Lleshi, nephew of a famous Dibran chieftain. After the surrender they were joined by the Firenze Division. With their combined forces Neel planned to occupy the old fortress town of Krujë, the birthplace of Skanderbeg, preparatory to an attack on Tiranë in conjunction with the troops of Myslim Peza.

They occupied the town, only to be driven out by a German attack powerfully supported with artillery. Neel himself narrowly escaped death when a shell hit the house he occupied, killing a woman in the next room. He told us that Abas Kupi, who had at first been reluctant to co-operate with the Italians, fought like a lion, killing a number of Germans with his tommy-gun and inspiring his tribesmen to a stubborn resistance that provided the only serious fighting of the battle; the Partisans, Neel added, fought indifferently and the Italians never fought at all. Soon after the Partisans and the Firenze Division entered the city four German soldiers drove up in a lorry; they got out and began to move among the Italians, disarming them with magnificent self-confidence and an insolent contempt for the Partisans. Nobody tried to stop them until Abas Kupi himself appeared on the scene and dispatched them with a few bursts of his tommy-gun. Neel was certain that if the others had fought as well as Abas Kupi's men they would have held Krujë. After the battle they had all suffered terribly from hunger, and were eventually reduced to killing their mules for food.

Neel went on to tell us that Abas Kupi was indignant with the L.N.C. Central Council, who had given him neither the arms nor the money they had promised him when he had joined them in 1942; Kupi was convinced that all the power in the movement was in the hands of the Communists, who were using the organization for their own political ends, regardless' of their country's interests. I was not entirely surprised when Enver Hoxha came to see me the following day to tell me, with a confidence surprising in one who had not been present, that the Partisans had borne the brunt of the battle and that Abas Kupi had done no fighting at all.

Having met Neel in Egypt I was shocked at the change in him now. His face was sallow and drawn, the skin stretched tight over the cheek-bones; his eyes were yellow, and he ran a temperature; there remained no trace of his old high spirits. Even to us it was evident that he had jaundice. Luckily we were able to find a competent doctor among the Italian troops in Arbonë, who treated Neel with such medicines as we could get by courier from Tiranë. The heavy, steamy heat that had lasted now for several weeks was affecting Seymour and myself; our room was close and airless, the plain and the encircling hills broiling under the harsh sun. Seymour's exhaustion increased with a sharp attack of dysentery, while I with a temperature and a sore throat squirmed also under the fiery irritation of prickly heat.

Upon this scene of distress Bill McLean entered unexpectedly a few days after Neel's arrival. He brought us the news that a brigadier would soon be arriving to co-ordinate the activities of all British Liaison Officers in Albania; McLean had just finished preparing a dropping ground and headquarters for him and his staff on the plateau of Biza in the wild mountains of Cermenikë, east of Tiranë.

The following day the weather broke in a deluge of rain which continued all day. Myslim now insisted that we move from our farm-house, where he said that we were no longer safe. We set up a temporary headquarters under canvas in a valley near the house occupied by the Central Council. While we were on our way there three German tanks swung off the main road about five miles west of Tiranë, debouched into the plain and for twenty minutes shelled a hamlet close by the farm-house we had just left. We had barely completed our move when Seymour went down with malaria. Luckily there was an Italian army doctor to look after him.

Weak and ill as he was, and badly though he needed rest, Neel refused to let us detain him more than five days; he insisted that his work in Mati could not wait, forgetting Chesterton's observation that cemeteries are full of indispensables. However, he asked me to accompany him as far as the village of Zall i Herrit in the hills five miles north of Tiranë, in order to meet two members of the Central Council of the Balli Kombëtar who were anxious to talk with me. Neel believed that my views had been influenced overmuch by the extremists of the L.N.C., and that now I ought to see the other side of the picture.

At dusk on the evening of 8th October Neel and I set out on foot accompanied by the eight men of his escort. We had the best part of fifteen miles to cover that night, working our way round to the west of Tiranë; we must cross two main roads and pass close by some well guarded petrol dumps and a German barracks; and so we had no time to waste if we wanted to reach the cover of the Mati hills by daylight. Neel was so weak from illness and lack of food that I wondered how he would manage the journey; nor was I very strong myself. But our guides refused to let us take horses, saying that only on foot could we hope to get through the German outposts.

It was a journey I still remember with distaste. We were hardly surprised that our guides were not ready to start at the appointed time, but we were indignant when they delayed us for two hours in Arbonë while two of them had a drink with Myslim Peza. Crossing the roads at night was not usually a difficult business, nor could we believe that we were in much danger from the German guards at the petrol dumps; but our companions regarded each of those obstacles as a major hazard and wasted a great deal of time in frequent pauses to work up their courage; they made much more noise hushing each other up than we should have made talking in our normal voices.

They seemed afraid of the dark, for they cheered up wonderfully soon as the moon rose, chattering happily to each other while Neel and I plodded on in grim, exhausted silence.

About one o'clock in the morning storm clouds hid the moon, enveloping us in thick darkness; heavy rain soaked our clothes and chilled our bodies as a violent thunder-storm broke overhead. For two hours we struggled on, unable to see anything except when a flash of lightning momentarily lit the sky. The storm passed but the rain continued in a steady downpour, turning the paths and fields into thick, slippery mud. Soon after half-past three we stumbled on a deserted shepherd's hut of clay and wattle. Our guides now told us that they had lost the way and suggested we should shelter in the hut until daylight.

As the first light paled the sky we staggered outside, damp and shivering, to continue our journey. From the south, beyond Tiranë, came the sound of gun-fire, a distant rumble of battle which continued all the morning. Luckily we had not gone far out of our way in the storm; we were now over the main roads and past the petrol dumps. Refusing to make a detour, we passed the barracks unchallenged in the early morning light. At ten o'clock we came in sight of the cluster of houses on a hillside that was the village of Zall i Herrit. We were taken to the house of a friend of Neel's, an ex-captain of gendarmerie who spoke English. He had prepared us a magnificent breakfast, which Neel was too ill to eat but which put new life into me.

In the evening a Rumanian doctor arrived from Tiranë to look after Neel; he ordered him to stay in bed for as long as possible, which Neel feared would not be very long. He ascribed my temperature to a local fever and kindly gave me a bottle of grappa, which he said might be taken at night with advantage.

I spent all the following day in conference with the Balli representatives, Halil Maçi and Vasil Andoni; the latter was the secretary of the Central Council of the Balli Kombëtar. I believed their assurances that they had never countenanced active collaboration with the Germans, notwithstanding Enver Hoxha's efforts to persuade me that they had; but I was unable to shake off the feeling that they intended to keep one foot in the German camp in order to conserve their strength for the real struggle for power with the Partisans. In the light of events it is impossible to blame them; but I could not feel much sympathy for them at the time. I did, however, exact from them a promise to send representatives to our brigadier at the end of October in order to discuss plans for operations against the Germans.

I had intended to return to Arbonë the day after the conference; but in the morning I awoke with a splitting headache and a high temperature. The Rumanian doctor thought it might be malaria but he had nothing to give me except aspirin. I spent the day in bed. Next day, 12th October, my temperature was down and so I decided to return that night. My host insisted on lending me a horse, overruling all the objections of my escort; for this solicitude I was soon profoundly grateful.

We left Zall i Herrit at half-past four in the afternoon. The malaria returned two hours later, striking with alarming suddenness so that my temperature seemed to soar in a matter of minutes. Soon I was unable to sit my horse without support; for the rest of the journey one of the escort walked on either side to hold me in the saddle. Fortunately there was no danger of losing our way, for the night was clear. I took no interest in the journey, concentrating only on trying to stay on my horse. Around midnight we stopped to rest at a farm-house, where I drank a cup of milky coffee. I remember that as I shivered and sweated in a feverish doze whole passages of Boswell's *Life of Samuel Johnson* flashed through my mind with extraordinary clarity, and I would jerk awake to find myself declaiming one of the magisterial pronouncements of the Great Cham.

About two in the morning we reached a village in the hills above the plain of Arbonë; here I told my escort that I must stop, for I felt too exhausted to continue our journey. But the villagers were too frightened to let me stay. It seemed that three days previously—the morning when we had heard the gun-fire—the Germans had attacked Arbonë; although they had been repulsed they were still patrolling these hills and would certainly find me if I stayed there.

I told my escort to return to Zall i Herrit immediately, for they would be taking a needless risk by accompanying me further; in any case we were too large a party to move in safety through an area infested with German patrols. Two of them, however, insisted on staying with me until I could find shelter. For another two hours we wandered through the woods, until we reached a lonely house whose owner was willing to take me in. He affirmed stoutly that he would never turn a British officer from his door, but admitted that he was very frightened, for he was certain that the Germans would be there in the morning. He carried me to a room at the top of the house, imploring me to be on my way by daylight. My two companions, seeing me safely lodged, turned back with my horse towards their own country.

I left the house at first light, thanking my host warmly for his courage and kindness; he walked with me for ten minutes to put me on the track that would bring me down to the plain. Revived by the fresh, chill morning air and spurred by the danger of my position I reached the edge of the plain in an hour. There was no sign of activity, German or Albanian. I crossed the plain without meeting anybody and reached Arbonë at about eight o'clock, only to find that Seymour had moved his headquarters back into the hills. However, a Partisan agreed to take me to the headquarters of Ulysses Spahiu's Third Brigade at the village of Haxhijas on the way to Grecë. After a three mile walk I staggered into Spahiu's tent, where I collapsed.

I rested for two or three hours while Spahiu found me a guide and a horse to take me on to Seymour's camp at Grecë. I have no memory of the ride there and only a faint recollection of my arrival and of Seymour's warm greeting as he hustled me into a comfortable camp-bed in his tent, while a small bearded Italian doctor fussed around with tablets of quinine and atabrin.

Seymour's camp at this time resembled a convalescent home rather than a military headquarters. He himself was recovering from the malaria he had started at Arbonë, but was still very weak; Roberts was just beginning to pull through his illness, and Hill was in bed with influenza. The Italian doctor worked tirelessly to look after us, making his rounds at all hours of the day to ensure that we took our medicines at the right time; through his conscientious care we all recovered remarkably quickly. Although the wireless traffic was no longer so heavy we still had to receive supply drops; however, we had collected a large body of Italian servants and camp-followers, who not only took much of the work off our hands but, unlike the Partisans, refrained from looting the stores.

From Seymour's account it was evident that the Partisans had put up a much better fight at Arbonë than they had done at Shtyllë. During the early hours of 9th October the Germans infiltrated strong patrols through the hills between Tiranë and the plain; Neel and I were very lucky not to run into them, and I felt ashamed of my contempt for our guides' caution. At dawn they crossed the river Arzen and were in Arbonë almost before the Partisans had woken up. After the initial shock, however, the Partisans rallied and held the Germans until Ulysses Spahiu's Third Brigade arrived, about eleven o'clock; Spahiu was a brave and competent officer who like Shehu had fought in the Spanish Civil War. By midday the Germans had been driven from Arbonë and were withdrawing northward, pursued by the Partisans. During the afternoon the Germans launched a second attack and retook Arbonë; again the Partisans counter-attacked and, after some close fighting, drove them from the village. By nine in the evening the Germans had fallen back into the hills, leaving thirty-five killed and twelve wounded. The Italians fought very well, showing discipline, courage, and an intense hatred of the Germans, but they suffered heavy casualties.

Seymour calculated that the enemy forces engaged were rather less than one battalion of infantry, supported by artillery, heavy mortars and a few tanks; the Partisans of course heavily outnumbered them, but had only a few mortars and two anti-tank rifles in support. They captured from the enemy seven machine-guns and six mortars. The Germans must seriously have miscalculated the numbers as well as the fighting spirit of the Partisans; we wondered how long they would be content to leave their defeat unavenged.

The heroes of the day, according to Seymour, were Spahiu and Gjinishi; the latter was in the thick of the battle the whole time and was twice wounded, fortunately not seriously. Gjinishi's example obliged the other members of the Central Council to come down from their retreat and join in the fighting, although not all of them showed his enthusiasm. At one moment Seymour found himself firing from a ditch with Enver Hoxha on one side of him and Ali Gostivari on the other; since he had recently quarrelled seriously with both of them, his predicament caused him some anxiety.

'They were damn funny to watch' he told me, 'when you remember the way they used to swagger around festooned with pistols, tommy-guns, and bandoliers. There was no swank in them that morning. Enver's fat cheeks were flapping like sheets in a wind and he could hardly hold his gun, while the Shop Assistant had a sort of crestfallen look as though his richest customer had just cancelled her account.

VIII

ON THE RUN

One morning a week later I was lying under the trees outside the tent I shared with Seymour, watching the dappled sunlight on the pine needles and happy to be feeling well again, when Roberts brought me a signal from Cairo which he had just deciphered. I read it with some satisfaction.

'George!' I called into the tent. 'The Brigadier wants to see me right away. From the wording of this signal it looks as though I may be going to Kossovo.'

'Good show, old boy! When will you leave?'

'The signal says as soon as I'm fit enough to travel—that's any time now. The Central Council have already left for Biza, so there's nothing more for me to do here. I'll have to leave Roberts and the wireless set with you because I've only got one mule; but I'll come back for them as soon as the Brigadier lets me have some more.'

That evening Seymour and I buried two canisters of gold in a secret hide-out, which we marked carefully. We had been visited every day by a German reconnaissance plane, and although we had done our best to camouflage the camp we could not be sure that it was invisible from the air. Lying in a rough triangle between three main roads, the area was peculiarly vulnerable to any German drive; if it came we should have neither time nor transport to remove the gold. Our efforts, however, were in vain, as Seymour told me much later; the gold was found, not by the Germans but by the people of Grecë.

After lunch on 21st October I began my journey to the Brigadier's headquarters at Biza with Stiljan and my Italian groom, a quiet young Florentine called Tomaso: he was an intelligent and reliable servant and a cheerful companion. I took my horse and mule with a minimum of personal kit for the three of us. On the way we stopped to have a drink with Myslim Peza and ask him for a guide to see me as far as the Tiranë-Elbasan road, the limit of Myslim's territory. He gave me a guide with a message to some friends who lived in a village near the road.

I spent the first night at Haxhijas in the house of a poor peasant; the guest-room was used as a store for maize—also, it seemed, as a breeding-ground for a million fleas, whose attentions made sleep impossible. Stiljan and Tomaso, who had the sense to sleep outside, were undisturbed.

The following afternoon we reached the tiny hillside village which was the home of Myslim's friends. These were three old men who shared a house but whose precise relationship to each other I could not determine. They gave us an enthusiastic welcome, plying us with raki and turning out a large room for our use. They gladly promised to see us across the road as they had been doing for Myslim's friends for many years; but they insisted we stay the night in their house while they reconnoitred the road to discover the latest positions of the German pickets; if all was well they would take us across the next evening. They added that the Central Council had passed their way two nights before with General Azzi and forty mules. They also warned me that the Germans were now operating in these hills in patrols of fifty men; but I could sleep easy because they were used to that sort of thing and would post reliable guards.

In the morning my new friends told me that they had made all their arrangements to take us across the road at dusk. Meanwhile, as I had so kindly expressed appreciation of their raki the previous night, perhaps I would care to see how it was made? We went down to a stream below the village, where a very small, wizened old man crouched over a crude pot-still, blowing with a bellows on a fire of wood shavings; on the ground beside him stood a number of small flasks filled with the clear spirit. Delighted at our interest the old man handed me a measure, explaining that the raki in it had just been distilled; he cackled with pleasure when he saw me choke over my first swallow. When I had recovered he handed me a measure from another flask; this, it seemed, was what they usually drank themselves—'not a drop is sold till it's two weeks old.' Finally, with enormous pride, he made me sample his oldest raki, thrice distilled and matured a full year; when, quite sincerely, I praised it he gave me a flask for the journey.

We crossed the road in the last faint twilight with a speed, efficiency and silence that I never saw before or since in that country. On the other side ran the river Arzen, spanned by a narrow wooden bridge; beyond, a steep track climbed into thickly wooded hills. Here our guides left us, embracing us with many assurances of friendship and begging us to return soon to try some more of their raki. We followed the track for two hours until we came to the village of Gurrë, a cluster of houses and a mosque, where we spent the night.

All the next morning we climbed steeply, until at midday we came out of the woods onto a bare, open ridge. We were now on the borders of Cermenikë, the most savage and inhospitable region of central Albania. Picking our way down a precipitous, winding track into a valley hemmed in by wild jagged peaks we followed the path that ran eastward beside the foaming Arzen; at half-past four in the afternoon we halted at the village of Shengjergj, sprawled in a hollow amphitheatre topped by frowning grey cliffs.

Shengjergj was disputed territory between the Partisans and the Balli Kombëtar; the lower half of the village had declared for the Partisans, the upper half for the Balli. Each side had built a line of rough fortifications facing towards the other. The Partisan commander, who lent me a guide to take me on to Biza, told me confidentially that he expected to clear the Balli Kombëtar from the village within the next few weeks.

Passing through the Ballist lines we climbed steeply for an hour to the top of the pass that led to Biza. On the bleak, windswept summit we crossed a disused motor road built by the Italians. At the cross-roads stood a small stone obelisk with an inscription in memory of the travellers who were frozen to death there a few years before. Darkness was falling and a fierce east wind numbed our faces as we came down the gentle incline on the other side onto a wide grassy plateau, at the far end of which lay the Brigadier's headquarters.

A fortnight previously the only habitation on the plateau had been a derelict shepherd's hut; but Smiley had set Italian soldiers to work on the preparation of a camp. In the course of two days they had built three large wooden huts, covered with camouflage parachutes, on the eastern edge of the plain at the foot of a thickly wooded mountain. Tents had also been improvised from parachutes to serve as sleeping and kitchen quarters, leaving the huts for the offices and mess. In the largest hut the Brigadier and his staff were sitting down to dine when I arrived on this evening of 24th October.

Brigadier Davies, usually known to us as 'Trotsky',[1] was a regular soldier of considerable seniority. His experience of guerrilla warfare had been, as it were, on the receiving end; for he had served before the war on the North-West Frontier and in Palestine. Stout and stocky, with a ruddy complexion and a bluff and friendly manner, he relied on his training and common-sense rather than on intuition or intellect to guide him through the complexities of Albanian military and political affairs. Though kind and considerate to his subordinates he tolerated neither inefficiency nor affectation. He detested sloppiness in dress or personal appearance, and discountenanced the wearing of beards—'None of that Wingate stuff here,' he would say. He listened carefully to the opinions of his officers, and once he had given them his confidence he was prepared to back them to the limit.

Resolved that his headquarters should function with strict military efficiency, even in such unpromising conditions, Trotsky had brought with him a formidable complement of staff officers, including a G.I, D.A.Q.M.G., Signals Officer, and Chief Clerk; their equipment comprised, among other things, several wireless sets, camp furniture for offices and mess, a typewriter, and two containers full of stationery. In the transport lines were more than a hundred mules.

The G.I, Lieutenant-Colonel Arthur Nicholls, Coldstream Guards, was an old friend of mine from pre-war days. Having been a staff officer at S.O.E.

---

[1] He had acquired this nickname as an officer cadet at Sandhurst from a reference in an instructor's report to 'a kind of disciplined bolshevism' in his character.

headquarters in Baker Street for the past two years, he had asked to be sent on operations, in the belief that every S.O.E. staff officer should spend at least six months in the field in order to understand the problems of those whose destinies he had to control. Tall, thin and very delicate he had not the constitution to withstand even normal conditions of service in a Balkan country in winter. From his first days in Albania he suffered continuously from dysentry, but his spirit and determination drove him to endurance far beyond his strength.

The D.A.Q.M.G. was Captain Alan Hare, Household Cavalry Regiment, a versatile young officer of outstanding ability and acumen. In charge of demolitions was Major Chesshire, R.E., of signals Lieutenant Trayhorn, an engineer who had lived in Istanbul and spoke Turkish. Other officers present at the time of my arrival were Major Alan Palmer, Captain Victor Smith, and Captain Smythe; Palmer and Smith left the morning afterwards to join the First Partisan Brigade in the south; Palmer later became senior British Liaison Officer with the Partisans. Among the N.C.O.s I found my paramilitary specialist, Gregson Allcott.

There was a fresh and friendly atmosphere among the officers and N.C.O.s despite the austere regime imposed on them by Trotsky and Nicholls, whose ideas of routine were suitable enough for a Brigade Headquarters but a little incongruous in a guerilla camp among the mountains. With touching consideration for my health the Brigadier excused me the most irksome of our duties—that of standing-to each morning an hour before sunrise, presumably in expectation of an enemy attack; at the time I ridiculed this piece of regimentation but within a few weeks I was to regret that I had not adopted it myself. Trotsky confided to me that his past experience of guerrillas had left him with few illusions about their fighting qualities; but even he was shocked when, two days after his arrival at Biza, all his Partisan guards vanished on receiving a false alarm of the approach of German troops. McLean and Smiley, who were still there at the time, assured him that this was their usual habit.

I was sorry to learn that I had missed McLean and Smiley by thirty-six hours; Trotsky was sending them out to Italy, where S.O.E. had established an advance base, to give a personal report on the situation and to enjoy some well-earned leave at home. I was sorry, also, that they had left behind Frederick Nosi to act as official interpreter. His natural arrogance, swollen by the importance of his new position, soon caused trouble in the camp. Encouraged by Nosi the Partisan guards, who had previously been willing and helpful even if not very efficient, suddenly refused to do manual work of any kind for the Mission; when asked for an explanation Nosi came out with the astonishing reply: 'Partisans do not work; their job is to fight.'

When the Albanian cook complained to Hare that the Partisans were openly stealing the rations he was warned by Nosi that as soon as the English had left he would be liquidated for his temerity; the poor fellow was so frightened that he asked to be released from our service. A few days later our N.C.O.s complained that Nosi had ordered them to salute him as 'an officer of the Albanian Army'; when they indignantly refused he called on the Brigadier to discipline them. It required all Nicholls's patience and tact to restore an appearance of harmony.

I spent my first morning at Biza writing a report for the Brigadier on the political situation in the country. When he had read it he sent for me.

'I have two pieces of good news for you,' he began. He indicated a large map on the wall. 'As you know, my parish includes not only the old frontiers of Albania, but the new regions incorporated into the country by the Axis; that is, the whole of Kossovo, the western fringe of Macedonia from the Vardar valley to Lake Ohrid, and a small corner of Montenegro. I'm going to send you to make a reconnaissance of those areas. I want you to be my eyes and ears. I want to know all about the political situation, with particular reference to the chances of starting resistance among the Albanian irredentists. I leave it entirely to you how you go about it. You will send your reports by wireless to Cairo in the usual manner for onward transmission to me; but I hope that later on we'll be able to arrange a courier service between us for letters.

'The second piece of news which I think will cheer you is that your majority has come through with effect from the first of the month. My best congratulations! Now I want you to be thoroughly fit before you start this job, so you'd better rest here while your interpreter goes back to Seymour's place for your wireless and kit.'

This was better than I had dared hope. I was still young enough to find a romantic glamour in the idea of exploring a disputed frontier, while the opportunity of studying at first-hand one of the most complex political problems in the Balkans made an irresistible appeal to one who was still attracted by the glitter of coffee-house politics; moreover, I was delighted to know that I should be working on my own. The next day Stiljan left for Grecë with Partisan guides and enough mules to transport Roberts and our kit. I never saw any of them again.

All the time I was at Biza Trotsky and Nicholls were fully engaged in conferences with the Central Council of the L.N.C., Abas Kupi, and the Balli Kombëtar representatives; I was not required to attend. The Brigadier was working for agreement between the three factions for a combined plan of operations. Kupi, whom the Brigadier liked and respected, was only too ready to agree; the Balli Kombëtar were with difficulty persuaded to sign a written declaration that they would immediately begin open hostilities against the Germans. But when, in order to commit them irrevocably, Trotsky wished to have their declaration broadcast by the B.B.C. Enver Hoxha flew into a rage and arrogantly commanded him to suppress it. At the same time he denounced the Mukaj agreement and issued orders to all Partisan units to attack and destroy the forces of the Balli Kombëtar wherever they could be found. The Civil War had begun.

Enver had repeatedly told us that he would gladly co-operate with the Ballists if they would give an undertaking to join in the War of Liberation. This flagrant duplicity therefore stupefied and shocked the Brigadier after all his patient work for reconciliation. Enver, however, seeing that the Germans were not trying to extend their control beyond the main towns and the roads, had decided to take advantage of his freedom from attack to liquidate his main political rivals.[1] With their superior armament, discipline and training the Partisans soon drove the Balli Kombëtar to take refuge in the towns under the guns of the Germans, so that Enver was able to represent the L.N.C. as the only effective guerrilla organization. For the moment he left Abas Kupi alone; his turn would come next.

The town of Dibra, or Debar, as it is called in Serbo-Croat, stands on the frontiers of Albania and Jugoslavia some thirty miles north of Lake Ohrid; part of Jugoslavia before the war, it had been incorporated into Albania by the Axis Powers. Flight-Lieutenant Hands had been the British Liaison Officer there until mid-October, when he had moved north, his place being taken by a new Mission under Major Riddell and Captain Simcox. At the end of October the Brigadier received disquieting reports of the situation in the area, which he ordered me to investigate.

After the fall of Mussolini, Haxhi Lleshi's Partisans had occupied the town, of which they were still in possession. At the same time some of the local Bajraktars[2] had formed a 'Committee of National Defence' with the avowed object of making war on the Italians, but with the real aim of preventing encroachment by the L.N.C. on the Bajraktars' territory. The headquarters of the Committee was the town of Peshkopijë, some thirteen miles north-west of Dibra; its leader was Colonel Fiqri Dine, formerly a Zone Commander in King Zog's Gendarmerie and one of the original quadrumvirate of chiefs that had helped Zog in his early days of power. There were also several volunteer bands, each numbering between fifty and three hundred men, under minor chieftains who belonged to neither faction and who had offered their services to the British.

The two rival factions had long been on the verge of hostilities; but Hands had achieved a precarious compromise whereby the authority of the Partisans was recognized in and around the town of Dibra and that of the Committee

---

[1] See also Amery, op. cit., p. 65.

[2] The word means 'Standard-bearer', an ancient hereditary title. Later it came to have virtually the same meaning as Chieftain.

in the country to the north. But from across the old frontier another danger threatened, in the shape of a certain Xhemal Gostivari,[1] an Albanian who had made himself powerful in Macedonia with Italian and German help. Riddell now reported that Gostivari was preparing an attack on Dibra with German support and—according to the Partisans—with the connivance of the Bajraktars' Committee.

When he heard the news Trotsky sent for me. 'I want a personal report on this situation as soon as possible. Riddell and Simcox are new to the country, so they may be glad of a bit of help. You'd better take Alan Hare with you—you'll find him very useful. I suggest you leave tomorrow.'

On 1st November Hare and I left the camp on horseback, accompanied by a local guide. Our route lay north-east over a high range of mountains to the village of Martanesh; thence it dropped into a valley where a disused motor road ran from west to east towards Peshkopijë. I had hoped that with good luck we might reach the valley by nightfall. Our guide had other ideas: determined that we should spend the night at the house of his uncle among the mountains he lost the way half a dozen times until, when darkness was falling and our tempers were becoming dangerous, he conveniently hit upon a track that led us straight to uncle's door.

We rode next morning through miles of silent beech forest over a carpet of gold and russet leaves beneath an ice-blue autumn sky. The air on these lonely uplands was clear and sharp; the pale sunlight filtering between the smooth boles, the soft gloom of the shadows and the stillness of the great woods induced a mood of quiet contentment and hushed our talk.

In the late afternoon we came down into the valley, forded a shallow river and climbed an embankment onto the old motor road. From now on the going was easy. Darkness found us at the village of Homesh, two or three miles from the west bank of the Black Drin. Here we heard that there had been fighting around Dibra for the past two days between the Partisans and Xhem Gostivari. We decided to spend the night at Homesh, and immediately sent a message to Fiqri Dine asking him to meet us next morning at the cross-roads of Maqellarë, five miles north of Dibra.

Next morning we forded the Drin without difficulty, and reached Maqellarë, a small village with a mosque, at ten o'clock. At first sight Fiqri Dine reminded me of an evil, black, overgrown toad; his manner was reserved and barely friendly, his speech patronizing. He denied any collaboration with Xhem Gostivari, adding that he had restrained his own forces from joining in the battle against Haxhi Lleshi; but he complained bitterly of the Partisans, saying that they terrorized the people of Dibra and were threatening to attack the Bajraktars.

[1] Xhemal, or Xhem, Gostivari, was the *nom-de-guerre* of one Xhemal Hasa; he must not be confused with the L.N.C. delegate, Ali Gostivari.

'Their aggressive behaviour will certainly bring the Germans upon us,' he concluded obscurely.

He told us that Simcox was in Peshkopijë and Riddell with Haxhi Lleshi in Dibra. He would give us an escort for a few miles down the road, but his men would have to leave ns at the approaches of Dibra, or they would certainly be fired on; we ourselves must carry sticks with handkerchiefs tied to them, which we must display prominently on approaching the town unless we wished to be shot. We took our leave after obtaining his promise that he would come to the help of the Partisans if they were attacked by the Germans; but he gave it so reluctantly as to inspire us with little confidence.

After parting from our escort about a mile from the town we rode along a straight, open road across the plain, feeling very foolish and conspicuous as we waved our white flags all the way. However, nobody fired at us and we met nobody until we came to the first houses of Dibra, where a Partisan picket challenged us. They took us through almost deserted streets to a barracks on the western edge of the town. In a third floor room crowded with people and thick with tobacco smoke we found Riddell and Haxhi Lleshi; among the party were Mehmet Hoxha—still wearing the same lounge suit that he had lent me for my Tiranë visit—and the Bektashi abbot, Baba Faja. Mehmet Hoxha was on his way to Kossovo to form a Partisan organization on the Albanian-Jugoslav border.

Our arrival broke up the meeting and Riddell took Hare and me to lunch at the hotel, a rickety wooden building kept by an Italian who gave us a most friendly welcome and a very good lunch. Riddell told us that Xhem Gostivari had attacked three days ago. He had driven the Partisans from the hills that overlooked Dibra on the east and had even occupied part of the town; after some street fighting he had withdrawn to his own territory, leaving the Partisans to celebrate a victory. He had been accompanied by a German officer and three or four other ranks. Riddell, who had been in Peshkopijë at the time, had tried to stop the fighting by persuading Fiqri Dine to send a letter to Xhem Gostivari, with whom he seemed to have some influence, asking him to withdraw; unfortunately the Partisans had intercepted the letter, which they were trying to use as proof that Fiqri Dine and his Committee were collaborating with Gostivari.

The fighting had prevented Riddell himself from entering Dibra until early that morning; but the previous evening he and Fiqri Dine had ridden to within a mile of the town under fire from both sides. For the whole morning he had been in conference with the Partisan leaders in a fruitless attempt to reach some compromise between them and Fiqri Dine's Committee; he had found them aggressive and intractable, much more ready to look on the Committee as enemies than as allies.

At five-thirty in the evening we reassembled for a conference with Haxhi Lleshi and his officers. After Riddell, Hare, and I in turn had stretched our eloquence to the utmost, Haxhi Lleshi agreed, rather in the manner of an indulgent schoolmaster humouring his backward pupils, to keep the peace with Fiqri Dine and co-operate with Riddell in his efforts to form a united front against Gostivari and the Germans. Privately we put little more faith in this promise than we had in Fiqri Dine's.

We did, however, obtain from Haxhi Lleshi one hopeful token of good faith: among the prisoners taken by the Partisans in the previous days' fighting was Helmi Beg Karasani, one of the independent minor chieftains who had put his men at Riddell's disposal. Helmi Beg, a cheerful little man with a fair complexion and a frank expression, swore that he had come to help the Partisans; but having lost touch with his men in the confusion he had fallen into the hands of a Partisan patrol. The Partisans swore that they had seen him firing on them, and they therefore intended to shoot him. Whatever the truth of the matter, it would clearly have the worst possible effect on Riddell's plans if they were to carry out their threat, for Helmi Beg was a popular figure with the chiefs and Bajraktars. After a good deal of persuasion, supported by some brilliant argument from Hare, we secured his release.

Although we had a good dinner and comfortable beds in the hotel I slept uneasily; for the night was disturbed by screams and short bursts of tommy-gun fire as the Partisans executed their opponents. Next day Riddell returned to Peshkopijë and Hare and I started our journey back to Biza. The autumn rains had been late this year, but they made up for it now as we rode slowly back over the mountains shivering and sodden. It was after dark on 6th November when, hungry and dispirited, we staggered into the Brigadier's mess, to be revived by Trotsky's formidable cocktails of raki and vermouth.

I was alarmed that there was no news of Stiljan and Roberts; Cairo reported that Seymour had been off the air since 30th October, and there were rumours of a German drive against Myslim Peza. For a week I waited at Biza while the rains deluged us with the sustained violence of a tropical monsoon and a murderous cold wind swept across the three thousand foot high plateau; thunder-storms burst among the mountains around us, echoing like artillery through the rocky gorges, while forked lightning lit the camp in brilliant violet flashes.

'Don't think I want to get rid of you,' Trotsky said to me one day, 'but if you're going to get to Kossovo this year you'd better start immediately—wireless or no wireless. Winter's coming on, and pretty soon the snow will stop you getting over these mountains.'

'Not only that,' added Nicholls, 'but once the Drin's in flood you'll never get across; I should think the water's high already.'

Both these points had occurred to me, but I wondered what use I could be in Kossovo without a wireless.

'If Roberts arrives in time,' said Trotsky, 'we'll send him after you. Meanwhile you'd better base yourself on Riddell and use his wireless; you can work your area from Dibra, starting with Macedonia.'

Summoning Gregson Allcott and Tomaso I told them to be ready to leave in twenty-four hours. I planned to spend the first night at Martanesh, the home of Baba Faja, whom the Brigadier wished me to see; it was a four-hour journey, and so I should have plenty of time if I left Biza immediately after lunch.

The next day, 13th November, I was standing outside the mess saying good-bye to Trotsky and his officers when somebody called our attention to a pair of figures limping wearily across the plateau towards us.

'Looks like Bulman and Corsair,' said Nicholls. 'Now we'll get some news of Seymour. They both look dead beat.'

Bulman and Corsair were two officers who had left Biza for Grecë about the same time as I had started my journey in the opposite direction; we had missed each other on the road. They had a grim story to tell. The Germans had cleaned up the Peza area, beginning their drive a few days after Bulman, Corsair, and Stiljan had reached Grecë. Seymour had immediately moved his headquarters to Myslim Peza's base in the hills, where he felt reasonably safe from surprise; Partisan guards were posted on all the heights commanding Myslim's camp. Early one morning, when the camp was barely stirring, they were alarmed by a single pistol shot close at hand; thirty seconds later the Germans opened fire with machine-guns and tommy-guns from the very hills where the guards were supposed to be stationed. Seymour's wireless operator, Bombardier Hill, was killed instantly; the rest of the Mission was forced to scatter, abandoning the wireless sets and all equipment. For six days, they were on the run; several times they were ambushed; but eventually all of them, including Stiljan, rejoined Myslim Peza, whom no trap was strong enough to hold. Now Roberts had pneumonia and was too ill to move; Stiljan had gone to Tiranë 'to tranquillize himself' and was unlikely to return.

The news of Roberts's death reached me two months later. He had been taken prisoner by the Germans but had escaped, shooting one of his guards with a pistol he had hidden in his stocking and pushing another over a cliff. But the ensuing days of hunger and exposure had proved too much for a frame that was never robust; if his physical strength had matched his gallant spirit he might still be alive.

I delayed my departure no longer, but set out for the mountains accompanied by Gregson Allcott and Tomaso. The Brigadier had given me a fresh supply of money and equipment and three mules to transport it, so that I need depend on Riddell and Simcox only for wireless contact. At Martanesh, where we arrived as darkness was falling, we were taken to the house of Baba Faja's Political Commissar, who sent a Partisan to warn the

Baba of our coming; the Baba did not like receiving visitors unannounced and his Political Commissar was equally averse to his doing so. By the time we had found lodging for the night the Abbot was ready to see me.

Baba Faja, or Baba Mustafa, as he was sometimes called, was one of the very few Albanian guerrilla leaders whose fame had reached the outside world before the arrival of McLean and Smiley; he had fought a vigorous and unrelenting war against the Italians from the first days of their occupation. A native of Martanesh, where his monastery had been burnt down by the Italians, he was revered by the people of Cermenikë more for his prowess than his piety. I found him sitting in a low, ill-lit, smoky room with a half-empty bottle of raki by his side and rows of empty bottles round the walls; his great black beard streamed over his battle-dress blouse. Rumour—not only the whispers of his enemies—credited him with two Partisan mistresses, but now he was alone. He was, as I had been warned to expect, very drunk.

Intoxication had not improved his temper. Returning my greeting with perfunctory courtesy he launched into a series of contentious questions and complaints: why had the English general given him no war material? How long had Abas Kupi spent at Shengjergj, and how much had the General given him? Why did we continue to help the Balli and Fiqri Dine when there was 'documentary proof' that they were working for the Germans?

I was amused to find that the 'documentary proof' was no more than the letter Fiqri Dine had written to Xhem Gostivari at Riddell's request. However, I made a careful note of each complaint, promising to retail it to the Brigadier; then I said good-night with my smartest salute, which he returned with a scowl.

It was half-past eleven next morning before the escort and guide promised by Baba Faja were ready to leave. We aimed to spend the night at Zerqan, a large village on the northern slopes of these mountains, a little way above the old motor road; the guide, who was a Partisan courier, told me that the journey would take at least eight hours and so we could not hope to arrive before dark; yet there was no shelter for the night nearer than Zerqan. The day was cold and cloudy with a threat of snow and I did not look forward to spending the night in the open at an altitude of six or seven thousand feet.

All day we scrambled up and down steep mountains covered in beech forests, climbing higher with each successive ridge. Dusk came upon us as we were crossing a wide, snow-covered plateau strewn with rocks and intersected by countless small streams; thick clouds were swirling around us, bringing a chilly rain. Our guide chose this moment to tell me that he was no longer certain of the way. We struggled on, past a smooth, black tarn onto a wooded ridge where darkness wholly enveloped us. Here the guide gave up; he was sure the track was not very far away, but he could never find it at night and so we must make up our minds to stay where we were until morning. It was hardly a suitable camping place that he had chosen—a steep slope exposed to a bitter wind that pierced right through our clothing. We unloaded and tethered the animals, lit several large fires and cooked a hot meal. Then, piling the fires with wood, we lay down and tried to sleep.

I had barely settled myself when the night was shattered by a violent explosion. I leaped to my feet, drawing my pistol, only to find that one of the Partisans, thinking he had heard a bear prowling around the camp, had thrown a grenade to scare it away. Sleep was impossible for any of us; whichever side we turned to the fire, the other, exposed to the icy wind, felt more miserably cold by comparison. Snow fell during the night.

At dawn I sent the guide to find the track; at seven he returned to tell us that after walking in circles for the last hour he had found it only fifty yards away. After a steep descent through the woods we came out onto open grassy slopes leading into Zerqan.

This was a pretty little village of modern white, red-roofed houses, in one of which the local L.N.C. Committee were waiting to receive us; all of them were followers of Abas Kupi. Their leader, a captain of artillery, showed us into a clean, well-furnished guest-room with a dais at one end and chairs as well as cushions to sit on. By the time we had washed and shaved an excellent breakfast was ready—tea, boiled eggs, a chicken, bread, butter, and jam; we felt ashamed to be eating what were probably their last supplies, but the laws of hospitality forbade to refuse what they offered. When we had finished the captain brought in three minor chieftains, each of whom commanded a body of a hundred men; they were anxious to help the British and asked me how they could best employ their men in our cause. After what I had seen on my previous visit to Dibra I could only advise them to join the Partisans, for I doubted that Fiqri Dine would use them against the Germans.

We left for Dibra at half-past two, warmed by the kindness and hospitality of our hosts; they lent us a guide to see us across the Drin and a horse for Gregson Allcott—a relief to me because I should no longer have to share mine. On the motor road we met groups of civilians coming from Dibra, the bundles on their backs and the grim, resigned expressions on their faces identifying them as refugees. Among them, riding by himself, I recognized a young man whom I had met on my last visit; he seemed a little drunk. He was on his way, he told me, to Biza, to put a safe distance between himself and the Germans.

'What Germans?' I asked.

'The Germans who are coming with Xhem Gostivari to take Dibra.'

'I don't hear any fighting.'

'You will tomorrow—they haven't arrived yet. Look up there!' He pointed to the sky above the Drin.

Looking through my glasses I saw two Me 109s flying up and down the valley between Dibra and Peshkopijë; they did not seem to be attacking any target and so I supposed they were simply showing the flag. Hurrying on we reached the river at dusk, to find it greatly swollen; we waited, therefore, on the near bank while the guide waded across to see if it was fordable. When he was satisfied he came back for us. We put the horses and mules to the stream, a man holding the head of each; in mid-stream the current tugged fiercely at us, the water foaming around the horses' flanks, so that for a few moments we feared we might be swept away. As we stood on the farther bank, while the horses shook the water from their coats, our guide said with a smile:

'Two or three days more and nobody will cross the river unless by boat.'

At half-past seven we dismounted outside the hotel in Dibra and paid off our guides. Riddell was dining at the hospital with some Italian officers, but I found Haxhi Lleshi seated at a table drinking raki with his Political Commissar, Ersat Ndreou, the brother of a powerful Dibran chieftain. They invited me to join them.

'You have come at a very interesting time,' said Ersat in English. 'We are expecting to be attacked any day now. We have information that Xhem Gostivari has arrived at a village on the other side of the mountains, only four hours' march from here, with a large force of Albanians and Germans.'

'But you need not worry,' interposed Haxhi Lleshi airily. 'We have concentrated our troops around here to meet the threat and we have taken all precautions against surprise.'

As we were finishing supper Riddell returned with his interpreter, Bungurri—a mournful-looking Dibran—and Captain Michael Lis, a lively, thick-set Pole who had been dropped into Albania recently to try and open an escape line from Poland through the Balkans; having found this task impossible he had attached himself to Riddell as an extra Liaison Officer.

Riddell did not share Haxhi Lleshi's confidence in the ability of the Partisans to hold Dibra in the face of a determined attack supported by German troops. He suggested that I send Gregson Allcott, Tomaso, and the mules with all our kit to Peshkopijë next morning, where they could set up a temporary base with Simcox; then Riddell and I could go to see Cen Elezi, the brother of Haxhi Lleshi's Political Commissar, whose house was in the hills north of Peshkopijë and who had valuable contacts across the frontier in Tetovo and Gostivar. I could then reconnoitre that area before going north to Kossovo.

I shared a room with Gregson Allcott and Tomaso, and slept solidly for ten hours. While we sat over the remains of our breakfast, Riddell recommended me to take a sulphur bath—a specialty of the town; he intended to inspect the aerodrome. As I sat there contentedly smoking a pipe, savouring the prospect of a few days' comfort after the hardship of the mountains and planning my forthcoming visit to Macedonia, a Partisan entered the room with a note for Riddell. When he had read it Riddell flicked it over the table to me. It was a message from Simcox at Peshkopijë, relaying an urgent warning from Fiqri Dine: 'It is dangerous to remain in Dibra after 10.00 on Tuesday, 16th November.'

'What's the date today?' I asked.

'Tuesday, 16th November. And the time is ten minutes to ten.'

'This may be a false alarm, but there's no harm in being prepared. I think we'd better find Haxhi Lleshi and tell him.' I turned to Gregson Allcott. 'Where's Tomaso?'

'Gone to feed and water the animals, sir.'

'Good. "When he comes back tell him to bring the lot here. Then you and he get all our stuff loaded and push off along the road to Peshkopijë. There's no point in your staying here, anyway.'

By good luck we ran into Haxhi Lleshi and Ersat Ndreou in the street outside the hotel, and took them inside to show them Simcox's letter. They were amused.

'We've told you there's no need for alarm,' they laughed. 'Every-thing is foreseen. The bridges over the rivers to the south and east are already destroyed, as you know; but in any case we have pickets there and scouts further down the roads to warn them. We have troops on those hills over there to the east. Every possible approach to Dibra is guarded. We shall get at least two hours' warning of an attack.'

I started to shrug my shoulders but was interrupted in mid-shrug. A spatter of bullets struck the walls of a neighbouring house as a machine-gun opened up from the eastern hills. The room emptied in a flash; Haxhi Lleshi and Ersat seized their tommy-guns and ran into the street followed by their guards. Riddell, Lis, and I stood in the doorway scanning the hills through our glasses. The sound of small-arms fire grew in intensity, a few bullets whistled over our heads or smacked against the walls and roofs of neighbouring houses, but the enemy was still invisible to us. From the direction of the barracks a pack gun began firing—one of two that the Partisans had captured from the Italians.

"While we were watching the hills Tomaso arrived with Riddell's Albanian servant, Myftar, and the horses and mules. I ordered Gregson Allcott to start for Peshkopijë as soon as the mules were loaded, leaving Myftar at the hotel to guard our horses. Then with Riddell and Lis I walked to the barracks to see Haxhi Lleshi.

Forcing our way through the crowd of armed Partisans and Italians who were standing round the doorway, we climbed to the third floor room which was Haxhi Lleshi's headquarters. We found him with Ersat and a mob of Partisan and Italian officers, commissars and guards, all of whom had plenty to say and were saying it volubly. I sat down by an open window which faced towards the sound of the fighting while Riddell, having with difficulty attracted Haxhi Lleshi's attention, explained to him the plan on which the three of us had agreed.

Riddell wanted me to go at once to Fiqri Dine and his Committee and urge them to fulfil their undertaking to help the Partisans with every available man; meanwhile he himself would rally his friends among the independent chieftains like Cen Elezi, Helmi Beg Karasani and Ramadan Kolloshi. With our combined forces we would attack and occupy the hills to the east of Dibra, cutting off Xhem Gostivari's retreat and, we hoped, inflicting on him a decisive defeat. We reckoned to be back with our troops about noon the next day if the Partisans could hold out so long; Lis gallantly volunteered to stay with them. Haxhi Lleshi replied that he could certainly hold out; but at first he refused to accept help from Fiqri Dine, whom he called a 'fascist collaborator'. However, recognizing the absurdity of his position, he at length agreed to Riddell's plan.

Back at the hotel we mounted our horses and, accompanied by Myftar and Shaban, a young French-speaking Partisan, rode northward out of the town. A few bullets came our way, none of them very near; the fighting was still confined to the hills to the east and there seemed no reason to suppose that this attack would be heavier than the last. After an hour we overtook Gregson Allcott and his party approaching the cross-roads of Maqellarë. At the entrance to the village we were accosted by two peasants who had come that morning from Peshkopijë; they warned us that German troops were already there. Soon afterwards we met Fiqri Dine's brother, who told us that Fiqri was in Peshkopijë with Simcox and Faik Shehu, another Dibran chieftain on whose help Riddell was counting. He had heard nothing about the presence of Germans in the town.

On our journey we heard more conflicting reports of German troops ahead of us. If indeed they were there and if they advanced on Dibra from that direction we should look very silly, caught on the road with a string of pack animals. We asked Bungurri and Shaban if they knew of a village off the main road where we could safely hide the mules and our heavy kit; they suggested the house of a friend of Haxhi Lleshi's near the village of Dovollan, which lay between the main road and the Drin, about two miles farther on.

We turned off to the left down a muddy lane and came after half a mile to a handsome house with a huge courtyard, where four Italians were working. The owner of the house willingly agreed to look after our mules, promising to hide them and our kit. We decided to leave Gregson Allcott and Myftar in charge of the animals while the rest of us went on towards Peshkopijë.

It was mid-afternoon when we rejoined the road. The noise of battle had been steadily increasing from the direction of Dibra, with a crescendo of automatic fire from which Riddell claimed he could distinguish the continuous chatter of the new German heavy machine-gun; the sound of artillery was louder and more insistent than could be accounted for by the two light pieces which were all that the Partisans possessed. From the top of a rise we looked back across the plain; I saw a series of flashes on the hills overlooking the town, followed a few seconds later by heavy explosions and puffs of smoke around the barracks; coloured ground flares, marking the positions of forward troops, showed where the German attack, creeping towards the banks of the river, was gradually enveloping the defenders. With the Germans so heavily committed I thought it very doubtful that Haxhi Lleshi would be able to hold Dibra overnight; he must either withdraw across the Drin under cover of darkness or be surrounded and annihilated. Clearly our help would arrive too late to turn the scales now. As we rode on our way there came to my uneasy mind some lines of Housman:

> *Behind, the vats of judgment brewing*
> *Thundered, and thick the brimstone snowed;*
> *He to the hill of his undoing*
> *Pursued his road.*

Poor Bungurri was in tears, wringing his hands and lamenting the destruction of his city and the fate of the women and children exposed to the shells and bullets. We did our best to console him but he would not be comforted. On the road we met groups of peasants who repeated warnings that the Germans were in Peshkopijë, one of them adding that they were on their way to Dibra. We decided to leave our horses at the next village and continue our journey on foot to give ourselves a greater chance of concealment or escape if we ran into trouble.

Before we had time to implement our decision matters were taken out of our hands. In the dusk we came to a bend where the road ran between high banks. As our party turned the corner a band of about a hundred armed men sprang from behind the banks on either side and with swift and silent movements surrounded us. They wore the peasant dress of Dibra—black coats, tight woollen trousers, broad, multi-coloured cummerbunds and fezzes of white felt; each man carried a rifle and bandolier. Their manner was determined but not menacing and they made no move to disarm us; yet, as I wondered whether we were in the hands of friends or enemies I saw Bungurri's ashen face, and my heart sank as I heard him mutter the name Halil Alija.

This chieftain had been mentioned to me by Riddell as one of a pair of 'robber barons' who—some said with Italian help—had risen from poverty to a position of local prominence and wide unpopularity; his partner was a certain Selim Kalloshi, cousin of Riddell's friend, Ramadan Kalloshi, with whom, however, he was at feud. The reasons for their unpopularity were not precisely known to Riddell—there were whispered stories of robbery and abduction—but he had made no response to their previous offers of help, fearing that nobody else in the neighbourhood would work with him if he took them for his allies. It was possible that Riddell's information, coming from prejudiced sources, had maligned them; in any case we could only pray now that they had not taken their rebuff to heart. With no chance either of resistance or of flight we must reconcile ourselves to the will of Providence and the mercy of the robber barons.

Such philosophical detachment came easier to us than to Bungurri. As our captors hustled us up the bank and off the road he gave way to unashamed tears of fright, convinced that they were going to shoot him; in reply to our reassurances, given with more confidence than we could feel, he gasped between his sobs:

'I know, and you don't know! I tell you, they are going to kill me. I am Faik Shehu's nephew and these men have *Hakmarjë* with my uncle!'

Our confidence was not increased by the hysterical behaviour of an ugly-looking fellow who stumped up to Riddell, waving his arms and screaming:

'Why did you never come to see our leaders—the chiefs of the People?'

Suddenly there was a murmur of 'Halil Alija!' and the hubbub died down. A small, sturdy man with a hooked nose and merry, dark eyes set in a fleshy face broke through the throng and, squinting up at us with a cheerful, roguish expression, shook us each warmly by the hand. Through Bungurri he told us that he was glad we had met at last; that we had fallen into the hands of friends, and that this was lucky for us because the Germans were even at this moment coming down the road from Peshkopijë. Now he would have us taken to a safe place while he and his men went on to Dibra to 'fight any Partisans or Germans we can find.' After this masterpiece of ambiguity he bade us an affectionate farewell and detailed a large escort to take us to the house of Selim Kalloshi.

Meekly we went with the escort, partly because we had no choice, partly because in the same village lived Selim's cousin Ramadan, on whose promise we were counting to raise men for the relief or recapture of Dibra. After telling Tomaso and young Shaban not to worry—quite unnecessarily, for they showed no signs of it——Riddell and I planned with them to shoot our way out at a given signal if it should seem likely that we were to be killed or handed over to the Germans.

Leading our horses we struggled for an hour across difficult country intersected with streams and gullies, until we saw the lights of Peshkopijë on a hillside ahead of us. For a moment I feared we were to be taken there; but our guides turned away to the left and led us over open country to a hamlet where we stopped for a drink of water. When we moved on we found that all but four of our escort had vanished; the prospect of murder or betrayal receded.

When we halted again Bungurri announced that we had reached the village of Helmi Beg Karasani, the chieftain whom Riddell and I had saved from a Partisan firing squad; but when we asked to be taken to his house our guards angrily refused, threatening to prevent us by force from going there. Irritated beyond distraction by worry and fatigue Riddell and I drew our pistols, swearing to shoot our way through them if necessary; their anger gave way to uncertainty but they begged us not to delay, pleading that they did not know the way to Helmi's house.

'That,' I shouted, 'is something we can easily find out. We will knock at the next door and ask.'

We knocked for nearly five minutes without answer. Then a shutter was slammed back; there was an orange flash, a deafening report and a bullet hummed past us into the darkness. After a moment's frightened silence Bungurri, Shaban and our guards broke out in angry complaint, apparently to some effect for the door was opened and an old man stood glowering at us, an ancient Turkish rifle in his hands. He lowered his gun, explaining none too graciously that he had thought we were bandits; he told us that Helmi Beg had left the village and added that it would be as well if we did the same.

Some time after midnight we reached the village where the Kalloshi cousins lived in mutual hostility. Standing in the little square in front of the mosque we began a bitter argument with our guards: we demanded to be taken to Ramadan but they answered that they could not go to his house, being at feud with him; nor would they accept our suggestion that we go by ourselves. They had the strictest orders to take us to Selim and to nobody else. When the quarrel was at its height their leader suddenly cocked his rifle and covered us. Provoked to a childish display of temper I dropped my horse's reins and ran at him, flourishing my riding crop. If I had struck him he would have shot me. Fortunately both Bungurri and Shaban intervened to tell us that we should be gravely offending against the custom of the district if we went to Ramadan; Halil Alija's men had brought us here safely, and we should be disgracing them if we left them now to go to his enemy.

This matter was settled by the appearance of Selim himself, pulled from his bed by the news of our arrival. He looked old and sick and limped heavily from a recent bullet wound received in battle against the Partisans; but his charm and friendliness calmed our seething tempers as he promised that we should see his cousin tomorrow. Even Bungurri had lost his former fear. We were taken to Selim's stronghold, a tall stone keep, well loop-holed for defence but too bare and grim for comfort; it was two o'clock when we lay down on the floor of the guest-room to sleep.

After four hours' sleep we were awakened with a breakfast of warm sweetened milk, bread, and goat's cheese; our host apologized that the milk was from a cow and not, as was usual, from a sheep. Having given us directions to find Ramadan's house, because his own men could not accompany us there, Selim bade us an affectionate farewell, gave us his besa—his pledge of friendship—and assured us that we should always find a safe refuge in his house.

Ramadan's home was quite different in appearance and atmosphere from his cousin's. It consisted of two long, low, white buildings, clean-looking and well designed, set in a spacious courtyard surrounded by a white wall; over the door of one building, the guest-house, hung a shield bearing the emblem of Albania—the black double eagle of Skanderbeg on a red background. Ramadan himself, a grave, dark, delicately-featured young man, led us inside to a cheerful and comfortable room with clean, white walls, furnished with brightly coloured rugs and cushions.

He was overjoyed to see us and laughed at our abduction by his cousin, for whom he seemed to feel contempt rather than enmity; but he warned us to put no trust in him. The Germans, he went on to tell us, were in Peshkopijë and Dibra; Haxhi Lleshi had withdrawn his men safely across the Drin in darkness, and Lis was with him. Simcox and Faik Shehu had gone to Cen Elezi's house in the hills at Sllovë, north of Peshkopijë. Ramadan suggested that we follow them and establish a new headquarters there; the house was comparatively secluded, and there was a suitable dropping ground near by. We agreed readily; Cen's house seemed an ideal base both for Riddell's operations against the Germans and for my expedition to Macedonia. Having dispatched messengers to bring Gregson Allcott and the mules to Sllovë, Ramadan made preparations to conduct us there himself.

In the early afternoon we set off across the plain with an escort of nearly a hundred men—Ramadan, Riddell, and I on horseback, the rest on foot; our numbers were swollen on the way as more of Ramadan's followers flocked to us from the countryside. He had wisely sent scouts ahead and detailed strong flanking parties to guard against surprise from prowling German patrols. However, the only sign of the enemy was a solitary Me 109 which flew over us very low and circled several times, apparently reconnoitring Kastriotë aerodrome. It was a bright autumn day with a fresh wind from the south-east and small, fleecy clouds in a pale blue sky; the disappointment and irritations of yesterday faded as I gazed across the brown fields to the majestic range of blue mountains that marked the old Jugoslav frontier.

After two hours we left the plain and climbed high into the hills. At dusk we came to a crest where a great valley lay spread before us, falling steeply to a river bed beyond which rose a formidable wall of mountains. Two hundred yards below the crest we halted at a large square stone house where we were greeted by Cen Elezi's brother, Xhetan; there we left Ramadan to spend the night. Xhetan apologized for not accompanying us to Cen's house but he showed us where it lay, only three hundred yards further down; although brothers and neighbours, Xhetan and Cen were not on speaking terms.

After crossing two fields and an orchard we entered a long, narrow yard covered by a trellis, where we were welcomed by a tall and sturdy man of about thirty who introduced himself as Cen's son, Xhelal; with him was Tony Simcox. I was touched by the obvious relief with which Simcox hailed Riddell's arrival; he had believed us dead or prisoners of the Germans in Dibra. Simcox himself had barely escaped from Peshkopijë, climbing the hills a few hundred yards away as the first Germans entered the streets. Warned by Fiqri Dine of their approach he had lingered to organize the defence of the town in the mistaken belief that the people would fight; on the contrary, it seemed that they had lined the streets to welcome the invaders. He had come straight here with Corporal Davis, the wireless operator; they had brought their wireless set but were obliged to leave everything else behind. In Dibra, we subsequently heard, the Germans had received a similar ovation; disgusted with the behaviour of the Partisans and grateful to the power that had united them with their kin in Albania, the Dibrans had turned their backs on the Allied cause.

Xhelal led us inside and up a narrow staircase to the guest-room, where his father was awaiting us. Cen Elezi was a thin, fierce-looking old man with white hair, bright blue eyes and a querulous, arrogant manner; his vigorous personality was reinforced by qualities of initiative and courage for which I was soon to be thankful. With him in the room were three more of his sons: Islam, tall, dark and cheerful; Gani, silent and morose, and a boy whose name I never learned. All were dominated by their father, whom they treated with a deep respect noticeably tinged with fear. 'You must understand' Xhelal confided to me, 'that in the mountains we follow a patriarchial rule of life.' The remaining guests were Faik Shehu and Corporal Davis, a cheerful youth whose fragile appearance concealed remarkable strength and resilience.

Removing our boots we settled ourselves cross-legged on the floor around the hearth while Xhelal, deputizing for his father, rolled cigarettes of fine Skopjë tobacco and tossed one to each of us in turn; Cen produced from inside his cummerbund a long cigarette-holder of chased silver with a large nicotine-stained bulb of amber for a mouth-piece. Our eyes smarted in the smoke that filled the room from the open fireplace, for the few slit-like windows gave little ventilation.

We were saved the usual difficulties of language because the three eldest sons spoke good English, having studied at the American College in Tiranë under the famous Harry T. Fulz. Unfortunately the conversation deteriorated into a prolonged dispute between Cen and Riddell over the deployment of the Elezi forces against the Germans, culminating in a preposterous demand by Cen that the British should recognize him officially as 'the only anti-German military commander in Dibra,' and should undertake to deal with nobody in the area except through him. I took no part in the discussion and was glad when the arrival of raki relieved the tension. Although Cen did not drink, the conviviality seemed to mellow him and he agreed to call up his men, evacuate his family and turn his house into a military headquarters.

After the raki a splendid meal was served, for our hosts had killed a sheep in our honour. The food was placed on an enormous circular wooden table, about six inches off the floor, around which we disposed ourselves with what comfort we could manage; according to custom Cen and his sons would not sit down to eat until we had finished. We all ate out of the same dish, using our fingers for the meat and rice, and spoons for the gravy and vegetables. Riddell, as the senior, was obliged to take the sheep's head to dissect as best he could. It was the custom for the host to give one of the eyes to an especially favoured guest; only by feigning a religious scruple could this delicacy be refused without discourtesy. A bowl of milk washed down the meal, after which we were brought a basin of hot water and a towel.

Xhelal showed great interest in my Macedonian plans. He had already sent for his kinsman and neighbour, Zenel Lita, who had many friends around Tetovo and Gostivar and who would himself accompany me on my journey there; he should arrive at Sllovë tomorrow. Xhelal stressed the many and grave dangers of the enterprise. 'And so', he concluded with a charming smile, 'you must be sure to give him a good present of money.'

Riddell and Simcox left the next morning with Faik Shehu and Ramadan Kalloshi to begin operations against the Dibra-Peshkopijë road, leaving me to await the arrival of Zenel Lita. While Davis made several unsuccessful attempts to get through to Cairo on the wireless I strolled outside the house, returning before lunch to share a flask of excellent Prizren slivovic with him and Xhelal.

Although larger than most houses in the Albanian highlands the home of Cen Elezi was built on a plan common to nearly all of them. Set in a walled courtyard, whose main entrance was barred by a stout timber gate, it commanded a wide field of fire in three directions; only on the southern side was it overlooked by the hills we had crossed the day before. The building consisted of two storeys, of which the ground floor was taken up by animals, fodder and women. We seldom saw and never spoke to the women. The top floor contained the men's sleeping quarters and the guest-room, which in every house was the largest and most important room—the only room a guest would normally see. There were no bathrooms in the mountains; the lavatory was usually a narrow hole in the planks of a tiny penthouse that projected over a yard in which fed poultry and, in the Catholic country, pigs.

These houses contained no furniture; the only concessions to comfort by day or night were cushions, rugs, mattresses, and quilts. Even the family valuables were usually stored in one wooden chest. Such simplicity was in part a legacy from the nomad instincts of the Turks; Sir Charles Eliot, describing a Turkish gentleman's house in the last century, wrote that it contained no more furniture than could be carried off at a moment's notice on a wagon into Asia. But it derived also from the perpetual insecurity of life in the mountains, especially on the frontiers; there were very few families whose houses had not been burnt at least once this century by Turks, Serbs, Greeks, Austrians, Germans, Italians, or fellow Albanians.

In the afternoon Gregson Allcott appeared, so exhausted that he could barely stand. His opening words to me were a severe shock:

'I'm sorry to report, sir, the loss of the rest of "Stepmother".'

At eight o'clock that morning, while he was crossing the plain with Ramadan Kalloshi's guide and our mules, a German patrol had spotted them and given chase; he naturally had to abandon the mules and flee. That was only the start of his troubles; no sooner had he and the guide shaken off their pursuers than they ran into another patrol. For four hours they were on the run, almost without rest and continually under fire from parties of roaming Germans. They had reached the safety of the hills at last, but Gregson had escaped with only the clothes on his back.

We were now in a serious plight for stores and money; I could not borrow from Riddell because he had lost nearly everything in Peshkopijë, and it would probably be a week or more before we could hope to receive a supply drop. I had a hundred gold sovereigns in my money belt, but after my talk with Xhelal I could not be sure how long this would last me in Macedonia. My Welgun was lost with the mules, leaving me with my pistol and only one magazine. I prayed that we should be allowed a little peace to replenish our stores.

I was therefore disturbed to hear later in the evening that a force of Germans from Peshkopijë had arrived at a village only two hours' march from Sllovë. About the same time Faik Shehu and Simcox returned, the latter in a black rage because Faik had refused at the last moment to send his men into action; however, he cheered up when he heard this latest piece of news and left again almost immediately with fifty of Faik's men on a reconnaissance towards the village where the Germans were supposed to be. He expected to be back in the morning.

At eight o'clock Zenel Lita arrived, a stocky little man whose appearance and manner reminded me of a friendly badger. He seemed pleased with the idea of accompanying me to Macedonia and suggested that he and I leave the next morning for his house across the valley, where we could plan the journey in detail. I packed a small haversack with a change of shirt and underclothes, socks, washing things, a few candles, and a pocket edition of *War and Peace* bought in London and still unopened.

While we were talking a sudden fusillade of shots brought us to our feet reaching for our guns; it proved to be a wedding in the village, which the guests were celebrating in traditional style with a *feu-de-joie*. When the excitement had died down Zenel, who was said to have the gift of second sight, tried to tell us the future from a sheep's bone—a method I never saw before or since; after a while he looked around with a grin and announced:

'I see a battle.'

I was dreaming that I was at an Investiture at Buckingham Palace, about to be made a Dame of the British Empire in recognition of outstanding services to Albanian agriculture; as I knelt to receive the Accolade I felt a touch on my shoulder and awoke to find the youngest Elezi bending over me:

'Your binoculars please, Mr. Major,' he whispered. 'There are some men coming over the hill.'

He took them off the floor beside me and hurried out of the room;

I turned over, still half asleep. Before I had time to drop off again Xhelal and Gani appeared in the doorway.

'Mr. Major, get up quickly! The Germans are here!'

For a moment I thought they were joking; but a volley of shots and the sound of bullets striking the wall outside soon jerked me to my feet. Rousing Allcott and Davis I pulled on my field boots without pausing to buckle them, struggled into my battle-dress blouse, fastened my belt and pistol and threw my haversack over my shoulder, blessing the impulse that had made me pack it the night before. Down below we saw Cen, holding a rifle in one hand and pointing with the other towards the back of the house; bullets were smacking into the courtyard all round us from the hills above, but no one was attempting to return the fire or improvise a defence. The surprise was so complete, I concluded, that our only chance lay in headlong flight. I was confirmed in my belief a moment later by Xhelal's shout:

'Follow me, Mr. Major! Quickly, this way!'

'Where's Tomaso?' I demanded.

'He is coming with my father. Please, Mr. Major, hurry!'

At that moment I caught sight of Tomaso; shouting to him to follow, I dived after Xhelal and Zenel, who were disappearing with the two N.C.O.s through a small postern in the wall. Ahead of us lay open ground sloping to a narrow, bushy ravine which seemed to offer the best hope of cover. As we came out of the gate we were challenged from both sides and I saw figures in grey uniform running towards us with pointed tommy-guns; Zenel fired his rifle from the hip and I took two running shots with my pistol at the nearest German; but I did not stop to watch the effect. From both directions bullets whistled past our ears or spattered on the rocks all round us; at such short range it seemed inevitable that one of us should be hit. Davis, I suddenly noticed with astonished admiration, was struggling to carry the heavy wireless set; I shouted to him to ditch it and save himself, but at that moment he tripped and fell headlong, smashing the set against a rock. He scrambled to his feet unhurt and threw the useless equipment into a bush.

The distance to the ravine could not have been more than two hundred yards; but it seemed like a mile as I laboured over the broken ground with

pounding heart, dry throat and bursting lungs. At last I reached the edge of
the gully and, throwing myself down among the bushes by a small stream,
looked around for my companions. Allcott and Davis were beside me,
panting but unharmed; Zenel was crouched a few yards away, smiling to
himself like a badger that has just dodged the dachshunds; but of Xhelal there
was no sign. Then I heard him shouting up on the right and, peering over the
edge of the ravine, saw him waving to us to join him.

As we broke cover and ran after him our pursuers caught sight of us and
opened fire, this time with a machine guns as well as Schmeizers. Plunging
down the hill amid the flying bullets I was pulled up by a stout wooden fence
beyond which was a tangle of brambles; with an athletic prowess that I have
never achieved before or since I vaulted clean over the fence but stumbled
on the other side and landed on my face in the brambles; sobbing with rage
and fear I scrambled to my knees and forced my way through, in the manner
of a swimmer doing the breast stroke. Davis cleared both obstacles in his
stride, but Allcott fell over the fence and, caught by his belt, hung upside
down for a few seconds before toppling on his head in the bushes. A minute
later we were all bunched with Xhelal in the safety of a piece of dead ground.
Together we hurried down towards the river valley.

We were joined by the youngest Elezi and two retainers, but there was no
sign of Cen, his other sons or Tomaso; they must have been trapped in the
courtyard, unable to break out before the German cordon closed. The house
was no longer in sight, but from above us came the rapid, intermittent firing
of machine-guns interjected with sharp explosions that sounded like mortar
bombs. Xhelal would not hear of our turning back. He was bound by his
father's orders and the traditional law of hospitality to escort us to safety; if
any thing were to happen to us now he and all his clan would be disgraced.
Zenel supported him and I yielded; in any case it was too late to help in the
defence. But I felt bitterly ashamed each time Xhelal stopped to look
backward, the tears running freely down his face.

Crossing a wide river bed at the bottom of the valley, we began a difficult
climb by a narrow track hewn almost perpendicular in the rocky face of the
cliff. Heavy rain began to fall, soaking us within a few minutes and almost
blinding us as we struggled upwards in the teeth of a fierce storm; the rolling
thunder and vivid lightning flashes added their infernal accompaniment to
this drama of battle and disaster.

After half an hour we halted at a small hamlet on the cliff top which
commanded a view across the valley; shivering and dispirited we sat in one
of the doorways and surveyed the ruin of our recent sanctuary. Cen's house
and his brother Xhetan's above it were in flames; otherwise the fighting
seemed to have died down except for isolated bursts of machine-gun fire and
a few mortar bombs exploding in the ravine we had recently traversed. The
rain had ceased; but the storm clouds still hung low over the valley. The

harsh, cold colours of that rain-washed landscape glowed luminous and steely in the lambent light. A pillar of smoke, dirty white and grey-brown, hung above the burning houses, blending into the sombre blackness of the sky. Lightning flickered on the mountain tops and thunder echoed menacingly along the dark ravines and watercourses. I seemed to be staring at some nightmare canvas of El Greco—a far ghastlier storm than the one he painted over Toledo.

I could not imagine how we had been so easily taken by surprise. But Xhelal explained that, counting on protection or at least warning from Simcox's patrol, he had not troubled to post any guards; so that the Germans were able to approach within a hundred yards of the house before the alarm was given. Much later I learned that the Germans had come by a different path from the one Simcox had taken, and Simcox knew nothing of our danger until he heard the sound of fighting; by the time he arrived the battle was over.

Remembering Shtyllë I reflected bitterly how much more dangerous and demoralizing were the German methods of pursuit than the Italian. The Germans were not afraid to penetrate into the hills with only a company of infantry and a few mortars; against such police tactics, directed with skill and vigour, we could take few effective precautions.

Gani Elezi, who joined us soon after midday, relieved some of our anxiety with the news that his father and Islam had shot their way through the enemy to safety; Cen had two bullet wounds—in the shoulder and wrist—but was not in serious danger. But Gani brought me bitter news as well: Tomaso was dead, shot through the heart at point-blank range as he ran out after us.

Both Gani and Xhelal swore that Halil Alija, despite the *besa* he had pledged us, had accompanied the Germans to Sllovë with a large force of his own men and some two hundred Dibrans. After looting and burning the Elezi houses the Germans had rounded up a group of villagers and their wives and children, lined them against the wall of the school and massacred them with machine-guns. This piece of *furchtbarkeit* seemed to me as stupid as it was sickening; it must have shocked the Germans' own allies, for even in their blood-feuds the Albanians would respect the lives of women and children.

We were now within the borders of Luma, the territory of the powerful Muharrem Bajraktar, one of the most important of all the Gheg chieftains. Zenel told me that Allcott, Davis and I must lie low for a few days because the Germans were sure to search the countryside for us; at this moment their patrols were probably on our track. His guides would take us to a hide-out in the mountains to the north, where we must remain until he sent for us. Before we parted he took pains to impress on me that we must on no account let it be known that we carried gold. Accompanied by two grim and silent tribesmen we walked for three and a half hours along an easy track following the line of beech-covered heights above the Black Drin. We met nobody; the distant calls of herdsmen were the only signs of human life in these wild, dark, precipitous mountains. In the evening we came to a small stone hut about fifty yards below the path, beside a ravine that ran steeply down to the deep river gorge. An old, emaciated shepherd met us in the doorway and bowed us into a bare and windowless room dimly lit by an oil lamp, where three blankets were spread on the floor for our beds. Without a word our guides departed.

We hid in the hut four days, getting up each morning an hour before dawn to take cover in the ravine until an hour after sunrise. Those were the hours of danger, when a German patrol might surprise us; at other times—or so we understood the shepherd to say—there were watchers who would warn us of the enemy's approach. It was said that the Germans never moved through the mountains by night; but I slept uneasily, jerking into wakefulness whenever a dog barked in the distance. Years afterwards that sound would still wake me from the deepest slumber.

We ate once a day, grateful for the coarse maize bread and skimmed milk that was all our host could offer us. Undismayed either by the danger or the discomfort of our situation Allcott and Davis joked or slept away the daytime hours. I read *War and Peace* by the light of a candle; absorbed in the problems of Pierre and Natasha I was able for a while to forget my own.

IX

THE MARCHES OF KOSSOVO

On the morning of 24th November our two guides returned to conduct us to Zenel. We retraced our steps along the track we had used five days before, past the hamlet from which we had watched the burning of the Elezi house to a village two hours' journey further east, beneath the black and snow-crowned mass of Mount Korab.

We found Zenel with Cen Elezi and his sons. Ceil greeted me with surprising cordiality seeing that I was largely responsible for his misfortunes; he looked very frail, sitting in a corner swathed in bandages, but his wounds were healing well under the usual local treatment, which was to plug the bullet-holes with goat's cheese. I asked Xhelal if they had any plans for the immediate future.

'As soon as my father is well,' he replied, 'we shall go to another part of Drin and raise men against the Germans.' Zenel's enquiries had convinced him that it would be folly for us to attempt a reconnaissance of Macedonia at the present; the Germans were on the alert and a great deal of time would be needed to prepare for such a journey. In the meantime he suggested that I accompany him to his brother-in-law, Muharrem Bajraktar, after which I might be able to visit Gjakovë, Prizren and other parts of Kossovo.

This plan suited me very well; the Brigadier had asked me for a report on Muharrem Bajraktar. Unquestionably the most powerful chieftain in eastern Albania he could, I had heard, raise at least a thousand fighting men from his own territory of Luma, and could probably call on as many more from his allies in Mirdita and the mountains further north; moreover, he was reported to have influential friends in Kossovo and Macedonia and to be in touch with Mihailović in Jugoslavia.

I was relieved to hear that Riddell and Simcox were safe with Ramadan Kalloshi somewhere near Peshkopijë; the Elezis promised to send Davis to join them as soon as possible. I decided to leave Gregson Allcott in their care with instructions to carry my report on the recent fighting to the Brigadier at Biza as soon as he could cross the Drin; although I was reluctant to lose him it seemed unlikely that I should need a paramilitary specialist in the immediate future.

Zenel and I started on our journey in the freezing blackness before dawn on 26th November; with us came his two cousins, Malik and Ismail Lita. Over my battle-dress I wore an old green Italian army greatcoat, with a tattered pair of puttees wound round my field boots; Zenel intended to pass me off to strangers as an Italian deserter seeking work with Muharrem Bajraktar. At the shepherd's hut where I had lain in hiding we halted for refreshment, and I was at last allowed to reward the old man for his kindness; even so, I could barely persuade him to accept the ten sovereigns which I pressed upon him. Afterwards we climbed steeply among woods of stunted mountain oak; through gaps in the forest we caught occasional glimpses of the Drin, brown and swollen, racing between the smooth granite walls of its narrow gorge far below on our left. The sky was overcast and heavy with the threat of rain, deadening the colours of earth and rocks and dulling the yellow of the maize stubble in the miserable scattered fields roughly terraced out of the stony mountain-side.

In the middle of the afternoon we stopped again, at a long, low, white house whose handsome, well-kept appearance contrasted strangely with the savagery of the surrounding hills; it belonged to Myftar Ahmedi, a vassal and close friend of Muharrem Bajraktar. Myftar, a lean, wiry man in early middle age with a mop of black hair and flashing, humourous eyes, received us joyfully and led us into a spacious guest-room with tall arched windows and clean, white-washed walls on which hung a horse's bridle, an old rapier, and an eighteenth century bayonet. We drank glasses of warm sweetened milk and smoked Bulgarian cigarettes with long, gilt cardboard mouthpieces while Myftar sent a messenger to tell Muharrem Bajraktar of our approach.

From this house we climbed through more oak woods until we came at evening to a crest that overlooked a broad valley sloping down towards the Black Drin; below us lay the village of Ymishtë, beyond it the fortress home of Muharrem. Hurrying through the village we came to a group of buildings surrounded by a high stone wall; on the battlements of the tower above the main gateway stood two armed sentries, who shouted the news of our arrival to someone in the court-yard below. As we entered I saw that all but two of the buildings had been gutted by fire. Before I had time to observe more a quiet voice greeted me in English, and I turned to see a small man with an olive complexion, a thin moustache and a wisp of beard; extending a frail and yellow hand with an ugly scar on the wrist he introduced himself as Muharrem's brother, Bairam. Leading the way across the courtyard he pointed to the gutted buildings and explained that they were the work of an Italian punitive expedition, as also was the bullet wound in his wrist.

Climbing a flight of stone steps we found ourselves in a dark, smoky room dimly lit by a small fire at one end; from the floor beside it a stocky figure rose and welcomed us with a stiff bow. I replied with the customary greeting of '*tungjatjeta*!' and he motioned me to a seat on the floor opposite him. He addressed me in French with short, jerky sentences uttered in a quiet, squeaky voice. When I mentioned my visit to Kossovo he pursed his lips and rose:

'Let us go upstairs where we can talk alone,' he ordered.

I followed him up a broad stone staircase into a spacious, well-lit room with a large open fireplace flanked by scarlet silk cushions, on which we sat facing one another. For the first time I was able to see him clearly, a short, middle-aged man with a ruddy, fleshy face, iron-grey hair and moustache, and small, very bright eyes. His manner was friendly if a trifle condescending, as befitted a powerful chieftain and experienced politician when talking with an ignorant and ingenuous young stranger.

I listened with respect, for I knew that he had played an important part in recent Albanian history and that he could be of great value to us in the future. Originally one of Zog's allies in the revolution of 1924 he had subsequently plotted to overthrow him and had been forced to flee the country. After a period of exile in Belgrade, Vienna and Paris he had returned to his house in Luma when the Italians occupied Albania in 1939; but he had stoutly refused to tolerate Italian rule in his own territory. After the surrender of Italy he had raised his tribesmen to occupy the important town of Kukës on the Scutari-Prizren road, at the confluence of the Black and the White Drin; within a few days, however, a strong German counter-attack had driven him into the hills.

He told me that the Germans had sent troops against him a week ago, shooting up some of his villages in what seemed a curiously inept attempt to persuade him to accept office in the puppet Tiranë government; he had spurned collaboration but had been sufficiently frightened to come to an agreement whereby he would not engage in hostilities against the Germans or allow his territory to be used as a base for operations against them, provided they did not again invade Luma. He was frankly terrified of their power and emphasized that we must not think of undertaking any action against them during the winter, but must build up our strength until the spring, when, he blandly supposed, an Allied invasion would drive them out.

His plans for the future, in contrast to his present fears, were coloured by a strange *folie de grandeur* which convinced him that he could unite the Balkan peoples in a federation under his leadership, to counter what he described as the twin dangers of Russian domination and Pan-Slav Imperialism; these two phrases recurred constantly in his talk during the evening. He admitted that he had received emissaries from Mihailović, who had proposed that they should join forces against the Partisans; negotiations, however, had foundered on the Kossovo question.

On the subject of my journey to Kossovo he was practical if not encouraging. At first he begged me to abandon the project, arguing that the area was overrun with German spies, that the Drin would be impassable and that, in any case, I could just as well study the Kossovo situation from his house. But when I persisted he promised to take me in person to his brother-in-law, Mehmet Ali, Bajraktar of Hass, the territory north of Kukës; there they would put me in touch with Hasan Beg Kryeziu, the influential Gjakovë landowner who had been one of the leaders of the abortive rising in 1941.

This was splendid news; Hasan Beg's had been the first of the names mentioned to me as valuable contacts in Kossovo during my Tirana visit, and I knew that he stood well with both nationalists and L.N.C. For the first time since the disaster at Sllovë I felt cheerful and confident; nor was I dismayed by Muharrem's frequent pauses in the conversation to look at me, shake his head sorrowfully and exclaim: '*J'ai beaucoup de peur pour vous!*'

Before dinner we were joined by Zenel and his cousins and by Muharrem's son Ibrahim, a solemn but friendly youth of twenty-two who brought us a bottle of slivovic; while we drank Muharrem sipped a cup of coffee and treated me to a dissertation on the perils of alcohol. At nine o'clock, after a very good meal, a mattress and quilts were spread for me on the floor and I was left alone to sleep.

Zenel and his cousins returned to their homes the next day; I was very sorry to see them go, remembering the risks they had taken to help me at a time when my fortunes were at their nadir. I spent the day resting and listening to Muharrem's account of Albanian history since the time of Philip of Macedon—a subject on which he claimed to have exhausted the authorities. He maintained that the Albanian language was still close to that of Philip and Alexander the Great; which of course I was in no position to dispute.

Muharrem and I left Ymishtë on Sunday morning, 28th November, accompanied by Myftar Ahmedi and an escort of twelve stalwart tribesmen dressed in short jackets and white woollen jodhpurs embroidered in black. Muharrem, wrapped in a long, dark blue cloak with a flat skull-cap of black silk on his head, bestrode a fine chestnut horse captured from the Italians; Myftar rode a grey cob, and I was mounted on a big grey mare which he had lent me for the journey. In addition to their rifles our escort carried a Fiat light machine-gun—picked up in Kukës, Muharrem explained with the complacent air of a collector exhibiting a fine piece of Chippendale.

We rode slowly up a steep, rough track climbing between high, jagged peaks to a broad plateau, which we skirted, following a line of hills along its eastern edge. Below us on our left was a disused flying field pitted with craters; beyond, on a hill across the river, was the ruined castle of the ancient Bajraktars of Tej Drinit. Muharrem evidently put little faith in his pact with the Germans, for he moved at a slow and cautious pace, throwing out scouts to front and flanks to watch for enemy patrols. At each village and hamlet the people turned out to give us a tumultuous welcome, saluting Muharrem with obvious affection and deep respect as 'Bajraktar'; as well as the title of a northern chief, Bajraktar was also the surname of Muharrem's family, deriving from some incident of medieval history.

We halted for two hours at the village of Shtiqën beneath the eight thousand foot peak of Mount Gjalicë. After a lunch of eggs fried in batter, followed by cheese and sour milk we descended towards the gorge of the

Luma, skirting the steep side of the mountain. Muharrem began to show signs of nervousness, shouting angrily at his men when-ever they bunched together, which was frequently; he explained that there was a German post a mile downstream from the ford. The Luma flowed swiftly between wide banks of shingle overhung by wooded cliffs down which we made our way with difficulty on foot, leading our horses. At the bottom we remounted and, led by Muharrem, trotted across the shingle into the river. Our mounts floundered in the deep and swirling water and Muharrem's was almost swept away in mid-stream; I felt that we should have done better to imitate the Tartars, who let themselves be ferried across rivers clinging to the tails of their swimming horses.

In the late afternoon we found ourselves on the top of the heights overlooking the town of Kukës, five miles to the west, where the Black Drin from Lake Ohrid joins the White Drin from Kossovo. Turning north-east we traversed open, rolling hillsides sloping towards the valley of the White Drin, and at dusk we came to a village where Muharrem announced that we should spend the night; the river ran beside the Prizren-Scutari road, and he wished his men to make a thorough reconnaissance of the crossing before we attempted it.

Our host, Rashid, killed a sheep in our honour, serving me to my disgust and embarrassment with the head and eye; before dinner I overheard Muharrem tell his men to find me some raki, but this they were unable to do. I was sufficiently stimulated, however, by listening to his interpretation of Albania's territorial claims—what he called the frontiers of an 'ethnical Albania'; they seemed to include most of the Balkan peninsula between Salonika and the Adriatic, between the Gulf of Corinth and the northern boundary of Montenegro.

In the morning Muharrem's precautions of the previous day proved justified, for we heard that a German patrol had visited Shtiqën soon after we had left; they had asked for information about 'British officers and Communists'.

At noon we sent a small party to watch the ferry over the White Drin; at half-past two we started ourselves. Moving at a leisurely pace, with frequent halts at houses on the way, we reached a grassy knoll above the valley as the sun was sinking behind the western mountains, splashing the snow-topped heights across the river with bars of delicate rose which faded while we watched to a dead and toneless white.

We paused while Muharrem gave instructions to his scouts. When they had gone he said to me:

'If anything happens while we are crossing the road, come back with me. If we are separated, see that you come back by the same route.'

We followed a steep spiral path down the hillside and came out of the trees suddenly onto an open grass bank. A few yards below us ran the road, a broad grass verge on either side; beyond raced the yellow, swollen river. We handed over our horses to Myftar Ahmedi and two tribesmen, and crouched behind the bank while Muharrem gave a series of orders and I scanned the road for possible cover; finding none I prayed that we should have an undisturbed crossing. The men listened to their orders quietly, but broke into a loud, excited babble as each explained and embellished them to his neighbour. Shouting them down, Muharrem launched into an angry lecture, apparently on the need for keeping silence; then he signed to Myftar and his two companions, who mounted and jogged down the path onto the road. As soon as they reached the tarmac they swung left and galloped for about two hundred yards before turning towards the river.

When they had vanished we followed at the double, leaving two men to cover us with the light machine-gun; we found Myftar and the horses in a clump of willows by the water's edge. From the opposite bank a broad punt was approaching, steered by an oarsman in the bow; it was attached by a pulley to an overhead cable slung across the river and so propelled by the force of the current. As we tried to scramble aboard Muharrem slipped on the muddy bank and slid into the water; I caught his arm and started to pull him out while two of the guards ran to help me, slinging their rifles on their shoulders as they bent to grasp him. In the excitement one of the rifles went off, singeing my face; the report rang down the valley echoing among the rocks on either side.

'If that doesn't bring the Germans upon us,' sighed Muharrem when he was safely on board, 'we can be sure that there are none around.'

Apparently there were none; for we ferried ourselves and the horses across in two journeys without hearing so much as a lorry on the road, although the operation lasted well over half an hour. On the other side we climbed a track up a steep, wooded ravine running towards the crest of the dark mountain mass that formed the northern wall of the valley. After an hour's journey we came to a poor village, whose inhabitants, however, received us hospitably and gave us food and shelter for the night.

We left next morning at ten, after a breakfast of maize bread and milk, and climbed slowly up the face of the mountain through woods of small oaks. The ranks of snowy peaks across the Drin glistened in the sunlight against the clear blue of the sky; the sharp, frosty mountain air brought the blood to our cheeks and put vigour into our limbs. On the road below us a column of horse-drawn artillery moved slowly towards Prizren with a platoon of infantry a few hundred yards ahead of the guns—a splendid target for an ambush.

Shortly before midday we came out upon a bleak plateau covered with coarse grass and studded with outcrops of rock and patches of snow. Above us loomed the squat bulk of Mount Bishtrik like a brown cottage loaf crowned with icing sugar; along the top ran the old Jugoslav frontier.

Shivering in the sudden cold I was glad when we stopped at a miserable hamlet for lunch. We entered the largest of the houses through the stable on the ground floor and climbed a ladder to a surprisingly clean and cheerful guest-room, where a bright fire blazed a welcome. We seated ourselves on a raised dais at one end of the room while the owner, an old man who had known Muharrem when the latter was commanding the gendarmerie in that region, brought us cups of camomile tea and showed us photographs of Muharrem looking very handsome in his uniform at the age of thirty.

When we left after lunch grey clouds were racing low over Bishtrik; on an upper slope of the mountain a splash of sunlight lingered on the grass beside a clump of pines in a lovely contrast of pale golden yellow and dark viridian. In the middle of the afternoon we reached the northern edge of the plateau and looked down upon a deep valley enclosed by high precipitous mountains; a steep, snow-covered track brought us down through thick woods to the head of the valley and the village of Vlahën, home of Mehmet Ali Bajraktar. His high stone tower stood on a mound, which we had barely started to climb when we were halted by a shout from above: a very tall, bent old man in a short black coat, white woollen jodhpurs and conical white skull-cap ran down the slope towards us flinging his arms wide in welcome. He embraced us each in turn, reserving a special hug for Muharrem, who introduced him as Mehmet Ali, the Bajraktar of Hass.

Friendliness and hospitality bubbled from him as he led us up the hill to his house where his son, a tall, dark man of about forty-five, was waiting to conduct us to the guest-room; the son, also known as Mehmet Ali Bajraktar, was married to Muharrem's sister. The old man, who combined the dignified appearance of a patriarch with the hearty manner of an English country squire, took pride in the fact that neither he nor his son could read or write; but he admitted that his grandson could do both, adding regretfully that the boy could even speak a little Italian.

In the guest-room, which contained, besides some fine Persian and Turkish rugs, the unusual feature of a table—although this, we were assured, was scarcely ever used—we were served with rich *mezë* and bottles of smooth but potent raki while father and son entertained us with stories of their embattled history. The old warrior had fought Turk, Montenegrin, Serb, and Italian with impartial vigour and enjoyment. On the last occasion, when they were hunted by the Italians, the whole family had taken refuge with thirty others in a cave in the Catholic country, where they had hidden for three weeks, existing on a little maize bread and water brought them each evening by the villagers.

'That Catholic bread nearly killed me,' chuckled the old man. 'I couldn't chew it with my ancient teeth!'

As the principal guest I must give my assent before the evening meal could be served. To have given it the first time I was asked would have been a grave discourtesy, for there was seldom any conversation after dinner; on this occasion I judged it tactful to delay a while longer than usual, because Muharrem and our hosts had much to discuss with each other and with me. During pauses in our talk an old man sang us harsh mountain threnodies to the accompaniment of the primitive two-stringed *çeteli*, and as a climax to our entertainment old Rasim Domë, the most ancient of Mehmet Ali's retainers, fuddled with the mellow raki, pranced and postured round the room, mouthing ludicrous grimaces from beneath his drooping black moustache, while his companions cheered his buffoonery and the *çeteli* screeched a faster, wilder rhythm.

Young Mehmet Ali told me there was a party of Englishmen at the village of Deg, near the bank of the river Drill, two days' journey to the west. This must be Flight-Lieutenant Hands's mission, which had moved north from Dibra in October. I decided to go straight there from Vlahën to refit myself with money and clothing and regain wireless contact with Cairo and Brigadier Davies; I should also need a properly equipped base from which to make my reconnaissance of Kossovo. I therefore sent word to Hands to expect me within the next few days, as soon as I had seen Hasan Kryeziu, whom Mehmet Ali had already summoned to his house to meet me.

On the evening of 2nd December, two days after our arrival at Vlahën, I was sitting over my raki talking with Muharrem and our hosts and trying to distract my mind from the activities of the colony of lice that had infested my clothes for the last month, when the barking of dogs and a clamour of voices outside announced the approach of strangers. A minute later there was a shout of welcome and a short, chunky man in a knickerbocker suit of grey pepper-and-salt tweed and stout leather gaiters stumped into the room, shook himself like a sheep dog and began to call out greetings in a deep, hearty voice. He extended his hand to me with a stiff bow:

'Kryeziu!' he boomed.

'Kemp!' I replied, coming stiffly to attention as I returned the bow and handshake.

With his white hair, square, heavy-jowled face, bulky figure and bluff good nature he looked like a prosperous farmer, which indeed he was. But I had heard also of his shrewdness, honesty and courage, of his friendship for the British, and of the wide affection and esteem he enjoyed on both sides of the frontier.

It was not until next morning that we were able to discuss the business that had brought us together. Ever since August, when I had heard that there was a chance of my going to Kossovo, I had set myself to study the problem of that disputed territory; I had questioned men of every shade of political opinion, but Hasan Kryeziu was the first Kossovar with whom I had been able to talk and the first person who enjoyed the confidence of nationalists and Partisans alike. Muharrem and Mehmet Ali were manifestly his close friends, and Enver Hoxha himself had told me that he was the 'unofficial president' of the L.N.C. in Gjakovë, whatever that meant. Kryeziu's views, then, should represent those of the great majority of Albanians.

The term Kossovo in its strictest application refers to the plain near Priština in Serbia where the great battle was fought in 1389 between the Serbs and the Ottoman Turks which brought Serbia under Turkish rule for more than four hundred years; more commonly—and in the sense in which I use it—it includes also Mitrovica and the region of Metohija—that is the towns of Peć, Gjakovë and Prizren. As the heart of the medieval Serbian kingdom the Serbs claim that it is indissolubly linked with the history of their nation; for which reason, more than any other, it was included in the frontiers of Jugoslavia. Albania s claims are based on two generally admitted facts: that it is her natural granary, and that the majority of the inhabitants are Albanians—the proportion is between seventy and eighty-five per cent. Jugoslav rule between the two World Wars unfortunately tended to suppress rather than encourage or even tolerate Albanian customs, religion, and language.

My principal task was to explore the chances of forming a resistance movement among Albanians in Kossovo. When I sounded him on the subject Hasan Beg warned me, as I had feared he would, that the majority of Kossovars preferred a German occupation to a Serb; the Axis Powers had at least united them with their fellow Albanians, whereas an Allied victory would, they feared, return them to Jugoslav rule. Therefore, although most believed that the Germans would eventually be beaten, few would risk their lives to help in the process without some combined declaration by the Allied governments, guaranteeing the Kossovars the right to decide their own future by plebiscite. I already knew from a previous interchange of a signals with Cairo that such a declaration was out of the question; instead, I had been advised to 'tactfully avoid the subject of the future of Kossovo'—not a very practical suggestion, as it proved. In my talks with irredentists the future of Kossovo was invariably the first point they raised; nor could I hope to arouse their enthusiasm or allay their fears by a vague reference to the terms of the Atlantic Charter, which was as far as I might commit myself.

Nevertheless, Hasan Beg seemed delighted that a British officer had come to Kossovo, and he promised to do everything in his power to make my visit a success. He emphasized the importance of my keeping in touch with him while I was at Deg, and to this end he detailed one of his retainers, Shpen Zeçeri, to act as courier between us. This Shpen Zeçeri was a tall, very silent man with undistinguished features whom I generally recognized by the way he wore his white 'egg cup' cap tilted well forward on his head. His master described him as exceptionally trustworthy; I certainly found him discreet, for I hardly ever heard him speak and only once saw him smile.

Hasan Beg also promised to arrange for me to visit Gjakovë in the near future; he would put me up in his house and invite a number of influential Kossovars to meet me. Afterwards we could plan a journey further afield. He would send Shpen to me at Deg as soon as he was ready.

Finally, he warned me that the Partisans were most unpopular in Kossovo and their influence was negligible; I should achieve little if I entered the area under their ægis, for they were regarded as agents of Tito, who, like Mihailović, was detested as an instrument of 'Pan-Slav Imperialism'. Coming from the 'unofficial president' of the L.N.C. in Kossovo this warning was not to be ignored.

Snow was falling heavily when I awoke the following day, obscuring the mountain tops, covering the roofs and blanketing the ground. Perhaps it was the weather that made Muharrem more than usually fussy. One of Mehmet Ali's servants arrived from Gjakovë with some shopping I had ordered; Muharrem seized the parcels from him and unwrapped them one by one, throwing the loose contents across the room to me and clucking anxiously as he inspected each item:

'Now look after this, and see you don't lose it!'

When the last parcel was open and I was sitting on the floor beside a pile of matchboxes, packets of cigarettes, candles and other odds and ends he sighed:

'Well! Now you have the things you wanted, but I'm afraid you'll lose them.'

I wondered whether he was thinking of my incompetence or the rapacity of his fellow-countrymen.

On 5th December we separated: Hasan Beg left for Gjakovë, Muharrem for his own territory, and I for Hands's headquarters at Deg. Before we parted Hasan promised to send me a reliable interpreter within a few days; Muharrem lent me one of his escort, Zenel Ahmedi, to act as my servant and bodyguard for as long as I needed him. Zenel's father had been a great warrior in his time and one of Muharrem's closest friends; in the end I was more grateful to Muharrem for this cheerful, loyal and courageous young man than for all his other kindnesses.

The morning was crisp and clear after the previous day's snow as I struck westward down the valley from Vlahën, accompanied by Zenel, Shpen Zeçeri and three of Mehmet Ali's men. At the far end the valley widened into open rolling grassland sloping towards the River Drin, beyond which the mountains of the Catholic country of Jballjë glittered frostily in the sunlight. At noon we met Corporal Brandrick, Hands's paramilitary specialist, with the messenger I had sent from Vlahën four days earlier. They brought with them two horses, a complete change of clothing for me, two tins of English pipe tobacco and a warm letter of welcome from Hands.

At five in the evening we reached a small village, where we decided to spend the night because darkness was already falling. Our escort brought us to a small house belonging to three young friends of theirs; in the tiny, stuffy guest-room there was barely enough space for the seven of us and our three hosts to lie on the floor. I had not been long asleep when I was awakened by the sound of three rifle shots in quick succession; grabbing their weapons Zenel and the others ran outside, to return in a few minutes with the comforting assurance that it was only a tribesman settling accounts with his blood-enemy.

After a small cup of acorn coffee—the usual breakfast in the poorer villages of these mountains—we left the open grasslands for the steep and forested marches of Bityç. At the end of a stiff three-hour climb we found ourselves on a high shoulder of rock overlooking the valley of Deg; behind us to the south-east stretched mile upon mile of shining mountain peaks. Zenel pointed to the horizon where a great mass of grey rock, scored with countless dark watercourses and barred with snow at the summit, swept proudly into the sunlit sky.

'There is Gjalicë of Luma,' he cried, 'and below it lies Shtiqën, my village!'

We walked down through thick beech woods along a track so steep and rough that I feared for the safety of our horses, until we came to a stream that flowed from north to south through the valley to empty itself into the deep ravine of the Drin. Deg stood about half-way down the glen, a few poor dwellings grouped around a small mosque.

Brandrick led us to a white farm-house surrounded by a low wall of brushwood and standing a little way apart from the other buildings; at the entrance stood Hands, a broad grin of welcome on his face.

When I had met him in Egypt in July he had seemed a cheery, self-confident fellow with a trace of brashness in his manner; five months of discomfort and insecurity in the mountains had drained much of his vigour and ebullience, etching deep lines of strain under his eyes and round his mouth. Almost his first words were of trouble.

'Old man, it looks as though you've walked out of one spot of bother straight into another. There's a blow-up expected here any day between the Partisans and the local chiefs.'

He led me up a rickety wooden staircase to a small, ill-lit, and dusty room in the centre of which was an improvised table of boards laid across parachute canisters, with more canisters to serve as seats. In a corner by the tiny window was a wireless set, at which the operator, Sergeant Smith,[1] was finishing a 'sked'; on the dirty floor were four old and greasy mattresses, one of which was for me. There was no other furniture. The remaining room in the house was used as a kitchen and sleeping quarters for the four Italians

---

[1] Not the Sergeant Smith who was with Seymour.

who waited on the Mission. The horses and mules were stabled underneath. The owners of the house had left or been ejected long ago.

Most of the other houses, including the mosque, were occupied by detachments of Partisans, who provided Hands with an inefficient and often troublesome guard. But there were a few villagers left; under the leadership of their *hoxha*, or priest, they maintained a precarious but apparently satisfactory livelihood by looting Hands's stores whenever he received a supply drop and stealing from his headquarters in the intervals; when such methods failed they would come to him and beg.

Their depredations, together with others on a larger, better organized scale by the Partisans who were supposed to help him receive his drops, had left Hands with scarcely enough food and clothing for his own needs. No supplies could be bought locally. Bad weather was holding up the sorties he expected and for which he had prepared a wide and level dropping-ground a few hundred yards below his house, where the valley opened into gently sloping meadows before tumbling into the Drin.

When we had finished tea Hands thrust a piece of paper at me with a sardonic laugh:

'You're dead, old man, in case you don't know it. We had this signal in from Cairo last night, but thought you might like to answer it yourself.'

The message simply said that I had been killed in street fighting in Peshkopijë. I drafted a brief reply:

'Still alive please refrain from wishful thinking.'

A year later I heard details of the rumour from Hare.

'A wounded Partisan turned up in our camp at Biza,' he explained, 'Saying that he had witnessed your death with his own eyes. Major Kemp, he told us, was creeping up a street, close to the wall, with his machine-gun (your Welgun, of course) at the ready; suddenly, round a corner he came face to face with a German, also with his gun at the ready. Both fired simultaneously and both fell dead. The others,' Hare concluded, 'were suitably impressed and sad. I alone knew the story couldn't be true: for one thing, you would never have been wide enough awake to fire at the same time as a German, and for another, your Welgun would certainly have jammed.'[1]

There were some three hundred Partisans grouped in *çetas* between Deg and the valley of the Valbonë about six miles further north; most were from Kossovo but a few had come from the Prefecture of Scutari, which they had made too hot to hold them. All were controlled by a newly formed organization, the 'Kosmet [*Kos*sovo and *Meto*hija] General Staff', under the military command of the renowned guerrilla leader, Fadil Hoxha, who had

---

[1] Brigadier Davies records that while he was a prisoner in Tiranë the Germans showed him photographs of dead bodies in British battle-dress which they alleged to be Riddell's, Simcox's, and my own. *Illyrian Venture* (The Bodley Head), pg. 171.

made a name for himself fighting the Bulgars in Macedonia; the political direction—and the effective power—was in the hands of the Chief Commissar, Mehmet Hoxha—the same man whose suit I had worn in Tiranë and whom I had last seen in Dibra. He in turn received directives from Tito.

The ostensible purpose of their presence was to establish a secure base for the winter; their real objects, according to Hands, were to co-ordinate operations with Tito's Montenegrin Partisans and to clear the frontiers of Montenegro and Kossovo of all 'reactionary elements.' Hands's view of their intentions was shared by most of the local Bajraktars and inhabitants, who regarded the Kosmet with undisguised suspicion and hostility—in which, unfortunately, they included Hands. He had been obliged to move his base twice in the last month under pressure from the chiefs.

It was useless for him to protest that he was only there to help anyone who would cooperate with him against the Germans, because nobody was prepared either to fight the Germans or invite their reprisals by allowing Hands to annoy them; even the Kosmet had rejected his proposals for attacking the Prizren-Scutari road. The local Bajraktars had gone further: after a conference presided over by a certain Mal Shabani the day before my arrival, they issued an ultimatum to the Kosmet and to Hands, either to leave their territory at once or be driven out—if necessary with German help.

If we had to leave Deg it was difficult to see where we could go. Beyond the Drill was Catholic country where the people, if not actively hostile, would certainly not receive us as friends; for they followed the lead of Gjon Marko Gjoni, the Captain of Mirdita and the most powerful chieftain in northern Albania, who was the ally of the Germans. Hands therefore asked me to mediate between himself and Mal Shabani and try to arrange a truce that would at least allow us to remain at Deg; he suggested that I should also have a talk with Mehmet Hoxha. I should find them both in the same village; Mehmet was staying with Salimani, *Bajraktar* of Krasniqi, the mountainous region beyond the Valbonë, and Mal Shabani's house was close by. Salimani was the only chieftain who supported the Partisans; I subsequently learned that he and Mal Shabani had long been at feud.

On 8th December I left for Krasniqi. A six hours' ride over difficult stony tracks brought me to the Valbonë, which I crossed by a flimsy wooden bridge, marvelling at the brilliant turquoise colour of the water pouring over the boulder-strewn river bed and the harsh grandeur of the bare limestone cliffs that frowned above the further bank.

I reached Salimani's house just before dark to find him celebrating the festival of Greater Bairam with Mehmet Hoxha and other officers of the Kosmet—an ironical situation, I thought. The eighty-year-old Bajraktar was the finest looking Albanian I had seen; six foot tall, lean and erect, with a fierce white moustache and silvery hair, he towered like some Homeric hero above the paunchy, puffy-faced Commissar.

The news Mehmet Hoxha gave me was disquieting: a force of six hundred Kossovar mercenaries under Xhafer Deva, the puppet Minister of the Interior, was poised on the frontier, ready to invade Krasniqi and Bityç and drive us into the Drin; of course they might not come this way if Mal Shabani and his friends did not invite them. It was too late for me to do anything that night, but I had better see Mal Shabani in the morning.

While Salimani was out of the room I told Mehmet of my plan to visit Hasan Beg in Gjakovë; he seemed to approve, warned me to be careful of 'fascist agents' and wished me a pleasant visit. I did not mention the matter in front of Salimani because he had a feud with the Kryezius, dating from the 1920s when the eldest Kryeziu, Cena Beg, had invaded Krasniqi with a force of gendarmerie to hunt down his outlawed rival, Bairam Curi. I heard more of this tale later.

After a good sleep in a large four-poster bed, damp with long disuse, I set out with Mehmet to tackle Mal Shabani. Apprised of my coming he was awaiting me with two of his confederates; the three of them eyed me with deep suspicion as Mehmet introduced me. I felt at a disadvantage in being dependent on Mehmet as interpreter and thought it probable that he was using me as a stalking-horse in his game of power politics; but I only realized the extent to which Hands and I were compromised when Mal Shabani, who spoke some Italian, told me bluntly that I was not a British officer but a Russian, because he knew that all British officers had been withdrawn from Albania, and in any case what would they be doing with Communists? It took me the whole morning to convince the three dour chieftains of my *bona fides* but I departed with an assurance that they would leave us in peace.

Mehmet Hoxha's report about the six hundred mercenaries proved to be a false alarm, one of many that kept us in a constant state of alert during the next two months. Despite Mal Shabani's promise we were several times asked to remove ourselves from Deg, and on one occasion Mehmet himself advised us to leave the district. Nevertheless, the Partisans remained and so did we; chiefly because, as I have said, we had nowhere else to go.

The next morning, while I was having an uncomfortable bath in one of the canisters that did alternative duty as chairs, Hands came into the room:

'Your interpreter's arrived from Hasan Kryeziu. Scruffy-looking bastard if you ask me.'

The description, though inelegant, was apt. Eles Yusufi was a dark, emaciated, untidy youth with a sallow complexion, shifty eyes and the furtive, apologetic look of an ill-used dog. He spoke little and in a quiet, frightened voice. He had only the sketchiest knowledge of English, but tried to conceal his ignorance by mistranslating what he could not understand. He would have been pathetic if he had been less incompetent and untruthful. Hasan Beg had sent him, I discovered later, because he was sorry for the boy and because there was no one else.

Later in the day I was approached by a young man in a blue uniform tunic, who gave his name as Sadri Dorçë and claimed to have served as an officer in the French Army in 1940; his father, who knew the Kryezius well, had told him to offer his services to me in any confidential capacity. Impressed by his command of French I asked him to stay as an extra interpreter; I felt the need of another to supplement the deficiencies of Eles. He agreed to take up his duties as soon as he had spoken to his father; for, he assured me, he did nothing without his father's approval.

On the evening of 13th December Shpen Zeçeri arrived from Gjakovë with two equally silent companions to escort me to Hasan Beg's house. Next morning I put on a civilian overcoat to hide my battle-dress and changed my green beret for a flat Bulgar fez of black lamb's wool. Our party consisted of Zenel, Eles, Sadri Dorçë, and his father, and a mule which Hasan Beg had considerately sent in case I wanted to ride; Dorçë *pere*, I thought ungraciously, might have been content to give his approval without adding himself to our already swollen numbers.

We had only gone a few paces when we were stopped by a body of Partisans under Rexheb, the Political Commissar of the Scutari *çetas*, an arrogant fellow whose manner and conversation, as well as his position, proclaimed him a sound Party man. He now demanded that I postpone my visit until I had seen Tito's delegate to the Kosmet, a certain Rada, who was expected shortly; he added insolently that the Kosmet had no interest in 'private individuals' like Hasan Kryeziu, and that if I went to Gjakovë I must go with Partisans and see only those people of whom the Partisans approved. I replied, as politely as my anger allowed, that I took orders from the Allied General Staff, not the Kosmet. After a long argument, watched by Shpen and his friends with silent disdain, I agreed, on the advice of Eles and Sadri, to take three Partisans for some of the way, though not into Gjakovë. Detailing three of his men—one of whom spoke French—to accompany us, the Commissar turned his back on me and stalked away.

I regretted bitterly my mistake in telling Mehmet of my plans; I had only done so because both he and Hasan Beg had led me to believe that they were allies, and because I did not want the Kosmet to accuse me of working behind their backs. In my innocence I had supposed them to be as interested as I in building up resistance against the Germans in Kossovo; whereas they were only concerned to consolidate their power at the expense of all other parties. Never again, I resolved, would I confide in them; but my wisdom had come too late.

It was mid-afternoon before we had climbed to the top of the water-shed between Deg and the grassy vale of Bityç. Skirting Vlad, a large village where there was a gendarmerie post, we arrived in the gloom of a wintry dusk at the foot of a steep slope, where we halted to eat the food we had brought from

Deg. It had been much too cold to ride but the mule had slowed our pace considerably; when I asked Shpen how far we were from Gjakovë he answered with glum satisfaction:

'Four hours by day; eight hours at night.'

Before I could make any comment a fruity voice hailed us out of the darkness; an intoxicated gendarme lurched down the track leading towards Vlad. He had only come to exchange gossip and so I kept out of sight, screened by Zenel and Sadri, until Shpen had satisfied his curiosity; he was unlikely to be hostile, but he would probably have spread the news of my presence if he had noticed me.

We climbed a steep and rocky path to the head of the pass, where a small stone pinnacle marked the old frontier between Albania and Jugoslavia. While we rested to get our breath Shpen and his two friends told me that they used to make a good living before the war smuggling tobacco across the frontier from Jugoslavia; now that Kossovo was part of Albania they had lost their livelihood.

The descent was precipitous and dangerous in the dark; several times we lost the track, but our smuggler guides seemed to feel their way back to it by instinct before we could stray far. Gradually the slope levelled and the track became a wide and muddy path running through woodland, easy to follow in the light of a rising moon.

At our next halt a heated argument broke out between Shpen and the three Partisans, at the end of which Shpen announced that he was going to take us back to Deg; it seemed that Rexheb had ordered the Partisans to accompany us into Gjakovë, and had told the one who spoke French that he must stay with me all the time I was there and be present at all my meetings. I was sorry for the three Partisans, who were only obeying orders, but I had not come all this way to have my plans upset by the duplicity of Rexheb; I ordered them to return to Deg at once, adding that the Kosmet could do what they liked about it. What they did, I soon discovered, was to send word to the Germans that I was in Gjakovë.

We left the foothills and, after fording a shallow river, came onto a dirt road running between hedges with what seemed to be hopfields on either side. We passed several isolated houses but met no one. The countryside was soft and peaceful in the moonlight; only the faint thud of the mule's hoofs and the distant barking of farm dogs disturbed the stillness.

We had been going for two hours across the plain when Shpen suddenly stopped and began whispering with his friends; I noticed some scattered buildings ahead, on our right. Eles sidled up to me and murmured:

'We must go very quietly now because we are entering the city and there are Germans in that white house on the right.'

Keeping well into the side of the road we advanced stealthily in single file; Shpen was in the lead, with Zenel and the mule bringing up the rear. We crossed a bridge over a river, lit by a lamp at each end; straight ahead ran a wide, well-lit street, which we avoided by turning right along a path by the river. After two or three hundred yards we turned sharp left again up a hill until we came to some large white barracks guarded by a pair of sentry-boxes. At this point our behaviour degenerated into burlesque. Shpen and his friends crept forward crouched over their rifles, which they carried at the hip with their fingers on the triggers—each one looking, to paraphrase a famous epigram, far more like a guerrilla than a guerrilla has a right to look. I wondered fearfully whether we were in greater danger of arrest as bandits or as lunatics. Fortunately the sentry-boxes were empty; the barracks housed only workers from the chrome mines.

Soon we were prowling through the twisting, cobbled streets of the town like small boys playing Red Indians. Shpen would stop at each corner, peer round it carefully, and hurriedly beckon us on; at every street lamp Eles, whose laboured breathing was heavy on my neck and whose Sten gun, I noticed unhappily, was pointed at the small of my back, would trot forward and steer me forcefully across the street in the full glare of the beam, until I told him irritably to leave me alone; and whenever one of the mule's iron-shod hoofs clattered against a cobblestone everyone stopped in his tracks and hissed 'sh-sh-sh!' so loudly and with such agonized urgency that the poor beast stood still and hung its head in shame.

But for the noise we made ourselves no sound disturbed the quiet of the sleeping city; nor did we see any movement other than our own shadows on the pale, moon-bathed walls of the houses. At midnight we came to a halt in front of a large wooden door in a high, whitewashed wall. Shpen knocked and called up to a lighted window in the house behind; a minute later the bolts were drawn back and a very old man with a long, drooping white moustache let us into a wide courtyard. At a doorway on the far side Hasan Beg was waiting.

He took me upstairs to a living-room furnished with armchairs, a large divan and a table; a double bedroom and a bathroom completed my luxurious quarters. I was too tired to eat but was persuaded to drink some unusually powerful home-distilled raki.

Hasan Beg had shed the breezy bonhomie of our first meeting; he was unmistakably nervous. His face darkened and his manner became more agitated as Shpen told him of our trouble with Rexheb; turning to me he reproached me sharply for having told Mehmet of our meeting at Vlahën. The Partisans had been trying for a long time to make him leave his house and join them in the mountains, seeking thus to deprive him of his contacts among the various Nationalist and Irredentist groups in Gjakovë; now they would spread the news of my presence, hoping that I should be discovered and he would be obliged to flee. Looking back I realize how simple-minded I must have been to suppose that because Hasan Beg was the unofficial president of the L.N.C. he would want to share his plans with official members; events were to prove him tragically justified.

I was horrified at Hasan's reproaches; he was already taking a grave risk in sheltering me, and the knowledge that I had thoughtlessly aggravated his danger was a heavy burden on my conscience. The old servant, on the other hand, who had been listening to our conversation, made light of our fears: 'If you want to play at politics, Hasan Beg,' he teased, 'you must be brave!'

I was roused next morning by Hasan himself carrying a flask of raki—to keep the cold out, he explained, while I dressed. He had recovered his good humour but warned me that I should have to curtail my stay in Gjakovë and postpone a journey to Prizren, Prištinä, and Peć which he had planned for me. There was another reason for his alarm, which he now confessed: the six hundred mercenaries who had threatened us in Krasniqi had imposed a reign of terror throughout Kossovo, and the memory of their executions was still fresh.

Despite his fears he kept me in his house for three days, treating me with a rare hospitality that I had not experienced in years; more important, he brought to see me some of the most influential of the Kossovar leaders. It was typical of Hasan's integrity that he included among them men who differed from him politically, and one or two who were his rivals; he had promised to help me in the formation of a common front of Kossovars against the Germans, and this object alone guided him in his choice.

Our talks convinced me that we should achieve no more than isolated military action in Kossovo without some Allied declaration on the future status of the Province; it was obvious that the Kossovars did not trust us. Nor might I use the one argument that would have appealed to them—that by fighting now they could obtain arms from us, which they could use later to defend themselves against Communists or Serbs. The most I obtained was a promise from the commander of the Albanian Army garrison at Peć to put his men at my disposal in the event of an Allied invasion or a German withdrawal, and an undertaking from the others to furnish me with military and political information in the meantime. One of my visitors was the Chief of Police at Peć, and so I should at least receive warning of any German operations against us. Two leaders of the Irredentist Party, Ejub Binaku and Professor Sulejman Riza, promised me a second visit to Kossovo with a wide itinerary; as soon as the situation improved they would send for me at Deg.

I left Gjakovë in the early hours of 17th December with the same escort and in much the same manner as I had entered, though without the embarrassing company of the mule. When I reached Deg I was told of the Kosmet's treachery. I smothered my resentment, not wishing to provoke an open breach; but I derived some consolation from the hypocritical enthusiasm with which Mehmet and Tito's delegate, Rada, congratulated me on my safe return.

With Hands I found Tony Neel, who had arrived the previous evening after a dangerous reconnaissance of the country near Scutari, followed by an equally hazardous journey across the Catholic territory west of the Drill. He would never have reached us safely but for the influence and diplomacy of his escort, Ymar Bardoshi, the Bajraktar of Pukë who, although a Moslem, had allies among the Catholic tribes.

'It was pretty rotten, you know,' Neel told us, 'to see how unpopular one was. The only time I was well received in a village was when old Ymar told them I was a Hun officer; then they were all over me.'

I had not been back at Deg twenty-four hours when Smith handed us a signal warning us to stand by that night for a sortie of three aircraft; as well as stores they would drop three parties, each consisting of an officer and a wireless operator.

As soon as we heard the engines in the distance we ran to the drop-ping ground, where Partisan guards were already stationed, and lit the signal fires. At the same time the villagers thronged from their houses in search of loot, while the tracks leading to Deg from all the surrounding countryside filled with shadowy, hurrying figures; some came on horseback, others on foot, the richer ones leading mules to carry their plunder. In some places men laid out their own patterns of fires in the hope that the aircraft would be deceived into dropping their loads.

It was a successful drop, executed with superb skill by the Royal Air Force pilots. The parachutists landed safely on the dropping ground, the containers not far away, but the 'free drops', of which there was a large number, gave us some bad moments; it was an uncomfortable experience to stand in the open in the chilly, moonless night and hear the bundles whistling through the air towards us. The greatest excitement came when a Partisan guard fired on a looting tribesman; the man fired back, frightening the Partisan out of his life, and vanished with his spoil into the darkness.

Instead of bringing the stores to our house the Partisans took them to the Mosque, where they rifled the personal kit of the men who had just landed and stole most of the food; our protests were useless, for they were acting on the orders of Commissar Rexheb, with whom my disobedience still rankled. On the intervention of Mehmet Hoxha next morning we recovered most of the military stores and some of the food; but the parachutists' introduction to Albania was the loss of all their belongings.

The new officers were Captain Hibberdine, Lieutenant Merritt and Lieutenant Hibbert; Hibbert was to join Riddell near Dibra, Merritt would work with Neel, and Hibberdine was attached to me. For the moment we were faced with an acute shortage of space, with twelve officers and N.C.O.s and four Italian servants in one very small house; although our Albanian staff had found themselves billets in the village there was no other house that we could requisition.

However, resolved that if our Christmas must be uncomfortable at least it should be merry, we sent couriers to Gjakovë and Prizren to buy food, drink, and cigarettes and to the Catholic country to bring us a pig. On Christmas Day we entertained successively representatives of the Kosmet, led by Mehmet and Rada, and of the villagers, led by their *hoxha*. The majority of the villagers stood outside in a body while I made them a speech of thanks, translated by Sadri Dorçë; but several came inside and wandered round the room, fiddling with the wireless and picking up anything they fancied to take away. One old man sat down with us and drank a whole bottle of cough mixture which Neel had put in front of him; he giggled weakly after each swig and reeled out at the end, apparently quite drunk.

X

BETRAYAL

On 27th December Eles Yusufi, who had been away on a visit to his family, returned with the news that Ejub Binaku was awaiting us in the house of the Sub-Prefect of Tropojë; this town was the district capital, lying some nine miles north of Deg and a mile or two from the frontier of Kossovo. Leaving Corporal Clifton, our wireless operator, at headquarters Hibberdine and I set off the same afternoon, accompanied by Zenel and Eles.

John Hibberdine was an officer in the Cameronians of slight but sturdy build and quiet, thoughtful manner. Several years younger than myself he combined great physical endurance with unusual intellectual maturity; his shrewd judgment, unruffled temper and dry sense of humour made him an invaluable partner in adventure and a strong stimulus to morale. That some such stimulus was needed became apparent to me from the frequency with which I found myself losing my temper over trifles.

Even Hibberdine's patience was strained on this journey; Eles, who was supposed to know the way, repeatedly lost it, bringing us at length to Tropojë angry, hungry, and exhausted, nine hours after we had started. The Sub-Prefect, a cheerful little man who had lived in the United States, soon revived us with food and raki. Although himself a member of the Balli Kombëtar he had protected the Kosmet so far as he could, even to the extent of sending an official report to the German authorities stating that there were no Partisans in his area and therefore no need for police action.

We stayed indoors next day until darkness had fallen on the town; then, taking leave of our host, we followed Ejub at a hurried pace through the streets and began the steep ascent of the Pass of Morina towards the frontier. The snow, which had been falling lightly when we left, increased as we climbed the pass to a full blizzard blown in our teeth by a howling east wind that froze our hands and faces and seared our lungs at every gasping breath; icicles formed in our noses, encrusted our moustaches, and hung from our eyebrows. As we neared the summit the snow lay deeper, until we were plunging above our knees in the drifts; every step was an effort. The shimmering flakes threw back the light of our torches in our eyes so that we frequently wandered off the path. As a little boy I had been thrilled by tales of trappers and Mounties in the Rockies or the forests of northern Canada, and in my day-dreams had sometimes pictured myself a member of an intrepid party of explorers crossing some wild and unmapped range of mountains. Now I found the reality hideously different, staggering blindly up the slope, my head bowed against the storm, my limbs numb with fatigue, my lungs bursting and my mind clouded with the fear that we should lose our way and perish horribly in this desolate, wind-swept waste of snow and darkness.

It was nearly midnight when we knocked on the door of a farmhouse at the mountain hamlet of Morina, on the Kossovo side of the frontier. We waited in the snow while Ejub and the owner whispered anxiously together for nearly ten minutes. There were visitors in the guest-room who must not see us, and so we were taken to sleep in a disused granary under the roof; but not even the attention of the vermin in which the room abounded could keep us awake for long.

By the time we were dressed next morning the other guests had gone, and so we moved into the comfortable guest-room. Ejub left for Gjakovë to discuss with Hasan Beg the final arrangements for our journey and reception there; he bade us await his return in patience and not on any account stir from the house without an escort—even then we must not wander far.

The fear of informers was so great that throughout our stay in Kossovo, even in the country districts, we were isolated from all contact with—and as much as possible from the sight of—people other than the family with which we happened to be staying and visitors specially summoned to meet us. When we wanted a walk to clear our heads—the guest-rooms were seldom ventilated, for the Albanians could not endure fresh air in their houses—someone would first make a reconnaissance to see that there was nobody about; we had always to take an escort, not so much for protection as for camouflage and in order to answer any awkward questions if we should happen to meet strangers. Lastly, Ejub insisted that we should always wear some kind of peasant head-dress and put on civilian overcoats to hide our uniforms; I wore my black Bulgar fez, but Hibberdine preferred the white Albanian half-egg'. To complete my disguise I usually wound puttees over my field boots.

Irksome though these restrictions were we could not reasonably refuse to obey them; for the consequences to our hosts and companions if we were taken would be far more serious than to ourselves. We were astonished at the unselfish courage of these people—whether powerful landowners like Hasan Kryeziu, intellectuals like Professor Sulejman Riza, government officials, small shopkeepers, or poor artisans—who risked their lives to accompany and shelter us in an area where even Albanian Partisans could not move in safety. Certainly people faced far graver dangers in other occupied countries, but in Kossovo there was no reason why men should expose themselves to any danger to help us. It may seem strange that we troubled to wear uniform at all when we must expect to be treated as spies if caught. The reasons were, first that we had a directive from Cairo not to remove our uniforms; secondly that Hasan and Ejub both thought the sight of them would have a useful effect on our visitors' morale.

Like most of the members of the Irredentist Party Ejub belonged also to the Balli Kombëtar. He told us very little about himself beyond the fact that he had been an outlaw since the Italian occupation of Kossovo in 1941 and that he had a wife somewhere. What his occupation was in peacetime we never discovered; but now he was military commander of the Irredentist *çetas*. They were still 'underground', but Ejub offered to call up a nucleus of two hundred men to act as our bodyguard in the mountains whenever we needed them. Despite his melancholy and secretive manner he was a simple man with a warm and generous nature who spared himself neither trouble nor risk in our service.

As chief bodyguard, guide, and constant companion on our journey Ejub appointed his closest friend, Ramadan, a dark, red-faced, thick-set highlander who spoke little and drank a great deal; he was friendly enough, although in his cups he was subject to fits of moroseness, when he would sit by himself with his head in his hands ignoring the rest of the company. But his story, which Ejub told us, proved him a loyal ally and a stout fighter. He had been an outlaw in these hills for twenty years, ever since the gendarmerie had killed his friend, Rustem Bairami; bound by his *besa* to protect Rustem he had fought a stiff battle with the gendarmes, killing six of them and only escaping himself after his friend had fallen. Since then he had been a hunted man without a home to shelter or a wife to comfort him. When there was nothing to do he would let his misfortunes prey on his mind; he would start drinking at seven in the morning and continue until lunch time, when he would pass out quietly until it was time to start the evening carouse.

New Year's Day 1944 found us still at Morina, impatient with the delay and worried by the continued absence of Ejub. He arrived without warning in the afternoon and told us to be ready to start for Gjakovë at dusk; he insisted that Eles and Zenel should stay behind, saying that they would make us too many to travel in safety. We should not need Eles because Ejub spoke French; but it required all my authority to persuade Zenel to return to Deg.

We left the house in the late afternoon and walked a few hundred yards down the hill to a narrow road, where an open fiacre was waiting. At our backs the gigantic bulk of Shkelzen, the eastern bastion of the North Albanian Alps, soared eight thousand feet above us, its southern face shimmering in the fading sunset with a pearly light. The name means 'shining'; and the people who dwell beneath it hold the mountain in deep veneration, investing it with a mythology of ghostly legends. A saint is buried on the upper slopes. In the calm yet menacing grandeur of that mighty massif looming through the twilight I saw embodied all the splendour and savagery of the Balkans; all the harsh nobility and fierce endurance of the land shone in the opalescent beauty of those ice-bound, snow-wrapped cliffs.

Well muffled against the cold Hibberdine and I climbed into the carriage; Ejub and Ramadan sat half on the seat, half on top of us. The driver, a cheery, deep-voiced fellow with a huge pair of moustaches, flicked his whip and the horse started down the slushy road at a spirited trot, in half an hour we had left the hills and were running across level, open country; we swept through the villages at a fast canter in a musical jingle of bells, the driver cracking his whip and shouting to clear the way. The carriage must have excited some comment, overloaded with the five of us and festooned with weapons; Ejub had brought a sub-machinegun for each of us in case we should have to fight, and the driver had a rifle slung across his shoulder.

We entered Gjakovë about seven o'clock, driving up the main street with a flourish that caused me acute alarm, which nearly turned to panic when we were halted at a control post manned by Albanian gendarmes; however, Ejub gave a signal to the N.C.O. in charge, who waved us on without a question though with several curious glances. We turned down a quiet side street, dismounted and began to creep through the streets like conspirators without, however, attracting attention from the few people we met. After a quarter of an hour we knocked on a wooden door in a wall, and were admitted to a courtyard leading to a discreet but comfortably furnished house. This proved to be the back premises of a small cafe and hotel of which our host was the owner.

Our first visitor, an hour later, was Gjakovë's Chief of Police, which accounted for our easy passage through the gendarmerie post. He told us over a glass of our host's smooth slivovitz that the Germans had reinforced their garrison by a thousand *Sicherheitsdienst* during the last few days and had considerably tightened their controls, both on the roads and in the towns. They knew of the parachute drop which had brought Hibberdine and the others, but their reports greatly exaggerated the numbers and they believed that a party of fifty British parachutists had arrived. Our friends thought they were planning an expedition against Deg, but they feared there would also be a house-to-house search through the town in the near future. The Chief of Police hoped to give us at least one hour's warning of any search, and Ejub had a small force of his men in readiness to fight our way out if the worst came to the worst; but we must always be ready to move at a moment's notice and must be prepared to change our lodgings every night.

Accordingly, we left the following evening for Hasan Beg's house, walking through the streets in pairs in a more sensible manner than usual; in the dusk no one seemed to pay us any attention, least of all the two or three German patrols that we met. This was just as well, for Ejub told us that the Kosmet already knew of my visit; only that morning he had met a schoolmaster belonging to the L.N.C. who stopped him in the street.

'How is Major Kemp?'

'I haven't seen him,' replied Ejub as innocently as he could.

'Oh yes, you have! We know he's in Gjakovë with you.'

Late that evening we listened on Hasan's wireless to the B.B.C.'s account of the sinking of the *Scharnhorst*; it was thrilling to watch the respect with which his guests heard the news. Hasan and Ejub we knew to be our friends and devoted to our cause, but the sympathies of the others were still in the balance; such an incident as this would impress them far more than any words of ours.

We moved house every evening for the next three days, covering the whole of the city in the course of our journeys. Ejub and Ramadan would point out the places of interest we passed—the Town Hall, the Prefecture of Police, and the German officers' mess among others. They had gained confidence since our first furtive entry into Gjakovë, but I was never entirely happy in the streets; Hasan Beg had impressed upon me that the German garrison had a most efficient counterespionage service among the civilians. The German soldiers we met seldom looked at us, but we attracted—I particularly—many curious stares and backward glances from Albanians. Only once did our guides show alarm—when Hibberdine unthinkingly pulled out a handkerchief to blow his nose. Ramadan whipped it from his hand, crushing it out of sight in his fist; while Hibberdine, realizing at once that no Albanian peasant would use a handkerchief, blew vigorously through his fingers, wiped them on the seat of his trousers and, to complete the picture, spat noisily on the cobbles.

During this time our hosts and most of our visitors were minor civil servants and small tradesmen, from which classes the Irredentist Party seemed to draw its greatest strength. The tradesmen made up to us in professional services what they lacked in political influence; for a barber arrived each morning to shave us, and at one house a tailor called to measure Hibberdine for a pair of breeches. Some of our visitors had come to see us from the farthest limits of Kossovo, so that we began to wonder how long it would be before the Germans came to hear of our presence. However, there was no doubt of the enthusiasm which our arrival had excited, for promises of help flowed in from every quarter.

From our conversations, especially from those with Army officers and government officials, our hopes grew of organizing a nucleus of resistance among Albanians throughout Kossovo. Our friends under-took, when they returned to their districts, to recruit their sympathizers into cadres which would receive clandestine training from officers of the Albanian Army, to choose sites for secret dumps of arms and food, and to reconnoitre suitable dropping grounds. In imagination we already saw ourselves controlling an underground army with cells in every town and large village from Gjakovë to Priština, from Mitrovica to the borders of Macedonia.

On the evening of 6th January we tramped for half an hour through snowy streets to the house of a leading member of the Irredentist Party, where we were to hold an important conference on the following day. I had a momentary pang of anxiety when I saw our reception committee, which consisted of our host and four uniformed gendarmes; however Ejub explained that one policeman would remain in the house with us for the whole of our visit while the other three kept watch outside. The one appointed as our personal bodyguard was a bibulous, red-faced fellow with an enormous 'Kaiser Bill' moustache; he spoke little but sat all day cross-legged on the floor, his rifle across his knees, regarding us with a benevolent and boozy leer which he interrupted at intervals to swallow raki from a flask by his side. Whatever use he might have been in an emergency there was no doubt that he took his duties seriously; for whenever either of us went to the lavatory he would follow across the courtyard and stand swaying and hiccupping in the cold until his charge was ready to return. It seemed that he was an equally conscientious husband, for he confided to us that he had begotten twenty children on his wife, although only seven of them had survived.

The conference which assembled the following evening was, in the hateful jargon of those wartime years, on a high level; there were present the Mayor of Gjakovë, the Colonel-Commandant of the Albanian Army in Kossovo, and Professor Sulejman Riza, the *Eminence Grise* of the Irredentist Party. Our purpose was to discuss the final arrangements for our journey through the rest of Kossovo—a matter which we had been pressing since our arrival in Gjakovë.

We were therefore bitterly disappointed to hear that we must postpone our journey for the present. Our friends at first pleaded the excuse that the recent heavy falls of snow had blocked the roads; but it was not long before they admitted the truth—German controls on the roads had been so severely tightened that they could not accept the responsibility of escorting us. Sulejman Riza, who did most of the talking, told us that the enemy knew of our presence and was on the look-out for us. Although we argued and pleaded, offering to absolve them in writing from any responsibility for our safety, the Irredentists were adamant; and we, knowing that these men were no cowards, were obliged in the end to give way. Reluctantly we agreed to remain a few more days in Gjakovë, and then return to Deg to await a better moment. We had to content ourselves with a promise from Sulejman Riza to prepare his party for immediate action against the Germans, and a further promise from the army commander to supply the Irredentists with weapons and instructors. It was midnight when the conference broke up; Hibberdine and I looked sorrowfully at each other.

'It's time to go home,' I sighed.

The next evening, sped on our way by the good wishes of our police guards, we returned to Hasan Beg's house; it was a short distance but Ejub, who seemed to have become much more nervous since our conference, took us on a long detour—in order, he said, to shake off any German agents who might be following us. Hasan welcomed us with unusual cheerfulness; we detected more than a little bit of 'I told you so' in his manner as he listened to the account of our disappointment.

We found a courier from Hands awaiting us with a parcel of books and tobacco from a recent sortie and a signal from Cairo blandly instructing us to keep Lake Scutari under observation. Forbearing all comment on the bizarre sense of geography displayed by Headquarters and hoping fervently that their message did not represent the true sum of their knowledge of the country or our whereabouts, we detained the courier until we had drafted a signal describing our present situation and future plans.

We stayed six days in the Kryeziu house, confined indoors during the hours of daylight but allowed to walk in a walled garden at dusk; we needed the exercise, for Hasan's rich pilaffs, strong red wine, and raki were taking the edge off our fitness. In the evenings we played poker with Hasan or listened to his wireless; and once, after he and his friends had heard the B.B.C. News in Serbo-Croat, we tuned in to Tommy Handley and shook with laughter under the solemn, uncomprehending gaze of our companions.

For all his kindness we noticed in Hasan's manner a rising tension as the days went by; his expression grew more harassed and from time to time he would mutter 'Gestapo! Gestapo!' under his breath. He was worried also by the indiscretion of our interpreter, Eles, who had followed us to Gjakovë and had been seen flaunting our gold in the cafes of the town. But although his fears for our safety increased with every day he would not let us leave until he was sure that we could circumvent the controls on the roads. We were all relieved when, on 13th January, Ejub arrived with the news that he had arranged for us to travel south on the morrow to Rogovo, a village half-way on the road to Prizren. Ejub admitted that he was not happy about the journey, but told us frankly that he dared not let us stay longer in Gjakovë.

I slept badly that night, waking often to fret about our escape from the town and the journey that lay ahead. These days I seemed to jump at shadows, but I was worried not only for our own safety but because we were risking the lives of so many good friends who had much more to lose than ourselves. Bright morning, however, scattered my fears and I relaxed happily watching the grey-and-white fan tail pigeons flash their wings among the bare trees in the garden under the pale blue sky. A pretty, dark-haired little girl carrying a basket on her arm trotted gaily along the path below our window, her tiny wooden shoes clattering like a pony's hoofs on the stones.

Hibberdine and I were left to ourselves all the morning. Hasan arrived to join us for lunch—an anxious but genial host. When the meal was over we prepared to depart: I wound puttees round my field-boots, donned an Italian army greatcoat and put on my black Bulgarian fez—an incongruous and ridiculous figure that could hardly escape attention; Hibberdine, in an old civilian overcoat and white skull-cap, should pass fairly well for an Albanian. Hasan, who was not accompanying me, found my appearance much more diverting than Hibberdine, who was.

At four o'clock Shpen Zeçeri came to fetch us, accompanied by Ismail, the old white-haired servant who had teased Hasan on my first night in the house; now the old man surprised me by taking my hand between his two withered claws and kissing it. Hasan said a hurried good-bye in the courtyard, promising to keep in touch with us. Shpen opened the gate, shooed away a crowd of small children who were playing in the porch and beckoned Hibberdine to follow; taking my arm Ismail hustled me after them, the two of us keeping about thirty yards behind.

After the semi-darkness in which we had lived for so long the glare of the afternoon sunlight on the white walls of the closely huddled houses struck painfully on our eyeballs; so that for a few minutes I was glad to let Ismail guide me by the arm. School-children with satchels over their shoulders were playing on an open space below Hasan's house; they let us pass without a glance. When we entered the narrow, twisting streets I bent my gaze on the cobbles, but even so I could not help noticing the curious stares that I attracted. Ismael, however, was quite unperturbed, even prodding me into calling a '*tungjatjeta!*' to a pair of gendarmes whom we passed on the outskirts of the town.

Half an hour's walking brought us to a broad dirt road where a fiacre was waiting, similar to that in which we had left Morina; standing beside it were Ejub and Ramadan. Taking an affectionate farewell of our two guides we squeezed into the back. While we rattled over the flat, snow-bound countryside, from which the colour was slowly draining as the sun sank in a fiery glow behind the western mountains, Ejub explained the reason for our hurried daylight departure: the previous evening the German garrison commander had ordered our friend, the Chief of Police, to put a cordon round the town and search every house. The Chief of Police gave Ejub twenty-four hours to get us out of the town, warning him that the search must begin at six o'clock tonight and that the *Sicherheitsdienst* would take part.

Ejub had scarcely finished his story when we came to a control post: turning a corner we saw, about two hundred yards ahead of us, a rough barrier across the road, guarded by a party of Albanian gendarmerie and two grim-looking figures in field grey. Ejub had evidently planned our journey carefully, for our driver, without checking his pace, turned down a rough track to the right which, after a few hundred yards, crossed a river and ran parallel to the road. Although they must have seen us, the Germans made no attempt to interfere. A mile further on we were met by a fine-looking man mounted on a spirited grey stallion with a high-pommelled saddle and scarlet and silver trappings. When he came up to us he wheeled his horse and shouted a greeting; Ejub told us that he was the owner of the house where we were to stay in Rogovo and that his name was Dobrushi. About eight o'clock we saw the white walls and lighted windows of a large farm-house gleaming through the darkness on our left. Following Dobrushi we dismounted in front of a handsome, two-storeyed house with broad bow windows protruding beneath thatched eaves. After food and raki in the guest-room we were shown into a bedroom with three wide and comfortable beds; despite our hosts apologies for what he called such inadequate accommodation I slept better and longer than I had done for many weeks.

The Dobrushis were a rich Albanian family with property in Gjakovë and Prizren as well as the large estate on which we were now staying. Their wealth, however, had brought them little happiness. Next morning we were shown the tomb of our host's elder brother, Rexheb, which lay in the garden beneath the windows of the guestroom. One day during the German invasion of Jugoslavia a party of Serbian soldiers came to the house; they were well received and entertained with food and drink. After their meal they ordered the whole family outside and shot Rexheb in front of them.

The suspicion and hostility in which Serbs and Albanians had for centuries held each other flared into open violence when the former saw their country and their power disintegrating under foreign attack; the Pan-Serb intransigence of successive Jugoslav governments between the wars, which had frustrated all hopes of unity within the kingdom, now expressed itself in the persecution of all minorities whose loyalties to the central power were suspect. The Mussulman populations in Bosnia, Montenegro and Kossovo provided the principal victims of this flood of fear and hatred. In their turn they reacted savagely against their former oppressors, under the benevolent protection of their new German and Italian masters.

The tragedy of the Dobrushi family deepened soon after Rexheb's murder, when the son of the house, conscripted into the Jugoslav Army, was taken prisoner and transported to Germany, since when there had been no word of him. Our host, shattered by this double blow, abandoned himself to a silent despair alleviated only by the temporary consolations of the bottle. With our guard, Ramadan, he would start drinking at daybreak and continue until both were unconscious; as soon as they awoke they would start again.

'He is always like this now,' whispered his mother to Ejub. 'Although he has a beautiful house in Gjakovë and another in Prizren he will not go near them; he just comes here with a few servants to drink.'

To escape from this stricken atmosphere Hibberdine and I each borrowed a gun and some cartridges and, accompanied by two servants, went duck shooting by the river. We killed no birds but the walk in the flat open country, the sunlight sparkling on the snow and the tingle of the sharp frosty air on our faces more than compensated for the lack of sport. Ejub, who complained of influenza, went to Prizren to see a chemist. He returned in the evening disgusted. The chemist had given him a draught whose nauseous smell and bright orange colour had aroused his suspicions, which were confirmed, he told us, when he saw that the chemist was a Serb. Leaving the draught untasted he stalked from the shop.

Much more serious was the confirmation he brought that the German authorities knew of our presence in the area; they were combing Prizren and Gjakovë for us, and had taken over all controls on the roads. If we stayed in Kossovo it would only be a matter of time before we were found. We decided to return to Deg until the hunt had died down.

We left Rogovo at dusk next day, 17th January, striking due west across country on foot until we reached the shelter of the foothills and a small village on the Jugoslav side of the old frontier. While resting there the following afternoon we received a courier from Hasan Beg with a long letter from Hands and a sheaf of telegrams from Cairo. From these we learnt the melancholy story of the death of Corporal Roberts, my wireless operator whom I had left behind with Seymour, and of the dispersal of Brigadier Davies's Mission by the Germans.

During the winter of 1943 the Germans launched a series of determined drives against areas known or believed to harbour British Missions or their allies. Those operations, combined with the fierce cold of one of the severest winters of the war, virtually paralysed the guerrilla movement for four months and forced British and Partisans high into the mountains, where they had a painful struggle even to survive. Trotsky was obliged to leave his camp at Biza and jettison his equipment, including essential supplies of food and clothing. Pursued by the Germans, abandoned by the swifter-moving Partisan General Staff—deserted even by the Partisan guards who were supposed to protect them—exhausted, starved, and frost-bitten, Trotsky and his companions were ambushed on the morning of 8th January by hostile Albanians while they were taking refuge in a high and lonely sheep-fold. Trotsky and two of his officers were wounded, captured, and handed over to the Germans; they remained prisoners until 1945. Nicholls and Hare, both suffering severely from frost-bite, escaped from the trap; but the former survived only three weeks before exhaustion and gangrene extinguished his incomparable spirit. He was awarded a posthumous George Cross. Hare, whose courage and steadiness throughout that terrible journey earned him the immediate award of the Military Cross, escaped to the south.[1]

A courier from Hasan Beg brought us another piece of grim news: our former host, the sub-Prefect of Tropojë, had been shot dead by Partisans

---

[1] A fuller account of Davies's disaster is given in his own book, *Illyrian Venture*, pp. 147-153, and by Julian Amery, *Sons of the Eagle*, pp. 68-70.

outside his own house a few days after our departure. His murder was the measure of the Kosmet's gratitude for the protection he had given them, nor did they ever try to justify it; it was a clear warning to other Albanians of the consequences of befriending us: to ourselves it was a scarcely concealed threat.

We recovered from total despair when we heard later in the evening that Hasan's brothers, Gani and Säid, had just arrived at his house in Gjakovë after escaping from their internment in Italy. This was thrilling news indeed. Devoted friend as Hasan had proved himself he did not pretend to the military qualities of Gani or the political ability of Säid. With these two new allies our chances of organizing an effective resistance movement in Kossovo were immeasurably increased. The recent messages from Cairo were enthusiastic over our progress in this direction and our plans for the future. I wrote at once to Gani asking for an early meeting.

Next day, 19th January, we moved further west towards the mountains of the frontier, walking across pleasant, gently rolling country under a bright sky. Ahead of us loomed the sugar-loaf bulk of Bishtrik; thirty miles to the south we could see the snowy bastion of the Sar Planina, a formidable line of white peaks, corrugated with deep black clefts, running away to the east—the barrier separating the plain of Kossovo from Macedonia; to the north the sunlight glanced on the top of Shkelzen, 'The Shining'.

We halted for the night in a large and isolated house where the guest-room had a curiously carved and painted wooden ceiling and a floor alive with fleas. We left early in the morning because there was a wedding nearby and we could not risk being seen by the guests—'Besides,' Ejub whispered to us, 'the food in this house is extremely bad.'

Inspired by Cairo's enthusiasm we spent the next two days reconnoitring the neighbourhood for a suitable base near the frontier. On the afternoon of the 21st we scrambled up the side of a steep, forested ridge, crossed the old frontier and came down into the valley where stood the house of the District Magistrate of Has, who was to be our host that night. As we sat over our raki before the evening meal Ejub pointed out a small man with long drooping moustaches who was standing by the window.

'That fellow,' he told us, 'has been in hiding from the gendarmerie for many years—ever since he killed a man who raped his sister.'

'Admirable. But how is it that we find him here in the District Magistrate's house?'

'But you see, he was a great friend of the District Magistrate; and of course the District Magistrate would have done the same thing himself.'

While we were preparing for bed a messenger arrived with a letter for me from Gani Beg Kryeziu, assuring us of his devotion to the Allied cause and his resolve to collaborate with us personally; he and Säid were leaving

Gjakovë that same evening for Vlad, where they would await us in the house of their friend, Halil Hoxha.

An eight-hour walk through splendid mountain scenery brought us late the following afternoon to Vlad. The courtyard of Halil Hoxha's house was crowded with Kryeziu retainers and friends who had come from town and countryside for miles around to bid them welcome; already, we heard, more than three thousand people had come to offer their congratulations to Gani and Säid on their escape. Inside the stifling guest-room the oil-lamps flickered mistily through a thick haze of tobacco smoke; above the continuous murmur of conversation rose the crackle of a brushwood fire and the coughing, hawking and spitting of the close-packed throng of neighbours and servants. We waited in the doorway while Ejub fought his way through the press to the group seated on the floor around the fire; a moment later Hasan Beg himself hurried forward to embrace us and led us to join his brothers by the hearth.

Gani Beg Kryeziu was short and sturdily built, with a high, prominent forehead, strong features and a candid, determined expression; he spoke clearly, without evasion or embellishment, in short, pungent sentences. Although he would make up his mind quickly and carry out his decisions with speed and vigour, he was at the same time a shrewd and careful planner. Säid was of lighter build, tall and dark, quiet and sparing of speech, by inclination a diplomat and scholar rather than a soldier. Detesting the methods and mistrusting the leadership of the Communists he had yet some sympathy for the political Left, with whose literature his French education had made him familiar. As an intellectual he had a passion for political philosophy and had many friends among the Partisans; as a politician he proposed the formation after the war of an Albanian Agrarian Party.

With them was sitting a quiet man with a gentle manner, a sallow face, delicate features and a melancholy expression who was introduced to us as Lazar Fundo, the Kryezius' companion in prison and in their recent escape. He had once been an important member of the Communist Party, with influential friends in Moscow, including the veteran Bulgarian Communist, Dmitrov; but a visit to Moscow during the great purge trials wholly disillusioned him and in 1938 he renounced all connection with the Party. Returning to Albania he was arrested by the Italians in 1939 and imprisoned on the island of Ventotene, where he was later joined by the Kryezius. His brilliant and objective mind, his integrity and his courage earned him their trust and admiration and led them to appoint him their chief political adviser in the field; his knowledge of seven languages, including English, made him particularly useful in this service.

All three carried on their worn faces and emaciated bodies the marks of extreme privation and suffering; Gani held a handkerchief to his lips, into which he coughed convulsively while he talked, and Säid's overbright eyes and waxy pallor were more suited to the sickroom than the mountains.

Their escape had indeed been remarkable. Transferred from Ventotene to the mainland when the Allied invasion of Italy seemed imminent, they had escaped to Rome in the confusion following the Italian surrender. There Mehmet Bey Konitsa, the Albanian Minister, had provided them with false papers and arranged their repatriation; they had travelled in a sealed carriage with other Albanian exiles in a German military train through Italy, Austria, and Jugoslavia. When, after a journey of three weeks, they arrived at Hasan Beg's house in Gjakovë the Germans were still ignorant of their real identities.

However, after a rest of three days they judged it prudent to leave the town; Hasan sent his family to a place of safety, shut his house and, with his brothers and Fundo, took to the hills, where he told me they intended to remain until the enemy should withdraw from their country. The immediate German reaction was to loot and burn his house.

While we listened to this story Hasan sat opposite us on the floor with a smile of pure happiness on his chunky face, occasionally leaping up to salute some new arrival who had come to offer congratulations. Despite the sufferings of more than two years' rigorous imprisonment and their present ill-health and anxieties Gani and Säid were in high heart and impatient to go into action with us against the Germans. At present they had with them about a hundred men under arms but they had already sent couriers to rally their friends and kinsmen and hoped soon to have a thousand men at their command. Gani listened sympathetically to my account of our journey in Kossovo and our disappointment when it was curtailed; after a moment's thought he said with decision:

'Do not worry, you will make your journey. I promise it. We will go together to Prizren, to Priština—even to Mitrovica. Only give me five or six days to make preparations while you are at Deg; then I will send you word. There is nothing I will not do for you; I have been waiting two years for this moment.'

Over the raki and goat cheese we talked late into the night—of suitable targets for attack, of the stores we should need, of a joint battle headquarters for the Kryezius and ourselves, of dropping grounds and arms caches, and of plans for a speedy and reliable intelligence service; we discussed the political situation in Kossovo and the measure of support we could expect from the people in each district; and, of more immediate importance, we debated the chances of active cooperation with the Kosmet Partisans. Gani and Säid were willing, even anxious, to sink all political differences and work with them, but from our own experiences Hibberdine and I were not optimistic about the Kosmet's response; however, we kept our doubts to ourselves.

When at last we had eaten we all settled down to sleep on the floor; but excitement and the incessant coughing of poor Gani gave me, at least, a disturbed night. I was thrilled at the prospect of continuing our journey through the whole of Kossovo, and I never doubted Gani's ability to perform what he had promised. Moreover, although the messages from Cairo had been warm in their praise I knew that military action was what our staff officers expected; now it seemed they were going to have it, for Gani convinced me—as he later demonstrated—that he meant to put all his energy and talent into the struggle.

Jubilant, Hibberdine and I set out next day for Berishtë, where Hands had established a new headquarters in a hamlet above the bank of the Drill, about three miles south-west of Deg. With us came the Kryezius, Fundo, and a large escort. We arrived in the afternoon to find Neel and Hands with the wireless operators, our two interpreters, and my servant, Zenel Ahmedi; Hibbert and Merritt had left, the former to join Riddell near Dibra, the latter to work with a Catholic chieftain near the Montenegrin border. I wasted no time in sending a signal to Cairo with the good news that we now had a formidable ally in the field, and asking that at least one of our supply drops be allocated to equip Gani Beg.

There was interesting news awaiting us: first, Hands told us that the Kosmet, enraged by what they called our 'defiance' of them in visiting Kossovo without their escort or permission, had threatened to 'report us to Tito'—a threat whose implications became clear to us soon enough; secondly, two days ago Neel had narrowly escaped capture by a party of fifty Germans.

On the other side of the Drin stood the Catholic village of Dardhë; about a mile further south Neel had his headquarters in the hamlet of Trun. Neel had thought himself safe from surprise, for although the Prizren-Scutari road lay no more than five miles south of Trun, the only paths across the wild and mountainous country that separated him from the road were guarded by the followers of his friend, the Bajraktar of Pukë. On this occasion, however, the guards were either too careless or too frightened to give the alarm. Swiftly and silently the Germans moved up the steep and twisting track towards the house where Neel was comfortably taking his lunch. He would certainly have been caught had not the commander of a gendarmerie post on the road received early notice of the German plan; a friend of the Bajraktar, he immediately dispatched one of his men to warn Neel. This man reached Trun half an hour ahead of the Germans, giving Neel and his staff just enough time to hide the wireless set and all traces of their presence and reach the cover of the hills before the first Germans surrounded the hamlet. Neel ferried his party across the Drin to Berishtë; the Germans, after spending the night in Dardhë and plastering the walls with anti-British slogans returned to their base.

The enemy was certainly taking an unhealthy interest in our movements. Next morning Hands received a letter from the Kosmet, warning him that German troops with strong forces of Albanian auxiliaries were massing around Plav and Gusinje on the Montenegrin border; their ostensible purpose was to attack the Montegrin Partisans in Andrijevica to the north, but the Kosmet feared that their real intention was to come down the Valbonë valley and attack us at the same time as the Germans in Kossovo launched a drive from the east.

From all we had heard such a plan seemed more than likely; if it were synchronized with a German advance from the Scutari-Prizren road along the path followed by Neel's fifty Germans we should have no way of escape. The Partisans claimed to be watching all the approaches from the east, but after Neel's recent experience and my own at Sllovë I felt we could hardly hope for much warning. I was a little reassured by Gani, who undertook to put his own guards on the tracks and send us word as soon as danger seemed imminent. He and his party returned to Vlad late the same evening.

I shall not easily forget that 24th January. The Parish priest of Dardhë came across the river to lunch, a quiet, taciturn figure who seemed to have little liking for our company. Hands and Neel had invited him in the hope that he might be persuaded to influence his villagers in our favour. Although Neel was protected at Trun by his friendship with the Bajraktar, Ymar Bardoshi, he was far from welcome in Dardhë, where the people would not even sell him food; indeed we had all been warned by the priest himself not to enter his village, even to go to church. But our lunch was not a success; although coldly polite to his hosts he would not listen to any of our arguments, quoting texts from the Pope's Christmas broadcast and twisting them to justify his own hostility to the Allies. To his mind we were clearly the agents of Communism. We escorted him back to the ferry in silence.

The signal that shattered all my hopes came over the evening wireless sked' from Cairo. Its opening words are fixed for ever in my memory 'Kemp to break tactfully all contact with Kryezius and Irredentists.' The message went on to explain that my activities in Kossovo were causing an 'unfavourable impression' among Tito's Partisans and ended with the sentence, 'Our relations with Jugoslav Partisans are of overriding importance.' Mehmet Hoxha's threat had produced quicker and more effective results than the worst we had feared.

With horror and incredulity Hibberdine and I read and re-read the decoded words on that dirty bit of paper. Only staff officers, we commented sardonically, would suppose that we could 'tactfully' abandon men who had risked their lives to help us; moreover, to desert the Kryezius at the very moment when, exhorted by Cairo and ourselves, they had taken up arms for the Allies, was not only base but foolish.

'And so,' I stormed to Hibberdine, 'we are to ditch Gani Beg, the one man in this part of Albania who really means to fight the Germans and has got the guts and ability to do it; the one man who can rouse the Kossovars to fight; a man who has just suffered two years' imprisonment for his loyalty to the British—just to please Mehmet Hoxha and his bunch of scheming thugs who hate the British anyway!'

'If Cairo's relations with the Jug Partisans are really so important,' added Hibberdine, 'why the hell didn't they warn us off before, instead of encouraging and praising us in everything we've done? After all, there isn't a step we've taken that hasn't had their approval.'

For all our anger we could not believe that these instructions had the approval of Philip Leake; and we proved to be right. We later discovered that Mehmet Hoxha's report was passed by Tito, with a strong protest, to the headquarters of the British Liaison Mission in Jugoslavia; in consequence, the order for our withdrawal came from a much higher quarter than the Albanian Country Section.

In desperation I drafted a 'Most Urgent' signal, begging at least to be allowed to keep in touch with Gani Beg now that he was in arms against the Germans; the answer was a categorical No. It was clear to me that my usefulness in the country was now over, my position no longer tenable. I was already discredited with the Kosmet Partisans, whose knowledge of their triumph would only increase their intransigence; besides, I did not believe that they contemplated any operations against the Germans, but were resolved to keep their forces intact for the subjugation of their own people, including those who had been my friends and protectors. On the other hand, if I could get out of Albania quickly it was just possible that I might be able to help both my country and my friends by personal interviews with our staff officers; thus naively I reasoned. Sadly I sent my last signal, asking permission to return to Cairo and report. Hibberdine, who was much less compromised than myself, was willing to remain.

He and I spent the next two days with Neel among the pine woods at Trun high above the swift flowing Drin, shaking off some of our depression in his cheerful company, and relaxing in the crisp mountain air and the splendid scenery that rolled away south of us towards the mountains of Luma.

At lunch-time on the 27th Hands arrived with a signal for me from Cairo approving my request to return and report. Hibberdine was ordered to remain and carry out general intelligence duties in the area—a vague assignment which I did not envy him.

Hands was very excited about a visit he had received the previous day from Mehmet Hoxha, who had arrived seething with rage against me for what

I had done in Kossovo; after a tirade against me and my dealing with 'traitors, collaborators, reactionaries, and enemies of the Albanian people' Mehmet had concluded with the revealing statement that if it had not been for his relations with Hands he would have 'taken measures against me'.

Hands suggested that I should join him at a meeting with the Kosmet General Staff the following afternoon at Deg, to which I agreed. We went on to discuss the question of how I was to get out of the country. I could not go south, for the Shkumbi was in flood; the only possible route was across the North Albanian Alps to Berane in Montenegro, where Tito's Partisans held an airfield from which I could be flown to Italy. But there was a difficulty here: in the words of Cairo's message, 'Berane Partisans have been receiving unfavourable accounts of your activities probably from Kosmet.' However, Hands believed that if I could avoid an open breach with the Kosmet at tomorrow's meeting, they would be so glad to have me out of the country that they would themselves arrange my journey.

After breakfast next morning Hands and I left Trun; we reached Deg in the early afternoon. At the entrance to the village we came upon a group of Partisans practising with an old Hotchkiss machine-gun under the supervision of a burly blond whose thick hair, beneath a brown fur Montegrin hat, reached to the shoulders; as we approached the blond turned round, revealing a fine pair of handle-bar moustaches that would have been the envy of any pilot in Bomber Command. He told us that the members of the Kosmet were assembling in the house of the village *hoxha*. Hands went on ahead of me to have a quiet word with Fadil Hoxha and Mehmet and soften the impact of my arrival.

So effective was his diplomacy that Mehmet and his colleagues greeted me more like an old friend and comrade than the Fascist beast of their denunciations. We maintained our facade of friendliness throughout the meeting; for the Kosmet were too happy at the thought of getting rid of me to be deliberately offensive, while I was determined not to be provoked into argument. There were, nevertheless, moments when I could hardly restrain my laughter; as when Mehmet propounded quite seriously the amazing theory that the civil war had been brought about solely by British encouragement of 'collaborationists and reactionaries,' and ended with a jewel of double-think: 'there was no civil war in Albania until the arrival of the British Military Missions.'

With genuine enthusiasm the Kosmet agreed to escort me to Berane, but warned me that the German and Albanian forces concentrated around Plav and Gusinje had started an offensive against the Montenegrin Partisans; a Kosmet patrol had been sent to report on the situation and should return within the next few days. If I would return to Hands's headquarters at Berishtë they would send for me as soon as it was safe to move.

While at Deg I received information that sickened me as much as anything I had heard in Albania: the miserable Eles, my interpreter, had been a frequent visitor to the German *Kommandatur* in Peć while Hibberdine and I were travelling in Kossovo. Instead of returning home when we left him at Molina at the beginning of January, he decided to earn some money by reporting our movements to the Germans; only Ejub's precautions had saved us from capture. I was at first unwilling to believe the story of his treachery, for I distrusted all evidence from Kosmet sources; but when, after examining the witnesses, I tackled Eles on my return to Berishtë, he burst into tears and admitted the charges. I was angry enough to have shot him on the spot; but I had no wish to start a blood-feud between his village and Berishtë. I sent him home feeling sure that either the Partisans or the Kryezius, whom he had also betrayed, would exact their own revenge.

From Berishtë I wrote a letter to the Kryezius, which I sent by the hand of my other interpreter, Sadri Dorçë: I tried to explain 'tactfully' that I had been recalled suddenly to Cairo for consultations, that I would never forget their kindness, and that I would do all in my power to secure them British arms and supplies in support of their operations. I felt too deeply ashamed to write more.

Our meeting with the Kosmet had taken place on 28th January; on the 31st, while I was still awaiting news of my journey, a signal came from Cairo informing me that there was a good chance of an aircraft landing at Berane airfield soon to pick up a party of British officers who had arrived there from Mihailović's territory. I decided to start immediately for Salimani's house in Krasniqi. There I should be much nearer the frontier, and I hoped that the old Bajraktar might have his own means of getting me across to Montenegro. After sending a fast messenger ahead to warn the Kosmet of my need for haste I left Berishtë at eleven the same morning; my servant, Zenel, mindful of Muharrem Bajraktar's charge, insisted on going with me.

We walked at a brisk pace in the cheerful morning sunlight across rolling hillsides above the gorge of the Drin. Although I was sorry to part from my friends it was a relief to turn my back on the disappointments and frustration of Berishtë. I was turning my back, also, on my six months' work in the country; but now that the decision had been made for me and I knew that I could do no more, I began to shed some of the gloom and apprehension which lately had almost overwhelmed me. I even looked forward to the adventure of crossing the frontier; and the prospect of leave and rest beyond was delightful.

We reached Salimani's house soon after dark, to find the Bajraktar seated in his guest-room among a group of Partisans, including Mehmet and Fadil Hoxha. They had received my message, and introduced me to their courier, Idris, who had just returned from Plav with his report on the offensive against the Montenegrin Partisans. An unassuming young man of slim and wiry build who spoke good French, he told me that the attacking 'reactionaries and Chetniks' had been routed, suffering extremely heavy casualties, chiefly from frost-bite and avalanches.

'In consequence,' he added, 'the repression up there is very severe.'

Mehmet, however, more affable than I had ever seen him, agreed to send me on my journey the following evening with Idris and two Montenegrin Partisans as escort. I must take only what kit I could carry easily on my back. Zenel, when told that he must stay behind, refused with such eloquence and determination that he persuaded Mehmet to let him accompany me as far as the frontier. We were warned to follow the courier's instructions without question; we should have to travel mostly by night, avoiding contact with people on the way. The frontier was closely patrolled by volunteer bands of Albanian 'reactionaries,' but we might be able to bribe one or two of their leaders to let us pass.

February 1st was a day of cloudless sky and brilliant sunshine in which the great peaks to the north beneath which I should have to travel that night shone in frosty but friendly grandeur. During the morning I reduced my kit to a small haversack, an overcoat and a couple of blankets; for defence I should have to rely on my .45 automatic and the rifles of my escort. Before lunch Fadil and Mehmet took their leave in the same sunny mood which at another time I might have thought suspicious.

In the late afternoon the five of us began our northward journey. It was safe to travel in daylight the few miles to the small town of Kolgecaj; but at a house on the outskirts we halted to eat and to await the fall of darkness. We left at eight and walked for an hour across open country until the track entered the deep gorge of the Valbonë, which runs north-westward along a narrow cleft through the mountains to within a few miles of the old frontier. Idris called a halt.

'Let us rest a few minutes,' he said. 'Ahead of us lies a march of six hours.'

Under a bright moon we resumed our journey, following a narrow path which wound along the cliff-face above the right bank of the river. Below us the torrent foamed and bubbled among the boulders and over the rapids, the roar and hissing of its passage echoed and amplified by the steep, confining walls; above, the moonlight glistened white on the mountain tops outlined starkly against the indigo sky and glinted evilly on the bare rock faces which plunged hundreds of feet into the shadows of the gorge.

On our side the overhanging wall of rock blotted out the light, so that we stumbled helplessly among the loose stones and boulders which littered the path. Soon the going became harder as the track dropped down to the river, then rose and fell again steeply in a series of vicious switchbacks. Hour after hour we struggled on, with only an occasional halt for a drink of water, until my eyes ached with the strain of following the track and I could no longer control the movements of my aching legs; as though drunk I began to stagger and lurch from side to side. I was painfully reminded of the local name for these mountains—*Prokletijë*, or Accursed.

The moon was already down when we came to a widening of the valley where a ravine ran in from the north. We forded the river and, after climbing several hundred feet up the opposite hillside in order to avoid a village, crossed the ravine and continued up the valley. If there was a track we failed to find it in the darkness; but after an agonizing scramble over broken, rocky ground, which drained my endurance, we suddenly found ourselves beneath the white walls of a farm-house. The owners were evidently expecting us, for the dogs were quickly silenced and we were hustled inside; Zenel and I were pushed into a small room by ourselves because there were strangers in the guest-room. The time, I noted, was a quarter past four.

Zenel awakened me to another bright morning with the news that the strangers had left. Soon afterwards Idris entered, followed by a giant of a man with huge black moustaches; tin's was our host's brother, a Capo Band or leader of one of the bands that had taken part in the attack against the Montenegrin Partisans. He greeted me warmly and told me that he would come with us to see me over the frontier.

'We have nothing against you English,' he added. 'Only we don't want the Communists here; and so we collaborate with the Germans, who help us to drive them out.'

Idris, I reflected, was an honest interpreter as well as a skilful diplomat.

After a brief lunch of sour milk and maize bread we left the house at half past three in the afternoon, retracing our steps as far as the ravine we had crossed the night before. Here we turned north and climbed steeply towards the head of the ravine, following a track which ran along the mountain-side through a forest of beeches above a narrow, stony stream. Throughout the afternoon we penetrated deeper into the heart of the North Albanian Alps. On every side rose great walls of shining rock pitted with crevices in which grew clusters of stunted pines. Darkness fell and a bright moon swung into the clear sky, glinting with a steely radiance on the naked rock and bathing the peaks in the still, white beauty that moonlight brings to deserts and mountains and all lonely places.

After four hours' march we crossed a wide, level valley carpeted in snow and began to climb a steep, beech-covered mountain—an exhausting business, for our feet slithered continually on the frozen track. Half an hour's climb brought us out of the trees onto an open, windswept crest where a small stone pyramid marked the old Montenegrin frontier. Here, while we rested, I looked back over the moonlit mountains and dark, deep valleys of Albania, so beautiful in that clear February night that all the fears and disappointments I had suffered there vanished from my mind; in that moment of rapture I felt a futile longing to return.

Led by our guide, the *Capo Band*, we set off downhill at what seemed to me a mad pace, for the narrow, twisting track of beaten snow was as slippery as an ice-rink; quite unable to control my speed or direction I continually slithered off to bury myself in the deep drifts at the side or land up hard against a tree. We progressed in a series of these terrifying descents, interrupted by arduous climbs up narrow paths on the side of mountains above sheer precipices, until at half past one in the morning we reached our destination, a wooden cabin at the bottom of a steep hill. Unable to keep my feet on the slippery gradient, I made the descent from the crest to the cabin on my bottom.

Our host, a fine-looking, dark Montenegrin, showed us furtively into a small room at the front of the house, apologizing in whispers for not being able to offer us the guest-room, which was occupied by strangers whom he dared not let us meet. Throwing myself on the floor without undressing or removing my boots I slept soundly until late in the morning.

We were now on the most dangerous part of our journey, Idris told me, in the heart of enemy territory. Through the little window of our room he pointed out to me a broad lake a mile or two below us, and beside it a cluster of houses among the trees; this was the lake and town of Plav. There was a German military headquarters in the town, he explained, and the country all around was thick with fascists. Our friend the *Capo Band* had already left for the new frontier to find out whether I could cross that night; meanwhile I must stay in the room, being careful not to show my face at the window.

At six in the evening the *Capo Band* returned to say that his friends would not be on duty until the following night, but that I could certainly cross then. I had resigned myself to another twenty-four hours of waiting and was preparing to go to bed after an excellent dinner when there was a loud knocking on the front door, and I heard a voice shouting for Idris. He hurried out, to return a minute later with a serious face, accompanied by the *Capo Band*, who looked a little frightened.

'Listen! We must hurry away from here! The German authorities in Plav know of our presence and are searching for us at this moment. We'll move to a village an hour's journey from here—back on the way we've come—please hurry!'

Wondering if one of our own party had betrayed us or if Mehmet's affability at our last meeting had been a mask for treachery, I hurried out of the house with Zenel at my heels. We scrambled breathlessly up the steep slope I had descended so fast the night before, until we came to a track running along the crest. From here we made good progress, only pausing at each bend in the path to send two scouts ahead. Keeping my eyes fixed on the track I lost all sense of direction and time; but at last we halted near a small cabin while one of our party went in to talk with the owner. Ten minutes later we were inside a dim, stuffy little room with grimy plaster walls

196

and a dirty wooden floor on which a young man and three small girls were lying in a jumble of dirty bedding. We threw ourselves beside them on the ground and slept.

Daylight revealed that our new hiding place had been well chosen, tucked away in a fold of the mountains at the head of a narrow valley with no other house in sight. Thick fir forests clothed the mountainsides, their foliage a soft green in the morning sunlight. In the afternoon the *Capo Band* appeared, accompanied by a tall, swarthy Albanian whose head and jaw were wrapped in cloths as though he had toothache; he was, it seemed, the *Capo Band* in charge of the sector of the frontier where I should have to cross.

Through Idris they told me that I could not leave until the following night, when the hue and cry should have died down. Then, for the sum of fifty gold napoleons, they would arrange my journey. This was more money than I had; but after some bargaining they agreed to accept thirty napoleons and my promise that I would commend them favourably to the Allied High Command. I handed over the money on the spot and took a note of their names, which I subsequently passed to a staff officer in Bari.

Next day it was snowing. Fearful that the weather would provide another excuse for delay I paced morosely all morning up and down the little room, my every movement followed by the grave, saucer eyes of the three little girls. Zenel and Idris joined me for lunch and Idris relieved my anxiety.

'Major,' he said, 'you leave for the frontier this afternoon. Zenel and I can accompany you no farther, but the two Montenegrin boys we have brought with us will escort you to Andrijevica, where Tito's Partisans will take care of you. The *Capo Band* and his friends will go with you as far as the new frontier. Between this frontier and Tito's territory is a wide no-man's-land infested by patrols of Albanians, Partisans and Mihailović's Chetniks—all hostile to each other. There will lie your greatest danger.'

In the early afternoon my escort arrived, shaking the snow from their clothes. There were six of them in all, including the two Montenegrin Partisans. Idris was leaving immediately for the south; Zenel, in tears, begged me to take him with me, even to Andrijevica, swearing that he could make his own way back through the mountains to Muharrem Bajraktar.

I knew as well as he did that he could not hope to survive such a journey alone. I sat down and wrote a letter to Muharrem thanking him for giving me so faithful a servant; sternly I ordered Zenel to take the letter to his master, telling him that it was a message of great importance. Only thus could I persuade him to leave me. Then, unable and unwilling to conceal my own tears, I took leave of that greathearted young man who combined in himself the finest qualities of the Albanian tribesman: patience, loyalty and courage. Every night he had lain down to sleep across the doorway of my room; on the march he had always placed himself where the first bullet from an ambush would be most likely to strike. Now, obedient to his *besa* and his chieftain's command, he wished to accompany me on a journey from which he knew he could not return.

We climbed steeply through the forest until we reached the top of the mountain behind the house. The thickly falling snow blotted out our view but the *Capo Band* set a fast and sure pace over the hills, along a very narrow track between high walls of frozen snow. At dusk we halted for an hour at a small house overlooking the lake of Plav and swallowed in silence a meal of eggs and milk provided by the Albanian owners.

It was still snowing when we resumed our journey in the darkness; but the moonlight, filtering through the clouds, was reflected from the snow to diffuse a weird, pale light over the landscape. Soon we descended from the hills into the broad valley of the Lina, following the course of the river northwards over open meadows bounded by hedges. Crossing the flat, snow-covered ground in single file we must, I felt, be easily visible to any hostile patrols or sentries. The two Montenegrin Partisans acted as scouts, moving about fifty yards ahead of us. Luckily they had sharp eyes. As we were crossing a field they halted suddenly, then signalled us frantically towards the cover of a hedge. Crouching in the ditch beside it I watched a file of men approaching on our left; I had counted a dozen of them when I felt a tug on my sleeve and found the *Capo Band* at my elbow:

'*Tedeschi!*' he hissed. 'Over there, too!'—he pointed to a field on our right, where I could make out another and larger party moving parallel with the first—'But they haven't seen us—not yet.'

Slowly, agonizingly slowly, the two German patrols stalked across the fields on either side of us. Silent and motionless we lay in the shallow ditch, holding our breath and sweating with anxiety. Once we were spotted we could not hope to escape across the open snow; nor could we fight our way out against such odds and without one automatic weapon between us. Fervently I prayed that they would not notice our footmarks.

They plodded steadily past us, seeming to look neither to right nor left. We lay hidden for a full five minutes after the last files had disappeared into the night; then we moved forward in a series of bounds from hedge to hedge, floundering across the open fields as fast as we could pull our feet through the deep snow. Nearly two hours later we came upon the main road from Plav to Andrijevica, a broad band of beaten snow between low banks.

After a brief rest we set off along the road at a good pace; our guides seemed confident that we should not run into trouble on this stretch of the journey—a feeling which, after our last experience, I could not share. But as it turned out they were right, for in two hours of walking we met no one.

Half a mile short of the frontier we turned up a steep track into the hills. We climbed slowly through thick pine woods, picking our way with difficulty in the darkness and striving to make no sound that might attract the attention of the frontier guards. Emerging suddenly from the woods we found ourselves on the top of a precipitous slope among some deserted earthworks. We stood now upon the frontier. At our feet lay a deep valley; a steep, bare hillside rose beyond—a no-man's-land of uncertain breadth and unknown danger.

For a moment we halted, crouched among the earthworks, while our Albanian guides held a whispered consultation with the two Montenegrins. Then, with a word of farewell to the Albanians, I sprang to my feet and launched myself downhill in the wake of the two Partisans. So steep was the slope and so slippery the snow that I was soon careering downhill quite out of control; unwilling to finish up with my head in a snowdrift I tobogganed on my bottom for most of the way, pulling up only when I came to a belt of trees beside a stream at the foot of the mountain.

I found the climb on the other side a nightmare, stumbling painfully upwards through the snow and tormented by the knowledge that our figures were clear targets against the bare hillside. However, although the ground was honeycombed with footprints we reached the top of the mountain without being seen. While I sat down to regain my breath the two Montenegrins added considerably to my alarm by lighting a fire in order to signal the *Capo Band* that we had crossed the valley safely. I made them put it out.

We walked for half an hour through the hills, seeing many more footprints but meeting nobody, until my guides, who knew the country well, brought me back onto the main road. We were now in Partisan territory, where our only danger lay in being shot by a trigger-happy sentry. We therefore kept to the middle of the road, walking in line abreast, singing and talking loudly with a confidence which I, at least, did not feel. Beside us ran the River Lim, swift and dark and noisy in the night. Suddenly, as we rounded a corner, a voice called peremptorily out of the darkness ahead.

'*Stoj!*'

We stopped in our tracks. My companions answered the challenge, exchanging a stream of words with the unseen sentry. At last we advanced slowly towards an improvised pill-box beneath an overhanging rock; two very young Partisans seized my hands and shook them over and over again amid a torrent of friendly greetings.

After a few minutes' rest and talk we continued down the road for two or three miles, challenged repeatedly by sentries, until we came to a collection of small wooden huts which formed Battalion Headquarters. In a narrow, smoky room, almost entirely filled by an incongruous four-poster bed, I found a crowd of soldiers, among them the Battalion Commander and his Political Commissar. The former, a lean, weather-beaten Serb, immediately subjected me to a sharp interrogation in Italian, strangely relaxing from suspicion into friendliness when he learned from my escort that I held the rank of major; the Commissar was a small, squat man with very bright eyes and a *Strumwelpeter* shock of black hair who sat on the bed swinging his legs and smiling into the light. I was handed a large piece of stale bread and an army water-bottle full of raki, from which I was repeatedly urged to drink, by the crowd of Partisans who pressed close around me. Overcome with relief at our safe arrival, exhausted by the journey, and stupefied by the heat, smoke, and fumes of alcohol I soon began to nod. Friendly hands removed my boots and carried me to the four-poster bed, where I lay beside the Political Commissar, scarcely aware of his presence.

At dawn I was shaken into consciousness by a very pretty girl wearing battle-dress and a Partisan forage cap; she gave me some soap and poured water over my hands, fluttering her eyelashes and giggling 'Aristocrat!' as I washed. At eight o'clock I took the road to Andrijevica, following the valley of the Lim, past burnt-out villages where the blackened shells of once prosperous farm-houses bore gloomy witness to the hatred bred by political cleavage and religious intolerance.

Soon after midday I reached Andrijevica, a cluster of brown and white houses with broad gables standing upon a hill above the river. In a house in the main street I lunched with a major and two captains of the old Royal Jugoslav Army, now serving on the Staff of General Peko Dapčević, Tito's commander in Montenegro; the walls of the room where we ate were plastered with such slogans as: 'Death to the Chetniks of the bandit Draža Mihailović—the general under whom my hosts had been proud to serve less than three years before. They told me that there was a party of British officers at Berane, eight miles up the road, awaiting evacuation by air to Italy, 'after escaping from Draža's territory.' I had, it seemed, arrived in time.

During the afternoon I received calls from various Albanians whom I had met with the Kosmet, among them a serious young schoolmaster who treated me to a long lecture in French on the 'ethnic identity of the Albanian and Montenegrin peoples'; Montenegro, he explained, his sad eyes enormously dilated behind the thick lenses of his glasses, was ethnically a part of Albania and would certainly be administered as such under the new Partisan regime. After dinner that evening I was treated to a similar lecture from a keen young Montenegrin Commissar, who explained to me that all Albania north of the Drin belonged economically and ethnically to Jugoslavia and would be so administered under the new Partisan regime. These fraternal sentiments did not seem to be shared by the people of Andrijevica; they pointed out to me the surrounding fields which had recently been the scene of fighting between the Partisans and. the attacking Albanians, and rejoiced that the former, even if they were Communists, had managed to repel the invading 'Turks'.

After lunch the following afternoon, 7th February, I started on the last lap of my journey to Berane. A walk of four hours through a thick snow-storm brought me in darkness to a sad and silent town straggling on either side of a broad main street in the middle of a valley dominated by high forested mountains. My guides left me at a dismal two-storeyed building with a courtyard opening off the street. Climbing a wooden staircase to the first floor I entered a dingy, ill-lit room furnished with a table, a few chairs and three narrow beds; through a thick haze of tobacco smoke I saw four or five men sitting round the table. A tall, lean figure in British Army battle-dress, wearing the badges of a lieutenant-colonel, rose and introduced himself with a charming smile.

'Good evening! You must be Kemp. I'm Hudson. We've been expecting you for some days now. Let me introduce Colonel Seitz of the United States Army, Captain Wade, Northamptonshire Yeomanry, and Sergeants Roberts and Ross, who operate our wireless. Have some raki. Do you play bridge?'

I never returned to Albania. Within the year the Communist forces of the L.N.C. and Kosmet had overrun the country. Implacable in their hatred of the British who had nursed them they were determined to destroy all those whom they considered to be our friends. In the eyes of the new rulers of Albania collaboration with the British was a far greater crime than collaboration with the Germans. The fury of the new regime was directed especially against those Albanians who, as our allies, had submerged their political differences with the Communists in a united effort to win their country's freedom. Such men were marked for destruction because their fighting record gave the lie to the Communist claim that the Communist Party alone represented the Albanian people in their fight for independence.[1]

From this murderous holocaust only a few of my friends escaped. The Kryezius, as I have told, declared open warfare against the Germans during my last days in Albania; and later conducted a brilliant campaign against them which nearly drove them from the town of Gjakovë. The Germans in reprisal burnt the Kryezius' house in Gjakovë, plundered their property and destroyed their fortune. But it took the Partisans to kill Hasan and Gani, torture to death their friend Lazar Fundo, and drive Saïd into exile.

Ejub Binaku, my companion and guide in Kossovo, escaped into Greece with his friend, Professor Sulejman Riza, when Tito's forces overran Kossovo and massacred or imprisoned all the Albanian Irredentists who fell into their hands. My servant, Zenel, returned to Muharrem Bajraktar in Luma; I have had no news of him since, nor do I know if he escaped to Greece with his master.

Of the Partisan leaders with whom I worked some have survived to enjoy power and privilege: others have been devoured by the monster they helped to rear. Mehmet Shehu, Prime Minister of the country, and Enver Hoxha, First Secretary of the Party, ride an uneasy see-saw for the supreme position; the ruthlessness and cruelty of the one matched by the treacherous subtlety

---

[1] For a detailed account of this sad saga see Julian Amery, *Sons of the Eagle*, p. 307 *et seq.*

of the other. Dušan Mugoša, alias Ali Gostivari, was murdered in Kossovo by an Albanian, who was afterwards hanged by Tito; Frederick Nosi, undismayed by his uncle's death at the hands of the Party executioners, was rewarded for his loyalty with the post of Chief Justice of Albania;[1] Baba Faja, the 'Whisky Priest', was shot dead by one of his own Bektashi Dervishes when he tried to impose obedience to the Communists upon his Order; Myslim Peza has found refuge if not peace under the Hammer and Sickle.

Albania, now the most abject of the Russian Satellites, was a totally unnecessary sacrifice to Soviet imperialism. It was British initiative, British arms and money that nurtured Albanian resistance in 1943; just as it was British policy in 1944 that surrendered to a hostile power our influence, our honour, and our friends.

---

[1] There is a rumour that he is now in disgrace.

XI

MONTENEGRO

I need not have hurried to reach Berane. It was nearly two months before an aircraft arrived to take us to Italy—two months of dispiriting inactivity during which we were confined within the limits of the town by the conditions of winter, rumours of an impending German attack and the hostility of our Partisan hosts. I was at least fortunate in my new companions.

The senior British officer of the party was Lieutenant-Colonel Bill Hudson. He was a man in his early thirties, of splendid physique and unusual powers of endurance, who had led an adventurous and exhausting life in peace-time and in war. I was to see a great deal more of him before another year was over. A South African by birth and a mining engineer by profession he had completed his technical studies in England before taking up a series of posts in some of the most unattractive and unhealthy parts of the world. The outbreak of war found him engaged in mining operations in Jugoslavia. When that country was invaded he was sent to Cairo, where his knowledge of the Balkans and command of Serbo-Croat immediately obtained him a commission in the British Army. According to the stories I have read about the fate of such people in the First World War, he should then have been posted to Iceland or Abyssinia; in fact, he was recruited by S.O.E. for service in Jugoslavia.

In the autumn of 1941 he was landed by submarine on the coast of Dalmatia—the first British officer to be sent into the country after the occupation. His orders were to get in touch with General Mihailović, at that time the only Jugoslav resistance leader known to the British Government. Slipping past the Italian coastal garrisons he arrived, after a long, hard and hazardous journey over the mountains, at the General's headquarters; his presence there as a British officer in uniform wonderfully stimulated the morale of that gallant but erratic soldier. Soon afterwards he met Tito, then an obscure guerrilla leader with a small but growing band of followers. Hudson was the first to report Tito's existence and potentialities to London, an achievement for which he was never given due credit by either party. Now, after two and a half years of unrelieved hardship and danger, he was looking forward to some leave in England.

Captain Bob Wade might have stepped straight from the pages of Surtees. About my own age, of medium height and broadly built, with a bright red face, a wide, humorous mouth and a rich throaty laugh he had a vitality and zest for life that no hardship or adversity seemed able to subdue. At the beginning of the war he left his farming and his horses to join the Northamptonshire Yeomanry and went with them to North Africa; there, after a period of regimental soldiering, he volunteered for service with S.O.E. In April 1943 he was dropped into southern Serbia to one of Mihailović's less reliable commanders. In that area the occupying forces were Bulgars— ferocious enemies whose treatment of the few B.L.O.s they captured was notorious and horrible. Wade had some narrow escapes from them, being surprised on one occasion literally with his trousers down. He was adored by the people of Berane. I can still see his stocky figure striding along the street, his face a glowing beacon against the snow, accompanied by two grinning, bearded Montenegrins, each with an arm round his shoulder.

Sergeant Roberts, who was Wade's wireless operator and worked the set which was our only link with S.O.E. headquarters in Cairo, and so with the outside world, was a quiet, competent young man who treated us all with an easy familiarity that was never offensive. Sergeant Ross, a perky little Australian with an irrepressible sense of fun, had been taken prisoner by the Germans in Greece in 1941 but had managed somehow to escape and join a band of Chetniks. He helped Roberts with the wireless.

Colonel Al Seitz of the U.S. Army was a regular soldier, a serious but amiable officer of considerable seniority. He had dropped to Brigadier Armstrong, the senior British Liaison Officer with Mihailović, in the previous autumn; for General 'Wild Bill' Donovan, the American O.S.S.[1] Commander, was anxious to attach American officers to S.O.E. missions in the Balkans. Seitz confessed himself no politician, but would listen with a fatherly interest to what we had to say before giving us the West Point angle. As time passed he fretted even more than the rest of us; for he was convinced that the 'boys in Washington' were gnawing their nails in their anxiety to have his report in time for what he continually referred to as the 'Spring Offensive'. I must admit that in those days we all shared a simple faith in the value of our reports to the architects of Allied policy.

There was another British officer in the area who sometimes paid us a visit; this was Major Anthony Hunter, Royal Scots Fusiliers, now acting as liaison officer to General Dapčević. He had long been away from his regiment, having commanded a troop of David Stirling's S.A.S. in the desert before he came to S.O.E.; but he retained the regular soldier's healthy horror of politics and, being a guileless young man, took at face value everything told him by the Partisans. Later on his innocent enthusiasm for his job nearly cost us our lives.

Berane was full of troops, Partisan and Italian; these were the 5th Partisan Brigade and the remnant of the Italian Army Corps that had occupied Montenegro in 1941 and surrendered in 1943 to the Partisans. The Italians

---

[1] Office of Strategic Services, the American equivalent of S.O.E.

carried arms and were supposed to fight beside their new allies, but they wore little of the look of fighting men. In tattered uniforms they shuffled about the streets, their sorrowful, starved faces gazing apathetically at the ground; the feathers stuck saucily in their dirty, shapeless Alpini hats seemed only a mockery of their wretched-ness. Whenever we spoke to one of them he would ask us the same sad question:

'When will the Allies come, so that we can go back to our lovely Italy?'

Their new masters treated them like helots; every morning a dismal procession of Italians would amble past our windows in the direction of the Partisan Brigade Headquarters, carrying logs the size of tree-trunks to feed the Comrades' fires. I sighed, remembering the gay *Vincitori di Málaga* whom I had seen swaggering about Spain during the Civil War. The humiliation of the proud ones may be a useful moral lesson, but it is not a pretty sight.

The Partisans, on the other hand, stalked haughtily about the town like men who owned the world—as indeed they did own this little part of it. The townspeople were terrified of them. The new regime had conscripted all the young men and women; the girls who declined military service were put to the hardest and most unpleasant work that the Brigade Commissar could find; for which, of course, they received no kind of payment.

Our own troubles were principally with the Partisan high command, represented by the Brigade Commander and his Political Commissar; the latter was a loud-voiced, dictatorial fellow with a shaven head, long drooping moustaches and a most aggressive manner. The two of them were never at a loss for some complaint against us.

We knew that the Partisans disliked and suspected us: myself for my activities in Kossovo, the others for their contacts with Mihailović, and all of us because of our nationalities; but we had not supposed that they would make their feelings so plain. They abused us to our faces as 'collaborators', 'Fascists' and 'reactionaries'; invited us to concerts where anti-British and anti-American songs were sung and insulting speeches made about our countries; watched our movements and put a guard on our house—officially to protect us but really to keep a check on our visitors. Alone of the Partisan leaders General Dapčević, on the one occasion when he came to Berane, showed us some courtesy. Small and dark, with a firm, handsome face, great personal charm and an alert, lively manner which gave the impression that he moved on springs, the General had won himself a name throughout the country for his leadership, skill, and courage.[1] Before the war he had commanded a battalion of the International Brigade in Spain; if he knew that I had fought on the other side he gave no sign of it.

Most of the time the weather was bitterly cold, with a dead grey sky and frequent falls of snow. The hideous modern town seemed to congeal into a

---

[1] He is now Marshal Tito's Chief of Staff.

gloom that matched our own; the harsh white mountains and the bare black skeletons of the forests hemmed us in, savage and hostile as the faces of our gaoler-hosts. We spent long hours in our cramped quarters playing endless games of bridge for stakes that were illusory, since we knew the winnings would never be collected; we had soon exhausted the few books there were among us. Except for Hudson, who had been in the country much too long, we really had little reason to complain; but it was not the disappointment or the boredom that irritated us—not even the needling of the Partisans—so much as the knowledge that we were sitting idle in a backwater while great things were happening in the war outside. I thank heaven that I was never so unfortunate as to become a prisoner of war.

As though to tantalize us, frequent signals arrived from Cairo assuring us of an aircraft to fly us to Italy as soon as the weather cleared. From time to time it did clear, giving us a day or two of brilliant sunshine; then we would listen all morning and afternoon for the sound of engines in the sky. On the first morning we heard them we ran into the street, to see a flight of old Savoia *trimotori* circling overhead, their Italian markings clearly visible through our glasses. We watched them descend slowly towards the airfield a quarter of a mile out of the town. We were about to run indoors and pack when from the belly of the leading aircraft fell a cluster of gaily-coloured parachutes; the red, yellow, and green canopies made a brilliant splash of colour against the sky and mountains. Each plane made several runs; then they climbed, circled once more over the town and flew off in the direction of the Adriatic.

The Savoias returned on several occasions to drop supplies; we always hoped until the last moment that they would land. In fact, the drops were badly needed, for they contained food, clothing, and medical stores, all of which were cruelly short in Berane. These supplies came from the Americans, but the Political Commissar used all his ingenuity to persuade his men and the peasants that they came from Russia. He went to the trouble of explaining that the initials, U.S. which were clearly stamped on the packages stood for 'Unione Sovietica'; had not the planes been Italian? Then of course the labelling would be in Italian.

The Partisans tried to discourage the local population from making friends with us, but in this they were unsuccessful. Peasants and townspeople would stop us in the street and invite us into a cafe for a glass of *rakija*; the bolder ones asked us to their houses. All told us that they were King Peter's men and hated the Communists. They told us, too, grim tales of night raids in the town by Partisan patrols and of men and women dragged screaming from their beds to the firing squad.

Generally, however, for the sake of our hosts, we avoided all talk of politics, especially when we were in a cafe; for the Partisans, knowing how little they were loved in Berane, employed a flock of *agents provocateurs*. These creatures were a persistent pest. One of them, a Croat, would follow us around from cafe to cafe, however hard we tried to shake him off; pretending to be drunk he would join our table and nothing would shift him because the proprietors were too frightened to make him leave. One day he overstepped himself by making a sickening pass at one of their daughters—a little girl of eleven—whom he had taken into a dark corner. Wade threw him into the street.

Sometimes, tiring of the ugly rectangular buildings of the new town, we crossed the river to the old Turkish quarter, a charming district of small white houses with glimpses of brown gables peeping through the snow. There we drank slivovic or rakija with two old Mussulmen who seemed to feel no more religious scruples about alcohol than their co-religionists in Albania. On other evenings we would join some of our older friends, who had fought in the Serbian Army in the first war, and listen to their stories of the great retreat through Albania to Corfu and their songs of the Salonika front. There was one song I still remember, about the lemon trees of Corfu; it had a sad and haunting lilt:

Tamo daleko, daleko kraj mora
Tamo je selo moi, tamo je lubov moia.[1]

We often wondered why the Germans never bombed Berane, for they must have known of the presence of so many troops. Presumably they had more important targets for their dwindling air force. But they sometimes sent over a reconnaissance plane, which strengthened the rumours of an impending attack from the north; it seemed unlike the Germans to leave a serviceable airfield for long in Partisan hands. We could not see how the Partisans could hold Berane, for they had neither the equipment nor the discipline to stand against the Germans, who could bring armour and artillery down the road from Bijelo Polje. We should have to take to the hills, which would mean leaving many of the sick and wounded to be massacred.

The Partisans and Italians maintained their own hospitals, over-flowing with casualties from the last few months' fighting. It was hoped to fly the most serious cases to Italy. Meanwhile, in the middle of February a new danger arose, more immediate and graver than the German threat: typhus broke out in the Italian hospital. Among the starved and debilitated patients it spread fast. Then it struck the town. There was nothing the civilian doctors could do to check it because, as one of them told us, the Partisans had requisitioned their entire stock of drugs. We ourselves trusted to luck and plentiful applications of delousing powder to keep off the disease; and we were lucky.

---

[1] 'There far away, far away by the sea, There is my village, there my love.'

On 20th February our relations with the Partisans exploded in an incident that nearly ended in murder. Although we resented having guards posted on our house we had never protested, because they had not interfered with us or our visitors. The sentry on duty stood on a landing at the top of an outside staircase leading up from the entrance courtyard of the building; his comrades usually lounged in the court-yard. On the morning of the 20th, hearing the sound of an argument from the landing, we went outside, to find the guard—a new man—refusing admission to the boy and girl who did our marketing. He explained to us, none too politely, that no one was allowed to see us without a written pass signed by the Staff at Brigade.

Hudson immediately sent Sergeant Ross to Brigade Headquarters. Ross returned with an apology from the Commissar, who said that the sentry must have misunderstood his orders. Hudson, Seitz, and I then went back to see the sentry, and Hudson passed him the Commissar's message. The sentry was unimpressed; leaning against the balcony with his hands in his pockets and puffing cigarette smoke in our faces, he replied contemptuously that he knew his orders perfectly well and nobody was going to get by him without a written pass.

Provoked beyond endurance by the deliberate insolence in his manner Hudson seized him by the scruff of his neck and booted him half-way down the stairs. Recovering swiftly from his surprise he turned on us, released the safety-catch of his rifle and pulled back the bolt—thereby ejecting a live round which he had forgotten was in the chamber; then he slammed another round into the breech and took up an 'on guard' position half-way up the stairs. He had the good sense not to level the muzzle at us; for Colonel Seitz had his .45 out and was squinting at him along the barrel.

There followed a few tense seconds. Seitz's face had turned a dangerous dark red and for a moment I feared for the sentry; then the other guards clattered up the stairs to see what was the matter. Hudson explained and asked for the guard to be changed.

'If we find this man on duty again,' he warned them, 'I promise you that we shall disarm him.'

Ten minutes later I passed the landing and saw the same man on guard. We had no difficulty in disarming him, for by now he was thoroughly scared. His rifle was laid on my bed, where it remained until the afternoon; then it was claimed in person by the Brigade Commander and the Commissar. I do not ever remember seeing two more angry men.

'That's all very well,' said Hudson when they had left. 'But it's obvious that the sentry's orders came from the Commissar and that he made no move to alter them. He just put Ross off with an excuse to get rid of him. I should never have gone for the sentry if he hadn't been so insolent. It's a terrible thing for a Montenegrin to have his gun taken from him. They have such exaggerated pride that even the peasants here refer to themselves as *junaci*—heroes.'

The question of passes for our visitors was never raised again. But Hudson was sure that we had not seen the end of Partisan hostility.

'You wait,' he warned us. 'The next thing they'll do is try to collar our wireless set. They knew that as long as we have a wireless link with Cairo there are limits to what they can get away with. So they'll find some excuse to get it from us. Then they can treat us like dirt.'

'Well, it's my bloody set,' said Wade, 'and they're damn well not getting it.'

A week later General Dapčević arrived in Berane. With great tact he asked us not to allow our recent misunderstandings with the 5th Brigade to spoil our relations with the Partisan movement; for a while we thought that the incident was closed.

On the afternoon of 15th March we heard the sound of aircraft overhead; someone ran into our room to tell us they were landing. In a few minutes we had packed and were on our way to the airfield, myself dragging behind the rest because I had another attack of gout. But when we arrived our hopes vanished, for there were only two Savoias on the ground; there would not be nearly enough room for all the wounded, let alone ourselves. The Italian officer in charge told us that his orders were to take only the worst cases, together with the Italian General and his secretary, but that we could have two seats. Hudson declined on our behalf; but after some discussion Colonel Seitz, who was in a state bordering on anxiety neurosis about his report and the 'Spring Offensive,' decided to go. He was not happy about going, but he believed it to be his duty.

By now the scene around the aircraft resembled a popular fair-ground; Partisans, Italians, peasants—men, women, and children—swarmed in a tightly packed circle to get a closer glimpse of the machines, ignoring the angry protests of the crew, who were trying to service them. More sightseers streamed towards them from the town until the field looked like an enormous wheel, with the aircraft as the hub and the converging lines of troops and villagers as the spokes. Everyone was screaming at once in excitement, anger or pure enjoyment.

Suddenly above the din I heard, close overhead, the unmistakable whine of fighters. I looked up in fear, for I knew that the Germans had fighters at Mostar, only a hundred miles to the north; I knew also that a German fighter had once before destroyed an aircraft on this field. Now I could see them—there were two of them—banking in a steep turn to bring them into a dive. People began to scatter in all directions to get away from the Savoias.

'This will be a bloody massacre!' shouted Wade to me as we made for the edge of the field.

Hitherto I had been hobbling slowly and painfully, for my foot was very sore and swollen; now, according to Hudson, I covered the ground like a racehorse. When I thought I was out of the danger area I looked round, just in time to see one of the fighters dive low over the Savoias, pull out and climb away. There was no shooting. My glasses, picking out the red, white and green markings, confirmed that we had made fools of ourselves.

The dive was a warning to the Savoias that the fuel reserves of the escort were running low. At this moment a dispute arose between the Commissar and the senior Italian pilot concerning the proportion of Italian to Partisan wounded in the aircraft. Disregarding the pilot's plea that he must leave at once or fly home without an escort, the Commissar kept the Savoias on the ground for another half-hour before he was satisfied. They took off at last, long after the fighters had gone, and their crew swore never to return.

I was forced to spend the next week in bed, for I could not get my foot into a shoe. My companions cheered me with the latest rumours of the expected German offensive. We should certainly have to take to the mountains, they smugly prophesied, and in a hurry too. How could I possibly come with them in my present state? There was no help for it, they would just have to leave me behind to be taken prisoner. It would provide Lord Haw-Haw with broadcasts for a week:

'Units of the Wehrmacht occupied Berane yesterday and captured a British major in bed with the gout.'

They found this hugely funny.

It was the afternoon of 25th March, and snowing hard outside, when Sergeant Roberts brought us the decoded message from Cairo:

'In view of misunderstanding between Partisans and yourselves reported by Hunter which may endanger British relations with Partisans in Montenegro you are instructed to hand your wireless set to Major Hunter within twenty-four hours of receiving this.'

The signal ended with the information that wireless contact with us would be broken off the following evening. For half a minute after Hudson had finished reading it to us there was complete, shocked silence. We could not have been more astounded if we had been ordered to hand ourselves over to the Germans.

It was not a pretty prospect. We needed little imagination to guess how the Partisans would treat us once the restraint of our wireless link was removed. Hudson was fairly certain that they would arrange an accident for us—or at least for himself, Wade, and me. Nothing could be easier for them, especially if the threatened offensive were to materialize: nothing, in their present mood, would suit them better. We cursed the innocence of Major

Hunter and the cynicism of the Staff in Cairo that had placed us in so dangerous a situation;[1] we could not feel that 'British relations with Partisans in Montenegro' were as important as our lives.

'We have a little over twenty-four hours,' Hudson pointed out, 'in which to get this order reversed. If we send a strong enough protest on our next sked, and send it highest priority, we should get Cairo's reply before the close-down.'

The signal he drafted was long and bitter. After listing the promises he had received from Cairo over the last two and a half years he concluded:

'At least refrain from treachery to your officers in the field. Such conduct is unworthy of prostitutes let alone S.O.E. Staff Officers.' He very rightly rejected my amendment, which would have read:

'Such conduct is unworthy of prostitutes or even S.O.E. Staff Officers.'

His anger must have roused some torpid conscience; for at noon next day we received the most abject apology I have ever seen from any headquarters. We were to retain our wireless, communications would be reopened and—a sting in the tail, but a welcome one—the next aircraft to land at Berane would take us all to Italy.

Two days later, on 28th March, three Savoias landed. While two of them embarked wounded we clambered aboard the third. We said good-bye to the Brigade Commander and the Commissar—one of the happiest partings of my life; a few minutes later the aircraft was climbing steeply towards the mountains. After half an hour's flying the dead black and white of snow and forest gave place to the deep blue of Lake Scutari; far away on our left the houses of the city gleamed in the sunlight. A few minutes later we were over the Adriatic.

To our uncritical minds the first few days in Bari seemed a paradise of gaiety and comfort. We were surrounded with friendliness and flattery; senior staff officers congratulated us, junior officers bought us drinks, and gorgeous secretaries and F.A.N.Y.s asked us to their dinner parties.

We were billeted in the S.O.E. holding camp at Castellana, a group of villas in open country a few miles south of Bari. There we met other B.L.O.s back from the Field, among them Anthony Quayle who had been on the Staff at Gibraltar when I was there in 1941. Quayle had just come out of Albania from the Valona area, where his life had been an uninterrupted nightmare in which the Germans had played only the smallest part. Persecuted alternately by Partisans and Balli Kombëtar, pursued, threatened, robbed, and on several occasions nearly murdered, he had been reduced to living like an animal in a

---

[1] In Justice to Major Hunter I must record that experience soon altered his view of the Partisans. When I met him in London a few months later he was even more virulent about them than I.

cave. He had been rescued by sea on the day that we had flown out of Berane; when I saw him he was suffering from malaria, jaundice, and nervous exhaustion.

There was also a tough little Canadian major, a veteran of the first war, who had been with the Partisans in Bosnia. He had taken to his work with such single-minded enthusiasm that the authorities in Cairo had decided to pull him out for a rest. It seemed that he used to preface his signals with the distribution order: 'Personal to Mr. Churchill following for President Roosevelt.'

Our party soon dispersed. Hudson and Wade flew to Cairo on their way to London, where Hudson's presence was required by the Foreign Office, Roberts and Ross went on leave, and I moved into Bari, where with the help of two patient secretaries I started work on my report.

When I entered the office of the Albanian Country Section the day after my arrival I found nobody there that I knew. Philip Leake was still in Cairo, although he was expected shortly in Bari; Mrs. Hasluck was in Cyprus. The officer in charge was Captain Watrous, an amiable young American with a commission in the British Army who took endless pains to ensure my comfort and peace of mind. He told me that Bill McLean and David Smiley were on their way to Bari to drop into Albania again, this time on a mission to Abas Kupi and the Zogist tribes; as their political officer they were bringing Julian Amery, whom I had met when he was a war correspondent in Spain. I was delighted at the news, for I reasoned that the British Government would not send so powerful a mission to Kupi unless it was intended to give them full support.

Another newcomer to the office was Lieutenant John Eyre, a serious young Communist whose courteous manner could not altogether conceal his disapproval of my Albanian record. Like his co-religionist, James Klugman, he was his Section's Intelligence Officer, and like Klugman and so many other Communists he had great sincerity combined with charm. I saw little of him in Bari but I heard a great deal of him later, when I was in Java. There, while attached to the 5th Indian Division in Soerabaja, he landed himself in trouble by editing a seditious newspaper for the troops; in consequence he was sent home by the G.O.C., General Mansergh.

In the intervals of writing my report I was conducted by Watrous on a round of official visits. The first of these was to the Major-General commanding S.O.M., or Special Operations, Mediterranean. S.O.M. directed, among other activities, all S.O.E. operations based on Italy. Its headquarters was in a village on the coast road south of Bari, where the Major-General had a suite of offices managed by four or five very tall, very beautiful F.A.N.Y.s known as the Potsdam Grenadiers. I have always been nervous of officers above the rank of lieutenant-colonel, and the Major-General did little to put

me at my case. For a minute he stared at me across his desk in silence; then he asked:
'Whereabouts were you in Albania?'
I told him. There was another pause.
'Were you with Hands?'
I said that I was.
'Humph! Well, I'm glad you got back all right.'
With that we were dismissed.

Watrous was most apologetic. 'I'm afraid the General is a little vague about Albania. I've shown it to him on the map, but . . .'

Much more friendly and useful were my interviews with the officers of P.W.B., the Psychological Warfare Bureau, an Anglo-American organization which gave valuable help to S.O.E. in the work of undermining enemy morale in occupied countries. One of its stars was the great Harry T. Fulz, who had been Principal of the American College in Tiranë and who was now reviled as a Fascist and a spy by the Albanian Partisans whose leaders included some of his own pupils, notably the ineffable Frederick Nosi. Another whose talents certainly lay in the right direction was my friend Archie Lyall. His work involved him closely with recent events in Albania, and I was disturbed to find him pessimistic about the future of Western influence in that country. He seemed to enjoy living in Bari although, like most British officers I met there, he could not stomach the inhabitants.

'I have an anthropologist friend in this office,' he told me, 'whose researches have convinced him that the *Baresi* are the authentic missing link between the Egyptians and Man.'

Personally I shall always associate Bari with the sharp lesson I learned there on the folly of indulging in outbursts of moral indignation. A short distance away was a rest camp for officers and men of the Eighth Army, where soldiers of Britain and the Dominions were sent to relax for a few days after the horrors of Cassino and the Sangro. For some of their relaxation they came into town, where the rough red wine and poisonous brandy supplied by the shopkeepers sent them literally spinning. It is scarcely an exaggeration to say that at this time the streets, pavements and gutters of the town were strewn day and night with inert khaki bodies.

I suppose that eight months in the Balkans can be lethal to anyone's sense of proportion. That must be my excuse, for it was certainly no business of mine. However, I took it upon myself to write a pompous letter to the Area Commander, in which I said that, having just returned from an enemy-occupied country to one under Allied occupation, I was horrified at the difference in behaviour of the occupying forces. Even today I blush at the memory. I sent the letter through the usual Army channels, and three days later it reached the General.

Meanwhile, for two days I sweated over my report, working well into the dog watches each night. On the third evening I put work aside and went to a party. It was late when I walked out of the Miramare Hotel and paused at the top of the steps to breathe in the cold night air. I took a pace forward, stumbled, and fell headlong onto the pavement, at the precise moment when a patrol of military police was passing.

In the D.A.P.M.'s office a young subaltern of the Brigade of Guards received me with a mixture of respectful courtesy and anxiety. After closely questioning the sergeant in charge of the patrol, who seemed particularly shocked that I had been found without my cap, he noted the details on a large sheet of official paper.

'I'm very sorry, sir.' he told me, 'but we shall have to send in a report on this incident to the Area Commander.'

'The Area Commander!' I exclaimed. 'But surely I didn't resist arrest or create any disturbance?'

'No, sir. On the contrary you were very quiet. But—' he squirmed with embarrassment—'you see, sir, a day or two ago we might have been able to overlook the matter. But since the General received a complaint about the behaviour of troops in Bari he has issued orders that all cases of drunkenness on the part of officers be reported direct to him.'

Luckily for me the General had a sense of humour. But I brooded bitterly on my humiliation—the story was soon known all over Bari—until the arrival of Philip Leake and, shortly afterwards, of Bill McLean and his party put an end to my gloom. I was disturbed to learn that Leake, in whom we all had such confidence, intended to drop into Albania in a last effort to persuade Enver Hoxha to sink his differences with his political opponents and call off the civil war.

'Why do you have to go yourself?' I asked him. 'After all, you're the only experienced Staff Officer we have in the Section.'

'Peter,' he sighed, 'for a year now I've been sitting on my bottom, sending other people into the field. Now I feel I must go in myself—and apologize.'

Six weeks after he dropped he was killed in a German air raid: an irreplaceable loss.

Bill McLean's mission was leaving on 16th April. Thankful as I had been to escape from the Balkans less than three weeks before, I now felt there was nothing I wanted more than to return to Albania with these old friends. McLean agreed to take me, but Leake would not hear of it.

'Certainly not until you've had some leave in England,' was his answer. But he said I might fly over with them in the aircraft.

We took off from Brindisi at nine in the evening in a U.S. Army Air Force Dakota with an American crew. As we were boarding the plane I asked the pilot:

'Who is doing the dispatching?'

'Why, you are, I guess,' was his reply.

'No, he damned well isn't!' chorused McLean, Smiley, and Amery. Not until one of the crew told us that he had dispatching experience could they be persuaded to climb aboard.

We flew over Tiranë and, less than an hour after take-off, saw the fires on the dropping zone where the mission's stores were to be jettisoned—near to the plateau where Brigadier Davies had set up his headquarters the previous October. It took us eight runs over the target to drop all the stores. This dropping zone was too small for parachutists, and so the party was to land on another one, a few miles away. When we arrived there we could see no fires. It turned out later that the officer in charge had lost his nerve and put them out.

For two hours we cruised around, sometimes approaching much too close to Tiranë for comfort or safety. It was not long before searchlights picked us up and the aircraft began to lurch and shake in the flak. We believed that the Germans had no night fighters in Albania, but the anti-aircraft fire was unpleasantly close, and so we raised no objection when at length the pilot told us that he was turning for home. We reached Brindisi at two in the morning and went straight to bed.

It was not until 19th April that the mission was able to drop, by which time I had been recalled to Bari.

XII

POLAND

Where war is holier than peace,
Where hate is holier than love,
Shone terrible as the Holy Ghost
An eagle whiter than a dove.
- G. K. Chesterton

Mr. Evelyn Waugh in one of his stories has referred to S.O.E.—though not by name—as an organization engaged in setting up hostile and oppressive governments in the countries of eastern and south-eastern Europe. There was, however, one Section of the organization to which his criticism never applied—the Section controlled by Lieutenant-Colonel Harold Perkins, who directed operations in Poland, Hungary, and Czechoslovakia. To him I reported in London in the middle of June, a month or so after my return from Italy.

Perkins and I had been friends at Weedon. When our course ended he was given the task of coordination with the Polish High Command the recruitment and training of Poles for S.O.E. work, their dispatch to Poland, and the planning of operations inside the country. Later on his responsibilities were extended to cover Czechoslovakia and Hungary. Having arrived back in England too late to take part in any operations connected with D-Day I hoped that Perkins would find me something to do in his territory.

I was not disappointed. He proposed to send me to Hungary to work with a non-Communist resistance group near Gyöngyös, north-east of Budapest. I should have to drop in the Tatra mountains in Slovakia, where the Slovak army was in revolt against the Germans, and cross the frontier to Hungary. It sounded an interesting assignment in a part of Europe that I had always wanted to visit.

Before releasing me to Perkins the Albanian Section suggested that I should meet King Zog, who was living near Marlow. Mrs. Frank Stirling, whose husband, in the course of his distinguished and adventurous career, had commanded the Albanian gendarmerie, took me there to tea. The ex-King lived in a large house above the river surrounded by woods patrolled by grim-faced bodyguards and Alsatian dogs famous for their ferocity and strength. He and the beautiful Queen Geraldine received me with extreme friendliness and almost excessive hospitality; for instead of a cup of tea I was given a tumbler of neat Scotch.

The courage, ruthlessness, and cunning that had raised King Zog from a small chieftain to be ruler of Albania were concealed in a mild manner, a soft voice, and considerable charm. Our conversation centred round the danger of Communist domination of his country—a danger of which I was only too well aware. He was disgusted with the Foreign Office, who had not allowed him to give McLean a letter to take back to Albania calling upon all Zogists to rise against the Germans.

Perkins sent me in July on a fortnight's refresher course in 'cloak and dagger' technique at the training school in the New Forest where I had been in 1941. There I found Hudson and Wade, the latter destined for the south of France, the former for Poland. The following month I spent in London trying to improve my German and learn a little Hungarian, and studying the brief prepared for me by Perkins's two assistants, Major Pickles and Captain Auster. My Hungarian studies were not a great success; the only words I learned were *Nem bezélek Magyarul* (I don't speak Hungarian).

Early in August, twenty-four hours before I was due to leave London, the operation was cancelled. I went on leave to Cornwall to get over my disappointment, but I had only been there a few days when a message from Perkins brought me hurrying back to London. On 1st August the Polish Underground Army,[1] commanded by General Bór-Komorowski, had risen in Warsaw. Perkins was sending them a British liaison mission under Bill Hudson, which he wanted me to join. This operation would be mounted from Brindisi and we must be ready to fly out there in a fortnight.

There were to be six of us, including Hudson and myself: the second-in-command, Lieutenant-Colonel Alim Morgan, was to meet us in Italy, where he had been engaged in liaison work with Polish agents. Next in seniority was Major Peter Solly-Flood, a quick-witted and quick-tempered young Irishman who had served with Hudson in Jugoslavia; a career diplomat, he had with difficulty persuaded the Foreign Office to release turn for the duration of the war. Captain Tony Currie, a British officer of Polish extraction, was to be our interpreter and signals officer; he was an amiable, studious young man who wore glasses and spoke in careful, precise accents; we immediately nicknamed him the Professor. Among his many valuable qualifications was that of a trained wireless operator, although the two wireless sets on which we should depend for our communications with London and Italy were in the care of Sergeant-Major Galbraith, a young and very competent N.C.O. of the Royal Corps of Signals.

We were ready to leave in a fortnight, but political difficulties arose with the Kremlin. In the years since the disruption of that curious manage a trois,

---

[1] In Polish 'Armja Krajowa' (Home Army), abbreviated to A.K.

the Anglo-American honeymoon with Russia, the various instances of Soviet treachery have faded from our memory, dulled either by the passage of time or by the frequency of repetition. The story of the Warsaw rising, however, provides a particularly odious example. In July the Red Army summer offensive across Poland was halted on the Vistula by the German Army Group Centre under Field-Marshal Model; on 1st August Russian forces under Marshal Rokossovsky—himself a Pole—were only five miles east of the capital. At this critical moment the Polish Home Army rose in revolt, joined by the entire civilian population of Warsaw.[1]

It may be that the rising was premature and that supply difficulties and heavy German reinforcements held up the Russians; perhaps the Poles were unduly sanguine if they forgot for the moment that it was the stab in the back from the Red Army in 1939 that brought about the final collapse of their resistance to the Germans, or if they expected Stalin to forget the great Polish victory on the Vistula in 1920 which drove the Red Army from their country. Nothing, however, can excuse the Russian failure to lift a finger in support of Bór-Komorowski; most infamous of all, the allied aircraft flying from Britain and Italy to drop supplies to the beleaguered Poles were refused permission to use the Russian airfields near the city. Knowing that the Armja Krajowa was opposed to Communism in Poland, Stalin was delighted to watch its destruction at the hands of the Germans; in the words of Dr. Isaac Deutscher, usually a sympathetic biographer, 'he was moved by that unscrupulous rancour and insensible spite of which he had given so much proof during the great purges.'[2] After a few weeks of lonely and heroic resistance, during which the Germans systematically reduced Warsaw to rubble, the remnant of the Polish garrison surrendered.

Having paralysed allied help to the Home Army by the denial of their airfields the Russians were equally adamant in their refusal to countenance our own small operation. Describing the Poles as 'Fascists' and 'bandits'—they could scarcely call them 'collaborationists'—they fiercely opposed the idea of sending a British mission to report on the fighting; for they rightly feared that the report would reflect little credit on themselves.

It was not until October that Major-General Colin Gubbins, now in command of S.O.E., was able to prevail upon the Cabinet to let us go without Russian approval. By that time General Bór was a prisoner and Warsaw—what remained of it—was again in German hands.

---

[1] Unlike the Hungarians who revolted in even more desperate circumstances twelve years later, the Poles had accumulated a stock of arms, partly from old Polish Army sources and partly from supplies dropped over the previous four years by S.O.E.
[2] *Stalin* (Oxford), p. 524.

The disaster proved, as the Russians hoped it would, the end of the Underground Army as an offensive fighting force. At the height of the insurrection the A.K. was able to mobilize, apart from its troops in Warsaw, some fifty thousand men throughout the country; but for the shortage of arms it could have mobilized more. In the middle of August these territorial units marched to the relief of the capital; none got through and few returned. The survivors remained mobilized until November, when the fighting formations were reduced to skeleton strength. Their main object during the winter was to maintain their existence.

There was one of these formations in the thickly forested country between Czestochowa and Kielce; Perkins decided that this was the most suitable area for our reception. Obviously much of the value of our mission was lost with the fall of Warsaw; but both the Foreign Office and S.O.E. still required independent information, to supplement reports from purely Polish sources, about the political and military situation in the country, in particular about the strength and morale of the Armja Krajowa. Our reports, it was hoped, would indicate how the British Government could best help the Poles in the face of increasing Russian pressure to abandon them. Perkins impressed upon us that our new role was simply to observe and report; we must not become involved in battle unless we should be trapped and have to fight our way out. He also passed on these instructions to the leaders of the A.K. The Russian Foreign Office and High Command were kept informed of our movements, because we should probably meet the Red Army on its next drive westward from the Vistula.

From the moment we received permission to go we had little time in which to complete our preparations for departure; most of it we spent in learning a new system of coding messages. The greater part of our operational kit awaited us in Italy, but we drew our personal arms from Baker Street; we chose American .30 calibre semi-automatic carbines, because they were light, easy to handle, and accurate up to three hundred yards—ideal weapons for forest warfare. We were also handed, in an atmosphere of grim and silent sympathy, a small supply of 'L tablets', each containing enough cyanide to kill a man in half an hour if swallowed, in a few seconds if chewed; the idea was that we might find ourselves in circumstances where suicide would be preferable to capture. Fortunately or unfortunately we somehow mixed them up with our aspirin tablets and so decided to destroy our store of both.

We flew to Italy in the middle of October; there we were quartered in the village of Selva, on the edge of the hills above the coastal plain between Bari and Brindisi. Had we arrived a few hours earlier we could have left for Poland immediately, for on that day the weather reports were good on both sides of the Carpathians—a very rare coincidence—and an aircraft was leaving to drop a party of agents near our area.

As it turned out, perhaps we were lucky, for the sortie was marked by an ugly accident caused by the inexperience of the dispatcher. While hooking up one of the agents to the wire strong point in the aircraft he somehow passed the static line through one of the straps that held the man's parachute to his back; when the agent jumped, the static line, instead of pulling open his parachute, held him swinging in the slip stream. Although the aircrew tried desperately to pull him back the slip stream was too powerful; he remained hanging in space until he froze to death.

Nevertheless, having missed that opportunity it was more than a month before we had another. At first it was the weather that defeated us. The flight from Brindisi to our target area took five and a half hours—eleven hours' flying there and back, excluding the time spent over the target; therefore the weather had to be good at Brindisi for take-off, clear over the target and good enough for landing at Brindisi on return. In winter this very seldom happened.

Soon, however, fresh political troubles intervened. When we left England the Polish Prime Minister in London was Mr. Mikolajczyk, in whom the British Government had the greatest confidence as a man who had done his utmost to co-operate with the Russians. His moderation, unfortunately, had met with no response from Stalin and had undermined his influence with his own countrymen. Russo-Polish relations were further embittered by Stalin's 'Curzon Line' declaration, when he annexed to the Soviet Union the territories in White Russia and the Ukraine from which Marshal Pilsudski had ejected the Red Army in 1920. Mikolajczyk therefore resigned in favour of Mr. Arciszewski, a Socialist as well known for his hatred of Russia as for his patriotism and integrity. As allies of the Russians the British Government naturally hesitated to accredit a military mission to an organization now under the direction of an acknowledged Russophobe. Stalin's reaction to Arciszewski's appointment was to denounce the Polish Government in London and give diplomatic recognition to a puppet government of his own, composed of Polish Communists and known at first as the 'Lublin Committee'.

It is a considerable nervous strain to have to sit for long in idleness when you are keyed up for an operation of great importance and some hazard; but it is an experience to which most officers of S.O.E. became accustomed. Throughout November we controlled our impatience while our future was fought out in London. We lived in a *trullo*, one of the beehive-shaped dwellings that are typical of the Apulian hill country. These quaint and cosy buildings, warm in winter and cool in summer, are said to date from pre-medieval times when taxation was levied on every house with a roof; their ingenious construction requires no mortar, the bricks supporting one another from foundations to ceiling, so that the roof could be quickly removed on the approach of the tax collector and as quickly replaced after his departure.

From the terrace of our *trullo* on the hillside we looked eastward over silver-green olive groves to the lead-coloured waters of the Adriatic. We had, of course, too much leisure. Some of it we spent learning Polish with the help of Tony Currie; sometimes we went to Bari to dine with Archie Lyall or drink at the Hotel Imperiale, the transit hotel, where we met our friends on leave from the Eighth Army. Nearly every day we drove to Monopoli on the coast-road halfway between Bari and Brindisi, where Perkins's advanced headquarters under Lieutenant-Colonel Henry Threlfall occupied two floors of a building in a muddy lane. An undistinguished village, Monopoli has one claim to recognition: it is the birthplace of Al Capone—'from mud hut to glasshouse,' as Lyall expressed it.

Occasionally Alun Morgan and I would take a jeep and drive into the mountains to buy wine for our mess. Morgan was an established civil servant who, like Solly Flood, had persuaded his Service to release him to the Army. At Oxford he had been an enthusiastic Socialist and, coming down from the University just before the outbreak of the Spanish Civil War, had all but enlisted in the International Brigades; electing instead to enter the Civil Service he had received a white feather from his girlfriend, a poetess who rowed stroke in the Oxford University Women's Eight.

We fretted, of course, at the erratic arrival, or failure to arrive, of our mail; I also missed the London newspapers. But one unfailing con-solation was the news-sheet Union Jack, published daily for the fighting services in the Central Mediterranean. Its editor was a well-known Fleet Street journalist, who with his anonymous staff of sub-editors managed to extract the spiciest headlines from the dullest items of news. Thus, soon after the liberation of Greece we were treated to GREEK PRIME MINISTER ADDRESSES TRIUMPHANT GATHERING OF LESBIANS IN ATHENS, while another small paragraph, tastefully headed 'DROIT DE SEIGNEUR', informed us that 'Field-Marshal Montgomery today accepted the freedom of Maidenhead'. The pearl of all headlines was found by my brother-in-law—and no doubt by many others—towards the end of the European war, on the front page of one of London's leading dailies: SOVIET PUSH BOTTLES UP ONE HUNDRED THOUSAND NAZIS IN LOWER BALKANS.

In Bari I found Bill McLean, David Smiley and Julian Amery back from their unlucky mission to Abas Kupi. Denied the support they had been promised in London they felt they had also been betrayed by their Country Section in Bari. They had reason to be bitter, because the staff officers of the Albanian Section had received them with undisguised contempt and had referred to them openly as 'Fascists'; worse still, messages which they had sent—and which under their terms of reference they were entitled to send—to the Foreign Secretary and to the Minister of State for Middle East Affairs had been suppressed by the office in Bari. Philip Leake's death in battle had proved a most fortunate accident for the Communists.

At last, early in December, we received permission to go. A few days afterwards, in the late afternoon, we boarded a Liberator of a Polish squadron at Brindisi. Wearing thick clothing under our flying suits—for the aircraft was unheated—and with our parachutes already strapped to our backs we climbed with difficulty through the narrow hatch under the fuselage and settled ourselves half lying, half reclining on the metal floor. I experienced again the claustrophobia I had first known when climbing into the Halifax at Derna; this time there was less room and I felt that we were being packed for immolation in a tin coffin.

The dropping zone, which we had settled in detail on the map, was a stretch of open country surrounded by forest near the town of Zarki, about twenty miles south-east of Czestochowa. We asked to be dropped from six hundred feet, which should give us plenty of time to look around on the way down. The two hazards of the journey, we were given to understand, were a German night fighter belt over Hungary and the possibility of icing up while crossing the great mountain barrier of the Carpathians. We must be careful, also, not to stray over territory held by the Red Army; for the Russians had given warning that they would fire on all aircraft flying to Poland.

When we were over Jugoslavia the two waist gun ports were thrown open and the gunners took up their positions behind the Brownings. One of the gunners started talking to Currie in Polish; he was a squat young man with long dark hair and a perpetual smile on his face, although when I heard his story from Currie I wondered what he had to smile about. His brother had been killed by the Germans in 1939 and his sister sent to a brothel; his mother and father had been arrested by the N.K.V.D. and deported to Siberia. He was the sole survivor of the family.

'Now I have only myself to worry about,' he told us with a little laugh; and he caressed the barrel of the Browning.

We met with no night fighters and we cleared the Carpathians without incident; but on the far side we ran into thick mist. The navigator, Wing-Commander Krol, who was also Captain of the aircraft, came aft and told us: 'It's just like flying through milk. I can't even see our wing tips.'

For an hour we cruised low over the target area, hoping to catch a glimpse through some break in the mist of the fires that would show us the dropping zone. Our fuel reserve allowed us to stay no longer; in deep gloom we resigned ourselves to another five and a half hours of cramp and cold. We landed at Brindisi at four in the morning, just twelve hours after take-off.

I have described this flight in some detail because it was typical of two more unsuccessful attempts we made that month, the last of them on Christmas Day. We had hurriedly swallowed a little cold turkey and plum pudding on the edge of the airfield and were on our way to the aircraft when two signals arrived from England. One was for Tony Currie, announcing the birth of his son; the other was an order to Alun Morgan to stand down and await transport to England, where he was urgently required for duty with his former Civil Service department. Morgan was so indignant that for a moment he seriously considered defying the signal and coming with us. It was as well that he didn't, because we were back in our *trullo* at dawn the next morning.

I had scarcely fallen asleep, or so it seemed, when I was shaken awake to see bright sunlight flooding the room and Hudson standing over my bed. It was half-past ten.

'Get dressed quick! The op's on again this afternoon. Weather reports are good everywhere, so we've an excellent chance of making it this time.'

Alun Morgan and Archie Lyall drove with us to the aerodrome. As we stood talking near the aircraft Morgan remarked cheerfully: 'The last person I saw off from here was Philip Leake. Six weeks later he was dead.'

Lyall shook my hand solemnly and said with impressive gravity: 'Well, good-bye, Peter. I trust you've made arrangements that if you croak I get your Spanish cloak.'

It was nine o'clock when the dispatcher came aft to open the exit hatch in the floor; he told us that the fires were clearly visible on the dropping ground.

'It is a beautiful night,' he smiled. 'Just like daylight, so bright is the moon.'

When it came to my turn to jump and the red light flashed for 'action stations' I sat on the edge of the drop praying that I might make a better landing than I usually managed, calming my fears with the thought that I should have at least twelve seconds in which to get ready for it, and repeating to myself the password Michal by which I must make myself known to the reception committee. According to our information the Germans had a garrison of eighty S.S. at a village six kilometres away and another of fifty gendarmerie ten kilometres away; if they had been alerted by our aircraft the night before we ran the risk of an unfriendly reception.

The red light turned to green, the dispatcher tapped my shoulder and two seconds later the slip-stream hit me as I cleared the exit. When I felt the pull of the opening parachute I looked down for the ground. To my horror I saw that it was very close and coming closer fast. I had just enough time to pull on my lift webs to break my fall before I crashed onto what felt like concrete. For a few moments I lay still, winded and shaken, on the ice-bound ploughland; my left knee hurt abominably and when I tried to get up I found that it would scarcely bear my weight.

At first I thought my parachute must have been late in opening; but it turned out that the pilot, either through an error of judgment or in the excitement of finding himself so close to his native land, had dropped us all from a little over two hundred feet. If any of our parachutes had failed to open immediately there would have been a fatal accident.

While I was pulling off my harness and flying suit two figures came running towards me across the dropping ground. When we had exchanged passwords they asked in French if I were badly hurt; after a moment's doubt I replied that I wasn't. Shaking my hand vigorously and slapping me on the back the two young men each put an arm round me and, laughing and chattering, helped me to hobble towards the trees that fringed the field. In fact, I had suffered no more than a severe bruising and a fright; for a while I forgot my pain in the exultation that swept over me as I realized that at last I was in Poland.

It was a fine, clear night, the air dry, bracing and intensely cold. The wide, level expanse of snow-patched fields where we had landed gleamed with a pale radiance under the glittering stars, in sharp contrast to the black outline of the surrounding forest. Gazing upward for a moment at the bright pattern of the sky I thanked God from my heart that despite all difficulties we had arrived and should now have the opportunity of helping these gallant people who had done so much to help themselves.

In a few minutes we came upon the rest of the party with a group of fifteen or twenty Poles. Hudson, who had knocked himself out on landing, was dazed and groggy from concussion; he wandered about, muttering in a bewildered, plaintive voice, 'I've wet my pants.' Solly-Flood had hurt his back, and Currie and Galbraith had minor injuries. Currie, who was the first to drop, had been dispatched too soon; arriving on the ground at the edge of the field he had found nobody there. Making his way through the woods he almost blundered into a village; luckily he met a party of youths on the outskirts who, although not members of the A.K., guided him back to the reception committee.

The leader of the committee told us that his men would collect all our kit and bury it in a hide-out in the woods in case the Germans, their curiosity aroused by the drop, should send troops to investigate; it would be delivered to us safely next day. Accustomed to the Balkans we were pleasantly surprised when it was. We lingered only long enough to recover our personal arms before setting off along a track through the woods for about half a mile, until we came to a long, low-built farm-house. We were shown into a large and well-lit room crowded with men and women of different ages, all of whom gave us such an enthusiastic welcome that I was unable to decide which were our host and hostess. The majority, we heard, were refugees from Warsaw.

Everyone sat down at a long table in the middle of the room loaded with plates of food and bottles of vodka and wine; I found myself next to a handsome middle-aged woman who encouraged me to drink more than was good for me and to eat more than I wanted; excitement or exhaustion had taken away my appetite. Fortunately she spoke French, for my Polish was unequal to conversation. A bright, intelligent woman, she was surprisingly well informed about events outside Poland. Although the Home Army maintained a news service its bulletins contained very little information and seldom reached the country districts; wireless receivers were almost unknown in the villages, so that most of the war news came from the German-controlled Press.

My neighbour, however, must have had some other source, for she challenged me on a matter which I was to hear raised frequently during the next few weeks and with some bitterness. Earlier in the month there had been a debate in the House of Commons on Poland and in particular on the Curzon Line. In his speech the Prime Minister, anxious to say nothing that might damage relations with Russia, had remarked that Stalin's action was largely a result of the intransigence of the Poles. Most people in Poland recognized that Britain could do little to restrain Stalin, since Russian troops were already on the Vistula; they were resigned to making the best of a bad job, for partition was not a new thing in their history, but they were indignant at being blamed for the treachery and rapacity of which they were the victims.

The meal ended with speeches of welcome, to which Hudson, somewhat recovered from his concussion, replied on our behalf. Soon after midnight we continued our journey northward, escorted by some twenty armed men and three girl partisans.[1] Nearly all wore some kind of uniform, usually an old army tunic—either Polish or converted German—with a leather belt and ammunition pouches, breeches, puttees, and boots; a few had British battle-dress. Most of the men wore Cossack hats of grey fur, sometimes with the Polish eagle and crown embroidered on the front.

My knee was too painful and swollen for me to walk, and so I was laid on a pile of hay in a farm cart pulled by an old horse. After three miles we stopped at a peasant's house in the village of Kacze Bloto, where an old man and his wife were awaiting us. Within a minute of lying down I was asleep.

Early next morning the leader of our escort woke us with the surprising news that two Russian officers were waiting to see us. We found a captain and a lieutenant, both of them quite young, who told us that they had been dropped three months before and were now living in this village. They spoke Polish and German, which Currie and Solly-Flood interpreted for the rest of us; although shy at first, they were friendly and freely answered all our questions. They were wearing civilian clothes, and almost their first words were to recommend us to do the same; advice which, as it turned out, we were wise not to take. It seemed that they lived on excellent terms with the villagers and with the Armja Krajowa, on whom they relied for their intelligence and for warning of German movements. They appeared to have no very active duties.

---

[1] The word 'partisans' in this chapter refers to any armed guerillas under military discipline, and has no political connotations.

It may be useful here to give a brief description of the paramilitary forces operating in Poland at this time. The Russians began to drop small parties of officers and N.C.O.s in the country west of the Vistula during the spring of 1944; although well equipped with arms and wire-less they were not supplied with food or money; they were obliged, therefore, to live off the country, requisitioning what they needed from the peasants. To the unpopularity thus imposed upon them they added the grave mistake of avoiding all contact with local resistance groups; in consequence they received no warning of German attacks and were soon destroyed or forced to abandon their equipment and go into hiding. Later the Russians dropped a few large parties, of a hundred men and upwards, who concentrated on railway demolition. These took care to cultivate good relations with Polish resistance, particularly with the A.K., establishing mutual warning systems against German attack; but like their predecessors they had to depend on requisitioning for their food. There had been two of the larger parties in this area, but they had moved east before our arrival.

Our Polish friends told us that all the Russian officers used to recite the same few words of propaganda, which they seemed to have learnt as a set piece; they make ironic reading against the background of subsequent events: 'We Russians have not come to occupy your country. We do not care what kind of regime you choose for yourselves, so long as it is not Fascist. We have only come to beat the Germans and then go home.'

It is well known, although it can bear repetition, that Poland alone among the countries occupied by Germany produced no Quisling. But Polish resistance was never united under a single command; there were several movements inside the country, each pursuing its own policy. Of these by far the most popular and powerful was the Armja Krajowa, which commanded the passive support if not the active participation of more than ninety per cent of the country. Originating at the end of 1942 with the fusion of four large resistance groups, each of which represented some political party of pre-war days, it was at first a purely underground movement, whose members remained in their homes but carried out secret military training. It was organized on a territorial basis in platoons of from thirty to a hundred men. Its principal objects were to prepare for a general rising at a suitable moment to expel the Germans; to weaken them in the meantime by sabotage and guerrilla actions on a small scale; and to protect the population against oppression. Later the A.K. developed its own political machinery, in collaboration with the exiled London Government, to administer the country after liberation. One of its leading politicians M. Retinger, parachuted in from Italy shortly before us, making the first drop of his life at the age of fifty-two.

Partisan units were mobilized as the need and opportunity arose for direct action; their ranks were swelled by young men who had fled from the towns and villages to escape conscription or forced labour. These units lived in the woods and, whenever possible, wore some trace of uniform. Their weapons were of all kinds: some came from old Polish Army stocks; others were dropped from Britain and Italy; a few were traded from Russian partisans for food, information or money, and many were captured or stolen from the Wehrmacht. The A.K. also maintained specialist sabotage groups, an elaborate intelligence system and its own nursing and courier services; the couriers were nearly always women and children. The higher ranks of the movement were drawn from officers of the Polish Army who had remained in Poland; some junior officers and many saboteurs and agents were sent by S.O.E., all of them Poles. As far as I know we were the first and only British officers to be dropped into the country.

Next in importance to the A.K., though greatly inferior to it in numbers, efficiency, and influence, was the A.L. or 'Armja Ludowa' (People's Army). As its name implies, this was a Communist organization, supplied and directed by the Russians. Its principal aim was to form a cadre capable of taking over the country's administration, with Russian help, after the arrival of the Red Army. In the meantime it attempted road and railway sabotage on a small scale and issued a great deal of propaganda designed to discredit all other resistance movements. Its partisan units wore red-and-white armbands and the Polish eagle without the crown. They were poorly trained and led, and their intelligence and warning systems were inadequate, with the result that their casualties were heavy. Moreover, having no funds they had to loot in order to live, and their levies pressed heavily on landowners and peasants alike. Relations with the A.K. were cold but correct; there was no fighting between them and they gave each other warning of enemy attacks. In Warsaw there were detachments of A.L. who fought very well, at least in the early stages of the rising.

Lastly, there was the N.S.Z. (National Armed Forces), a small political and paramilitary organization derisively nicknamed 'The Colonel's Party'; politically it was so far to the right that even the A.K. called it reactionary. Its members were sometimes accused, especially by the A.L., of collaboration with the Germans, but they fought gallantly enough in Warsaw. Relations between the N.S.Z. and Armja Ludowa were as bad as they could be; they fought each other whenever they met, taking no prisoners.

The Germans treated members of all three organizations as rebels, so that any Pole taken in arms was likely to be executed. But our friends in the A.K. told us that they stood some chance of survival if captured by the Wehrmacht, none at all if taken by the S.S.

Most savage of all were the German auxiliary troops belonging to the army of the renegade Russian General Vlasov. Vlasov was a Cossack who was captured at the beginning of the German offensive against Russia in 1941 when, according to some figures, eight hundred thousand Russian soldiers were taken prisoner. From these Vlasov recruited an army of Cossack,

Ukrainian, Turkoman, Mongol, and other Asiatic troops, which the Germans employed chiefly on garrison and security duties in occupied countries. Knowing that they would receive no quarter if taken, these men fought to the last; such was their barbarity towards the civilian population that they were feared and detested throughout occupied Europe. In this part of Poland there were Ukrainian and Turkoman divisions on the river Pilica and Cossack patrols everywhere. The A.K. shot any of Vlasov's men whom they captured, as they also shot all S.S. men; prisoners from the Wehrmacht were usually deprived of their arms and uniforms and then released.

The country here was not well suited to guerrilla warfare. It was quite flat and, at this time of year, covered in snow. The Germans could bring tanks, armoured cars and lorried infantry to almost any part of the area with very little warning; the partisans, on the other hand, were seldom more than five miles from a German garrison. The great fir forests, carefully cultivated for their timber, were intersected at regular intervals by long, straight, broad rides which could be swept by machine-guns; there was scarcely any scrub or undergrowth and the trees were bare of branches from the ground to a height of more than twelve feet. They gave concealment from a distant enemy but little protection from close range. The only dense cover was to be found in plantations of young firs that had not yet been thinned.

German operations against the Poles took two forms; the *pacyfikacja*, a punitive expedition against partisans, and the *lapanka*, a round-up of young men and women in the towns and villages for work in Germany; Cossack and Ukrainian troops were usually employed in both. The tactics of the *pacyfikacja* were as simple as they were frightening. The area of forest in which the partisans were hiding was tightly cordoned; tanks, armoured cars and heavy machine-guns were stationed where they could command all the rides; then infantry in close formation beat through the woods, driving the partisans, like game, onto the guns. The A.K. claimed that their warning system usually gave them time to leave the threatened area, or that their knowledge of the terrain enabled them to slip through the cordons by night. The *lapanka* was harder to counter, in winter especially, because the partisan units were then reduced to skeleton strength and could provide neither food nor protection for the fugitives.

We left Kacze Bloto at dusk on the 27th with an escort of twenty men under a Lieutenant Twardy;[1] I was still unable to walk far and rode again on the farm cart, which also carried our heavy kit. It was a fine but freezing night and despite my American army windbreaker jacket, heavy whipcord trousers, and thick gloves and socks I was soon numb with the cold. The creaking of

---

[1] Nearly all the names of A.K. officers mentioned in these pages are *noms-de-guerre*.

the wagon, the crunch of footsteps in the snow and the gusty whinnying of the old horse sounded as if they must carry for miles in the stillness. Propped upright against a pile of rucksacks, my pipe in my mouth and my carbine resting on my knees, I fancied myself an early settler travelling into the heart of some unknown continent; I certainly felt jumpy enough, for whenever the men at either end of the column called out directions or orders in their loud, harsh voices I found myself gripping the carbine with my thumb on the safety catch and peering anxiously from side to side into the dark and silent forest.

At length we came to a cottage on the fringe of forest and open fields. Here we were welcomed by a middle-aged Pole who wore the armband of the German-controlled Forestry Service, a taciturn but hospitable fellow. In his small but comfortable parlour his wife gave us a warm greeting, which she immediately reinforced by making us sit down and drink two bottles of cherry vodka. An enormous meal followed; and we slept in clean sheets.

We were surprised at the quantity and excellence of our food, for we had understood that the severity of the German agricultural levies had left the peasants on the verge of starvation. However, we learned that the peasants, with the help of the A.K., contrived to evade the levies, or at least to mitigate their effect; and an ingenious system of barter and black market in the surplus produce ensured that, in the country districts at least, the people did not go short.

We stayed the next two days in the forester's cottage, but we were not idle. Most of the first day we spent encoding telegrams to Italy, which Galbraith immediately dispatched, announcing our arrival and recording such of our first impressions as we thought might be useful. We had visits from A.K. officers, including the local battalion commander and an officer who had recently returned from a campaign of sabotage in northern Silesia—a dangerous area owing to the hostility of the population. A young lieutenant was attached to us to act as our liaison officer with the A.K.

In the early afternoon we heard the sound of machine-gun fire about two miles away across the fields. Lieutenant Roman, the liaison officer, immediately sent out a patrol and posted double guards on the approaches to the house. In the evening he told us that a troop of Cossacks had been carrying out a *lapanka* in a village nearby.

'One or two villagers were shot, and I hear that a girl was raped.' He smiled and shrugged his shoulders.

However, he was sufficiently worried to suggest that we should move away from this area; he told us that the Germans had heard our aircraft two nights ago and were already making inquiries, and that the partisans here were not strong enough to protect us. He proposed to take us the following evening to the neighbourhood of Radomsko, where they were more numerous.

Next morning, 29th December, Currie and Galbraith, accompanied by Roman and his men, carried all our heavy kit except the two wireless sets and their necessary equipment into the woods and buried it in a concealed dugout. We could send for it later when we were more securely established. In fact we never saw it again; Roman was killed by the Germans a fortnight later while he was trying to recover it for us.

We began our journey at dusk, accompanied by Roman, Twardy and the escort. Nearly all our journeys in Poland were made at night, because the enemy had too healthy a respect for the partisans to venture into the country after dark; the dangerous hours for us were from dawn until late afternoon. Even so, we moved carefully as a small tactical unit, with scouts ahead, an advanced section and a rearguard. On this occasion two hay carts accompanied us and carried not only our kit but our entire party and all of the escort who were not required for scout or guard duty; for the paths were deep in snow and if the Germans were searching for us we should be wise not to leave too many tracks. As a further precaution we had to remove our badges of rank and parachute wings; in order to keep our identity from the peasants our guards were going to pass us off as escaped prisoners of war. There was little, I reflected, that the Poles did not know about their favourite word, *kotispiracja*.

We travelled all through the night, sometimes along forest tracks scarcely wide enough for the carts to pass, sometimes across open country over fields shining in the snow, with the faint lights of distant villages blinking at us through the dark. Three times on the way we stopped at peasant houses— twice for a glass of vodka and something to eat, and once when a cart broke an axle in a deep rut. Dawn was near when we came to a group of farm buildings, part of a large estate. Here we had hoped to sleep, but the manager would not have us; Cossacks came there every morning, he told us, to collect hay and so we should be well advised to move on quickly.

It was bright daylight when, tired and frozen, we stopped at a peasant's house in a village five miles further on. The two small rooms were already filled with people sleeping on the floor, all of them refugees from Warsaw. Indeed, all the country districts in this part of Poland were overcrowded with fugitives from Warsaw and from the eastern provinces occupied by the Red Army; it was a serious problem, which had already caused one epidemic of typhus and a general deterioration in health, aggravated by an acute shortage of medical supplies.

Late in the morning, after we had slept, we made our first wireless contact with London, who had the kindness to pass on to us a few messages from our families and friends. We left again in the evening and marched all night. There was no need now to hide our tracks, and so we walked beside the carts, glad enough to be able to keep warm rather than sit and freeze as we had done on the last journey; luckily we had all recovered from our parachuting injuries. Marching along with these cheerful Poles I began to feel a sense of security such as I had never known before in enemy country; their infectious self-confidence, their efficiency and their inspiring record convinced me that they would neither lead us into unnecessary danger nor fail us if we ran into trouble. In the latter belief I was soon enough proved right.

In cold grey twilight we skirted the small village of Wlynica and approached a large country house standing on a rise in open parkland surrounded by woods. We were evidently expected, for lights were burning in the windows downstairs. Roman went ahead to announce us. In a few minutes he returned and led us up a flight of stone steps into a large high-ceilinged hall dimly lit by oil lamps and filled with the scent of pine logs; there our hostess was waiting. In many countries over many years I have never seen a more beautiful woman than the slim, dark-haired girl who stepped from the shadows to meet us. Her great, dark eyes set in the face of a mourning Madonna smiled a welcome that brightened the gloom of the dying lamps and coloured the ugly neutral light of invading morning.

She greeted us in a soft, clear voice and led us to a small room where a meal was waiting. While we ate she asked us about the progress of the war. Her husband, an officer in the Polish Army, had been a prisoner of the Germans since 1939 in an Oflag in Posen; she counted the days till she could see him again.

We awoke late, relaxed and content. The war seemed very far away in this large and gracious house. Solly-Flood and I shared a room; we had bathed and were finishing dressing, savouring the luxury of comfort and leisure, when Hudson came in.

'There are some men coming up to the house,' he told us cheerfully. 'They're in uniform, and they look to me like Huns. But no one seems to be worrying and so I suppose it's all right.'

'Lots of the A.K. wear Hun uniforms or bits of them,' I pointed out. 'Are we in time for some breakfast, or do we go straight on to the vodka?'

Before he could answer, Roman and Currie hurried into the room, their faces tense.

'The Cossacks are here! We've got to hide. Hurry!'

Behind them I saw our hostess looking anxious but calm; she beckoned to Roman and murmured a few words to him before walking towards the hall.

'Follow me,' Roman ordered and led us at a run up a flight of stairs, along a corridor and up more stairs to a small, bare room with a single high window.

We sat on the floor not daring even to whisper, our cars strained for the sounds of a search; all I could hear was a murmur of voices and the muffled tread of boots in the hall below, but even those sounds seemed faint in comparison with the hammering of my own heart. I did not dare imagine what would happen to Madame Rubachowa if we were discovered in her house; I could not bear to think of her rotting in the horrors of Ravensbruck or Oswiecim—supposing Vlasov's ruffians let her get so far. As for ourselves, we should be lucky to meet no worse a death than a firing squad; Hitler had ordered the execution of all captured parachutists, and we could not hope to pass for long as escaped prisoners of war.

The tension grew in the tiny, dim room as the long drawn-out minutes passed and we listened to the shouts and clatter of boots on the two lower floors. Suddenly, with a wild rush of panic, I heard heavy steps on the stairs leading to our hide-out; I unbuttoned my holster and gripped my automatic as with agonizing deliberation they approached. The door was flung open and two grinning figures stood in the entrance beckoning us out. With almost sickening relief I recognized two of the servants who had waited on us the previous night.

Madame Rubachowa was an excellent hostess and went to a great deal of trouble to ensure our comfort and entertainment. Knowing that we wished to meet as many of her countrymen as might be useful to us in our mission she arranged a large luncheon party, to which she asked a few senior officers of the A.K. and some younger friends of hers who lived or were staying in the neighbourhood. I suppose the latter could be described as a mixture of local landowners and refugee intellectuals from Warsaw. We commented on the lack of interest that all of them, old and young, showed in the personalities of the exiled Polish Government in London—an indifference which we found everywhere in Poland. Mikolajczyk alone seemed to have a considerable following. It has often been remarked that governments in exile tend to lose touch with the people they claim to represent; they tend also to lose their respect.

Among the A.K. officers present was a certain Major Stefan, commanding the 25th Infantry Regiment. This unit, which was disbanded after Warsaw, retained one detachment of about forty men under arms, commanded by a very young and enthusiastic subaltern, Lieutenant Warta; he and his men were to be our escort in future, replacing Roman and Twardy.

That evening, the last day of the year, we left the house of Madame Rubachowa while it was still light; we were to see her again before long, in sadder circumstances. As we plodded across the fields towards the forest I was filled with a curious despondency, I might almost say a premonition of disaster; at the time I put it down to the melancholy of parting from Madame Rubachowa, intensified by the chill of the dead and snow-bound countryside and the grim, cold blackness of the fir trees rising out of the thickening gloom. I tried to shake it off during the three-mile journey through the woods which brought us to the village of Katarzyna; but my apprehension deepened as we approached the outskirts and came upon a wide, straight road whose hard, snow-covered surface was clearly designed to carry motor traffic.

In the village we were led to the house of a Madame Dembowska, a middle-aged widow with a shock of white hair above a mahogany face who fussed unceasingly about our food and comfort. The house, which resembled a small chalet, stood apart from the village, among open fields separating two areas of forest, and was surrounded by stables and outbuildings; the rooms were furnished in the heavy, gloomy style usually associated with aspidistras and antimacassars.

Our escort, whose quarters were in a group of huts on the edge of the nearest woods, invited us to join them after dinner to see in the New Year. When we arrived the small mess room was packed with cheerful, noisy partisans and heavy with the reek of sweat, tobacco and unwashed clothing; the lamplight flickered on the strong faces and sparkled in their fierce, eager eyes. At midnight we all stood to attention and sang the Polish National Anthem, a noble tune with brave words worthy of that heroic and indestructible people.

'*Jeszcze Polska nie zginela póki my zyjemy,*' (Poland is not yet lost while we are alive) we roared in chorus with more feeling than tune.

Next we sang the *Warszawianka*, the stirring call to battle written for the Warsaw rising of 1830—the rising whose defeat a year later inspired Chopin's 'Revolutionary' study. Bottles of vodka and plates of *zakaska* were passed round; we drank toasts to Poland and Britain, to Anglo-Polish friendship, to His Majesty the King of England, to Mikolajczyk, Churchill, and Roosevelt, and to the damnation of our common enemies; our hosts shook us by the hand, slapped us on the back and warmly if unsteadily embraced us all in turn. The smoky, overcrowded room rang with shouts: 'Down with the Curzon Line!' 'We want Wilna and Lvóv!' 'To Hell with the Lublin Committee!'

The party culminated in a series of *feux-de-joie* from the rifles of our escort. It was this final gesture, I am sure, that brought us trouble in the morning.

Before we went to bed Hudson made it clear to Lieutenant Warta that we should have to depend on him for all instructions concerning our security. He replied that his men made a habit of rising at five every morning and standing to until at least an hour after daybreak; he did not think it likely that the Germans would be very active on the morning of New Year's Day, but he would see that we were alerted just the same. And so ended the year 1944.

I awoke soon after seven with a bursting bladder, a natural consequence of the previous evening. I went outside to relieve it and was on my way back to the house when I heard a dull rumbling from the direction of the road we had crossed the previous evening; distant at first, it became noticeably louder as I listened. It was a sound I had first heard in the days of the Spanish Civil War: the sound of approaching tanks. Hurrying into the room where the rest of the party were sleeping I shook Hudson awake.

'Bill, I don't want to alarm you, but I'm jolly sure I hear tanks. And they're coming closer.'

I had hardly finished speaking when one of our escort burst into the room to confirm my fears. We threw on our clothes, grabbed our carbines and slung over our shoulders the small haversacks containing our signal codes and essential personal kit. Currie and Galbraith seized the smaller of our two wireless sets and the portable hand generator; it would be calamitous if we were to lose our own wireless links with London and Italy. If the Germans were indeed coming after us there was no hope of saving our heavy, more powerful set or any of our equipment that we could not carry ourselves.

We were not left long in doubt. While we made our preparations for flight the sound of the tanks grew louder; we could also hear the roar of heavy lorries grinding along in low gear. From close at hand came Warta's voice rapping curt orders to our escort. Solly-Flood and I ran out to see what was happening. Turning right outside the door I ran for the shelter of a barn and peered round the corner in the direction of the noise.

I saw four medium tanks, their guns pointing straight at us, moving at a tangent across a field three or four hundred yards to my front; behind them, in a clump of trees, several large lorries were disgorging green-uniformed soldiers. Fascinated by these preparations for our destruction I was brought sharply to my senses by the crack of an exploding shell in a ditch a few yards away; at the same time a burst of machine-gun fire spattered the walls of my barn. As I jumped back into cover I heard, from my left, the clatter of a Bren; with astonished admiration I saw that a detachment of our escort had emplaced itself behind a low bank and was firing on the tanks and the advancing infantry: some twenty-five Poles with rifles and one light machine-gun were taking on four tanks and at least a hundred well-armed Germans.

I heard my name shouted and, turning, saw Warta and the rest of our party beckoning to me from the door of the chalet. Warta was talking to Currie in short, urgent sentences; he ran to join his men and Currie translated his instructions.

'We're to make for those woods,' he told us, 'while Warta holds off the Germans. Once we've got clear he will break off the action and try to join us. We have to cross some open ground first, so we must run.'

The patch of open ground between the house and the woods was some three hundred yards wide; we should be crossing it in full view of the enemy and clearly outlined against the snow. Half-way across was a thin plantation of young firs; we sprinted for this, darting from the cover of the chalet like flushed rabbits and sweating with fear as we forced our heavy feet through the clogging snow. If there is any more disagreeable experience in warfare than that of running away under fire I hope I never meet it. There is none of the hot excitement of attack, but much more of the danger; the blood trickled icily in my veins and with each step my muscles contracted, anticipating the impact of a bullet; my throat felt dry and constricted and I had a violent urge to vomit. Bullets in plenty sang over our heads and smacked into the ground all round us as we ran. But fortunately the tanks were concentrating their attention on the heroic Bren-gunner and his companions; one machine-gun would have finished the lot of us. As it was, we were beyond the effective range of Schmeizers, and the riflemen seemed to be poor shots.

We reached the fir plantation without a casualty and paused a moment for breath, sitting in the snow because the saplings were not tall enough to hide us when we stood. Here we dumped the hand generator in a ditch; it was much too heavy for a running man and Currie had done well to bring it so far. It was cunningly hidden and Currie retrieved it himself later the same day.

From behind us broke loud on our ears the sound of battle: long bursts of machine-gun fire, the vicious crack of tank shells and the faint popping of rifles.

'Jesus!' sighed Solly-Flood, 'aren't we the brave boys? Running off to the woods while the Poles stand and take the rap. This is a shit's job.'

'You know our orders,' snapped Hudson. 'What's more, so do the Poles. Come on, let's go.'

All together we broke cover, spreading out as we ran across the last hundred and fifty yards that separated us from the shelter of the great forest. But the fighting now was in Katarzyna village, around the house of poor Madame Dembowska, and no one paid attention to our flight.

Ten minutes later, when we had hidden the wireless at the rendezvous Warta had indicated, we returned to the edge of the wood to peer through the trees at Katarzyna. The firing had died away; thick smoke was rising from Madame Dembowska's farm buildings, and above the roar and crackle of the flames we heard the Germans calling orders in that half-bellow, half-scream which in their army was the voice of command.

Dismally we wandered back to the large plantation of saplings where we had left the wireless. We were sure we had seen the last of Warta and his men, and it was bitter to feel that but for our presence they could have faded into the forest without a fight. Madame Dembowska, too, would be in trouble when the Germans found all our equipment in her house. The fact that she had not invited us was unlikely to be accepted as an excuse.

These painful thoughts occupied us in silence for half an hour. We were the more astounded, therefore, as well as delighted when Warta himself appeared with the greater part of his detachment—the rest, he explained, were on guard or patrol duties. In the whole action he had lost only one man—the Bren-gunner, who had certainly courted death and who had been killed instantaneously by a machine-gun burst from one of the tanks; his body had been recovered and would be buried in the morning. Warta had broken off the action after ten minutes, rightly considering that he had given us plenty of time to get away. He claimed to have inflicted casualties on the Germans, and he must have given them a mauling, because they had not cared to pursue him. By any standards his performance was an epic of skill, self-sacrifice, and valour—those qualities that had forged the grand and tragic drama of Warsaw.

We stayed in the woods for most of the day, with guards posted to warn us if the Germans should return. Now that they knew there was a party of British parachutists in the neighbourhood they might well conduct an intensive pacyfikacja and beat us out of our hiding place; we must therefore be clear of the district before morning.

In the late afternoon we went back to Katarzyna. Madame Dembowska's house was deserted but undamaged; the Germans had confined their destruction to the out-buildings. As we feared, our unhappy hostess had been taken to Czestochowa; we learned later that she was released next day frightened but unharmed. After the battle the Germans had brought their casualties into her house, and Warta pointed with grim satisfaction to the blood-spattered dining-room table on which they had been laid for operation.

All our equipment, of course, had gone; Solly-Flood, who had been a Brigade Intelligence Officer, treated us to a graphic description of German Security Officers examining with painstaking thoroughness each article of our kit and evaluating its military and political significance. From our point of view the most serious losses—we did not then appreciate how serious— were our heavy wireless set and petrol generator; the smaller set had not the necessary power, and the hand generator that Currie had saved gave continual trouble. We were soon reduced to handing our encoded signals to the Home Army for transmission; only when we returned to London did we learn that neither Perkins nor Threlfall had received any of them.

We never discovered what had brought the Germans to Katarzyna. Warta suspected that members of the Armja Ludowa, of whom there were several in the village, had informed on us in the hope that we should be captured and their rivals consequently discredited. There was no evidence to support his theory, and it seems more likely that the *feux-de-joie* on New Year's Eve attracted the enemy's attention.

We did not linger in Katarzyna, but in the last daylight began our journey through the woods. We marched fast and with few halts or rests; although it was unlikely that we should meet Germans abroad at so late an hour we took no chances and moved in our usual formation. Warta's senior sergeant had found himself a fine horse and rode up and down the column all night, checking the distances between the main body and the advance guard and rearguard, keeping an eye on the scouts and encouraging us all in his strong, cheerful voice. He was a man of fine physique and commanding presence with a long experience of partisan warfare; in his fur hat, with his cavalry bandolier and his rifle slung across his back, he looked to me like some famous Cossack hetman—a Mazeppa or a Stenka Razin—as he rode along the line in the thickening dusk.

In the small hours of the morning we reached our destination, the village of Dudki. We had brought with us the body of the gallant Bren-gunner, and at daybreak we assembled to give him burial. There was no priest, but the service was read by the Battalion Commander, whom we found awaiting us at Dudki. As we stood around the open grave on a bare, windswept mound outside the village, blinking our red-rimmed eyes against the harsh and hostile light of that snowbound dawn, I wondered, as I think we all did, how we could hope to justify this man's sacrifice for our safety. When the body, wrapped in a Polish flag, was lowered into the ground, when the volley was fired and the earth sprinkled, then we felt the full shame and bitterness of our flight. On the wooden cross that marked his grave I wished I could have written Simonides's epitaph on the Spartan dead at Thermopylae, who also died defying hopeless odds.

Afterwards Warta told us sadly: 'We can not even tell his family, because they live in eastern Poland—beyond your Curzon Line.'

We left Dudki immediately after the funeral and tramped for two hours through the forest until we came to a collection of scattered farm-houses known as Maly Jacków. In one of these we prepared to spend the day, but at noon Warta hustled us outside and led us at a run into the woods: detachments of *Feldgendarmerei* had arrived at the next village and were asking if any British officers had been seen. Although they did not visit Maly Jacków we remained in the forest until twilight, nursing our ragged nerves among the fir trees.

Our guest at dinner that night was a very senior officer of the Armja Krajowa, the colonel in command of the Czestochowa Inspectorate. A friendly person and anxious to put us at our ease, he frequently assured us that nobody in Poland felt bitterly towards our country because Britain was too far away to give much help to Poland; but, he added fiercely, the Poles would fight to the last man to preserve their independence from Russia. We forbore to ask him how they could hope to fight so powerful a neighbour without a single aeroplane or piece of ordnance at their disposal. At that time, of course, the whole problem seemed academic and unreal; none of us could foretell the hideous future, none of us remembered Stalin's pledge to Hitler in 1939 that Poland should never rise again; least of all could we suppose that those apostles of freedom, Britain and the United States, would underwrite by treaty such an odious conspiracy.

In the middle of our conversation the Colonel quietly informed us that the following afternoon we were to meet the Commander-in-Chief of the Polish Home Army—the successor to General Bór-Komorowski. This romantic and mysterious figure, whose very name was concealed from us until our return to London, was travelling swiftly and secretly throughout the country, reviving and reorganizing those shattered remnants of the A.K. that had survived the catastrophe of Warsaw. Tomorrow he would be staying nearby; twenty-four hours later he might be in Kraków, Lódz, Póznan, or even Warsaw.

In the early afternoon of 3rd January we set off from the farm-house with a strong escort under the command of Warta's senior sergeant; a horse-drawn sledge came with us to bring us home in the evening. It was still light when we arrived at a large and comfortable mansion surrounded by tall trees. Inside we found a blaze of lights and a crowd of people, nearly all of them in civilian clothes; among them I recognized an old acquaintance, Colonel Rudkowski, a close friend of Perkins, whom I had met several times in London and once, briefly, in Italy.

Rudkowski was already a senior officer of the Polish Air Force when war broke out in 1939. He was a short, square man of about fifty-five who combined the fierce patriotism and mature cunning of his race with the irresponsible ana disarming sense of fun of a preparatory schoolboy. His courage was attested by his two ribbons of the Virtuti Militari, the Polish Victoria Cross: his skill by the post he had held until recently of Air Officer Commanding of the Polish Fighter Group in Britain, and by his present assignment, which was to build the foundations of a new Polish Air Force. He had parachuted into Poland on the night of our arrival in Italy.

Looking in his civilian clothes more like a character out of Murder Incorporated than the gallant and distinguished officer he was, Rudkowski pounced on us in the hall and led us directly to a small, trim library where we were presented without formality to the Commander-in-Chief.

Of General Okulicki's appearance I can recall little, and that would probably be inaccurate because I only met him this once; of his history I knew only that he had commanded a Polish division in the field under General Anders. What I do remember well is his soft voice, his courteous, almost deferential manner, his quiet, convincing self-confidence, and his passionate sincerity and belief in his own people and his mission among them. He had no illusions about the difficulties ahead of him and meagre hope for their solution; but as I listened to him I knew that this man would make any sacrifice to nourish the starving spirit of his shattered army, caring nothing for his own safety in the cause of his country's freedom. With his life he was to prove me right.

The details of our talk are no longer important: the German Army order of battle in Poland, the morale of the Armja Krajowa after Warsaw, the military and political intentions of the Russians—all these have long reposed in the waste paper basket of history. But one sentence of General Okulicki's still stays in my mind: despite their treachery at Warsaw, he told us, he would continue to treat the Russians as allies and would do all in his power to co-operate with them; but he could not trust their word. Later, in his anxiety to save his country, he trusted them too much.

After the Russian occupation of Poland and the end of the war Stalin invited the leaders of the Armja Krajowa, who had gone into hiding, to come to Moscow for discussions on the future government of Poland; the invitation was issued through the Chief of the Russian General Staff, who publicly gave his word of honour as a General Officer of the Red Army that the delegates would come to no harm in Russia and would be allowed to return to Poland without interference. In spite of their natural misgivings General Okulicki and the other leaders of the Home Army felt it their duty, in the interests of Poland, to accept this invitation. On arrival in Moscow they were all immediately arrested and imprisoned in the Lubianka. They were brought to trial on charges of sabotaging the communications of the Red Army in Poland and operating clandestine wireless stations; on evidence which in Britain would not even have secured their committal for trial they were convicted and sentenced to penal servitude for life. General Okulicki has died in prison; there is no news yet of his companions.

After the conference was over I found Rudkowski again. He escorted me to a large buffet laid out in a room leading from the hall, and pointed to a pair of decanters, each filled with a clear spirit.

'Which do you like?' he asked me, 'Vodka or bimba?' Bimba is an inferior kind of vodka made from potatoes; it has a filthy taste, a violent kick, and a horrible effect on the head and stomach. But it is cheap and plentiful and so, out of politeness, I asked for bimba. Rudkowski gave me a wicked grin as he handed me my glass.

'I never touch bimba, only vodka.' And he poured himself a drink from the other decanter.

We left Maly Jaków long before dawn, and after a five-mile march reached Redziny, a few small houses on the edge of a great forest.

Our hosts, an old peasant and his wife, moved with remarkable good humour into their kitchen, leaving the other two rooms for ourselves and our wireless equipment. While we were there we worked late every night, drafting and encoding signals to London reporting the action at Katarzyna, our meeting with General Okulicki and information we acquired from our numerous visitors—unaware, of course, that we were losing our sleep to no purpose.

At five o'clock each morning Warta routed us out of bed and led us into the forest, where he kept us until two in the afternoon. This was the usual pattern of our lives for the rest of our time with the Home Army; there were many German and Cossack foraging parties around, and the Poles were taking no more chances after Katarzyna. Throughout the daytime we remained in a perpetual state of alert, ready to move at a minute's notice; we slept, of course, in our clothes.

Our first visitors were two junior officers of the Home Army, Lieutenants Jerzy and Alm; they were to be attached to us in future as liaison officers with the Home Army command. Alm was an intelligent young man with a fresh complexion and reddish brown hair who came from Western Poland; a lively, friendly companion he was gifted with unusual courage and resource, as his story showed. In order to secure the release of his father, who had been sent to Dachau, he had volunteered for the German army and had soon won himself a commission. As an officer he had little difficulty in persuading the authorities to free his father, who went into hiding. Alm then obtained a posting to the Russian front, where he skilfully—or luckily—contrived to get wounded just badly enough to be sent to Poland for convalescence; once he was back in his own country he deserted and joined the Armja Krajowa. Jerzy was a very tall, thin young man with a quiet, serious manner; a brother of the beautiful Madame Rubachowa, he had all his sister's gentle charm. Both officers proved themselves invaluable during the next ten days.

M. Siemienski, our next caller, was a prominent landowner from the neighbouring town of Zytno; he was a saddened, soft-spoken man in his middle or late fifties whose principal interest was farming but who looked more like a university don than a squire. His only son had been killed four months earlier with the A.K. in battle against the Germans. With him came two young women who worked in the courier service of the Home Army; one of them was his daughter, a gay, pretty, dark-haired girl of about twenty; the other was married to a Polish officer now in a German prisoner-of-war camp. Siemienski was a member of the *Uprawa*, an organization of landowners whose principal object was to keep the Home Army supplied with food, money, clothing, and shelter.

On the third evening of our stay at Redziny we were in the middle of supper when there was a commotion outside and the sound of urgent whispering; Warta swept into the house, followed by Jerzy. The latter spoke without preliminary greeting.

'Please hurry with your meal. We have just heard there is to be a *pacyfikacja* in this area tomorrow morning. We are leaving at once.'

We marched all night in grim silence, for we were all short of sleep and only too liable to snap at one another when we spoke. At first light we arrived, grey-faced and bleary-eyed, at a small settlement of poor peasant houses. Before the war the place had been a colony of *Volksdeutsche*—German settlers—but after the occupation these had been moved to richer holdings near Radomsko and the dispossessed Poles resettled here. Our house was filthy and almost bare of furniture and we slept on grubby pallets on the earthen floor; but the owners, a small family reduced to a state of apathy by poverty and suffering, did their best to make us comfortable. In return for their hospitality we gave them a few sovereigns, which they accepted courteously but with apparent indifference; adversity had drained them of all feeling.

During the three days of our stay we became infested with the most prolific and ferocious crop of lice that I at least have ever encountered. For the Spanish, Albanian, and Montenegrin louse I had learnt to acquire a certain tolerance, even affection; but these creatures bit with an increasing and fanatical fury that excluded all hope of sleep and comfort.

On 11th January we returned to Redziny. The Germans, having caught no one in their net, had withdrawn; but we did not relax our security measures during the five days we were there. Any temptation towards slackness that we might have felt was soon dispelled by the regular appearance every morning and afternoon of a pair of Storch reconnaissance aircraft; they flew steadily back and forth over the village, and it was soon clear to us that they were trying to locate our wireless by D/F. General Okulicki had warned us of this very danger. We had plenty of traffic for Galbraith's skeds—every day we received fresh reports from different sources on military, political, and economic conditions; but we could not risk operating the set while the aircraft were around, and so we were obliged to hand most of our messages to Jerzy or Alm to be sent on Polish links.

The presence of the two aircraft seemed to confirm our suspicions that the Germans already had a good idea of our whereabouts; we braced ourselves for an unpleasant period of *pacyfikacja* and pursuit. It never came. Instead, on the night of 13th January we were startled to hear the sound of heavy gunfire rolling towards us from the east. As the hours passed the barrage intensified to such a climax that we knew it could mean only one thing: the Russians were attacking on the Vistula; a new offensive had begun.

Neither the Poles nor ourselves—not even, it seemed, the Germans—had expected the Red Army to begin its drive towards the Oder before the spring; nor could we foresee that it would meet with so little resistance. The bombardment continued all night without interruption. During the next two days numbers of enemy fighters and bombers flew overhead, but the Poles told us that the Germans were withdrawing. Warta kept us in the woods from early morning until dusk, for we were so close to the battle now that he had every reason to fear an intensive round-up by Security forces; but so swift was the German retreat that we were left in peace.

On the 15th we heard that Russian tanks were in Maluszyn, on the western bank of the Pilica, which meant that they had breached the last line of defence before the Oder and the German frontier; we could expect them to reach us within twenty-four hours. Our standing orders, when this happened, were to present ourselves at the nearest Red Army headquarters.

The same afternoon Jerzy brought us an invitation from his sister to a party at Włynica. We should not be returning to Redziny, and so we piled all our kit onto one farm cart and ourselves onto another and set off soon after dark. We travelled slowly and with extra caution, every man on the alert for signs of trouble; we avoided all villages and roads, keeping as much as possible to the forest and pausing for a thorough reconnaissance whenever we had to cross a patch of open country. The district was crawling with enemy patrols, and we had no desire at this stage for a brush with desperate Cossacks or S.S.; nor could we be certain of the temper of any Armja Ludowa forces we might meet at this moment of their masters' triumph.

We did in fact run into an A.L. patrol soon after we had started, in the depths of a very dark wood; they were belligerent at first and called on us to surrender. We leaped off our wagon and took up battle stations at the sound of peremptory shouting and the menacing clatter of rifle bolts; but after a brief parley they decided that we outnumbered them, and so they let us pass.

Madame Rubachowa's party was going briskly when we arrived.

Her guests included almost everyone we had met there before, and many more of her friends from the district. The atmosphere was much less restrained than on our previous visit; there was music and dancing, and tables laden with vodka, champagne, and food of every kind. But the evening sparkled with a forced, determined hilarity that was terrible and tragic; the underlying tension and anxiety crackled from room to room.

We had hoped for a final interview with General Okulicki, and Hudson had accepted tonight's invitation partly in the hope of meeting some representative of the G.O.C. But he was disappointed, for the only two senior officers present were our old friend Major Stefan, Warta's commanding officer, and the deputy commander of the Czestochowa Inspectorate, neither of whom could—or would—give us any idea of the General's whereabouts. They had received no fresh instructions and therefore proposed to carry out those they had been given several months ago—to disband all partisan units on the arrival of the Russians and go into hiding. Home Army formations were making no attempt to harass the Germans. After Warsaw they could hardly be expected to, even if they had been given warning of the offensive; besides, the hostile tone of recent Russian broadcasts can have left them in no doubt of the treatment they might expect from the Red Army.

As the evening progressed, the pace of the party quickened to a macabre and frenzied gaiety whose implications could no longer be concealed. However much these people hated the Germans—and there was not a man or woman in the room who had not lost at least one close relative fighting against them—they literally dreaded the Russians. Tonight they were saying good-bye to the world they had always known. The German occupation had brought unbelievable hardship and tragedy to their country and their class: Russian rule, they foresaw, meant extinction for both.

The dancing grew faster and wilder: waltzes and foxtrots were abandoned for the whirling, stamping folk dances of Poland—the Krakowiak, Oberek, and Kujawiak; glasses were filled, emptied at once and immediately filled again as people drank with an intense, desperate urgency, as though they would never be drinking again, as though they must not leave a drop for the invading Russians. Beautiful and solitary among these fantastic bacchanals wandered our hostess, her air of gentle melancholy dissolving in a gay and friendly smile as she talked to each of her guests. She told me that she would leave for the north as soon as the party was over, and make for Poznan, where she hoped to find her husband.

It was after midnight when we left Wlynica and took the road to Katarzyna, as we had done on New Year's Eve; Warta and his men accompanied us, for they had been ordered to remain with us until the arrival of the Russians. We stayed in a small cottage near the village: at such a time it might be wise to sleep away from large houses.

We awoke to a noisy morning. From the north, where the main road ran west towards Czestochowa, came the rumble of tanks and the continuous roar of motor transport, often punctuated by bursts of machine-gun fire and the thunder of artillery; the sky above us was filled with the whine and drone of aircraft, and to east and west the air vibrated with the thud of heavy bombing.

Our hand generator had finally broken down, but Galbraith's batteries had just enough charge left in them for a last contact with London; this contact brought us a brief signal, confirming our orders to hand ourselves over to the Russians and reassuring us that our names and location and the nature of our mission had been communicated to the Russian political and military authorities and to the British Military Mission in Moscow.

At noon we learned that Russian armoured spearheads were already well to the west of us; there seemed no reason to keep our escort with us any longer—indeed there was every reason to let them disband and hide themselves while they could. They had refused to leave us the day before when we had made the same suggestion, but now it was easy to convince them; they left us the same afternoon, each one shaking us firmly by the hand and giving us a cracking salute before he marched away proudly into his future of hazard and doom. Sorrowfully we took our leave of these men who had hazarded their lives for so many years to uphold the imperishable honour of their country.

Our problem now was to find the Russians without running into any of the large groups of defeated Germans, Turkomen, and Cossacks that were wandering about the country; Vlasov's troops, especially, would be in an ugly mood. Hudson decided to send Currie and Solly-Flood to try and make contact with a Russian divisional or corps headquarters; they left soon after the Poles, telling us to expect them back in the morning.

Much to our surprise we received an invitation to dine that night with Madame Dembowska; we had thought that after New Year's Day she would want no more of our company. Hudson, Galbraith, and I set off for her house before it was quite dark, keeping a careful look-out on the way. It was well that we were vigilant, because we saw the Russian patrol before they saw us—in a wood a few hundred yards from Madame Dembowska's house; there were two soldiers moving slowly through the trees, their tommy-guns at the ready. It was unnecessary as well as dangerous to try to avoid them, and so we stood still and called to them, waving in what we hoped would seem a friendly, carefree manner.

They came towards us slowly and suspiciously, their guns pointed straight at our stomachs and their fingers on the triggers. When they were close Hudson, who spoke some Russian, explained who we were and showed them a card, with which each of us had been issued in London, displaying a Union Jack and a message in printed cyrillic letters which began, I remember, 'Ya Anglichanin.'

They shed some of their hostility and accompanied us the rest of the way, still keeping us covered in a manner suggesting that they would stand no nonsense. I hate to speculate on Madame Dembowska's feelings when she opened the door to us; first we had brought the Germans to her house: now we were bringing the Russians. Perhaps she had expected them anyway, and hoped that our presence would have a restraining influence; because she welcomed us with warmth and even affection. One of our guards now left us to fetch his officers, while his companion made himself comfortable squatting on the floor of the dining-room. There were three or four other guests for dinner, all of them farmers or professional men from the district.

We were starting to eat when a Russian captain and two lieutenants walked into the room and saluted smartly; they were all from one of the armoured formations which had been leading the advance and were for the moment resting in reserve. The captain, who acted as spokesman for the others was a rangy, fair-complexioned young Ukrainian with a frank and humorous face; Madame Dembowska asked them rather nervously to join us for dinner—an unnecessary invitation, for they told her in a firm though friendly manner to fetch a lot more vodka and be quick about it.

At the end of the meal we toasted each other and the British and Russian leaders; the captain himself proposed the health of President Roosevelt—as well he might. He then launched into a long set speech, obviously carefully rehearsed because he paused from time to time to ask his colleagues whether he had omitted anything.

In outline his argument was the same as that of the Russian parachutists of whom our friends in the Armja Krajowa had told us: there was a long defence of Russia's attitude to the Curzon Line, coupled with a statement that the Poles would be well compensated on their western borders; there was much praise of the Lublin Committee, and there were repeated assurances that the Russians would make no attempt to impose Communism but would leave Poland as soon as the Germans were beaten.

His concluding words were directed at us: in the most charming way he told us that the Red Army had been holding three hundred German divisions for the greater part of the war, while the British and Americans were even now containing only sixty-seven. When Hudson gently reminded him of the enormous material help Russia had received under Lend-Lease he smiled and admitted that of course Lend-Lease had been very useful, graciously adding that the tanks supplied by Britain had been especially valuable and that one of the Brigades in this offensive was equipped entirely with British tanks.

In fact it was a very successful party for all except poor Madame Dembowska, whose entire store of vodka was drunk in the course of the evening—without, I must add, producing any noticeable effect on her Russian guests. Before we left, the Captain invited us to drink in his mess the following evening.

There was no sign of Solly-Flood and Currie all next day; although anxious about them we thought they had probably been detained by the Russians and would show up in due course. Our party with the tank officers that night was brief but memorable. Their mess was in a small wooden house on the outskirts of the village; about a dozen officers stood at a long table laden with bottles of what appeared to be cherry vodka and plates of zakaska—small pieces of cheese, smoked ham and sausage. When we were seated our glasses—half-pint tumblers—were filled almost to the top with vodka by the Ukrainian captain, who indicated that he expected no heel-taps. We rose as the first toast was called: '*Pobeda!*—to the victory of the Allies!' Jauntily I raised my tumbler and poured the contents down my throat; a moment later, if I had had any voice left, I would have screamed.

Mr. P. G. Wodehouse once described a certain drink as having an effect— I quote from memory—'as though someone had touched off a bomb in the old bean and then taken a stroll through the stomach with a lighted torch.' That is a fair description of what we had just swallowed; it burned like molten lead and tasted strongly of petrol. It was in fact a mixture of the neat spirit used as the basis of vodka, and the petrol on which they drove their tanks— camouflaged with fruit juice.

In fairness to our hosts I must add that they drank the same liquor and seemed to love it; moreover they swallowed several glassfulls, whereas we surreptitiously emptied our refills on the floor. I cannot say what was the ultimate effect on them because we left after half an hour, but I know that I did not recover my voice that evening.

XIII

CAPTIVITY

Early next morning, 18th January, a Dodge truck arrived outside our house to take us to the Russian Army Corps headquarters at Zytno; in it were Currie, a Russian major and two soldiers. The major was far from friendly, and curtly ordered us to pack up our things and get into the truck.

Currie warned us that our reception at headquarters was not going to be an affair of handshakes, vodka and caviare. He and Solly-Flood had been received with arrogance and suspicion; they had been taken before a major-general and subjected to a long interrogation; the general had called them liars, made them hand over their arms and identity cards and sent them under guard to the house of M. Siemienski, where Solly-Flood was now detained.

As soon as we turned into the main road we came upon a continuous stream of Russian trucks, guns, and tanks rolling westward in the opposite direction to ours; all the way to Zytno we passed the same column of vehicles driving nose to tail with scarcely a break. On this and on subsequent journeys we observed that at least two thirds of the motor transport of the Red Army was of American or British Commonwealth manufacture; the fighting vehicles, on the other hand, and the artillery were almost all Russian. It is fair to say that without this aid from Lend-Lease the Russians would not have had the mobility to follow up their victories even if they had been able to achieve them.

The armour was mixed indiscriminately with administrative and supply vehicles, jeeps, civilian cars, and a surprising amount of horse transport. But traffic control seemed to be well organized; road forks and junctions were already clearly signposted in Cyrillic, and traffic police—usually enormous girls in military uniform—were stationed at the major cross-roads.

Apart from a brief delaying action on the Pilica the Germans had put up little or no resistance; their object had been to withdraw their forces intact behind the line of the Oder. They seemed largely to have succeeded, because we saw very little destroyed or abandoned equipment and only two columns of German prisoners, of about fifty men each.

Corps H.Q. at Zytno occupied two small rooms of a peasant's cottage. Forcing his way through a crowd of lounging guards and orderlies, who stiffened to attention as he passed, the major led us to the inner room, where a lieutenant-general and several staff officers were standing before a large coloured wall map of the front. The general, a lean, dark man of thirty-five or forty with a grave, intelligent face and a very quiet voice, courteously acknowledged our salutes and pointed to some hard chairs round a small table; his interest was con-fined to the course of the battle. An officer with a field telephone in one hand passed a series of reports to the Corps Commander, who commented briefly on each, while another officer marked the map with coloured pencils. The General gave his orders confidently and without hesitation; nothing seemed to be put in writing.

We rose to our feet as the door opened to admit a square, thick-set officer with a pale, flabby face who wore on his greatcoat the gilded epaulettes of a major-general. He made no attempt to acknowledge our salutes, but sat down across the table from us and stared at us for a while without speaking; a faint sneer twisted the corners of his mouth.

He brought with him a Polish-speaking subaltern, who interpreted for him, as Currie did for us. Hudson explained who we were, adding that Moscow had already received all our particulars; he showed his identity card, but the major-general refused to look at it, saying that it was probably a German forgery. We were then subjected to a barrage of questions: What was the name of our organization in London, and who commanded it? What were the times of our skeds, what frequencies and what codes were we using? Most sinister of all, who were our Polish contacts?

Hudson answered politely that we were not allowed to give this in-formation, but that our bona fides could easily be verified from Moscow; the general laughed unpleasantly and said that this was a fine way to treat allies. We felt the same. It was clear to us that he did not seriously doubt our story but was going out of his way to be offensive; it was also fairly certain that he was not an officer of the Red Army, but of the N.K.V.D.[1] He concluded the interview by ordering us to hand over our arms, documents, and wireless equipment; our protests were contemptuously dismissed and we were obliged to comply. Hudson's parting threat to take up the matter with higher authority in Moscow met with a very nasty laugh.

We were sent under escort to Siemienski's house, which seemed to have been taken over as the administrative headquarters of the Army Corps. Troops thronged the building; in the grounds were parked vehicles, guns and 'Katiusha' multiple rocket batteries, which we were never allowed to approach. We found Solly-Flood, still seething from his treatment of the night before, and Siemienski and his daughter, his mother, and his niece, who welcomed us with joy and relief—either because they had feared for our

---

[1] *Narodny Komisariat Vnutrennik Dyel* (People's Commissariat for Home Affairs) formerly known as the OGPU and now the MVD. This organization controls not only the secret police and forced labour camps, but all the forces of public order, such as the municipal police and militia. It is independent of the fighting services and has its own aircraft, infantry, artillery, and armour, in which a large proportion of the rank and file are Asiatic troops.

safety or because they hoped for our protection; perhaps both. Siemienski's niece was an attractive blonde of about the same age as her cousin; Madame Siemienska, a small, white-haired old lady with fine, delicate features, walked erect and proud among the noisy Mongol soldiers as though she was not even aware of their presence. As well as their uninvited guests they were housing some forty Polish refugees, most of them from Warsaw.

We lived, ate, and slept in a large ground-floor room at the front of the house, formerly the drawing-room but now denuded of most of its furniture. We were committed to the charge of a Russian major, who in the three days that we stayed there never let us out of his sight. There was, of course, no privacy for any of us—the Siemienskis or ourselves. They bore their humiliation with a fine dignity and good humour.

Apart from the uncertainty of their future, their sufferings were already considerable. Siemienski owned an estate of between four and five thousand acres—most of it timber, the rest farmland; if he was lucky he might be allowed to retain twelve acres and a few rooms in his own house. A committee had been formed of his own estate workers to manage the property, but they depended entirely upon his technical skill and experience. The Russians had requisitioned all the livestock in the district without compensation, and so there would be no means of cultivating the land in the spring; the Red Army's method of living off the country during an advance was as devastating as their 'scorched earth' policy in retreat.

These troops belonged to Marshal Koniev's Second Ukrainian Army; among them was a high proportion of Mongols. I believe their behaviour was no worse than that of other Soviet armies in occupied territory; there seemed to be little difference between their treatment of the peoples they were supposed to be liberating and those they were conquering.

The soldiers quartered on Siemienski behaved towards him and his family with calculated brutality and contempt. They broke up his furniture for firewood, they pilfered every article of value and marked or spoilt what they did not care to take away; they urinated and defecated in every room, sparing only our living quarters because the major in charge of us stopped them; the hall, the stairs and the passages were heaped and spattered with piles of excrement, the walls and floors were splashed with liquor, spittle, and vomit, the whole building stank like an untended latrine. It is a pity that those Communists in France and in Australia who declared a few years ago that they would welcome the Red Army as liberators never saw that army at its work of liberation.

Towards the girls, whenever they were out of our sight, they showed a deliberately boorish and arrogant manner, insulting, threatening, and sometimes hitting them. The officers behaved better; the girls could always put them to shame by the use of the phrase, *nie kulturny*, for the Red Army officer is very touchy about his 'culture'. But the officers had no authority over their men off duty. On parade and in action I am told that orders are obeyed instantly and to the letter; here, however, the officers seemed to mix with their troops without distinction of rank, and their few attempts to check indiscipline and hooliganism were either ignored or—as we ourselves observed—answered with ridicule and defiance. To us they made no pretence of being friendly; one bumptious little captain told us with spiteful conviction:

'Don't worry. When we've beaten the Germans we're going on to fight the British.'

He at least did not doubt our nationality.

For Madame Siemienska, however, the troops displayed a reluctant respect; she was, I have said, an old lady of formidable personality, and her obvious indifference to whatever fate might overtake her, coupled with her unconcealed scorn for her captors, filled them with surprise and awe. On the evening before we left she came into our room and, sitting down at the piano, began to play some Chopin; soon the Russian officers, and then the little Mongols, gathered round until there was scarcely room to move in the close-packed circle. With superb skill and with a fierce, exultant pride she played the *Révolutionnaire*, the 'Death of Poland', the Polonaise and the first two Ballades. She ended with the *Warszawianka* and the Polish National Anthem. Then, with a stiff little bow she wished us good-night and, looking straight ahead of her, walked quietly away through the ranks of applauding Russians.

On the afternoon of 21st January we left Zytno in a truck, escorted by the major and an armed guard. We spent that night in Radomsko, where we dined with two Russian colonels who noted with apparent sympathy Hudson's complaints against our treatment as prisoners instead of as allies. Prisoners, however, we remained and were even prevented from speaking to the owners of the house in which we slept.

Our status was made clearer the next day. In the town of Jędrzejów, some sixty miles to the south-east, we were handed over to a major of the N.K.V.D. and two subalterns, who kept us confined under guard for five days in a small and dirty room; only once were we allowed outside the house, when we were taken for a brief walk under the supervision of one of the subalterns, a supercilious young man with very close-set eyes who wore a Cossack hat and talked German to us in tones of studied insolence. We were firmly segregated from all contact with the Poles; our protests were disregarded and when we asked to speak to a senior officer the major simply laughed and told us to shut up. He was a swaggering, loud-voiced ruffian, clearly happy in his work.

The final humiliation came on 26th January. We were crammed into the back of a lorry with a dozen Russian soldiers and a glum, tubby little man with a red face who wore the blue uniform of General Vlasov's army; he seemed to be an officer and spoke fluent Russian. He sat on the floor in deep gloom, his head on his chest and his hands plunged in the pockets of his greatcoat. The soldiers addressed him as 'Vlasov' and from time to time prodded good-humouredly at his tummy with their rifles, which did nothing to cheer him up. A few miles from Czestochowa, which was our destination, the lorry stopped beside a long, low stone building, and all but two of our escort climbed down.

'Come on, Vlasov!' they shouted cheerfully. 'This is you.'

I felt sorry for the little man as he climbed very slowly and deliberately over the back of the truck, lost and lonely and afraid; his guards marched him through the gloomy prison gates while we drove on our way.

I was beginning to feel quite sorry for myself.

The lorry stopped outside a grim stone building surrounded by a high wall with a gateway guarded by two sentries. The major and his Cossack subaltern led us through, across a courtyard and into a gloomy, dim-lit stone passage with doors along one side. Here they handed us over to a sergeant, who signed a receipt for us and led us to one of the doors, unlocked it with an enormous key and motioned us inside; the guards urged us forward at the points of their tommy-guns. We stepped into the cell, the heavy door crashed to behind us and from the other side we heard the laughter of our captors.

'Well, boys, this is it,' sighed Solly-Flood. 'There's only one question now: which is it to be—Siberia or the firing squad? Personally, I'm not sure I wouldn't choose the firing squad.'

The cell was about twelve feet long, nine feet in breadth and twelve feet high, with a stone floor and bare, whitewashed walls; stout boards nailed across the window shut out the daylight, but a powerful naked bulb hung from the ceiling, throwing a hard bright glare in our eyes day and night, for we had no means of turning it off. Against the wall on each side of the door was a triple tier of bunks with mattresses of straw covered by pieces of old sacking; they were alive with vermin. Through a slot in the door, cut at eye-level and fitted with a shutter on the outside, the guards peered at us and mocked our helplessness.

'*Soyusniki!*' they jeered, 'how are you feeling—*you allies?*'

Seated on the bunks we discussed our fate with indignation and anxiety, in which I am not ashamed to admit that anxiety predominated. We had the greatest confidence in Perkins and General Gubbins, but what could they do if the Russians chose to deny all knowledge of our existence, or to report us as dead? While we were debating, we heard from a few yards down the corridor, a woman crying out in anger and despair; with horror we recognized the voice of the Home Army courier, married to a Polish officer, who had visited us at Redziny with Siemienski and his daughter. We heard her give her name to the interrogating officer or N.C.O.; then we all broke spontaneously into loud and random chatter, for we wished to hear no more. . . .

At six in the evening we dined; that is to say, a pair of guards stood in the doorway and handed us each a piece of stale rye bread a little larger than the average restaurant roll, and a filth-encrusted tin canteen half-filled with lukewarm water in which floated a few grains of barley. This was the staple prison diet, and we had it twice a day; when I asked the sergeant of the guard for some vodka he slammed the door with a volley of abuse which unfortunately I could not understand.

Worry, lice, and the unrelenting glare from the ceiling kept me from sleep for most of the night; a thunderous banging on the door, accompanied by shouts and more abuse, roused us in the morning. The door was thrown open and a couple of guards with levelled tommy-guns ordered us outside. Led by an N.C.O. and prodded on by the guards we were hurried along the passage to wash in the courtyard. On the way we met a group of Poles, among whom we recognized two who had been our fellow-guests at the Wlynica party; we passed them with-out a sign. In the yard each of us was given a bucket of water, in which, after breaking the ice, we washed superficially and with haste, for the temperature at this early hour was well below freezing. After our wash we were escorted to the latrine, a shallow trench surmounted by a wooden pole and only too evidently never cleaned; we had to use it under the cynical stares of our guards. Then we were locked in our cell for the day.

Such was the routine of our prison life. The N.K.V.D. had taken over the building from the Gestapo only two days earlier—with all fittings. Luckily we still had two packs of cards and so were able to vary the monotony, as once before in Montenegro, with endless rubbers of bridge; I have never played the game since. Poker was impossible because we did not even have matches for chips; somebody suggested using lice, but that proved impracticable because they would never stay put.

From time to time, usually at night, we would be called out for interrogation; this burden fell principally upon Hudson—and upon Currie who accompanied him as interpreter—because he had given all of us the strictest orders to answer no questions of any kind. He himself firmly and fearlessly refused to speak to any Russian officer below his own rank, which was full colonel; in the face of threats from the bullying major and his colleagues he remained stolidly silent, to their appeals to reason dourly indifferent. Finally, with our help he drafted a personal letter of protest to Marshal Koniev, which he persuaded the major to forward to Army headquarters.

We never knew whether this letter reached the Marshal; but Hudson's intransigence impressed the Russians and our treatment began to improve. The food remained the same, but we were lodged in a larger, brighter cell upstairs with bars across the windows but with glass to let in the light. The junior officers who visited us were sometimes polite; we even overheard one of them telling an N.C.O. that he considered our previous treatment scandalous. Finally Hudson was interviewed by a Russian colonel—or by an officer dressed as a colonel—who showered him with sympathy and wholly unconvincing excuses.

The guards also became quite friendly; they were Asiatics who felt no embarrassment at being required to switch suddenly from their former hostility. One of them, a cheerful, wiry little peasant from the Soviet Republic of Azerbaijan beside the Caspian, told us that he had thirteen brothers and as many sisters; such was the efficiency of the Soviet school system, he added, that all of them had received as good an education as he.

'What is the capital of England?' asked Hudson.

He scratched his head. 'I know...it is...it is...' for a moment he looked puzzled, but then his face cleared: 'Of course, *jep twaya match*, it is London!'

'When did Lenin die?' asked Currie gently.

Without a moment's hesitation the boy replied: 'On the 21st of January 1924, at six-fifty a.m. precisely.'

On 12th February we were driven to the aerodrome and embarked in a Dakota of the Soviet Air Force; with us came the major—now a model of courtesy and consideration—and his two subalterns; also, we noted, all the equipment we had been made to hand over at Zytno; our identity cards were returned to us.

We flew at five hundred feet, following the course of roads and rail-ways eastward to Mielec beyond the Vistula, where we spent a night; then on to Lvóv in the newly-incorporated Russian territory and thence to Kiev in the Ukraine. All the way the major fussed over us like an old hen, anxious lest we should slip away long enough to speak to any of the inhabitants. At Kiev, a city still in ruins, we were taken early in the afternoon to the station to await the Moscow express, due to leave at midnight. We changed our Polish zlotys into roubles and bought at an inflated price enough food to last the three days' journey ahead of us. We had a second class compartment to ourselves—and the major; it was fitted with bunks and so we slept for most of the way.

At nine o'clock on the morning of 17th February we reached Moscow. After a long wait in the draughty station in a temperature of about ten degrees Fahrenheit an N.K.V.D. police van appeared and whisked us at high speed through the snow-bound streets. None of us knew Moscow, but we all recognized the grim facade of the Lubianka when the van drew up outside its heavily guarded gates. At that moment I think we all tasted the dregs of despair.

Perhaps this was only the Russian idea of a joke; for our driver disappeared into the guard house to return a few minutes later with an envelope, which he handed to the major. We sped off again and stopped ten minutes later in front of another large building—the *Narkomindyel* or Ministry of Foreign Affairs. We were taken up several flights of stairs and shown into a long, narrow room furnished with a green baize-covered table and high-backed chairs. Here the major stammered an embarrassed good-bye and left us.

Two or three hours later we abandoned our game of bridge and sprang to our feet as the door opened to admit a Russian general; he motioned us to sit down and stood staring at us for five minutes in silence. Then all our worries rolled away as a British Army captain stepped briskly into the room, followed by two Russian officers. Our names were read out and checked, salutes were exchanged and a few minutes later we were being driven in an army station wagon to the headquarters of the British Military Mission.

The Mission headquarters was in the street called Ulitza Kominterna; although Stalin had decreed the dissolution of the Komintern nearly three years ago, the memory obviously lingered on. The building itself reflected a freer, possibly happier and certainly quite irresponsible society. Constructed to the plan of a rich merchant at the turn of the century its stone walls were crowned with crenellated towers and battlements, its halls and stairways paved with the rarest marble. The merchant's mother, when invited to inspect the completed product of her son's wealth and genius, simply remarked:

'My son, before you built this only I knew what a fool you were: now all Moscow knows.'

In the entrance hall we were greeted with a warm and dazzling smile by Natasha, the blonde young Russian receptionist who was married to a sergeant in the Mission. Dirty, lice-bound, and unshaven we were rushed to the M.I. Room, where we shed our filthy battle-dress and were deloused under the sympathetic supervision of a young major of the R.A.M.C.; bathed, shaven and dressed in clean, if ill-fitting, uniforms we presented ourselves in the mess before lunch, to be plied with vodka, red caviare, and an endless series of questions.

At no time did we receive either explanation or apology from the Russians for our detention; but at least a part of the true reason became clear to me when I met General Bob Laycock in the mess, on his way back to England from the Yalta Conference. The future of Poland had been one of the subjects under discussion, and so the Russians had made sure that it should not be complicated by any report we might have to make.

We remained in Moscow exactly a month while the applications for our exit visas went through the tortuous channels of the *Narkomindyel*. For the first few days we stayed in the already overcrowded headquarters in Ulitza Kominterna. The Mission at this time was commanded by Admiral Archer, a short, broad-shouldered sailor with an inexhaustible good nature and a refreshing sense of humour, qualities he badly needed in the discharge of his official duties; his chief of staff was a Grenadier officer, Colonel Napoleon Brinckman. They and their subordinates spared no effort to make up to us for the discomforts of the past month; indeed, they succeeded so well that I really believe we were in more danger of death from alcoholic poisoning during those days than we ever had been from enemy or Russian action.

Very much to our surprise we were allowed to move freely about the city, although we were warned that we were probably being kept under discreet observation and that we should be unwise to talk to strangers in the streets or in cafes—more for their sakes than our own. There were a few girl students from the university who were allowed to mix freely with officers of the Mission and were often seen dining in the mess; they were attractive and friendly and spoke good English, but they were all considered to be unofficial agents of the N.K.V.D., and so conversation with them was somewhat restricted. Four years of war—or twenty years of Stalin—seemed to have reduced most of the civilian population to a state of empty-eyed apathy; they shuffled along with downcast faces drained of all interest or hope. With fascinated horror I watched an old man who had lost both his legs at the groin, crossing a street in the snow and slush on his elbows and his stumps. Nobody paid the slightest attention.

We admired from every angle the smooth straight lines of the Kremlin walls and the multi-domed church of St. Vassili in Red Square, whose architect, according to legend, the Tsar rewarded by having him blinded lest he should design another like it. The tall narrow gateway leading from the Kremlin into Red Square was a formidable hazard to cross; a bell would ring and then, with no further warning, one of the long black government limousines would race into the Square at fifty or sixty miles an hour, carrying some high official of police or Politburo safe behind armour and dark, bullet-proof glass.

We were vividly reminded, however, that there was another aspect to this Russia, when we went to the Bolshoi Theatre to see the bewitching Ulanova dance *Giselle* or watched the exquisite Tartar ballet, *Fountain of Bakhchisarai*, or thrilled to the Tartar dancing in *Prince Igor*, led by a pair of Krim Tartars, brother and sister, who whirled round the stage in a symmetry of flashing colour and fierce, ecstatic movement that brought the whole audience to its feet in hysterical, uncontrollable applause.

The difficult problem of our accommodation was solved by Brigadier Hill, the S.O.E. representative in Moscow; he put up Hudson and Currie in his own flat and arranged for Solly-Flood and me to share the suite he kept at the Hotel Nazional. As a young man the Brigadier had been engaged in intelligence work in Russia during the first world war, both before and after the Revolution, and had been a friend of the fabulous Sydney Reilly; between the wars he had published his memoirs in a book called *Go Spy the Land*—a mistake, he told me, that he had never ceased to regret. Whether to atone for his past activities or because he thought it good policy in his present position, he now adopted towards the Soviet government an attitude of uncritical approval and would allow himself no sympathy for our complaints.

Nevertheless Solly-Flood and I were grateful enough for his hospitality. Our suite, which was really a vast double bed-sitting-room with a bathroom, looked across Metropole Square to the Kremlin. There was a legend that from its windows it was possible, with the aid of a telescope or binoculars, to watch Stalin shaving; we had a pair of binoculars, but we caught no glimpse of Stalin.

Life was never dull in that room. We had been warned that the walls were wired for microphones and that all our conversation would be recorded; if that is so the N.K.V.D. must have heard some plain if hardly novel criticism of themselves. When either of us was at home in the evening the telephone was sure to ring; whoever picked it up would hear a husky female voice vibrant with desire—the approach was always the same, though not the voice:

'Darling! I see you today and you are so attractive! Let me come to your room now, please, darling.'

Young and foolish and sex-starved we may have been; but we were old enough not to fall into that trap.

We received our visas in the middle of March; at six o'clock in the morning of the 17th we boarded a Soviet Air Force Dakota bound for Baku. None of us had been to bed; for our farewell party, including a boisterous dinner with the Mission, had lasted all night and we had barely time to pack and get to the airport. I was in particularly bad shape and so I remember with undying gratitude the kindness of one of our Russian fellow-passengers, a diplomatic courier on his way to Johannesburg. For a while he listened to my groans and watched my contortions with a sympathetic smile on his smooth round face. Then he tapped me on the knee.

'Butter!' he whispered with a friendly grin. 'A piece of bread, much butter and red caviare. Then I give you a glass of vodka and you will feel wonderful.'

I cried out in my misery and begged him to let me die in peace. But he opened his black brief case and brought out a long roll of fresh French bread, cut off a large hunk, spread it thickly with butter and piled on most of the contents of a tin of caviare; he handed me the *bonne bouche* with one hand and a bottle of vodka with the other.

'First you drink a little vodka—from the bottle because we have no glass. Then you eat this.'

I remembered how one of Tolstoy's characters in *The Cossacks* used to cure her husband's hangovers with platefuls of red caviare, and so I did as I was told. Within the hour I had recovered.

Another example of the many faces of Russia.

We stayed two nights in Baku's wilderness of abandoned oil derricks; we had, of course, a Soviet officer as escort, but he was more guide to us than gaoler and found us rooms in the comfortable In-tourist hotel overlooking the dull grey waters of the Caspian.

The next lap of our journey, and our last in Soviet aircraft, was over the massive range of the Elburz to Tehran; first-class pilots were employed on this run, for it was dangerous in winter. It was a memorably disagreeable experience. We flew at twenty-two thousand feet through thick cloud, without heating and without oxygen. Ambulances met us on the airfield at Tehran and carried away our fellow-passengers—three Field Officers of the Red Army and their wives; very proud of our inexplicable and undeserved stamina we climbed into our waiting staff car and were driven to our hotel.

In Cairo five days later I found David Smiley, *en route* to the Far East on a mission to Siam. Over lunch in a small Arab restaurant he told me that Bill McLean was already on his way to Kashgar in Chinese Turkestan and Julian Amery was in Chungking as political adviser to General Carton de Wiart. Siam appealed to me, and so we agreed that I should apply to join Smiley as soon as Perkins had released me.

There was nothing for us to do in London. We handed in our report to Perkins and General Gubbins; dined at the Rembrandt Hotel as guests of the Polish Government in London—now no longer recognized by the British Government—who decorated us with the eagle and wreath of the Polish Parachute Corps; and prepared to drop into Czecho-slovakia to make contact with some partisans discovered north or north-west of Prague. VE-Day and Perkins had intervened, instead we watched the celebrations in front of Buckingham Palace.

There still remained the war with Japan.

Alms for Oblivion

Peter Kemp

TO THE MEMORY
OF MY FRIEND
COLLIN BROOKS

We shall all meet again in the great
tavern that lies at the end of the world
G.K. Chesterton

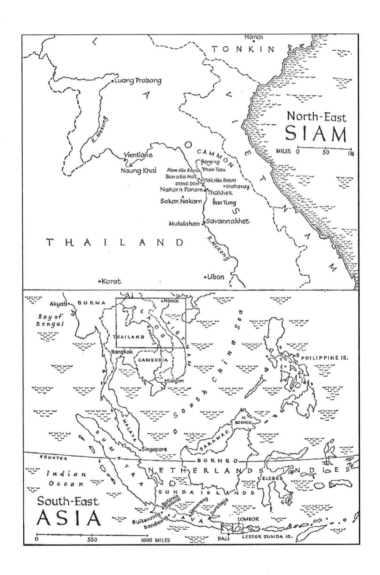

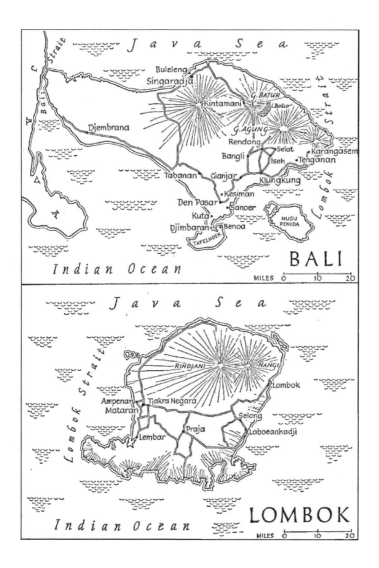

ACKNOWLEDGEMENTS

My particular thanks are due to the following friends:

Colonel David Smiley, M.V.O., O.B.E., M.C., for access to his valuable diaries covering the period August to November 1945; Major the Lord St. Oswald, M.C., for his useful advice and for permission to quote from his signals; General Sir Robert Mansergh, G.C.B., K.B.E., M.C., and General Sir Geoffrey Evans, C.I.E., for details of military operations in which I had the honour to serve under them; Major Daan Hubrecht, Royal Netherlands East Indies Army, for putting at my disposal his unique knowledge of the island of Bali; Lt.-Col. John Shaw, M.C., Royal Horse Guards, for his help in the preparation of the chapters on Bali and Lombok, where we served together; and to Mrs. John Etty-Leal and Mrs. Elizabeth Moore for their indispensable advice and collaboration in the preparation of my typescript.

The quotation from 'Mad Dogs and Englishmen' by Noel Coward is printed by permission of Chappell & Co. Ltd.; the extract from *Island of Bali* by Miguel Covarrubias is printed by permission of Cassell & Co. Ltd.

PETER KEMP

Time hath, my lord, a wallet at his back,
Wherein he puts alms for oblivion

Troilus and Cressida
Act III, Scene 3

TABLE OF CONTENTS

PROLOGUE

GO EAST, YOUNG MAN

'Well now,' grinned the fat man as he finished his third pint of bitter, 'after your five years' holiday I hope you'll be thinking of settling down to a decent job of work.'

Like many others in uniform I was getting used to this old joke; I made a polite but unconvincing effort to smile. Something, I realized on this May morning in 1945, was gravely wrong with my sense of humour. Outside the stuffy, overcrowded bar with its wrought glass mirrors, enamelled pump handles and remnants of Victorian bric-a-brac, London sparkled in the midday sunlight. The fireworks of V.E. day were barely cold. But already the wine of victory had turned to vinegar; disenchantment had set in. Europe was a desert of rubble whose embittered, starved and disease-ridden population watched with apathy the preparations for a hideous peace. While Russian soldiers raped and murdered in Vienna, Prague and Budapest, Englishmen talked with admiration and affection of good old Uncle Joe, and on V.E. night I had heard voices in the crowd before Buckingham Palace call out, 'Joe for King!'

In truth my own 'holiday' had lasted a good deal longer than five years, for I had first gone to war soon after leaving Cambridge in 1936; I had spent the greater part of the next three years in Spain, serving in the Nationalist armies—at first in the Carlist Militia and later in the Spanish Foreign Legion. I had joined the Nationalists to fight against Communism, which I believed— and still believe—would have engulfed Spain if the Republicans had won the Civil War. However, in Britain General Franco had not enjoyed a good Press and in the eyes of some of my intellectual friends, for whom an uncritical enthusiasm for everything Russian was, since 1941, the indispensable equipment of a patriot, I was little better than a Fascist; I found it useless to point out that nearly all my companions in Spain had been either monarchists, whose loathing of all totalitarian systems was as strong as my own, or professional soldiers who viewed all politics with suspicion and contempt.

By the end of the Civil War I had seen enough fighting to last me a lifetime and, after severe injuries to my jaw and hands from an enemy mortar bomb, I was temporarily unfit for any more. For the first four months of the European war, therefore, I had been a civilian. But as a result of a chance meeting with a friend in the War Office, followed by an interview in one of the dustier and more depressing rooms of that cheerless building, I soon found myself commissioned into the British Army, in the service of a paramilitary organization that has since became famous under the title of S.O.E. or Special Operations Executive. This organization, whose purpose was to promote subversion in enemy and enemy-occupied territories, has in recent years aroused considerable controversy, attracting from different quarters some excessive praise and much unmerited abuse. For me it proved a first-class travel agency, sending me at His Majesty's expense to countries that I could never otherwise have hoped to visit.

Thus, after taking part in a number of small raids on the coast of France, I had dropped by parachute in the late summer of 1943 into southern Albania; I had travelled on foot and horseback the length of that country until, some nine months later, I was flown from Montenegro to S.O.E. headquarters in southern Italy. Arriving back in England with frayed nerves, corns on my feet and a useful experience of political intrigue, I had dropped in December 1944 into south-western Poland, a member of a small mission to the Polish Underground Army—or what was left of it after the heroism and tragedy of Warsaw. For a month we had eluded German pursuit, owing our lives to the courage and self-sacrifice of our Polish friends: then we had witnessed the sickening spectacle of the Red Army's progress through Poland and its subjection of that incomparable nation. There had followed a month in an N.K.V.D. prison and another month in Moscow before I had returned by slow stages to England, the end of the European war, and the welcome of my fat friend in the pub.

I was worried and ill-tempered as I walked down Piccadilly on my way to lunch with a brother officer. It was all very well, I reflected sourly, to talk about settling down to a decent job of work; but the work we had started in 1939 was not yet done. Large areas of south-east Asia and the Far East were in the hands of an enemy less efficient, perhaps, than the Germans, but still formidable. In any case I was not yet due for demobilization. There was nothing to keep me in England. My marriage had collapsed; I was in the process of a divorce. My private life was an ugly mess. There were plenty of married men in our Far Eastern forces who had not seen their families for years; what conceivable justification could I have for staying at home? I had, too, a more positive reason for going.

On my way home from Russia I had spent several days in Cairo, where I had renewed an old friendship. Major David Smiley, a regular officer in the Household Cavalry, with whom I had worked closely during my first months in Albania, was passing through on his way to the Far East. A year younger than myself, short and wiry, with very bright blue eyes, an alert, inquisitive manner and a jerky, often abrupt style of speech, he concealed behind a disarming modesty and shyness a shrewd, objective mind, a cool judgment and the stoutest heart I have ever known.

Over a delicious lunch of shishkebab and Turkish coffee in a small Arab restaurant he had told me that he was bound for Siam to train and lead guerrillas in operations against the Japanese lines of communication between Indo-China and Malaya; if I cared to join him, all I need do when I reached London was to send him a signal from our office in Baker Street.

Although born in India I knew nothing of the Far East, and had previously felt no urge to go there; but Siam appealed to me as a romantic and little known country, and the prospect of such important and interesting work with Smiley attracted me still more. By the time I reached the club where I was lunching I had made up my mind to go.

The two lieutenant-colonels in the Far Eastern Section of our office in Baker Street were cordial and co-operative.

'We'll signal Smiley right away,' they promised. 'But in any case you needn't worry. There'll be plenty of man's work in Burma and Malaya as well as Siam. Give us a couple of weeks to arrange your transfer to this Section and fix you up with an air passage to India; but you needn't be in too much of a hurry because the monsoon is well under way out there and nothing much is likely to happen in the field just yet. Why don't you take a bit more leave? You could probably do with it after Poland and that Russian prison. Meanwhile, here's Juliet, who's just back from our headquarters in Calcutta— she can probably give you a few useful tips.'

Juliet was a trim and self-possessed young woman with soft brown hair, faultless curves and inviting dark blue eyes. Most of her advice on the Far East proved inaccurate; she did, however, give me a few tips of more lasting value, and she was a sparkling, even bewitching companion and partner in pleasure.

From this exhausting diversion I soon felt obliged to take a short rest; and so I invited myself to stay with some cousins near Dublin. Whether that was the best way to restore my health will be doubted by anyone who remembers the generous hospitality of the southern Irish to members of His Majesty's armed forces on leave in their country. It needed more than a vigorous walk in the Wicklow Hills to work off a heavy drinking session in Davy Byrnne's or the Royal Hibernian; on the other hand there was no breath of disenchantment in the wind that kissed the bracken on the Sugar Loaf, no gleam of cynicism in the sunlight that gilded the stones of Trinity, no suspicion of reserve in the welcome extended me by everyone I met, from the great John McCormack, his vitality undimmed by age and illness, to the porters in the Shelbourne or the peasants in the country around Bray. Most of them, I remembered, had close friends or relatives in the fighting services of the British Commonwealth.

Back in London I stayed in St. John's Wood with Collin Brooks, at that time the Editor of *Truth*; he and his family were old friends of infinite kindness, patience and stamina who had often given me shelter during and before the war. From their house I made daily visits to Baker Street. Juliet was busy giving instruction to another officer; but the two lieutenant-colonels greeted me as cordially as before.

'We've had a signal back from Smiley,' they told me. 'He's dropped into Siam and wants you to join him. You'll have to report first to our base at Kandy; they'll send you on to Calcutta, where you'll find the Siamese Country Section. We've applied for your air passage and we'll let you know as soon as it comes through. Meanwhile, here's Geraldine who's just back from Kandy—she'll probably give you some useful tips.'

Geraldine also had a trim figure. . . . The remainder of my time in London was a frenzied round of parties, bars and night-clubs, which did nothing to restore a constitution already weakened by the two extremes of Russian and Irish hospitality. One morning, fearing that I was sickening for something, I decided to consult a doctor whom I had known for some years. After examining me and asking a number of questions he reached for his prescription pad, scribbled a few words and pushed the piece of paper across the desk.

'I think this should fix you,' he observed drily.

It read simply: 'Say no thank you three times daily.'

Young man, I told myself severely, Go East. A week later I was in India.

I

'EVEN CARIBUS LIE AROUND AND SNOOZE'

My destination was Ceylon: to be exact Kandy, where S.O.E., under its Far Eastern disguise of Force 136, maintained its own headquarters staff among the many that contributed to the glory, and variety, of South-East Asia Command. But my aeroplane would take me no farther than Karachi, where I was consigned to a transit camp on the edge of the Sind Desert, along with a large number of other officers who were southward bound.

Before leaving London I had been well endowed with that sacred gift, Priority, and so it is unlikely that I should have lingered in Karachi had I not, with my faultless genius for putting spokes in my own wheel, developed an acute and laming attack of gout. In the cool and beautifully run R.A.F. hospital I soon recovered; I also learned some disturbing things about the habits of this new enemy I was going to meet.

Among the patients with whom I became friendly was a young subaltern of an Indian infantry regiment, who had been wounded and taken prisoner by the retreating Japanese in Burma; they had tied him to a tree and detailed one of their number to shoot him. Luckily the man detailed was a young soldier and nervous; the bullet struck my friend in the shoulder, the Japanese ran off to rejoin his fellows, and my friend was released later by his own men. He urged me most seriously not to let myself be taken by the Japanese at this stage of the war.

I reached Kandy on the ominous date of Friday, 13th July and spent the week-end in that delightful mountain capital. The morning after my arrival I had an interview with Brigadier John Anstey, the senior officer, who endorsed with enthusiasm my request to drop into Siam; he pointed out that the campaign in Burma was drawing to its close, and when the great attack was mounted against Singapore and Malaya S.O.E. would have a vital operational role to play in Siam, through which country ran all the Japanese lines of communication with French Indo-China. Although, under Japanese military pressure, Siam had declared war on Britain, there was strong anti-Japanese feeling in the country, and many high officials and officers of the three armed services were secretly working for the Allies. A guerrilla organization, known as the 'Free Thais', was already in existence and British officers were required to train and arm these irregulars and prepare airstrips and dropping grounds in the jungle.

The Siamese Country Section was in Calcutta, where I should probably find Smiley. He had been dropped into north-east Siam in the last days of

5

May, but had been terribly burnt three weeks later by the premature explosion of one of S.O.E.'s new toys—an incendiary brief-case designed to burst into flames and destroy the documents inside in the event of enemy ambush or surprise; Smiley was packing documents into it when there was a short-circuit and five pounds of blazing thermite spread all over him. For a week he lay in agony, unable to sleep, with first-, second- and third-degree burns and a hole in one arm full of maggots; he was, of course, without medical attention. At last he was picked up by an aircraft of the Siamese Air Force and taken to an airstrip, where a Dakota landed and flew him to Calcutta. By now he should be nearly well enough to return to the field.

Among the brigadier's staff officers at dinner that evening I found an old friend, Major Alan Hare, who had distinguished himself in Albania during the terrible winter of 1943-4; he had emerged with severe injuries from frostbite and the immediate award of the M.C. for outstanding initiative and courage. Like myself he was part of the *Drang nach Osten* by S.O.E. officers that had followed hard upon the end of the war in Europe.

There was a curious incident before dinner. While we were having drinks on the palm-thatched veranda I was talking to Wing-Commander Redding, who used to run our Air Transport Section in Baker Street; suddenly I heard a faint plop and saw with horror that a gigantic black scorpion had fallen from the roof on to his head. With commendable presence of mind he jerked his neck smartly, so that it fell on to his shoulder, whence he brushed it to the floor. A young bull terrier and a small black puppy made a concerted dive at it, and were only just restrained in time from rushing to certain death when somebody inverted a half-pint tumbler over the creature; the glass was barely wide enough to contain it. The officer with whom I shared a hut at the training camp a few days later had an even greater shock when he found a Russell's viper in his shirt.

In the holding and training camp on the plains near Colombo where I was sent to await an aircraft for Calcutta I found a wide variety of races, white, brown and yellow; there were British, French and Dutch officers; there were Javanese, Siamese, Burmans, Karens and Gurkhas, and there were Malayan Chinese and Annamites, all waiting or training for operations by parachute, submarine or canoe. I spent my time trying, unsuccessfully, to learn a little Siamese; listening to blood-curdling lectures by the Medical Officer on the treatment of malaria, cholera, typhus, smallpox, snake-bite and syphilis; and politely declining offers to send me on a jungle-training exercise, carrying a fifty-pound rucksack. A heavy rucksack, I told the training staff, was a white man's burden that I was not prepared to tote; a small haversack such as had served me well in Albania and Poland was the most I would allow to aggravate my prickly heat; anything bulkier must be carried by mule, pony, bullock-cart or local labour—or abandoned. I never had cause to change this view.

It was almost the end of July when I reached Calcutta, arriving in that ugly fetid city on a sticky evening at the height of the monsoon. In the office of the Siamese Country Section—two stifling, noisy rooms in a dingy house on a dusty street full of pot-holes—I was received without enthusiasm by a sweaty, irritable and overworked staff officer; his appearance, like my own, was in squalid contrast to the cool serenity of the neat, pretty young secretaries who flitted in and out among the desks and the clattering typewriters. Smiley, it seemed, had gone to Simla to finish his convalescence at Viceregal Lodge as the guest of his friends the Wavells; I had better find myself a billet in the Transit Hotel until he returned—and now would I kindly get the hell out of the office and keep out of everyone's way.

This discouraging welcome, not unusual in my experience of reporting for duty in a strange theatre of war, left me nettled but not unduly depressed; for in the same office I met another old friend from Albania, John Hibberdine, a young Captain of the Cameronians who had been my close companion during the gloomy and hazardous days of my reconnaissance of the marches of Kossovo. After my departure for Montenegro early in 1944, Hibberdine had suffered appalling hardship and danger, being chased across north Albania in a series of determined German drives aimed at clearing the country of British Liaison Officers; while lying up in the inhospitable forests of Mirdita he had contracted typhoid, which all but killed him; eventually his companions managed to carry him to the coast, where an M.T.B. took him to Italy. His experiences seemed to have made little impression either on his health or his resolution; for now he was waiting to drop into southern Siam, to the Isthmus of Kra on the Burmese and Malayan borders. In his urbanely cynical company I spent the next two days exploring the restaurants and clubs of Calcutta. The European business community, we noticed, while extending to us the privilege of membership of their clubs, viewed our uniforms with a mixture of resentment and contempt which, as newcomers, we found hard to understand; at times we wondered if they would have preferred the Japanese.

Forty-eight hours after my arrival I received an urgent summons from Smiley to go to Simla to discuss plans. It was accompanied by an invitation from Lady Wavell to stay at Viceregal Lodge. I flew to Delhi and reached Simla on the morning of 3rd August. The next five days were among the happiest of my life. Although the marks of his burns were terribly evident, Smiley had made an astonishing recovery; strolling among the dark green, fir-covered hills, with the gigantic Himalayan snows nacreous and opalescent on the distant skyline, we planned in eager detail the course of our future operations in the field.

We very nearly did not get into the field. The bomb on Hiroshima shattered our pleasant pipe-dream and sent us scurrying back to Calcutta as soon as Smiley had been passed fit by a medical board. We heard the news at luncheon from a very sweet old lady, the wife of a distinguished lawyer. '*Isn't* it wonderful?' she beamed. 'They've dropped a bomb on Japan which has the force of *ten thousand* tons of high explosive! Isn't science *marvellous?* Truly civilization progresses from day to day!'

I could only recall the bitter words of Colin Ellis's epigram:

'Science finds out ingenious ways to kill
Strong men, and keep alive the weak and ill,
That these asickly progeny may breed:
Too poor to tax, too numerous to feed.'

It is fair to add that five years later I was to owe to science my own recovery from tuberculosis.

We did not have to linger long in Calcutta. Because of the prevailing uncertainty the Siamese Country Section decided to send in its operational parties as fast as possible. Smiley, now a lieutenant-colonel, left immediately in a Dakota that was going to land on the Siamese airstrip from which he had been flown out the previous month; with him went Brigadier Victor Jaques, commanding all Force 136 Missions in Siam. Jaques was a lawyer who had practised in Bangkok before the war; he had continued to live there during the Japanese occupation, sheltered by the Regent in his palace, where, under the noses of the enemy, he had maintained wireless communication with Calcutta and built up a subversive organization inside the country.

I was delighted to learn that I was to drop in with an old friend, Major Rowland Winn, 8th Hussars, who was also joining Smiley. I had first met Winn when I was a Carlist officer and he a correspondent for the *Daily Telegraph* in Spain. The outbreak of the Civil War found him in Madrid, but his dispatches on events there during the first few weeks were too candid for the liking of the Republican authorities, who clapped him into gaol and sentenced him to death; his life was saved by the intervention of the British Chargé d'Affaires, but he judged it prudent thereafter to report the war from the Nationalist side. In the winter of 1943 he parachuted into Albania, breaking a leg on landing; for a month, until a doctor could reach him, he lay in great pain in a shepherd's hut among the wild mountains of Cermenikë.

He held the strongest convictions on most matters of importance, especially on the subject of bullfighting, and would defend his ideas with a pugnacity in argument that was only matched by his courage in the field; a generous and loyal friend, he possessed a keen wit that made him an excellent companion and a devastating critic.

Short and stocky, with a pronounced limp from his parachute accident, he showed in his personal appearance a remarkable blend of fastidiousness and neglect; thus he seldom brushed his hair, but neither in Albania nor in

Siam was he ever without a bottle of Trumpet's after-shaving lotion. His independence of dress and manner sometimes shocked more orthodox soldiers. Just before the end of the European War he was stationed at a holding camp near Virginia Water, waiting to be sent on an operation into western Germany: bored with the inactivity of the camp he went to London for a few days' relaxation; he omitted the formality of asking permission, but left a note for the Brigadier:

> As there is nothing for me to do here I am proceeding to London. If required for operations I can be found at the Cavalry Club.

I was taking no wireless, but Winn had a set and a first-class operator, the amiable Sergeant Lawson, usually known as 'Spider', a light-hearted young man who had served with S.O.E. in Greece; he was also taking an interpreter, a giggly little Siamese, friendly, intelligent and helpful, whose *nom-de-guerre* was Toy. We left just forty-eight hours after Smiley, in a Liberator christened Vernon the Villain; it was to be a daylight drop, and so we took off at 11.30 in the morning. I was in poor shape, suffering from a mild attack of bacillary dysentery and a slight recurrence of the malaria I had contracted in Albania. However, a kindly R.A.F. doctor on the airfield dosed me heavily with sulphonamides and mepacrine, and during the flight Winn generously poured down my throat the entire contents of a flask of Courvoisier which he had brought from Europe and had saved up to drink in celebration of his arrival in Siam; his Christian action not only mitigated the squalor and discomfort of dysentery in an aircraft that had no lavatory, but took my mind off the hazards of monsoon flying among cumulonimbus clouds that could—and sometimes did—tear an aircraft apart.[1]

We flew over the Bay of Bengal, turned east near Akyab and crossed the jungle-covered hills that separate Burma from Siam.

Our dropping zone was in the north-east, near Sakon Nakorn, a town about fifty miles west of the Mekong river, which forms the frontier between Siam and French Indo-China; the area is covered in forest. At six in the evening we were over the target, and in the clear light we soon picked up the smoke signals on the dropping ground; we put on our parachutes and prepared to jump.

'Jump' is not really the right word, for since my last drop a new way of leaving the aircraft had been invented; this was a wooden chute, similar to those in swimming pools, which was lowered from the roof of the fuselage to the exit aperture. When the red light flashed 'Action Stations' the

---

[1] Our missions in Siam owed much to these aircrews, who were for long our only means of supply and who flew in the most frightening weather conditions and across the most dangerous mountain country in order to deliver our stores.

parachutist swung his legs into the trough and lay on his back with his hands gripping the sides; when he received the order to go he simply brought his hands together on his chest and, helped by a push from the dispatcher, slid down the chute and out of the hole.

We were dropping in pairs; first Winn and Lawson, and then, on the next run, Toy and myself. When we had dropped our load of containers and packages Winn took up his position on the slide. I noticed that his lips were moving as though in prayer; he caught my eye and, thinking that he might have some last message for me, I bent down to listen. He was in fact intoning Noël Coward's refrain:

In the mangrove swamps where the python romps
There is peace from ten till two.
Even caribous lie around and snooze
—There's nothing else to do

The light flashed green and he slid away, mumbling the next verse.

When it came to our turn, a few minutes later, I waited until Toy's head had disappeared before releasing my hold and laying my hands on my chest; it was all I could do to keep them there during the next two or three seconds. Then I was clear of the exit and swinging gently in mid-air with an acute pain in my crotch, which had taken most of the strain as the parachute opened. Having satisfied myself that I was not irreparably damaged I turned my attention to the ground; for a nasty moment I thought I was going to hit the roof of a wooden hut, but I missed it and landed with a great splash in a paddy-field. Soaked to the skin and temporarily blinded by mud and water, I was helped to my feet and out of my harness by three Siamese. Looking around, I was rewarded by the spectacle of Major the Honourable Rowland Winn, spattered all over with mud and paddy stalk, standing erect while he adjusted with infinite care the green and gold forage cap of the 8th Hussars which he had pulled from inside his bush shirt.

He introduced me to the leader of the reception committee, a handsome young Siamese policeman who, under the pseudonym of Kong, held a captain's commission in the British Army. Kong led us to the hut on whose roof I had so nearly landed, where the packages and containers were now assembled.

'Please sort out your kit as quickly as possible,' he asked us, speaking in quick, jerky sentences. 'We ride from here ten kilometres through the forest. There are Japanese around; their patrols are very active still, and last night they burnt a village only a mile away.'

Mounted on small, sturdy ponies we rode across the paddy towards the forest; the four of us, accompanied by Kong and another Siamese, went ahead while the rest followed with our kit. These Siamese ponies—all of them were stallions because, so Smiley told us later, it was considered bad form to ride a mare—moved like Andalusian horses, with a curious gait that was a blend of walk, trot and gallop. They went at a surprisingly fast pace and, for a short person, were comfortable to ride; but my long legs reached almost to the ground and, when I forgot to keep them clear of the pony's feet, received some painful kicks.

It was already dark when we entered the forest, but the half moon shining through the trees cast a pale, dappled light on the muddy track that wound through the tangled undergrowth. Our horses splashed, and sometimes swam, through deep pools and across swollen streams; once we crossed a creek on a wooden bridge whose posts and railings alone showed above the water, and once we swam a broad river. Twice only did we halt: when the unhappy Lawson was thrown from his pony into a dark and slimy puddle, and when Winn's forage cap was swept off by an overhanging branch. Otherwise we rode in silence at a steady pace, inhaling the heavy, scented warmth of the sodden forest while glow-worms and fireflies flashed in the misty darkness; at intervals the rain showered upon us, cool and soothing.

It was nearly ten o'clock when we arrived at the village of Akat, where we were to spend the night. At the point where the path debouched into the clearing we found the headman awaiting us surrounded by a curious and whispering crowd of men and women carrying lighted brushwood torches; joining the palms of his hands before him he bowed us a graceful welcome. He led us to a long, narrow building raised on wooden piles to a height of twelve or fifteen feet above the ground and approached by a flight of steps leading to an open veranda. This was the school-house, where we were going to sleep.

In construction and design it resembled many other houses in north-eastern Siam. From the veranda we passed into a large room, bare of furniture except for a table and benches down the centre; the table was laid for a meal and mattresses were spread against one of the walls. The floor was spotlessly clean, the boards scrubbed almost to a polish. Food was set before us—cold boiled rice with pieces of chicken, meat balls, eggs and chilies; also a bottle of what Kong called 'Siamese whisky'—a potent rice spirit with a sour, not unpleasing flavour. Already comatose from illness and fatigue I could not bring myself to eat or drink more than the mouthful that politeness demanded; the effects of the doctor's pills and Winn's brandy had long worn off, leaving me weak and sick and feverish. During the last hour of the journey I had been barely conscious, and at the end I had been unable to dismount without help. Winn and Lawson undressed me, laid me on a mattress and heaped blankets upon my shivering, sweating body.

We rested all next day; by the evening, although still weak from loss of blood, I was beginning to recover. The following morning we left Akat and rode all day through the forest, keeping up a fast pace along a broad but marshy track; we spent the night in a village with the charming name of Ba Wa, where a squad of guerrillas, lined up in front of the school, greeted us with a shout of '*Knio!*', repeated three times, and a smart present arms. They carried British service rifles and looked keen and fit.

We made an early start and covered ten miles before breakfast and another ten before noon; then we came to a wide expanse of water, a river in flood, where *pirogues* awaited us—hollowed tree-trunks, each one a masterpiece of skilful workmanship. We were paddled silently over the surface of the water, the half-submerged forest around us reminding me of pictures I had seen of the Florida Everglades; after two miles we landed at a house beside the water and had lunch.

Kong had received a message from Smiley saying that a lorry would be awaiting us that afternoon about a mile from this house; while we rested he sent a scout to look for it. I reflected that, whether or not the Japanese surrendered, we should be pretty safe from them as long as we stayed in the forest. Our Siamese friends made extensive use of scouts, and their intelligence systems seemed excellent; we ought to have plenty of warning of Japanese movements, and in this vast area of forest we should have no difficulty in hiding.

Kong's scout returned to say that the lorry was waiting. We set off on foot, but mid-afternoon in the tropics is not a good time for a walk, especially during the monsoon; and so, when an old man driving a bullock cart offered us a lift we climbed up thankfully beside him. Our escort of guerrillas trudged along on either side, apparently quite content.

We found Smiley's truck, a bright red Chevrolet, parked beside a rough track that ran from the verge of the forest through a wide expanse of waterlogged paddy-field. We climbed into the back, where we were soon joined by the twenty men of our escort, and tried to stave off bruises and abrasions as the vehicle lurched and plunged in the ruts and pot-holes. At length we came on to the straight, brick-coloured *piste* that was the road between Sakon Nakorn and Udaun; Japanese military transport used this road and police patrols were frequent, and so our guards made us lie on the floor and covered us with a tarpaulin. After a quarter of an hour the lorry stopped and we were allowed to emerge from hiding, sweaty and half-suffocated. We were hustled off the road on to a forest track, which led us in a few moments to another village with an enchanting name—Phannikom. There we found Smiley with his wireless operator, Sergeant Collins, and a wiry, lightly built Siamese with a gaunt, tormented face, whom Smiley introduced to me as Pluto.

I had already heard of this man. Tiang Sirikhand, alias Pluto, was one of the founders of the Free Thai movement and its leader in north-eastern Siam, where he had been born of an influential family about thirty-five years before.

Parliamentary Deputy for Sakon Nakorn, close friend and staunch supporter of the Regent, Pridi Panomyong, he had given valuable service to the Allies and in particular to Smiley, who liked and admired him for his kindness, competence and integrity. He was a forceful if humourless personality, with great powers of organization and leadership; his enemies accused him of Communist sympathies, I think unfairly.[1]

His grim, swarthy face relaxed in a smile of unusual warmth and charm as he greeted us and, turning to me, remarked:

'Smiley tells me it is your birthday today. We have arranged a celebration for you.'

In the excitement and fatigue of the last few days I had forgotten that this was indeed my thirtieth birthday, 19th August 1945.

It was now about four o'clock. Over mugs of tea we discussed plans for the future. Although it seemed likely that the war was coming to an end there had as yet been no surrender, and we could not be sure of the reactions of local Japanese commanders if we should fall into their hands; there were some grim rumours of the fate of British officers in Burma who had been captured in the last few days. We knew that the enemy had been preparing a drive against this area, and it was still possible that they might launch an attack on the guerrillas—although they would find it hard to catch us in these miles of forest, where our men knew every path. Calcutta's instructions were that we should remain underground until we received the code word 'Goldfish', authorizing us to approach the Japanese.

'Meanwhile,' Smiley continued, 'I want you, Rowly, to go to Naung Khai, north-west of here, and Peter to go to Nakorn Panom, to the east. Both towns are on the Mekong river, which, as you know, forms the frontier between Siam and the province of Laos in Indo-China; each is the capital of a *changvad* or province. You'll meet the two Provincial Governors here tonight and leave with them tomorrow; I myself am going to Sakon Nakorn with Pluto. Peter, you'll be the worst off, having no wireless contact; but Calcutta have promised to drop in a set and operator for you as soon as they can.'

'I'm afraid that, until we get orders from Calcutta, I can only give you the vaguest instructions. Find out all you can about your districts, and about the places across the river in Laos—that means Vientiane for Rowly, and for

---

[1] *The Times* of 6th January 1955 carried a report from its Bangkok correspondent to the effect that Nai Tiang Sirikhand, who was described as a 'well-known Communist sympathizer', was organizing an 'army of liberation' of Siamese in northern Laos and that he was receiving Viet-minh support. On the other hand, his close friend, General Phoumi Nosavan, the Laotian anti-Communist leader, recently assured me that Pluto was no Communist. The question, alas, is now purely academic, for Pluto himself was murdered in Siam a few years ago, allegedly on the orders of the Chief of Police, General Phao.

Peter Thakhek and Savannakhet farther south; especially get all the dope you can about Japanese and prisoners of war. We can keep in touch through the Siamese, who can be trusted not to open our letters—unlike the Albanian Partisans!'

At seven o'clock, after toasting our reunion with a few whiskies, we walked over to the school-house for my birthday party. If I describe it in detail this is because it was typical of almost every party I attended in north-east Siam—and they were many, for the Siamese are a friendly and laughter-loving people. A great crowd of men and girls was gathered there to greet us and a roar of welcome hailed our entry into the large classroom, where long tables loaded with food and drink displayed the magnificence of Siamese hospitality. Seeing the roast sucking pigs, ducks, chickens, plates heaped with meat, vegetables and fruit, and the huge tureens of rice I found it hard to believe that we were in a small village in a rain-soaked tropical forest.

Before dining we were led out on to the veranda, where stood several great earthenware jars filled with rice beer; a thick layer of rice floated on the top of each jar and from each protruded several thin bamboo drinking straws; the jars were colloquially known as *changs* (elephants) and the bamboos were their tusks. All this we were told by Pluto, who, beaming with enthusiasm, made us drink plentifully from each *chang*; the beer tasted slightly sweet and deceptively mild.

On the veranda, also, we met the Governors of Naung Khai and Nakorn Panom. The former was small and slightly built with an impressively quiet but friendly manner; the latter, named Ta Win, was taller, broader, stouter and more effusive than his colleague. He had very thick lips and an excited, bubbly way of speaking. Although he knew a little English, he had with him his interpreter, Sang-a, an emaciated little man with a hoarse, nervous giggle and a twitch, a man who seemed to me a little too anxious to please everyone.

We dined standing at the tables, as at a buffet, and helping ourselves. There was a remarkable variety of food; in addition to what I have mentioned there was pork, water buffalo, barking deer, fish, eels, snails, frogs, bamboo shoots, coconuts and every kind of tropical fruit; and there were small dishes of a chili sauce so powerful that anything flavoured with it turned to fire in the mouth.

While we were eating, girls brought us glasses of *lao kao*, a fierce rice spirit, which they offered with a charming little bow. As soon as our glasses were empty they were refilled, the girls taking it in turns to serve each of us; Siamese women are uncommonly pretty, and in the face of their bewitching smiles and mischievous dark eyes I found myself unable to refuse, with the result that my head was swimming and my eyes were a trifle glazed by the end of the meal. It was foolish of me, so soon after dysentery, to drink so much; but the warmth of my welcome made me forget my illness.

14

When we had finished we were led to a row of chairs at one end of the room; more *changs* were placed in front of us, from which we were continually pressed to drink. The tables were removed, and an orchestra assembled to play Siamese tunes for us on stringed instruments and what looked like large bamboo pan-pipes. The notes were sweet and pure and the music had, to our western ears, an attractive if somewhat monotonous melody. Local folk-songs followed, Then, to my horror, Pluto called for a song from each of us; worse still, as the guest of honour I had to start. Smiley urged me to sing something Polish, and so, in a voice hoarse with *lao kao* and thick with rice beer, I gave them the Warszawianka, explaining with alcoholic exuberance that it was a song of revolution against a foreign oppressor. My performance met with courteous applause from the Siamese and hoots of ribald laughter from our party.

Then began the Siamese national dance known as Ramwong, in which partners shuffle round the room in a double line, moving arms and hands to a slow, sinuous rhythm. It was a joy to watch the beautiful figures and graceful gestures of the Siamese girls, but when we were asked to join in, even my well-fortified spirit quailed; Smiley by constant practice had become quite competent, but personally I felt I resembled an inebriated camel slowly swaying its neck and limbs from side to side. Sergeant Lawson, however, was troubled by no such inhibitions; he whirled round the room like a dervish, arms and legs flying, and so much did he delight our hosts that for a while he held the floor alone.

I suffered no more than a hangover for that night's intoxication. Smiley comforted me.

'Don't worry. You're pretty well expected to get plastered on these occasions. Even I have been carried home to bed.'

II

'A FATE WORSE THAN KEMP'

The inhabitants of the fifteen provinces of north-east Siam differ from those of the rest of the country in that they have close ties of race and language with the Laotians beyond the Mekong. Although a little impatient of the authority of Bangkok and of the civil servants sent from there to administer them they had, and I believe still have, no inclination towards separatism;[1] commerce with Laos, however, is frequent and virtually unrestricted.

The area is a plateau averaging live hundred feet above sea-level, most of it covered in forest of a type which geographers call 'dry monsoon forest' and the Siamese call *padeng*; this forest assumes in the dry season a stark and lifeless appearance because the trees shed their foliage and only the undergrowth retains a certain tarnished green. It is for the most part a forlorn and desolate region, whether sodden under the monsoon rains or dusty and desiccated in the winter months, monotonous to the eye, with scarcely a break in the colourless forest landscape save for the few acres of paddy-fields near the villages. Only under bright moonlight have I seen it beautiful.

The soil is poor and so, therefore, are the people, who supplement their income by breeding water buffalo, oxen and pigs for export to other parts of the country. But poverty has not brought discontent; most of the land is owned by the peasants who till it, and those twin vultures, the absentee landlord and the money-lender, cannot prey here as in India and in Lower Siam.

All but three per cent of the population live in villages, most of which lie some distance from the road and are approached by torturous tracks through the forest.

Their villages, surrounded with bright green ricefields, are built in the thick shade of lofty mango trees, groves of bamboo and coconut palms. The wooden houses are on stilts, with cattle and water buffalo often living under them. Almost every village has a Wat, which is a Buddhist religious enclosure containing a temple, a pavilion, and a

---

[1] See an excellent article on north-east Siam by Professor Charles Madge in *The Times* of 7th January 1955, to which I am much indebted. But Pluto had to flee from Siam in 1949, accused of attempting to form a separate state in the north-east (*The Times*, 6th January 1955).

16

residence for the monks. The village communities are socially homogenous and in their easy-going way they hang together and help each other. There are no divisions of religion, caste or language. The position of women is traditionally good and family life is traditionally happy and united.[1]

One object of hatred these people shared with their Laotian cousins; the Annamese. Indeed, Smiley told me that Pluto's guerrillas shot any Annamite they caught, suspecting him, often with good reason, of spying for the Japanese.[2] There were Annamese colonies in many towns of the north-east; in Nakorn Panom they had their separate village. The Chinese, on the other hand, though not loved were tolerated; they owned all the hotels and eating houses and, together with the Indians, all the shops.

Such was the land in which for the next five months I was to make my home.

Nakorn Panom was a clean-looking little town, consisting of a muddy main street, lined on either side with shops and running north and south beside the Mekong, and a few small side streets leading down to the river or dwindling away westwards into country tracks. To the west the ground rose gently from the river bank and the town, past open fields and scattered houses to a small landing strip on the verge of the forest; on the other two sides were banana plantations and coconut palms. The Wat lay half a mile to the south; about the same distance to the north lived the Annamese, earning their livelihood chiefly on the river. There was one hotel, owned of course by Chinese.

I arrived at half past five on the evening of 20th August in a rickety old bus with Governor Ta Win, Sang-a and a small party of guerrillas. On the way from Phannikom we had passed several lorries full of Japanese troops, who had paid no attention to us, looking straight ahead with blank, unseeing faces.

Among my companions on this journey was a lean, handsome Lao of about twenty-five, with a very soft voice and an unusually charming smile. He told me that he had been in charge of what he called the 'Free Lao' resistance against the Japanese in the Savannakhet area; what he did not tell me was that he was on his way back there to organize a similar resistance movement against the French. His name, which he gave simply as Phoumi, meant nothing to me at the time, and it was more that fifteen years before I

---

[1] Professor Madge, op. cit.
[2] It should not be forgotten that President Ho Chi Minh, like President Sukarno of Indonesia, was awarded a high decoration by the Japanese.

was to see him again. Now he is the most powerful figure in Laos and the bitterest enemy of his former allies the Viet-minh.

We turned left in the main street and bumped slowly through the pot-holes, past the stucco fronts of the Governor's office and 'Flail of Justice' to the Governor's house, a yellow, plaster-fronted, two-storey building in European style, with a cool green garden shaded by coconut palms. It faced on to the Mekong, at this season nearly a mile wide and flowing swiftly over hidden sandbanks in a series of swirling eddies and whirlpools. On the other side the white houses of Thakhek showed clearly, picked out amid a blaze of green. Behind them rose the first ranges of the Chaine Annamitique—dark, jungle-covered mountains, grim and threatening, their summits swathed in black, grey-streaked clouds, lit at intervals by jagged, purple flashes of lightning; the thunder rolled to our ears across the mud-brown river.

The following day passed uneventfully. The Governor, who seemed to think I was a confirmed alcoholic, produced throughout the day a succession of strange new drinks for me to sample; with the exception of a light golden rum from Indo-China they were all disgusting. In the afternoon he took me to the club, where I met the local officials; the Deputy Governor, the Police Captain and Lieutenant, the Sheriff, Harbourmaster, Chief Customs Officer, Doctor, and a quiet, shy little man who astonished me by introducing himself as 'the Director of Humanity'. He turned out to be the schoolmaster.

Japanese troops seldom came to Nakorn Panom—only when crossing to or from Thakhek; we should have plenty of warning of their approach, and there was a company of our guerrillas in the town. On the second day after my arrival the Governor thought it would be safe for me to set up my own headquarters. The place he had prepared was known as the Officials' Rest House, a large bungalow on the open, rising ground behind the town, like all Government buildings it had walls of cream-washed laterite; a wide, cool veranda led to a long dining-room and several bedrooms. The house backed on to the airfield. Commanding a wide view across the town and river to Thakhek and the mountains of Laos it was an ideal headquarters. I moved in there the same evening. I was given a staff of servants, assisted by convicts from the local prison, to see to my comfort, and a guard of two police and four guerrillas to ensure my safety.

During my first week I was able to gain some idea of the situation on the other side of the river. I sent agents to Thakhek, men who had relatives over there; and I drove with Governor Ta Win to Mukdahan, some fifty miles south of Nakorn Panom, to brief others to bring me news from Savannakhet. My inquiries established that there was in Thakhek a number of French civilian internees but no prisoners of war; that there was a force of French and Laotian guerrillas living in the jungle south of Thakhek, commanded by a certain Lieutenant Tavernier; that there was a similar force near

Savannakhet under a Lieutenant Quinquenel, and that all were in urgent need of food, money and medical supplies. I received also a great deal of information that turned out to be false. The problem of sifting true from inaccurate reports was one that I was never able to solve the whole time I was on the frontier; I was at the mercy of my agents, who turned out as often as not to be double agents.

This question of double agents became more difficult when the struggle began between the French and the Viet-minh, because the Siamese, on whose advice I was largely dependent for my recruiting, were hostile to the French cause.

My most disastrous experiment was in October, with an Indian agent—a Sikh merchant who was well recommended to me. The day after I had recruited him and given him his instructions, together with a sizeable sum of money, I received a signal from our office in Bangkok, ordering me to arrest him as an ex-agent of the Japanese; before I could do so he had disappeared.

I was soon obliged to disobey my orders to stay underground. On 25th August the Police Lieutenant brought me a message that two Frenchmen in Thakhek had been condemned to death by the Japanese and were about to be executed. To save their lives I felt I must act at once. Calling on the Governor I asked him for transport across to Thakhek, intending to present myself to the Japanese commander, a Captain Nakajima, and dissuade him from carrying out the sentence. The Governor and the Police Captain, who was with him, implored me not to go; almost in tears they protested that if anything happened to me the consequences to themselves, and perhaps to their country, would be disastrous. I could, they pointed out, achieve as much and probably more through a letter, which they promised to deliver in Thakhek immediately.

Their arguments seemed reasonable, and so I abandoned my original idea—not unwillingly, I may add. Instead, I wrote to Captain Nakajima, warning him that he would be held personally responsible for the safety of his prisoners, and asking to be allowed to visit them. The Governor added a letter of his own. He agreed that if we did not receive a satisfactory reply by the following morning I might go in person. I also relayed the news to Smiley, who had moved from Sakon Nakorn to Ubon, about 150 miles down the Mekong.

I spent an anxious day. About seven o'clock in the evening I was sitting on my veranda watching the green and lilac colours on the hills of Laos deepen to purple and indigo in the twilight; at intervals the cackle of a gekko lizard on the ceiling broke in upon the stillness to jar the rhythm of my thoughts. I sprang eagerly to my feet as the Police Lieutenant approached with the two messengers who had delivered my letter to Thakhek. They brought me an answer from Captain Nakajima, written in good English and courteously phrased, regretting that until he received instructions from his superiors he must decline my request for an interview and for the release of the prisoners; but he assured me that in the meantime they would come to no harm. After a further exchange of letters, in which I was joined by Smiley, who paid me a visit the next day, the two condemned men were released from close arrest.

Dining with the Governor one evening I met the American Dr. Holliday, a Presbyterian missionary who had lived in Siam for fifteen years before the war, and previously for thirteen years in China. Having left the country before the Japanese occupation he had been dropped back there in April to form an intelligence network for the American O.S.S., and he now held the rank of major in the U.S. Army. He was one of the very few O.S.S. officers in Siam, this theatre of operations being the agreed responsibility of the British South-East Asia Command. A stocky, well-built man in the early fifties, with a bronzed square face, a strong jaw and a quiet, friendly manner, he was held in great affection and respect by the Siamese people, whose language he spoke fluently.

He explained to me the reason behind the Governor's anxiety that I should not cross the river.

'These people are terribly afraid for their independence. They feel they're in bad with the Allies—even though it wasn't their fault they were sold out to the Nips. They are responsible for your safety and they think that if at this critical time something should happen to you, or to any British officer in Thailand, they would lose their independence.'

'But surely if I put it in writing that I take full responsibility myself, that I've gone against their advice . . . ?'

'That makes no difference. They still feel they would be blamed.'

It was becoming difficult to avoid the Japanese on my tour of the area; it also seemed unnecessary. While visiting the Sheriff of Mukdahan I was embarrassed to find myself in a street crowded with their troops. I received some dirty looks from the officers; by the men I was ignored.

On 29th August Smiley passed me the code word 'Goldfish'; on 2nd September came the news of the Japanese surrender. By that time the Japanese forces in my area had moved south to Ubon, where Smiley immediately found his hands full. Outside the town there was a large prisoner-of-war camp, full of British, Australians and Dutch. Although the efficient and tactful administration of the famous Colonel Toosey relieved him from responsibility inside the camp, Smiley had the task of receiving and sorting the daily parachute drops which supplied it, and of ensuring the smooth cooperation of the Siamese civil and military authorities which was so necessary for its welfare.

Another of his duties was to supervise the disarming of some eleven thousand Japanese and the shooting of their horses, which were in terrible condition, having been shamefully neglected by their masters. He was astonished, therefore, to see the Japanese soldiers in tears as they shot their horses, and then to watch them remove their caps and bow for two minutes before filling in the graves, which they covered with flowers.

My attention at this time was occupied almost wholly with events around Thakhek. Two days after my arrival at Nakorn Panom I had seen a Dakota flying low over the opposite bank; soon afterwards I received reports that it had dropped two French parachutists, a man and a girl. On 29th August one of my agents brought me a letter from the former, Lieutenant Klotz, addressed to 'The British Officer at Lakhon',[1] saying that he was in difficulties and would like to meet me. He suggested a rendezvous at the Catholic mission house on the island of Dong Don, a few miles north-west of Thakhek, in two days' time.

The Governor would not hear of my crossing to the island, which was not in Siamese territory; mindful of Dr. Holliday's words I did not press the point. Instead, we arranged that the Governor should take me in his launch to the village of Ban A Sa Mat, opposite Dong Don, where we could wait while the launch fetched Klotz from the island.

We started after lunch on 31st August—the Governor, Sang-a and myself, with a small escort, all bristling with Stens and carbines; even I was asked to bring my carbine, for what purpose I cannot imagine. The launch, an ancient open boat with a canvas canopy on stanchions to protect us from the broiling sun, puffed and spluttered noisily up the tawny river, making slow progress against the current. Keeping near to the bank, a steep cliff of red laterite with banana plantations and a few huts on the top, and passing close beneath the squalid dwellings of the Annamites, who stared at us with surly curiosity, we reached Ban A Sa Mat in the sweltering heat of mid-afternoon. We waited on the veranda of a hut while the launch went to find Klotz.

Half an hour later he appeared, a dark, thick-set young man of about twenty-five with strong, heavy features and a sombre expression; his speech was slow, his voice hoarse but soft, his command of English nearly perfect. By birth he was Alsatian. He was very tired.

He belonged to a French organization similar to our Force 136.

Together with his wireless operator—'who is a she', he explained—he had been dropped by the Dakota we had seen on the 22nd, into the hills about ten miles north of Thakhek.

'For the first few days we lived in a cave,' he told me. 'But now we have moved to a village. Since our arrival my operator has been unable to make contact with our base at Rangoon, although she has been trying six skeds a day. She is very disheartened. Now my hand generator is broken and I cannot recharge my batteries.

---

[1] Alternate name for Nakorn Panom.

'On the 27th I went to Thakhek—in uniform of course—to ask the Japanese to let me see the French prisoners. The Japanese commander was very correct—gave me lunch but would not let me see the prisoners. He mentioned your name, but without comment. Afterwards he drove me in a car outside the town, and I went back to my village.'

He added that there were very few Japanese left in Thakhek and none, except deserters, in the country around.

It seemed to me that Klotz would be much more comfortable, and would be able to operate more effectively, if he set up his headquarters in my house. The Governor readily agreed and promised to charge his batteries at Nakorn Panom; in any case I was expecting a wireless set very shortly. We arranged, therefore, that Klotz and his operator should join me in the course of the next few days.

We brought him back with us to dine and stay the night. Next morning we took him in the launch to Dong Don, where he had a *pirogue* waiting to ferry him back to the far side. The Governor, reassured by the news that there were no Japanese outside Thakhek, landed with us on the island. We followed a muddy, slippery track through the jungle until we came to a small Laotian village, where Klotz led us to the house of his piroguier. The young Lao lived with his mother and wife; all of them welcomed us warmly, going down on their knees to us and clasping their hands in greeting. The Governor and I had to return immediately, but for Klotz, who was staying there to eat, his host lolled a chicken, and in a manner I had never seen before. Taking a wooden crossbow from the wall he fitted to it a slim bamboo arrow. With his bow at the ready he sidled down the steps to a patch of beaten earth in front of the house, where a few hens were scratching at the soil; selecting his victim he shot it through the middle of the body. The wretched bird screeched and flapped, splashing the ground with blood, until he seized it and wrung its neck.

On 3rd September I had a message from Smiley asking me to meet him at Ubon, where he had a wireless set and operator awaiting me. There was much excitement that day, for the names of the new Siamese government had been announced. Pluto had been nominated Minister Without Portfolio; Marshal Phibul, the 'Strong Man' of the country, who had declared war against us, was under arrest, awaiting trial as a war criminal.[1]

In the evening I had a visit from a Lieutenant de Fay, one of Tavernier's officers, who commanded a group of Laotian guerrillas at Pak Hin Boun, on the Mekong above Thakhek. He gave me a very clear picture of the situation, which I was soon able to confirm for myself.

---

[1] It was not so very long before he became once more the Strong Man, and Pluto and the Regent Pridi Panomyong were fugitives. Now, of course, Marshal Sarit is the Strong Man and Phibul an exile.

Although the capital of the Laotian province of Cammon, Thakhek had a very large Annamese population, which in fact outnumbered the Laos; in the countryside, on the other hand, there were comparatively few Annamites, for they tended to congregate where there was some form of industry to give them employment. There was no love lost between the two races. The majority of Laos stood by the French, whereas the Annamites detested them and, having collaborated actively with the Japanese, were now organizing themselves into a Communist movement, with the declared intention of expelling the French from the whole of Indo-China; this movement was the Viet-minh. Now the Annamites, having obtained large supplies of arms from the Japanese, would, after the departure of the latter, control Thakhek. Tavernier's troops were too weak and poorly armed to drive them out; indeed, they would be lucky to hold their own.

Tension was increasing. The Viet-minh were mustering their forces and had already attacked isolated groups of Franco-Laotian guerrillas, protesting in the usual Communist manner that it was the French who were attacking them. Most serious of all at the moment was the position of the French internees in the town, some forty men, women and children who had been confined in the convent under Japanese guard. Now, however, Captain Nakajima had withdrawn his guards, leaving the prisoners in the care of the *Chaokhoueng*, the Laotian Governor of Cammon. This official had no means of protecting them, being himself at the mercy of the Viet-minh, whose leaders—or Delegates, as they chose to style themselves—had declared their intention of holding the internees as hostages against the French. The attitude of the Viet-minh towards these defenceless people became so menacing that one of the women wrote a letter to de Fay, which he showed me, imploring him to intervene at once.

As a Frenchman de Fay could do nothing; and I could do little enough. However, I immediately wrote to the Annamese Delegates warning them not to harm the French civilians; I gave myself the arrogant title of 'Allied Representative at Nakorn Panom', for I knew that the Viet-minh were hoping to enlist Anglo-American support. I wrote also to Captain Nakajima, asking him to put some troops at the disposal of the Chaokhoueng. Clearly the only solution would be to transport all the internees to the Siamese side of the river, where the Governor readily agreed to receive them. This was a situation which I must discuss with Smiley. I resolved to go to Ubon next day.

A message to Pluto secured me a car and driver for the journey; early the following evening I reached the large wooden bungalow on the outskirts of Ubon where Smiley had established his headquarters. Impressed with the gravity of the situation he agreed to follow me to Nakorn Panom and accompany me across the river to try and evacuate the internees.

In the morning I went with him to visit the prisoner-of-war camp. Talking to those men who had suffered so much, I was filled with admiration for their high morale; for the calm, detached manner in which they talked of their years of misery, overwork and starvation and described the brutalities of their guards, particularly the Koreans—the savage beatings and the horrors of the 'water torture'. They seemed to feel no bitterness, no urge to indulge in reprisals against their former gaolers.

Among the Japanese some discipline still remained; the officers who took orders from Smiley continued to exact obedience from their men. But in the evenings there was a good deal of drunkenness among all ranks; a few days before my visit the Colonel commanding Japanese troops in Ubon, who was unpopular, was badly bitten by an intoxicated private in a brothel.

I left for Nakorn Panom after lunch, reinforced at last by a wireless set and operator and a code name with which to preface all my messages to Calcutta—'Sackcloth'. Jock Rork, the operator, was a tall, rangy, red-haired sergeant in the Royal Corps of Signals with nearly twenty years of service behind him. A man of independent, even contentious character with more than a streak of obstinacy, he was expert at his job, warm-hearted, loyal and fearless. We travelled in a three-ton lorry which Smiley had given me and reached Nakorn Panom after dark. There I found François Klotz and his operator, Edith Fournier, a cheerful, fresh-faced, buxom young woman clothed like the rest of us in olive-green battle-dress and jungle boots and wearing the badges of a second lieutenant of the French Army. They had arrived that morning.

I was awakened next day by a messenger with a letter from Captain Tavernier, written from the village of Ban Tung, about twenty miles south of Thakhek. He told me that he had been appointed civil and military governor of the province of Cammon, with the task of restoring order there as quickly as possible, and asked my help in persuading the Japanese commander in Thakhek to allow him and his troops to occupy the town immediately; to this end he suggested a meeting with me and named a village on the far bank of the Mekong, where some of his men would await me and take me to his headquarters. He also begged me to send him arms, medical supplies— especially for malaria and dysentery—and money; all of which he needed urgently.

When the Japanese occupied French Indo-China in 1940 they did so with the acquiescence of the Vichy authorities who at that time ruled the colony; the French Colonial Army had orders not to resist. Until March 1945 the Japanese were content to use the country as a base, leaving the administration in the hands of the French, whose soldiers retained their arms. But on 9th March they struck. They arrested every French official and officer they could lay hands on; and they murdered the great majority of those they caught. Pockets of the Armée Coloniale resisted and were overwhelmed. In Tonkin a large body of troops fought its way towards the Chinese border but, cut off from outside help, it suffered heavy losses from fever and dysentery and soon ceased to be an effective fighting force.

With few exceptions the Annamese units surrendered or deserted; but the Laotian troops remained loyal to their officers and went with them into the mountains or the jungle to continue resistance. Short of arms and ammunition, with little food and less medical equipment, plagued by every form of tropical disease, those gallant, great-hearted little men stood by their splendid officers and N.C.O.s, who were the flower of the French Army. Actively, they could do little against the Japanese; they could hardly remain alive. But they survived; now they meant to recover Indo-China for France.

Tavernier's needs were urgent; but more important was the danger threatening the French civilians in Thakhek. I wrote back to Tavernier, saying I would meet him as soon as our hands were free of this problem.

Smiley arrived in the afternoon. The Governor was so impressed with the necessity for action that he said he would accompany us to Thakhek in person. While he busied himself organizing food and housing for the evacuees Smiley and I drafted letters to Captain Nakajima and the *Chaokhoueng*, asking for interviews with him and with the Viet-minh Delegates. Nakajima did not answer, but next morning we received a polite note from the *Chaokhoueng* asking us to meet him at the Residency in Thakhek at two o'clock in the afternoon.

Soon after noon on 7th September we embarked in the Governor's launch—Smiley, Klotz, the Governor and myself; two Annamese servants came with us, a mechanic and a pilot. At the Residency gate, opposite the landing-stage, the *Chaokhoueng* awaited us, an unhappy little figure in a white shirt and baggy, purple silk pantaloons reaching half-way down his legs. After a brief talk, in which it became clear that the poor man was much too scared to intervene with the Viet-minh leaders, we persuaded him to take us to see his charges.

Ignoring the groups of scowling Annamites who sauntered through the streets with slung rifles, we came, after a walk of ten minutes, to the convent, a long, low, wooden building beside a white-washed chapel. A thin, fair woman of about forty came out on to the veranda to greet us; this was Madame Collin, widow of the French Resident who had been beheaded in March. She was the acknowledged spokesman of the rest by virtue not only of position but of character, for she was a woman of indestructible serenity, kindliness and courage.

We were at once surrounded by a pathetic throng of women and children, wretchedly clad in worn and shapeless garments little better than rags; they threw their arms around us, clasped and held our hands or simply stared in apathetic or bewildered disbelief. Some, in an agony of fear, called on us to protect them from the Annamese; others kept silence, only betraying by the tears that poured down their cheeks and the spasms that shook their bodies the desolation of their hearts. All of them begged for news of their husbands; we had to say we knew nothing, for we could not tell them that we believed all their men to be dead.

There were eighteen women and fourteen children—boys and girls between the ages of four and fourteen; there were five nuns, whose steadfast faith and devotion had sustained them all through the past grim months, and there were some forty Eurasian orphans whom they had taken under their care. All these lived, sleeping on the floor, in a long dormitory that had been, I think, the refectory.

Living with the priest, in a room adjoining the chapel, were three men, all civilians and very lucky to be alive. One of them, the electrician in charge of the power station, had been under sentence of death. On 22nd August the Dakota which dropped Klotz had flown over Thakhek to drop leaflets. The electrician unwisely waved to it, was seen by an Annamite and reported to the Japanese; that evening he was arrested, together with his wife and child, and taken by car to the fourth kilometre stone on the road south of the town. Realizing that they were going to be executed he warned his family to run for safety as soon as the car drew up; they leaped out and ran towards the jungle but the woman and child were quickly recaptured and shot. They were buried beside the kilometre stone. He himself wandered for two days in the forest until, driven by hunger and exhaustion, he approached the hut of an Annamese charcoal-burner and begged for help; the Annamite, after hacking him about the arms with a machete, handed him over to the Japanese, who were going to kill him when our letters reached Captain Nakajima. The slashes on his arms were open to the bone.

'I think, gentlemen, you have only just arrived in time,' said Madame Collin in her quiet voice. 'The Annamite guards who have replaced the Japanese have become extremely menacing. They show us their knives and make gestures of cutting our throats.'

We looked across the courtyard to the gateway, where a group of villainous-looking young men in grey topees squatted in the dust, their rifles between their knees, while others wandered up and down casting furtive glances in our direction.

'We'll go and see the Annamese Delegates now,' announced Smiley. 'Then we'll take all these people across to Nakorn Panom tonight.'

While he and Klotz were conducted to the Delegates, and the Chaokhoueng and Governor Ta Win went to the quay to organize boats and crews for the evacuation, I stayed at the convent in case the guards should take advantage of their absence to make trouble.

It was two hours, and nearly dusk, before Smiley returned to say that all was ready. He and Klotz had had a stormy session, alternately cajoling and threatening the Delegates, who had protested vehemently against this interference and had raised the astonishing argument that France was not a signatory to the Peace Treaty. But at length Smiley had overridden their objections, and now everything was prepared for the move; the Governor awaited us by the river.

Under the direction of Madame Collin and the nuns the packing began in a bustle of excitement and relief. Suddenly there was an interruption: we heard a bark of orders as a Japanese patrol marched through the gate and halted beneath the veranda. An N.C.O. beckoned to Smiley, Klotz and me. As we reached the bottom of the steps, the patrol fell in on either side of us and at an order marched us away amid the despairing wails of the women. We turned and waved to them, shouting that we should soon return, but the Japanese jammed their rifles in our backs and snarled at us to keep moving. Several of them were obviously drunk.

We were marched to a house on the waterfront, up a flight of stairs and into a bare room furnished only with a desk, at which sat a young Japanese captain with straight, dark hair and a handsome, strangely Latin cast of face. He bowed to us and introduced himself as Captain Nakajima. In jerky, broken English he explained that he had not yet received the precise terms of the surrender treaty, and that without orders from his superiors he could not let us evacuate the French civilians.

Angrily we protested against the manner of our arrest and the behaviour of his patrol. Smiling thinly, the captain apologized and promised that the offending soldiers would be punished; but, although he would place no further restriction on our movements, he bluntly refused to let us remove the French. Smiley undertook to get him the necessary orders from the Japanese colonel at Ubon; meanwhile he demanded that the Annamese guards at the convent should be replaced at once by Japanese, and that the captain should hold himself responsible for the safety of its inmates. Nakajima agreed and, while we waited, detailed the guards and ordered them to escort us back. Gravely he bowed us out.

'Obviously,' growled Smiley, 'he's been tipped off by the Annamese and is scared of them because they outnumber his men.'

Back at the convent we watched the mounting of the Japanese guard and the expulsion of the Annamese, who left with surprising docility. But our troubles were not yet over. A commotion on the veranda brought us running, to find a drunken Japanese soldier trying to tear a wrist watch off one of the nuns. Smiley, who arrived first, tried to remonstrate with him, whereupon the Japanese, an ugly look on his face, drew his bayonet; I felt for my pistol. At that moment the Corporal of the Guard walked up to us, took the soldier by the arm and spun him round, hissing at him angrily; the soldier lurched and muttered, but the corporal slapped his face and continued to slap until the man staggered away, grunting.

'Stay here,' ordered Smiley, 'I'm going back to report this to the captain.'

A quarter of an hour later he returned with a grim-faced Nakajima and another patrol; the offending soldier, after a further bout of slapping, was marched away, his place being taken by an evidently sober guard. Smiley and Klotz returned to Nakorn Panom, the former on his way to Ubon to secure the necessary authority for the release of the refugees, the latter to ask Calcutta for an immediate drop of food, clothing and medical supplies on my airfield. I remained in the convent—where I stayed with the priest, who opened two bottles of his Communion wine in my honour—in order to reassure the refugees; or, as Rowland Winn described it in a subsequent signal, 'to protect the women from a fate worse than Kemp.'

Next day Klotz relieved me at the convent, for I still had work to do at Nakorn Panom. We had heard that there were some French families stranded at the Bartholony tin mines at Phon Tiou, twenty-five miles north of Thakhek, and so I've arranged that I should come back on the morrow, by which time Klotz hoped to have found a car to take us both to the mines. When I returned on the morning of the 9th he had borrowed from the *Chaokhoueng* an old and dilapidated Citroën, whose engine popped and spluttered alarmingly as we drove through the neat, shady streets and out on to the laterite surface of the Route Coloniale 13. At first we followed the course of the Mekong, but after passing through Pak Hin Boun we turned due north and soon began to climb into the hills. The road ran through thick, overgrown forest, intersected by numerous tracks and varied occasionally by bright green patches of paddy or banana plantations; ahead the distant mountain tops shone blue and clear on the horizon, the patches of jungle on their slopes glowing emerald in the sunlight.

We met several convoys of lorries carrying armed Annamese to Thakhek. Each truck displayed a large red flag, and the young men riding behind gave us the clenched fist salute as we passed. Approaching the mines we were stopped several times by control posts, also decorated with the red flag and manned by youths in grey pith helmets; when I said I was a British officer they let us through without argument.

It was getting on in the afternoon when we reached the small cluster of bungalows that formed the living quarters of the mine officials. As we stepped out of the car a grey-haired Frenchwoman ran towards us gesticulating and sobbing piteously; her face was ravaged with lines of horror and despair. Taking us each by the arm she led us into one of the houses. Lying on a bed, wearing only a nightdress, was a girl of seventeen or eighteen; she was a very pretty girl, but now her face was sunken and waxy, her dark eyes hollow and lustreless.

'My daughter,' said the woman. 'Look!'

She lifted the girl's nightdress and pointed to the bluish puncture of a bullet wound about two inches below the navel. The girl looked at us without speaking, without interest. Her mother led us to another room, where lay a man of about fifty, a sallow death's-head who gazed at us in silence, but with tragedy and terror in his eyes.

'In God's name, madame,' said Klotz, 'what has happened?' Pulling herself together the woman told us the dreadful story.

She and her daughter had lived alone in this house since March, when the Japanese had taken her husband; the wounded man lived in the next bungalow with his wife. On 22nd August a party of Japanese, probably deserters, had burst in upon them, looted their houses and, in a fit of wanton cruelty, shot her daughter in the stomach with a pistol, put two bullets into their neighbour and murdered his wife.

'Obviously we must move them at once to Nakorn Panom,' said Klotz. 'But how can we take two badly wounded people, as well as this woman and ourselves, in our small Citroën? They won't survive the journey.'

'Let's try and borrow or hire something from the Annamese,' I suggested. 'Even a truck would do, and they seem to have plenty of those. I know they aren't friendly, but there must be somebody among them with a spark of humanity.'

I was wrong. We tried for an hour, approaching every lorry we saw and begging at least the kindness of a lift for one of the wounded and one of ourselves. At best we met indifference, at worst hostility.

'We can't leave them here, François,' I said. 'There's no alternative but to take a chance with the Citroën. Let's ask them how they feel about it.'

'But of course, gentlemen,' whispered the girl. She gave us a charming smile; only her eyes betrayed her fear.

'As for me,' murmured the man, 'I care nothing if only I can get out of here.'

They told us that there were some half-dozen more French civilians at the tin mines of Boneng, a few miles up the road. At the moment we could do nothing for them, but we resolved to come back with sufficient transport as soon as possible.

Gently we carried the girl into the car and placed her on the front seat; she made no complaint, despite her obvious suffering. Klotz took the wheel and the rest of us squeezed in behind. It was nearly dusk when we started; before we had covered five miles we were in darkness. The lights made a faint, ineffective glow.

'This battery is *kaput*,' Klotz called over his shoulder. 'I can hardly see the road, and if we run off it and have to stop we'll never get her started again. We must look for a village, or even a hut, where we can lie up for the night. In the morning we can find villagers who will push her until she starts.'

We drove at barely more than walking pace for another two miles until, across a paddy-field on the left of the road, we saw a light that seemed to indicate some dwelling.

'Keep the engine running, François, while I go and see if we can stay there.'

Although not usually a provident person I had remembered to bring a lamp. I made my way along a narrow path beside the field until I came to a small hut on the verge of the forest. A wiry, middle-aged Lao came down the steps carrying a torch of flaming brushwood. I pointed to the road and beckoned him to follow me, which he did without the least sign of surprise. When we reached the car he listened quietly while the wounded girl's mother, who spoke his language, explained our trouble. Then he smiled, and she translated his reply.

'He says we must stay with him for the night. He is a poor man and has little to offer us, but he will do his best to make us comfortable. There is a village four kilometres down the road to Thakhek. Tomorrow you can walk there and hire men to push the car.'

Very slowly, with the greatest care, we carried the girl along the path, the Lao preceding us with his torch; the wounded man followed, supported by the girl's mother. Even when we carried her up the steps of the hut the girl gave no sign of the pain she must have felt. There was only one room but it was spotlessly clean, as were the straw mats which were all our host could provide for bedding. I have seen many wounded in my life, and have been seriously wounded myself; but never have I met such fortitude, such indomitable spirit as that young French girl showed throughout her ghastly journey. Whenever either of us tried to sympathize or to apologize for her discomfort, she answered gently, 'It is nothing, monsieur,' and gave her soft, enchanting smile. The man, also, must have been in terrible pain; but he seemed too sunk in misery to care.

In the morning Klotz and I set off on foot down the road to get help, leaving the others in the care of the Lao. We found the village on a track about half a mile off the road. The headman, who spoke pidgin French, procured us the men we needed; but it took time to assemble them, for hurry is a word unknown in the Laotian vocabulary. Klotz decided to make his way separately to Thakhek, to send help to us in case we could not start the car.

He took a *pirogue* down the Nam Hin Boun, a small river which flows into the Mekong at Pak Hin Boun, and reached Nakorn Panom in the evening.

It was afternoon before we started the car and bowled down the road to Thakhek. Although light-headed from relief that our troubles were nearly over, as well as from lack of sleep, I took the journey very slowly, to avoid jolting the wounded. When we arrived at the quay I was thankful to find Smiley and Rowland Winn supervising the embarkation of the convent refugees and their very considerable quantity of luggage. Smiley had returned the previous night from Ubon with his order to Nakajima, and with a Japanese officer to see it carried out; on his instructions Nakajima's men had cleared the streets of Annamites who, despite their superior numbers, seemed to have a healthy respect for the Japanese. Winn had arrived from Naung Khai for a party which I had arranged but had forgotten in the emergency to cancel.

With the help of the Japanese, who carried the baggage, we finished the embarkation before dark; on the other side the Governor, Chief of Police and doctor were waiting with a large party of labourers, several lorries and a dozen bullock carts. Within two hours all the refugees were installed in the hospital, which the Governor had requisitioned for them; they were, naturally, almost hysterical with relief, and poured out their thanks to us all in such profusion that I thought we should never be allowed to leave.

The doctor examined the two wounded and made them as comfortable as possible; but he could not operate on them, lacking the instruments, anaesthetics and—by his own admission—confidence. We sent an urgent signal, asking for a Siamese Air Force plane to land on my airstrip and take them to Bangkok. The aircraft arrived ten days later; when I saw them again in Bangkok, in early November, they had both made a complete recovery.

Winn, too, had been busy at Naung Khai. At Vientiane the Franco-Laotian forces, under the veteran Commandant Fabre, were faced with stiff opposition, not so much from the Viet-minh, although they were active enough, as from the 'Free Lao' movement. This organization, in alliance with the Viet-minh, had declared an independent State of Laos, free from all French control, and had nominated a provisional government under the premier ship of Prince Phetsarath, a member of the royal house of Luang Prabang. Winn, who was working closely with Fabre, giving him what help he could, had to leave us next day to arrange the evacuation of French civilians from Vientiane.

The situation gave him scope for his impish and astringent wit. When Calcutta asked him for the names of the Provisional Free Lao Government he sent them the complete list, starting with Prince Phetsarath and ending with the words: 'But my favourite is Excellency Phoui repeat Phoui, Justice and the Arts.' Our staff officers in Calcutta were nearly always sympathetic and helpful; but on occasions they would send us the most senseless or irritating instructions. One of them, I remember, was to report on the number of elephants in our respective areas and their condition—some of the senior staff officers of Force 136 had interests in the Bombay-Burma Company; to this it was easy enough to reply that the only elephants we had seen were pink. But now, when they knew that we all had our hands full with the emergency in Indo-China, they chose to signal us:

'On leaving Field Finance Branch will require detailed accounts in ticals[1] and gold.'

---

[1] Siamese currency.

It was the timing we resented rather than the content. Winn drafted a bitter reply, concluding with the *cri-de-coeur*: 'Uncomplaining gravest difficulties here but how long oh how long must we continue to kick against the pricks in your office.'

It was late on that night of 10th September before we went to bed. We rose early to prepare for our journey to Boneng to rescue the remaining French civilians. Smiley, Klotz and I re-crossed the Mekong and went immediately to see Nakajima. That young officer was now only too anxious to help. At Smiley's request he provided us with a lorry and a Japanese escort with a light machine-gun, under the command of a lieutenant.

On the road we met few signs of life except an occasional water buffalo with a small boy perched upon its back, and a few peacocks which flitted across the road, gay and glorious in their bright plumage of blue and green. At the Bartholony mines we were stopped by some Annamese guards, who told us that there was a battle going on at Boneng between their troops and the French, and begged us to stop 'this French aggression against our people.'

As we approached Boneng we heard, above the noise of the engine, the sound of rifle and machine-gun fire. We left the lorry on the outskirts of the village and advanced through the town in battle order, the Japanese looking very grim behind their machine-gun, and the three of us doing our best to look resolute and undismayed.

The fighting was centred round the village school; there a small Franco-Laotian force was holding out against some hundred and fifty well-armed Annamites, who with four machine-guns were pouring an intensive if inaccurate fire into the wooden building. We approached the Viet-minh commander and Smiley ordered him to cease fire; after a moment's hesitation and a long look at our escort he obeyed. It now remained for us to parley with the French.

Telling Klotz and me to stay where we were and ignoring our anxiety for his safety, Smiley broke cover and walked boldly towards the school-house, waving a white handkerchief and calling out at intervals, '*Ne tirez pas, je suis officier anglais.*' With our hearts thumping we watched him walk slowly up the steps to the barricade across the door. He spoke for a few moments to someone inside, then beckoned to Klotz and me to join him.

We found a young French officer of Force 136, Lieutenant Gasset, a Eurasian sergeant and ten Lao soldiers. Gasset told us that he had entered the mines to rescue the French civilians there, but had been fired on by the Annamites, who had taken the civilians as hostages; he had evidently fought a good action, for his casualties were only two men wounded, whereas we saw, lying in the road outside, the dead bodies of four Annamites, and there were four more wounded.

Returning with Gasset to the Annamese lines we began to discuss with their commander some way of ending the conflict. During our talk the

Annamese insisted on producing for our close inspection the very messy bodies of their dead—as Smiley commented, they must have been unattractive enough when alive. Eventually we persuaded the Annamese to hand over their hostages and Gasset to return with his men to the mountains, leaving his two wounded Laos in our care.

The hostages were a man, four women and two children, all of them naturally very frightened. We lost no time in packing them and the two Laos into our lorry and driving away with our escort, happy in the fond belief that we had completed our work on that side of the Mekong.

III

MURDER ON THE MEKONG

Smiley returned to Ubon the next day to make arrangements for the transport of the prisoners of war to Bangkok and to disarm a Japanese division. Now that all the French civilians were safe we were ordered to interfere no more in Indo-China. I had, therefore, to leave Tavernier's problems to Klotz, who had already asked for a parachute drop of supplies and money for him.

Our refugees soon adapted themselves to their new life. In the single bare room that ran the whole length of the hospital they spread their mattresses and scanty possessions on the floor, grouping themselves by families in defiance of all the good Sisters' efforts to segregate the sexes. A few days of rest, decent food and, above all, freedom from fear, worked amazing changes in their appearance, especially among the women. After observing the effects of a little make-up and a lot of ingenuity on one or two of the girls, I began to regret that present circumstances did not allow me to cash in on my position as their liberator and protector.

The Siamese authorities did everything they could for them, and on 15th September we received our first drop—food, medical supplies and clothing. The refugees remained with us until the beginning of October, when all but the nuns and their orphan charges left for Ubon; there a French liaison officer met them and accompanied them to Bangkok. The nuns preferred to stay with us until conditions in Thakhek should permit them to return to their convent. An eighteen-year-old Eurasian girl, whom we called Jeannette, attached herself to my headquarters to help Rork and Edith Fournier with the very heavy cipher work, which was more than they could tackle by themselves. I had to ask permission from Calcutta to employ her, and somewhat to my surprise they agreed.

Pluto gave us a monkey, who lived on our veranda; he was very savage at first, having been badly teased by Pluto's young son, but Rork and I gradually tamed him, and he seemed to become very fond of us. He had some disgusting sexual habits which he usually indulged in the presence of young girls; Jeannette, who went about in shorts and bare legs, used to rouse him to a pitch of hysterical fury, and she could never go near him in safety. Later on we acquired from Indo-China two young male gibbons. They were enchanting creatures whose soft fur smelt deliciously of musk; they would cling to us, put their arms round our necks and pick imaginary parasites from our hair. One, whom we christened Toby, was black with a white face; the

34

other, who was white with a black face, we called Smift. The origin of his name needs some explanation. We frequently received signals ending with this obscure word; it was some time before we learned that it stood for 'See My Immediately Following Telegram'.

A few days after Smiley's departure a signal from Calcutta advised us of the decisions that had been taken at' highest level' about the immediate future of Indo-China. South of the sixteenth parallel the country was in the S.E.A.C.[1] theatre of operations. As soon as their troops arrived, which would be in October, the French would take over the responsibilities of restoring law and order and disarming the Japanese; at present the only Allied military organization there was an Indian Division under General Gracey at Saigon. North of the sixteenth parallel, which included all the country adjoining our areas, those duties would be undertaken by Marshal Chiang-Kai-Shek's Kuomintang Chinese, whose troops were now advancing from the north and might be expected in Vientiane and Thakhek at any moment.

This news caused grave alarm among the Siamese, who had always feared—and still do—that their own large and unassimilated Chinese population might one day be used by China as a pretext for invading their country. Units of the Siamese Army and reinforcements of police began to move into our areas. The Governor looked worried and repeatedly stressed to me his anxiety. Although since the last century, when they had annexed Cambodia, the French had been the immediate object of Siamese fear and suspicion, always there had been the remoter but much more formidable menace of China.

In these new circumstances Force 136 lifted the ban on our intervention in affairs across the river, stipulating only that we should be accompanied wherever possible by French officers, and that we should tread very warily in our dealings with the Chinese; there was considerable danger, we were warned, of friction between the Chinese and the French. The British, on the other hand, were working very closely with the French, who needed our support badly in view of the American attitude to Indo-China. This signal concluded with a sentence so typical of the staff officer's mind that it is worth recording: 'You will give French all possible assistance short of becoming involved yourselves.'

The American attitude was summarized by the late Mr. Chester Wilmot, who wrote, 'Roosevelt was determined that Indo-China should not go back to France.' Mr. Graham Greene, who visited the country early in 1954, wrote of American intervention:

In 1945, after the fall of Japan, they had done their best to eliminate French influence in Tongkin. M. Sainteny, the first post-

---

[1] South-East Asia Command, under Lord Mountbatten.

war Commissioner in Hanoi, has told the sad, ignoble story in his recent book, *Histoire d'une Paix Manqée*—aeroplanes forbidden to take off with their French passengers from China, couriers who never arrived, help withheld at moments of crisis.

We were shortly to witness even worse. Like ourselves the French had been accustomed to thinking of the Americans not only as allies but as friends; it never occurred to any of us simple officers that the most powerful country in the free world would deliberately embark upon a policy of weakening her allies to the sole advantage of her most dangerous enemy. We have learnt a lot since, but in those days it all seemed very strange.

Towards the end of the third week in September I paid Winn a visit at Naung Kai; Smiley had procured me from Bangkok a jeep, a three-ton lorry, two motor bicycles and several drums of petrol, so that communications were no longer a problem. The occasion for my journey was a party for Winn's twenty-ninth birthday, but its real object was to discuss in the light of our new instructions the problems facing us across the river.

Winn had evacuated from the other side a large party of French civilians, who were now under the care of the Governor of Naung Khai pending their departure to Bangkok; they were going by air, because the aerodrome at Naung Khai was large enough for Dakotas. Commandant Fabre's troops were in occupation of Vientiane, but they were not allowed to remain there long. At the end of the month the Chinese arrived in strength. Almost their first action was to invite all the French officers to a dinner-party. At the Chinese headquarters in the Residency, where the tricolour was flying in their honour, Fabre and his companions were courteously shown into a room and immediately surrounded by Chinese soldiers with levelled tommy-guns. They were relieved of their arms, equipment, money and watches and ordered to quit the town instantly, on pain of arrest. After some argument Fabre himself was allowed to stay, together with his wireless set and operator; but he had to send the rest of his force ten miles away, for he had been ordered to avoid incidents with the Chinese.

Defenceless and surrounded by enemies Fabre was vitally dependent upon help from Winn, who received parachute drops, including arms, and smuggled them across the river by night to a rendezvous with the Franco-Laotians in the jungle; more than once he had to smuggle not only arms but parachutists, for the French had no suitable dropping ground at their disposal. It was fortunate that the Governor of Naung Khai was sympathetic.

Winn's visits to confer with Fabre exposed him to grave personal risk. The distance from the landing-stage opposite Naung Kai to Vientiane was nearly fifteen miles—it was impracticable to make the journey direct by boat owing to the distance and the strength of the current; the Chinese had requisitioned all transport, and so Winn had to walk or bicycle. On the way he often found himself a target for Free Lao or Viet-minh snipers.

When, later on, he received a jeep his journeys became easier; but at the beginning of November he ran into an ambush and nearly lost his life. He was driving towards Vientiane with Fabre, a Lieutenant Larroue and two Lao soldiers when they were fired on at a range of fifty yards by about twenty Annamese with light machine-guns. He accelerated through the hail of bullets, but the jeep was hit, ran off the road and overturned; Winn broke a wrist, Fabre a shoulder and one of the Laos a leg. While the two uninjured men ran to get help Winn and his companions crouched for two hours in a ditch behind their vehicle, waiting for the enemy, whom they could plainly hear moving and talking in the undergrowth, to close in for the kill. But the enemy seemed to have no stomach for close fighting and kept their distance until a lorry arrived full of friendly Laos, who took the wounded men to safety.

A few days before my visit an American O.S.S mission of ten officers and N.C.O.s, under a Major Banks, had dropped without warning on the aerodrome at Naung Khai. Ignoring Winn they had established themselves in the town and prepared to receive supply drops. They had no authority from S.E.A.C. to be in Siam. Although perplexed and a little irritated by their discourtesy Winn was much more worried by their behaviour to Fabre and his officers, who at this time had not yet occupied Vientiane. From his base at Naung Khai Banks crossed the river on several occasions and in the most insulting manner ordered the French to keep out of the town and to 'cease their aggression' against the Annamese and Free Laos.

Determined to get rid of this nuisance Winn hit on the brilliant and comradely idea of persuading Banks that he would find a more interesting situation and greater scope for his activities at Thakhek.

'They left for Nakorn Panom yesterday,' he told me amiably when I arrived. 'You should find them there on your return.'

It is only fair to add that he would never have done it if he could have foreseen the consequences.

The birthday party took place in the Governor's house, where Winn had his headquarters; this was a tall white building over-looking the Naung Khai waterfront and the broad brown flood of the Mekong that swirled westwards from Vientiane in a great curve beneath the low red cliffs and bright green jungle of the Laotian bank. The Governor and his handsome wife, who had both taken a great liking to Winn and Lawson, had been at pains to provide the best food, unlimited liquor and the prettiest girls from the neighbourhood to make the party a success; Winn had also invited the French refugees from Vientiane. He had changed for the occasion into what my friend Hardy Amies might have called a daring and original number: a pair of black satin Chinese trousers, surmounted by a broad, multi-coloured silk cummerbund of Laotian design, an open-necked white silk shirt, and a green and white spotted silk scarf. I was unable to persuade him to wear his green forage cap as well. He had omitted to brush his hair but he smelt deliciously of Trumper's after-shaving lotion.

After the anxieties of the past weeks I was more than ready to enjoy myself; with the result that not all the events of that evening are clear in my memory. I have a blurred recollection of a totally uninhibited Spider Lawson causing some eyebrow-raising among those of the refugees who spoke English, with a spirited rendering of a famous soldiers' version of the Egyptian National Anthem; also of inflicting my attentions on a shapely and evidently nubile blonde, only to discover that she had formed an unshakable attachment to Lawson—'*Ce Spidair, donc,*' she kept whispering to me, '*croyez-vous que c'est un Homme Serieux?*'

Next morning we went to Vientiane for a meeting with H.H. Prince Phetsarath, self-styled Prime Minister of the Free Lao Government; he had promised to provide us with transport from the landing-stage, but for safety's sake we each took a pistol and an American .30 calibre carbine. Commandant Fabre met us at the landing-stage, a tall and silent man whose strong, determined features were drawn and sallow from months of malaria, dysentery and strain. A rickety old bus with a small escort of apathetic Chinese soldiers took us to Vientiane, a well-laid-out town of imposing white villas in spacious, shady gardens. In the largest, most luxurious, lived His Highness.

A swarthy, heavily built man in early middle age, he received us in a cool and comfortable room where the strong morning light filtered faintly through sun-blinds; his beautifully manicured hands and smart white linen suit matched the opulence of his surroundings. He had an unfortunate manner compounded of shiftiness, complacency and arrogance; nor were we impressed by his contemptuous references to our French friends or his exaggerated claims of the support he enjoyed among his people. But he mixed us a really excellent rum cocktail, which he described—with unconscious humour—as something between a *Cuba Libre* and a *Presidente*.

In the afternoon I drove back to Nakorn Panom full of anxiety about the O.S.S. mission Winn had wished on me. My fears were justified. Banks had set up his headquarters there, and had already received a drop on the airfield. He had also taken it upon himself to scare my French refugees out of their lives by telling them that they were going to be returned to Thakhek. But he was not seriously interested in Nakorn Panom, except as a base, and in me not interested at all. It was in Thakhek that he had made his presence felt. The Japanese had gone, leaving the town in the hands of the Viet-minh. In conferences with the Annamese Delegates, Banks assured them that he was determined to put an end to what he called French aggression; also that Chinese troops would shortly arrive to disarm the French and take over the administration of the country pending the establishment of a 'national and democratic government' in Indo-China, free from the rule of France.

In proof of his intentions he sought out Tavernier, whom he found holding a road block to the north of the town and brusquely ordered him to withdraw. To avoid incidents Tavernier complied, but afterwards he complained to me bitterly of Banks's tone and language.

'He spoke to me as I would not dream of speaking to a servant—in front of my own soldiers and the Annamites, all of whom understand French. He called me a pirate, and threatened that if I did not withdraw my men he would send Chinese troops to disarm us.'

By the same methods he had forced Quinquenel to abandon Savannakhet, which that officer had recently occupied.

The Annamese, of course, were delighted and immediately launched a series of sharp attacks on the French posts around both towns, forcing them to withdraw farther into the forest. I signalled Calcutta for instructions. They replied that Banks had no right to be in Siam, which came under S.E.A.C., we could not stop him making trouble in Thakhek, but he must do so from that side of the river. I should request him, tactfully, to remove his party. In the meantime Calcutta would take up the matter with S.E.A.C.

As diplomatically as I could I gave Banks the message. He was a spare, well-knit man in his early thirties, with a dark complexion, a thin, sneering mouth and flickering, close-set eyes; his manner was furtive and he seemed reluctant to look at me as he spoke. He told me curtly that he had his orders and meant to carry them out; he would stay at Nakorn Panom as long as it suited him and would make his own arrangements to receive drops on the airfield—he saw no need to give me warning of them.

I begged him to desist from encouraging the Annamese, who had been truculent enough before his arrival.

'After all,' I pointed out, 'the French are our allies. Tavernier and his men have held out with great endurance against the Japanese, to whom the Annamites gave their whole-hearted collaboration.'

'So did the French collaborate,' he snarled, his narrow eyes glancing around my feet. 'Why, I was betrayed myself by a traitor in France! It damn nearly cost me my life.'

Suppressing a wistful sigh I returned to my headquarters, where I drafted gloomy reports to Calcutta and Smiley.

Banks did in fact move within the next few days to Thakhek, where the Annamese were only too happy to find him a house. From time to time I received reports of his speeches, encouraging them in their 'struggle for freedom'. I must add that the others in his party were very different from their commander, being courteous, friendly and—on the few occasions when they were allowed—helpful; but they seemed overawed by Banks.

They had been gone two days when Klotz and I decided to visit Tavernier to hand over some medical stores; Klotz wrote to him to expect us. We should pass through Thakhek on the way, to pick up a car for part of the journey and carry out some commissions for the French. Banks had told Klotz to keep away, but he had replied with some heat:

'I can certainly go to Thakhek if I wish! I am a French officer and Thakhek belongs to France.'

We borrowed the Governor's launch with his two Annamese boatmen; the American Lieutenant Reese, who had come over that morning, was our only other companion. We started across the Mekong after lunch on 27th September. It is a date I am unlikely to forget. The monsoon was coming to an end; the afternoon was cloudless, still and warm; the hills behind Thakhek smiled peaceful and welcoming, a bright quilt of green and gold. The houses on the waterfront seemed deserted and asleep. We jumped ashore and walked up the ramp.

As we stepped on to the road we heard a high-pitched command, 'Halt!' From a doorway on the left issued a platoon of Annamese led by a short, lightly built officer with a drawn pistol, whom I recognized as one of the Viet-minh Delegates, known as Tu, formerly an employee of the electricity plant. In different circumstances he would have been a ludicrous figure with his dirty khaki shorts, the grey composition topee that seemed to be the uniform of his kind, and his self-important pseudo-military manner. He strutted up to us and made a signal to his men, who spread out facing us with levelled rifles.

'*Bien*,' he yapped, grinning to show a mouthful of uneven blackened teeth rotting in red, betel-stained gums. He turned to me. 'Who are you?'

'I am a British officer, as you know.'

'And you?' to Reese.

'American.'

'You,' he said to Klotz, 'are French?' Klotz nodded.

'Very well. The British and American officers may go free. They are our allies. The Frenchman is under arrest and will come with us. The French declared war on us yesterday in Saigon.'

'Don't be ridiculous,' I protested, trying to sound calm and confident. 'The British, Americans and French are all allies, and we are certainly not going to let you arrest our friend. Isn't that so, lieutenant?' I called to Reese, who had made his way through the rank of Annamese and was now leaning against the wall of a house across the road.

Reese shuffled his feet and looked unhappily at the ground. 'I don't know,' he muttered. 'I guess we're neutral.'

He looked miserable. I was and still am convinced that he was acting under orders; certainly he showed the next day that he had abundant moral courage, and I am certain that it was not physical cowardice that made him withhold his help from us at this moment.

I do not believe I have ever felt so utterly defeated. With Reese on one side of him and myself on the other it would have been possible to conduct Klotz back to the launch; I was sure the Annamese would not risk harming a British or American officer, and in this way we could have screened Klotz from their fire without much danger. Now I must try to do it alone, for it was unthinkable to leave him to certain murder and probable torture. What I would have given at that moment for just one section of British or Indian troops!

'François,' I said quietly in English, 'you and I are going back to the boat. There doesn't seem any future in staying here.'

He smiled and took his hand off his pistol holster. I turned to the Delegate, trying to keep my voice steady and conceal my fear.

'Monsieur Tu, since our presence here is unwelcome to you, my friend and I are returning to Siam. Au revoir.'

I made him a stiff bow and, putting my arm around Klotz and trying to keep myself between him and his enemies, turned and started to walk towards the ramp.

'No!' screamed Tu. 'You may go, but he stays here.'

'Keep moving,' I whispered, 'and pretend we haven't heard.'

Klotz nodded, his face expressionless, his eyes calm. I do not like to imagine his real feelings during those moments: I remember too vividly my own. But he gave no sign of the fear that must have been tormenting him; his frame beneath my arm was unshaking and relaxed. Behind us we heard the rattle of rifle bolts as the Annamese closed in. Please, dear God, I prayed, look after us now.

There was a shout from Tu, followed by a fusillade of shots about our ears. I felt the blast of a rifle on my right cheek and realized with a sudden surge of elation that they were firing past us or into the air. It was, after all, a bluff. Only a few yards ahead of us lay the launch under her dirty canvas awning; she was deserted, but if we could reach her safely and cast off from the bank, the current would take us downstream with enough steerage way to reach the Siamese side. I was now walking almost directly behind Klotz to give him the maximum of cover; it seemed that we had got away with it.

There was a fresh burst of firing; a figure ran up on my left, thrust his rifle under my arm into Klotz's back, fired once and disappeared. Klotz staggered and let out a terrible, despairing gasp.

'Oh, Peter,' he whispered. 'Oh, Peter!'

A wide crimson stain spread thickly over the front of his shirt; a torrent of blood poured from his mouth. I tried to hold him but he swayed forward out of my arms and lurched with weakening steps down the ramp on to the landing-stage; there he dropped on all fours and began to drag himself towards the launch. I ran after him and lifted him over the thwarts on to the raised after deck; he lay there face downwards, the blood trickling from his mouth. Within half a minute he was dead.

Nearly hysterical with anger and grief I ran back up the ramp. Tu and his men had vanished, but Reese was where I had left him, leaning against the wall; he had been joined by a major who was Banks's second-in-command and by two N.C.O.s.

'I hope,' I said, trying to keep my voice under control, 'I hope you're proud of your Annamite friends. 'That'—I pointed to the corpse on the launch—that is the direct result of your work!'

'Gee!" squealed a small dark boy, the younger of the N.C.O.s, 'Gee, this is terrible! Let's get the hell out of this place.'

'I guess,' said the major slowly, 'we better have a company of Chinese paratroopers down here right away. I'll go call Hanoi.'

Having failed to save Klotz's life I must at all costs rescue his body before the Viet-minh came to claim it as a token of their triumph. I was thankful to see the dowdy, sorrowful, figure of the *Chaokhoueng* approaching with the two Annamese boatmen who, not unnaturally, had run away when the trouble began. While they started the engine and swung the bows into the stream I sat down beside Klotz, brushing away the flies that were already clustered on his bloodstained mouth and back and on the congealing pool on the deck; they rose in a cloud with a low, resentful buzz.

All the way across I sat watching the poor dead face of this gallant, warm-hearted young man who in such a short time had become so close a friend. It seemed a tragic waste that after fighting throughout the war he should die now with a bullet in the back. I could not know how many thousands of his countrymen were to follow him in the next ten years. At that moment I felt only a bitter anger and a shattering sense of loss.

> So smothers in blood and burning
> And flaming flight
> Of valour and truth returning
> To dust and night.

Remorsefully I thought of how he had trusted my judgment when his own instinct had been to draw his pistol and stand his ground. If I had stood with him, threatening to shoot the first Annamese to lift a rifle, might he not, I now wondered, yet be alive? I am still haunted by the thought that it might have turned out better that way.

At Nakorn Panom I sent one of the boatmen with a note to the Governor, asking him to have the body delivered to the nuns, and to arrange a military funeral for the following afternoon; leaving the other man on guard at the wharf I walked to my headquarters.

Rork and Edith Fournier were on the veranda waiting for me; they had heard the shooting.

'Where is François?' Edith's voice was very low.

I could hardly bring myself to look at her: 'François is dead.'

She stood quite still and silent while the tears flooded into her eyes and fell in great glistening drops slowly down her cheeks. When I had told her what had happened she whispered, '*C'est la deuxième fois, mon Dieu, c'est la deuxième fois!*' On her last mission, in occupied France, her chief had been taken by the Gestapo. There was nothing I could say to her. Leaving her with Rork I shut myself in my room, fell upon the bed and for a few minutes gave in to my own misery and despair.

Pulling myself together I asked Edith to come with me to the hospital and break the news to the refugees and nuns before Klotz's body arrived. We covered the quarter of a mile distance without speaking. At the hospital we were surrounded by an anxious crowd, who stared in horror at my blood-stained clothes. When they heard that Klotz was dead there was a stunned silence, followed by a chorus of cries and sobs from the women; but their sorrow gave way to a rising clamour of indignation when I told them of Lieutenant Reese's neutrality.

While we were talking, the Governor arrived with the Chief of Police and the doctor. The doctor had already examined the body, which was now on the way to the hospital; he said that Klotz had been shot through the base of the heart and no power on earth could have saved him. The Governor was almost in tears himself with distress and anxiety. It appeared that the messenger to Tavernier had been intercepted by the Viet-minh, who had read Klotz's letter and prepared the ambush to meet us; by the time the Governor knew, Klotz had been killed. The order for Klotz's detention had been given by the Chief Delegate, Long, alias Le Hoq Minh, who had entrusted its execution to Tu. I asked the Governor to have them both arrested if ever they came to Nakorn Panom; but he could not do so without instructions from Bangkok, which despite my repeated efforts never arrived.

I gave him a telegram to send Smiley, asking him to come as soon as possible; with his rank and authority I felt that he might have some influence on Banks.

The nuns would lay out the body, and we would keep vigil over it in watches during the coming night. The funeral was arranged for the following afternoon, at the Catholic cemetery north of the town; the police would provide a guard of honour.

I spent the earlier part of the night drafting two long signals to Calcutta, one in clear giving them the facts, the other in code embodying my suggestions for bringing Klotz's murderers to justice and for helping Tavernier; I also wrote a detailed report on the incident and the events preceding it. The effort at least made me concentrate; I could not eat and it was useless to try and sleep.

At midnight we left for the hospital. I had ordered Rork not to stay long, for he had a heavy signal traffic in the morning; but Edith insisted on staying the rest of the night, and I could not prevent her. Klotz was lying on a camp bed, dressed in a clean uniform; he looked serene and peaceful, his strong features softened in the dim candlelight. We took our places among the shadowy figures thronging the small bare room. I found myself standing beside the Sheriff; all the officials of Nakorn Panom came to stand guard for a part of the night.

As the silent hours passed and I watched the calm, still face on the camp bed, I found I was no longer tortured by the terrible memory of that blood-drenched figure staggering down the ramp at Thakhek. Instead, I remembered François gently lifting in his strong arms the wounded girl at the mines; François reading me passages from Descartes and patiently and unsuccessfully trying to explain what Frenchmen meant when they described themselves as Cartésiens; both of us sitting over our rum on the veranda in the cool night, singing French Army marching songs. Into my mind came suddenly a verse from our favourite—sung, I believe, by the troops of General Juin in North Africa:

Il n'y aura plus de pierres,
Il y aura des fleurs dans les jardins,
Il y aura des oiseaux sur les branches légères
—Il y aura des filles sur tous les chemins.

We were about to leave for the funeral when Lieutenant Reese arrived at the house, grim-faced but very smart in his uniform. He saluted me gravely.

'I've come, major, to attend Lieutenant Klotz's funeral.'

Edith turned and walked out of the room.

'That's very good of you, lieutenant, I'm sure. But—but—do you know what you may be letting yourself in for? The French here are pretty indignant and—'

'I know. But I'd like to be there.'

He walked with us to the cemetery. There he stood alone, his eyes on the ground, while the silent, fierce tide of hatred welled all round him. At last the priest began the service and everyone turned towards the open grave. When the coffin had been lowered, wrapped in the tricolour, the volley fired and the earth shovelled over, Reese turned to face the trench, saluted and marched away. Whatever may be said about him he showed that day no lack of dignity or courage.

The grave was marked with a plain wooden cross inscribed with Klotz's name and the date of his murder. It was not allowed to remain there long.

The Annamese, whose town adjoined the cemetery, could not let their hatred rest with his death; time and again during the next three months they uprooted the cross and took it away, leaving a few splinters to mock his trampled grave. Each time we replaced it they would do the same: an easy revenge, but what a people that could find it sweet.'

When we had thanked the Governor and all his officers, Edith, Rork and I walked slowly homewards along the road by the Mekong bank. Gazing at those hateful hills above Thakhek which only yesterday I had thought so beautiful, I felt Edith's tight grip on my arm. 'Nous le vengerons,' she whispered fiercely, '*nous le vengerons!*'

Before we reached the main street we met Smiley, driving a large Cadillac saloon which he had taken from a Japanese general. My telegram had found him at Mukdahan, where he had gone to take over the Japanese ships on the Mekong; he had driven here at full speed.

When he had heard my story he wrote a note to Banks asking for an interview in Thakhek the next morning and for an escort to take him from the boat to O.S.S. headquarters. He ordered me to stay behind, and in the circumstances I could not argue. But I tried to stop him going alone, because I had heard that the Viet-minh had announced that any officers, of whatever nationality, who had been helping the French would be arrested if they came to Thakhek.

I was very glad to see him back in the afternoon.

'What did you think of Banks?' I asked.

Smiley made a rude gesture. 'Apart from everything else, he can't tell the truth. He swore to me that he had never called the French officers bandits or ordered them to give themselves up to the Annamese; but he didn't know that I had in my pocket a letter written by him to the French at Savannakhet in those very words. By the way, Peter, you're not to go to Thakhek again. The Viet-minh are after your blood and they've put a price on your head.'

'How much?'

'I can't quite make out. It's either five hundred pounds or half a crown, depending on the rate of exchange.'

IV

PERILS OF A GUN-RUNNER

At the beginning of October I had news from Calcutta that S.E.A.C. were pressing for the withdrawal of Banks and his party. I was ordered to tell him that the Viet-minh had just shot up O.S.S. headquarters in Saigon and killed Colonel Dewey, the Commander.

To my surprise the news made no impression on him, he had already heard it. He simply repeated that he had his orders. However, at the end of the week his entire party left for Ubon; I never saw them again. At this point I must make it clear that Major Banks was quite unlike any other American officer I have ever met; moreover, the other members of his mission seemed a friendly and well-intentioned body of men. If I have been unable to hide my bitterness against Banks it is because he was largely responsible for the murder of my friend and for the strengthening of Viet-minh resistance around Thakhek which was to cause the French so many casualties in the next six months. What I cannot explain is how he was able to use Siamese territory as a base in contravention of a clear agreement between the British and United States governments.

That Smiley had been right about the Viet-minh attitude towards me was soon apparent. Interested in locating their positions facing Tavernier south of the town, I borrowed the Governor's launch one afternoon and cruised up and down close to the other bank of the river, studying the shore through my field glasses. This pleasant pastime came to an abrupt end when, without warning, several machine-guns opened up on us, fortunately firing short. Sang-a, the only other passenger, threw himself on the floor—wisely—and lay there gibbering. I did not have to tell the helmsman to turn away; before I could give the order he had the launch headed at full speed for home. I reflected that if it were true, as we had heard, that the Viet-minh had Japanese deserters in their ranks, it was lucky for us that none of them was behind those guns.

On various occasions during the next four months I and the officers attached to me were sniped on the road; but the Annamese were not sure enough of themselves to pursue their vengeance very vigorously in Siam— or so, at least, I thought.

One of the suggestions I had made in my signal on the night of Klotz's death was that supplies of arms should be dropped to me to smuggle to Tavernier; two days later Calcutta agreed, and told me to stand by for a drop on 3rd October; I had also asked to receive French parachutists, as Winn had been doing at Naung Khai, and transport them across; but this was not agreed until some weeks later. I was particularly warned not to divulge the fact that I was smuggling arms; I was to pretend that the containers held medicines, food and clothing—as indeed a few of them would. I decided to visit Tavernier immediately to plan our gun-running operation.

Tavernier's headquarters was still at Ban Tung. I asked him to have men and horses waiting for me at a small village on the far bank of the Mekong, about ten miles south of Thakhek. On 1st October I borrowed the Governor's launch and crossed over in the morning. Tavernier's men were waiting—six young Lao soldiers under a French N.C.O.

We rode along narrow winding tracks through thick undergrowth, frequently having to lean over our ponies' necks to avoid branches and creepers that overhung our path. After half an hour we began to climb gradually into the hills. We had covered about ten miles and climbed a thousand feet when we came suddenly upon the familiar banana plantations that marked the outskirts of a village; here we were challenged by an outpost of three Lao soldiers with an old Hotchkiss light machine-gun. A few minutes later we came into a wide clearing dotted with huts and a few small houses, which was the village of Ban Tung. Laotian soldiers—barefooted little men in shorts and dark blue berets—walked between the huts in twos and threes, or squatted in groups in the doorways, chatting and laughing; all had the same alert, expectant look. Dismounting, I followed the N.C.O. to the largest of the houses, which was Tavernier's command post, and waited on the veranda while he announced me with an impressively smart salute.

Lieutenant Ferdinand Tavernier was a tall, dark officer of about my own age; lean and ascetic in appearance, prematurely bald, with tired eyes blinking behind thick horn-rimmed glasses, he seemed a good deal older. He spoke in a quiet, rather high voice and he very seldom smiled; he had no English.

I had brought with me a few medical stores and told him that there were more waiting for him at Nakorn Panom. He was pathetically grateful.

'You know, major, there is not one of us here who is not sick. All of us have recurring malaria, most have amoebic dysentery, and our small stock of medicines was long ago exhausted. We have had no supplies since the Japanese coup in March.'

Making a note of his most urgent needs I asked, 'Have you had any cases of bacillary dysentery?'

'Oh yes, plenty. But they all died.'

We arranged that he should come to Nakorn Panom the day after the drop; we would load his stores on to one of my lorries and drive to a point about fifteen miles south of the town, where he would have men and *pirogues* waiting to transport them over the river.

'This is wonderful news!' he exclaimed. 'We are really desperate here. Since our Major Banks gave them such encouragement the Annamites have been pressing us hard; with the few weapons I have I cannot stand up to them, and now I am running out of ammunition. I could, of course, retire deep into the mountains, but that would mean leaving the population here, who are our friends, to be massacred.

'Do you think you could also get me some money to buy food? We cannot continue to live indefinitely on the charity of these good people. And of course my soldiers have not been paid since March. It is wonderful the way they have stood by us, when they could so easily have deserted.'

There was no other officer with Tavernier, but I was introduced to his N.C.O.s. Sickness, undernourishment and fatigue made them look like walking corpses, but they were all cheerful and full of hope and enthusiasm. The most impressive figure was the padre, a short, square Frenchman with a huge black beard, a deep voice and an apparently inexhaustible fund of energy and good humour.

On the way back to the launch I was riding at the head of the party; as I leaned forward to pass under an overhanging branch I heard a sharp cry from the man behind '*Attention, Commandant!*' Looking back I saw, coiled along the branch I had just passed, a large snake. That was the only live snake I saw in the Far East, outside the pits of the Pasteur Institute in Bangkok.

My carefully disseminated cover-story about the arms was shattered during the drop by one of those pieces of bad luck which always seem to catch me out when I embark upon deception. The two Liberators made their dropping runs from west to east, turning at the end of each run when they were over Thakhek. Owing to a fault in the release mechanism one of the containers stuck underneath the aircraft, falling a few seconds later on the far bank; it was retrieved by the Viet-minh, who thus received a present of eighteen Stens, as well as valuable material for propaganda, of which they made immediate use.

The next morning the Governor came to see me in a state of extreme indignation, forbade me to move the arms I had just received, and placed a police guard over them. Even Smiley was unable to mollify him; the most he would allow poor Tavernier to take were the containers that actually held only food, clothing and medicine, and the money which I had received on his behalf.

I sent an urgent signal to Calcutta, asking for instructions to be sent from Bangkok for the release of the arms; but it was a fortnight before they arrived. Even then the Governor insisted that the operation should be carried out at night, and well away from the town. I therefore wrote to Tavernier asking him to send *pirogues* and men to a small village on the Siamese bank of the river, a little way upstream of our original rendezvous; they were to await me there at midnight on 20th October. I decided to accompany the arms across the river and see them delivered personally—partly to satisfy myself about their condition, and partly because it would give me the opportunity of having a further talk with Tavernier and assessing his future requirements.

I could scarcely hope for complete secrecy in smuggling the arms, after the publicity that had attended their arrival; the Governor, however, tactfully removed our police guards at dusk on the 20th, and so gave us the chance to load the containers on to our lorry under cover of darkness. It was a slow and exhausting business but, exhilarated by the thought that we were doing something, however small, to avenge poor Klotz, we quite literally put our backs into the work.

Leaving Edith Fournier behind to operate the wireless sked Rork and I set out for the rendezvous shortly after eleven, with Rork at the wheel.

'I hope to God the French are there on time,' I commented as we bumped over the pot-holes on the road leading southwards from the town and left the last huts and plantations behind. 'I shan't feel happy so long as this stuff remains on Siamese soil. Those Annamite bastards must have a pretty good idea of our plan, and I wouldn't put it past them to try and intercept—in which case I don't at all care for the thought of waiting around on our own in the dark in the middle of the countryside.' 'No more do I, sir. D'you really think they'll try something here? I don't think the Governor would like that much.'

'No, he certainly wouldn't. But I don't want to take chances, just the same. Of course, they may try to catch us on the river—they ought to be able to see all right with this moon. 'That reminds me,' I went on. 'In my letter, I gave Tavernier to understand that I should be returning tomorrow by the same route, and you'd be picking me up in the truck at this same village. Now of course that would be a dotty idea. If the Annamese are really out to get us, it's the obvious place they'd choose to lie in wait.'

'But how will you really get back?'

'Quite simply. Before we left home tonight I wrote a line to the Governor—I have it on me now—asking him to send his launch tomorrow morning to collect me from the other side and take me direct to Nakorn Panom. You will please deliver it to him personally first thing in the morning.'

'I will, sir. But will he agree?'

'Certainly, he'll agree. I've explained that I'm afraid of trouble from Comrade Tu and his pals, and that's something he's as keen to avoid as we are.'

We drove on in silence until we came to the track leading to the village where I was to meet Tavernier's men; it ran off to the left, just before the road crossed a narrow wooden bridge over a watercourse. Rork slowed down.

'Better turn her round,' I said, 'so that we're facing homewards in case of trouble.'

'We're a bit late for that, sir. Look!'

In the moonlight I saw two figures standing by the posts on either side of the bridge; at the same moment two more appeared from the bushes at the entrance to the track. I fumbled for my pistol and was about to shout to Rork to put his foot on the accelerator when, with an almost sickening flood of relief, I noticed the berets and uniform shirts of Tavernier's Laotians.

There were more than a dozen men awaiting us, not all of them soldiers; in command was one of the N.C.O.s I had met on my first visit. Under his direction they set to work swiftly and quietly, opening the containers and carrying the weapons and boxes of ammunition down the few hundred yards of track to the river. When the last empty container had been replaced in the lorry I gave Rork my note to the Governor.

'Mind you hand it to him personally,' I repeated.

'I will, sir, never fear. Good luck to you now.'

He drove off into the night. Slinging my carbine on my shoulder I followed on the heels of the French sergeant, picking out the pale ribbon of the winding path between dark clumps of thorn bushes. Once or twice I stopped and looked around uneasily, to reassure myself that we were not being followed; but the fields lay still and peaceful in the milky moonlight. We slowed our pace when we entered the coconut plantations on the outskirts of the village, making a wide detour to avoid the houses. A gentle breeze rattled the palm fronds overhead and brought to our nostrils the heady, sweet scents of the tropical night mingled with the reek of wood smoke from dying fires; from close by came the snarling bark of a dog, followed by a brief chorus of yelps that gradually died away into silence.

Six or seven large *pirogues* were lying at the water's edge. The work of loading was completed with the same speed and silence as before. There was no sign of life from the village as we climbed aboard and paddled away from the bank; even the dogs had ceased their howling, and the only sounds in the still night were the gentle splash of our paddles, the gurgle of water against the hulls and the faint whispers of the Laotian crews.

Reclining in the centre of my canoe on top of some salvaged parachutes and propping my back none too comfortably against a small pile of ammunition boxes in the stern, I gazed at the stars and abandoned myself to some sardonic reflections on the many unmilitary disguises I had been called upon to assume during my employment with S.O.E. In my time I had played the part of a journalist, a commercial traveller, a diplomat, a politician, a brigand, and even a gigolo—I did not care to dwell on that desperate occasion in a neutral country when a cynical superior had ordered me, in the interests of the King's Service, to seduce a lady suspected of dealings with the enemy: an experience so shattering that I still sweat with embarrassment at the memory. Recently I had been a sort of District Commissioner, and now I was a smuggler. This last, at least, was respectable; moreover, the operation had gone without a hitch. It seemed too good to be true: indeed it was.

For the first part of the journey we set a course slightly upstream, to take advantage of the current later on. From my position, roughly in the middle of the flotilla, I kept an anxious watch for our enemies, but the only signs of human life other than ourselves were an occasional *pirogue*, obviously engaged in fishing, and one or two lights on the farther bank—probably the fires of charcoal burners; the only movement that caught my eye was the shimmer of the moon on the swiftly gliding water and the dancing points of light where the river raced over the shoals among the blue and silver shadows of the sandbanks.

In the middle of the river, a little more than half-way across, lay a small island, a long, low strip of jungle whose tree-fringed shore showed dark against the distant background of the Cammon hills. As we approached it we began to alter course to pass below its southern tip.

'Who lives there?' I asked the French sergeant, who was sitting immediately in front of me.

'Oh, nobody. The fishermen use it sometimes, and we too, when we cross the river, halt there to rest ourselves a while. But tonight,' he flashed me a smile over his shoulder, 'with this valuable cargo perhaps we had better hurry on our way.' I was to thank my guardian angel for the haste.

As I watched the trees glide past I strained my eyes to peer into the gloom of the undergrowth, wondering if any hidden enemies were lying in wait for us; but I could see no movement in that strip of silent jungle. I lay back with a sigh, and marvelled again at the moonlit beauty of this mighty and mysterious river which ran for nearly three thousand miles from the Tibetan Plateau to the South China Sea. What a romantic setting, I gloated, for a smuggler!

We were rounding the tip of the island, less than two hundred yards from the shore, when an abrupt challenge rang out from the darkness, shattering my reverie; I clutched at my carbine as a burst of machine-gun fire ripped up the water a few yards away. A second burst slammed into the leading canoe, toppling the bow paddler straight over the side; the steersman slumped slowly forward and sideways and, as he fell, the canoe heeled over and capsized with a great splash and flurry of foam. The third occupant appeared for a moment in the water, grabbing frantically at the slippery bottom of the dug-out as it spun away on the current; but he stood no chance, and in a few seconds was swept from our sight with a sickening cry of terror and despair.

The sergeant bellowed an order in Lao, and our *pirogue* swung sharply downstream, almost tipping me overboard as the crew drove their paddlers into the water to speed us away from that murderous and cunning trap. The little island, which had seemed a moment earlier so quiet and aloof, was now erupting with the ragged crackle of rifle-fire and the vicious stammer of the machine-gun; the sound of the fusillades rolled across the river to echo back to us from the distant hills.

I imagine that a smuggler can have few more disagreeable experiences than that of coming under heavy fire at close range in a flimsy canoe on a fast and turbulent river. As the bullets smacked into the water around us, or zipped frighteningly past my ears, or whined in angry richochet among our scattering flotilla I let go of my carbine and lay back as far as I could, gripping the gunwales tightly to brace myself against every lurch and twist of our plunging craft. I was acutely conscious, also, of my proximity to the ammunition cases, and wondered unhappily whether it would be more uncomfortable to be blown to glory or downed in the Mekong. Were there crocodiles in the Mekong, I asked myself; I had heard there were some in the tributaries. And hippopotami? No, you bloody fool, they're in Africa. But there may be crocs; they'll be lying on the sandbanks disguising themselves as logs of wood. I began to giggle foolishly until I saw the sergeant give me a worried glance.

Thoroughly ashamed, I picked up my carbine and, wriggling over on to my stomach facing the stern, began to shoot back at the island. There was not the least likelihood, of course, of my hitting anybody—except perhaps the paddler in the stern, whose nervousness increased noticeably with each shot I fired—but I thought it showed the right spirit, and at least it made me feel better. It was obviously having the opposite effect on the poor paddler, who, with bullets flying past him from both directions, was rapidly approaching hysteria; moreover, my efforts were endangering the balance of the boat. I rolled over again on to my back and tried to lie still, praying feverishly that we should soon be out of effective range.

Fortunately the enemy's fire, after that early unlucky burst, was not very accurate. Untrained troops, as the Annamese were, tend to fire high, especially at night: fortunately, also, they seemed to have only one machine-gun, and they had no tracer to help them correct their aim. They had probably hoped to take us by surprise on the island. Clearly visible as we had been at first in the moonlight, now that we had scattered we presented more difficult targets; moreover, the strong current, combined with the efforts of the paddlers, was rapidly increasing the range. Their shots went wider with each minute of our flight, and soon they ceased to trouble us, although they continued to blaze away sporadically in our direction almost until we landed.

It was indeed a miraculous escape, and I poured out my thanks to providence for the sergeant's decision not to stop for a rest on that island. In the capsized canoe we had lost two Lao villagers and one soldier, as well as a number of Stens and some food and clothing; otherwise our only casualties were two men slightly wounded, both of them able to walk.

As I checked the stores next morning with Tavernier, he said to me: 'In future I think it is better if we use no couriers but mine to carry letters concerning the delivery of arms. The Annamites will always try to intercept our correspondence, and in Lakhon you do not know who you can trust. But

I can always send men of proved fidelity. So next time you have some material for me, send me word and I will send you a courier to whom you can entrust the details of a rendezvous. It will take a little longer, but it will be much safer.' I could only agree.

As had expected, the Governor's launch arrived to take me back, and a very worried Governor came to meet me at the landing-stage at Nakorn Panom. I tried to make light of the incident, although I knew he would learn the full story soon enough. But when I reached home Edith Fournier was looking 'very grave.

'I hear you had trouble on the river, Peter.'

'Yes, a little. There was some treachery, I'm afraid.'

'There was indeed. It is as well you did not come back the same way this morning. The *curé* of the church by the *ville annamite* was here. Although he is an Annamite himself he is a good friend of ours, and he hears a lot of things. He was very worried because the Annamites had arranged another little reception for you at that village where you and Rork went last night.'

A few days later I received an enthusiastic letter of thanks from Tavernier. The Viet-minh had launched a heavy attack on Ban Tung the night after I had left. Thanks to the arms, and more particularly the ammunition, I had brought him he had been able to hold his ground; but for their timely arrival lack of ammunition would have forced him to withdraw. In the following weeks I took him several more consignments; some of the arms I received by parachute drop, others came from Smiley, who was able to draw on Japanese dumps. Each time we varied our rendezvous, using Tavernier's couriers as we had arranged; there were no more incidents.

I celebrated my reconciliation with the Governor by inviting him to a dinner party; I thought it an appropriate occasion to ask also the Chinese colonel at Thakhek and his staff. From the colonel I received a most courteous letter thanking me in flowery language for my invitation and ending sadly with the words, 'We are sorry we cannot come because we have a sore foot.'

During this time I made one visit to Savannakhet, by night, for a clandestine meeting with Quinquenel to discuss arms deliveries. Crossing the Mekong by *pirogue* I was met at the landing-stage by two Laos soldiers, who led me through silent and empty streets, flooded in moonlight, to a large house at the back of the town. I knew that Quinquenel had evacuated Savannakhet, but it seemed that the Viet-minh had not been able—or had not bothered—to occupy it themselves. However, we were taking no chances, and padded swiftly and noiselessly through the streets, keeping, wherever possible, to the shadows.

Awaiting me with Quinquenel was a thick-set, broad-shouldered Laotian who was later to exercise a profound influence on the history of his country.

Chao (Prince) Boun Oum of the royal house of Champassak—the old southern Laotian kingdom suppressed by the French—had the intellectual outlook of a European superimposed on the instincts of a Laotian patriot.[1] A passionate Francophile who had received his education in France, he had played a leading part in the resistance against the Japanese. Now he was preparing to throw the full weight of his very considerable influence in this area behind the French and against the Viet-minh.

Thereafter, as long as I remained on the frontier, a large part of my time was spent in running arms to the French—both to Tavernier and to Quinquenel, with whom I arranged a secluded rendezvous on the river south of Mukdahan. These officers needed everything we could send them; they were continually engaged in savage battles against superior forces, and their own Command in Saigon was in no position to help. But on 19th October they received their first reinforcements: sixty-four French parachutists dropped on my airfield and, after an enormous lunch which Tavernier attended, were ferried across the river in *pirogues*. By the time our missions left the area, at the end of January 1946, the French were able to take the offensive; two months later they were in possession of Thakhek and Savannakhet.

Apart from gun-running my principal duty was the filing of intelligence reports, known as 'sitreps', to Calcutta and later to the G.O.C. in Bangkok, General Evans. There was, in fact, much more work than I could tackle alone; and so I was delighted when, towards the end of October, two officers arrived to help me. They were Major Cox and Captain Maynard, and they brought with them a wireless operator, Corporal Powling. They installed themselves at Mukdahan.

Cox was a clever and experienced officer who had served with Force 136 in Burma; his gift for extracting the maximum amount of quiet fun out of life made him a delightful companion. Maynard was a young man of twenty-two whose ingenuity and enthusiasm more than compensated for any lack of maturity. Powling, a tall, quiet, very young soldier, most efficient at his job, unfortunately died the following January from virulent smallpox.

One of Maynard's first actions was to design and build a motor *pirogue* to help us with our gun-running. He recruited a squad of skilled Siamese workmen and a competent mechanic, and bought from a Chinese merchant an outboard motor in excellent condition. In a remarkably short space of time we had a stout and swift little craft, fitted with a half-deck forr'd; in the bows we mounted a Bren gun. We now felt able to deal with any attempt by the Annamese to interrupt our convoys on the water. In deference to the Viet-minh's Radio Hanoi, which had been denouncing us a 'brigands and pirates', we persuaded the nuns to embroider us a silken ensign with a skull

---

[1] He is, at the moment of writing, Prime Minister of Laos.

54

and crossbones, which streamed proudly in the breeze above the puttering outboard motor. We had to be careful, however, because the very sight of our toy gunboat would rouse the Annamese machine-guns to a fury of activity; they would open fire on us even when we were cruising close in to the Siamese shore.

On 26th October a medical officer was attached to my headquarters. Captain Donald Gunn, R.A.M.C. was quiet, most conscientious and extremely efficient, he was about twenty-six and had previously worked behind the Japanese lines in Burma. His confident, unruffled manner, dry sense of humour and abundant common sense vastly increased his value to our party. Sickness and enemy action took a constant toll of the French forces; to Nakorn Panom, Mukdahan and Naung Kai they brought their casualties for treatment and evacuation by air to Bangkok. Gunn's life was an exacting round of journeys between the three stations; after driving all night to attend a batch of wounded he would often have to drive back sleepless through the following night for further work elsewhere. In the intervals he found time to help us with the problems of administration and the reception and disposal of parachute stores; he did not seem to need rest.

Smiley had cultivated excellent relations with the Siamese Air Force, especially with the station commander at Korat, Wing-Commander Manop Souriya, who was known even to his brother-officers as Nobby; the Wing-Commander, who had passed through West Point and served an attachment to the R.A.F. before the war, proved himself a firm and valuable friend. Aware of our difficulties with communications, he obtained permission from his superiors to send an aircraft and pilot to Ubon for Smiley's personal use. The aircraft was a dual-control Mitsubishi Advanced Trainer, an obsolete monoplane of doubtful reliability, with seating for one passenger in comfort and a precarious perch for a second in the tail; it did not prove as useful as we had hoped, because it spent most of the time on the airfield at Ubon or Korat undergoing repairs or awaiting spare parts. We were none too happy to learn that the pilot's name was Pilot Officer Prang.

My first flight in the machine was on 31st October, when Smiley and I were summoned to Bangkok, he for a conference with General Evans and Brigadier Jaques, I for my first meeting with the Brigadier. We took off from Nakorn Panom after breakfast, with Smiley sitting behind the pilot, and myself squatting on a discarded parachute, a prey to acute discomfort and claustrophobia. Our first call was at Udaun, thirty-five miles south of Naung Kai, where we had an appointment with Winn. We reached it in an hour, flying at a thousand feet and following the narrow pink strip of laterite road that ran almost straight through the feathery carpet of forest.

Planning to lunch at Korat, nearly two hundred miles to the south, we left Udaun at noon and climbed to five thousand feet, to cross a high range of mountains. After an hour's flying we saw them beneath us—jagged outcrops of rock thrusting malevolently up towards us through the bright green profusion of hostile jungle; deep-shadowed gorges twisting sharply between the peaks. If the engine fails now, I thought, we haven't a hope of making a landing.

Of course it did fail, in a series of sharp, angry backfires while Prang fiddled furiously with various switches on the instrument panel; then it cut and left us gliding through the air in a grim and fearful silence. Smiley turned round in his seat to catch my eye, the corners of his mouth twisted comically downwards as he pointed to the savage mountains below. R.A.F. pilots had told me that if your engine failed while flying over jungle, and there was no paddy in sight, the best chance was to land on top of bamboo.

'Do you see any bamboo down there?' I asked. Smiley shook his head, obviously thinking that terror had deprived me of my wits.

At that moment the engine spluttered into life and we breathed again. But not for long. Five times in the next half-hour this terrifying performance was repeated, while we steadily lost height, until, at two hundred feet above the ground, clear at last of the mountains, we saw ahead of us the comforting expanse of Korat aerodrome. There was no safety margin for a circuit, and so we came straight in, landing with the wind in a frightening succession of vicious bumps, breaking off a wheel and slewing sideways on the starboard wing in a cloud of choking red dust. Leaping from the aircraft Smiley and I stood shaking and sweating on the runway while Prang climbed slowly down and gazed at us in silence with a bashful, apologetic and wholly disarming smile.

Strong drinks and lunch with Nobby restored our nerve sufficiently to fly on with Prang in another aircraft. We reached Bangkok in the last daylight and in time for a spectacular party given by Force 136 in the palace of one of the royal princes. I had never thought our frontier life uncomfortable, but I was staggered by this sudden projection into luxury, and felt awkward and scruffy in my faded battledress beside the trim little Siamese officers and the British in their well-tailored uniforms. The women dancing under the coloured Chinese lanterns or gliding across the lawns in the clear, warm, scented moonlight seemed each one an Aphrodite of voluptuous grace and sensuality. Sadly I noted that none of them showed the least interest in me.

The following day passed in an endless succession of conferences. Force 136 was going into liquidation but a few of our missions in Siam, including those on the north-east frontier, were being retained in a new organization, Allied Land Forces Paramilitary Operations, under the direct orders of the G.O.C., General Evans. Smiley and Winn were returning to England at the end of November, the former to attend his Staff College course, the latter for demobilization. I was asked to take over Smiley's command, an offer which delighted me; I should be the only remaining officer with experience of the north-eastern frontier and, having no urgent reason to return home, I felt that I must stay to give all possible help to our Franco-Laotian Allies who had so deeply inspired me by their devotion and courage.

We left Bangkok after lunch on 2nd November and landed at Korat without incident; when we took off again Smiley, who had flown his own aircraft before the war, was at the controls. We were gaining height over the aerodrome when there was a violent jar on the port wing; as the aircraft shuddered and banked at a dangerous angle I peered over the cockpit, to see a long, deep gash in the leading edge, about half-way along. Smiley quickly adjusted the trim and returned to land safely. It turned out that we had collided with a very large bird, which fortunately had struck the wing and not the propeller; but the dented metal had jammed the connecting wires to the ailerons and we were lucky to have avoided a crash.

After a half-hour's delay we left in the machine which had brought us to Korat two days before. By now we were both thoroughly apprehensive of Siamese aircraft, or at least of Advanced Trainers, and we only began to breathe freely when we saw to starboard the hill above Sakon Nakorn, a round furry pimple in the forested plain, and flew over the reed-fringed lake where in August I had tried to shoot duck. The mountains of Laos loomed closer through the haze, and I sighed contentedly when I caught sight of the houses of Nakorn Panom straggling down towards the mudbanks exposed by the subsiding waters of the Mekong. I was not even alarmed when, as we swung in to land, the engine spluttered once or twice and cut. We glided in and bumped gently over the landing-strip to a halt.

'What was the cause of that?' I asked Smiley a little later.

'Oh, it seems they forgot to fill her up at Korat. She was clean out of gas when the engine cut. Aren't we the lucky ones?'

I had a better chance of seeing Bangkok in the middle of November, when I was summoned there for a detailed briefing by the G.O.C. on the duties of my new command. We flew no more in Siamese aircraft, but depended for our air communications on a flight of R.A.F. L5s based on the racecourse on the outskirts of the capital.

Brigadier Jaques had already gone, although Smiley and Winn were in Bangkok awaiting transport home. The new office of ALFPMO was controlled by two majors, Tom Hobbs and David Muirhead; they were able and conscientious officers, grossly overworked and understaffed, but with their anxiety to help and their rare skill at extracting precious stores from the harassed Q branch, they were to prove invaluable allies during the ensuing two months. From them I graduated through the offices of the GI Operations and the GI Intelligence to the presence of my new master, Major-General Geoffrey Evans, commanding 7th Indian Division and British Troops Siam.

Robustness, which Lord Wavell considered the most important quality in a modern commander, was evident both in General Evans's military record and in his personal appearance. As a brigade major in 4th Indian Division he had served in the first Western Desert campaign in 1940 and afterwards at the storming of the Keren heights in Eritrea—the most arduous battle, he told me, he had ever fought. As a brigadier in 5th Indian Division he had commanded the Sinzewia box in the bitter Arakan fighting of 1944, when 5th and 7th Indian Divisions were surrounded and narrowly escaped annihilation. After commanding a brigade at the siege of Imphal he had become G.O.C. successively of 5th and 7th Indian Divisions. A short, solidly built man in his middle forties with close-cropped greying hair and moustache, firm features in a rounded face and a determined thrust to his jaw, he combined with a gruff, sometimes abrupt, manner of speech, a cool, alert mind, a shrewd judgment and a dry, ironic wit. With none of the suspicion and dislike of paramilitary operations sometimes found in regular soldiers he showed a clear understanding of the situation on the frontier and of our difficulties in meeting it; and he promised me his full support in our efforts—a promise which he fulfilled beyond all my hopes.

Our principal task, he explained, would be the gathering and grading of intelligence, especially political intelligence; we must pay particular attention to the situation across the frontier because the French High Command at Saigon had very little contact with their forces in Laos, and we should be the only sure means of getting information from that region as well as of sending help into it. I was to signal to G.H.Q. a weekly 'sitrep' covering the whole of my command, and for this purpose I was given, in addition to my wireless link with Bangkok, direct links with my sub-stations at Naung Khai and Mukdahan. We were forbidden to undertake any operations in Laos without the General's express authority, except for the purpose of smuggling arms and supplies to the French and succouring their sick and wounded.

Theoretically I was responsible for an enormous area, comprising some fifty thousand square miles and well over five hundred miles of frontier, from the sixteenth parallel to the northern border; we had hoped to establish a new sub-station in the north, opposite the Laotian capital of Luang Prabang, but SEAC vetoed the idea, thus confining our effective influence to the vicinity of the three existing missions. We were the only British forces in the country north and east of Korat[1]; and so was able to convince the General that I should need a few more officers and wireless operators.

To Naung Khai, therefore, I sent Captain Hubart, a young officer who had won the D.S.O. as an agent in France; Ubon, although within my territory, was too far from the frontier to require our close attention. Maynard

---

[1] Most of 7th Indian Division was concentrated around Bangkok and in the south. ALFPMO maintained a few missions in southern Siam and Cambodia.

was posted from Mukdahan to Nakorn Panom to act as my second-in-command and deputy in my absence; Cox unfortunately I lost, for he was needed urgently in Cambodia. In their places Major Victor Wemyss and Captain Harry Despagne took over the station at Mukdahan. Despagne, like Hubart, had won a D.S.O. in France; Wemyss, having managed tin mines in Siam before the war, knew the country and the language. He proved an admirable intelligence officer, able, hard-working and quietly efficient, although he sometimes shocked his more sensitive acquaintances by his rugged earthy manner of speaking. He was a fine natural drinker, with a head that no type or quantity of alcohol could turn, and every visit of his to my headquarters was an occasion for a special party; the next morning he would appear at our breakfast table, a little green in the face, to complain to the company: 'My God! I feel as though a whole Portuguese family just moved out of my mouth.'

During my fortnight's stay I had time to relax and absorb the glamorous and corrupting atmosphere of this gaudy, fetid and fantastic capital. Bangkok was a startling contrast of extravagance and poverty, squalor and splendour. There were broad, clean, well-paved streets lined with tall, fresh-fronted shops and blocks of flats; palaces and temples whose graceful curling roofs gleamed gaily with tiles of red and green; and pagodas whose soaring spirals threw back the sunlight in sheets of dazzling gold. There were other streets that were narrow lanes of mud and filth between rows of festering hovels with sacking hung across the doorways; and stinking canals on whose stagnant waters huddled the miserable sampan dwellings where the crowded Annamese families sweated and starved in indigence and ordure.

To my shame I must confess that I ignored the seamy side and, in the company of Smiley and other friends, devoted my spare time to the full enjoyment of this novel life. Almost every evening there was a reception or dinner party given by some Siamese notable, or a cocktail party in an Army mess. There was a variety of gay and noisy night-clubs, each providing a band, a wide selection of pretty, doll-like hostesses and an inexhaustible supply of the local whisky—a rice spirit coloured and pleasantly flavoured with brown sugar and labelled 'Mekhong' or 'Black and White Cat'. Diluted with soda-water it gave a satisfying and lasting glow for the evening, and left no hangover the next morning beyond an indefinable feeling of tension around the eyes; prolonged indulgence, however, induced a noticeable shake, increasing in some officers to the appearance of locomotor ataxia.

The little Siamese dance-hostesses took a liberal view of their duties, and after closing time were happy to extend more intimate favours to their clients. This practice caused a certain headstrong young officer in my hotel a moment of acute embarrassment. Arriving back in his room very late at the end of a bibulous evening in the night-club across the road, he suddenly realized that he had with him not one but two girls. It was, of course, strictly against standing orders for an officer to bring any woman to his room; but such puritanical restrictions made no sense to the simple minds of the Siamese hotel staff, who turned a blind eye to their infringement. My friend therefore found himself faced with a delicate problem: he had sobered up enough to realize that he was in no condition to deal with two girls; yet he could not send one of them away without giving grave offence. His solution has always seemed to me a masterpiece of tact and ingenuity. He signed to them both to strip; having made his own choice and waved her towards his bed, he gently led the other girl down the corridor to a room he knew to be occupied by a very senior visiting officer. He knocked loudly and, hearing a gruff and sleepy voice from within, opened the door a fraction and propelled his companion through into the darkness; then he softly closed the door and returned to his own room. There were, he assured me, no complaints.

Among the gayest and most hospitable of our Siamese friends was a middle-aged nobleman who had rendered valuable and hazardous service to the Allies during the Japanese occupation. A fervent Anglophile—he had lived in England before the war—he took pleasure in entertaining his British friends in Bangkok with lavish generosity and tireless exuberance. He would invite three or four of us to dinner, usually in some house on the distant outskirts of the city either owned or rented by himself to which he would drive us in his own car. There we would find awaiting our enjoyment not only plenty of food and drink but a selection of ravishing girls. That these last were designed, in the words of Gibbon, for use rather than ostentation he left us in no possible doubt. When a decent interval had elapsed after the end of the meal he would somehow manage to fade unnoticed from the party and drive himself away, leaving each of his guests deliciously stranded, like Ulysses on Calypso's island, with a glamorous and enthusiastic partner.

The girls were not prostitutes; they would take no money from us, but gave themselves over with uninhibited abandon to the pleasures of the night. Their attitude was not untypical, in my experience, of the Siamese outlook on sex which seemed to be compounded of equal parts of sensuality and humour.

There was in Bangkok a thriving business in pornography of the 'feelthy pictures' type; but what to my mind distinguished those pictures from the majority of their land was the blatant cheerfulness on the faces of the protagonists and their manifest delight in the pastime at which they were being photographed.

I was lucky to be given a room in the Ratanakosin hotel, a luxurious modern building on the main street, supposedly reserved for senior officers and distinguished civilians. It was in theory run by the government, in practice by a very attractive young Siamese receptionist whose name, as well as I can spell it, was An-Kna. She spoke perfect English and adopted towards her younger military guests an attitude of amused and sympathetic tolerance. To a friend of mine who came to inquire for me she replied with only the faintest flicker of a smile:

'If you mean Round-the-Bend Kemp, he is in.'

I flew back to Nakorn Panom at the end of November. My work during the rest of the year differed little from that of previous months, except that there was more of it. There were no Japanese troops to disarm; on the other hand the activity across the frontier was increasing and scarcely a day passed without a clash between French and Annamese or Free Lao forces. I spent much of my time on the road visiting Naung Khai and Mukdahan, but my job was made much easier for me by the enthusiasm of my staff and the confidence in us shown by General Evans, who was content to leave most decisions to me, within the framework of his original directive.

Unhappily, relations rapidly deteriorated between Captain Tavernier and the Governor of Nakorn Panom. There was certainly justification for Tavernier's repeated complaints that the Siamese authorities were giving aid and comfort to the Viet-minh; but it was seldom possible to find proof to support them. All I could do was to remonstrate with the Governor, listen as patiently as I could to his transparently false denials and counter-accusations, and relay to G.H.Q. an account of each incident; for this reason my popularity in Nakorn Panom began to wane. It is difficult to say whether the provocative behaviour of the Siamese was due to a resurgence of their old suspicion of France or to the left-wing sympathies of the Government in Bangkok; but it was a short-sighted policy, for which the French were quick to take reprisals as soon as they regained control of Thakhek.

Meanwhile Franco-Laotian soldiers visiting their friends or relatives in Nakorn Panom disappeared without trace or, when returning by *pirogue*, were intercepted and kidnapped in Siamese waters; if we ever heard of them again it was to learn that they had been beheaded. Ambushes were laid for us on Siamese territory; there was an ugly moment one evening, while we were sitting out on our veranda after dinner, when we were sniped on from the darkness, which resulted in my spilling a glassful of good Indo-Chinese rum over my newly washed, khaki drill slacks. We suffered no casualties, however, for the shooting was wild and our enemies never pressed an attack. I sometimes wondered if the object was not simply to embitter our relations with the local authorities and alarm Bangkok; the police were noticeably reluctant to pursue investigations.

Morally I was not in a very strong position to complain. For a long time I had treasured hopes of revenge upon the murderers of Klotz; against Le Hoq Minh and his subordinate, Tu, in particular, I nursed a blinding hatred and spent much of my time working on schemes for their assassination. Both, I knew, crossed often to the Siamese bank of the river, and I had information that Le Hoq Minh made periodic visits to Bangkok; if only I could get accurate information in advance it should be possible to intercept them when they passed through my territory. Having laid hands on them with the help of a few of my officers and N.C.O.s, I planned to transport them to Ban Tung and leave them to the justice of Tavernier; if that should prove impossible we would kill them and throw the bodies in the river. I suppose I must seem no better myself than the men I was pursuing, but so bitter was my hatred for those two that I could not feel I was contravening the teachings of my education and religion.

In Bangkok I had managed to obtain cautious and unofficial approval of the idea, provided I could carry it out without attracting too much attention from the Siamese. The difficulty, of course, was to get the necessary information in time. Tavernier, who was naturally enthusiastic, put his own agents at my disposal, and one day we had our chance.

I learned that Le Hoq Minh was to pass through Nakorn Panom on the following evening; the message, which was from a highly reliable source, gave enough details to make it easy for me to intercept him. I immediately sent a 'Most Urgent' signal to Bangkok, asking permission to carry out the operation. Back came their refusal, in one word of cabalese. 'Unoffbump.'

On 1st January 1946 the peace treaty was signed between the United Kingdom and Siam. The most important consequence to us was an order, a week later, to prepare for the withdrawal of all my missions. Now that they were masters in their own house the Siamese were not going to tolerate in it activities such as ours. General Evans and his superiors were no longer in a position to resist their pressure, because by now the French in Laos had begun to receive support from Saigon; moreover, the grave political consequences that would result if one of us were murdered far outweighed any value we might still possess. On 20th January I left Nakorn Panom for the last time.

My orders were to take my two parties from Nakorn Panom and Mukdahan in lorries as far as the railhead at Ubon, together with all our stores; there we were to hand over the lorries and stores to Major Hedley of the British Military Mission to the Siamese Army, and travel by train to Bangkok. The Governor and his officers saw us off from Nakorn Panom in the morning; although we parted with expressions of mutual esteem and affection they can hardly have been sorry to see us go, for our support of the French had caused them continual vexation and embarrassment. Tavernier, on the other hand, seemed genuinely distressed, even shattered; he showed little confidence in the support of his superiors at Saigon.

Ubon, about thirty miles from the frontier of Indo-China, was the headquarters of an important military district and of a division of the Siamese Army; Johnny Hedley, whom I had already met with Smiley, was living in a wing of the barracks on the outskirts of the town. A spare, sun-baked figure with unblinking light blue eyes and a slow, elaborate drawl, he gave the impression that he found all conversation tedious. He was an Old Etonian and an Old Burma Hand who had spent his happiest days in the teak forests and despised the comfort and frivolity of city life; even for official parties or government receptions in the capital he refused to vary his style of dress—a battered old bush hat, a shapeless bush shirt, slacks and jungle boots, and an old .303 Lee Enfield service rifle, which he carried slung from his shoulder or propped in a corner of the room, heedless of his hosts' astonishment, indignation or alarm. He was not always tactful with senior officers. When the Brigadier commanding his mission, an amiable old gentleman whom he had not met before, flew up to Ubon on a visit of inspection, Hedley greeted him without the formality of a salute.

'Have you brought my mail?' were his opening words.

'Er-no-er, I'm afraid I didn't bring any mail,' stammered the surprised Brigadier.

'Humph! Somebody in Bangkok ought to pull their fingers out.'

However, his welcome to us was friendly enough. There was a train leaving for Bangkok in three days' time, he explained—only a goods train, but he would fix us up with some wicker chairs in one of the waggons; in the meantime he had plenty of room for us in his quarters.

It was on the second night of our stay that a very curious incident befell me, one which might have brought my adventures to a painful end. It is fixed for ever in my memory as The Night I Lost My Trousers. We had spent most of the evening drinking and playing poker with Hedley, a young Australian captain from the War Graves Commission, and some Sappers who had arrived on a road reconnaissance of north-eastern Siam; Hedley, who drank little himself, had nevertheless laid in a large supply of Siamese whisky and Indo-Chinese rum; and we, after weeks of hard work and worry, were in the mood to relax. The party broke up about midnight, but before turning in I decided to take a short walk in the cool night to clear my head of the fumes of smoke and liquor. When the others had gone upstairs to bed I stepped outside into the darkness.

I have no idea how long afterwards it was when I came to. At first I was aware only of a splitting headache, a dim and flickering light in my eyes, and a rancid, smoky smell; the last two, I soon saw, came from an old and dirty lamp on the ground a yard away from my face. The lower part of my body felt cold and bare.

I lay still for a while, hoping the pain would go from my head and wondering apathetically where on earth I was and what had happened to bring me there. I could remember nothing after walking out of the room at the barracks, but I seemed to have a distant recollection, as though from a dream, of hearing voices whispering near me as I was regaining

63

consciousness; but it was only the faintest impression, perhaps no more than imagination. Very slowly I opened my eyes; painfully I raised myself on an elbow and looked around.

I was lying on a heap of filthy sacking on the floor of a squalid, smoke-filled peasant's hovel, bare of any kind of furniture. I was quite alone, and my loneliness and the dark, empty silence around me began to fill me with a frightening sense of desolation and foreboding. Then fear gave way to astonishment as I saw the reason for the chilly feeling round my lower limbs. I was still wearing the bush shirt I had put on before dinner, but below the waist I was naked; my trousers, underpants, socks and shoes had vanished. I looked carefully round the room, but could see no place where they might be hidden. Desperately I tried to concentrate and remember what had happened.

My last clear memory was of walking out of that room at the barracks. Was it possible that during my walk in the fresh air I had picked up or been picked up by some woman? I quickly decided that I was safe in rejecting that explanation; I might have had too much to drink, but certainly not so much that I should have forgotten all about it if it had happened. Had I, then, been robbed? I examined the pockets of my bush shirt. My wallet was still there, stuffed with money, and so were my military identity card and all my documents; even my wrist watch was intact. The pockets of my missing trousers had contained nothing more than an old pipe and tobacco pouch. Evidently I had not fallen among thieves.

Reluctantly I forced myself to stand up, ignoring the stabbing pains in my head, and padded barefoot round the room in search of my missing clothes. There was no sign of them; the hut had only one room and only one door, which opened out into the darkness of the night. I returned to my pile of sacking and tried to think again.

I was now quite sure that, whatever had brought on my loss of memory, it was more than mere excess of alcohol; apart from a headache and a cloudy mind I had none of the symptoms that usually attend a hangover. And then I remembered: I knew just when I had last felt like this. In August 1943 I had parachuted into Albania; the pilot had dropped me too late and I had landed half-way up the side of a mountain, knocking myself out on a boulder as I fell. When I regained consciousness it was with this same muzzy, disembodied feeling and a similar gap in my memory.

This train of thought had unpleasant implications. Had I simply fallen down outside the barracks and hit my head on a stone—in which case why wasn't I back there in my own bed? Or had I been slugged on the head and—I began to tremble—kidnapped? At this point I was interrupted by a shuffling sound outside the door of the hut. Naked and unarmed—for I had left my pistol at the barracks—I cowered back on the sacking to await the intruder; all my courage had evaporated in my humiliation, embarrassment and alarm.

64

He was an ancient peasant, bent and emaciated, with a wrinkled, yellow-brown face; the bones of his ribs and chest showed skeleton c ear through his skin above the dirty white and grey chequered loincloth that was all his clothing. He sidled slowly across the floor and bent over the lamp, his face expressionless, while I watched him through half-closed eyes. When I saw he was alone; whispered good evening in Siamese, forcing an ingratiating smile. His reaction was hardly reassuring. He turned on me a brief, hostile look and padded swiftly from the room.

Pain and dizziness forgotten, I was on my feet in an instant. I was thoroughly frightened. Whoever had brought me to this hut had not done so for the good of my health; if, as seemed likely, the old peasant had gone to tell them I was awake, they would not be long in returning. It was then that I remembered the Viet-minh and the price on my head.

Nothing so concentrates a man's mind, observed Dr. Johnson, as the knowledge that he is going to be hanged. My own mind instantly became clear: I must get away from this hut, and quickly. Shivering with disgust I snatched up a piece of the sacking I had been lying on, and wrapped it round my middle. I padded across the earthen floor to the doorway and peered cautiously outside. There was no sign of a guard. With a muttered prayer I plunged, for the second time that night, into the darkness.

There was no challenge or sound of pursuit as I ran blindly on in my terrified resolve to put as much distance as I could between myself and that sinister hut. After a few minutes I stopped for breath and took a quick look around, trying to get my bearings. There was no moon, but the bright stars gave a little light. I had no idea where I was, nor how far or in which direction lay the barracks. The only plan I could think of was to continue walking, taking a rough course from the stars, until I should come upon some familiar landmark or some lights that might show me the way.

Hitherto I had been too frightened to worry about anything except my escape; but now, as I plodded on in my bare feet, I began to think of snakes and scorpions and to strain my eyes in an effort to see what I was treading on. I padded forward with infinite caution, shuddering in anticipation each time I put my foot to the ground.

Every few minutes I halted and crouched down to listen for sounds of pursuit. Once I heard the hum of muffled voices getting rapidly louder. I froze in terror until I realized they were coming from the opposite direction; even so, I decided to take no chances, and kept down until they had passed out of earshot.

I had been going about twenty minutes when I heard a new sound behind me; the clink and clatter of arms and accoutrements. A party of police or soldiers was approaching, and for the first time in that ghastly evening I felt a surge of hope; in all probability they were making for the barracks. Of course it would never do for them to find a British officer of field rank wandering about the countryside at half past one in the morning without his trousers; but there was no reason why I should not let them overtake me and then follow them home at a discreet distance. As they drew closer I crouched low on the ground, holding my breath and praying that they would not see me. However, they loped past within a few yards, chattering unconcernedly in their high, sing-song voices. I rose to my feet and followed them silently, keeping my eyes fixed on their dim silhouettes and forgetting at last the dangers of snakes and scorpions.

It must have been ten minutes later, though it seemed an hour, when I saw in front of us a line of lights and recognized them as the barracks. I almost cried out in my relief. I let my guides draw ahead to a safe distance, and made my way cautiously towards the buildings until I had picked out the wing where we were billeted.

I paused for a moment to make sure there were no sentries around, and to collect what remained of my courage; then, with a prayer on my lips, I girded my sackcloth-encased limbs and sprinted across the barrack square. In a few seconds I was through the doorway out of which I had sauntered so carelessly an hour or two—or was it a year or two?—earlier. I raced up the stairs and collapsed on my bed, shaking and sweating with exertion and relief. Suddenly I began to laugh, hysterically and uncontrollably, until the tears poured down my face. I had just remembered the code name of my mission: 'Sackcloth'.

My companions received my story the next morning with a mixture of incredulity and delight; they produced several theories to account for it, the simplest and by far the most popular being that I had left my trousers in a brothel. Hedley alone looked thoughtful.

'We'd better find that hut,' was his comment.

But we never did find it. In the first place I could not be certain how far or in what direction it lay; secondly, there were any number of peasant huts of the same description in the neighborhood. Much later, however, from discreet inquiries of the Siamese authorities and from some fragments of information I picked up in Bangkok I pieced together the story of what must have happened that night. Although the details are largely surmise the outline seems pretty certain; in which case I am indeed lucky to be alive.

It seems that Viet-minh agents had been keeping us under observation even at Ubon. When I stepped outside for my breath of air, one—or more probably two—of them had spotted me. Seeing a chance of collecting the large reward offered for me, they had knocked me on the back of the neck— I had wondered why there was no bump on my head—and dragged me away. It would have been too risky for them to murder me on the spot, but easy to drag me off to the hut. Probably they bribed or frightened the driver of a bullock cart into taking us to his hut; or perhaps the hut belonged to one of their sympathizers. It is impossible to say.

In the hut they were faced with a dilemma. In order to collect the reward they would have to hand me over to the Viet-minh, preferably alive; but there was no one at hand competent to take delivery of my body. They must therefore have decided to leave me in the care of the old peasant while they went to find the local Viet-minh commander. Presumably they had no rope, or they would have tied me up; instead they took away my trousers and shoes in the belief that I should be unable to move very far without them.

Obviously something upset their plans. Perhaps the Viet-minh commander was away; or the old peasant took fright when he saw that I had recovered, and fled without warning them; or perhaps they themselves lost their nerve. Whatever the reason, I am heartily thankful for it; I have heard too many stories of Viet-minh irregulars disembowelling their prisoners.

My intention had been to apply at once for the demobilization to which I was now entitled. But while waiting in Bangkok I was offered and immediately accepted the command of a mission to the islands of Bali and Lombok in the Netherlands East Indies. There the Japanese garrisons had not yet surrendered, and the situation in both islands was obscure; SEAC therefore decided to send in a small advance party of British troops before committing the Dutch forces of occupation. On 15th February I flew to Singapore; two days later I was in Java.

V

JAVA

Bright sunlight, soft breezes and a blaze of tropical greenery was the picture I had formed of the islands of Indonesia, described by the Dutch writer Multatuli as 'a girdle of emerald around the Equator'. Reality, when I stood forlornly beside the sodden runway of Batavia[1] airport at half past ten on the morning of 17th February, was grotesquely different. A thick, warm curtain of rain, falling from a blanket of puffy grey clouds and whipped across the airfield by the violence of the monsoon, blotted out the horizon and drained all colour from trees and grass and buildings. My fellow-passengers from the Dakota were driven away to their various units, leaving me standing in the open—bewildered, dripping and alone.

After a quarter of an hour an open jeep splashed up, driven by an apologetic young subaltern who took me to the Hotel des Indes, a large sprawling building once the queen of hotels in the Far East. War and the ensuing emergency had deprived it of its former extravagant splendour. Gone were the enormous meals of *rijsttafel*, each requiring a posse of fifteen waiters to carry the dishes, which had sent so many colonial administrators and business men to their early graves; and the high, airy suites with their wide verandas were stripped of most of their furniture and crowded with extra beds.

The situation in the capital was quiet but tense. Troops were required to carry arms in the streets, there was a strict curfew at midnight, and some quarters of the town and port were out of bounds; but the hours of daylight generally passed without incident. The nights were full of danger for the foolhardy; almost every morning patrols would retrieve from the drainage canals the dismembered bodies of British or Indian soldiers who had defied the curfew in search of liquor or women; girls indeed made a practice of enticing troops into their houses to be set upon by their menfolk.

The sudden end to the war brought about by the bombs on Hiroshima and Nagasaki found South-East Asia Command quite unprepared for the problems of policing and administration that immediately followed. For the Dutch East Indies, which had only been placed within the British sphere of operations by the Potsdam conference in July, there were scarcely any troops available. In Java the nationalists, encouraged by Japanese propaganda during

---

[1] Now called Jakarta, the capital of the Netherlands East Indies was at the time still known by its old Dutch name of Batavia.

the occupation and armed after the surrender by the Japanese Sixteenth Army on the orders of its commander, seized control of most of the country, proclaimed their independence and organized a provincial government under the leadership of Dr. Sukarno. With their own demand for freedom they identified, illogically, their claim to sovereignity over all the peoples of Indonesia, many of whom differed widely in language, religion and culture from the Moslem Javanese, of whose influence they were bitterly resentful and afraid. The various nationalist groups, many of them little more than robber bands admitting no loyalty to the Sukarno government—they included the Communists under the Moscow-trained Tan Malaka—were united only in their hostility to the Dutch and to the British, who attempted to restore order in the Dutch name.

British and Indian reinforcements landed and, by the time I arrived, had secured perimeters defending the towns of Batavia, Buitenzorg, Bandaung, Semarang and Surabaja.[1] Only between Batavia and Buitenzorg was communication possible by road, and then only in convoys, which often had to fight their way through ambushes at a heavy cost in casualties. The nationalists did not spare their prisoners, whom they usually put to death by hewing in pieces to the greater glory of *Merdeka*;[2] a risk which added to the hazards of a forced landing when flying over that jungle-covered, mountainous and enchantingly beautiful country.

Tolerance and mercy are qualities seldom found in twentieth century revolutionaries. Towards their own people the Javanese nationalists behaved with extreme ruthlessness, maintaining their grip upon the countryside by an effective apparatus of terror. For example, they forbade the peasants, on pain of death, to trade with the Allies or even to possess the guilders issued as currency by the Allied military administration. Villagers who lived near towns occupied by the Allies were faced with the alternatives of defying the ban, or letting their produce rot and starving themselves; most of them chose to trade, and many were executed for it by their liberators. But the full fury of Javanese chauvinism was reserved for the Eurasians. Devotedly loyal to the Dutch Crown—they provided some of the best officers of the R.N.E.I. Army and some of the ablest officials in the administration—those unfortunate people, wherever the nationalists were in control, fell victims to barbaric persecution and atrocious massacre.

Formerly among the richest countries of Asia, with a happy and prosperous people, Java in 1946 presented a melancholy spectacle of

---

[1] The Royal Netherlands East Indies Army, destroyed by the Japanese, was being slowly reconstituted with Dutch, Eurasian, and native troops from the prisoner-of-war camps throughout South-East Asia.

[2] The nationalist slogan. Malay for that much abused word, Freedom.

neglected paddy-fields and derelict plantations abandoned by an impoverished and terrified peasantry.

Two days later, in the warm, wet darkness before dawn, I stood once again on Batavia airport, talking to the crew of the Dakota which was to fly me to Surabaja on the next stage of my journey. The general nature of my mission had been explained to me at AFNEI[1] Headquarters: to lead a small British reconnaissance party to Bali, and afterwards to Lombok, and prepare for the landing of the main occupation force, which would be Dutch. We should go in by sea. The operation would be under the direct control of General Mansergh, commanding 5th Indian Division at Surabaja, who would brief me in detail.

With me was my second-in-command, Captain John Shaw, attached to me from the staff of SEAC Intelligence. Shaw and I had trained together at Weedon in 1940, after which he had joined the Royal Horse Guards in Palestine and won the M.C. in the Syrian campaign. A tall, solidly built Yorkshireman, he combined a placid, easy-going attitude with a sound knowledge of his job, shrewd common sense and a thorough attention to detail. Often in the next two months I was to praise the good fortune that had brought us together. In addition to his many other duties, he performed with conscientious efficiency and patience the exacting task of getting his erratic commanding officer to the right place at the right time.

We were joined on the airfield by a party of three Japanese officers, led by a Major-General Ando; he was a short, slight, solemn man with a fussy but deferential manner. He had with him a major and a lieutenant interpreter. They were coming with us to make the first contacts with the Japanese garrisons of the islands and to act as liaison officers. We never came to know them well because our orders forbade any but the most formal relations with them—we were expressly forbidden even to shake hands with them or any of their countrymen; but they carried out our instructions faithfully and proved themselves invaluable on both operations.

We took off into the sunrise in a lull between the rainstorms and flew along the coast, gazing at the flattened cones of the great volcanoes that rose out of the jungle against the southern skyline. After a brief halt for breakfast at Semarang we landed at half past ten at Surabaja. Until a few days previously the Indonesians had been able to sweep the airfield with small-arms fire; now they had been pushed back, but they could still shell the runway, and I was relieved when we had taxied safely to the dispersal point and were driven off in a large green Chevrolet to Divisional Headquarters in the centre of the town.

---

[1] Allied Forces Netherlands East Indies, at that time under the command of General Sir Montague Stopford.

Surabaja at the end of the previous October had been the scene of some of the bloodiest fighting against the Indonesians. At that time the only Allied force there was rather less than one brigade of 23rd Indian Division, deployed in the dock area under the command of that very fine and gallant soldier, Brigadier Mallaby. While attempting to negotiate the release of a large number of Dutch and Eurasians interned in the town, the Brigadier was murdered by a hysterical crowd of Indonesians. This incident was the signal for a general attack on his brigade, which, hopelessly outnumbered in men and weapons, was only saved from annihilation by the arrival of General Mansergh's 5th Indian Division, hurriedly transported from Singapore; even so, one battalion was wiped out; brigade headquarters was overrun, and every man in it slaughtered. Several hundred Eurasian men, women and children were hideously butchered in the lavatories of the Officers' Club.

Mansergh immediately issued an ultimatum to the Indonesian leaders to hand over the rest of the internees and to lay down their arms. When they refused he launched a full-scale assault with artillery, tanks and aircraft. He was only just in time: the Indonesians had herded their Dutch and Eurasian prisoners—some sixteen hundred men, women and children—into the prison, and were pouring petrol over the roof and walls preparatory to burning them alive. Mansergh opened fire on the prison with an anti-tank gun loaded with armour-piercing shot; through the narrow hole blasted in the wall a company of an Indian regiment entered two abreast, shot down the Indonesians who were in the act of setting fire to the building, and freed the prisoners. Nearly three weeks of bitter fighting followed before the town was cleared. A fortnight later Mansergh and his officers had the civil administration, the public services and even the schools functioning—a remarkable achievement in the face of repeated Indonesian attacks on the perimeter defences.

We met with a most friendly welcome from Colonel Carroll, the GI, who had planned our operation, and the G2, Major Armour. They apologized charmingly for the temporary absence of the General.

'At the moment he's out on the perimeter inspecting some new positions. He spends most of his time out there, poking around the hot spots. The troops think the world of him, but he causes us a lot of worry.'

We were to embark in three days' time aboard H.M. Frigate *Loch Eck* (Lieut.-Commander Peter Hoare, R.N.), now lying in the harbour, and we should arrive off the port of Benoa in South Bali on the morning of the 23rd. The Dutch force would land exactly a week later. Our party would consist of an escort of eight Buffs under a sergeant; six signallers with two wireless sets; an R.A.M.C. sergeant and a naval officer, Lieutenant Neville, who was a qualified beachmaster; he was, in a way, the most important member of the mission, because the Dutch force was to land in assault craft on to an open beach.

My first task would be to accept the formal surrender of the Japanese naval and military garrisons; my second to establish law and order and some sort of administration in the island, and my third to deploy the Japanese forces to cover the beachhead and the Dutch landing. I should have to rely on the Japanese for the maintenance of security; it was assumed they would be prepared to surrender and place themselves under my orders. The most uncertain factors were the attitude of the Balinese population and the strength of nationalist feeling among them; my report on these points would be of especial interest to 5th Indian Division.

'In other words,' Armour concluded cheerfully, 'if they chop you up we'll know we'll have to be more careful with the next lot.'

The following morning we met the Divisional Commander. General Mansergh was a widely experienced soldier of about forty-five who had greatly distinguished himself with the Fourteenth Army in Burma. He was an impressive figure, tall and broad-shouldered, with an alert intelligent face, firm features and an easy, informal manner; to me he always conveyed the feeling that he had every situation or eventuality under perfect control. Towards his subordinates he was invariably courteous and sympathetic, and he earned every bit of the affection and respect in which they held him.

When he was satisfied that we understood all the points of his plan he said to me:

'Until the Dutch arrive you chaps frankly are going to be out on a limb; there's little we can do to help you if you get into trouble. You will be my representative and, through me, the representative of the Supreme Allied Commander; as such you must make it quite clear from the start to the Japanese and to the locals that your orders are to be obeyed implicitly. There is one point which is vitally important; no word must leak out that the main landing will be carried out by the Dutch. You must not reveal this information even to the Japanese commanders, and you must impress on all your party the need for absolute security. It is essential that the landing should take place without opposition, but there may well be trouble from the locals if they hear that the Dutch are coming. If you're asked about the composition of the main landing force you will say that they will be Allied troops, but you don't know what nationality. Is that clear?

'Another point: you may well have to resort to force to keep order, and you have plenty of it in the shape of the Japanese, if you need it. But I do ask you to use it only as a last resort. There's a great deal of opposition in certain quarters at home to our role here in the N.E.I.—they say we're using troops to bolster up Dutch colonialism; whenever I have to give orders to clear out a nest of snipers that's been harassing my men I seem to feel the hot, angry breath of Socialism on the back of my neck. So for God's sake be careful how you use the Japanese in Bali. Of course you will keep in close touch with me through your wireless, but, as the man on the spot, you will have to make most of the decisions yourself. Keep me informed. I will back you up.' And so he did.

Shaw collected our stores from Colonel Waddilove, the A.Q., and supervised their lodging aboard *Loch Eck* Waddilove and his assistant, the Judian Major Kannah, went out of their way to provide us with everything we could possibly need, including fifteen gallons of 'operational rum' and plenty of beer and whisky.

I spent most of my time plaguing General Mansergh's hard-worked but ever helpful staff officers for information about the topography, history and politics of Bali.

I had long talks with the commander of the Dutch landing force, Colonel Ter Meulen, a bluff, amiable veteran of the R.N.E.I. Army who had commanded its 'Bali Korps' in pre-war days; unlike most of his troops, who had recently emerged from Japanese prison camps, he had been captured in Holland in 1940. He flattered me by listening to my suggestions with a respect he can scarcely have felt. His Intelligence Officer, Captain Daan Hubrecht, was a delightful and uninhibited eccentric. The son of a Cambridge astronomy professor who had also served as Dutch Minister in Rome and Madrid and who owned large sugar estates in east Java, Hubrecht had benefited from the most liberal cosmopolitan education and upbringing of anyone I have known; a handsome, carefree person of unusual intelligence, sensitivity and charm he had taken his Degree at Trinity and his pleasures in the sophisticated pre-war society of the major European capitals. Coming east to enter the family business in Surabaja he had immediately responded to the proximity and lure of Bali; in the course of frequent and protracted visits he had fallen in love with the island and its beautiful, fascinating people. Three years of captivity in Changi gaol in Singapore had sharpened his anxiety to return. His knowledge of Malay—the *lingua franca* of the Archipelago—his experience and his popularity with the Balinese made him during the next three months an indispensable and most stimulating companion.

We boarded *Loch Eck* on the 21st, after a lively farewell lunch with Carroll, Waddilove and Armour, at which one of our fellow guests, I remember, was the intrepid Colonel Laurens Van Der Post. In the evening, when we had seen our party settled into their accommodation and the three Japanese quartered in a petty officers' mess—to the indignation of the evicted P.O.s.— Commander Hoare invited us to drinks in the wardroom. This short, bearded, energetic sailor had the reputation of a martinet with his officers but, like them, was unfailingly hospitable and helpful to us. We were to sail at dawn, but in the midst of all this festivity I found it difficult to realize that I was entrusted with a complicated mission whose failure would cost many more lives than my own.

At least, I reflected, we could not have asked for more co-operation and support than we had received from 5th Indian Division. At this point perhaps

I should mention one item of our stores that was later to cause me considerable embarrassment. Pointing out that I was responsible for the health as well as the safety of my party the A.D.M.S.[1] I had insisted on handing to me, over and above the supply carried by our medical sergeant, several gross of those contraceptives usually known as French letters. They were thrust into the pockets of my rucksack and forgotten. Soon after my return to London I was invited to tea by a much loved aunt, who also asked me to bring along my rucksack, which she wished to borrow for her son to take on a holiday in Switzerland. Only when I was in the taxi on my way to her house did I remember what that rucksack still contained. Useless, I knew, to attempt any explanation. Sweating with anxiety and keeping a furtive eye on the driver, I lowered each of the spare passenger seats in turn, loaded it with the contents of the pockets and gently released it to its normal position, where it effectively concealed them. I have often wondered about the reactions of the driver and his next fare.

---

[1] Assistant Director of Medical Services.

VI

ARRIVAL IN BALI

Closed up at action stations *Loch Eck* steamed safely past the Indonesian batteries commanding the narrow strait between Madura and the mainland. Afterwards I strolled on deck watching the mountains of Java slip slowly by, distant grey outlines in the muggy haze. Our troops seemed to look forward to the venture with a mixture of mild curiosity and amusement; they showed no signs either of excitement or anxiety. The Buffs, very brisk and soldierly and very young—the oldest was their sergeant, not yet twenty—were invariably cheerful and gave an impressive display of smartness and efficiency on all ceremonial occasions; the signallers, much less tidy, took full advantage of their traditional right to grumble, but also put into their work all their traditional skill and energy. The father of the party was Sergeant Hopkins, R.A.M.C., a grizzled old regular soldier of inexhaustible patience and good humour; such was the men's respect for him that during the two operations we only had one case of sickness—a mild attack of bronchitis.

I was awakened early on the morning of the 23rd by the lowering of the anchor; we were lying in Benoa Roads, a mile off the tiny harbour built by the Dutch which is the only port in South Bali. About half past seven a Japanese landing-craft drew alongside, under the command of an ugly little naval lieutenant who told us sourly that Sixteenth Army had omitted to warn the garrison of our arrival. We sent Ando's party ashore to tell the commanders that we should land in the afternoon for an unofficial visit of inspection.

Another landing-craft came for us at noon. With Peter Hoare, Shaw, Neville and the Buffs escort I took my place in the stern and prepared for my meeting with the officers whom we could see awaiting us on the jetty; I wondered anxiously if we were right in our easy assumption that they would obey me, or if our reception was going to be warm rather than friendly.

It was a fair afternoon with a soft, fresh breeze to temper the midday heat; the sun sparkled on the clear blue water and struck bright on the limestone cliffs of the bare Tafelhoek peninsula as we nosed our way slowly between the double line of buoys that marked the channel through the hidden coral reefs. Ahead of us lay a beach of dazzling white sand, rising in a gentle slope to a fringe of palm trees whose foliage gleamed a startling vivid green against the indigo shadow of the hinterland.

A company of infantry was drawn up on the jetty. As we stepped ashore there was a bellowed command, the officers' swords flashed in salute, and with smart precision the troops presented arms; returning the salute I reflected that now at least we were over the first fence. There followed a brief conference with Captain Okuyama, the senior naval officer, who was in command of the garrison, and his military colleague, Colonel Tsuneoka; Okuyama was a short, grizzled officer of dignified bearing with intelligent, sensitive features. They had brought with them their own interpreter, Miura, a smooth and shifty-looking official of the Japanese Civil Affairs Administration, obsequious and spotless in a well-pressed white duck suit. I told them to report aboard *Loch Eck* at 0930 next morning to sign the terms of surrender; the full surrender ceremony would be taken by General Mansergh himself about a week after the main landing, until which time officers and men would retain their arms—at this last statement a look of profound relief crossed both commanders' faces. This relief became more pronounced as I passed on General Mansergh's instructions that my orders were to be obeyed implicitly; it began to dawn on me that these officers had not been enjoying their equivocal position of responsibility in isolation. We passed on to discuss troop concentrations and the organization of naval patrols in the Bali Strait to prevent the infiltration of terrorists from Java—a very difficult task owing to the narrowness of the strait and the length of the coastline.

A large and comfortable staff car took us the seven miles to Den Pasar, the capital of South Bali and pre-war centre of the island's tourist industry, where we were to establish our headquarters. The Japanese warned us that this town was the centre of extremist feeling, the countryside being for the moment comparatively quiet. When I asked if there had been any incidents Captain Okuyama answered in precise tones:

'On 13th December last the islanders unlawfully attacked our troops. The object of this attack was to gain possession of our arms. We suppressed the attack and detained the headmen responsible. They are now in custody.'

A great improvement on what happened in Java, I said to myself, making a mental note to visit those headmen in prison as soon as I had the time.

All along the straight tarmac road, lined with tall palms and flanked by rich green paddy-fields, we passed groups of Balinese—slight, well-built young men whose muscles rippled above their brightly coloured loincloths; slender, golden-skinned girls with firm, bare breasts; old men and women with emaciated bodies and skeleton ribs who still retained their dignified and graceful bearing, and children wide-eyed with bewilderment and surprise. Some stared at us in silent curiosity; others, especially the women and children, smiled and waved; a few of the men gave the *merdeka* salute, but hesitatingly, as though uncertain whether it was the right thing to do.

South Bali, separated from the north by a wild range of high volcanic mountains—one of them, Batur, is still active—is by far the more fertile and thickly populated part of the country; indeed it supports the great majority of

76

the million and a half inhabitants which the Balinese genius for rice cultivation enables to live without hardship on an island of only five thousand square kilometres.[1] Den Pasar had therefore been selected for our base in preference to Singaradja, the capital; it was, moreover, close to the beach where the Dutch force was to land.

The town, covering an area no longer or broader than a man could comfortably walk in fifteen minutes, centred round a large grassy square named the Alun-Alun,[2] planted with trees along the edges and resembling a public playground—on which model, indeed, it seemed to have been designed. Around it in their trim little gardens stood the neat white bungalows of the former Dutch officials; the largest had previously been the Residency and was now the Japanese naval headquarters. To the east a road ran to the village of Sanoer and the beach where we were expecting the Dutch to land; to the west a street Lined with squalid modern shops led to the markets and the Javanese and Chinese quarters. On either side of the road leading north stood the luxurious buildings of the Bali Hotel and its annex; beyond them, surrounded by a mud wall pierced with thatched gateways lay the old Balinese village of Badung, from which the local Rajah took his title.

Leaving the Bali Hotel for Colonel Ter Meulen and his staff, we ordered the Japanese to prepare the Residency for our occupation the following afternoon; a single-storey but roomy bungalow with a large courtyard and garden at the back and a short, crescent-shaped sweep of drive in front leading from the road and the Alun-Alun, it could easily accommodate my entire party. Our last action before returning to Benoa was to requisition three staff cars from the Japanese, one each for Shaw, Neville and myself.

A light breeze ruffled the blue-green waters of Benoa Roads and swayed the feathery tops of the palm trees beyond the line of breakers on the shore; inland, dark banks of grey cloud threatened heavy rain, but overhead the morning sun beat warm upon the canvas awning spread above the frigate's quarterdeck. Even in the shade the paintwork gleamed a spotless light grey, the brass shone, the deck was holystoned to a faultless white; Commander Hoare had prepared an impressive setting for the ceremony that was about to begin.

The after bulkhead was draped with the Union Jack and Stars and Stripes; beneath the flags was ranged a line of chairs at a long table spread with a green baize cloth. Here Commander Hoare, my officers and I took our seats;

---

[1] Owing to a remarkable increase in the population since 1946 there is now, I believe, some shortage of food in Bali.

[2] The Dutch did me the honour of re-christening the Alun-Alun 'Kemp Platz', but since their departure I understand it has reverted to some more suitable and doubtless more euphonious Indonesian title.

facing us, at a short distance, was another line of chairs, as yet empty. Aft, in ceremonial white dress, were assembled the men of the ship's company; the officers, immaculate in Number Tens, lined up on our left against the starboard rail. At the gangway head, on the port side, stood Mansell, the First Lieutenant, with a Chief Petty Officer and, very impressive in their smartly pressed green uniforms and scrubbed and blancoed webbing, the armed guard party of the Buffs.

On the blotter in front of me lay a five page roneo document entitled 'Formal Instrument of Surrender', which the Japanese Commanders would have to sign. In brief, its terms empowered me to assume command of the Japanese naval and military garrison; to use Japanese forces as I thought fit for police and labour duties, in particular for the preparation and protection of the landing beaches; and to take over the civil and military administration of the island until the arrival of the Dutch. On my left Hoare was studying a shorter paper, which he would read out at the opening of the ceremony, embodying certain immediate naval requirements. Although this was to be only a formal surrender, and the official surrender of the garrison would be taken by General Mansergh after the main landing, I could not suppress a surge of pride at the thought of the small but historic role I was allowed to assume.

> Is it not passing brave to be a king,
> And ride in triumph through Persepolis?

As the time drew on to half past nine a tense, expectant silence descended on the ship; the slapping of the waves against the hull broke strangely loud on our ears.

A shout from Mansell at the gangway head announced the approach of the Japanese Surrender Commission. A few minutes later they climbed aboard—Captain Okuyama, Colonel Tsuneoka, two staff officers and the interpreter, Miura; when Mansell had relieved each officer of his sword, which he placed on a table by the gangway, the party approached us, came smartly to attention and bowed gravely to Hoare and me. In accordance with our orders from General Mansergh we remained seated, and told Mansell to lead them to their places. Followed by General Ando and his two officers, they sat down facing us.

When Hoare and I had read out the surrender terms Okuyama asked our permission to withdraw and discuss them with his colleague; Mansell led them to Hoare's cabin. Half an hour later they returned to tell us they would sign. Each of them came up to the table, affixed his signature in ink with a thin brush, and sat down. While Hoare was dictating to Miura final orders for our disembarkation that afternoon, I happened to glance at Okuyama. He was sitting quite still with his hands upon his knees, his head bowed and his lined old face puckered in grief; tears dripped slowly down his shrunken cheeks. As I watched him my heart was filled with an overwhelming pity, and the glamour and glory of my position faded to a shadow. Perhaps I ought not to put my feelings on record for I had suffered nothing at the hands of the Japanese. Their callousness and cruelty, the brutality of their prison camps, and the horrors of the Burma-Siam railway were things I had heard of but not experienced. I had never met Japanese in battle, the most I had had to do was keep out of their way. Now in my unearned hour of triumph I felt ashamed to watch this veteran sailor, who had spent his life in a service with a great fighting tradition, weeping openly over his humiliation at the hands of a jumped-up young lieutenant-colonel who had never even fought against him.

We disembarked that afternoon, and by the evening had established ourselves in the Residency; *Loch Eck* remained at anchor off Benoa for another twenty-four hours with a landing-party ready to come to our assistance if we should fire a Verey light. We posted a pair of sentries on the gates in front of the house, more for the sake of appearances than from fear of attack. Whatever undercurrents of hostility might be flowing beneath the surface, there had so far been nothing but friendliness in our welcome from the Balinese; nevertheless I ordered Colonel Tsuneoka to station a platoon of infantry on the Alun-Alun to cover our headquarters against a sudden attack. Our signallers installed their equipment in the entrance hall of the Residency, and before midnight I had sent my first message to 5th Indian Division.

While Shaw and Sergeant Hopkins busied themselves with the accommodation of our troops and the stowage of our stores, I sat down in the office which had been prepared for me in the front of the house to study the intelligence reports I had received from the Japanese and compare them with the information I had collected Surabaja. From time to time, as the night wore on, we went outside and stood listening in the heavy, scented air for any sound of trouble from the town; we heard nothing but the soft tread of the sentries m their rubber-soled canvas boots. Those young men seemed strangely indifferent to their lonely situation in a strange and possibly hostile island.

I was still at my desk when dawn broke. I was appalled at the amount of work that lay ahead of us in the short time before the arrival of the main force, and at the loss of life that would follow any failure or mistake on my part. The civil administration of the island was in chaos, and I should have to build it up from scratch; the few Balinese officials who remained at their posts were, it appeared, too frightened of the extremists to give us any help or even advice.[1] The beaches where the Dutch proposed to land were at present unfit for any craft much larger than a canoe; we should need a considerable Japanese labour force to prepare them for D Day, and we must deploy other Japanese formations to cover the landings. There was a disused airstrip at Kuta in the south of the island, which we were required to make serviceable for Dakotas. Lastly, and of prime importance, I must find out the strength of the extremists, especially around Den Pasar, and, if possible, the names of their leaders; and I must make contact immediately with a number of influential Balinese who, I had been told, were well disposed towards us and capable of assuming the responsibilities of government.

I had heard that there were three Europeans still at large on the island, all of them artists: the well-known Belgian painter, Le Mayeur, who lived with his Balinese wife at Sanoer; the Austrian Strasser, somewhere in the mountains of the north, and an eccentric Swiss, Theo Meier, whose house was near Selat in eastern Bali among the foothills of the great volcano, Gunung Agung. They should be able to give us valuable and unprejudiced information about local conditions.

There would be little rest or even sleep for any of us, I reflected; but at least I was fortunate in being able to delegate with confidence much of the work to my officers. Over breakfast the three of us discussed the situation. I decided to concentrate on the political problems; Neville would be responsible for the beaches, Shaw for the airstrip. The tactical disposition of the Japanese formations to cover the landings was, of course, my personal responsibility; but Shaw, who had much more experience of tactics in this war than I, undertook to work out the details with Colonel Tsuneoka.

We immediately called the Japanese commanders and General Ando to a conference, which lasted for the rest of the morning. They impressed on us again that there was a strong element of extremism and lawlessness in Den Pasar, although at present it was latent and ill-armed. With some indignation I asked why, if they knew of it, they had taken no steps to suppress it; they replied uneasily that they had been without instructions, which indeed seemed to be true. They could tell us little of the situation outside Den Pasar, but believed that there were a few small bands in the countryside, especially in the west, who were supplied with arms by sea from Java; although they had established an effective blockade of the ports they could not hope, with their limited forces, to control the entire western coastline. Indeed, as I

---

[1] By the term 'extremists' I mean the Javanese-controlled, terrorist, independence movement which had as its object the removal of all Dutch and Allied control in the islands of Indonesia; despite the difference in religion and the mutual antipathy between the two peoples this movement had active supporters in Bali, particularly among the youth. They were also known as *Pemudas*, from the Malay word meaning 'youth'.

signalled General Mansergh, it was impossible to prevent the shipment of arms and agents from Java when the Bali Strait was only two miles wide.

As they were about to leave, Okuyama said to me, 'If the troops who follow you are British you need have no fear of trouble. But if they should be Dutch, then there may be incidents—although even then it would only be a few snipers.'

Refusing to be drawn by this obvious bait I answered that I knew nothing of the composition of the main force, but that in any event I expected his troops to see that there were no incidents. However, I sent a signal to Colonel Ter Meulen warning him of the danger and asking him to take precautions on D Day to ensure that one or two isolated shots should not develop into a major engagement.

Speaking neither Malay nor Balinese,[1] I badly needed an interpreter, and so I asked for Miura, whose Malay was as good as his English, to be attached to my staff. In addition, the Japanese gave me a chauffeur-mechanic to maintain our three staff cars. His name was Shimada, a simple, smiling lad of twenty-two who came from Yokohama and had been a merchant seaman before the war. He was a competent mechanic though an erratic driver, and he was a useful interpreter too, for he had a smattering of English and a good deal of Malay. He was a genial, carefree fellow with a perpetual grin on his ugly little pock-marked face; but he was a tireless and willing worker and, as we soon discovered, he had plenty of courage.

In the afternoon Neville went to inspect the beaches and Shaw drove to Kuta to examine the airfield. I made Miura take me to the prison where the Japanese were holding the headmen who had led the revolt of 13th December. My instructions gave me no authority to order their release, and if, as the Japanese maintained, they were dangerous terrorists, they were better in custody; but at least I could ensure that they were decently treated.

That evening Shaw and I drove the five miles to Sanoer to pay our respects to the famous Adrien Le Mayeur. He was a painter well known in south-east Asia, whose fame had already penetrated to Europe before the war. He had lived and worked in Bali for many years, and had built and furnished his own house; it stood on the beach, looking east across the lagoon to the line of white breakers on the coral reef that encircled those smooth

---

[1] There are three Balinese languages—high, low and middle, the last being a hybrid of the first two. High and low Balinese are not different dialects but separate languages, yet every Balinese must know both. For their rigid caste system dictates that, to take an example, a peasant addressing a rajah must speak to him in high Balinese, but the rajah would reply to him in low Balinese. Low Balinese is the native language of the island, whereas high Balinese is of Javanese or Sanskrit origin. Malay, which is the Hindustani of the Archipelago, is understood in Bali but is not spoken by the people amongst themselves.

and shallow waters and kept them clear of shark and barracuda. We had heard also of his beautiful Balinese wife, Polok, in her childhood a famous Legong dancer and afterwards the model for many of his best paintings.

Leaving the car at the end of the track we walked across the soft, shell-strewn sand past the white hulls of the fishing boats, carved in the shape of the mythical 'elephant fish' with eyes painted in their prows to enable them to see in the dark; through the fringe of palms and undergrowth on our right filtered the rays of the setting sun, etching rivulets of gold on the calm surface of the lagoon. Out of the silence ahead there appeared two figures plodding towards us: a slight, emaciated man whose age I judged to be near seventy, wearing only an old pair of shorts and sandals, and a tall, well-built, even husky girl with a golden skin and an expression of singular sweetness and serenity. She was wearing a magenta skirt with a green silk sash and a deep blue, gold-embroidered breast cloth.

'Le Mayeur,' the man introduced himself in a thin, reedy voice. 'Allow me to present my wife, Polok. We are very pleased to welcome you to our home.'

The house was built in Balinese style, of palm wood and bamboo, with a well-thatched roof of grass. There were no outside walls to the rooms; they were left open to the cooling breezes, the soft night scents and the murmur of the breakers on the reef. All the furniture was of bamboo. The house was filled with a profusion of Balinese carvings in wood and stone—gods and demons, animals and men; two squat stone demons with scarlet hibiscus flowers in their ears stood guard upon the porch. The walls were hung with Le Mayeur's paintings, most of them portraits of Polok and her friends. A cool and spacious living-room gave on to a veranda which overlooked a long, narrow compound enclosed by thorn hedges and bright with scarlet and yellow hibiscus and canna lilies; nearby stood a simple open summer house with a raised matting floor, where Le Mayeur and his guests usually took their meals.

While we sat talking on the veranda in the last of the daylight, Polok's two handsome maidservants brought us *arak* and small dishes of rice and meat with it.

'I hope you will come often,' said Polok in her halting, sing-song English. 'You can bathe and then eat with us. I will make you the special Balinese *bébé guling*.'[1]

We asked Le Mayeur how he had fared under the Japanese occupation.

'It was very worrying, of course,' he told us, 'but not really bad. At first they were very strict, but afterwards they left us alone. In the beginning, when the Dutch went away, the Balinese came and robbed my house; they took away many of my things, even the furniture, but later on I got some of them

---

[1] Roast sucking pig and rice.

back. They are great thieves, the Balinese,' he laughed, 'but they are like children, not really vicious.'

'Are we going to have a lot of trouble here, do you think?'

'Trouble? Yes, you can have some trouble. The Japanese of course were not popular, but they excited the people against you; and now that they see what is happening in Java some of the young men have big ideas and want to get rid of all foreigners. However, the older people are more sensible and want things to go slowly, and if you are firm with the troublemakers you will have their support.'

In the week that followed, whenever our work permitted, we would drive to Sanoer about seven in the morning, bathe in the lagoon and breakfast afterwards with the Le Mayeurs. Their knowledge of the district and people around Den Pasar was of the greatest help to us in those early days; and our affection grew daily for this kindly, easy-going couple and their two servants whom they regarded as part of their family.

One day, after a lunch of Polok's *bébé guling*, we sat on the veranda and listened to a *gamelan*[1] of musicians invited by Le Mayeur to play us Balinese music. The orchestra of some twenty young men squatted beside their instruments, forming a hollow square in the compound; the instruments were all percussion, which the musicians struck with light mallets. There were metallophones with polished bronze keys of different pitch; heavy gongs to play deep notes; two sets of twelve and ten bells each, arranged in a wooden frame; a pair of drums—a large 'male' and smaller 'female'—wrapped in chequered black and white cloth to shield them from evil vibrations; sets of cymbals, and bells, metal tubes and a small, light gong held in the lap and beaten with a stick.

The music was unlike any I had heard either in Europe or the East. Above the distant sound of the breakers on the reef it beat upon our ears—the pure, ringing notes of the metallophones, the soft, sweet chimes of the bells, the deep, mellow boom of the gongs, all superbly controlled by the throbbing pulse of the double-headed drums; now a gentle, soothing melody, now a wild, fast, exultant rhythm, the notes came to us like drops of clearest water through the still and heavy air.

Later we persuaded Polok, not without difficulty, to show us some of the movements of the *Legong*. She explained that this, the finest of Balinese dances,[2] must be performed by young, unmarried girls and so it was a long

---

[1] The orchestra of Bali and Java. The Balinese, strangely enough, have no written music.

[2] But it does not seem to be among the most ancient. For a full account of this dance and its origins see *Island of Bali* by Miguel Covarrubias, Cassell, 1937, pp. 224-30, and *Dance and Drama in Bali* by Beryl de Zoete and Walter Spies, Faber & Faber,

time since she had been able to dance it; moreover, it properly required three girls—two principals, the *legongs*, and their attendant, the *tjondong*. However, she wrapped herself in the heavy, tightly constricting, gold and crimson brocade garments of a *legong*, fastened on her head a golden diadem interwoven with fresh frangipani blossoms and, clasping a small fan in her right hand, stepped on to the floor.

Legong has been described as 'the flower of bodily movement at its utmost intensity of vibration.'[1] Although, as she said, Polok could give us no more than a bare idea of what it should be, the grace and vitality of her movements held us entranced. Now she stood poised with knees flexed, stamping her foot at each accent of the music, the vibrations spreading to her thigh, up her whole body and even to her neck, shaking the flowers in her hair; now she glided across the floor, one arm outstretched with the fingers tense and quivering. Her face was expressionless, even melancholy; but her eyes, darting from side to side in quick, sudden flashes, and her long, fluttering fingers gave life and warmth to this symphony of movement, colour and sound. The tense, absorbed faces of the musicians glistened in the afternoon sunlight, which flooded the flowering garden in a blaze of green and yellow and scarlet; between the notes of the orchestra we heard the fainter, unceasing music of the surf.

From the moment of our arrival our house became the centre of interest for the population of Den Pasar, especially for the women and children. From early morning until dusk there was a crowd gathered around our gates: handsome, bronze young men strolling up and down, hand in hand;[2] children staring wide-eyed and solemn or grinning shyly, then turning away or hiding their faces in sudden embarrassment; old women squatting on their haunches chewing betel nut and spitting streams of the scarlet juice on to the ground; golden, bare-breasted girls with baskets of fruit, walking with rippling muscles and superb, erect carriage and smiling lazily and seductively at the smart young sentries. The latter, without concealing their appreciation of the beautiful bare flesh exposed to them at such close quarters, contrived to preserve a soldierly decorum in the face of temptation; the signallers, true to their independent tradition, affected a cynical indifference and deplored the absence of a cinema.

1938, pp. 218-32. The dance tells a story, or variations of a story, from ancient Javanese legend.

[1] *Dance and Drama in Bali*, p. 218.

[2] In Bali this is a usual practice and is not considered in the lease effeminate.

VII

BALI AND THE BALINESE

To give an adequate picture of the island and people of Bali is beyond the scope of this work or the ingenuity of its author. The infinite variety of Balinese life, religion and culture has exhausted volumes of literature on art and anthropology with which I have not the knowledge, the skill or the impudence to compete.[1] A very brief outline is all I can attempt.

Lying between eight and nine degrees south of the Equator Bali naturally enjoys a warm climate and an even temperature throughout the year; there is in fact less than ten degrees variation between the warmest and coolest months. Sea winds preserve the island from the burning heat of other equatorial lands, but from November until April the north-west monsoons bring heavy rainfall and the discomforts of a high humidity; the pleasantest months are from June to September, when a cool, dry wind blows from Australia.

The island is mountainous, with high volcanic peaks on the north, east and west; the highest of them, the great volcano Gunung Agung, which rises over ten thousand feet, is sacred to all Balinese, who regard it as the navel (*puséh*) of the world. In the south the foothills drop gradually to the sea, intersected by steep, wooded ravines and watercourses; the slopes are terraced with superb skill in tier after tier of *sawas*, or small paddy-fields, that produce each year two crops of the finest rice in South-East Asia. The north-western corner of the island, which unfortunately I was never able to visit, is very little populated because of the lack of running water; there are found tiger, wild boar and giant lizards, which exist nowhere else on Bali. Elephants, incidentally, have never existed on Bali, and their appearance in Balinese art is due to Indian and Javanese influence. The average density of population over the whole island is 1,000 per square mile, but in the Gianjar district of South Bali it is 2,300, making a total of a million and a half inhabitants.

To the Balinese the mountain-tops are the homes of the gods and of the spirits of their ancestors, whom they worship and who descend to earth on feast days; the sea is the haunt of evil spirits and demons. The land between

---

[1] Foremost among works in the English language I would commend to readers, Miguel Covarrubias's valuable and informative *Island of Bali* and the more technical study, *Dance and Drama in Bali* by Beryl de Zoete and Walter Spies. John Coast's *Dancing out of Bali*, Faber & Faber, 1954, gives a fascinating account of more recent conditions on the island.

85

is, to them, the whole world. They recognize, of course, that other countries exist, but those countries mean nothing to them, and they regard their inhabitants as unfortunates whose past or present imperfections have rendered them unfit to live in Bali; exile for a Balinese is far worse than death, and Miss Emily Hahn records an ordinance of the old Dutch East India Company forbidding the importation of Balinese slaves into Java because they so often ran amok.[1]

In their fear and hatred of the sea the Balinese are exceptional among island peoples. At Sanoer I saw men wading in the lagoon a few yards off shore with casting nets, or putting to sea in canoes with triangular sails and curiously carved and painted prows, to hunt the sea turtles that are a favourite delicacy at banquets; but most Balinese avoid even the coast and the beaches. In the words of Covarrubias 'they are one of the rare island peoples in the world who turn their eyes not outward to the waters, but upward to the mountain tops.'[2]

Here it is perhaps worthwhile quoting Covarrubias again on another peculiarity of the Balinese—their attitude to death, or rather to the ceremony of cremation. 'It is in their cremation ceremonies,' he writes, 'that the Balinese have their greatest fun. A cremation is an occasion for gaiety and not for mourning, since it represents the accomplishment of their most sacred duty: the ceremonial burning of the corpses of the dead to liberate their souls so that they can thus attain the higher worlds and be free for reincarnation into better things.'[3]

Although a strange, even a unique people, the Balinese are not a pure race; they are a mixture of the ancient Indonesian inhabitants of the islands with Hindu-Javanese, Chinese and Indian colonists. Hindu dynasties flourished in the Archipelago from the seventh to the fifteenth or early sixteenth centuries, the most famous of them being the Srivijaya in Sumatra and the Madjapahit in Java. For much of this period Bali was under the rule of Hindu-Javanese kings. On the collapse of the Madjapahit dynasty about the end of the fifteenth century, under the pressure of Islamic penetration, the surviving Hindu-Javanese aristocracy of priests and warriors migrated to Bali, where they established their rule and their culture. The son of the last Madjapahit ruler styled himself *Dewa Agung*[4] or supreme ruler of Bali, and divided the island into principalities to which he appointed rajahs. These principalities gradually developed into independent kingdoms, though theoretically

---

[1] *Raffles of Singapore*, Alder, 1948. On the other hand, the Balinese conquered Lombok in 1740 and established a prosperous colony there, ruled by a rajah.

[2] Covarrubias, op. cit., p. 10.

[3] Ibid, p. 359.

[4] Literally 'Divine Great'. When I was in Bali this was still the title of the Rajah of Klungkung, the paramount rajah of the island.

acknowledging the supremacy of the *Dewa Agung* before the arrival of the Dutch they were perpetually at war among themselves.

'It was of extreme significance for the cultural development of Bali that in the exodus of the rulers, the priests, and the intellectuals of what was the most civilized race of the Eastern islands, the cream of Javanese culture was transplanted as a unit into Bali. There the art, the religion and philosophy of the Hindu-Javanese were preserved and have flourished practically undisturbed until today. When the fury of intolerant Islamism drove the intellectuals of Java into Bali, they brought with them their classics and continued to cultivate their poetry and art, so that when Sir Stamford Raffles wanted to write the history of Java, he had to turn to Bali for what remains of the once great literature of Java.'[1]

The Hindu-Javanese princes established a feudal, often vicious and oppressive dominion over the native Balinese; they claimed and tried to enforce absolute power over the persons of their subjects. The Dutchman Dr. Julius Jacobs, who visited South Bali in the early 1880's, mentions a particularly savage example.[2] Every adult male Balinese, he says, was obliged to contribute a tax to his rajah in the form of work; if a man died without leaving a son old enough to take over this work, his widow and female children became the rajah's property. Old women were employed in the palace, the middle-aged put to heavy manual labour; but the young girls—often before the age of puberty—were forced to become prostitutes and pay as much as nine-tenths of their earnings to the rajah. In Badung, the old principality of Den Pasar, Dr. Jacobs met several of these prostitutes under the age of puberty. Each rajah owned between two and three hundred of these unfortunate girls—a considerable source of income.

Nevertheless, the Balinese, in their self-governing village communities, were often able to mitigate the oppression of their rulers by the threat of boycott and passive resistance. Moreover, in the mountains there are still a few villages of pure descendants of the ancient Indonesian inhabitants, who live in strict isolation and have protected the purity of their stock by the most rigid taboos against marriage outside the community; the most interesting and the most exclusive is the village of Tenganan near Karangasem in East Bali. These people, who style themselves Bali Aga, or 'original Balinese', have never accepted the Hinduism of the Javanese invaders, but cling with fanatical devotion to their ancient traditions and beliefs. The Hindu-Balinese aristocracy seem to have respected them and left them alone.

---

[1] Covarrubias, op. cit., p. 28.
[2] *Eenigen Tijd onder de Baliërs*, Batavia, 1883, a most fascinating work unfortunately not published in English; for the translations quoted here I am indebted to my friend Daan Hubrecht.

The statement that the Balinese are Hindus requires considerable qualification. It is impossible to give here a satisfactory account of Balinese religious belief and custom; but the Balinese seem to have absorbed a little from each of the sects and cults that reached their island, adapted the new teachings to suit their own habits and ideas, and superimposed them on their own primitive animistic religion. Indeed, 'it is not unlikely,' says Covarrubias,[1] 'that in the future "Sanghyang Widi", the exalted name that the missionaries have adopted for Jesus, will become a first cousin of Siva and Buddha and will enjoy offerings and a shrine where he can rest when he chooses to visit Bali.'[2]

Of far more religious importance to the Balinese than the imported Hinduism of their conquerors are their own traditional rites connected with the worship of their ancestors' spirits; of the gods of fertility; of the gods of fire and water, earth and sun; of the mountains—the two great volcanoes, Batur and Gunung Agung, have their shrines in every village temple—and of other lesser gods and demons. This worship, as Covarrubias points out, is The backbone of the Balinese religion, which is generally referred to as Hinduism, but which is in reality too close to the earth, too animistic, to be taken as the same esoteric religion as that of the Hindus of India. ... It is true that Hindu gods and practices are constantly in evidence, but their aspect and significance differ in Bali to such an extent from orthodox Hinduism *that we find the primitive beliefs of a people who never lost contact with the soil rising supreme over the religious philosophy and practices of their masters*. . . . Religion is to the Balinese both race and nationality. . . . The religious sages, the Brahmanic priests, remain outsiders, aloof from the ordinary Balinese, who have their own priests, simple people whose office is to guard and sweep the community temples, in which there are no idols, no images of gods to be worshipped. The temples are frequented by the ancestral gods. . . . *The Balinese live with their forefathers in a great family of the dead and the living. . . . The religion of Bali is a set of rules of behaviour, a mode of life.*'[3]

When, therefore, the Balinese speak of their gods they do not mean the gods of orthodox Hinduism—indeed, the only Hindu god actually worshipped in Balinese temples is Surya, the Sun, who has somehow achieved the dignity of head of the Balinese pantheon; they mean a wide variety of protective spirits, all of them connected in some way with the cult of ancestry. Into this family they have also absorbed certain characters from Hindu mythology to whom they have taken a fancy. However, I might

---

[1] Covarrubias, op. cit., p. 263.

[2] It is not true, as is sometimes asserted, that the Dutch excluded missionaries; it was the religious outlook of the Balinese that proved unresponsive to missionary zeal.

[3] Covarrubias, op. cit., p. 260-1. (My italics.)

mention that when I questioned the Swiss artist Theo Meier on the number and variety of Balinese deities, he laughed.

'There are only two gods in Bali—*takut* and *malu*! Those two rule the lives of all Balinese; the old rajahs ruled through them, and you will find you must do so too.'

Takut means fear; *malu* is shame, embarrassment or 'face'. Of the power of *takut* over the Balinese we were to have immediate and almost daily experience.

Like the Manichaeans the Balinese believe that there is perpetual war between the equally powerful forces of good and evil; between their gods and protecting spirits on the one hand, and on the other the demons and *leyaks*, or witches, whose purpose and joy it is to destroy humanity. It is necessary to propitiate both to avoid arousing the wrath of either. On its ability to preserve a proper balance between the two depends the physical and spiritual health of each community and family. Certain acts or conditions of individual members can make the whole community *sebel*, or unclean, and therefore vulnerable to evil forces. Such acts extend beyond the unpardonable crimes of suicide, bestiality, incest and the desecration of a temple, to quite innocent or unavoidable breaches of taboo; a menstruating woman, for instance, is *sebel* and must be secluded, and parents who have twins will render their village *sebel*. To such a people, in the words of Mr. Raymond Mortimer, 'sin is not a disregard for conscience but a breaking, no matter how unintentional, of a taboo; and the resulting pollution can be removed only by ritual cleansings and sacrifice.'[1]

The Hindu caste system, which is an essential feature of Balinese society, was not established in its present form until the middle of the fourteenth century, when Bali was overrun by a famous Madjapahit general, Gadja Mada. Previously the old Balinese aristocracy had their own caste system, which still survives among the Bali Aga.

There are four main castes, of which more than ninety per cent of Balinese belong to the lowest, the Sudras. The three noble castes are the Brahmanas, the priests; the Satrias, the princes, and the Wesias, the warrior caste. All three claim divine origin—from Brahma, the Creator—which is probably why the common people hold them in such respect. The Brahmanas are theoretically the highest, although the Satrias are inclined to contest their superiority; their influence is religious rather than political, but they serve as judges in the courts; their own laws forbid them to engage in commerce. Brahmana men carry the title *Ida Bagus*, and the women are styled *Ida Ayu*, both meaning 'Eminent and Beautiful'. The two principal titles of the Satrias are *Anak Agung*, 'Child of the Great', and *Tjokorde*, Prince. Most of the nobility,

---

[1] Review in the *Sunday Times* of 7th September 1958.

however, belong to the Wesias and carry the title, *Gusti*; they have considerable political influence.[1]

There do not seem to be any 'untouchables', as in India, but certain professions are 'unclean' and will pollute a village if practised within its boundaries; among them are, strangely enough, pottery, indigo-dying and the manufacture of arak—a powerful, fiery spirit distilled from the juice of the sugar palm.

An important survival from the pre-Hindu castes are the pandés, or blacksmiths, descendants of the ancient fire priests, who worship the volcano Batur. They enjoy great respect among all Balinese because they have the magical powers to handle with impunity the holy elements of fire and iron; even a Brahmana must address a pandé in high Balinese. The pandés make the magic krises, symbols of a family's virility; a man will invest much of his fortune in his kris and the jewellery decorating it, for the richness of his kris determines his economic status.[2]

While it is untrue to say that the Balinese are 'caste-ridden', they are intensely—and proudly—caste-conscious. Relations between the castes are distinguished by an elasticity and friendliness unknown in India, but the Balinese pay careful attention to caste etiquette and to the rank conferred upon a man by his birth; this respect for rank, strange among so easy-going a people, is as much a matter of good manners as of duty. When strangers meet upon the road the first question they ask each other is 'What is your caste?' Thereafter the higher caste will continue the conversation in low Balinese, and the lower caste will reply to him in high. It is unthinkable for a man of low caste to place himself at a higher level in a room than someone of higher caste. For example, a Sudra would never stand upright in the presence of a seated Brahmana or Satria, but would immediately sit down at a lower level, probably on the floor; and the common people—who are not ashamed to think of themselves as such—would always bow their heads when passing a nobleman. I remember an occasion when I was staying in the house of the Swiss painter, Theo Meier, and a Brahmana came to visit him; as soon as the visitor was seated Meier signed to me to sit down. 'You see' he explained to me later, 'it would have been the insult for you to have remained standing. You would have made yourself higher than the *Ida Bagus*.'

Only the laws of marriage are inflexible between the castes. A man may marry a woman of an equal or lower caste, but never may a woman marry a

---

[1] For example, a famous Balinese terrorist and hero, killed in battle with the Dutch soon after I left, was Gusti Ngurah Rai; Ngurah is a title assumed by some nobility to indicate the purity of their descent.

[2] Covarrubias, op. cit., p. 199. When a rajah marries a girl of low caste she is often married ceremonially to his Kris, the prince not attending the ceremony.

man of lower caste; even sexual intercourse between the two is forbidden, and in former times was punishable by the death of the guilty pair.

The life of the Balinese is concentrated in their villages. Each village is a small, independent republic with its own council of Elders and officials who are elected by the community, who are generally unpaid, and who govern as representatives of the ancestral spirits; all villagers have equal rights and obligations. Each *desa*, as these independent villages are called, will have three temples: the civil temple, or *pura desa*, where the Elders meet in council and where the main feasts take place; the 'temple of origin', or *pura puséh* the ancient village shrine, dedicated to the founder of the community; and the *pura dalem*, the temple of the dead, outside the village in the cemetery. Balinese cemeteries are desolate and forbidding spots, shunned by the people, especially after dark when they are haunts of the abominable *leyaks*; these malignant witches, under their terrible queen, Rangda—a hideous creature with lolling tongue, long fierce fangs and monstrous drooping breasts—bring plagues on the island and live off the blood and entrails of young or unborn children and the blood of pregnant women.

Usually a village consists of a number of family compounds, each containing several pavilions housing relatives or related families; every compound is surrounded by a low wall of whitewashed mud, pierced by a narrow thatched gateway with a raised doorstep. A wide avenue, shaded by great trees and flanked by deep irrigation ditches, runs through the centre of the village in the direction of the Balinese cardinal points—'from the mountain to the sea', or from north to south. They are a lovely sight, these villages, with their long, beautifully proportioned walls and thatched roofs half-hidden in cool, shady groves of banana trees, mangoes and tall, slim, plume-topped coco-palms.

The work of the village, in particular the cultivation of the rice-fields, is organized on a communal or co-operative basis; *subaks*, or village water boards, control the vitally important irrigation. Every villager who owns a ricefield is obliged to join the *subak* and to carry out its orders. The objectives of the *subak* are to give the small agriculturist the assurance that he will not lack water, to police the dams effectively so that strangers will not divert the water supply, to settle disputes, and to attend to the communal rice festivals. In the village the society assumes full social, technical, and administrative authority in all matters concerning irrigation and agriculture. Like other Balinese associations, the spirit of the *subak* is essentially communal; all members abide by the same rules, each one being allotted work in relation to the amount of water he receives. Certain stipulations are made to prevent individuals from holding more land than would be convenient to the community. A man 'who has more land than he can work is compelled to share the produce with people appointed to help him.'[1]

As I have said, the Balinese are primarily a nation of agriculturists whose standard of rice cultivation is the highest in the Far East. Rice itself is treated with extreme reverence and there is an elaborate religious ritual connected with all aspects of its cultivation; it must be handled with great respect, and must be collected from the granaries in silence and only in the daytime. Except in the north and west, where the soil is barren and water scarce, the whole island is intensively cultivated; people who live in those arid districts grow corn and sweet potatoes, which are considered inferior foods to rice. Only men may plant and attend to the rice, but women and children help with the harvest.

The rajahs had no voice in the councils of these self-governing village republics, although they appointed *pungawas* as provincial governors and tax-collectors; the *pungawa* was usually a relative of the rajah. 'Bali presents the amazing spectacle of a land where the deeply rooted agrarian communalism of the people has continued to exist side by side with the feudalism of the noble landlords.'[2]

The administration of justice is largely in the hands of the village councils; moral sanctions and the weight of public opinion are more effective than imprisonment or fine. The most terrible of all punishments for a Balinese is expulsion from the village, when the offender is publicly declared 'dead' to the community; when the Dutch abolished the death penalty this became the capital punishment. 'A man expelled from his village cannot be admitted into another community, so he becomes a total outcast—a punishment greater than physical death to the Balinese mind. It often happens that a man who has been publicly shamed kills himself.'[3]

Dutch relations with Bali date back to the end of the sixteenth century, when a fleet of their ships visited the ruler. The ill-famed Dutch East India Company engaged in trade—and political intrigue—in the island until its dissolution in 1798. In the mid-nineteenth century the Dutch Government obtained from the Balinese princes a vague recognition of its sovereignty; but it was not until 1882 that the Dutch, provoked by some stupid acts of Balinese pirates and 'wreckers' against their shipping, launched a military expedition against North Bali and occupied the states of Buleleng (Singaradja) and Djembrana. At the same time they concluded treaties with the rajahs of South Bali under which the rajahs renounced piracy and

---

[1] Covarrubias, op. cit., pp. 72, 73.
[2] Covarrubias, op. cit., p. 83.
[3] Covarrubias, op. cit., p. 64.

'wrecking', and promised to abolish slavery and *suttee*.[1] According to Dr. Jacobs, who visited South Bali shortly afterwards, the last two promises were not honoured.

During the following years the rulers of South Bali engaged in perpetual civil war; in 1900 the Dutch, appealed to for help by the local rajah, annexed the principality of Gianjar. In September 1906 they occupied Badung and Tabanan, and in 1908 they annexed the last independent state, Klungkung; these last three occupations were accompanied by the mass suicides of the rajahs, their chiefs, generals and the women of their households, who threw themselves with spears and krises against the bullets of the invading army.

The army continued in occupation until 1914, when a police force took over its duties. The Dutch placed the administration of the island in the hands of two Residents, one in Singaradja, the other in Den Pasar; but they continued to govern through the Council of Rajahs—the eight rulers of the old autonomous principalities—attaching to each Rajah a Controller as adviser, or rather supervisor. The village councils they left alone, contenting themselves with the appointment of their own *pungawas* in place of those of the Rajahs. This system continued until the Japanese occupation of 1942.

The physical beauty of the Balinese has been proverbial for hundreds of years, and at one time Balinese women were in great demand in the slave markets of the East and West Indies. This reputation, we soon discovered, was no myth; handsome looks, fine physique and dignified bearing are characteristic of both men and women. Nowhere in the world have I seen girls so perfect in the flawless texture of their golden-brown skins, their narrow waists, full, firm breasts, slender arms and delicate hands and feet; the men are small but lithe, quick but graceful in their movements, gentle in their manner yet alert and quivering with vitality; even the elderly retain their dignity of bearing and grace of movement.

'Childlike' is the label attached in this hideous age to a people unresponsive to the language of the demagogue, the high-pressure salesman and the advertising hound; it is a label that bears no resemblance to the character of the Balinese, although they prefer their traditional way of life to that of the modern world, which, they would certainly agree with Pierre Louÿs, '*succombe sous un envahissement de laideur.*'

They have neither the ignorance nor the innocence of childhood, although they give an impression of its simplicity. They are, as I have said, the most skilful agriculturists in Asia, they are painters, craftsmen, poets, musicians and dancers; and their art has aroused the envy of a civilization to whose arrogance, ugliness and brutality they are largely indifferent.

---

[1] The immolation of a nobleman's widows, concubines, and slaves on his funeral pyre. In Bali *suttee* was never compulsory; the victims of this grisly practice were volunteers, not only in theory but in fact.

They take little thought for the sufferings of animals, but they are indulgent to children and would never think of beating them, preferring to coax them into obedience as equals; on the other hand they do not pamper them but are inclined to leave them from their earliest years to the care of older children. In this way the young quickly acquire a sense of responsibility, self-confidence and poise seldom found before maturity in Anglo-Saxons.

They have a refreshingly bawdy sense of humour and a Rabelaisian turn of wit; women and even children are permitted to make jokes which in Europe would be received in shocked silence. There is no prudery in the Balinese, but behaviour between the sexes in public is characterized by extreme modesty; for example, although men and women frequently bathe naked in pools or rivers by the roadside, it would be the grossest bad manners for a man to look at a woman bathing, let alone to take photographs as tourists used to do.[1] They are resourceful, sensitive, intelligent, extremely courteous and usually good-humoured. Though naturally timid they have a fierce pride, and when roused are capable of excessive cruelty; of this darker side to their character I was to have some grim experience.

The Balinese pay careful attention to cleanliness and the care of their bodies. They bathe regularly every morning and evening and frequently during the day, scrubbing themselves with pumice stone to cleanse and stimulate the skin and remove the hair. The traditional everyday dress of both men and women is the simple *kamben*, a cloth skirt reaching from the hips to the feet on women, to the knees on men. In addition to the *kamben*, women wear a bright-coloured sash round the waist and a long scarf thrown over one shoulder or tied round the head to hold the hair in place; men wear a headcloth tied as a turban in different styles to suit the wearer's taste. Although the Balinese normally go bare above the waist, both men and women cover the breast in the company of superiors. Priests wear white, and a high priest or *pedanda* goes bareheaded and carries a staff surmounted by a crystal ball.

For temple feasts, weddings and other ceremonial occasions the Balinese dress much more elaborately, wrapping themselves in rich cloth and brocade from armpits to feet and adorning their hair with beautiful and scented flowers. Although it is customary for men to put flowers in their hair, over each ear, only a Satria may wear the scarlet hibiscus; infringement of this rule by a man of lower caste carried in former times severe penalties. According to Theo Meier the offender was tied to a post in the market-place while groups of old men stood in front of him spitting peppers into his eyes.

---

[1] I hear from a recent visitor that in the new airport building on Bali there is a prominent notice informing visitors that 'It is forbidden to photograph native women without breast coverings, whether on purpose or by accident.'

Women in North Bali wear a hideous garment called a *badju*, a tight-fitting and usually dirty cotton blouse originally forced upon them, I understand, by the Dutch authorities in the 1880's to lessen the temptation to their troops;[1] by the end of the last war, unfortunately, the fashion had begun to spread to the rest of the island. European dress has become increasingly popular since the war, especially among the young men, who consider a shirt and slacks or shorts much smarter than the *kamben*.

While there are fine artists among them, and their sculpture, particularly in wood, is famous, it is in music, dancing and the drama that the Balinese take their chief delight; every community has at least one orchestra—many have two or three—and a troop of dancers; the villages vie with each other in the excellence of their musicians and dancers, all of whom, of course, are unpaid. 'There is not *one* music in Bali,' writes Beryl de Zoete. 'There is an appropriate music for every occasion, and an appropriate type of *gamelan*: for birthdays, tooth filing [at puberty], weddings, cremations, for temple feasts and processions to the sea with the holy images, for purifications and the driving away of disease and demons. There is naturally also an appropriate music for every kind of dance. . . .'[2] According to Covarrubias the Balinese attribute a divine origin to music and dancing.[3]

Elaborate dramatic performances, shadow-plays, and opera, are regular features of every festival, every wedding, birthday and cremation; they often last the entire night. The themes are ancient legends, a favourite being the struggle between Rangda and her *leyaks*, and the *Barong*, a kind of giant pekinese who champions the people of Bali and tries to protect them from Rangda's plagues.[4]

The Balinese are also devoted to gambling and cockfighting, although the Dutch government used to restrict both. The cocks are carried to the meeting halls, where the fights are held, in curious round baskets of coconut leaves which have handles and are woven round the bird's body, leaving the tail outside. For the fight the spur on the right foot is removed and replaced by a wicked steel blade five or six inches long, with a needle-sharp point; this practice, of course, shortens the fight, which is to the death. When a cock is wounded its owner will often revive it by massage and by blowing his own breath into its lungs.[5] The enthusiasm of the Balinese for this sport is as

---

[1] Covarrubias, op. cit., p. 111.

[2] Dance and Drama in Bali, pp. 6 and 7.

[3] Covarrubias, op. cit., p. 216.

[4] It is obviously beyond the scope of this book to attempt any description of the various fascinating plays and dances of Bali; for a concise account see Covarrubias, op. cit. pp. 205-55, and for a full study I recommend *Dance and Drama in Bali* by Beryl de Zoete and Walter Spies.

[5] Covarrubias, op. cit., p. 114.

intense as that of the British for football or the Spanish for bulls; in ancient times, indeed, men would sometimes gamble away their whole fortunes in cockfights, even staking their wives and children. It was for this reason that the Dutch government intervened.

It is only too easy to fall in love with Bali and to blind oneself to the vices which, though not immediately apparent, are an essential part of the people's character. Only the cantankerous Dr. Julius Jacobs, who visited the rajahs of South Bali in a semi-official capacity, seems to have had no difficulty in penetrating the veneer of Balinese charm; indeed he finds a sour satisfaction in exposing their faults. Contrary to the general impression of authors, he says, who represent the Balinese as patient, hard-working and courageous, he found them extremely egotistical, effeminate, cowardly, cynical, revengeful and jealous; a Balinese, according to him, has no feeling for the sufferings of others, and will undertake nothing that does not hold out some profit for himself. But he does admit that the women have unusual charm, and that they accept with loyalty and without complaint the selfish and callous ill-treatment of their menfolk.

Between these two extreme opinions—that of Covarrubias and that of Dr. Jacobs—I confess I find it difficult to judge; certainly there is an element of truth in both, and, though the picture I shall always cherish is nearer to Covarrubias's than to Jacobs's, I came myself into unpleasantly close contact with the seamy side of the Balinese character. Of their jealousy and cruelty the story of the dancer Sampih is a terrible but typical example.

In the autumn of 1952, when the Javanese Central Government were in control of Bali, Sampih left the island with a troupe of dancers organized by John Coast to tour Europe and America; they met with resounding success, and their star was Sampih. At the end of the tour he returned to Bali to enjoy, as he no doubt thought, the envious adulation of his people. The envy he experienced all too soon. At the end of February 1954, he disappeared, and it was three days before his remains were found in a river bed; his jealous fellow-countrymen had cut his throat, chopped his body into pieces and thrown them in the river.[1]

To return to the brighter side, the Balinese have a passion for clubs; even more than the British the men are 'clubbable', although their women resent it less. There are *sekehe*, as they are called, for every conceivable purpose, some more frivolous in our eyes—though not to the Balinese—than others. Thus there are *sekehe* for fire-lighting and for hunting squirrels, who eat the coconuts; and there are *sekehe* for drinking *tuak*, and for sitting on bridges on Sunday mornings. Meetings are regular and a member who fails to turn up pays a fine in money or in kind. There are no mixed or ladies' *sekehe*.

---

[1] The story is told in John Coast's Dancing Out of Bali, p. 227.

The little grey squirrels that infest the coconut plantations are a serious nuisance to the villagers, causing devastation to the crop; the method of hunting them is a primitive stratagem with echoes of the brain-washing techniques of today. Armed with sticks and tin cans the members of the sekehe surround a plantation; gradually they close in, beating the tin cans with their sticks and making as much noise as they can. The squirrels, alarmed by the din, hop from tree-top to tree-top in panic. As the circle narrows, the squirrels become so nervous that they lose their footholds and fall to the ground, where they are quickly dispatched by the sticks of the villagers.

Tuak drinking is a favourite pastime of the elderly men.[1] *Tuak*, or toddy, is brewed from the juice of the sugar palm; it looks and tastes somewhat like farm cider and, though not so intoxicating, makes a most refreshing and mellowing drink. It should be drunk within forty-eight hours of being tapped, for it soon turns to vinegar; and so when people talk of 'old' or 'young' tuak they mean a difference only of a few hours. The *tuak*-drinking *sekehe* gather every evening before sundown; a member who fails to appear for a meeting must bring an extra 'bamboo' of tuak the next time—in fact he buys a round. The popularity of these clubs was the reason I found it so hard to get good tuak in the island. In Den Pasar I used to have a posse of small boys and girls scouting for me to find a good brew; when I passed in the street they would call out to me: *'Tabé* (hallo), *Tuan Tuak!'*

The Balinese begin their love life early, in fact they seldom delay it long after puberty. The attitude of the Sudras towards virginity is as 'progressive' as that of our most advanced Western civilizations; neither by law nor by custom is there an 'age of consent', the generally accepted principle being, in the words of the old west-country proverb, 'if they're big enough they're old enough'.

For example, it is not customary to say of a girl, 'She is still a virgin'; rather they say, after her first menstruation, 'she is *already* a virgin'—implying that she is unlikely to remain one.[2] Widows, therefore, and divorced women have no difficulty in remarrying; but adultery, especially by a woman, is a serious offence in their eyes, and used to be punished by death.[3]

Every Balinese considers it one of his first duties to marry and raise a family of sons to perpetuate his line and do honour to his spirit after his death. Men usually marry at eighteen, girls at sixteen, but since in those latitudes they mature at a much earlier age it is usual for both to have love

---

[1] In general the Balinese are moderate drinkers; I only met one who wasn't—a priest. Incidentally, the consumption of opium, very heavy in Dr. Jacobs' time, had almost disappeared in mine.

[2] The Bali Aga, on the other hand, consider that sexual intercourse carries pollution, and do not encourage it before marriage.

[3] Infidelity by the husband seems to be taken for granted.

affairs before; the idea of platonic love is foreign to the Balinese, who prefer to consummate their desire by sleeping together. In public, however, lovers behave with extreme discretion and decorum.

According to Dr. Jacobs,[1] who appears to have considered them as little better than sex maniacs, the Balinese are addicted to every conceivable form of sexual aberration; certainly in their paintings and temple reliefs they show some ingenious variations of the normal positions for intercourse. Much of what the doctor says on the subject is irrelevant to this work, impossible of verification by this author, and, even in the present state of the law risky to print. But he states categorically—in contrast to the opinion of Covarrubias[2]—that male and female homosexuality and Onanism were prevalent; he concludes with a sniff of disgust, 'cucumbers and bananas are used by Balinese girls not only as food'.

A couple will often live together before their wedding in a legal form of trial marriage known as *gendak*; the laws governing it protect the girl against desertion by her husband and legitimize children born during this period. The most usual form of marriage, however, is elopement or the more spectacular kidnapping of the bride by her suitor and his friends. The girl, though not of course her parents, is a party to the plot; she arranges to have her belongings taken secretly to her new home, and plans with her future husband the place—usually on the road or in the fields—where he and his friends will waylay her. She usually puts up the pretence of a fight, and any of her relatives who happen to be with her at the time are expected to try to prevent her abduction; but no other witnesses would dream of interfering, even to the extent of informing the girl's parents.

As soon afterwards as possible representatives of the husband will call upon the girl's outraged parents—they must pretend to be outraged even if they really approve of the marriage—to obtain their formal consent and fix the price the father will receive for his daughter. But a man who kidnaps a girl by force and against her will is liable to severe penalties, unless she chooses to remain with him.

The marriage is made binding in the sight of the gods by certain offerings which await the runaway couple at their new home; and it is an important point of law that the pair must consummate the wedding there before the offerings have wilted.[3] A public ceremony and feast usually follow a few weeks later. After marriage a girl leaves her own ancestral gods and worships her husband's.

In families of the higher castes a formal betrothal is more usual, often arranged by the parents. To the aristocracy a bride's virginity is important,

[1] Jacobs, op. cit., pp. 134-5.
[2] Covarrubias, op. cit., p. 145.
[3] Covarrubias, op. cit., p. 148.

and in old-fashioned weddings there is a barbaric ceremony in which the husband announces the defloration of his bride to the assembled guests while her women attendants verify the evidence.[1] Until recent times a rajah might order a subject to reserve him his daughter when she came of age; but children, though they may be betrothed very young, never marry before puberty.

Among the peasantry, though not among the aristocracy, women enjoy a degree of freedom unusual in Eastern countries; their rights are well defined and recognized by law and custom. They have the right to dispose of their own income and property without the consent or even the knowledge of their husbands; they manage the family finances and often contribute to them; nearly all the marketing is controlled by women. Moreover, unlike the Common Law of England, Balinese law does not hold a husband responsible for his wife's debts.

There are strict rules defining the work and duties of each sex. 'All heavy work requiring manly attributes—agriculture, building in wood or thatch, the care of cattle—as well as most of the trades and crafts ... is the work of men. Women own, raise, and sell chickens and pigs, but only men care for cows, buffaloes, and ducks.'[2] Similarly, the cooking of everyday meals is the task of women; but it is the privilege of men to prepare the food at the great banquets that mark all Balinese festivals. In the home women usually prefer to eat after their men have finished; but this does not imply any inferiority in their status.

Such, then, is the complicated, alluring and unpredictable race which, with no experience or qualifications and with none of the knowledge I have just recorded, I was called upon to govern.

[1] Covarrubias, op. cit., pp. 150-51.
[2] Covarrubias, op, cit., pp. 81-82.

VIII

TERRORISTS

The slight brown figure in the creased white linen suit shifted uncomfortably in his chair; his fingers, interlocked on his lap, twisted in an agony of nervousness and indecision while his flickering, frightened eyes, heavily pouched with fatigue and strain, darted round the veranda of his house, resting fearfully now on the compound at the back, now on the road and the front gate, where a pair of Buffs stood on guard. The Tjokorde Gdé Rake Sukawati was not ashamed to admit that he was badly scared; he had, it seemed, good reason.

A trusted friend of the Dutch and a most able statesman who by his education and rank enjoyed considerable influence and respect around Den Pasar, Sukawati was the first local dignitary with whom I had tried to make contact; I had lost no time in sending a message to his house, which was not far from my own headquarters, asking him to call on me. My messenger returned with a letter from the Tjokorde welcoming me to Bali, assuring me of his warmest sentiments but regretting that he dared not visit me in person. Taking a small escort I hastened to call on him myself.

Placing my men in positions where they could command all approaches to the house, I climbed a flight of steps to the open wooden veranda which ran round the outside. The Tjokorde received me alone, the few servants who had been with him vanishing at my approach; there was no doubt that my visit was causing him acute embarrassment and alarm. He spoke very softly, little above a whisper, trying to keep the tremor out of his voice.

'Forgive me, colonel, that I do not appear more hospitable. You do not know how dangerous is my situation. I am friendly to the Allies, and the leaders of the *Sukerela*—the terrorists—they know this. Once already they have taken me away—yes, kidnapped me from my own house! They did not kill me then, for I have many friends among the people; but others that they took have been killed or have disappeared. They kept me for two weeks, and when they let me go they warned me to have nothing to do with the Allies when they should come. Then, when you arrived three days ago, they threatened me again. Colonel, this time they will kill me. I am sorry I cannot help you. I am afraid.'

It was obviously difficult for me to reassure him; I knew too well the power of determined terrorism. As it was, he probably owed his life only to his popularity and to the terrorists' reluctance to outrage public opinion by the murder of a Satria. Others apparently had been less fortunate. But even if I could no longer expect him to help me, I must still protect him as a friend of the Dutch and a valuable ally in the future.

'I am going to put a guard on your house,' I told him, 'both by day and night—sentries at the back and the front; they will have orders to shoot on sight anyone trying to break in here. When you want to leave the house please let me know, and I will provide you with an escort.'

'What guards can you give me?'

'By day a pair of British soldiers and a pair of Japanese; by night a section of Japanese. Is that sufficient?'

'Can you trust the Japanese?'

I smiled. 'At this moment they are only too anxious to do all they can to help me.'

He seemed a little relieved and went on to tell me something of the situation around Den Pasar. In general, he said, the people were well-disposed towards us—this much I must have gathered from my reception among them in the last three days. But there was a small, well-organized body of extremists, many of them Javanese, who by murder and kidnapping had so terrorized the district that nobody would dare to collaborate with me openly; let me deal promptly and firmly with them, and he was sure that people would hasten to me with offers of help.

I asked if he would give me the names of the leading terrorists After some persuasion he gave me a few, fearfully and in a whisper, and told me the places where I might search for them. As I rose to go he spoke in a more earnest and resolute voice than he had used before:

'Believe me, you have many friends in this island. The people are sick of the Japanese—when they heard you had arrested that criminal sergeant-major of the *Kempeitai*[1] as soon as you arrived, everyone was delighted. They want to return to normal times and finish with the Japanese and with terrorists. But I tell you this: if the people are going to help you, they must see you rule.' He struck the arm of the chair with his fist. 'If they see you are weak they will be afraid. One more thing. Let us hope that you have come to stay. In 1942 the Allies fled and left us to the Japanese; now we are afraid you will go away again and leave us to the Javanese.'

How often during the following months was I to hear those same opinions voiced by Balinese of every caste and rank! In my naive ignorance it never occurred to me that they had any ground for such fears, let alone that they were speaking with the voice of prophecy.

The guards I posted must have looked formidable enough to deter Sukawati's enemies, for there were no more attempts on his safety. He remained in seclusion until the arrival of the Dutch, when he put his exceptional qualities at their disposal, rendering great service to them and to

---

[1] Japanese Security Policy. The arrest was ordered by the 5th Indian Division.

his own people. When the Dutch handed over power in 1947 to the Indonesian Federation he was elected President of the State of East Indonesia, which included Celebes, Bali and Lombok, with the capital at Macassar. But after the suppression of this State by the Javanese Central Government of Dr. Sukarno—in flagrant breach of the treaty with the Dutch—Sukawati retired from political life; when I last heard of him he was doing very well as a motor-car salesman in Djakarta.

As soon as I had given orders for the posting of the guards I signalled General Mansergh, asking for authority to arrest the terrorist leaders and hold them until the arrival of the Dutch; also to publish a proclamation I had drafted inviting the co-operation of all Balinese in the maintenance of order. Permission came back immediately for the arrests, with the express proviso that they must be carried out by Japanese troops. I was categorically forbidden to issue any proclamation.

The arrests, however, proved far from easy to achieve. Whether they foresaw my intentions or whether, as is very probable, they had allies among the Japanese, many of the wanted men disappeared; some fled to remote villages, others went into hiding in the neighbourhood. In the meantime, from Den Pasar and from Tabanan to the west came more reports of the murder or disappearance of Balinese officials and headmen supposed to be unsympathetic to the extremists. Our own servants became frightened to work for us, and one or two left our service, although the crowd of sightseers outside our gates never seemed to diminish. In time we laid hands on some of the men we wanted, and the example of a few arrests brought a rapid improvement in the situation.

I had given orders to the Japanese that these prisoners should be well treated; that they might see their families, who could bring them extra food; but that they might receive no other visitors or have any other contact with the outside world. One evening I walked round to the prison with Miura to see how my orders were being carried out. Each of the prisoners had a cell to himself. When I interviewed them in the courtyard they greeted me with smiling politeness and assured me that they had no complaints to make of their treatment. However, when I remarked that I was sorry to meet them in such circumstances their reply was scarcely reassuring.

'We do not at all mind being here,' laughed their spokesman. 'We know that we must suffer to win our freedom. After all, the great leaders of the Russian revolution were often in prison before they came to power.'

'Do you then mean to follow the examples of Lenin and Stalin,' I asked, 'when you win this freedom you talk about?'

They smiled again, but gave me no answer.

I pondered sadly on the strange contradiction whereby men who will gladly become martyrs in the cause of freedom will invoke the name of freedom, when they themselves achieve power, to persecute their own people. The result in Indonesia was to impose a heavier oppression than any endured under the Dutch.

With a heavy heart I strolled back in the twilight to the more cheerful atmosphere of the Residency, where Shaw with the help of fresh limes was converting some of our operational rum into a badly needed drink.

In the afternoon, a few hours after my visit to Tjokorde Sukawati, I was sitting in my office, drafting a long signal and pausing occasionally to look longingly out of the window at the sunlight glistening on the palm fronds still dripping from a rain-storm, and to sniff the damp, heavy-scented air that drifted in from the garden; Shaw was discussing with Colonel Tsuneoka the location of supply dumps; Neville was at the beach-head. From the hall outside came the burr and tapping of the wireless.

This quiet scene of industry and application was suddenly interrupted by a series of sharp, urgent commands in Japanese from the drive; a moment later there was a quick knock and a young lieutenant stood saluting in the doorway. He spoke rapidly to Colonel Tsuneoka. Miura turned to me.

'Sir, we have heard that rebellion has broken out at Gianjar: the Rajah has just telephoned to one of our posts. He says that a force of three hundred extremist elements has assembled south of Gianjar and is marching against him; they have some rifles and spears. The Rajah is very alarmed and asks your help.'

I turned to Shaw. 'This, I imagine, is the kind of situation General Mansergh had in mind when he warned me against the indiscriminate use of force. Somehow we must settle this affair without bloodshed, and I see only one way to do it—to go there ourselves and try to parley with the rebels. I only hope they won't be in the mood to shoot first and parley afterwards! Now will you collect a couple of Buffs and tell Shimada to get the Chevrolet ready? I'll get Tsuneoka to send round a lorry-load of Nips with a light machine-gun to keep us company.'

By four o'clock we were ready to start. Shaw and I sat in the front of the staff car with Shimada; the two Buffs, as happy as schoolboys on a treat, sat with Miura in the back, one armed with a Sten, the other nursing a rifle. Ten solemn-faced Japanese infantrymen under a subaltern followed in their lorry.

Infected with the cheerfulness of our two soldiers I felt a thrill of excitement at the thought that now I was really on my mettle, and that on the decisions I might have to make in the next few hours would probably rest the peace and security of the island. On the other hand I could not suppress a twinge of dismay when I contemplated the possible cost in lives if a mistake or misjudgment on my part should let this revolt get out of hand; I cannot deny that I was also daunted by the ignoble thought of how my own reputation would suffer in the eyes of General Mansergh and the world if I should fail—although I was unlikely to survive to endure the disgrace. What, after all, did I yet know of these people? In particular, what did I know, beyond a vague report by telephone, of the situation I was driving so lightheartedly to meet?

It was this last thought that steadied me, with the reflection that there was nothing more I could do or plan to do until I arrived on the spot and saw the situation for myself. I should have to play it off the cuff; meanwhile, I had better relax and enjoy the scenery.

We passed through Kesiman with its low mud walls and thatched gateways, where men squatted in groups by the roadside idling and gossiping; the women were returning from the market carrying loads in baskets on their heads, the girls proud and erect as goddesses, graceful as nymphs, each with an arm raised to balance the weight of the basket. Beyond the village, as we drove east, the palm trees gave way to ricefields, where the vivid green of the young paddy blended with the rich gold of the ripening crop. War and rebellion seemed far away.

'I find it encouraging,' Shaw broke in upon my thoughts, 'to see people on the roads and in the fields. In Java you always knew there was trouble afoot if the countryside was deserted and the men were not working in the *sawas*'

'Yes, but we've still a fair way to go. What I'm wondering is whether we're going to find that this is the start of a full-scale revolt by the *Pemudas*, which is what the Rajah would have us believe, or whether it's just a local riot by some of the lads who don t like the Rajah or don't want to pay his taxes; Gianjar, you remember, was one of the few Rajahs whom the Dutch allowed to retain most of their feudal rights after the conquest of South Bali. Anyway, I don't suppose we'll be left long in doubt.'

We climbed gently among the terraced fields, on a well-constructed metalled road shaded by great sugar palms. Approaching Gianjar we saw immediately that something was wrong. Groups of young men carrying long spears and heavy *koloks*, or chopping knives, thronged the road, padding silently in the direction of the Rajah's Palace; they were naked except for their loincloths girt up above their knees, and they looked resolute and grim. They paid no attention to us whatever.

Puzzled as to whether we were among enemies or friends, I told Shimada to drive on slowly to the palace; the throng of Balinese made way for us reluctantly but without sparing us more than a glance. I felt the tension rising as we drove through them, and wondered whether at any moment we were to meet the fate of poor Brigadier Mallaby. Quite suddenly, as the last group parted before us, I saw ahead the square of Gianjar and the carved gateway of the Rajah's *puri*, or palace. Under the broad, cascading *waringin*[1] in front of

---

[1] The giant banyan tree, sacred to the Hindus; its great branches droop to the ground, where they form new roots to spread the girth of the tree. In every Balinese

it stood a slight figure in a grey uniform with a Sam Browne belt and a pistol holster; the pistol, a Luger, was in his hand. We halted as he hastened towards us.

His Highness Anak Agung Gdé Agung, 'Child of the Great Grand Great', acting Rajah of Gianjar and eldest son of the old ruler, was a slim, handsome man of about thirty, with a sensitive face, bright, intelligent eyes, dark, curly hair and small, sad moustache; his nervous manner seemed inappropriate to his smartly cut military tunic and breeches. As I stepped from my car to salute him he replaced his Luger in its holster—to my great relief—and shook me warmly by the hand.

'I think you have come only just in time.' His English was careful but fluent, his voice soft and hesitant. 'The concentrations of Pemudas have increased since this morning, and now there are at least two thousand of them. My own people are loyal to me—you passed many of them just now on the road, coming here to defend me—but there are not enough of us; besides, the enemy have rifles, while I am the only one here to possess a gun. I have been trying to warn you since midday, but it took me so long to get a message through.'

'How did this trouble start?' I asked.

'It has been in preparation for a long time, but I think your arrival in Bali hastened the event. It is organized by the *Sukerela*, the extremist leaders in Den Pasar. You see, Gianjar is the richest, and most populated part of Bali, and if they can gain control here they think they will be too powerful for you to overthrow them. So they have assembled men from Badung and Tabanan to attack me and my people. But we will resist them to the end!'

'Where are they assembled?'

'If you follow that road southward through the *sawas* you will come upon my outposts; I will send a man with you that far, to see they let you pass. When you have passed them you will see the Pemudas within a few hundred metres—but please be careful, because I fear they will shoot at you before they know who you are.'

Leaving the *Anak Agung* to complete the organization of his defences we turned down the road he had indicated; his guide perched on the mudguard. As we passed more groups of spearmen I recalled the stories I had read of the palace retainers who had thrown themselves with their gold-tipped spears upon the Dutch riflemen when the Rajahs of South Bali went down in mass suicide before the European invaders.

We came into a countryside of open paddy-fields on either side of the road. On a corner a small group of spearmen barred our way, waving to us

---

village square there are *waringin*, beneath which are performed the plays and dances at festivals.

with urgent gestures. Miura and our guide exchanged a few words with them, then Miura said to me:

'This is the last of the Rajah's outposts. They say that we shall find the *Pemudas* a short way down the road. They ask us not to go on, because we shall be attacked.'

I ordered the Japanese to get out of their lorry and precede us along the road in open file; at the same time I told their subaltern that there was to be no shooting unless we were fired upon. When they were fifty yards ahead I told Shimada to drive on slowly. Leaving the Rajah's guide with the picket looking gloomily after us, we continued our journey; I was feeling far from happy, but it was clearly essential for us to make contact with the Pemudas, and quickly.

We made it quicker than I had expected. At one moment there was nobody in sight; at the next we were confronted with a road block of felled trees and, behind it, a mob of sullen-looking Balinese; most were armed and clad like the Rajah's retainers, but a few among them were dressed in green shirts and slacks and I noticed with misgiving that these men, whom I assumed to be the leaders, carried rifles or pistols. Many more Pemudas were dispersed among the paddy on either side of the road.

The Japanese halted and took up action stations; the subaltern hurried back to me for orders, his concern showing plainly on his face. As Shimada stopped the car I scrambled out, followed immediately by Shaw, the two Buffs and, more slowly, Miura.

'This is where we parley—I hope.' I smiled to Shaw and started to walk towards the road block. The lieutenant stood in front of me, saluting and talking urgently in Japanese.

'He begs you not to go forward, sir,' translated Miura. 'He says he is responsible for your safety.'

'Tell him he's also under my orders. He's to stay here with his men until I tell him to move.'

Leaving the Buffs by the car Shaw and I approached the *Pemudas*; we put on the most nonchalant air we could muster, but for my part I know that my stomach felt full of butterflies and, as the Spaniards so prettily express it, my testicles were in my throat. Once again I thought of Brigadier Mallaby and the appalling massacre that had followed his murder; as always in moments of acute peril, I found myself praying to the God I usually neglected.

There was a stir in the ranks behind the barricade and my tortured stomach contracted again as I saw the spearmen stiffen at their leaders' commands; there was a murmur of voices, in which I caught the words '*Orang Puteh*'[1] Then quite suddenly and without warning relaxation spread like a ripple along the lowering faces in front of us; there were cries of '*tabeh, tuan!*'

---

[1] 'White men'—in Malay, not Balinese

and several men gave us the Merdeka salute. Two youths in European dress climbed nimbly over the road block and ran up to us with hands outstretched in greeting; others followed until we were the centre of a crowd, who studied us with silent but apparently not hostile interest.

I had been turning over in my mind what I should say, and had improvised a simple speech on the lines of the proclamation I had wished to publish. The details would make dull reading at this distance, but in essence it was a plea for the co-operation of all Balinese in the maintenance of peace, an assurance that we would do all in our power to restore prosperity to the island and a veiled threat that I would not hesitate to use force if I found it necessary; I concluded with the platitude that on their co-operation depended the quick removal of the Japanese forces, and urged them to disperse to their homes without delay.

When I had finished there was silence for a few moments. Then came the expected question.

'Will the Dutch come back, or shall we be allowed to govern ourselves?'

I knew the answer to that one. 'The Allied governments will decide in consultation the future of Bali in the best interests of the Balinese people.' I made Miura repeat the last three words, while I looked pointedly at the half-dozen Javanese we had noticed among the leaders.

There was a brief discussion among the *Pemudas*; soon they began to drift away southward in small groups, giving us their salute as they went. I was not so sanguine as to suppose that they were going home.

'I think I'll stay in Gianjar,' I told Shaw, 'in case they attack during the night. Miura and the Nips will have to stay too, and I'll have another platoon sent here at once from Klungkung. Will you take our party back to Den Pasar and send a signal to Surabaja giving all details? Shimada can come back to collect me in the morning.'

'You ought to go back and send the signal,' protested Shaw, 'and let me stay here. If it comes to a battle I know much more about soldiering than you do.'

'Maybe. But if it comes to a battle I dare say the Nip commander is a reasonably competent infantry officer. I want to be here to watch how the situation develops.'

We found the *Anak Agung* pacing anxiously before the palace; his men were ranged in lines around the square, squatting on the ground with their long spears held upright before them. He was grateful but far from reassured.

'I am certain they have not gone away,' he declared gloomily.

'They are sure to attack during the night.'

He cheered up when I suggested that I should stay, and disappeared into the palace to see personally to my comfort. I said good-bye to Shaw and two almost mutinous Buffs, who clearly felt themselves cheated of their fun; Shaw's parting handshake was a little too firm and 'stiff upper lip' for my comfort, and I watched the Chevrolet disappear in the twilight with a curious feeling of desolation. It was going to be an anxious night. The telephone between Gianjar and Klungkung had broken down—more probably it had been cut—and so my demand for reinforcements would have to be sent by radio from Japanese headquarters in Den Pasar. It was unlikely that help would arrive before morning; meanwhile we had only the small force I had brought with me, and about two hundred of the Rajah's retainers, to oppose at least ten times as many *Pemudas*, some of whom were armed with modern rifles. Having stationed the Japanese in the square outside the palace, where they would be under my immediate control in case of attack, I went inside to have supper with the *Anak Agung*.

Although it was an excellent meal neither of us felt like eating; but courtesy obliged us both to try. The *Anak Agung* was the most intelligent and best educated of the Rajahs—in fact about the most intelligent Balinese I met.[1] We talked, inevitably, of nationalism and the future of Indonesia, on which I was particularly anxious to learn his views. He praised the efficiency of pre-war Dutch administration and the selfless devotion of their best Residents and Controllers; but he was critical of some aspects of their educational policy, in particular their suppression of all political activity, which had provided the Japanese with a useful field for exploitation.

'We hope for independence, of course,' he explained. 'But not the kind of *merdeka* preached by those hot-headed boys in Den Pasar!'

He spoke of the Council of Rajahs, through which the Dutch had to some degree governed Bali; and it occurred to me then that the Council might prove the answer to my own problem of establishing a temporary civilian administration. I decided to explore the possibility as soon as the present trouble was over.

When we had finished eating we went to bed; the Rajah led me to the guest pavilion, a miniature bungalow on the opposite side of the courtyard from the main building of the palace; its single room was plainly but comfortably furnished.

'I hope I shall wake up if there is an attack.' I tried to put on an air of indifference. 'I should be ashamed to sleep through a battle!'

'Do not worry. If there is an alarm we beat the *kulkul*—the great drum in the tower above. Nobody can sleep through that noise.'

I took off my belt and pistol and boots, and stretched out on the divan bed. For all my pretence to the *Anak Agung* I felt no inclination to sleep. My thoughts were chaotic, my mind torn between anxiety over the hazards of

---

[1] Subsequently he became Indonesian Foreign Minister under Sukarno; he has also held appointments of Indonesian Ambassador in Paris and in Brussels. Later he quarrelled with Sukarno, but he still has a desk in the Ministry of Foreign Affairs in Djakarta.

the coming night and a childlike, even snobbish elation at the glamorous circumstances in which I found myself—a guest in the palace of a powerful feudal prince, surrounded by enemies from whom I was pledged to protect him. I began to wonder whether the Anak Aging's hospitality would extend to providing me with a beautiful Balinese girl to share my bed; I had heard such stories before,[1] and confess that I kept my ears pricked for some sound that might herald the arrival of a concubine. . . .

It was a different sound that woke me a few hours later: the deep, urgent throbbing of the *kulkul*, its fast, panicky beats bursting through the heavy pall of my unconsciousness. A blaze of light appeared in the doorway, where I saw a servant in a girded loin-cloth carrying a flaming resin torch and beckoning me urgently to get up; I struggled into my boots and ran out after him, buckling my belt on the way.

Outside, the great *waringin* threw its dark, domed shadow across the moon-drenched square; its smooth leaves reflected the soft silvery light in a thousand tiny stars. The Anak Agung was giving orders to a group of his chiefs and *pungawas*; most of his retainers had vanished—I hoped to battle stations—but a small bodyguard remained by the tree. I walked over to the Japanese, who sprang to attention at my approach. The subaltern looked at me attentively, awaiting orders; Miura stood beside him, looking at the ground. Having satisfied myself that they were ready to go into action at once, I joined the *Anak Agung*. Despite his obvious anxiety he preserved an admirable self-control and when he spoke his tone was calm and resolute.

'The attack is coming in from the south, from the direction of the road block you saw this evening; they have been concentrating there for the last half-hour—I could see the lights of their torches from the tower. We must be ready to fight. I have sent my men to their posts.'

I called Miura and the Japanese subaltern, explained the situation to them and told the subaltern to take up a position commanding the enemy line of advance. As soon as the *Pemudas* came within easy range the machine-gunner was to fire three separate bursts over their heads; if they still continued to advance the whole section would open fire to kill.

'We may be few,' I tried to reassure the *Anak Agung* as the soldiers trotted off into the darkness, 'but I doubt if the *Pemudas* will stand up very long to machine-gun fire.'

'Let us hope,' he answered glumly.

We stood together in silence, listening for some sound that would tell us the attack had started. But no human voice or noise of battle broke the tense, uneasy stillness of that lovely night; only the shrill humming of the cicadas

---

[1] There was truth in them, too. Dr. Jacobs records that during his visit to Gianjar in 1882 the women of the harem were instructed to make themselves agreeable to him and his party every night. Some people have all the luck.

strummed a ceaseless accompaniment to our gloomy thoughts. Moonlight flooded the countryside that sloped away to the south-west in numerous narrow ravines, and glittered silver on the smooth sheets of water covering the terraced ricefields; the air was soft and heavy with the sweet, intoxicating fragrance of champaka flowers—the strong, heady smell of the Balinese night.

From close at hand came a burst of machine-gun fire, followed five seconds later by another, and then a third; in the ensuing silence we looked at one another long and hard.

'We are about to see,' I smiled grimly as I moved towards the Japanese, 'whether what I told you just now was right.'

Suddenly I halted in my tracks. From the east, faintly at first but rapidly growing louder, I heard the sound of engines: motor transport approaching at speed from the direction of Klungkung; in a few moments the lights of a convoy came into view. At the same time a runner padded up from the Japanese lieutenant with the news that the enemy had halted after the three bursts from his machine-gun; on the approach of the convoy they had begun to withdraw. A long line of lorries drove into the square and ground to a halt; instead of the platoon I had demanded, there was a full company of infantry, well equipped with light machine-guns and mortars. Clearly somebody had been using his initiative. The danger was over; half an hour later I was back in bed.

Before leaving in the morning I gave orders that a company of Japanese should be stationed permanently in Gianjar; it was as well that I did, because next day there were two separate attacks on the town. The Japanese garrison repulsed them, but did not prevent the *Pemudas* from pillaging and burning houses in several villages around; the Japanese commander, misinterpreting my instructions, had been reluctant to open fire and had preferred to withdraw his troops into the town. Thereafter I amended my orders to allow him to open fire on all *Pemuda* concentrations that did not disperse after one warning volley.

IX

PAINTERS AND PRINCES

My first action on returning to Den Pasar was to signal General Mansergh asking permission to entrust the civil administration of the island to the Council of Rajahs; my second was to summon the Council to meet at Klungkung the following afternoon. Late the same night I received a reply from the General giving his full approval to my plan; another signal warned us that the Dutch would land at 8 a.m. on 2nd March.

Apart from the visit to Gianjar our duties had hitherto confined us to the Den Pasar area; it was time, I judged, for us to see what was going on in other parts of the island. We had less than three days before the landing, and so could only hope to cover the more important districts. I therefore decided to visit Singaradja that same afternoon, the 27th, for as yet I knew nothing of the situation in North Bali; on my way back I would call in at the village of Kintamani, on the rim of the volcano Batur, and see the Austrian painter Roland Strasser, who had lived there throughout the Japanese occupation. Meanwhile I asked Shaw to take the other staff car to Klungkung and Karangasem in the east; he could combine the journey with a visit to the Swiss artist Theo Meier, who lived at Iseh in the foothills of Gunung Agung.

As soon as I had dealt with the signal traffic I set out, taking a few sandwiches to eat in the car in order to save time. We drove through Gianjar, then turned north towards the mountains along a straight, palm-fringed avenue that rose in a gentle gradient among terraces of paddy. Above the neat and peaceful village of Bangli, at a height of nearly two thousand feet, the lush vegetation and rich *sawas* gave way to rough hill pasture; poinsettias grew thickly by the roadside, winding up the hill in a ribbon of scarlet. Soon we began to climb steeply. The air grew suddenly colder and the sky overcast; to the east a dark mass of lowering cloud hid the gigantic cone of Gunung Agung.

A fierce and bitter wind howled across the mountainside, hurling great gusts of rain against our windscreen; with every mile the stony landscape became bleaker, the few villages more miserable and dirty. Shivering in my thin clothes I could scarcely believe that we had only just left the tropical exuberance of South Bali. Above three thousand feet the pass was in cloud, which limited our vision to fifty yards and hid the great bulk of Batur and its crater lake. Round a corner we came upon two wild-looking men riding scraggy ponies—the first travellers we had met in this desolate region; they pulled hurriedly off the road and, huddled and hooded in their thick blankets, watched us go by, neither acknowledging our greeting nor showing any sign of interest in our appearance.

'Not very friendly, are they?' called out Sergeant Hopkins from the back; he had asked to come with me for the ride. 'Do you think they know who we are?'

'No, and I don't suppose they care either. It must be all the same to these highlanders whether the Dutch, the Nips, the British or their own people are in power. Nobody seems to have bothered about them; they look as if they live pretty near the starvation level, and I'm sure they wouldn't recognize a social conscience if they saw one.'

The head of the pass marked the boundary with North Bali—the Residency of Singaradja and the ancient State of Buleleng.[1] From this point the road wound steeply down towards the north coast; the mist dispersed and the grim mountain landscape gave place to terraced paddy-fields, their crops a lustreless green under the overcast sky. We entered Singaradja along a broad, straight avenue flanked by the neat but neglected European bungalows of the old Colonial administration, and turned in, through stone gateposts adorned by two enormous carved snakes, to the drive-way of the Residency.

Here the Rajah, warned by telephone of my visit, was awaiting me with his brother. Both of them spoke English and both, I believe, were graduates of the University of Leyden. The Rajah, who seemed a man of initiative and intelligence, told me that he had already taken command of the native police and, with the co-operation of the Japanese, was keeping order in his territory; there were no incidents to report. He welcomed me warmly and promised me all the help in his power; but, like Sukawati a few days before, he was frankly apprehensive about the future course of Allied policy.

'I am afraid you are going to hand us over to the Javanese,' he predicted. And his brother added with a wry smile, 'Bali has been called "the last Paradise". Will it become "the lost Paradise"?'

The clouds were still down over Batur when we reached Kintamani. The house of Roland Strasser, built in the style of an Alpine chalet, stood a little way apart from the village, alone and cheerless in that rain-soaked mountain scene. Despite their friendly greeting, I was shocked by the forlorn appearance of the artist and his Hungarian wife; in contrast to the carefree, ebullient Le Mayeurs they seemed worn out by illness, adversity and fear. Their nationality and status as 'friendly aliens' had given them little protection from the venom of the Japanese, who had subjected them to ceaseless petty

---

[1] Although Singaradja was the Dutch administrative capital of the island, the adjacent port of Buleleng was the seat of the Balinese Rajah.

persecution, and none from the rapacity of the local villagers, who had taken advantage of their distress and loneliness to pillage and insult them.

'I *hate* these people!' Strasser's rugged features twisted with indignation and disgust. 'They are *despicable*—vicious, treacherous and cruel!' His tall, bowed frame shook and the tufts of grey hair at the side of his bald head stood out like the wings on a Norseman's helmet.

'Now all we want is to go away from here,' murmured his wife, a gentle, slim blonde whose pretty face was marred with the pallor of sickness. 'We should like to go to America, or even back to Europe—anywhere outside Asia, and especially away from Bali with its hateful memories.'

Privately I thought that I too might come to hate Bali if I had chosen to seclude myself among these dark and storm-swept hills. But Strasser took me aside and whispered urgently, 'Erica is very ill indeed. She must have an operation—a very serious operation you understand—as quickly as possible. I implore you, colonel, to do something to get us away from here.'

Overcome with pity by the urgency and despair in his voice I gladly undertook to do what I could for them. As soon as the Dutch arrived and we had the Kuta airstrip in use, I thought it should be possible to fly them to Java; meanwhile I offered to send a truck in the morning to bring them to the comparative comfort and safety of Den Pasar, where at least we had better medical facilities than they enjoyed at Kintamani. But they would not hear of leaving their house and possessions to be looted, and preferred to remain for the moment at Kintamani. Later on, however, they made their way to Den Pasar, where I was able to introduce them to General Mansergh during his visit; he immediately had them flown in his personal aircraft to Surabaja and thence to Australia. The operation on Frau Strasser was successful, and they now live happily in California.

The mood of despondency brought upon me by my visit to this stricken pair evaporated as we came down from the mountains and the mist, and saw below us in the evening light the richly coloured pattern of ricefields and palm groves falling away towards the sea in tier after tier of green and gold. By the roadside between Bangli and Gianjar men and women were bathing in the ditches and streams, splashing, laughing and chattering happily. Less pleasing were the numbers of miserable dogs, with mangy coats and ulcerous backs, that thronged the approaches to each village—the outcast, scavenging offspring of the watchdogs kept by every Balinese household; at night their howling chorus keeps away the witches.

Near Gianjar we saw a file of ducks strutting across the fields, making their way homeward in neat and orderly column behind an old man who carried an improvised flag—a bamboo topped with a bunch of white feathers. Balinese ducks are curiously well trained: every morning, soon after sunrise, they march out from the village to feed in the ricefields, following in perfect formation behind their herdsman, an old man or a child carrying a white flag; when they reach their feeding place the herdsman plants the flag in the ground and returns to his other duties. The ducks will stay near the flag all day, eating the weeds and insects that damage the rice but never touching the shoots. In the evening, half an hour before sundown, the herdsman returns and picks up the flag; the ducks assemble round him and strut off in solemn procession behind him to the village.

Here in Bali, as in the Greece of Sappho, evening was gathering in all that bright morning scattered. Huge water buffaloes, dark grey or pale pink, lumbered and slouched their way home, each of them led or ridden by a tiny, naked urchin in a preposterously large straw sun-hat shaped like an inverted shallow bowl. These powerful and treacherous brutes never seem to turn their ill-temper against the little boys who look after them; but to adults, and to Europeans in particular, they are notoriously dangerous—which may account for the saying, once popular in India, that 'the ugliest creatures in the East are water buffaloes and British officers' wives'.

Shaw reported extremely satisfactory interviews with the Rajahs of Klungkung and Karangasem; both had promised us their full support, the Dewa Agung adding that he was 'looking forward eagerly to the day when the Dutch should return and restore normal conditions', a remark on which Shaw had wisely declined to comment. From the Swiss painter at Iseh he brought me enthusiastic messages of welcome and a pressing invitation to pay him a visit.

'I should certainly go when you get a chance,' he added. 'Theo Meier's an extraordinary little man—full of energy and vivacity. Knows a lot about Bali too, and is extremely popular with the villagers. He runs a sort of amateur clinic at Iseh, and has his own Home Guard to protect him from the *Pemudas*; he also has his own home-made arak, which he calls "Swhisky"—and I reckon you need something to protect you from that! In fact he seems to do pretty well, one way and another; he has the most glamorous collection of girls in his house, not the least glamorous of them being his wife.'

'She's Balinese, isn't she?'

'Yes, she comes from Sanoer. I don't quite know who the rest of them are—in-laws, servants or concubines, I suppose. But seriously, Peter, you ought to go and take a look for yourself. They're well worth the journey on their own account.'

'How's the political situation up there?'

'Quiet, for the moment. Theo's given me a long document to pass on to you, explaining his views on the state of Bali and how we ought to run the place. I don't know if you'll be able to make head or tail of it; it runs on, rather like his conversation, in a mixture of English, French, German, and Malay, with a few Balinese phrases thrown in for luck.'

'Well, I'll certainly drop in on him as soon as I see an opportunity. Quite apart from the Swhisky and the harem—and don't think I'm not keen to have a taste of the one and at least a glance at the other—he sounds as though he would well repay a visit. But I don't see how we can fit it in before the landing the day after tomorrow.'

I sat down to digest the twelve closely written pages of fool-scap which Theo Meier had sent me—not an easy task in view of the strange mixture of languages in which they were written and the very curious syntax and spelling of the English. However, I read them carefully, because I knew from Daan Hubrecht that Meier had lived eight years in the island; that he had acquired an intimate knowledge of the folklore and customs of the people; and that he enjoyed the friendship and confidence of all castes and classes, being one of the few Europeans who had taken the trouble to learn their language—or rather languages. In general his thesis served to confirm what I had already heard from other sources—that we must lose no time in asserting our authority and showing the people that we meant to rule. I will quote a few extracts.

'I have nothing to do with ruling Bali,' he wrote, 'but I learn from the facts that are happening in Den Pasar today. Please learn it too and take the tragic consequence—*and be strong now*. . . . Being strong now means no bloodshed, but in a week it may be impossible without. . . . Oriental people have no respect for weakness in cases like these [the murders around Den Pasar], and your land "humane" behaviour is just *mistaken as weak*, and no oriental people trusts or believes in or even honours weakness. All my Balinese friends are afraid about your weakness. . . . Act now, rule as strong as possible and then make *for ever* friends in keeping your word of giving them freedom, when there is peace.'

I was disconcerted to learn that I had given such a widespread impression of weakness; there was little I could do about it in the two days still left to me before the arrival of the Dutch. But at least, it seemed, we were not unpopular.

'Freedom not believed [sic],' he went on. 'But 99% of Bali wants you, believe in you. A high Pedanda[1] told me today: "If you like Bali, come and rule in its greatest moment of *susah* [trouble], and when is *aman* [peace] give us the present of our country. But conquer first." My friend the Pungawa of Selat said nearly the same. . . . Don't ask any more if the Balinese officials want to work with you and the

---

[1] Brahmana high priest.

Rajahs now. Take it for normal that they do and make it plenty hard known to them that they stand trial for murder—or helping murder—if not working. Every day lost means that most of the loyal Balinese functionaries lose confidence in your, the Rajahs', and their own power and influence. After a few years of Japanese terror most functionaries' nerves are near a breakdown, and only medicine is immediate personal contact with you and strongest actions against crime.'

This absorbing document impressed me by its humility no less than its sincerity: 'As I am no man with any knowledge of economic and without any education for administration, I cannot give you "logique" advises, but just the result of my artist-mind.' There was a touching postscript: '*Now take no risk more!* Take Theo Meier the ink and paper away; give him brush and colour and buy his paintings.'

In the morning, accompanied by the Japanese commanders, we went to inspect the beach-head, which Neville had pronounced ready for the assault landing. I was astonished at the transformation his ingenuity had wrought, in so short a time, on that rock- and boulder-strewn beach and scrub-covered foreshore; now, with every natural obstacle cleared or blasted away, it might have formed part of some fashionable Lido. Connecting the beach-head with the road from Den Pasar Neville had built a wide dirt track suitable for motor traffic. When I had given my final orders for the deployment of the Japanese troops guarding the approaches we returned to Den Pasar to prepare for the Rajahs' conference that afternoon.

It was in a state of considerable anxiety that I set out for Klungkung, after an early and hasty lunch which I had no appetite to eat. So much depended on the outcome of this conference. In my optimistic plan for presenting the Dutch, on their arrival, with an efficient and smoothly-working civil administration I had taken it for granted that all the Rajahs would support me. But would they? It was just as likely that some of them would be hostile, and even more likely that some would hedge; they might be sympathetic to this new spirit of xenophobic nationalism, or unwilling to risk the wrath of the terrorists, who had already shown that they were not afraid to strike at the great. Of one thing only could I be sure—that in the game of statecraft and political manoeuvre these princes would have forgotten more than I should ever learn.

Xenophobic nationalism, of course, might equally operate in my favour; my impression was that the majority of them, like most of their subjects, feared Javanese more than European rule, and there was no doubt that the terrorists took their orders from Java. The Japanese, on the other hand, were universally un-popular, and I could expect opposition to the use of Japanese troops in support of our government. I hated the idea myself, but what alternative did we have? The native police were unarmed and it would take time to arm them in sufficient numbers; nor did I know how many of them were reliable. For the moment, however distasteful the thought, the Japanese were my only means of keeping order. I was still reviewing the situation when we drew up outside the palace at Klungkung.

Only two out of the eight members of the Council were absent: the Rajah of the western state of Djembrana had sent a message pleading illness, and the aged and infirm Rajah of Badung (Den Pasar) was represented by his eldest son. When the introductions were over we took our seats at a long table; the *Dewa Agung* of Klungkung, a dignified and portly figure in white robes, sat at the head, with me and my interpreter on his right. Behind each rajah stood a court official, presumably of Brahmana caste, in the role of secretary. Some of the older men wore richly embroidered Balinese dress, in contrast to the carefully pressed white shirts and trousers of the emancipated young.

Striving to control my nervousness I rose to address them. Speaking slowly, with long pauses at the end of each sentence to allow the interpreter to translate and my audience to assimilate what I was saying, I began with a brief explanation of the purpose of my mission; I outlined the main problems, as I saw them, and my reasons for inviting the rajahs to take over the civil administration in their respective areas; and in conclusion, with all the force and eloquence I could command, I launched my plea for their support.

A long debate followed, in which the principal point of argument, as I had foreseen, was the weakness of the native police and the necessity for making use of the Japanese. In the end it was the *Dewa Agung* who swayed the meeting to my side.

'Will you promise us,' he asked me, 'that you will give us arms for our police?'

'Tuanku *Dewa Agung*,' I answered, 'I will signal my headquarters tonight, asking permission from my general.'

'Very well then,' he continued. 'As the English colonel said earlier, it will take time to have our own police armed and ready. In the meantime order must be preserved. It is regrettable that we should have to use the Japanese; but surely, my friends, it is better to use them for a little while than to watch Bali disintegrate before our eyes in bloodshed, anarchy and civil war!'

One by one the others rose to speak their approval. There was only one voice raised in opposition: the young son of the Rajah of Badung sprang to his feet and delivered a violent attack on me, my policy and my methods.

'It is shameful to use Japanese soldiers to suppress the *Pemudas*, who only ask for freedom!' he shouted. 'The *Pemudas* would not be active if the Japanese did not hunt them all the time. I want no Japanese guards in Den

Pasar!' He glared at me out of bright and angry eyes. 'Take away your soldiers, bring the *Pemudas* into the administration, and you will have no trouble!'

He spoke with such passion and sincerity that, despite my indignation, I could scarcely refrain from clapping when he sat down. However, much as I admired his courage I could not ignore the implications of his speech, especially when I learned that he was a leader of one of the extreme revolutionary groups in Den Pasar. Fortunately his outburst seemed to have little effect on the other Rajahs, who agreed to give the necessary orders to their *pungawas* immediately.

After the conference was over the *Dewa Agung* took me to see the famous Kerta Gosa, the court-house of Klungkung. This ancient building, a simple but beautifully carved and decorated pavilion, stood at a crossroads in the centre of the town. A stair-case guarded by two stone serpents led to a raised platform covered by a roof and fenced by a stone balustrade along each side, the ceiling was covered with paintings illustrating the tortures of the damned in hell—evidently the work of an artist, or artists, of a sadistic turn of mind.

The *kertas* are the courts of the Rajahs, and the judges are usually Brahmana priests; but the people only appeal to them as a last resort, in cases of particular complexity or bitterness, preferring to settle their disputes within the village community. I never witnessed any proceedings before a *kerta*, but I am told that their rules and technical language resemble those of the cockfight which is such an important feature of Balinese life. There is, however, nothing lighthearted about the ritual of swearing-in. The oath is administered to only one of the contesting parties—the judges determine which one—in an elaborate and extremely solemn ceremony, and invokes appalling calamities upon the person and family of a perjurer. The judges also pay particular attention to the bearing and mannerisms of the litigants during the trial, noting any signs of nervousness, hesitation or anxiety.

I returned to Den Pasar in a mood of considerable satisfaction, bordering upon elation, very different from the gloom in which I had left earlier that afternoon. With the exception of Badung and possibly Djembrana, who had been absent, I felt I could now depend upon the Rajahs' support; the Dutch should find at least a foundation on which to build. My first action on reaching my headquarters was to put the eldest son of the Rajah of Badung under house arrest in his father's palace, and to instruct the Japanese to keep him under surveillance. I regretted having to take this step against a sincere and courageous young man, but he was already suspected of helping the terrorists in the town and of organizing the movement of *Pemudas* towards Gianjar which had caused trouble earlier; he was obviously in a position to cause further trouble, and I could afford to take no risks at such a time. In the circumstances I could hardly be accused of undue severity. I also told the Japanese to increase their day and night patrols in an effort to stop the movement of *Pemudas* to Gianjar, and to increase their watch on the Javanese in the town, from whom I was sure we had most to fear.

There was a signal in from Surabaja informing me that we were to remain in Bali for a week after the arrival of the Dutch, during which period I was to act as political adviser to Colonel Ter Meulen; General Mansergh would arrive in *Loch Eck* on the 8th to accept the official surrender of the Japanese forces at a ceremonial parade on the Alun-Alun.

Both Shaw and I had been impressed by the excellent discipline of the Japanese in Bali; on this particular evening I caught a glimpse of the methods by which it was maintained. Walking past a building occupied by Japanese troops near the Residency I was amazed to see the sentry, instead of springing to attention at my approach, remain standing at ease, watching me with an unmistakably impudent leer. I had been warned in Surabaja to be particularly strict in enforcing the orders requiring all Japanese ranks to salute Allied officers, and so I could not possibly ignore this lapse. I walked straight into the house and shouted 'Guard Commander!' at the top of my voice. My meaning must have been clear, because a subaltern appeared immediately with two N.C.O.s. I pointed to the sentry, who unaccountably had not moved from his slovenly attitude; he was disarmed on the spot and marched away.

Colonel Okuyama had him confined in a bamboo cage so constructed that he could neither stand upright in it nor he down; he was fed like an animal through the bars. When I asked the colonel how long this punishment was to last, Miura translated his reply.

'We have sentenced him to a fortnight in the cage. But if you wish that we should execute the fellow, that can be done afterwards.'

'No,' I answered, suppressing a shudder. 'That will not be necessary.' But I had no authority to alter the sentence, and the poor man was still in his cage when I left for Surabaja.

The next morning, Friday, 1st March, passed in a fever of final preparations. Neville hurried off to the beach-head, while Shaw and I toured the whole area, inspecting troop dispositions and checking the billeting arrangements for the Dutch; the buildings of the Bali Hotel and its annex had been cleared to house, in addition to Colonel Ter Meulen and his staff, sixteen war correspondents of various nationalities who were arriving at the same time and who, we had been warned, would expect, and must receive, V.I.P. treatment.

We spent the latter part of the morning studying and collating the intelligence reports which poured in from the Rajahs and the Japanese garrisons in various parts of the island. Things seemed to be quiet everywhere, for the moment at least; I could only hope that they would remain quiet and that the gods of Bali, who had watched so many invasions in the past, would look kindly upon this one.

'I really don't think there's much more we could have done,' commented Shaw, 'in the very short time at our disposal. You realize, don't you, that we haven't been here a week yet?'

'It's incredible! I seem to have lost all track of time since we arrived—there've been so many other things to think about. Let's see, today's Friday, isn't it? You're quite right—it was only last Saturday that we anchored off Benoa and caught our first glimpse of Bali. It seems ages ago.

'I suppose everything will be all right tomorrow,' I continued doubtfully. 'But I'm not absolutely happy about Tabanan. After Den Pasar it's the worst area of the lot, and the Rajah is old, weak and scared.'

'I know, but you've got it pretty well sealed off by the Nips, haven't you? For heaven's sake stop fussing, Peter! Just relax for a change. You've been like a bloody old hen with chicks—flap, flap, flap! What about going to see Theo this afternoon?'

'Damned good idea. Can we get to Iseh and back before dinner?'

'Easily, now I know the way. We might do worse than take him one of our gallon jars of rum. We've got plenty here, and he'll certainly appreciate it. It'll probably save our own lives as well—otherwise we'll have to drink that lethal Swhisky.'

We reached Klungkung in the height of the afternoon and, turning left at the crossroads by the Kerta Gosa, began to climb into the foothills of Gunung Agung. After ten miles, at the sprawling, untidy village of Rendang, we turned to the right and travelled eastwards along a mountain road which soon dropped into a broad and fertile valley. On our left rose the mighty flank of Gunung Agung; on the right the paddy-fields stretched level to a line of low but steep and thickly wooded hills, among which we could see the lighter green of coconut plantations and the palm-thatch roofs of a few buildings.

'There,' said Shaw, 'is Iseh.'

We branched off to the right along a rough track across the fields towards the hills; as we approached, they seemed to rise sheer above us, the terraced ricefields meeting the rich green jungle where a wide path climbed at a gentle angle across the hill-side. We roared up the winding track, which came to an abrupt end in a tiny market-place among a few poor dwellings, little better than hovels; on our right the path led up the hill to a neat wooden house with a wide veranda.

From that direction, as we climbed out of the car, came a loud and cheerful greeting.

'Ho, ho, ho, *mon colonel*! I turned to see a figure in a striped singlet, dark blue shorts, and sandals running down the hill towards us with arms waving in welcome. 'Ho, ho, ho! Theo Meier makes you welcome to his house!' A moment later a dark, tubby little man with twinkling eyes and an enchanting mischievous smile was standing in front of us, vigorously shaking hands alternately with Shaw and me and patting Shimada on the shoulder, while a group of grinning villagers stood by, bowing and murmuring '*tabé, Tuan Besar!*' His merry eyes lit up when he saw us pull the wicker jar of rum from the car and start to carry it up the hill.

'Ho, ho, ho! *Ausgezeichnet!*' he chuckled. 'Now we drink together. *Patut, patut!* But first you try my Swhisky.' Shaw caught my eye and gave a faint shudder.

Theo Meier's home was almost a village in itself. In addition to the house there were several bales, or pavilions, for his servants and dependents, and one, containing a single room, for the exclusive use of his wife; there she would go to worship her household gods and there, so Meier told me, she would seclude herself from the sight of all men, including her husband, during the periods when she was *sebel*—unclean. The house was a fine, compact building of wood and brick, built by the artist himself with the help of the villagers; perched on the hillside between the ricefields and the jungle, it looked across the valley of Selat to the scrub-covered slopes and cloud-wrapped crater of Gunung Agung.

A flight of steps led from the path up to the veranda; at the top stood two of Meier's retainers, a slim, good-looking boy in a loin-cloth who saluted us with a cheerful grin, and an old man with a straggly, drooping moustache and a fringe of grey-flecked stubble round his chin, wearing a green robe. 'I call him the Monkey-Man,' said Meier, indicating the boy. 'When we go hunting the monkeys on the hill up there, to keep them from robbing the plantations, he is my shikar.' He chuckled to himself. 'He is fantastic, that one, at finding monkeys,' The other man was probably younger than he looked at first sight; but his slack, half-open lips and red-rimmed watery eyes indicated a constant and heavy drinker. He mouthed us a slobbery greeting, his shaven head bobbing up and down as he mumbled his words.

'He used to be a priest of Siwa,' Meier explained, 'at the temple of Besakih over there on Gunung Agung—the most holy temple in Bali. But, as you see, he is always drinking. He used to appear drunk at all the ceremonies and sacrifices, and so they sent him away. Now he lives here and is my very devoted friend.' The old man's face lit up in a fond and childish smile that was strangely moving.

From the shadow of the doorway three girls were watching; their ages ranged from about twenty-one to a bare thirteen. Gravely and gracefully they bowed us welcome, and then, at a sign from Meier, stepped forward each in turn. Shaw had not exaggerated: they were indeed beautiful.

'This is Madé Pegi, my wife.' Meier put an arm round the shoulder of the eldest. 'Now she only speaks Balinese and Malay, but soon we teach her to speak English, we three together.'

'Of course,' I answered. 'But first we must learn,' I broke off, staring in wonder at the beauty of this slender girl. Her dark eyes gazed steadily back at me from an oval face beneath a smooth, broad forehead from which the hair was combed back in the shape of a high arch; a soft, shy smile curved the corners of her fine and sensitive mouth. In a gentle voice she murmured some words of Balinese, which Meier translated; but I scarcely heard him. I was conscious only of that exquisite face and slim figure and the swell of the young breasts beneath their covering of gold and crimson brocade. There seemed a certain wistfulness about her serenity but in those lovely eyes and delicate lips glowed a disturbing intensity of passion.

'And this is Njoman Pespes,' Meier's voice, faintly amused, brought me to my senses; with an effort I turned to smile back at a stocky but comely girl of fifteen or sixteen. 'Pespes,' he continued, 'means riches in Balinese. But her family, who live in Iseh, are very poor, and so she lives here and helps Madé Pegi.'

'Now this one,' he patted the youngest, 'we call Hungry Eyes.' She was a mischievous, slant-eyed urchin, as bright as a bee. 'She is living with us also, since six or eight months,' He lowered his voice confidentially, 'At first I would not permit myself to go to bed with her. But afterwards,' he grinned impishly, 'I find the Monkey-Man with her—*et alors*, she is no longer vierge!' He pinched the little girl's cheek; she answered with a little crow of laughter and a saucy wink.

We sat on benches at a long table while the girls fetched us glasses and bottles of Meier's home-distilled *arak*—'as drunk by the Swiss mountain sailors'—the labels assured us. Our host kept up an incessant flow of chatter, darting sharp glances at each of us in turn, his brown eyes flashing merrily and his head jerking from side to side like an agitated jackdaw. He raised his glass.

'*Selamat minum!* That is how you say "Cheerio!" in Malay. *Selamat minum, tuan besar!*' And he drained his glass.

I drained mine too, but I was unable to reply '*selamat minum*' or anything else for several minutes; my voice seemed to shrivel in my throat and my eyes were blinded with tears as I swallowed that dose of liquid fire. Not since I had been obliged to drink a mixture of raw alcohol and petrol with some friendly officers of a Russian armoured division in Poland had I administered such a painful shock to my system.

'*Tjumpol!*' he went on, fortunately without observing my distress. He smacked his lips appreciatively. '"*Tjumpol*" is *wunderbar* in high Balinese. You must learn these words. To say *tjumpol* or *patut*—very right—to these peoples makes great fun all over the place.' He picked up the jar of rum from the floor. 'Now we drink some of this. It is good you bring me the rum, it is more safe than *arak*. I like also the *arak*, you understand, but now since a few days I find *des jolis cristaux dorés dans mon pipi* and I must be prudent.'

'Herr Meier,' I began as soon as I could find my voice; but he cut me off.

'Oh no, *mon colonel*, please! You must call me Theo. Everybody in Bali is calling me Theo. It is many years since any man calls me Herr Meier. *Patut!* So now you call me Theo.'

'Where did you live before you came to Bali, Theo?'

'In the Marquesas.'

'I see. Like Gauguin.'

'Ah, Gauguin! Gauguin is my master—all I know of painting I learn from his work. Always I hope I paint like Gauguin.'

'And why did you leave the Marquesas?'

'I was not happy. The Marquesas is not like when is there Gauguin. And so I come to Bali, where is much better for me.'

'You came at once to Iseh?'

He shook his head. 'At first we live near Sanoer by the sea, my friend Schlager and I. Dr. Ernst Schlager, he is Director for the Orient of the Sandoz chemical *fabrik*; he comes from Basle like me. He has made the study of the Bali music and has transcribed it in European tones, and we both together make the study of the custom and religion; also we drink plenty *arak* and most—that is *tuak*—and make great fun all the time! Then Schlager is going to Switzerland, and I come here.'

'And you are happy here alone?'

He jerked his head towards the girls and smiled.

Our talk turned inevitably to the state of Bali. 'What did you mean,' I asked, 'when you wrote me that "freedom is not believed" here?'

He smiled. 'You know about lontars,'[1] Good. Well, in one important *lontar* is written, "It is fair to lie to wives and enemies." And so no Balinese man believe you when you promise freedom.'

'But why should they think of me as an enemy?'

'Why? Four years' miserable life, four years' first-class Japs' propaganda, and many serious patriots—not only the Bali-Nazi terrorists—created the *unum idea* that every foreign country is enemy as soon as they land.' He laughed shortly. 'Silly public idea is often fact more real than *verité!*'

'My friend Schlager and I find out that we are in front of a primitive people with *high culture* and *high standard* of life in its way. Moral don't exist here—not in our way of thinking. Don't speak to primitive peoples in abstract, logic way—they are never ready to be moved by it; but they are immediately moved by their way of thinking. Like this: you are Rajah, you are strong, you trust them, you don't make speeches, you can rule, you forbid *ribut*—violence, you are the *tuans*, you know everything!' His earnest little face relaxed in a wide grin.

---

[1] Ancient manuscripts, written on the leaves of the lontar palm, recording the history and literature of Hindu Java.

123

'I see,' I answered, not quite truthfully. 'But I have no authority to promise them freedom. My duty is simply to keep the peace.'

'Listen, please. You know what is *Eid-genossenschaft?* Well, Switzerland is a country with several different native populations living together as *Eid-genossenschaft*. Up to its present form was much organic development—through hundreds of years. It started small and was in time of seven hundred years enlarged. Religion and foreign wars unified us. Now Bali has never been a *Eid-genossenschaft*. Since always one county—one state—has fighted the others, and if for a certain time the *Dewa Agungs* kept most of it together, it was by *definite ungentle pressing.*' He ground his fist on the table. 'Yes, the Rajahs' power was merely on *takut* and rarely on *malu* based. The Holland government unified almost the land of Bali and the Japs kept on. But the chaotic structure of Balinese country has had not enough time of organic development towards peaceful understanding one the other. There are many—there are more as is ordinarily known—village-republics and sippen-verbände going criss-cross through Bali, and religious differences too.

'The greatest part of Bali is just now quiet—at least looked upon from far—but the organic joining together of the last thirty years is exhausted and needs immediate friendly kind help in administrative matters. This is the cause of the murders in Badung and Tabanan.'

'You mean,' I asked, somewhat confused by his efforts to explain a difficult problem in a language he had not spoken for at least four years, 'you mean that these murders are the result of personal or family feuds, not the work of political terrorists?'

'Terrorists? Yes, without doubt many of them are made by politic terrorists—*Bali-Nazis*, I call them. But many killings also are for *adat*,[1] because the breaking-up of organic unity.'

He sat back and swallowed a glass of rum. I was silent for a while. I understood what Shaw had meant when he described Theo's writing as rambling on like his conversation. Whatever the value of his opinion it was clearly too late for me to profit from it. But the Dutch might find it useful, and so I readily accepted his invitation to visit him again as soon as possible after the landings; I would bring with me his old friend, Daan Hubrecht.

Before leaving I asked Theo if there was anything we could bring or send him from Den Pasar. His own needs, he replied, were simple: canvases, paint and brushes. They would probably have to come from Singapore, but I promised to order them at once. However, he begged me to send him immediately a supply of medicines for the clinic which he held every morning in the village; he had virtually nothing to give his patients, who suffered, as far as I could gather, chiefly from skin complaints, gonorrhoea and trachoma; the last two were common sources of infection to the children's eyes.

---

[1] Village law and custom—a word adopted from the Arabic.

124

'When did you start this clinic?' I asked, wondering also where he had acquired his medical knowledge.

'My friend Schlager and I, we start it when we come here. Schlager is doctor of *pharnacopoea*. Also our good friend Dr. Hausman from Java has given us much help. From them,' he smiled proudly, 'I learn all my skill.'[1]

The entire household accompanied us to the car. We found Shimada chatting with a group of villagers armed with spears. 'These are my guards,' explained Theo. 'Some of them do the service every night to protect me from the Pemudas; so you see, I am quite safe here.'[2]

---

[1] According to Covarrubias (op. cit., p. 351), the Balinese have no faith in Western medicines, believing that they can only cure the people who invented them; they will only accept treatment out of politeness or when everything else has failed them. However, as I later saw for myself, Theo's 'clinic' was well attended by villagers, who seemed to hold him in great reverence as well as affection.

[2] But four years later even Theo had to flee from another outburst of anti-European terrorism.

X

THE LANDING

In the cool freshness of a brilliant morning I stood with Shaw and Neville on the beach-head, gazing seawards through my glasses at the two large landing-ships of the Royal Navy as they discharged through the gaping ports in their hulls a swarm of soldiers and equipment into the smaller craft that were to ferry them ashore; beyond I could make out the long, low silhouette of a Dutch destroyer. A mile to the west the sparkling blue sea creamed in breakers on the reef of the Sanoer lagoon, but here in the shallow little bay the waves lapped quietly along the stretch of shining sand.

Behind us, in the scrub-covered hinterland that separated the foreshore from the road, Japanese troops had been in position since the previous evening. Small groups of infantrymen crouched silently at action stations in the sandbagged weapon-pits that formed a wide semi-circle protecting the beach-head; others were posted in strategic positions all along the roads leading to Den Pasar. These military precautions that intruded so grimly on the lazy, colourful, sun-drenched landscape were a chilly reminder of the menace that lay hidden but still alert beneath the sensual tropical beauty of this enchanting island.

I looked around uneasily. The landing-craft had begun their run to the shore; the leaders, riding smoothly over the calm water, were already inside the bay. A few groups of villagers and fishermen watched the scene from a distance, but with curiosity rather than excitement, and certainly not with any evident hostility. Surely we had done everything conceivable to prevent bloodshed on this morning? At my side Shaw gave a gasp of surprise.

'Look who's here!'

Forgetting the traditions of Eton and the Royal Horse Guards he extended his arm to point at a couple of figures hurrying with short steps along the beach towards us; I recognized Polok's green sash and magenta kamben.

'What's brought you here?' I asked Le Mayeur when we had exchanged greetings. He pointed out to sea.

' When we saw those ships at sunrise I knew it must mean that the Allies were going to land. So we came along to watch. You do not mind?'

'On the contrary. My one fear has been that some trigger-happy Dutchman might loose off at one of those groups of Balinese and cause an incident. But now I can relax. The sight of your lovely Polok is just what we need to ease the tension.'

I turned to watch the first wave of the assault come in. The landing-craft ran on to the gently shelving beach; the ramps came down and the troops, in full battle order, splashed ashore; the operation was proceeding with the smooth precision of a well-run training exercise—which indeed was what it most resembled. The green-clad, steel-helmeted figures—tall, sun-tanned Dutchmen and lithe, dark-skinned Eurasians—swept forward up the beach, their faces set and grim, their bodies bent forward over their levelled tommy-guns. Then they caught sight of Polok, bright-clad, Junoesque and smiling. For a moment they paused. Their mouths sagged open in amazement; the barrels of their guns wavered uncertainly, and swung towards the ground; and then with a great cheer and flourish of hands they surged forward off the beach to their assembly points round the bridgehead.

I gave a great gasp of relief and turned to greet Colonel Ter Meulen, who was stepping ashore with his staff; with him was that amiable and distinguished soldier, Brigadier Geoffrey Bourne, C.R.A. to 5th Indian Division, who was accompanying the invasion force as observer on behalf of General Mansergh. From this moment Ter Meulen was in command on Bali, and I was only his adviser; I could almost feel the weight of responsibility roll from my shoulders as I shook his hand.

'Mission completed!' Shaw sighed happily and poured another round of rum sours. The three of us were sitting with Brigadier Bourne in my office at the Residency in the cool of the evening before dinner. We had reason to feel content. The entire Dutch force, consisting of two battalions and numbering some two and a half thousand men, had landed without incident and, for the moment at least, without encountering any sign of hostility; the Japanese had provided all the necessary transport and, as *The Times* correspondent wrote in his dispatch, 'by midday Dutch convoys were pouring into the interior taking over vital points from the Japanese, and the allied military administration was in control.'[1]

Even the journalists, who included such formidable American personalities as Martha Gellhorn and Bob Sherrard, seemed satisfied with our arrangements for their reception, although there was an indignant outburst from Miss Gellhorn when she was asked by the management of the Bali Hotel to share a room with an Eurasian girl; there was no other room available in the hotel, but I solved the problem by giving her my bedroom at the Residency, and moving my own bed into my office.

Now that the operation was over I could not help wondering why the Dutch had chosen to make an assault landing instead of coming ashore, as we had done, in the harbour at Benoa. When, long afterwards, I put this question to Colonel Carroll he chuckled.

---

[1] *The Times*, 4th March 1946.

'Nothing would convince them, up to the very last moment, that they weren't going to be opposed.'

'By whom? The Japanese or the locals?'

'The locals. It seems that Japanese propaganda had made its mark even on the Dutch High Command. You know, the landing-force had strict orders to withdraw on the first sign of opposition.'

'I notice,' observed the brigadier, 'that the people here have developed that odious Nip habit of bowing three times from the waist when we pass.'

'The Japanese taught them that,' I explained. 'We tried to stop it, but we couldn't in a week cure them of a habit they've learnt—and learnt the hard way—over a period of three years.'

'I suppose not. Let's hope the Dutch will put a stop to it. By the way, Ter Meulen seems most grateful to you all.'

'I only hope he feels the same way after a week or two.'

'You think they're going to have trouble, then?'

'I don't honestly know, sir. I believe that the great majority of Balinese don't want trouble. What they want above all else is peace and the chance to till their ricefields and follow their old, delightful, easy way of life without interference and without fear. But when have the great majority—especially in the East—ever been able to make their wishes felt against the determination of a ruthless, well-organized minority? As long as we were here on our own the terrorists were content to lie low and watch, confining their actions to a few carefully selected incidents in order to demonstrate their power—to show the flag, you might say. It's possible that if this force that landed today had been a British, or even an inter-Allied force, they might have remained comparatively quiet. But now they know the Dutch are back they may start serious guerrilla warfare—and the country's ideal for that.'

'You don't think they'll get much help from the mass of the population?'

'No, but they won't get much opposition either. Some of the population, I'm sure, really welcome back the Dutch; others are just indifferent. But all of them are much too frightened of the terrorists to give the Dutch any help, even if their Rajahs told them to—which they certainly won't in Den Pasar or Tabanan.'

'These terrorists, are they Balinese mostly, or Javanese?'

Shaw intervened. 'Numerically, they would be mostly Balinese, wouldn't they, Peter? But we're convinced that the inspiration, the leadership and the organization of the movement is Javanese; it is directed and controlled from Java—hence, of course, its lack of popular support.'

'Do you think the terrorists are getting any help from the Japs here?'

'We can find no evidence of it,' I said. 'Of course, they probably have informers among them, but we'll never know who they are.'

'How many Javanese would you estimate there are in Bali?'

'Only a few thousands, of whom about three hundred are active and dangerous; I'm talking of those in the towns and villages—I don't know how many there are with the gangs in the hills.'

'Oughtn't you to have done something about the dangerous ones?'

'We certainly ought—looking back on it now. We should have clamped down on them the moment we arrived. But we didn't have the information or the resources then; also, I wanted to avoid anything that might savour of repression. But now I'm convinced that one of the first things the Dutch should do is to round up those three hundred and either deport them to Java or keep them here under strict surveillance.'

The Brigadier laughed. 'Well, it's no longer your problem. You can talk to Ter Meulen about it in the morning.'

Although released from the pressure of the previous weeks, I had during the following days neither the opportunity nor the inclination to be idle. With Brigadier Bourne or with Sherrard and Miss Gellhorn we toured the island from Karangasem in the east to Djembrana in the west and northwards to Singaradja. I spent long hours in conference with Colonel Ter Meulen. Whether out of courtesy or because he really thought it useful, he sought my advice on almost every aspect of the political and military problem; and, to give us the benefit of that remarkable officer's ability and experience, he attached Daan Hubrecht to us for liaison duties between the two headquarters.

The day after the landing, 3rd March, we accompanied Ter Meulen to Klungkung for his first meeting with the Council of Rajahs. After a simple and informal lunch given by the *Dewa Agung* the business of the conference proceeded smoothly, without any of the tension of the previous meeting; the Rajahs pledged their full support to Ter Meulen, and he in return promised to reorganize and arm their police. In this atmosphere of friendliness and confidence some of my anxieties began to disperse.

This was the first day of the feast of *njepi*, marking the spring equinox, the end of the rainy season, and the Balinese New Year;[1] on this day every community in the island clears out its devils and evil spirits. 'It is believed,' says Covarrubias, 'that then the Lord of Hell, Yama, sweeps Hades of devils, which fall on Bali, making it imperative that the whole of the island be purified.' The festival lasts two days—the *metjaru*, the day of purification, and the *njepi* proper, the day of silence.

In Den Pasar that morning we had seen men carrying fighting cocks in their curious coconut baskets to the meeting halls for the cockfights which

---

[1] *Njepi* is the only festival of the old Hindu *saka* calendar still celebrated throughout this island; this calendar was superseded in Madjapahit times by the *wuku* calendar divided simply into weeks.

are an essential part of the celebrations; for the land is cleansed by the spilling of blood upon it. The purification rites take place before sunset, when the devils and evil spirits are lured to the *metjaru*—the 'great offering'—for the ceremony of expulsion; the *metjaru* is a strange assortment of objects laid out on the ground in the form of an eight-pointed star and surrounded by a low palm-leaf fence: there is every kind of food and strong drink, money and household utensils, samples of every seed and fruit growing on the island, and a piece of the flesh of every wild and domestic animal in Bali. A low-caste priest, the *sunguhu*, dedicates these offerings to the evil spirits, who converge all unsuspecting upon the sacrificial ground; once assembled there, they are expelled in a body by powerful *mantras* chanted by the waiting High Priests.

The populace take over the work where the priests leave off, and in Den Pasar we were treated to a noisy night. To the accompaniment of the furious throbbing of the *kulkuls* and the sharp explosions of firecrackers groups of men roamed the town carrying torches, beating drums, gongs, empty petrol tins, the ground and the trees, and shouting at the tops of their voices to frighten away any lurking devils, any *kalas* or *butas* that might have evaded the curses of the priests.[1]

In normal times the day of silence was most strictly enforced. No fires might be lit, for cooking or any other purpose—it was unlawful even to smoke a cigarette; there was no traffic on the roads; no work and no sexual intercourse were permitted on this day. Under present circumstances the last was the only prohibition we felt ourselves bound to observe; nevertheless we remained in Den Pasar, where there was plenty to keep us busy in conference and office.

On 5th March Brigadier Bourne flew back to Surabaja, taking off from the airstrip at Kuta which Shaw's Japanese working parties had made serviceable; he would return to Bali in three days' time with General Mansergh.

Den Pasar seemed to settle down peacefully enough under the new occupation. The townspeople, cautious at first, soon welcomed the Dutch troops, and shops and market-vendors did a brisk trade. Ter Meulen formed a defended perimeter around the town, with check points and road blocks covering all approaches; no European was allowed to wander outside without an escort. The terrorists had not yet shown their hand, but neither were they idle. Their first move was to impose a boycott on Den Pasar, and they were able to interfere seriously with the supply of food from the countryside; Ter Meulen soon found himself with a food shortage on his hands, and he had to call upon Surabaja for help.

---

[1] For a detailed description of this ceremony see *Island of Bali*, p. 279-282.

The focus of terrorist activity was Tabanan. Whatever the feelings of the Rajah, he was much too frightened of the terrorists to take any action against them, or even to ask Ter Meulen for protection. Murders continued on a large scale, so that no Balinese suspected of sympathy with the Dutch could consider his life safe; the civil administration had virtually collapsed. That this was an unfriendly district was made clear to Ter Meulen on his first visit. 'The attitude of the people along the roads towards us,' he wrote in his report, 'was mistrustful and without any sign of welcome.' And he concluded: 'The situation in Tabanan is most alarming.' It was not long before the trouble spread.

To divert ourselves from this depressing picture Shaw, Hubrecht and I drove up to Iseh to see Theo Meier, taking with us another jar of rum—and, on Ter Meulen's orders, a substantial escort. The little man was ecstatic to see his old friend again, and the beautiful Pegi shed tears of joy, exclaiming that now everything was going to be the same as it had been in the days before the war. When the time came for us to leave, Theo insisted on accompanying us back to Den Pasar; he wanted to see Van Burger, the new chief of civil administration, and give him advice on how to govern the island. I gladly offered to put him up.

'Ho, ho, ho!' he chorded as he skipped down the path to our jeep, while Pegi and the two girls waved us good-bye. 'Ho, ho, ho! Tonight we make the celebration in the headquarters of *mon colonel* Peter—the conqueror of Bali!' I prayed he would not talk like that to Van Burger.

We certainly made a celebration, and it was a noisy one, lasting late into the night; unfortunately it disturbed my other guest, whom in the excitement I had temporarily forgotten. Miss Gellhorn's furious protests broke in upon our revels, sobering me instantly as I remembered General Mansergh's strict instructions on the importance of the Press. Seeing my crestfallen expression Theo patted me reassuringly on the shoulder.

'Do not worry, Peter,' he whispered. 'Now I make everything all right with her.' He tiptoed across the room.

'Where are you going?' I asked anxiously.

He gave a devilish leer. 'I go to her now, and I make love to her. Yes?' And he padded through the door.

'Theo, come back at once!' I stopped him in his tracks with a voice of command I had not used since my arrival in Bali. 'I don't mind your getting your face slapped, but I'm not going to end my military career with a court martial.'

Shaw and I stood in silence on the quarterdeck of *Loch Eck* as she glided over the calm water towards the sunset. The previous day had seen the culmination of our work in Bali, when, at an impressive ceremony on the

Alun-Alun, General Mansergh had officially accepted the surrender of the Japanese garrison.

The next morning he had flown back to Surabaja with Brigadier Bourne; in the afternoon I had embarked my party in the frigate to follow them and prepare for our mission to Lombok.

Warmed by General Mansergh's praise and the effusive thanks of Ter Meulen and his officers, I had good reason to bless my luck; especially I blessed the two officers on my staff who had done most of the work for which I was getting the credit. But as I watched the land fade into the dusk astern I wondered uneasily whether our work there was going to prove so useful in the long run as it might seem at the moment; I was afraid Ter Meulen's stay in Bali would not be so peaceful as his landing.

Except for Surabaja the Indonesian nationalists held the whole of East Java; it was too easy for them to infiltrate arms and agents across the narrow waters of the Bali Strait. They had already shown that in Bali they had an organization efficient, cunning and ruthless enough to impose their will on large sections of the people, while the Dutch had nowhere near enough troops to winkle them out from that difficult, well-wooded, broken country. With foreboding I remembered the words spoken to me in Singaradja: 'Bali has been called "the last Paradise". Will it become the "*lost* Paradise"?'

XI

LOMBOK

Lombok is smaller than Bali, measuring some thirty miles from east to west and forty-five from north to south. The Lombok Strait dividing the two islands is one of the main waterways for shipping between South-East Asia and Australia; it holds some uncomfortable memories for Allied submariners of the Pacific War, who suffered much from Japanese patrols in its deep but narrow waters. It is also, according to the naturalist Wallace, the demarcation line between the flora and fauna of Asia, still found on Bali, and those of Australia, which begin to appear on Lombok; there have been various modifications of 'Wallace's line' during the ninety years since its promulgation, but Professor Dobby has noted that the drier climate of east Lombok has 'an almost Australian aspect, with prickly pears and cockatoos indicating the migration of Australian flora and fauna.'[1]

The north of the island is bare and mountainous; it rises steeply from the sea to the cloud-topped and still active crater of the great twelve thousand foot volcano, Rindjani, where, so the simpler islanders believe, dwells the spirit of the well-loved Lieftinck, first Dutch Resident of Lombok, forever keeping watch over his people. In the south is a barren limestone massif, about a thousand feet high, waterless and almost uninhabited, covered with scrub and bamboo thickets. Across the centre of the island, beneath the gentle southern slopes of the volcanoes Rindjani and Nangi, runs a fertile, well-watered and intensely cultivated belt of terraced ricefields and plantations, which produces enough food for the entire population of nearly a million.

Almost nine-tenths of this population are Sasaks, a simple agricultural people of Malay stock without the highly developed culture of the Balinese but with an infinite capacity for enjoyment and a remarkable aptitude for clowning. By religion they are what is called 'lax Moslems', and indeed Islam rests so lightly upon them as to be recognizable only in a few of their names. They are exceedingly promiscuous in their sex life, bringing to the pleasures of love a skill and enthusiasm unsurpassed by any people in my experience. Although given overmuch to robbery—but not to murder—they are an irresistibly lovable and friendly race, and they nurse remarkably little resentment for the wrongs they suffered under their former Balinese overlords.

---

[1] *South-East Asia*, University of London Press, 1950, p. 275.

The Balinese completed their conquest of Lombok in 1740, and for more than a century and a half a line of semi-independent Rajahs ruled the island from their fortress palaces at Mataran, the capital, and Tjakra Negara. In 1885 the Sasak chiefs rebelled and asked the Dutch for help against their Balinese governors; but it was not until 1894 that the Dutch sent an expeditionary force to occupy the island. After a bloody campaign, in which the invaders suffered one severe defeat, the Balinese fortresses were destroyed, Mataran was razed to the ground, and the old Rajah was sent to die of a broken heart in Batavia; the Dutch allowed his successors a limited jurisdiction over the forty thousand Balinese in Lombok, but they annexed the island and governed it through their Resident in Mataran. Friction between Balinese and Sasaks died down, although the Balinese, who remained in possession of the richest ricefields, naturally attracted some jealousy, especially from the old and impoverished Sasak nobility.

In addition to Sasaks and Balinese there is a small but commercially active Chinese community in the port of Ampenan, an Arab colony, and a few villages of Bugi traders.[1]

There was nothing complicated about the orders I received for this new operation; they ran as follows: 'You will land in Lombok to transmit latest military and political information and prepare for the landing of Dutch troops on Lombok.' But the written brief that accompanied them was far from reassuring. 'Japanese forces, totalling 409 Naval and 1945 Army personnel [sic] are concentrated in Mataran. They cannot be expected to control the civilian population in the event of a major disturbance, except in the immediate vicinity of Mataran. The Japanese garrison is in possession of only a limited amount of arms, left to them by an Australian surveillance party.'

It was explained to me in Surabaja that the Australian party had turned up some months previously from one of the islands farther east, disarmed the Japanese and sailed back whence they had come; they had acted on their own initiative and without authority. My brief concluded with the encouraging forecast that 'the landing may well be opposed by the local inhabitants, who are known to possess a number of weapons.'

To keep the peace, therefore, until the Dutch arrived I must rely on a virtually disarmed and almost certainly demoralized Japanese garrison, reinforced by General Ando and his two officers, and on my own formidable party, consisting of Shaw and Neville, Sergeant Hopkins, six signallers, one

---

[1] Natives of Celébes, the Buginese are stricter Moslems than either Sasaks or Javanese. 'The Bugis and Mascassaris,' says Professor Dobby, 'were historically one of the most active Muslim seafaring peoples of the Indies, acquiring a notoriety as pirates and slavers; they now rank as an inter-island trading people whose little sailing ships may be found anywhere between Singapore and Port Moresby.'

cook and my escort of one N.C.O. and five troopers of the Royal Berkshire Yeomanry. I had been obliged, reluctantly, to leave our Buffs behind in Surabaja; but this new escort, though all of them equally young, were all just as enthusiastic as their predecessors, and would, I was certain, give a good account of themselves in trouble.

'One thing's for sure,' I observed to my two officers as *Loch Eck* carried us across the smiling blue waters of the Lombok Strait towards the gleaming white houses of Ampenan. 'We don't repeat the mistake we made in Bali. One squeak out of any agitator, and he goes straight inside. Once we let trouble spread in this set-up we haven't a hope of controlling it.'

With this amiable resolution I stepped ashore on the little pier at Ampenan on the morning of 19th March, to receive the salute of a Japanese guard of honour and drive the four miles inland to my new headquarters in the Residency at Mataran, where servants and interpreters were already waiting.

Ampenan, though the principal port of Lombok, was too exposed to the westerly monsoon to be suitable for an assault landing; the Dutch had therefore decided to come ashore at the small, land-locked harbour of Lembar, about fifteen miles farther down the coast. I sent Neville there immediately with a Japanese working-party of two hundred and a strong armed guard; he seemed to enjoy himself, for the work of preparation was much simpler than at Sanoer, and the local inhabitants gave him an enthusiastic welcome.

After my ominous briefing I was agreeably surprised at the friendliness of the people of Mataran and Ampenan—Balinese and Sasaks alike. From the moment of our arrival, whenever we went out, groups would gather round us in the streets, calling out greetings in Malay and asking us whether we intended to remain; they seemed genuinely delighted to hear that we did. There were a few truculent shouts of '*Merdeka!*' from young men in European dress, but they were almost pathetic in their isolation.

On our first evening in Mataran the leaders of the Balinese, Sasaks and Eurasian communities presented themselves in turn at the Residency to offer us their support.[1] The Balinese warned us to be very careful of the Sasak leader; the Sasaks advised us to have no dealings with the Balinese. The Eurasian urged us to trust no one. They were followed by an urbane and well-groomed Chinaman bearing an invitation to dinner with the Chinese Association of Ampanan; he gave us no advice or promises of support, but wished to present me with a typewriter—purely, of course, as a token of esteem.

---

[1] The Balinese representative was not Rajah, but an official in charge of the Balinese civil administration.

We enlisted the Eurasian as an extra interpreter, for besides excellent English he spoke Dutch, Malay, Balinese and Sasak. He was a soft-voiced, desiccated man in late middle age, with thin, silvery hair, a pronouncedly European cast of features and a melancholy, timorous expression; with his emaciated body, lean, sad face, and long, scrawny, undulating neck he reminded me of some weary and disillusioned old vulture. He had been a senior police official under the Dutch and his name was Mr. Smith.

Despite their suspicion of each other, Smith and the Balinese and Sasak leaders all agreed that there was on the island a small but potentially dangerous movement, under Javanese leadership, pledged to resist occupation by the Allies; they assured me that it had little support among the population, whose interest was in farming rather than politics, but they hinted that the Japanese were giving it clandestine help. Moreover, the day before our arrival a certain Kumenit, an agitator from Manado in north Celébes, had addressed a public meeting in Mataran, exhorting the people to 'oppose the Allies to the last drop of their blood.' There had also been some attempts at intimidation, but as yet no kidnapping or murder. I decided on an immediate show-down, to dispose of the malcontents and at the same time test the loyalty of the Japanese garrison.

I recognized my cue the following afternoon, when a party of four young Javanese presented themselves at the Residency and demanded an immediate interview in the name of the "National Independence Committee,' Their leader, I afterwards learned, was a clerk in a government office; the other three were schoolmasters. Trooping into my office they brusquely declined my invitation to sit down, and stood stiffly in front of my desk glaring at me with an angry self-assurance. Smith, looking more than usually woebegone and frightened, acted as interpreter. They wasted no time on courtesies.

'We have come,' declared their leader haughtily, 'to lay before you the people's demands for the civil administration of Lombok.'

I asked mildly by what right they, who were Javanese, claimed to speak for the people of Lombok. Quite unabashed he replied simply, 'We have been appointed.' He then launched into a fierce indictment of the Allies for their 'repression' in Java; demanded my assurance that the Dutch would not land in Lombok, and concluded by ordering me to hand over the civil administration immediately to his committee and confine myself to getting rid of the Japanese. His companions hung on his words with rapt attention, nodding their heads eagerly as he made each point.

Controlling my temper I heard him out to the end; then I stood up and coldly invited them to leave. It would be impolitic, as well as unethical, to detain them while they were technically my guests in the Residency; but that evening I told the Japanese to arrest their leader. I gave the same orders about his treatment and privileges as I had given for my prisoners in Bali. Two days later I visited him in prison and found him in excellent spirits; he seemed amused when I apologized for having to curtail his liberty, and clearly bore me no ill will. Shorn of his arrogance he seemed a delightful fellow.

I made the Japanese give me a copy in translation of their prison records, stating the name of each prisoner and the charge on which he was being held. I observed that in several cases the charge was listed simply as 'fornication'. After consultation with Balinese and Sasak officials I ordered the release of these men. 'I should feel extremely uncomfortable,' I explained to Shaw, 'to be holding anybody in gaol for that particular offence. Besides, even if it is a crime under Moslem law, it certainly isn't under Balinese or Sasak custom.'

Touring the island with Smith and the Sasak and Balinese leaders, Shaw and I interviewed the principal officials and head-men of every district, and soon had a clear picture of the situation. It was a great deal better than in Bali. From the information we collected I was able to identify the most dangerous characters; within four days I had ordered some thirty arrests, including three officers of the Japanese *Kempeitai*, one of them a war criminal and the other two *agents provocateurs* who had busied themselves in stirring up trouble between the Balinese and Sasaks.

With these arrests all sign of opposition ceased; it was quickly evident, in the cheerful faces of the people and the enthusiastic welcomes we received wherever we went, that a new and happier atmosphere prevailed in the island. Every day the Residency was thronged with deputations of villagers and headmen, come to declare their loyalty; they brought presents of pigs, ducks, eggs and *brom*, a potent wine made from black or red rice. The live-stock was something of an embarrassment, for their numbers threatened to overcrowd the small Residency compound; yet we could not hurt the feelings of our visitors by refusing their gifts. Sergeant Hopkins, whose medical duties were fortunately light, appointed himself chief swineherd, but we had to leave most of his charges to our Dutch successors.

The Japanese at first were slow to co-operate, especially in carrying out the arrests I ordered; we soon traced the fault to the attitude of their commander. He was an elderly colonel of slovenly manner and untidy appearance, whose attitude in our presence was a studied blend of apathy and insolence; at conferences he would sit sprawled in his chair with his jacket unbuttoned and his hands in his pockets, staring at the ceiling and occasionally yawning, and he carried out our instructions—when he carried them out at all—with unconcealed reluctance and ill grace. It was probably *ennui* that was affecting him rather than malice, but I could not afford to make allowances; and so I relieved him of his command and sent him under close arrest to Bali. We had no trouble from his successor.

Although we had less cause to worry now than when we were in Bali, we still had an extremely heavy load of work, and neither Shaw nor I had much time to sleep or to relax and enjoy the exuberant loveliness of this gaily coloured landscape. In addition to our daily tours of inspection, which took us all over the island, Shaw was busy with his old problem of Japanese troop concentrations to protect the Dutch landing at Lembar—for we dared not neglect any precautions—and the preparation of a landing-strip for aircraft on the east coast; while I was absorbed in a host of minor but still important matters—questions of civil administration, local law and custom, and village economy that were far outside my capacity or experience. Acting on the principle that it is better to give a wrong decision than none at all, I almost certainly gave a lot of wrong decisions.

On the morning of 27th March Colonel Ter Meulen led his troops ashore at Lembar, to be greeted by a crowd of cheering villagers; he brought with him his own motor transport, and by noon had occupied the capital. Mataram and Ampenan—indeed every village on the route from Lembar—came out in a rash of Dutch flags, which must have been concealed since before the war; the warmth and enthusiasm of the people's welcome far exceeded our brightest hopes. Indeed Brigadier Bourne, who once again accompanied Ter Meulen, signalled to General Mansergh: 'People's welcome both spontaneous and vociferous. Those who saw welcome to British in Malaya compare it equally.'

'That briefing we had in Surabaja,' I remarked to Shaw, 'was the most inaccurate appreciation of a situation I've ever come across.' We were standing outside the Residency with Ter Meulen and Jacobs, the new Dutch Resident, watching the happy, excited crowds that thronged the long, wide main street.

'It wouldn't have been,' he answered, 'if we hadn't learnt our lesson in Bali and muzzled the opposition here right away.'

'What will you do with them?' I asked Ter Meulen.

He shrugged his shoulders. 'Nothing. They will have to stay in prison until everything is normal here. Then they will be allowed to leave.'

The next morning, at an assembly of all the heads of district, the Balinese *pungawas*, the Sasak chiefs and the principal village headmen, Ter Meulen and Jacobs formally announced the return of Lombok to the Dutch Crown. At the end of the ceremony there were prolonged cheers, led by the Dutch but echoed enthusiastically by the people, for Queen Wilhelmina. The British and Dutch flags were hoisted over the Residency.

In the afternoon we watched a remarkable display of Sasak games on the great open space where the assembly had taken place in the morning. It consisted chiefly of a series of mock combats between two men armed with long, pliant rattan rods and wooden shields. Naked, save for their girded loincloths, the combatants pranced warily round each other, their shields raised over their heads, their right arms extended, trailing the rattans on the ground behind them; suddenly one of them would leap forward, swinging his staff in a high arc over the opposing shield at his adversary's head, or in a wide sweep round the shield at his ribs. Usually the shields parried these murderous blows, and nobody was hit on the head, but sometimes a sideways swipe would land with a sickening whack, loud as the impact of a bullet, on a man's bare ribs. When this happened there was a brief lull; the striker would execute a small dance of triumph in the middle of the arena, while his victim capered round the ring of spectators, grimacing horribly, pointing to the rapidly swelling weal on his flank and in turn giggling, crying with pain and shouting to his friends to admire his pluck. When they had finished their clowning they would resume the battle. The victims seemed to get more applause than the victors—but no shred of sympathy—from the delighted crowd; I never saw a man show the least sign of temper, although some of the bruises almost turned my stomach and the pain must have been excruciating.[1]

By contrast with this virile spectacle the dance we gave in the Residency that night for the Dutch officers and nurses was a pallid affair; but Shaw and I had no longer any worries to inhibit our enjoyment, and the fifteen gallons of 'operational' rum which 5th Indian Division had given us for this operation, and which we had scarcely broached since our arrival, proved an ideal lubricant. The Chinese Association had provided us with the elements of an orchestra; in the manner of Chinese merchants all the world over, they had dug up out of nowhere a piano, a trumpet and drums. The piano was a little out of tune, but so also was the pianist—Brigadier Bourne's soldier servant, who had learnt by correspondence course during his service in the Far East; a Dutchman played the trumpet, and the drummer was a Japanese sailor, who in peacetime had been the champion tap dancer of Tokyo.

At Ter Meulen's request we remained another week on Lombok, although there was very little for us to do. There was no serious opposition to the Dutch, and it seemed unlikely now that any would develop. The people, the Sasaks especially, were well disposed towards them; moreover, the island was not suitable for guerrilla warfare, for the cultivated area was too small, the mountains too bare and desolate to shelter bands of terrorists. Ter Meulen decided to hand over to Jacobs and return to the much more serious problems of Bali. On General Mansergh's orders I sent my party back to Surabaja, but Shaw and I, who had been granted a week's leave in Bali, left with Ter Meulen in an M.T.B. on 3rd April.

One of my last actions in Lombok was to make a farewell call on the Balinese Rajah in his palace. He welcomed me with warmth, remarking that I had come at a most auspicious moment; although seventy-five years old, he had that day been presented with a son by his youngest wife, a girl of

---

[1] These contests are very similar to the *Gebug* or *Ende*, performed as a dance in certain districts of East Bali (see *Dance and Drama in Bali*, pp. 265-7).

seventeen. To mark the occasion he gave me a fine *kolok* with a beautifully worked wooden sheath.

'I can't imagine what he thinks *you* had to do with it,' grumbled Shaw.

XII

AND FAREWELL GOES OUT SIGHING

Shaw and I had agreed with the Le Mayeurs and Theo to divide our leave between them; while he was staying with one I should stay with the others, and we should change round after three days. And so, when we landed at Karangasem on 3rd April Shaw took the road to Iseh, while I went straight to Sanoer, to the bamboo house beside the murmuring sea, and exchanged my uniform for a *kamben*, and slept a great deal, and bathed in the lagoon before breakfast, and lounged on the veranda watching the bright hibiscus in the garden glowing in the early morning sunshine, and listened to the sea breeze whispering in the tall sugar palms.

And yet I was not happy, for all the kindness of Le Mayeur and Polok. For the first time, almost, since I had dropped into Siam I had no responsibilities or urgent problems; I had plenty of time to think, and my thoughts were heavy and full of misery and self-reproach. In Lombok I had received a letter telling me that my wife had remarried. There I had been too busy—or I could make myself too busy—to think about it; but now I felt the full pain and desolation—mixed, let me be honest, with a large dose of hurt pride—of this news which I ought to have expected but somehow had never foreseen. Bitterly I cursed the selfishness and obstinate determination to go my own way that had wrecked my marriage and destroyed our love. And so I took no pleasure in this paradise, but brooded in a deep pit of loneliness and despair, and abused my fate, and hated myself, and wept a little, and drank too much, and wept some more.

This discreditable exhibition of *Angst und Schaden* was aggravated, though I did not recognize them at the time, by the early symptoms of the tuberculosis which eighteen months later almost ended my life. Apart from the usual persistent cough, to which I paid no attention, I became noticeably neurotic, short tempered and snappy, with spells of overpowering lassitude that seemed to deprive me of all my energy and will. At the time I put everything down to war-weariness and alcohol.

Ter Meulen, too, had his troubles, more serious than mine. On my way to Sanoer I had called at the hospital in Den Pasar to visit Van Burger, the Resident, who was lying in bed with a bullet wound in his stomach; terrorists had fired on his jeep as he was driving back from Singaradja. Luckily the wound was not dangerous, but this attack proved to be the first of many; emboldened by early success and the inability of the Dutch to retaliate, the terrorists embarked on more ambitious operations, until they were ambushing troop convoys on the road to Tabanan.

On the 5th I took my leave of the Le Mayeurs and drove up into the cool green hills of Iseh. I arrived in the early evening, and all of a sudden my heart lifted at the welcoming light in Madé Pegi's lovely eyes. Theo and Shaw had gone to shoot monkeys in the plantations above the house; they came back just before dark with the Monkey-Man carrying five or six pathetic little furry bodies slung on a pole over his shoulder.

'I can't say I enjoy shooting them,' Shaw told me as he cleaned his carbine. 'It's too like shooting human beings, and they give a terribly human scream when they're hit.'

We had brought Theo another two gallons of rum—for our own sakes as much as his—and now, while he went to prepare our food, we lingered over our drinks on the porch, watching the deepening darkness spread from the valley up the lower slopes of Gunung Agung. Theo was a superb cook and was happy to spend hours in the kitchen, applying to his work a rare skill and a fine inventive flair; his specialty was *bifstek tartare*, which he would let no one make but himself—'for here in Bali,' he warned us, 'you can easily have some worm.' That night he gave us a curry which still lives in my memory, and not only for its flavour; when we asked him what was this delicious and tender meat, he smiled softly at Shaw.

'You have just shot them.'

The Dutch had lent us each a staff car, and so when Shaw left for Sanur I drove with Theo to visit the curious village-republic of Tenganan in the hills south-west of Karangasem. This is the most conservative of the Bali Aga communities, pure descendants of the ancient Indonesians who colonized the islands nearly two thousand years ago. Socially and economically it is entirely cut off from the rest of Bali, and its physical isolation is emphasized by a solid wall surrounding the village, pierced only by four very narrow gates; the life and customs of these Bali Aga have remained untouched by the religion and culture of the later Hindu Javanese conquerors.

The people of Tenganan are fair-skinned, with slender, fragile bodies, small bones, and the carefully cultivated, artificial manners of an effete and over-leisured aristocracy; they look down on other Balinese, and are themselves forbidden, on pain of exile, to marry outside the community. Their village is ruled by a council of Elders, who are also priests, and they worship the spirits of nature and of their ancestors. Their society is a form of patriarchal Communism, for they do not recognize the individual ownership of property; even the houses are all built alike, intersected in an austere, geometrical pattern by long straight avenues paved with stone. On the other hand, they are not permitted to work the rich and extensive ricefields and plantations owned by the village, but hire Balinese from outside as labourers.

As an indication of their superiority to manual work they grow their fingernails to an extraordinary length, those of the *perbekel*, or headman, who received us measuring at least four inches.

Strangers are not usually welcome in Tenganan, and we owed our invitation to Theo's friendship with the *perbekel*, a faded ghost of a man in his middle thirties who greeted us with formal courtesy and an air of well-bred languor. After he had escorted us through the village we sat down to sample a delicious fresh tuak from the local plantations—the preparation of this drink is the only agricultural labour the villagers allow themselves; Theo pointed out to me an old man who hovered in the background with a watchful, anxious expression.

'It is that one's duty,' he whispered, 'to sweep the village after we have gone, to brush away our footprints.'

In the clear, sweet air of Iseh, cooled by the dry wind that blew steadily from the east to fan those lush green hills and ricefields, my lethargy and my cares dissolved. Nobody, indeed, could remain gloomy for long in the company of Theo, with his bubbling vitality and lust for life, his warm humanity, and his bright and bawdy wit. Usually I saw more of Madé Pegi during the daytime than of Theo. During the morning, when he had finished with his clinic, he would retire to one of the hales to paint; in the afternoon he would visit a neighbouring village where the pungawa or pedanda was his friend, to return in the evening, breathless and flushed with excitement, followed by a retinue of servants staggering under the weight of heavy bamboo jars.

'Ho, ho, ho!' he would shout. '*Venez, venez*, Peter! *J'ai trouvé un* EXCELLENT *tuak! Nous allons goûter de ça!*'

Later, after we had eaten, we would sit with the girls on the terrace in the still, cool darkness, rich with the scent of frangipani and champaka, drinking tuak and talking while the full moon threw dappled shadows among the ricefields in the valley and bathed the slopes of Gunung Agung in grey and silver light. As the hours wore on the girls crept silently to bed; but I remained listening to Theo's stories of Bali and the Marquesas, till the darkness paled and dawn revealed the great mountain rising from the valley mists, its flattened cone outlined against a pearly sky.

One day we had a visit from a fellow-countryman of Theo's who had known him in Bali before the war; his name was Andoregg and he was working for the International Red Cross. Short and slight of build, with humorous eyes blinking behind thick horn-rimmed spectacles and a slow, hesitant manner of speech, he had the appearance of a benevolent but emaciated tortoise. He spoke good Malay and was popular among the Balinese, with whom he believed himself to have some special affinity; it was over-confidence in this belief that was to lead him to a terrible end.

Theo confessed to me that his married life had not always been easy. Madé
Pegi was his second wife, and both she and her predecessor came from
Sanoer, a village famous for the power of its priests and witch-doctors and
the hysterical temperament of its women. He had kidnapped Madé Pegi,
following the established Balinese custom, and for a while had lived with the
two girls in his house by the sea. But his first wife had resented the intrusion,
and her persistent jealousy had broken up his comfortable ménage; after she
had made several skilful attempts to poison him and Madé Pegi he had felt
obliged to send her away. She had gone to live in Den Pasar and Theo had
brought Madé Pegi to Iseh. Although not actively inclined to homicide Madé
Pegi was also capable, so Theo told me, of extravagant outbursts of
indignation and he bore many bruises as evidence of the strength of her
displeasure.

'You would not credit it, *mon cher*,' he assured me with wistful admiration,
'the force with which that little girl strike me.'

'She has the appearance of a passionate nature. But Theo,' I added
impulsively, 'I have never seen a more beautiful girl and she is so wonderfully
sweet to me!'

'Oh, yes,' he murmured with a sly grin. 'She is quite in love with you.' He
giggled and wagged a finger in my face. 'Mais prenez garde, mon vieux! Je
suis devenu amoureux de ma femme. Elle n'est plus couchable avec!'

Our leave was up on 10th April, but when I arrived in Den Pasar I was
greeted with a request to report to Colonel Ter Meulen. Beneath his usual
courteous manner I could see that he was very worried. A certain Colonel
Tweedy, a British officer on the staff of A.F.N.E.I. who was spending his
leave in Bali, had disappeared. He had wandered off on his own, most
unwisely, to take photographs in a village north of Den Pasar; that was four
days ago, and he had not been seen since. Ter Meulen suggested that Shaw
and I might like to remain in Bali to help with the search; we readily agreed,
and General Mansergh immediately signalled his approval.

We persuaded Ter Meulen to let Hubrecht join our party, and to lend us
a jeep, together with our old chauffeur, Shimada. Hubrecht brought with him
a Eurasian lieutenant, Jack Hagemann, one of the keenest and most efficient
young officers I ever met, who spoke not only Dutch and English but perfect
Malay—I never knew how beautiful a language Malay could be until I heard
Hagemann speak it.

Our search for Colonel Tweedy developed into a search for leading
terrorists or terrorist sympathizers who might know something about the
murder—that he had been murdered there was little doubt. We obtained
from the Dutch, from Theo and the Leo Mayeurs, and from our Balinese
contacts the names of suspects or possible informants in the area between
Den Pasar, Tabanan, Bangli and Gianjar, and these we set out to find and

interrogate; we operated principally by night, partly because we could hope to surprise them sleeping, partly because at such a time they would show less resistance to questioning, but partly, I am sorry to admit, in the belief—naive and childish as it now seems—that our sudden appearance in a hostile area in the dead of night would have a profound effect on the morale of the terrorists.

We ran into trouble on the first evening. Driving back from Kesiman, where we had been questioning the *pungawa*—an old man high on our list of suspects who pleaded ignorance to all our questions—we came upon a large tree felled across the road; as we slowed down a heavy machine-gun opened fire on us from a plantation on the outskirts of Den Pasar. Fortunately the aim was high, and we were able to remove the road block and drive on, without lights, until we met a Dutch picket; they too had heard the firing, but by the time they had arrived on the scene the enemy had vanished.

We patrolled the whole area systematically, planning each operation carefully beforehand on our maps. We would drive to a point near our objective and walk the rest of the way, leaving Shimada, with a heavy service revolver in his hand and a broad, happy grin on his face, to guard the jeep. I had the greatest admiration for his courage when I thought of him standing there alone for two hours or more in the silent, hostile darkness; but someone had to stand guard, and Shimada begged so insistently to come on every operation that we hadn't the heart to leave him in Den Pasar. I am thankful that he came to no harm.

I felt pretty scared myself as we padded silently through the night along narrow paths through thick undergrowth, or among the tall, black trunks of palm trees that looked cold and evil and menacing in the pale light of the moon; by nature a timid person I imagined an army of dangers, real or ghostly, lurking in the surrounding darkness, and I would halt suddenly, gripping my carbine in a sweat of terror, ready to shoot at some shadow that I thought had moved.

I cannot pretend that we met with much success. The few suspects we caught either knew or would tell us nothing; but usually they had vanished before we arrived. The countryside was broken up into deep, narrow ravines between perpendicular walls of rock, overgrown with vegetation, where even in daylight fifty men might hide while we passed within a few feet. Once or twice, indeed, we had an encounter with a terrorist outpost or patrol—a brief, wild exchange of shots, the quick shadow of a running figure, and then silence in the empty night.

Looking back on it now, it all seems a most amateur, schoolboy performance and an irresponsible risk out of all proportion to anything we could hope to gain. The wonder is that we never met serious trouble; we must have been so easy to ambush. Years later some of the terrorist leaders told Hubrecht that on many occasions they had watched us and sometimes they had had us in their sights. Why they made no attempt to kill us all is something I can only attribute to Hubrecht's personal popularity with the Balinese, and to the well-known Oriental affection for lunatics and children. After two weeks Shaw was summoned to Singapore, where a new post awaited him in SEAC, and early in May I received orders to report to General Mansergh, now Commander-in-Chief A.F.N.E.I., in Batavia. Tweedy's murderer was caught by the Dutch military police, trying to dispose of the poor man's watch. The motive of the murder was not political after all; it was plain robbery. Tweedy was carrying the three possessions most coveted by a Balinese: a watch, a camera, and a pistol; it was for these he was killed. The murderer, a man with a bad criminal record, stalked him and struck him down from behind; then he rolled the body into an irrigation ditch about a kilometre north of Den Pasar, cut off the flow of water with an improvised dam of earth, covered the body with stones, and let the water flow over it again. If there were any witnesses they never talked; it was the watch that gave the criminal away.

This murder led indirectly to another tragedy. Theo's friend Andoregg, who had visited us at Iseh, decided to look for Tweedy on his own. Trusting in his knowledge of the Balinese and in their affection for him, and disregarding all the warnings and entreaties of Ter Meulen, Hubrecht and even Theo himself, he put on Balinese dress and set off on foot alone into the countryside. He wandered from village to village, staying at night with the various *pungawas* and headmen whom he knew, and following any leads they could give him; every two or three days he would turn up in Den Pasar to report. Then he too vanished; for ten days nothing was heard of him. By that time I was in Java, and I was on the point of returning to Bali to look for him when news arrived that he had been found by a Dutch patrol: he was lying dead in a ricefield with a rope round his neck and more than thirty sword slashes in his poor mutilated body. I shuddered to think how very easily his fate might have been our own.

Lying on my stomach in the perspex nose of a Mitchell bomber, I shaded my eyes from the full glare of the declining sun and peered down to let them linger for the last time upon the lovely island dropping away beneath me as the aircraft straightened on her course towards Java. I was ashamed to feel the prickle of tears against my eyelids, and suddenly I could no longer stifle my sobs. On the airfield at Kuta, in front of Theo and Pegi, the Le Mayeurs and Hubrecht, I had just been able to control my feelings—although the sight of Shimada standing a little way behind the others with the tears streaming freely down his ugly face brought a sudden shock of pity and surprise; he must have enjoyed himself with us more than I had realized, and now he would have no more fun. But when I came to say good-bye to Madé Pegi I could scarcely hide my misery; I felt her trembling, too, as she kissed me. Theo put his hand gently on my own.

'You will come back to us,' he said. The others echoed his words, but I could not believe them. I felt I should never again find the peace and happiness I had experienced in that house among the bright green hills of Iseh, or be able to forget the moonlight on the slopes of Gunung Agung above the shadowed, silent valley.

I stayed only twenty-four hours in Surabaja, where I found the atmosphere less hospitable than before. This was due to the recent arrival of two Dutch marine brigades who had just completed their training in the United States; they were ill-disciplined, truculent and trigger-happy, and nursed against the British, whom by some curious process of reasoning they seemed to hold responsible for the collapse of their empire, a resentment scarcely less violent than their hatred of the Javanese. The following evening at dusk I landed at Batavia, and was driven straight to the Hotel des Indes, where some kindly Staff Officer had booked me a suite.

The standard of luxury for which this hotel was once so justly famous had, as I have already remarked, deteriorated since the war; one symptom of its decline became immediately clear to me on arrival, when I opened the door of my sitting-room, switched on the light and started to carry my luggage through to the bedroom. Half-way across the room I was arrested by the sound of agitated scuffling and, turning my eyes to the wall on my right, I saw a large brass-posted bed draped with a mosquito curtain suspended from the ceiling; the bed was shaking violently, from behind the curtain came the sound of heavy breathing, and dimly through the gauze I discerned the outline of a struggling figure.

I dropped my bags and stared in open-mouthed, speechless amazement as the curtain parted and there emerged not one but two figures, both of them as naked as—though in every detail more striking than—on the day they were born. The man was broadly built, with thick, short arms; he was deeply tanned and covered all over with black, curly hair. The girl was a young giantess, a round, vacant, pink and white doll's face on the smooth, glistening body of a whale; after ten years of war I was no longer squeamish, but my stomach fairly heaved when I glanced at those huge suety thighs.

'Well, hello!' called the man in a hearty, nasal voice. 'Come right in.' He fished out a pack of Lucky Strike from the pocket of a uniform jacket hanging on a chair by the bed; I noticed the four rings of a captain of the mercantile marine. He put a cigarette between the girl's fat lips, took another himself and threw one to me. 'Got a light?'

They sat side by side on the bed, smoking quietly and looking me over with a friendly curiosity while I struggled with my voice. At last in desperation I snatched a flask of whisky from my rucksack and passed it to them; then I took a long, deep pull myself. Never had I so badly needed a drink.

'Oh boy!' sighed the captain ecstatically. 'That was real Scotch!' Then he appeared to remember his manners. 'Gee, I'm sorry!' he apologized. 'I never introduced you.' He laid an enormous hand on the girl's bare shoulder. 'Honey, meet Colonel...'

'Kemp. Peter Kemp.' I bowed awkwardly, for I was still badly shaken. He heaved himself to his feet and shambled towards me, stretching out a hairy arm and beaming like some friendly forest gorilla.

'Hiya, Pete! This is just great! Now you call me Mike, see?'

I looked down at my dirty, sweat-sodden bush shirt and slacks, and came out with probably the silliest sentence of my life. 'I'm most terribly sorry,' I began, 'to be looking so untidy. You see, I've been travelling all day. . . .' I dived for the shelter of my bedroom.

A few minutes later, as I was about to take a shower, the captain appeared in the doorway. 'Mind if I come in?' He didn't wait for my answer; as he had put on a few clothes our positions were now reversed. He lowered his voice to a hoarse whisper. 'See here, Pete, Greta and me we've been havin' a little talk about you, and she thinks you're swell. Now I'm sailin' tomorrow, see, so why don't you kinda take over from me, see what I mean? She's a great girl,' he added with unconscious humour.

'Well now, Mike, that's awfully kind of you,' I began, hoping my face wouldn't betray the mounting horror inside me. 'But-'

'Aw, hell!' I winced as he slapped me on my unprotected back. 'You don't need to thank me, Pete. We're all pals out here. You'd do the same for me. She'll be at one of those tables out front of the hotel after lunch tomorrow, and she'll be lookin' for you.'

'Thanks for the tip, Mike,' I said with deep feeling.

'O.K., Pete. Bye now. Greta and me we're for another shack down.'

In order to escape I arranged to fly up to Bandaung, about a hundred miles inland, as the guest of an Indian Cavalry regiment. In this cool and picturesque mountain resort, surrounded by my genial and hospitable friends, I felt safe. Bandaung, held by 23rd Indian Division, was invested on all sides by hostile Indonesians, and the only safe approach to it from Batavia was by air; several convoys had been ambushed on the road with very heavy casualties. The Indonesians made no attempt to attack, at least while I was there, but there was a good deal of sniping in the town and it paid to be wary. Social life, however, was brisk, beginning after sundown and continuing, despite the curfew, late into the night. Even a sharp attack of gastritis, probably alcoholic, did little to spoil my pleasure.

Returning to Batavia a week later I learned that I was at last to go home; the War Office had written to A.F.N.E.I. pointing out that I was well overdue for demobilization. I reported for the last time to General Mansergh, who greeted me with his usual warmth and kindness.

'You've earned an air passage,' he said at the end of the interview. I'll sign an order now to give you priority.'

On 15th June I took off from Batavia for Singapore, on the first stage of my homeward journey. As the Dakota circled low over the city and turned out to sea across the harbour I gazed back sadly on my last view of Java. I knew I was bewitched forever by the strange, sultry beauty of those islands, and I felt a deep and painful longing for Bali and Lombok, for the charm of their people and the easy peace of their life—above all for the gaiety and kindness of Pegi and Theo and my friends at Sanoer. Europe, I thought, will seem a drab place after all this colour. It occurred to me now that I was just two months short of my thirty-first birthday and for ten years I had been almost continuously at war; I wondered how I should make out in peace.

ABOUT THE AUTHOR

Peter Kemp was an English soldier and writer. Educated at Wellington College and Trinity College in Cambridge, Kemp was preparing for a career as a lawyer before, alarmed by the spread of Communism, he volunteered to assist the Nationalists during the Spanish Civil War. Kemp saw extensive combat in both the Requetés militia and later the Spanish Foreign Legion. After the Civil War ended, Kemp was recruited as an agent for the British Special Operations Executive, taking part in numerous commando raids and other irregular warfare activities in France, Albania, Poland, and several colonial territories throughout the Pacific during and after the Second World War. His adventures are recorded in the books *Mine Were of* Trouble, *No Colours or Crest,* and *Alms for Oblivion.* After that war ended, he worked as an insurance salesman and international journalist, continuing his life of distinction and courage. He died on October 30, 1993.

Made in the USA
Coppell, TX
06 December 2024

41787121R30331